A PALI READER AND PALI GLOSSARY

A PALI READER AND PALI GLOSSARY

A PALI READER
WITH NOTES AND GLOSSARY
(TEXT AND NOTES)

DINES ANDERSEN

IN TWO VOLUMES
VOL. II

GYAN

Published by

Gyan Publishing House
5, Ansari Road
Daryaganj, New Delhi-110002
Phone: 011-47034999, 9811692060
E-mail: books@gyanbooks.com

Distribution Network
gyanbooks.com
India, USA, Canada, UK, Australia, France

ISBN : 978-81-212-4489-3 (Set)
ISBN : 978-81-212-4652-1 (PB)
First Published, 1907

2nd Impression 2020

Printed at: Gyan Press, Delhi.

A Pali Reader and Pali Glossary Vol. II
Author: Dines Andersen

PREFACE.

In issuing the present part of the Pāli Reader I ought to express my sincere regret that various circumstances have so much retarded the final revision and printing of the glossary, the conclusion of which I know has been expected long ago by not a few scholars. As has been promised in the preface to Part I. this glossary includes the vocabulary of the whole text of Dhammapada, and I have upon the whole done my best to make it as complete as possible. It has been my aim by this to supply the young student with a sufficient help for the first years' study, untill he will be able to work inpendently, and I have therefore above all striven to arrange the materials so that every passage in the texts which might be supposed to present even the slightest difficulty to the beginner should not be passed by in silence. Whether I have succeeded in my explanations in such cases, where I differ from the usual interpretation, I must leave to my critics to judge of. With regard to the lexicographical system introduced into this glossary I need not to say much; it is of course, as to the outer form, in many respects different from that of the Dictionary of *Childers*: in addition to the Indian order of the letters I have introduced all declinable words in their stems (only with a few exceptions, e. g. pronouns like ahaṁ, bhavaṁ, etc.); where the stems are ending in consonants these have been printed in Italics, the reason for which I hope will be understood: ghosava*t*, ceta*s*, muddha*n*, gandhi*n*, pita*r* (the latter I have considered more practical than pitu). The verbs ought in my opinion to be given in their present indicative (3. sing.), as has also been done by *Childers*, together with reference to the Sanskrit roots; so I have not paid any attention to roots or forms given by the native Pāli-grammarians, my task only being to deal with the texts themselves, and nothing has been quoted, that cannot be traced in the litterature. In many single cases I have had an indispensable support in the exhaustive lexicographical collections of *V. Trenckner* (now in the Copenhagen University Library), especially where my own collections were not sufficient to state a certain signification, form, or gender of a word; the abbreviation (Tr.) added here and there in the glossary will show that also on other accounts I have derived some benefit from suggestions of his accidentally occurring among the vast number of his quotations. With regard to typographical arrangements I beg to remark that asterisks have been put before those Pāli words to which no Sanskrit equivalents can be traced; likewise generally before compounds not found in the Sanskrit Dictionary of Monier Williams, the new edition of which has been of great help to me during the whole work; certain forms of the Pāli words are put within parentheses in order to show that they do not occur in the Reader or the Dhpd., whilst brackets put to a heading-word (e. g. [samāsati]) denote that this particular form of the word is not traced. Of the English translations it ought to be observed that those within double inverted comma are simply quotations from my predecessors; other typographical indications, abbreviations, etc., I hope will easily be understood. Before using the book my readers are earnestly requested to insert the corrections and additions given on the last pages into the text of both parts.

In conclusion I wish to address my best thanks to my young friend Mr. *Joh. Eyser*, Assistant Librarian at our University Library, to whom I am indebted for his kind assistance in correcting the proofs.

Copenhagen, September 1907.

DINES ANDERSEN.

TO

MY TEACHER AND FRIEND

PROFESSOR DR. PHIL. V. FAUSBØLL

IN COMMEMORATION OF

THE 50TH ANNIVERSARY OF HIS FIRST EDITION

OF THE

DHAMMAPADA

Copenhagen, March 15., 1905

DINES ANDERSEN

A.

a-[1], the base of *pron. gen.* assa, assā, *v.* ayaṁ.

a-[2], the *prp.* ā-, shortened before double cons. *v.* akkamati, akkosati *etc.*

a-[3], the augment originally prefixed to the verbal root in the formation of the *impf.*, *aor.* & *cond.* tenses, in most cases dropped after mā (*q. v.*) and generally omitted in ordinary prose. List of augmented forms occurring in the texts of the Reader & the Dhp.:

a-kā, a-kari, a-kāsi, a-kaṁsu, a-karamhase, *v.* karoti.

a-kārayi, *v.* kāreti.

a-gañchi, a-gamā, a-gamāsi, a-gamaṁsu, *v.* gacchati.

a-ggahi, a-ggahuṁ, a-ggahesi, *v.* gaṇhati.

a-ghātayi, *v.* ghāteti.

a-cāri, *v.* carati.

a-cāvayi, *v.* cāveti.

a-cchidda, a-cchindi, *v.* chindati.

a-jali, *v.* jalati.

a-jini, *v.* jināti.

a-ṭṭhā, a-ṭṭhāsi, a-ṭṭhaṁsu, *v.* tiṭṭhati.

a-tari, *v.* tarati.

a-dā, a-dāsi(ṁ), a-daṁsu, *v.* dadāti.

a-desayi, *v.* deseti.

a-ddakkhi, *v.* dakkhati.

a-ddasa, a-ddasā, a-ddasāma, a-ddasāsuṁ, *v.* dissati.

a-passi, *v.* passati.

a-pucchi, a-pucchiṁsu, *v.* pucchati.

a-pūjesuṁ, *v.* pūjeti.

a-plaviṁ, *v.* p(a)lavati.

a-bravi, a-bruvi, *v.* brūti.

a-bhavissa (*cond.*), *v.* bhavati.

a-bhassatha, *v.* bhassati.

a-bhāṇiṁ, *v.* bhaṇati.

a-bhāsi, a-bhāsatha, *v.* bhāsati.

a-vaca(ṁ), a-voca, a-vocuṁ, *v.* vadati.

a-vadhi, *v.* vadhati.

a-vādesi, *v.* vādeti.

a-saṁsi, *v.* saṁsati.

a-sakkhi(ṁ), *v.* sakkoti.

a-ssumha, *v.* suṇati.

a-hāyatha, *v.* hāyati.

a-hāsi, *v.* harati.

a-hū, a-huṁ, a-huvā, a-huvattha, a-huvamhase, a-hosi(ṁ), a-hesuṁ, *v.* hoti.

âsiṁ, *v.* atthi.

acc-a-gā, acc-a-gamā, *v.* a[illegible]-gacchati.

ajjh-a-gā, ajjh-a-gū, *v.* adhi-gacchati.

ajjh-a-bhāsi, *v.* adhi-bhāsati.

ajjh-a-vāsayi, *v.* adhi-vāseti.

anu-pariy-a-gā, *v.* anu-pari-gacchati.

anv-a-gā, *v.* anu-gacchati.

apâ-nayi, *v.* apa-neti.

ud-a-pādi, *v.* up-pajjati.

upacc-a-gā, *v.* (upāti-gacchati).

upâ-gami, *v.* upa-gacchati.

upâ-visi. v. upa-visati.
pacc-a-ssosi, pacc-a-ssosum. v. paṭi-suṇāti.
pâ-mado, v. pa-majjati.
pâ-yāsi, pâ-yiṁsu, v. pa-yāti.
pâ-vassi, v. pa-vassati.
pâ-visi, v. pa-visati.
pâ-hesi. v. pahiṇati.
vyapâ-nudi. v. vyapa-nudati.

a-[4], negative particle, prefixed to the following words, *1*) to nouns (*subst.*, *adj.*, *adv.*), *2*) to verbal forms (mostly to *part.*, *grd.*, *ger.* or *inf.*, rarely to finite verbal forms). In *comp.* with words beginning originally with two consonants the first cons. is generally doubled (*v.* a-ppaṭivattiya. a-paccakkhāya), and before vowels it has always the form an- (*v.* below). As to the signification it is often *opp.* to sa- (*q. v.*) and synom. with the particles na-, nir-, vi- (vinā-?). Sometimes this particle is found repeated: an-a- (as a kind of stronger negation (?), *cp.* an-a-bhāvakata [but an-a-kāma, not unwilling]). It is doubtful whether this particle is contained in comp. like phalāphala. maggāmagga *etc.* (*q. v.*). [*R. Otto Franke:* a-pacasi. ZDMG. XLVIII,84 (*cp.* a-sakkoti. Dhpd. (1855) p. 102,14. a-sakkhi, Jāt. I, 382,24. an-abhirami, Jāt. III, 30,20). *G. Bühler:* ZDMG. XL, 544 (*cp.* Jāt. I, 171,17. 385,16)].

a-kakkasa, *mfn.* free from harshness. Dh. 408. (~aṁ, *acc. m.*).

a-kata, a) *mfn.* not done, left undone, Dh. 50. 165. 314. b) *n.* the uncreated (*s.* Nibbāna): a-kataññu[1], *mfn.* Dh. 97. 383. (~ū). knowing the uncreated.

a-kataññu[2], *mfn.* ungrateful, 14,1.

a-kattar. *m.* who does no good. 14,1 (*acc.* -araṁ).

a-katvā, *v.* karoti.

a-kathaṁ-kathin. *mfn.* free from doubt (kathaṁ-kathā). Dh. 411. 414 (-ī, *m.*).

a-kathetvā, *v.* katheti.

a-karaṇa. *n.*, omission, avoiding of, Dh. 183. 333.

a-karonta, *v.* karoti.

a-kāma, *mfn.* unwilling, reluctant, 104,10. (~assa, *m. gen.*).

a-kāraṇena. *instr. adv.* without (reasonable) cause, 34,17. 58,11, *v.* kāraṇa.

a-kāriya, *mfn.* not to be done, that may not be done, 106,15 — Dh. 176. *v.* karoti.

a-kāla, *m.* wrong time, or *mfn.* unseasonable, 25,21. 37,16, *v.* kāla.

a-kicca, *mfn.* not to be done, Dh. 74. 293. *v.* karoti.

a-kiñcana, *mfn.* without anything, calling nothing his own, disinterested, Dh. 88. 221. 396 — 431.

a-kiñci, *adv.* not a little, Dh. 390, *v.* koci (*cp.* na).

a-kujjhitvā, *v.* kujjhati.

a-kutobhaya, *mfn.* (= *sa*, from kuto + bhaya. *q. v.*), knowing no fear, secure, Dh. 196 (~e. *acc. pl. m.*).

a-kuddha. *mfn.* not angry. 11,17 (~assa. *gen.*), *v.* kujjhati.

a-kubbato. *gen. m.*, from *part.* kubbaṁ, (*v.* karoti), who does not act, Dh. 51, 124.

a-kulin, *mfn.* (*fr.* kula, *q. v.*), of base extraction, 102,4 (~ino rājāno, *nom. pl. m.*).

a-kusala, *mfn.* evil. 75,24 (yathā ~aṁ, *acc. m.*); *n.* ~aṁ, evil deed, demerit, 97,13. Dh. 281.

a-kkodha. *m.* mildness, 44,8 — Dh. 223 (~ena, *instr.*), *v.* kodha.

a-kkodhana. *mfn.* free from anger, 104,21. Dh. 400. *v.* kodhana.

a-kkhara. *q. v.*

a-gaṇhantī. *v.* gaṇhati.

a-gata, *mfn.* not gone to, 48,11: not frequented, Dh. 323. *v.* gata.

a-gantvā, *v.* gacchati.

a-gandhaka, *mfn.* (*fr.* gandha. *q. v.*). without odour (*opp.* sa-gandhaka), Dh. 51 (~aṁ pupphaṁ).

a-gahetvā, *v.* gaṇhati.

a-guṇa. *m.* fault, ~o. 43,4, ~aṁ, 43,7. ~a (*pl.*) 44,5; °-gavesaka. *mfn.* seeking his own faults, 43,16 (~o); °-vādin, *mfn.* telling one of his faults, ~ī, ~iṁ (*nom. acc. m.*) 43,5. 43,6.

a-caritvā. *v.* carati.

a-carima, *mfn.* not subsequent, not last; ~aṁ, *adv.* 99,26 (*cp.* a-pubba).

a-cala, *mfn.* immovable, firm, 110,7 (~ā bhūmi).

a-cira, *mfn.* short, brief; ~aṁ, *adv.* soon, before long. 107,5 = Dh. 41; °-ppakkanta, *mfn.* 70,13 ~e, *loc.* soon after he was gone (*cp.* pakkamati).

a-ccuta, *mfn.* not fallen, permanent, unchangeable, Dh. 225 ~aṁ ṭhānaṁ, Nibbāna (*cp.* cuta & cavati).

a-cchidda, *mfn.* uninjured, faultless, blameless; °-vutti *adj. m.* Dh. 229 (~iṁ. *acc.*) of blameless conduct.

a-chinditvā, *v.* chindati.

a-jañña, *mfn.* not to be produced (*v.* jāyati); *n.* a portent; purisājañño. *m.* Dh. 193, *q.v.*

a-jānanta (*gen.* a-jānato), **a-jānitvā**, *v.* jānāti.

a-jhāyato (*gen.*), *v.* jhāyati.

a-ññāṇa. *n.* ignorance, 94,21 (~aṁ. *acc.*), 94,24 (~āya. *dat.*) *cp.* ñāṇa.

a-ññāta, *mfn.* unknown (*v.* jānāti). ~aṁ, *nom. n.* 92,25. ~ ānaṁ, *gen. m. pl.* unknown persons, 90,32.

a-ññātaka. *mfn.* (aññāta *w. suff.* -ka) *id.* °-vesena. *instr.* in disguise 43,13 (*cp.* vesa).

a-ṭṭhāna, *n.* wrong place or wrong time (*v.* ṭhāna), 34,22 (~e, *loc*); an impossible thing, that cannot take place 76,26 (~aṁ, *nom.*).

a-takkāvacara, *mfn.* being beyond the sphere of thought, 94,25 (takka + avacara, *q.v.*).

a-tandita. *mfn.* not slothful, unwearied, Dh. 305. 366. 375.

a-titta. *mfn.* unsatisfied, insatiate, 52,24 ~aṁ (*acc. f.*) kāmesu, insatiate in pleasures; Dh. 48.

a-tula, *mfn.* unequalled; *m. nom. pr.* (*q.v.*) Dh. 227.

a-daṇḍa, *mfn.* [1]) without stick, 77,13 (~ena. *instr.*) — [2]) exempt from punishment, innocent, Dh. 137 (~esu. *loc. pl.*).

a-datvā. *v.* dadāti.

a-dassana. *n.* not seeing (*w. gen.*); piyānaṁ ~aṁ, 106,26 = Dh. 210; ~ena (*instr.*) morassa. before the peacock had appeared, 18,32; Dh. 206; ~aṁ gacche, will not see, Dh. 46.

***a-dātukāmatā**; *f.* (*fr. inf.* dātuṁ *v.* dadāti) + kāma *w. suff.* -tā) unwillingness to give, ~aṁ (*acc.*) 16,11, ~āya (*instr.* „because you do not wish to give it") 23,36.

a-dinna, *mfn.* not given; ~aṁ ādiyati, to take what is not given, to steal, 97,10, Dh. 246. 409; a-dinnâdāna, *n.* stealing. 81,22 (~ā, *abl.*); a-dinnapubba, *mfn.* not given before, 15,30 (*cp.* pubba).

a-disvā, **(a)-dissamāna**, *v.* dissati.

a-duṭṭha, *mfn.* not guilty, innocent, Dh. 399.

***a-dūbha**, *mfn.* not treacherous (or *s. m.*(?) not deceiving) 111,29: a-dūbhatthāya (*dat. cp.* attha[1]) „in order that she might not prove herself treacherous" (*cp.* dūbhati).

a-ddhuva, *mfn.* not fixed, uncertain, 86,15 (*cp.* dhuva).

a-dhamma, *m.* injustice, Dh. 248; ~ena (*instr. adv.*) unjustly, Dh. 84.

***a-dhammika**, *mfn.* unrighteous, impious, ~ā (*m. pl.*) 102,6.

***a-dhammikatā**, *f.* unrighteousness. ~āya (*instr.*) 102,6.

***a-nikkasāva**, *mfn.* not free from impurity, impure, Dh. 9 (*cp.* kasāva & kāsāva).

a-nicca *mfn.* (*v.* niccaṁ) not eternal, transitory, impermanent, perishable, ~ā saṁkhārā 80,28; 107,11 = Dh. 277; a-niccâdi-vasena (*instr.*) 88,32 „on account of the instability *etc.* of this world" (?) (*cp.* ādi & vasa).

a-niccatā, *f.* transient existence, instability, mortality, ~ā (= a-niccatāya, *instr.*) 95,32.

a-niṭṭhita, *mfn.* not finished, not completed, 87,11.

a-nindita, *mfn.* (*v.* nindati), not blamed, Dh. 227.

***a-nibbisaṁ**, *part. adv.* uselessly, fruitlessly, 108,16. Dh. 153. (*v.* nibbiṭṭha; SBE. X, 43.)

a-nimitta, *mfn.* causeless, groundless, ~o vimokho (*q. v.*) = Nibbāna, Dh. 92. 93.

***a-nimisatā**, *f.* not winking; ~āya (akkhīnaṁ) 59,5 „on account of her not winking".

a-niyata, *mfn.* not fixed, uncertain, ~aṁ jīvitaṁ, 86,17.

***a-niyata-gatika**, *mfn.* whose path (through the numerous forms of life, *v.* gati) is uncertain, ~ā, *f.* 87,29.

***a-niyyānika**, *mfn.* unprofitable, 9,29.

a-nivattana, *n.* not turning back, not fleeing: °-dhamma, *mfn.* having the nature of not fleeing, 39,10 ~ā mahāyodhā (*m. pl.*).

a-nivesana, *mfn.* homeless; inaccessible to desire, free from attachment (?) Dh. 40. (*cp.* SBE. X, 14.)

a-nissita, *mfn.* not dependent on, Dh. 93 āhāre ~o, „not absorbed in enjoyment".

***a-nīgha**, *mfn.* scatheless, harmless (?) Dh. 294. 295. (*Sa.* ***a-nighna**, *Morris* JPTS. '91—93, p. 41 ff.; ***a-nyagha** (= an-agha), sinless, Fsb. *cp.* SBE. X, 71 ff. The natives derive this word from *nīgha „suffering" and explain it by niddukkha; *cp.* also *sa.* an-ehas (√īh)).

a-paccakkhāya, *v.* paccakkhāti.

a-pañña, *mfn.* not intelligent, Dh. 372.

a-paṭikkamitvā, *v.* paṭikkamati.

a-pada, *mfn.* footless *i. e.* having no footing in the existence (saṁsāra), Dh. 179. 180.

***a-pabbajana**, *n.* 47,5: °-atthāya (*dat. v.* attha[1]) „to keep him from a religious life".

***a-para-ppaccaya**, *mfn.* not dependent of others, ~o sāsane (— „for the knowledge of the doctrine") 69,14; aparappaccayā, *abl. adv.* ~ñānaṁ, intuitive knowledge, 96,14.

a-pariggaha, *mfn.* unmarried, 56,4 (~ā, *f.*); °-bhāva, *m.* the unmarried state, 56,7 (*cp.* pariggaha).

a-parighaṁsanta, *v.* parighaṁsati.

***a-parisuddha**, *mfn.* dirty, 41,1.

a-parihīna-jhāna, *n.* uninterrupted meditation, 45,15 (*v.* parihāyati).

a-passanta, a-passitvā, *v.* passati.

a-pāra, *n.* not the opposite bank, Dh. 385 (*v.* pāra).

a-puccha, *mfn.* not to be asked about, ~aṁ (*acc. n.*) 91,13 (*v.* pucchati).

a-pujja, *mfn.* not to be revered, not deserving homage, 30,21 (*v.* pūjeti).

a-puñña, *n.* demerit, 76,3 °-lābha, *m.* acquisition of demerit, Dh. 309. 310.

***a-puthujjana-sevita**, *mfn.* which common people cannot enjoy, Dh. 272 (*cp.* sevati).

a-pubba, *mfn.* not first, unpreceeded (*opp.* a-carima); ~aṁ, *adv.* 99,25: apubbam acarimaṁ, „not before and not after", „simultaneously" (*Morris* JPTS. '87 *p.* 101; *Rhys Davids* SBE. XXXV *p.* 64).

a-ppagabbha, *mfn.* not arrogant, modest, quiet, Dh. 245 (*v.* pagabbha).

***a-ppaṭicchanna**, *mfn.* not covered, naked, 10,15 ~o ahosi, „he exposed himself" (*v.* paṭicchanna).

***a-ppaṭipuggala**, *mfn.* unequalled, 80,24 (*v.* paṭi-puggala).

a-ppaṭibaddha-citta, *mfn.* one whose mind is not turned to (*loc.*), kāmesu ~o, „not bewildered by love", Dh. 218 (*v.* paṭibaddha).

a-ppaṭivattiya, *mfn.* insubvertible, 110,7 ~ā (*f.* bhūmi). (*v.* paṭivatteti).

***a-ppatikaraka**, *mfn.* ungrateful, 14,1: katassa ~aṁ (*acc. m.*), one who does not return what has been done. (*v.* patikāraka).

***a-ppatissavāsa**, *m.* anarchy, 10,31. (*v.* patissava).

a-ppatta. *mfn.* not having obtained (*acc.*) Dh. 272. (*v.* patta[3] *cp.* SBE. X, *p.* 67).

a-ppaduṭṭha, *mfn.* harmless. Dh. 125. (*v.* paduṭṭha, *cp.* dussati).

a-ppamatta, *mfn.* not slothful, earnest, zealous, strenuous, ~ā (*m. pl.*) 104,9. Dh. 21. (*v.* pamatta, pamajjati; *cp.* appa-matta).

a-ppamāda, *m.* earnestness, strenuousness, ~o Dh. 21; ~e & ~amhi (*loc.*) Dh. 22; ~ena sampādetha, „work out your salvation with diligence" (*instr.*). ⁰-rata, *mfn.* delighting in earnestness, Dh. 31. 327. ⁰-vagga, *m.* the second chapter of Dh. ⁰-vihārin, *mfn.* living strenuously, Dh. 57 (~inaṁ, *gen. pl.*) (*cp.* pamāda & pamajjati).

a-ppameyya. *mfn.* immensurable, 95,13. (*v.* pameyya).

a-ppasanna. *mfn.* not quiet, unbelieving, without faith, 76,30. (*cp.* pasanna & pasīdati).

a-ppiya, *mfn.* unpleasant, disagreeable; ~ehi (*instr. n. pl.*) 67,9. 106,25 = Dh. 210; ~ānaṁ (*gen. n. pl.*) 106,26 = Dh. 210; *m.* ~o, an enemy, Dh. 77. (*v.* piya).

a-phala. *mfn.* without fruit, improfitable, vain, ~ā vācā Dh. 51. (*opp.* sa-phala, *cp.* phalāphala).

***a-phāsuka**, *mfn.* unpleasant, uneasy; *n.* sickness, 46,5. 49,24. 28. kiṁ te ~aṁ, what ails you? 49,25.

a-bala. *mfn.* weak; *a-bal'-assa, *m.* a weak horse, a hack (*opp.* sīghassa), Dh. 29.

a-bbaṇa. *mfn.* having no wound (vaṇa, *q. v.*) Dh. 124.

a-bbata, *mfn.* undisciplined, not observing the religious duties (vata, *q. v.*) Dh. 264 (*cp.* subbata).

a-brahmacariya, *n.* unchastity, impurity, ~ā (*abl.*) 81,22.

a-bhabba, *mfn.* (*v.* bhabba & bhavati) unable, *w. inf.* 69,26: ~o Yaso kāme paribhuñjituṁ, „it is impossible that Y. should enjoy pleasures"; *w. dat.* ~o parihānāya, „cannot fall away (from holiness)". Dh. 32.

a-bhaya (*fr.* bhaya, *n.*) [1]) *mfn.* free from fear, Dh. 258. [2]) *n.* safety, security, immunity, ~aṁ, *nom.* 7,6. *acc.* 6,18. ~e, *loc.* 7,14. Dh. 317. *a-bhaya-laddhaka, *mfn.* 7,35. who has obtained immunity = *laddhâbhaya, *mfn.* 7,3 (*cp.* laddha). *a-bhaya-dassin, *mfn.* seeing no danger, Dh. 317 (~ino, *m. pl.*).

a-bhāva, *m.* absence, non-existence, ~ā (*abl.*) 42,30. 63,31 & ~ena (*instr.*) 59,18. 88,31, on account of the absence of (*gen.*); an-abhāvakata, *q. v.*

a-bhāvita, *mfn.* (*v.* bhāveti) [1]) not produced, not practised, not realized, ~ā (*f.* maraṇasati) 86,18. [2]) not trained, not versed in religious practise, ~aṁ (cittaṁ) Dh. 13 „unreflecting" (*opp.* su-bhāvita).

a-bhūta, *mfn.* that has not happened, ~aṁ (*acc. n.*) 9,29. *⁰-vādin, *mfn.* delighting in lie, ~ī (*nom. m.*) 74,1.

a-bhejja, *mfn.* unconquerable, ⁰-varasūra-, 39,12.

a-magga, *m.* the evil path, Dh. 403 (maggâmagga).

a-maṅgala, *mfn.* unauspicious, ungracious, impolite (?), ~aṁ (*n.* paṭikkhipanaṁ) 56,23.

a-mata, *mfn.* immortal; *n.* the immortal (= Nibbāna), Dh. 374; ~aṁ padaṁ (*n.*) Dh. 114 = a-mata-pada, *n.* Dh. 21, the immortal place, Nibbāna (*opp.* maccuno padaṁ). *a-matogadha, *n.* (?) (*cp.* ogadha) the depth of Nibbāna, Dh. 411.

***a-mattaññu**, *mfn.* immoderate (*w. loc.*) Dh. 7.

a-madhura, *mfn.* not sweet, sour, bitter, ⁰-saṁsaggena, „by the company of the sour (plant)", 37,21.

a-manussa, *m.* not a human being, *pl.* ~ā. 68,3 (*cp.* a-mānusa).

a-mara, *mfn.* immortal, imperishable, *n.* ~aṁ, 56,12; *f.* ~ā, *nom. pr.* = Amarādevī, *q. v.*

a-mātu-hadaya, *n.* not a mother's heart, 59,12 (*v.* mātar).
a-mānusa, *mfn.* not human, superhuman; *m.* ~o (saddo) 27,6; *f.* ~ī (ratī) Dh. 373 (*cp.* a-manussa).
a-mārenta, *v.* māreti.
a-mitta, *m.* an enemy, ~enêva, (*instr.*) Dh. 66. 207 („as with an enemy", *cp.* iva).
a-yasa, *m.* infamy, disgrace, *acc.* ~aṁ 73,8.
a-yutta, *mfn.* unfit, unright, wrong, *n.* ~aṁ 38,19.
a-yoga, *m.* not meditation, lack of devotion or religious exertion, *abl.* ~ā Dh. 282, *loc.* ~e Dh. 209.
a-yojayaṁ, *v.* yojeti.
a-rakkhita, *mfn.* 9,10, = a-rakkhiya, *mfn.* 52,8, difficult to watch (*v.* rakkhati).
a-rati, *f.* discontent, 103,25 (dutiyā senā Mārassa).
a-rājika. *mfn.* (*sa.* a-rājaka), having no king (*v.* rājan), *n.* ~aṁ raṭṭhaṁ, 31,12.
a-roga, *mfn.* free from disease, healthy, *m. pl.* ~ā, 105,5 (*cp.* ārogya).
a-lajjitāya, *mfn.* what one ought not to be ashamed of, Dh. 316 (*v.* lajjati).
a-laddhā, a-labhanta, a-labhantī, a-labhamāna, a-labhitvā *v.* labhati.
a-lasa, *mfn.* (= *sa.*) without energy, lazy, slothful, Dh. 280 (*cp.* ālasiya).
*a-līna, *mfn.* free from attachment, *instr.* ~ena, Dh. 245 (*cp.* allīyati).
a-lola, *mfn.* unagitated, not desirous, not wanton, *f.* ~ā (gopī) 104,33.
*a-vajja, *mfn.* to be avoided, *n.* sin, fault, *loc.* ~e Dh. 318; °-dassin, *mfn.* seeing no sin, *m. pl.* ~ino Dh. 318.
a-vaṇṇa, *m.* blame; ~aṁ uppādeti, to bring reproach on (*gen.*) 72,32.
*a-vatthu-kata, *mfn.* pulled out of the ground, tālâ-° 95,11. *q. v.*
a-vatvā, *v.* vadati.
a-vassaṁ, *adv.* necessarily, inevitably, 86,16 (*sa.* a-vaçyaṁ, *cp.* vasa & vasi).
a-vijānat, *v.* vijānāti.
a-vijjamāna, *v.* vijjati.
a-vijjā, *f.* ignorance, *gen.* ~āya 66,12; °-paccayā, 66,6, *q. v.*
a-vijjhāpita, a-vijjhāpetvā, *v.* vijjhāpeti.
a-vitiṇṇa-kaṁkha, *mfn.* who has not overcome desires, Dh. 141.
a-vidūre, *adv.* not far off, near, 1,26; *prp. w. gen.* 5,30. 36,30. 75,17, *w. abl.* tato ~ 61,15 (*cp.* vidūra).
a-viddasu, *mfn.* ignorant, Dh. 268.
*a-vināsana, *mfn.* imperishable, *m. acc.* ~aṁ 110,1.
*a-vinipāta-dhamma, *mfn.* not liable to be born in a lower state of existence (*v.* vinipāta), 79,33.
a-viruddha, *mfn.* compatible, tolerant, Dh. 406 (*w. loc.*).
a-visahanta. *v.* visahati.
a-vihaññamāna, *v.* vihaññati.
*a-vera, *n.* abstinence from hatred or anger, mildness, *instr.* ~ena 106,24 = Dh. 5.
*a-verin, *mfn.* free from hatred, *m.* ~ī Dh. 258. *pl.* ~ino Dh. 197.
a-vyākata, *mfn.* not explained, not elucidated, 93,2 (*v.* vyākaroti).
a-saṁvara, *m.* lack of self-restraint, *instr.* ~ena 85,19.
a-saṁvuta, *mfn.* not controlled, intemperate, indriyesu ~aṁ (*acc. m.*) „whose senses are not controlled", Dh. 7.
a-saṁsaṭṭha, *mfn.* not mixed with, who keeps aloof from (*instr.*), *acc. m.* ~aṁ Dh. 404.
*a-saṁhīra, *mfn.* not to be shaken, immovable, *m. pl.* ~ā 109,27.
a-sakkonta, *v.* sakkoti.
*a-saṁkuppa. *mfn.* immovable, *m. pl.* ~ā 109,27.
a-sajjamāna. *mfn.* not attached to (*loc.*), Dh. 221 (*cp.* sajjati, satta[1]).
a-sajjhāya. *m.* (*sa.* a-svādhyāya)

non-repetition: °-mala, *mfn.* Dh. 241 (*v.* mala. *n.*).

a-saññata, *mfn.* unrestrained, intemperate, 107.2 = Dh. 308; *pl.* ~ā Dh. 248; *w. instr.* vācāya ~o, 84.29.

a-saññā, *f.* non-perception, 80,8 (in *comp.* neva-saññā-nâsaññā-°, *q. v.*).

a-sat, *mfn.* (*cp.* a-santa) [1]) not being, not existing, false; *instr.* asatā socati Dh. 367, *loc. abs.* sāmikamhi asati 31.9 (without husband). [2]) bad, *pl.* asant(o) Dh. 304 (bad people), *gen. pl.* asataṁ Dh. 73. 77, ~ sannivāsena 37,35 („by bad company"); a-sad-dhamma. *m.* bad quality, fault, *instr. pl.* ~ehi samannāgato 18,16; wickedness 51,26 (asaddhamma-samannāgatā itthiyā); sexual intercourse 52,29 (~aṁ patisevi).

a-satta, *mfn.* not clinging to the world, free from desires, Dh. 419 (*cp.* sajjati *&* saṅga).

a-sattha, *mfn.* weaponless, unarmed, *instr. m.* ~ena 77,18.

a-saddahitvā, *v.* saddahati.

a-saddhamma, *v.* a-sat.

***a-santa**, *mfn.* (*cp.* a-sat), not being, unreal, imaginary. — a-santapaggaha, *m.* taking or accepting for real what is only imaginary, ~aṁ katvā 29.29 („because he imagined himself saluted"); ~-kārana, *n. id.* (naiveté?) 29.27.

***a-santasana**, *n.* intrepidity; ~-bhāva, *mfn.* intrepid, *m. pl.* ~ā (mahāyodhā) 39,10.

***a-santāsin**, *mfn.* who does not tremble, *m.* ~ī, Dh. 351.

a-sabbha, *mfn.* unfit, improper, *abl. n.* ~ā. Dh. 77.

***a-samāhita**, *mfn.* not collected, whose mind is not composed (*opp.* jhāyin). Dh. 110.

a-sampajjanta, *v.* sampajjati.

***a-sampavedhin**, *mfn.* not to be shaken, ~ī (= ~ino, *m. pl.* (khilā)) 105,17.

a-sarīra, *mfn.* bodiless, incorporeal, ~aṁ cittaṁ. Dh. 37.

a-sallakkhetvā, *v.* sallakkheti.

***a-sallīna**, *mfn.* not depressed, resolute, ~ena cittena (*instr.* „with unshaken mind") 80.34.

a-sassata, *mfn.* not eternal, transient, ~o loko 89,26.

a-sahanta. *v.* sahati.

***a-sāta**. *mfn.* unpleasant, noxious, 37,21 (°-amadhura-).

a-sādhu. *mfn.* not good, bad, evil; *n. pl.* ~ūni, bad deeds, Dh. 163.

a-sāra, *m.* (or *mfn.*) what is not essential, Dh. 11. 12 (*v.* sāra); a-sāradassin, *mfn.* considering anything as unessential, *m. pl.* ~ino, Dh. 11.

a-sāhasa, *n.* non-violence; *instr. adv.* ~ena, not arbitrarily, Dh. 257 (*cp.* sahasā).

a-suci, *mfn.* impure; *m.* impure matter, phlegm, semen *etc. instr.* ~inā 62.25.

***a-suddhin**, *mfn.* impure, *nom. m.* ~ī Dh. 165 (*cp.* suddha).

a-subha. *mfn.* not beautiful, disagreeable, inauspicious, bad, *n.* ~aṁ Dh. 350, subhâsubhaṁ Dh. 409. *a-subhâsupassin, *mfn.* not looking for what is agreeable, *acc. m.* ~iṁ Dh. 8.

***a-sūra**, *m.* not a hero, na ~o „none but a hero" 103.32.

a-sesa, *mfn.* without remainder, perfect, complete; °-virāga-nirodhā (*abl.*), by a complete annihilation that leaves no track, 66,12. (*cp.* virāga).

a-soka, *mfn.* free from sorrow, Dh. 28. 412.

a-ssaddha, *mfn.* [1]) unbelieving, *m.* ~o 22.14. *pl.* ~ā 76,30. [2]) free from credulity, Dh. 97 (*v.* saddha *&* saddhā).

a-hata, *mfn.* not beaten, uninjured; °-vatthāni (*n. pl.*) 27,18, °-vattha- 61,28, new (unwashed or not worn out?) clothes.

a-hiṁsā, *f.* (= *sa. cp.* hiṁsati) not injuring anything, harmlessness, compassion or pity on all beings, Dh. 261; ~ā (= ~āya. *instr.*) Dh. 270; ~āya. *loc.* Dh. 300. a-hiṁsaka, *mfn.* not injuring, *m. pl.* ~ā. Dh. 225.

a-hita. *mfn.* not good, unadvantageous; *n.* disadvantage, damage, ~āya (*dat.*) 90,27, ~āni (*pl.*) „evil deeds", Dh. 163.

a-hirika or a-hirīka, *mfn.* (*fr.* hiri, *q. v.*) shameless, *m. pl.* ~ā, 54,13; *instr.* ~ena (*varr.* -hiri-, -hīri-) Dh. 244.

a-heṭhayaṁ. *v.* heṭheti.

an- (only before vowels, = a-[1]) in the foll. *comp.*:

an-akkosaṁ, *v.* akkosati.

*an-akkhāta, *mfn.* not described, ineffable; *n.* — Nibbāna, ~e, *loc.* Dh. 218.

an-agāriyā, *f.* (*sa.* an-agārikā, *cp.* agāra) houseless life, *acc.* ~aṁ. 68,4.

an-aggha. *mfn.* priceless, invaluable, *m.* ~o (manto) 32,10; °-manto 53,14.

*an-aṅgaṇa. *mfn.* free from lust, without sin, Dh. 125. 236. 351.

an-atikkamanta. *v.* atikkamati.

an-atta, *mfn.* (*v.* attan) destitute of a soul or a self; sabbe dhammā ~ā (*m. pl.*) 107,15 — Dh. 279.

*an-attamana, *mfn.* (*fr.* atta[1] + manas, *q. v.*) displeased, *m.* ~o, 74,30.

an-attha, [1]) *m.* (*v.* attha[1]) non-value, harm, a bad or worthless thing; atthaṁ ~añ ca (*acc.*) „right and wrong" Dh. 256; *dat.* ~āya „to harm" Dh. 72; °-saṁhita, *mfn.* profitless, 66,27. [2]) *mfn.* worthless, senseless; °-pada-saṁhita, *mfn.* „made up of senseless words", Dh. 100.

an-anta, *mfn.* endless, (*cp.* ānañca); *°-gocara, *mfn.* whose sphere (of perception) is unlimited, Dh. 179 (~aṁ Buddhaṁ).

an-antara, *mfn.* having no interval, next following; °-gāthā, *f.* 26,7 (~āya, *instr.*); *cp.* ānantariya, samanantarā.

an-antarahita. *mfn.* not concealed, open, bare; *loc. f.* ~āya bhūmiyā. 83,19 (*v.* antaradhāyati).

an-antavat. *mfn.* infinite; *nom. m.* ~vā loko. 89,28.

*an-anvāhata-cetasa, *mfn.* whose mind is not perplexed, Dh. 39 (*cp.* cetas).

an-apāyin, *mfn.* not going away. *f.* ~inī (chāyā) Dh. 2.

an-apekkhin. an-apekhin, *mfn.* without desire, regardless, indifferent, *m. pl.* ~ino. 47,28 — Dh. 346. 347 (-kh-).

*an-appaka, *mfn.* not a little, considerable, great, *f.* ~ā (lābhā) 105,23; *n.* ~aṁ (dukkhaṁ) Dh. 144.

*an-a-bhāva-kata. *mfn.* become not existent, annihilated, *n.* ~aṁ (rūpaṁ Tathāgatassa). The often recurring phrase „anabhāvaṁ gameti", to annihilate, seems to infer that we have to take an-a- in a negative sense, as a kind of stronger negation (*cp.* Tr. PM. 64,25, who considers °-kata an error for °-gata, due to the preceeding tālāvatthukata). In Prākṛit a similar use of aṇa- has been traced in not a few instances, (*cp. Pischel*, Gramm. d. Prākṛit-Spr. § 77). I should, however, be inclined to think that this phenomenon is only a secondary development, having no true base in the original language; thus *sa.* anabhāvakṛta would mean „made not non-existing" ɔ: brought into a state in which it can neither be said to exist nor not to exist; in this case an-abhāva would be *adj.* „free from annihilation" (a-bhāva being taken in a kind of positive value, as *Fausbøll* suggests), and °-kata would be correct. *cp.* anamatagga.

*an-abhirati, *f.* not delighting in, discontent (*w. loc.*), *acc.* ~iṁ. 47,24 (agāra-majjhe).

*an-abhirata, *mfn.* not taking pleasure in (*loc.*), *m.* ~o (naccādisu) 64,32 (*cp.* abhiramati).

*an-amatagga, *mfn.* endless, *loc.* ~asmiṁ saṁsāre „in the endless revolution of being“ 89,13; °-kathā, *f. acc.* ~aṁ kathesi „he instructed him about Saṁsāra“ 89,15. This word has generally been taken as = *Sa.* *an-amṛta + agra „which does not end in Nibbāṇa“ (*cp.* a-mata above), or *ana-mata (√man) + agra, „whose end is not known“ (*Alwis*, Buddhist Nirv. p. 21., Tr. PM., p. 64, with the negative prefix doubled, like ana-bhāva-kata). *Weber*, Ind. Str. III p. 150 refers to *Sa.* an-āmṛta, „without end or beginning (*cp.* an-āmataṁ „immortal“ Jāt. II 56, 3), but *Jacobi* and *Pischel* have shown that anamatagga must be identical with Prākrit: aṇavadagga or aṇavayagga and have taken it = *Sa.* *a-namadagra (√nam) „dessen Anfang sich nicht verändert, endlos“ (*Jacobi*, Erzähl. 33,17. *Pischel*, Gramm. §251. *cp.* an-abhāvakata above).

an-ariya, *mfn.* ignoble, low, *m.* ~o (anto) 66,27.

an-allīyanta, *v.* allīyati.

an-avakāsa, *mfn.* that cannot take place, impossible, not occurring, *m.* ~o yo . . (*w. pot.*) „it cannot occur that one should . .“, 76,26.

an-avaṭṭhita-citta, *mfn.* unsteady-minded, *gen. m.* ~assa, Dh. 38.

*an-avassuta-citta, *mfn.* whose mind is free from lust, *gen. m.* ~assa. Dh. 39. (*cp.* avassuta, āsava, SBE. X p. 13—14).

an-āgata, *mfn.* future, *acc. m.* ~aṁ (atthaṁ) 112,4; *loc.* (*adv.*) atītânagate, in the past and in the future, 56,11; ~vaṁsa, *q. v.*

*an-āgamana, *n.* not coming, not returning; pacchato kassaci °-bhāvaṁ ñatvā „seeing no one pursuing“, 40,11; asurānaṁ °-atthāya, „to prevent the A's from coming back“, 60,26.

an-āgāra, *m.* houseless, a mendicant, *instr. pl.* ~ehi Dh. 404.

an-ācāra, *m.* misconduct, immorality, *acc.* ~aṁ 9,15. 52,30.

an-ācikkhitvā, *v.* ācikkhati.

an-ātura, *mfn.* free from suffering, *m. pl.* ~ā Dh. 198.

*an-ādāna, *mfn.* free from affection or desire, *m.* ~o Dh. 352, *acc.* ~aṁ Dh. 406 (*opp.* sādāna).

an-āyanta, *v.* āyāti.

*an-ālaya, *m.* not desiring, aversion, doing away with, *nom.* ~o (taṇhāya) 67,16.

an-āvila, *mfn.* clear, pure, undisturbed, *m.* ~o (rahado) Dh. 82, *acc.* ~aṁ Dh. 413.

an-āsakā, *f.* (*sa.* anāçaka, *n.*) fasting, Dh. 141 (*cp.* āsa).

*an-āsava, *mfn.* free from passions, *m. acc.* ~aṁ Dh. 386, *gen.* ~assa, Dh. 94, *pl.* ~ā Dh. 126.

an-āhāra, *mfn.* having or taking no food, being without nutriment, *m.* ~o (aggi) 95,8.

an-ukkaṇṭhamāna, *v.* ukkaṇṭhati.

an-uṭṭhahāna, *v.* uṭṭhahati.

an-uṭṭhāna, *n.* the act of not rising, want of energy or firmness; °-mala, *mfn.* whose taint (fault) is bad repair, *pl.* ~ā gharā „houses are useless, if they are in bad repair“ Dh. 241 (*cp.* mala).

an-uttara, *mfn.* best, highest, unsurpassed, *m.* ~o (sīlagandho) Dh. 55, *acc.* ~aṁ (yogakkhemaṁ) Dh. 23.

an-uddhata, *mfn.* 'not lifted up', calm (in speech), *m.* ~o (bhikkhu) Dh. 363.

*an-upakkamena, *adv.* not by attack (from external enemies) 76,27 (*opp.* parūpakkamena, *v.* upakkama).

an-upagata, an-upagamma, *v.* upagacchati.

an-upaghāta, *m.* not striking, not abusing, *nom.* ~o Dh. 185.

*an-upaddava, *mfn.* uninjured, safe, *loc. n.* ~e (mūle) Dh. 338.

*an-upadduta, *mfn.* not annoyed, not oppressed, *n.* idaṁ . . ~aṁ „here is no distress", 68,14.
*an-upalitta, *mfn.* not besmeared, free from taint, *m.* ~o Dh. 353 (anū–).
*an-upavāda, *m.* not blaming, not abusing, ~o Dh. 185.
*an-upassaṭṭha, *mfn.* not afflicted, not plagued, *n.* idaṁ . . ~am „here is no danger", 68,14.
*an-upahāra, *m.* not presenting, aññassa ~ā (*abl.*) „because it can get no other (fuel)" 95,8.
an-upādā = an-upādāya. & an-upādiyāna, *v.* upādiyati.
*an-upāyena, *adv.* by misguided means, 34,17 (*v.* upāya).
an-uppāda, *m.* not coming into existence; °-dhamma, *mfn.* not liable to come into existence again, *n.* ~aṁ (rupaṁ) 95,11 (*cp.* dhamma).
an-usuyyaṁ, *v.* usuyyati.
an-ussuka, *mfn.* not eager, free from greed, *m. pl.* ~ā Dh. 199.
*an-ussuta, *mfn.* free from lust, *acc. m.* ~aṁ Dh. 400 (= an-avassuta, *q. v.* (Fsb.); *fr. sa.* *an-udsruta (Child.)).
an-ūpalitta = an-upalitta, *q. v.*
an-ūhata, *mfn.* not destroyed, *loc.* ~e Dh. 338 (*v.* ūhaññati).
an-eka, *mfn.* many; °-âkāra, *mfn.* multiform; °-vokāra, *mfn.* containing many disadvantages, *acc. m.* ~aṁ (ādīnavaṁ) 86,8; °-âdīnava, *mfn.* full of dangers, *m.* ~o (samuddo) 23,7; °-jāti-saṁsāra, *m.* a course of many births, *acc.* ~aṁ Dh. 153; °-pariyāyena, *instr. adv.* in many ways, 69,18; °-sūpa-vyañjana, *mfn.* richly supplied with sauce & condiments, *n.* ~aṁ (bahubhattaṁ) 57,11.
*an-eja, *mfn.* free from lust (ejā, *f. q. v.*) *m.* ~o (muni) 80,33, Dh. 414; *acc.* ~aṁ Dh. 422.
an-enta, *v.* eti.
an-oka, *m.* a houseless state, *acc.* ~aṁ (*adv.*?) Dh. 87; °-sārin, *mfn.* wandering about homeless, *acc. m.* ~sāriṁ Dh. 404.
an-okkanta, *v.* okkamati.
*an-odaka, *mfn.* without water, dry, *f.* ~ā (nadī) 31,12.

aṁsa, *m.* (— *sa.*) [1]) a shoulder, *instr.* ~ena paṭicchituṁ nâsakkhi „could not get hold of him by his shoulder" (ɔ: dropped him? or have we to take aṁsena — in part (*adv.*)? and translate „could not thoroughly get hold of him). [2]) (*sa.* aṁça) a part, portion; *v.* ekaṁsa, sukkaṁsa.
akka, *m.* (*sa.* arka) name of a plant (Calotropis gigantea, „swallow-wort" (Child.); *gen.* ~assa (jiyā), made from that plant, 92,16.
akkamati, *vb.* (*sa.* ā-√kram), to tread upon (*acc.*); *ger.* ~itvā 3,21.
akkamma (*sa.* ā-kramya) 108,29.
akkosa, *m.* (*sa.* ākroça) abuse, reproach, *acc.* ~aṁ Dh. 399.
akkosati, *vb.* (*sa.* ā-√kruç), to abuse (*acc.*) *pr. 3. sg.* ~ati (bhikkhū) 84,29; *part.* an-akkosaṁ (*m.* — ~anto, not abusing) 14,4, *m. pl.* ~antā, 73,34.
akkha, *m.* (*sa.* aksha) an axle (of a chariot), *nom.* ~o 98,4.
akkhara, *n.* & *m.* (*sa.* akshara, *n.*) a letter, *gen. pl.* ~anaṁ Dh. 352.
akkhātar, *m.* (*sa.* ākhyātṛ) a preacher, a teacher, *pl.* ~āro (Tathāgatā) „(only) preachers", Dh. 276.
akkhāti, *vb.* (*sa.* ā-√khyā), to tell, communicate; *imp.* ~āhi (taṁ me) 54,37; *pp.* akkhāta, *m.* ~o me maggo „the way was preached by me", Dh. 275; sv-ākkhāto dhammo „well taught is the doctrine", 70,16 (*cp.* su-); samma-d-akkhāta Dh. 86. *v.* sammā; an-akkhāta *q. v.*
akkhi, *n.* (*sa.* akshi) the eye; *pl. nom.* ~ini 3,17; *abl.* ~īhi 5,14; *gen.* ~īnaṁ 59,5. mandakkhī, *adj. f.* 20,27. *v.* manda.
agāra (& āgāra), *n.* (— *sa.*) a house; *nom.* ~aṁ 106,31 = Dh. 14;

pl. ~āni Dh. 140. ²) a household life, *acc.* ~aṁ 61,32. *abl.* ~ā 61,33, ~asmā (pabbajjā) 68,4; °-majjhe „amid a householders life", 46,17. 47,21 (*v.* majjha). — bandhanâgāra, a prison, *v.* bandhana. — suññâgāra, an empty house, *v.* suñña. (*cp.* an-āgāra, an-agāriyā).

*agārika, *m.* (*fr.* agāra) a householder, a layman; °-bhūto, *m.* „while he lived in his house", 69,26 (*cp.* bhavati).

agga, *mfn.* (*sa.* agra) ¹) foremost, first; ~aṁ saṁgahaṁ (*acc.*) „the first collection" 109,29; agga-nikkhittakā (therā) „original depositaries (of Buddha's doctrine)" 109,11; agga-vādo the first or original doctrine = theravādo, 109,30. — ²) highest, topmost; agga-sākhā (*acc. f. pl.*) „the topmost branches" 62,11. — ³) excellent, best, chief, principal; *m.* ~o dhutavādānaṁ „the chief propounder of the Dhutanga" 109,6; agga-dhamma, agga-mahesī, *q. v.*; agga-rasa-, *v.* nānā; agga-rājā „the chief King" 98,13; agga-santike „from the first (among teachers)" 109,28. — ⁴) *subst. n.* top, tip, point: ~aṁ (*acc.*) „the best part" 111,35; at the end of *comp.*: āragge (*loc.*) on the point of a needle (*v.* ārā) Dh. 401; kusaggena (*instr.*) „with the tip of a blade of Kusa-grass", Dh. 70; kūpagge (*loc.*) on the top of the mast, 18,6; rukkhagge, 11,25; sākhagge, 13,22 and sākhaggesu (*loc. pl.*) 1,25 (*v.* sākhā); dumaggamhā (*abl.*) down from the top of the tree, 13,4; -vettaggaṁ 62,17 (*v.* vetta); lābhagga-yasagga-ppatta, *mfn.* having obtained the highest gain and glory, 18,16 (*cp.* patta³); rūpagga-ppatta, *mfn.* of extraordinary beauty, 49,12 (~āya, *gen. f.*) (*cp.* ajjatagge, anamatagga.)

*aggatā, *f.* (*fr.* agga *w. suff.* -tā) superiority; guṇaggataṁ (*acc.*) „the summit of perfection" 109,3.

*agga-dhamma, *mfn.* most excellent in the knowledge of the true doctrine; ~ā tathāgatā (*pl.*) the T-s are the chiefs in the truth, 109,28.

agga-mahesī, *f.* (*sa.* agra-mahishī) a queen, the chief-queen, 19,7. 46,21; *gen.* ~iyā 38,9.

*Aggāḷava, (*m.* or *n.*?) *nom. pr.* a sanctuary at Āḷavī; *loc.* ~e cetiye 86,13; °-vihāraṁ (*acc.*) 87,4. A. seems to be a *comp.* agga + Āḷavī (*q. v.*), but might possibly be a false etymology for *Aggālaya (*sa.* agnyālaya?).

aggi, *m.* (*sa.* agni) ¹) fire; ~i 16,7. 95,8. Dh. 202. 251; aggiva 26,5. Dh. 31; *acc.* ~iṁ kareyyāsi „make a fire" 35,8. ~iṁ jaletvā „to light a fire" 100,24. ~iṁ datvā „to set light to" 51,11; *instr.* ~inā 16,2. 35,4; padīpaggi, the fire of a lamp, 101,7. — ²) a pyre, a funeral pile; ~iṁ pavisitvā 51,10 (as an ordeal). — ³) the sacrificial fire; ~iṁ paricare „to worship Agni" Dh. 107. — ⁴) *metaph.* „passion": dosaggi, mohaggi, rāgaggi (*q. v.*) „the fire of anger, ignorance & lust".

*aggikkhandha, *m.* (aggi + khandha) a great body of fire; ~o 26,3 (pajjalita-°).

aggidaḍḍha, *mfn.* (aggi + daḍḍha, *pp. v.* ḍahati) burnt by fire; ~o Dh. 136.

*Aggimāla, *m.*(?) *nom. pr.* (aggi + māla = mālā?) name of an ocean; *acc.* ~aṁ 26,3. — *Aggimāli(n), *m.*(?) *id.* (= „fire-garlanded") 26,8.

*Aggi-Vacchagotta-suttanta, *n.* the title of a dialogue between Buddha and Vacchagotta, MN. 72.

aggisikhā, *f.* (*sa.* agni-çikhā) a flame; °-sikh'ūpama, *mfn.* „like flaming fire", ~o (ayoguḷo) 107,1 = Dh. 308 (*cp.* upama).

aggihutta, *n.* (*sa.* agni-hotra) oblation to Agni; *acc.* ~aṁ juhato, sacrificing to Agni, 103,8. — ²) the sacrificial fire, Dh. 392.

aggha, *m.* (*sa.* argha) value, price; in *comp.* an-aggha, *mfn.* *q. v.* beyond all price, invaluable; appaggha. *mfn.* of little value, 26,2; mahaggha (*v.* mahā) *mfn.* of great price, *n.* ~aṁ 25,5.

*agghati, *vb.* (*sa.* √argh), to be worth (*w. acc.*); *pr. 3. sg.* na ~ati (mama sāmikassa padarajaṁ) 58,5; nâgghati (kalaṁ soḷasiṁ) Dh. 70. *caus.* agghāpeti, *q. v.*

*agghanaka, *mfn.* (*fr.* agghana, *n.* (√argh) valuation, *w. suff.* -ka) worth; satasahassagghanakaṁ (muttāhāraṁ. *acc. m.*) worth 100,000, 64,25.

*agghāpaniya, *m.* (*fr.* agghāpana, *n.* (agghāpeti)) a valuer; °-kamma, *n.* the office of a valuer, *loc.* ~e 24,18.

*agghāpeti, *vb. caus.* (*fr.* agghati), to appraise; *pr. 3. sg.* ~eti 24,20 (*acc.*).

aṁka, *m.* (— *sa.*) a side, breast, hip; *instr.* ~ena uddharī (maṁ), lifted (me) up unto her hip, 20,35; dārake aṁkenâdāya, with their childs on their hips, 21,2; *loc.* ~e nisinnaṁ puttaṁ „a baby boy“ 38,15.

aṁkura, *m.* (— *sa.*) a sprout, a shoot; °-nibbattana-ṭṭhāna, *n.* the place where the sprout develops, 37,5.

aṅkusa, *m.* (*sa.* aṅkuça) a hook to guide an elephant with, a goad; *instr. pl.* ~ehi 77,12. — aṅkusa-ggaha, *m.* (*sa.* aṅkuça-graha) an elephant-driver, Dh. 326.

aṅga, *n.* (— *sa.*) [1]) a limb, member, a part of the body; uttamaṅga, the head, °-ruha. *mfn.* growing on the head, *pl. m.* ~ā (ɔ: the hairs) 45,11; aṅgavijjā, *q. v.* — [2]) a part or portion; aṅga-sambhārā (*abl.*), bringing together the various parts, 98,30; sabbaṅga-sampanna, *mfn.* complete in every part, 110,13. — [3]) a point or a constituent part of a system of rules; uposathaṅgāni (*pl.*), the holy day wows, 61,7; bojjhaṅga, sambodhi-aṅga, & Aṅguttara (*q. v.*). — [4]) a quality, attribute, *instr. pl.* dasah(i) aṅgehi, 82,14. — [5]) *comp. w. num.* ~ -fold (*cp.* aṅgika & aṅgin), navaṅga, *mfn.* nine-fold, ~aṁ Jinasāsanaṁ 109,22. — [6]) *comp. w. vb.*: aṅgī, *v.* sam-aṅgī-bhūta.

aṅgaṇa, *n.* (*sa.* aṅgana) an open space before a house; rājaṅgaṇa, the king's courtyard, *loc.* ~e 8,1. 42,30. — [2]) *metaph.* (only in comp. with the prefixes an-, nir-, sa-) the mean or vulgar life ɔ: lust, sin; an-aṅgana, *mfn.* (*q. v.*) [cp. *Böhtlingk*, Ber. d. sächs. Ges. 1898. p. 77; *Rhys Davids*, JRAS. 1898. p. 193 & 462.].

aṅga-vijjā, *f.* (*sa.* aṅga-vidyā) the science of prognostication, chiromantia etc.: *loc.* ~āya 48,16.

aṅgāra, *m.* (— *sa.*) charcoal, burning coals, fire; *loc.* ~e 15,32; °-gabbhe, amid the fire, 15,33 (*v.* gabbha); °-rāsi, *m.* a heap of burning coals, *acc.* ~iṁ 16,3.

aṅgika, *mfn.* (*sa.* aṅgaka) *comp. w. num. v.* aṭṭhaṅgika, pañcaṅgika (*cp.* aṅga [5]) & *next*).

aṅgin, *mfn.* (— *sa.*) *comp. w. num. v.* caturaṅgin (*cp.* aṅga [5]) & *prec.*).

*Aṅguttara-nikaya, *m. nom. pr.* (*fr.* aṅga + uttara ɔ: one part more, „the add-one collection“, cp. *Morris*, preliminary remarks, AN. vol. I. p. IX.), name of a canonical Pāli-work, the fourth of the five Nikāyas; comm. Manoratha-pūraṇī (*q. v.*); ~o 102,14.

aṅgula, *m.* (— *sa.*) a finger, the measure of a finger's breadth, an inch; *v.* catur-aṅgula, *mfn.*

aṅguli, *f.* (— *sa.*) a finger; *v.* pañcaṅgulika.

*Aciravatī, *f. nom. pr.* a river in India (Rapti); °-tīraṁ, *n.* the bank of A. 28,4.

accagamā & accagā, *v.* atigacchati (*cp.* upaccagā).

accanta, *mfn.* (*fr.* ati + anta, *sa.* atyanta), excessive, perpetual; *adv.* ~aṁ, in perpetuity, absolutely: nâccanta[ṁ], not always, 5,21. — °-sukhumāla, *m.* „an exceedingly delicate prince" 97,34. — °-dussīlya, *n.* „very great wickedness" Dh. 162.

accaya, *m.* (*sa.* atyaya, *cp.* atigacchati). [1]) passing away, lapse (of time), end, death; *instr. adv.* ~ena „at the end of" (*w. gen.* or *in comp.*): pitu ~ena „when his father died" 24,13; mam' accayena 79,5; tassā rattiyā a-° „at the end of the night" 78,1; ekāha-dvīha-° „in one or two days" 32,24; katipāha-° „a few days later" 49,33; satt'-aṭṭha-divas'-a° „seven or eight days later" 35,1; māsaddhamāsa-° „at the end of one and a half month" 20,11. — [2]) transgression, sin; ~o mam accagamā „transgression has overcome me" 75,23; tassa me Bhagavā accayaṁ accayato paṭigaṇhātu „may Bh. accept the confession I make of my sin" 75,25; the words accayaṁ accayato (*acc. & abl.*) may originally be due to phrases like ~aṁ ~ato passati (Vin. I, 315) „to see the sin in its sinfullness", or ~aṁ ~ato deseti (SN. I, 239) „to confess, to apologize. — [3]) overcoming, conquering; dur-accaya, *mfn.* difficult to be conquered, *acc. f.* ~aṁ (taṇhaṁ) 108,1.

acci, *f.* (*sa.* arci(s), *m. n.*), a flame; *nom.* yā acci 99,21.

acchati, *vb.* (*sa.* √ās) to sit, stay, remain; *pr. 3. pl.* ~anti 76,29. The *pr.* acchati seems to be a later formation from aor. acchi (*sa.* *ātsīt) *cp.* Tr. PM. 61,3; *K. F. Johansson*, Idg. F. III 205. (= *sa.* ṛcchati, *Pischel*, Gr. § 480.)

*accharā, *f.* a snap with the fingers; °-sadda, *m.* ~ena (*instr.*) „at the snapping of the fingers" 18,17.

acchariya, *mfn.* (*sa.* āçcarya) marvellous, wonderful, astonishing; *f.* ~ā (Buddhānaṁ kathā) 86,24; *n.* ~aṁ (in exclamations) how wonderful! 79,25. 98,32; *s. n.* a wonder, a marvel; *acc.* ~aṁ 3,22. 5,19; *pl. acc.* ~āni 25,9. (*cp.* accheraka).

acchādana, *n.* (*sa.* ācch-°) covering, clothes; ~aṁ 31,3-9. — sāmika-° the protection of a husband, ~aṁ (*acc.*) 31,7-8.

acchādeti, *vb. caus.* (*sa.* ā-√chad) to array in (*acc. & instr.*), to put on (clothes, *acc.*); *ger.* ~etvā (taṁ dibbavatthehi) 20,8; ~(ahatavatthāni) 33,3.

*accheraka, *mfn.* (*fr.* acchariya *w. suff.* -ka). ati-acch-° *mfn.* admirable, extraordinary; *n.* ~aṁ 3,29.

aja, *m.* (= *sa.*) a goat, a ram; ~o 54,8; *voc.* aja, 54.12; *pl.* ~ā 54,12. — aja-rāja (*voc.*) 54,26. — ajikā, *f.* a she-goat; *acc.* ~aṁ 54,8. (*cp.* ajina).

Ajātasattu, *m. nom. pr.* (*sa.* Ajāta-çatru ɔ: having no enemy) a son of king Bimbisāra (*q. v.*). °-kumāra, *m.* the prince A. ~o 75,1; ~aṁ (*acc.*) 75,2.

ajikā, *v.* aja.

ajina, *n.* (= *sa.*) a skin (of a goat (?) *esp.* of the black antelope, used by ascetics). °-sāṭī, *f.* a garment of skins; *instr.* ~iyā 106,10. = Dh. 394.

ajja, *adv.* (*sa.* adya) to-day, now, 2,30. 3,14; ajjâpi tâva „until this day" (*w. pr. of the verb*) 10,13; ajj'eva „this very day" 65,13; ajj'ahaṁ Dh. 326.

*ajjatagge, *adv.* (*fr.* ajjato [*sa.* *adya-tas] + agge, *v.* agga[4])) from this day forth, henceforth, 69,30. (*cp. Weber*, Ind. Str. III. 150.).

ajjatana, *mfn.* (*sa.* adyatana) of to-day, modern (*opp.* porāṇa); *n.* ~aṁ Dh. 227 (*metri causa* ~āṁ). ~āya, *adv.* (*dat.* or *loc. f.*?) to-day 70,10.

ajjhagā, ajjhagu, *v.* adhi-gacchati.

ajjhatta, *n.* (*sa.* adhy-ātman) the soul, individual thought. °-samuṭṭhāna, *mfn.* originating from internal (intellectual) cultivation. *f.* ~ā (hiri) 10,16 (*opp.* bahiddhā-samuṭṭhāna). — °-rata, *mfn.* delighting inwardly, *m.* ~o Dh. 362.

ajjhattika, *mfn.* (*sa.* adhy-ātmika), belonging to the soul or to the individual; *n. pl.* ~āni āyatanāni, the internal senses, 82,11.

ajjhabhāsi, *v.* adhi-bhāsati.

ajjhavāsayi, *v.* adhi-vāseti.

ajjhāya, *m.* (*sa.* adhyāya) reading, *v.* sajjhāya.

ajjhā-vasati, *vb.* (*sa.* adhy-ā-√vas) to inhabit (*acc.*); *fut. 3. sg.* ~issati (agāraṁ) „to live a household life" 61,31.

*ajjhāsaya, *m.* (*fr. sa.* adhi + āçaya (√çi)) meaning, intention; sabbesaṁ °-gahaṇatthaṁ (*cp.* attha), in order to hear the meaning of the assembly, 11,4.

*ajjhokāsa, *m.* (*fr.* adhi + okāsa, *q. v.*) the open air, an open place; *loc.* ~e (caṅkamati) 68,9.

*ajjhottharati, *pr.* (*fr.* *adhi-ava-√stṛ) to strew about, to throw on the ground (*acc.*) *ger.* ~itvā (turiyāni) 65,3.

*ajjhoharati, *vb.* (*fr.* adhi-ava-√hṛ) to eat, to swallow (*acc.*) *inf.* ~ituṁ (ambaphalaṁ) 37,35.

añjana, *n.* (— *sa.*) black pigment. °-vaṇṇa, *mfn.* black-coloured, *gen. pl.* ~ānaṁ (kesānaṁ) 44,24.

añjali, *m.* (— *sa.*) the two palms joined; *acc.* ~iṁ paggayha, raising (their) joined hands (as a mark of supplication) 22,4; ~iṁ pagganhitvā. *id.* (respectfully) 30,6; ~iṁ paṇāmetvā, *id.* 74,20.

añña, *pron.* (*sa.* anya) *m.* ~o, *f.* ~ā, *n.* ~aṁ, *acc. mfn.* ~aṁ, *instr. m. n.* ~ena, *gen. m. n.* ~assa, *f.* ~issā; *pl. m.* ~e, *instr. m. n.* ~ehi, *gen. m. n.* ~esaṁ, *loc. m. n.* ~esu. [1]) other, another (not the same, different or similar) 6,35. 7,3. 61,28. 74,3; 7,9 (~assa, *opp.* ekassa), 99,2 (~o, *opp.* so eva); Dh. 158 (~aṁ, *opp.* attānaṁ), *cp.* Dh. 252. 355; añño pi. 5,31; ~assa purisassa (a paramour) 9,13, ~aṁ (*sc.* purisaṁ, *id.*) 9,28; ~ena pariyāyena, 91,11 = ~enâkārena, 91,32 (in another way o: wrong); *comp.* añña-purisaṁ 48,12. — [2]) another, a second, a new (by way of addition) 4,23. 18,9; ~ehi dvīhi (still two) 34,9. — [3]) the rest, the others (*pl. & n. sg.*) 33,16. 34,24; ~esu divasesu (on the preceeding days) 13,10. 65,21; aññe sattā (other mortals) 62,25; *n.* aññaṁ (everything else, *opp.* idam eva) 89,35. — [4]) *with a negation:* the only one, none but; ~o gamanamaggo n'atthi, 3,14; ~ā patiṭṭhā n'atthi (ṭhapetvā tīṇi saraṇāni) 28,35. — [5]) *pleonastically:* ~aṁ saṁvaccharaṁ (a whole year) 33,17; ~aṁ aphāsukaṁ n'atthi (no sickness) 49,28. — [6]) *repeated:* [a]) one, . . another (in different way) 67,29. 67,30. 99,10; ~aṁ jīvaṁ ~aṁ sarīraṁ (*opp.* taṁ) 89,28. *cp.* Dh. 75. [b]) *reciprocally:* one-another (one towards or with another *etc.*) ~o ~aṁ Dh. 165; often *comp.:* aññamaññaṁ, *adv.* 11,20. 11,27. 19,14. 33,20-21. 74,5. — [7]) *combined with other pron.:* yo añño (every other who) 34,21; ~aṁ kiṁ (anything further) 41,7; na añño koci (nobody else) 51,8; ~aṁ kiñci kāthetvā („told some lie") 53,9; mā ~aṁ kiñci āsaṁkittha („you ought not to suppose that there is anything behind this") 7,11; ~aṁ kiñca yathicchitaṁ („every other service according to your desire") 111,28. — *cp.* para, apara, itara, aññatara.

*añña-khantika, *m(fn).* (*fr.* añña + khanti) „belonging to another faith"; *instr. m.* ~ena (tayā) 94,26.

aññatara, *pron.* (*compar. fr.* añña, *sa.* anyatara). [1]) a certain, some; *m.* ~o 32,9; *acc.* ~aṁ 3,30; *gen.* ~assa 9,9; *loc.* ~asmiṁ 30,23; *acc. f.* ~aṁ 30,28. — [2]) one of a certain number (*w. gen. of the numeral*) Dh. 137. 157. — [3]) another; *gen. m.* ~assa purisassa (another man's) 100,11; aññatara-vesena 55,29 („in disguise" *cp.* vesa; perhaps we have to read: aññātaka-° as 43,12).

*añña-titthiya, *m(fn).* (*sa.* anya + tīrtha), heretical; *pl.* ~ā, the heretics, 72,26; *instr.* ~ehi 74,9 *cp.* titthiya).

aññattha, *adv.* (*sa.* anyatra) elsewhere, to another place, 12,35. 49,15 (*cp. next*).

aññatra, [1]) *adv.* (= *prec.*) elsewhere, except, save; aññatra Tathāgatassa

(„save by the T.", the *gen.* being due to the prec. tassa) 78,17. — [2]) *prp.* besides (*w. acc.*) 97,28. — *aññatra-yoga, *m(fn).* having another discipline; *instr. m.* ~ena (tayā) 94,27. (*cp.* yoga).

aññathatta, *n.* (*sa.* anyathātva *cp. next*) variation, difference; ~aṁ 114,22.

aññathā, *adv.* (*sa.* anyathā) otherwise. — *aññathācariyaka, *m(fn).* having another teacher (*cp.* ācariya); ~ena (tayā) 94,27.

***añña-diṭṭhika**, *m(fn).* belonging to another sect (*cp.* diṭṭhi); ~ena (tayā) 94,26.

aññamaññaṁ, *adv. v.* añña[6])

***añña-rucika**, *m(fn).* having another inclination (*cp.* ruci); ~ena (tayā) 94,26-27.

aññā, *f.* (*sa.* ājñā) knowledge. — samma-d-aññā-vimutta, *mfn.* who has become free through perfect knowledge; *gen.* ~assa Dh. 96. *pl.* ~ānaṁ, Dh. 57. (*cp.* ājānāti).

aññāya, **aññāsi**, *v.* ājānāti.

aṭavi, *f.* (= *sa.*) a forest; *loc.* ~iyaṁ 30,30; ~i-mukhe „on the outskirt of a forest" 30,29. (*cp.* mukha).

aṭṭa[1], *mfn.* (*sa.* ārta, *cp.* aṭṭiyati, √ard.) afflicted, pained, suffering. — aṭṭassara, *m.* a cry of pain or distress, ~aṁ (*acc.*) 40,21 (*cp.* sara[3]). — vedanaṭṭa, *mfn.* oppressed by pain, *m.* ~o 50,30.

aṭṭa[2], *m.* (*sa.* artha, *cp.* attha[1] & aṭṭha[2]), case, cause, lawsuit, litigation; *acc.* ~aṁ 59,4; aṭṭatthāya (uparavo) on account of litigations 42,30. — kūṭaṭṭa, false suit (*q. v.*).

aṭṭaka, *m.* (*dimin. fr.* aṭṭa, a watchtower, — *sa.*) a tower, a platform; *acc.* ~aṁ 73,32. cp. *Morris*, JPTS. '86,104.

***aṭṭiyati**, *vb.* (also written attiyati or addh°-, add°-, *denom. fr.* aṭṭa[1], *cp.* √ard & √ṛt) to feel annoyed or bored, to be incommodated or tormented; *part. f.* ~mānā 50,1. [*cp. Morris*, JPTS. '86,104-05.].

aṭṭha[1], *num.* (*sa.* ashṭa-) eight. [1]) *indecl.* 23,22. 82,12. — [2]) *comp.* aṭṭhūsabha-matta, *mfn.* of a measure of 8 usabhas (*q. v.*) ~aṁ ṭhānaṁ 27,27 (*acc.*). — satt'-aṭṭha-divas'-accayena (seven or eight days) 35,1. (*cp.* aṭṭhaṅgika, aṭṭhama, aṭṭhārasama).

aṭṭha[2] — attha[1] (*q. v.*) *in the comp.* *aṭṭha-kathā, *f.* a commentary, the commentary on the Buddhist holy scriptures; *nom.* ~ā (*opp.* Pāli) 113,26; *acc.* ~aṁ 114,7; *instr.* ~āya 114,25. — *comp. w. the prefix* sa- (*adj.*): sāṭṭhakathā pāli (the text with the commentary) 102,3. — parittaṭṭhakathaṁ (*acc.* a concise or compendious commentary) 113,24. — Sihalaṭṭhakathā (the Sinhalese A.) 113,28; *acc. pl.* ~ā (sabbā) 114,27. (*cp.* aṭṭa[2]).

***aṭṭhaṅgika**, *mfn.* (*fr.* aṭṭha[1] + aṅga *w. pref.* -ka, *cp. sa.* ashṭāṅga) consisting of 8 parts, eightfold; *m.* ~o (maggo) 67,3. 82,12. Dh. 273; *acc.* ~aṁ (maggaṁ) Dh. 191.

aṭṭhama, *mfn.* (*sa.* ashṭama) the eighth; *m.* ~o 103,28 (ɔ: aṭṭhamī (*f.*) senā Mārassa).

aṭṭhārasa, *num.* (*sa.* ashṭādaça-) eighteen. — aṭṭhārasama, *mfn.* (*sa.* ashṭādaça) the eighteenth; *m.* ~o (Malavaggo) Dh. XVIII.

aṭṭhi, *n.* (*sa.* asthi) [1]) a bone; *nom.* ~i 13,11; *coll.* (bones) 82,3 — 97,30; *acc.* ~iṁ 13,14; *pl.* ~īni Dh. 149; *gen.* ~īnaṁ Dh. 150. — [2]) the stone of a fruit; ~i 37,6; *acc.* -iṁ 36,35; *abl.* ~ito 37,5. — aṭṭhi-koṭi, *f.* the end of a bone; *acc.* ~iṁ 13,30. — aṭṭhi-miñjā, *f.* (*q. v.*) (*cp. next*).

aṭṭhika, *n.* (*sa.* asthika) a bone; hanukaṭṭhikena (*instr.*) by the jawbone. 40,18 (*v.* hanu(ka)).

***aṭṭhi-karoti**, *vb.* (*perhaps fr.* artha, *cp. sa.* kad-arthī- √kṛ, (Tr.)) to attend, to pay attention to (*synon. w.* manasi-karoti, *q. v.*); *ger.* ~katvā 71,23. [*cp. Morris*, JPTS. '86,107; *Fausböll*, Sn. vol. II,28 (*fr. sa.* ashṭi (√aç) „reaching"); *Windisch*, Māra, p. 100 (= *sa.* āsthāṁkṛtvā „Acht geben");

Warren, Buddhism, p. 349 „to be convinced"].

*aṭṭhi-miñjā, *f.* (*sa.* *asthi-majjan) the marrow of bones, 82,5 = 97,20. [*cp. Morris*, JPTS. '85,29-30.]

aṭṭhūsabha-matta, *v.* aṭṭha[1].

aḍḍha, *m. & n.* (also written addha (*q. v.*), *sa.* ardha) a half. °-nālika-matta, *mfn.* of the measure of a half nālika (*q. v.*), *acc. m.* ~aṁ (taṇḍulaṁ) 57,18. – °-ratta-samaye (*loc.*) at midnight, 40,8. *cp.* upaḍḍha, diyaḍḍha & *next*.

aḍḍhatiya, *mfn.* (a shortened form of aḍḍha-teyya, or from *aḍḍha-tatiya with elision of -ta- (like viññāṇañca-, *q. v.*)) two and a half; *n. pl.* ~āni (purisa-satāni) 33,20. – aḍḍhatiya-sata, *mfn.* „250"; *m. acc. pl.* ~e (jane) 34,7.

aḍḍhateyya, *mfn.* (a prakritic formation from *sa.* ardha-tṛtīya) two and a half. – °-sata, *mfn.* „250"; *m. pl.* ~ā 21,31, *acc.* ~e 21,33.

aṇu (or anu) *mfn.* (= *sa.*) fine, small (*opp.* thūla). *aṇuṁthūla, (*mf*)*n.* small and large, Dh. 409; ~aṁ (saññojanaṁ) Dh. 31; *n. pl.* ~āni (pāpāni) Dh. 265.

aṇumatta, *mfn.* (*sa.* aṇu-mātra) small, atomic. *m.* ~o pi (vanatho) „even the smallest" Dh. 284 [anu-]; *acc.* ~aṁ (dubbhāsitaṁ padaṁ) 110,12; *instr. n.* ~ena (puññena) „even the least (good work)" 103,14 [but here the Birman reading aṇumatto (*sc.* attho) ought to be preferred].

aṇḍa, *n.* (= *sa.*) an egg. °-bhūta, *mfn.* (*cp.* bhavati) fragile, weak; *f.* ~ā (bhatā bhariyā) „from her childhood" 51,4. – Aṇḍabhūta-jātaka, *n.* 52,11. (*cp.* andha-bhūta).

ati, *indecl.* (before vowels usually acc-, *v.* accanta, accaya *etc.* = *sa.*) prefix [1]) to verbs, expressing „beyond, over"; [2]) to nouns „excessive(ly), extraordinary(-ily), too much" (= ativiya, *q. v.*).

*ati-accheraka, *mfn.* ~aṁ (*n.*) a very wonderful thing, 3,22.

*ati-karuṇa, *mfn.* very pitiable or miserable; *m.* ~o (ravo) 60,10; °-sara, *m.* (*v.* sara[3]), *acc.* ~aṁ 27,14.

atikkama, *m.* (*sa.* ati-krama) overcoming, conquering; *acc.* ~aṁ (dukkhassa) „the destruction (of pain)" 107,19 = Dh. 191.

atikkamati, *vb.* (*sa.* ati-√kram) [1]) to pass, cross. [2]) to surpass, overcome (*w. acc.*). *part. m. pl.* ~antā 26,32; an-atikkamanto (*m.*) not surpassing o: accompagnying (gītassaraṁ tantissarena) 19,32. *pot. 3. sg.* ~eyya (saññojanaṁ sabbaṁ) Dh. 221. *pp. n. pl.* atikkantāni (tīṇi saṁvaccharāni) 21,11. *ger.* ~itvā (samuddaṁ) 26,2; (simaṁ) 39,18; atikamma (Kāsiraṭṭhaṁ) „having left" 38,21. *caus.* atikkameti (*q. v.*)

atikkamana, *n.* (*sa.* atikramaṇa) overstepping. – *atikkamanaka, *mfn.* exceeding (*w. acc.*): paṇṇasaññaṁ °-migo, 8,10.

atikkameti, *pr.* (*caus.* atikkamati) to cause to pass or to be passed over; *imp. 2. sg.* ~ehi (mayhaṁ vāraṁ) 6,31. *fut. 1. sg.* ~essāmi (te vāraṁ) 7,2.

*ati-khīṇa, *mfn.* (*fr.* ati + khīṇa, *pp.* √kshi?) destroyed, broken; capâtikhīṇā va (*m. pl.*) „like broken bows" Dh. 156.

ati-ga, *mfn.* (= *sa.*) overcoming, surmounting. *m.* pañca-saṅgâtigo (bhikkhu) Dh. 370; *acc.* saṅgâtigaṁ, Dh. 397.

atigacchati, *pr.* (*sa.* ati-√gam & √gā) to overcome. *aor. 3. sg.* acc-a-gamā (maṁ) 75,23; acc-a-gā (mohaṁ) Dh. 414.

ati-gāḷha, *mfn.* (*sa.* ati-gāḍha, *pp.* √gāh) very tight or close, intensive; *f.* ~ā (kappanā) 65,21.

*ati-citra, *mfn.* (*sa.* *ati + citra) excellent, brilliant; *n. pl.* ~āni (pañhapaṭibhānāni 98,33.

*ati-tuṭṭhi, *f.* (*fr. sa.* ati + tushṭi) extreme joy; *instr.* ~iyā 10,13.

ati-dūra, *mfn.* (= *sa.*) very distant, too far; *loc. n.* (*adv.*) ~e 12,29. 83,2 (nâtidūre).

*ati-dhona-cārin, *mfn.* 'wandering in transgression', sinful; *acc. m.* ~inaṁ 106,20 = Dh. 240. (The etymology of this word is a little doubtful, but it seems to be preferable to take it = *ati-dhāvana-cārin (√dhāv[1], to run). *Morris.* JPTS. '87,100 and *Franke.* WZ. 1901 derive it from *dhona (pure, √dhāv[2] to wash) *sa.* dhauta: „practising impurity, transgressing purity", „der wider die Reinheit verstösst").

atipāta, *m.* (= *sa.*) neglect, transgression, injuring. pāṇātipāta, destroying life (*q. v.*)

*ati-bahala, *mfn.* (*fr.* ati + bahala) very thick; *f.* ~ā yāgu? „is the rice-gruel thick enough?" 56,29 (the questioner seems to think that the rice-gruel is very thin or weak (nâtibahalā) and gets that enigmatical answer: udakaṁ na laddhaṁ „it has not got any water").

*ati-bhagini-putta, *m.* (*fr.* ati + bhagini-putta, *q.v.*) a very dear nephew (ironically), ~o 5,5.

atimaññati, *vb.* (*sa.* ati-√man) to despise; *pr. 3. sg.* ~ati Dh. 366; *pot. 3. sg.* ~eyya Dh. 365 (*w. acc.* salābhaṁ).

*ati-manorama, *mfn.* (*fr.* ati + mano-rama, *q.v.*) very charming; *instr. n.* ~ena (sirisobhaggena) 64,10.

*ati-mahanta. *mfn.* (*fr.* ati + mahanta (*sa.* mahat)) very great (big or large); *loc. m.* nâtimahante (sare) 3,32.

*atimāpeti. *vb.* (*caus.* *ati-√mī (māpayati)) to injure, to destroy (*acc.*); *pr. 3. sg.* ~eti Dh. 246 (pāṇaṁ).

*ati-muduka, *mfn.* (*fr.* ati + muduka, *q.v.*) very soft, mild or feeble; *m.* ~o (rājā) 38,24.

atirocati, *vb.* (*sa.* ati-√ruc) to shine forth; *pr. 3. sg.* ~ati Dh. 59.

ativattati, *vb.* (*sa.* √vṛt) to overcome (*acc.*); *pr. 3. sg.* ~ati (diṭṭhaṁ) 3,27.

*ati-vasa, *mfn.* (*fr.* ati + vasa (*sa.* vaça)) thoroughly subject to or dependent on (*gen.*); *m. pl.* ~ā (mama) Dh. 74.

*ati-vākya, *n.* (*fr.* ati + vākya, *cp. sa.* ati-√vac) abuse; *acc.* ~aṁ Dh. 320.

ativiya, *adv.* (*sa.* atīva) very, excessively; ~sūro hutvā 38,31; ~dhammiko rājā 39,8; ~pabbajjāya cittaṁ nami 65,12.

*ati-sītala, *mfn.* (*fr.* ati + sītala (*sa.* çītala)) very cold; *m.* ~o (aggi) 16,10.

atiharati, *vb.* (*sa.* ati-√hṛ) to carry over, to bring; *aor. 3. sg.* ~ri (dhuttaṁ māṇavikāya santikaṁ) 50,5.

atīta, *mfn.* (*sa. pp.* ati-√i) [1]) past, passed away, dead; atīta-jāti, *f.* a former existence, *loc.* ~iyaṁ 85,12; *atīta-satthuka, *mfn.* having no master more, *n.* ~aṁ pāvacanaṁ („the holy word has no announcer more") 79,3; khaṇātīta, *mfn.* who allows the right moment to pass, *m. pl.* ~ā 108,7 = Dh. 315. — [2]) *act.* who has neglected or transgressed, *m. gen.* ~assa (ekaṁ dhammaṁ) 106,14 = Dh. 176. — [3]) *subst. n.* the past, an event of the past, a tale; *loc.* (*adv.*) atīte, formerly, in the times of past, 1,3. 2,17 *etc*; atītânāgate (*opp.* etarahi) in the past and in the future, 56,11 (*cp.* an-āgata); *acc.* ~aṁ āhari (told a tale of the past) 28,17.

Atula, *m. nom. pr.* an Upāsaka; *voc.* ~a Dh. 227.

atta[1], *mfn.* (*sa.* ātta. *pp.* ā-√dā) seized, *v.* atta-daṇḍa, atta-mana.

atta[2], *in comp.* = attan („self") *q. v. cp.* sayaṁ.

*atta-kilamatha, *m.* (*fr.* atta[2] + kilamatha (*sa.* klamatha)) mortification; °-ânuyoga. *mfn.* given to mortification, *m.* ~ 66,27 (*cp.* anuyoga).

*atta-gutta, *mfn.* (*fr.* atta[2] + gutta (*sa.* gupta, *pp.* √gup)) self-protected; *m.* ~o Dh. 379.

*atta-ghañña, *n.* (*fr.* atta[2] + ghañña (*cp. sa.* ghānya, √han)) destruction of one's self; *dat.* ~āya „to his own destruction" Dh. 164.

atta-ja, *mfn.* (*fr.* atta[2] + ja, *sa.* ātmaja) born from one's self; *n.* ~aṁ (pāpaṁ) Dh. 161.

***atta-daṇḍa** *mfn.* (*fr.* atta[1] + daṇḍa, *q. v.*) using the stick, violent (*opp.* nibbuta); *m. pl. loc.* ~esu Dh. 406.

***attadattha**, *m.* (*fr.* atta[2] + attha[1], with d euphonically inserted) one's own advantage, what is useful to one's self (with regard to one's moral improvement or to the development of one's spiritual faculties; *opp.* parattha. *q. v.*); *acc.* ~aṁ Dh. 166 (*cp.* SBE. X 46). *cp.* sadattha-pasuta.

***atta-danta**, *mfn.* (*fr.* atta[2] + danta, *pp.* √dam) having tamed one's self; *m.* ~o Dh. 322; *gen.* ~assa (posassa) Dh. 104.

attan (*in comp.* atta-) *m. sg.* (*sa.* ātman) [1]) the individual soul, self, person, the Ego (the real existence of which is denied, *cp.* puggala, nāmarūpa, jīva); *nom.* attā 55,2. Dh. 62. 104. 160; 'attā me'ti „a so-called (imagined) myself" or „thinking that I have a soul" 96,13; *instr.* attanā Dh. 161; attanā sudantena „by his own welltamed self" Dh. 160. 323; *abl.* attanā añño piyataro n'atthi 54,33. — [2]) *instr.* attanā is frequently used like *nom.* (in apposition to the grammatical subject) = „himself" (*lit.* „by himself") : 34,16 (attanâpi) 34,23-25. 38,18. 42,1. 49,21. 54,8. Dh. 379. — [3]) *acc.* attānaṁ (contracted attaṁ) and the other oblique cases (*esp. gen.* attano) are used as *pron. reflex.* referring to the gramm. subject in all persons, genders, and numbers = myself (ourselves), yourself (~selves), himself (herself, itself, one's self, themselves). attānaṁ : *3. sg.* 12,27. 54,31. 55,1 (attaṁ) Dh. 159. 355 (attanaṁ metri causa) 379 (attaṁ); *1. sg.* 3,15. 27,22; *3. pl.* 106,28 — Dh. 80. *instr.* attanā : *3. sg.* 17,4 (kata-kammaṁ) 20,27 (maṁ uddhari); *1. sg.* 29,2 (dinna-dāne). *gen.* attano : *3. sg.* 2,14. 10,5. 52,32. Dh. 160; *2. sg.* 9,23. 12,35; *1. sg.* 7,9; *3. pl.* 5,9. 73,24; *2. pl.* 17,1. 41,22. attano attano („each . . . his own") 14,11-14 (*3. pl.*); 41,23 (referring to the gramm. object). — atta-vetana-bhata, *mfn.* „supporting one's self by one's own earnings" 105,5. — an-atta, *mfn.* destitute of a self (*q. v.*). — ojit-tatta, *mfn.* having secured one's self (*v.* ojita). — paccattaṁ, *adv.* by one's self (*q. v.*). — pahitatta, *mfn.* whose mind is intent upon (*v.* pahita, *cp.* padhāna). — bhāvitatta, *mfn.* having trained one's self (*v.* bhāveti). — atta-kilamatha *etc.* (*qv.*). — Atta-vagga, *m.* name of a chapter of Dhammapada. Dh. XII.

atta-bhāva, *m.* (*fr.* atta[2] + bhāva, *sa.* ātmabhāva) [1]) proper or peculiar nature, body, figure; *acc.* ~aṁ 52,29. 64,16. — [2]) birth, existence; *nom.* ~o (pañcasatimo) 17,8; pañcasu [0]-satesu „in 500 of my former existences" 17,7.

atta-mana, *mfn.* (*fr.* atta[1] + manas, *sa.* āttamanas) joyful, delighted, happy; *m.* ~o 93,18. Dh. 328. *f.* ~ā 62,24. — an-attamana, *mfn.* displeased, *m.* ~o 74,30.

atta-sambhava, *mfn.* (*fr.* atta[2] + sambhava, *sa.* ātmasambhava) originating from one's self; *n.* ~aṁ (pāpaṁ) Dh. 161.

***atta-hetu**, *adv.* (*fr.* atta[2] + hetu (*q. v.*)) for one's own sake. Dh. 84 (*opp.* parassahetu).

***attānuyogin**, *mfn.* (*fr.* atta[2] + anuyogin) who exerts himself in meditation, Dh. 209 (*gen. pl.* ~inaṁ).

attha[1], *m.* (*sa.* artha) [1]) aim, purpose, sake, reason; *instr.* yen' atthena idhâgato 103,13 („the reason for which you have come here", corresponding to the foll. attho (?); but „yena" is probably an error for sena (*sa.* svenârthena)); *dat.* atthāya and *acc.* atthaṁ are frequently used at the end of *comp.* (*adv.*) = „for the sake of, on account of, for" : (*dat.*) 3,5.

9,11. 15,30. 16,12. 21,28. 28,5. 32,29. 41,3. 42,30. 47,5. 58,1. 60,26. 111,29. (*acc.*) 8,7. 11,4. 21,3. 31,11. 57.23. 61,13. 62,31. 91,25; kimatthāya („why") 33,1. kimattharh (do.) 3,12. 15,10. 33,8; *dat.* atthāya also separately (*adv. w. gen.*): 49,11. 57,1. 60,14. 65,1. 108,21 (*cp.* 3) below). — 2) need, want, desire (*w. instr.*) *nom.* ~o 18,9. 22,17-20. 33,2. 35,3-4. 55,15. 83,25. 103,14. 104,31; usīrattha, *mfn.* „he who wants Usīra" (*q. v.*) 108,4 (*m.* ~o); *cp.* atthika & atthin. — 3) use, utility, advantage, gain, wealth; *acc.* ~aṁ icchati 34,20; ~aṁ karissaṁ 47,8; ~aṁ anāgataṁ (pekkhaṁ) „foreseeing future advantage" 112,4; bahūnaṁ ~āya (*dat.*) 108,21. — attha-saṁhita, *mfn.* useful, *n.* ~aṁ 93,7; an-attha-saṁhita, *mfn.* & an-attha, *m*(*fn*). (*v. h.*); nir-attha-(ka), *mfn.* useless (*q. v.*); sattha (= sa + attha) *v.* appa-sattha & sātthaka. *cp.* attad-attha, *m.*, parattha, *m.* & sadattha-pasuta, *mfn.* — 4) thing, object, matter; *acc.* imam atthaṁ „this" 2,8. 105,22; tam atthaṁ „the matter" 7,1. 13,14; *gen.* imassa ~assa 31,10; atthavasaṁ (*acc.*) „the meaning of this" (*v.* vasa) Dh. 289. — uttamatthaṁ (*acc.*) a precious thing, 54,29, the best thing, Dh. 386 — 403. — 5) = aṭṭa[2], case, cause; *acc.* ~aṁ 101,9. Dh. 256; *loc.* ~amhi Dh. 331. — 6) sense, meaning, signification; ~o 52,7. 85,10. 89,3; *acc.* ~aṁ 90,30. 113,11-15; *abl.* (*adv.*) ~to („according to the meaning") 114,20. — attha-pada, *n.* a word of sense (*opp.* vācā anatthapada-saṁhitā) Dh. 100; antogadha-hetu-attha, *mfn.* containing a causative meaning, ~aṁ padaṁ 85,9; paramatthato, *adv.* (*abl.*) „in the absolute sense" 98,27 (*cp.* Paramatthadīpanī). For the comp. aṭṭha-kathā (a commentary) *v.* aṭṭha[2]. — 7) the right, the truth; *acc.* ~aṁ an-atthañ ca, right and wrong Dh. 256; ~aṁ hitvā, leaving the real (aim of life) Dh. 209; in this sense attha is often *opp.* dhamma („duty"): ~aṁ dhammañ ca, 11,13. Dh. 363, *cp.* 58,25; hence the name *attha-dhammânusāsaka, *m.* of a royal counsellor or secretary (he must give the king information of what is 'attha' (ɔ: the real state of the case) and advice concerning the 'dhamma' (ɔ: what ought to be done)), a counsellor of right and justice, *nom.* ~o 37,26.

attha[2] *m.* (*sa.* asta) disappearance, destruction; atthaṁ (*acc.*) gacchati, to disappear, to cease, to perish, Dh. 226. 293. 384; *loc.* suriye atthaṁ gate, at sunset 32,29. (*cp. next*).

attha[3], *pr. 2. pl. v.* atthi.

***atthagama**, *m.* (*fr.* attha[2] + gama) perishing, vanishing, destruction; rūpassa ~o 94,9.

***atthañgama**, *m.* (*fr.* atthaṁ, *acc.* attha[2] + gama) = *prec.*; *dat.* ~āya (dukkha-domanassānaṁ) 90,18.

atthato, *adv.* (*sa.* arthatas) *v.* attha[1] (6).

***attha-dhammânusāsaka**, *m. v.* attha[1] (7).

***attha-pada**, *n. v.* attha[1] (6).

***attha-vasa**, *m.* (*sa.* *artha-vaça) *v.* attha[1] (4).

***attha-saṁhita**, *mfn. v.* attha[1] (3).

***Atthasālinī**, *f.* (*sa.* *artha-çālinī) *nom. pr.* name of a commentary (by Buddhaghosa) on Dhamma-saṅgaṇi, the first book of the Abhidhamma-Piṭaka; *acc.* ~iṁ 113,23.

atthi, *vb.* (*sa.* √as, *pr.* asti) to be, to exist; *pr. 3. sg.* atthi 2,32, 96,16; n'atthi 3,14. 87,33; atth' 1,10. 43,26. 92,30. *2. sg.* si 2,7-13. 3,12-13. 4,11. 98,13; asi 54,20. 88,9. *1. sg.* amhi 12,11. 92,10; 'mhi 4,4. 28,14. 45,4. 88,10; asmi 16,12. 104,31; 'smi 7,13. 49,29. 98,3. *3. pl.* santi 11,14. 110,32. *2. pl.* attha 21,9. 73,5 (atthā 'ti). *1. pl.* amha 21,3 (amhā 'ti). This verb is often used as copula with an *adj.* or *subst.* 2,7. 98,13, and esp. with a *pp.* 2,13. 12,11. 21,3-9. 92,10 etc. The *3. sg.* atthi is frequently used in the sense of „to belong to" (*gen.*): 12,1. 16,1-5. 105,11 (atthi *sc.* me), and this form may also be combined even with the *pl.* of the subject (— santi) : 3,25. 12,1. 18,5. 43,2. 53,31. 82,2. 105,11. 109,11. Dh. 255 etc. tassā kira taṁ divasaṁ maraṇato mutti nāma n'atthi, „she could not be delivered from death that day" 87,32. – *imp. 3. sg.* atthu : namo ty-atthu „homage to thee" (*voc.*) 13,26. 108,11; dhi-r-atthu „shame on" 103,33 (*acc.* jīvitaṁ), 63,13 (*gen.* jātiyā); astu (— *sa.* astu) 114,33. – *pot. 3. sg.* siyā (*sa.* syāt) 38,27. 79,16. 104,14; sakkā ~ „it would be possible" 56,5; vatthabaṁ ~ „ought to have been said" 88,6; in the phrase siyā kho pana (*w. pot. of the foll. verb*) we have siyā used adverbially like the Latin *forsitan* „it may be that", 79,2-23. Besides siyā we often find an older form assa (*sa.* *asyāt?) : tad assa (*w. dat.* dukkhāya) 90,26 = bhaveyya 91,17; avyākatam assa 92,6 foll. (*cp.* atha); suddho assa (sālarukkho) 95,24; Dh. 124 (nâssa), 260; *w. gen.* tumhākam evam assa. (perhaps) you will think, 79,3; tatr' assa „suppose there were (in that town)" 90,32 (*cp.* seyyathā). *pot. 3. pl.* assu (*sa.* *asyus) Dh. 74. – *aor.* (*impf.*) *1. sg.* āsiṁ 85,15. 85,17 („āsin"ti = ahosiṁ), 108,24. – *part.* [1]) sat, being; *loc.* sati (in *loc. abs.*) : ekaṁsena maritabbe sati (*n. sg.*), if (their) death is necessary 6,24; mahārājassa ruciyā sati, at the king's command 39,11; diṭṭhiyā sati. if you hold that view, 92,27-30; niccaṁ pajjalite sati, as (everything) is always burning, Dh. 146. [2]) santa, *mfn. m.* ~o 13,29. 94,25; *loc. n. sg.* evaṁ sante, in this case, 6,28. 99,7; evaṁ sante pi, yet, notwithstanding this, 37,28. 44,28. 62,30; *loc. m. pl.* ~esu (khandhesu) 98,31 („when the groups appear to view"). [3]) samāna, *mfn. m.* ~o (andho) 25,15. (manussabhūto) 41,33. (puṭṭho) 90,1. (vutto) 98,16-17; *acc. m. pl.* ~e (matte) 59,26. The *part. fr.* atthi is frequently used as *adj.*, *v.* sat, santa[3] (santaka) & samāna, (*cp.* a-sat, a-santa). – atthibhāva, atthitā & sotthi, *q. v.*

atthika, *mfn.* (*fr.* attha[1], *sa.* arthika) wanting anything; rajjatthika, *mfn.* who covets the kingdom, *m. pl.* ~ā 39,17. (*cp.* atthin).

atthitā, *f.* (*fr.* atthi, *sa.* astitā) being, existence, reality (*opp.* natthitā); *acc.* ~añ c'eva natthitañ ca. to be and not to be, 96,7; (lokanirodhaṁ passato) yā loke ~ā sā na hoti, (to him) there is no reality in existence (the world) 96,10.

atthin, *mfn.* (*fr.* attha[1], *sa.* arthin) desirous, wanting anything; *v.* mantatthin, vādatthin. (*cp.* atthika).

***atthi-bhāva**, *m.* (*fr.* atthi + bhāva, *q. v.*) existence; *acc.* ~aṁ (sarassa) 4,12; ~aṁ ñatvā, having known this being the fact. 48,26; na no koci ~aṁ jānāti, nobody knows that we exist, 72,31.

atthu, *imp. v.* atthi.

atha, *indecl.* (— *sa.*) [1]) and, further, Dh. 55. [2]) then, now (continuing the tale) 1,5. 3,15. 3,18 (ath'); atha kho 66,3-5 *etc.*; atha kena, why then? 54,27. [3]) then (*corresp. w. a prec.* yadā), 66,31. 107,12-16 = Dh. 377–79. Dh. 69. 119–20. 384; (*after prec.* paṭhamaṁ :) Dh. 158. [4]) but, 107,25 = Dh. 387. Dh. 85. 136; atha kho [khv'] on the contrary 90,36. 91,4; atha ca pana, but on the other hand, 3,4 (*cp.* ca). *cp.* atho *& next.*

athavā, *indecl.* (— *sa.*) or (*corresp. w. prec.* vā, *q. v.*) Dh. 140. 271.

atho, *indecl.* (= *sa.*) and, also, likewise, Dh. 151. 234. 332. 423.

aduṁ, *pron. n.* (*sa.* adas) *v.* asu.

addha — aḍḍha, half (*q. v.*); °-māsaccayena, at the end of a half month, 20,11; °-yojana, *n.* a half yojana (*q. v.*) 63,19.

addhagu, *m.* (*fr.* addhan + gu = ga, *sa.* adhva-ga) a traveller; *nom.* ~ū, Dh. 302 (*sg. & pl.?*)

addhan, *m.* (*sa.* adhvan), a road, a journey, life-time, time; *acc.* ~ānaṁ 44,21. 110,5. Dh. 207 (addhāna). –

***addha-gata**. *mfn.* one who has accomplished his journey ɔ: old, *m.* ~o 74,21 = gataddhin, *mfn.* (*q. v.*). *cp.* addhika & *prec.*

addhā, *adv.* (= *sa.*) certainly, truly; probably, 3,10. 60,20.

***addhika**, *m(fn)*. (*fr.* addhan) travelling, a traveller; *gen. pl. m.* kapaṇaddhikānaṁ, poor travellers, 38,14 (*v.* kapaṇa).

adhama, *mfn.* (= *sa. superl. fr.* adho, *q. v.*) lowest, vilest; purisâdhame (*acc. m. pl.*) low people, Dh. 78. (*cp. next.*)

adhara, *mfn.* (= *sa. compar. fr.* adho, *q. v.*) lower. adharoṭṭhe (*loc.*) the lower jaw 13,19 (*v.* oṭṭha. *cp. prec.*).

adhi, *indecl.* (= *sa.*) prefix to verbs & nouns expressing 'above, over, on, at, to'; before vowels (except „i") it takes the form ajjh-, *e. g.* adhibhāsati, *aor.* ajjhabhāsi.

adhika, *mfn.* (*fr.* adhi. = *sa.*) exceeding, superior. — *compar.* adhikatara, *mfn. id.*; *n.* ~aṁ (assuṁ) *w. abl.* (catunnaṁ samuddānaṁ udakato) 89,14.

adhigacchati. *vb.* (*sa.* adhi-√gam) 'to go to', to attain, obtain, find, understand (*w. acc.*); *pr. 3. sg.* ~ati (ratiṁ) Dh. 187, (samādhiṁ) Dh. 365; *3. pl.* ~anti (sāraṁ) Dh. 11—22; *pot. 3. sg.* adhigacche (padaṁ santaṁ) Dh. 368, ~eyya (seyyaṁ, one who is better) Dh. 61; *aor. 3. sg.* (a)dhigā (atthaṁ). could not understand, 113,15; *w. augm.* ajjhagā (taṇhānaṁ khayaṁ) Dh. 154; *aor. 3. pl.* ajjhagū (= ~gu) (vyasanaṁ) 34,21; *cond. 1. sg.* otāraṁ nâdhigacchissaṁ „I should never find faults", 104,12 (*cp.* upessaṁ, vicarissaṁ. *v.* upeti & vicarati; Pāṇ. III, 2,112 & the use of the Greek ἔμελλον).

adhigama, *m.* (= *sa.*) attainment, acquisition; *dat.* ~āya (*w. gen.* ñāyassa) 90,18.

***adhi-citta**, *n.* 'the higher thought', meditation; *loc.* ~e (āyogo) Dh. 185.

adhiṭṭhāti, *vb.* (*sa.* adhi-√sthā) [1]) to stand (on); *ger.* ~āya 54,8. [2]) to practise, to perform, to devote oneself to (*acc.*); *pr. 3. sg.* ~āti (upāyupādānaṁ, *q. v.*) 96,12; *ger.* ~āya (uposathaṅgāni) 61,7.

adhiṭṭhāna, *n.* (*sa.* adhishṭhāna) [1]) determination, resolution. [2]) adhering to, clinging to the world, *comp. w. the synon.* abhinivesa (being a paraphrase to upāyupādāna, *q. v.*) : adhiṭṭhānâbhinivesânusayaṁ (cetaso), that inclination (of the mind) which consists in clinging to the world, 96,12 (*cp.* anusaya).

adhipa, *m.* (= *sa.*) a master, lord; *v.* ādhipacca.

***adhipanna**, *pp.* (adhi-√pad) assailed, seized; *gen. m.* ~assa (antakenâ-⁰ „whom death has seized") Dh. 288.

***adhippāya**, *m.* (*fr.* adhi-pra-√i, *cp. sa.* abhi-prāya) intention, meaning; *nom.* ~o, 114,6.

***adhibhāsati**, *vb.* (adhi-√bhās) to speak to, to adress (*acc.*); *aor. 3. sg.* ajjhabhāsi 77,2.

adhimutta, *pp.* (*sa.* adhi-mukta (√muc)) inclined to (*w. acc.* or *comp.*); *m.* vanâdhimutto, who gives oneself to desires, Dh. 344 (*cp.* vana[2]); *gen. m. pl.* ~ānaṁ (nibbānaṁ) „who strive after Nibbāna", Dh. 226.

adhivattha, *pp.* (*fr.* adhi-√vas) living, inhabiting (*loc*); *f.* ~ā, 5,19.

***adhivāsana**, *n.* (*fr.* adhivāseti) consent, acceptance of an invitation; *acc.* ~aṁ, 70,11.

***adhivāseti**, *vb.* (*caus.* adhi-√vas) [1]) to wait, to wait for; *imp. 2. sg.* ~ehi, 53,25; *2. pl.* ~etha, 33,15; *ger.* ~etvā (*w. acc.* dve sāvanā) 11,5. — [2]) to bear, endure (*acc.*); *ger.* ~etvā (tayo pahāre) 55,15; *aor. 3. sg.* ~esi (tā *sc.* vedanā) 78,25 = ajjhavāsayi (vedanaṁ) 80,24. — [3]) to consent; *aor.* ~esi, 70,10 = 77,29; *esp.* to accept an invitation to dinner (bhattaṁ) : *imp. 3. sg.* ~etu, 70,9 = 77,28. (*cp.* adhivāsana). — *caus. II:* adhivāsāpeti, to cause to wait; *pr. 2. sg.* ~esi, 33,17.

adhiseti, *vb.* (*sa.* adhi-√çī) to

lie upon (*acc.*); *fut. 3. sg.* ~sessati (paṭhaviṁ) 107,5 — Dh. 41.

adhunā, *adv.* (— *sa.*) now. ⁰-âgata, *mfn.* a new-comer; *m.* ~o (uyyānapālo) 37,15.

adho, *indecl.* (*sa.* adhas) down (*w. acc.*); adho Gaṅgaṁ, down the river G. 14,24 (or perhaps better *comp.* adhogaṅgaṁ, *adv.*?) — *compar.* adhara, *mfn.*, *superl.* adhama. *mfn.* (*q. v.*).

an-, ana-, negative prefix, *v.* a-[4].

*Anāgata-vaṁsa, *m.* 'history of the future', name of a non-canonical Pāli work („the Buddhist Apocalypse"), from which an extract is given 102,2-28.

Anāthapiṇḍika, *m. nom. pr.* (— *sa.*) 'giver of food to the poor', name of a rich merchant; *gen.* ~assa, 71,20.

anīka, *m. & n.* (— *sa.*) an army. balânīka, *mfn. q. v.*

anu[1], *indecl.* (— *sa.*) before vowels except „u" usually 'anv-' (*v.* anvāya *etc.*), prefix to verbs and nouns, expressing 'after, along, near to, according to' etc. Inserted in a dvandva-comp. of the same word repeated, *v.* khuddânukhuddaka (*cp.* paṭi).

anu[2], *mfn.* — aṇu (*q. v.*) *cp.* anumatta.

anukantati. *vb.* (*sa.* anu-√kṛt. 6.) to cut (*acc.*); *pr. 3. sg.* ~ati (hatthaṁ) Dh. 311.

anukampā, *f.* (— *sa.*) compassion; *instr.* ~āya (*w. gen.* tava) out of pity (for you) 55,4.

anukkama, *m.* (*sa.* anu-krama) succession, order; *instr. adv.* ~ena, gradually, 38,22. 48,9; ti ~ena „and so on by degrees" 34,8. sahanukkama, *mfn.* (*q. v.*).

anukkamati, *vb.* (*sa.* anu-√kram) to follow, to go along (*acc.*); *part. med. m.* ~māno (-pathaṁ) 90,34.

anukhuddaka, *mfn. v.* khuddânukhuddaka.

anuga, *mfn.* (*sa.* anu-ga) following; sattâmacca-satânuga, *mfn.* followed by 700 companions, 110,23 (*m.* ~o).

anugacchati, *vb.* (*sa.* anu-√gam) to follow (*acc.*); *aor. 3. sg.* ~gamāsi (taṁ yeva) 68,33; *w. augm.* anv-a-gā (taṁ) 111,3.

anuggaha, *m.* (*sa.* anu-graha) favour, kindness, help. assistance; *acc.* ~aṁ 6,36.

anucara, *m.* (= *sa.*) a companion, follower. — sânucara. *mfn. v.* sa[1].

anuciṇṇa, *mfn.* (*sa.* anu-cīrṇa, *pp.* anu-√car) having attained (*acc.*); *m. pl.* ~ā (samādhijhānaṁ) 109,21.

*anucchavika, *mfn.* (*fr.* anu + chavi) suitable. fit; *m.* ~o (*w. inf.*) 24.24; (*w. gen. pers.*) 25,3 (rañño).

anujānāti, *vb.* (*sa.* anu-√jñā). [1]) to permit, allow; *pr. 1. sg.* ~āmi (ekena (bhikkhunā) dve sāmaṇere upaṭṭhāpetuṁ) 81,16. [2]) to prescribe (*acc.*) 81,20 (dasa sikkhāpadāni). (*cp. next.*)

anuññāta, *mfn.* (*pp.* anujānāti, *sa.* anu-jñāta) permitted, allowed, having attained the permission of (*instr.*); *m.* ~o (ñātih(i)) 11,11. 11,13-15; *m. pl.* ~ā (raññā) 73,24.

*anuññātatta, *n.* (*sa.* *anu-jñāta-tva) the being permitted; *abl.* ~ā, 11,12 („granting him leave to speak").

anutappati, *vb. pass.* (*sa.* anutapyate. √tap) to suffer, to repent; *pr. 3. sg.* ~ati Dh. 67. 314. (*cp.* tapati[2].)

*anutīre, *adv.* (*fr.* anu[1] + tīra (*loc.*)) near the banks of a river (*gen.*) 104,21.

*anutthunati, *vb.* (*fr.* *anu-√stan) to deplore, bewail (*acc.*); *part. m. sg.* ~unaṁ (purāṇāni) Dh. 156 (— anutthunantā (*pl.*) Comm.). The discordance between the *sg.* anutthunaṁ and the *pl.* of the verb is probably due to the fact that senti has been influenced by cāpâ-'tikhīṇā (like jhāyanti in the preceeding verse); *cp.* also the use of *sg.* anutappati Dh. 314.) *cp.* Tr. PM. 76,10.

*anuddayā. *f.* compassion, mercy; in *comp.* this word generally takes the form anuddaya- (*cp.* muttā): khantimettâ-'nuddaya-sampanna, *mfn.* (*q. v.*) 7,12. 38,15. (*fr.* *anu + dayā, although it is generally spelt with double 'd', perhaps from analogy with niddaya?).

*anu-dhamma-cārin, *mfn.* living according to the law; *m.* ~ī Dh. 20 (*cp.* dhamma-cārin).

anudhāvati, *vb.* (*sa.* anu-√dhāv[1]) to follow, pursue, seek (*acc.*); *pr. 3. sg.* ~ati (tīraṁ) Dh. 85; *aor. 2. sg.* anu-dhāvi (kālikaṁ) 47,10.

anupakkamena, *v.* an- (*cp.* upakkama).

*anupakhajja, *ger.* encroaching on (*acc.*) 83,33 (there bhikkhū). This word seems to be *ger. fr.* *anu-pra-√skand (-skadya) = to enter together with, disrespectfully pushing oneself forward (= anu-pavisati, *comm.*). Hence the *vb. denom.* anupakhajjati (Vin. V 163,4). *Morris*, JPTS. '86,115. '89,201, derives it from √khād.

anupatati, *vb.* (*sa.* anu-√pat) to run after, to follow (*acc.*); *pr. 3. sg.* ~anti (sotaṁ) Dh. 347; *pp.* ~ita, followed, *m.* dukkhānupatito. Dh. 302, *pl.* dukkhānupatit' (o: ~ā addhagū) ib.

anuparigacchati. *vb.* (*sa.* anu-pari-√gā) to walk (fly) round (*acc.*); *aor. 3. sg.* anu-pariy-agā (pāsāṇaṁ) 104,13.

*anupariyāya, *m.* (*fr.* anu-pari-√i) going round along; °-patha. *m. acc.* ~aṁ 90,33 — anupariyāya-nāmakaṁ maggaṁ, 91,28 (the path round the town).

*anupassin, *mfn.* (*fr.* anu-√paç) looking after, looking for; para-vajjâ-°, looking after the faults of others, Dh. 253 (*gen. m.* ~issa); śubhâ-°, looking for pleasures. Dh. 7 (*acc. m.* ~iṁ), Dh. 349 (*gen. m.* ~ino).

anupucchati. *vb.* (*sa.* anu-√prach) to inquire after (*acc.*); *pr. 2. sg.* ~asi (jīvaṁ) 103,17.

anupubba, *mfn.* (*sa.* anu-pūrva) regular; *instr. adv.* ~ena, gradually, by and by, in course of time, 18,11. 37,20. 42,24. 81,8. 87,4. Dh. 239.

*anupubbikathā, *f.* (*fr. prec.* + kathā, *q. v.*) a regulated exposition; *acc.* ~aṁ kathesi „preached in due course" 68,19.

anuppatta. *pp.* (*sa.* anu-prāpta, anu-pra-√āp) arrived to, having reached, having attained (*acc.*); *m.* ~o (vayo) 74,21. (Laṅkaṁ) 110,28. *acc.* ~aṁ (uttamatthaṁ) Dh. 386. *loc.* ~e (Āḷaviṁ).

anubandhati, *vb.* (*sa.* anu-√bandh) to follow, to pursue (*acc.*); *aor. 3. sg.* ~i 11,19. 12,28; *1. sg.* ~iṁ 104,11; *ger.* ~itvā 33,18.

anubodha, *m.* (= *sa.*) comprehension, understanding. – dur-anubodha. *mfn. q. v.*

*anubrūheti, *vb.* (*sa.* *anu-√vṛṇh) to 'increase', to devote oneself to (*acc.*); *pot. 3. sg.* ~aye (vivekaṁ) Dh. 75 (*cp.* brūheti).

anubhavati, *vb.* (*sa.* anu-√bhū) to feel, to experience, to obtain (enjoy, suffer) (*w. acc.*); *pr. 3. pl.* ~anti (dukkhaṁ) 23,16; *aor. 3. sg.* ~i (dibbasampattiṁ) 23,17; *inf.* ~ituṁ 23,25; *ger.* ~itvā 23,24; *part.* ~anta, *m.* ~o 63,18; *part. med.* ~māna, *f.* ~ā 61,5 („taking part in", -kīlaṁ); *pp.* anubhūta : kiṁ me dukkhena ~ena (*instr.*) „why should I suffer this pain?" 32,32.

*anubhavana, *n.* (*fr.* anubhavati) partaking of (enjoying, suffering). – dukkhânubhavanatthāya 23,18 (in order to endure their punishment, *cp.* attha[1]); kamma-karaṇânubhavanaṭṭhānaṁ 23,27 (a place where one has to endure the results of his bad deeds).

anubhāva, *v.* ānubhāva.

anubhūta. *pp. v.* anubhavati.

anumatta, *mfn.* Dh. 284, *v.* aṇumatta.

anumodati. *vb.* (*sa.* anu-√mud) to rejoice in (*acc.*), to accept with joy, to thank; *part. med.* ~māna, *m.* ~o (dānaṁ) Dh. 177; *pr. 1. sg.* ~āmi („I thank you") 29,3.

anumodana, *n.* (= *sa.*) acceptance, benediction, thanks (*esp.* the words pronounced by the Buddhist priests at the end of the meal, or after receiving gifts or offerings to the fraternity); *acc.* ~aṁ karonto 86,15; ~aṁ karissāmi 87,20; °-atthāya 87,18 (in order to hear the benediction). (*cp.* Dhpd. (1855) p. 168,7. foll.)

anuyuñjati, *vb.* (*sa.* anu-√yuj) to practise, to give oneself up to (*acc.*); *pr. 3. sg.* ~ati (bhāvanaṁ) 97,9; *3. pl.* ~anti Dh. 26 (pamādaṁ), Dh. 247 (surā-meraya-pānaṁ); *pot. med. 3. sg.* mā pamādaṁ ~etha, Dh. 27. — *pp.* anuyutta, *m.* ~o „in the enjoyment of" 74,22 (diṭṭha-dhamma-sukha-vihāraṁ *q. v.*).

anuyoga, *m.* (— *sa.*) study, meditation, application to. — kāmasukh'-allika-°, *mfn.* whose application is wholly concentrated in pleasure and lust, *m.* ~o (*sc.* anto) 66.26. — atta-kilamatha-°, *mfn. q. v.* (*cp. prec.*).

anuyogin, *mfn.* (*fr.* anuyoga). *v.* attānuyogin.

anurakkhati, *vb.* (*sa.* anu-√raksh). to guard. to watch (*acc.*); *imper. 2. pl.* ~atha (sacittaṁ) Dh. 327.

***anurakkhin**. *mfn.* (*fr.* anurakkhati) watching. — vācā-°, *mfn. q. v.*

Anuruddha, *m. nom. pr.* (= *sa.*) name of a cousin of Gotama Buddha, one of his great disciples; *nom.* ~o 80,30. 109,17 (mahāgaṇī). 109,8 (dibbacakkhumhi [aggo]); *acc.* ~aṁ 80,11; *voc.* ~a, ib.

anurūpa. *mfn.* (— *sa.*) conformable, adapted to, fit, suitable; tadanurūpa. *mfn.* 57,21. *q. v.*

anulitta, *pp.* (*fr.* anu-√lip, *sa.* anulipta) anointed, scented. — nahātānulitta, 41,9. *v.* nahāta.

anuloma, *mfn.* (= *sa.*) 'with the hairs', in natural order (*opp.* paṭiloma). — °-paṭilomaṁ (*adv.*?) „forward and back" 66,6. (*cp.* loma).

anuvattin. *mfn.* (*sa.* anu-vartin) following. — dhammānuvattino (*m. pl.*) following the law, Dh. 86.

anuvicarati. *vb.* (*sa.* anu-vi-√car) to wander or roam through, to explore (*acc. cp.* vicāreti); *pr. 3. pl.* ~anti (samuddatīraṁ) 21,17; *ger.* ~itvā (thala-jala-pathaṁ) 19,33.

anuvicinteti, *vb.* (*sa.* anu-vi-√cint) to meditate upon (*acc.*); *part. m.* ~ayanto (tam eva) 47,25; ~ayaṁ (dhammaṁ) Dh. 364.

anuvicca, *ger.* discovering, attending to, observing, examining(?) Dh. 229 (viññū pasaṁsanti). This word is generally explained in the commentaries by anuviditvā, jānitvā, *etc.*; it is perhaps *ger. fr.* anu-vi-√ci (*anuvicitya, *anuviciya. *cp.* Sn. v. 530 and viceyya ib. v. 529) or *fr.* anu-√vid (= anu-vijja, Tr. MN. I 379,3 (Note p. 562) *cp. Morris*, JPTS. '86. p. 121.). but it can hardly be derived from anu-√i or anu-√vṛt. *cp.* Dhpd. (1855) p. 368.

anuvijja, **anuvijjati**, *v.* anuvicca.

anusañcarati, *vb.* (*sa.* anu-saṁ-√car) to walk along (*acc.*); *part. med. m. pl.* ~mānā (kipillikā viya thambhaṁ) 60,2.

***anusandhi**, *m.* (*cp. sa.* anusandhāna) application, conclusion, connexion; *acc.* ~iṁ ghaṭetvā („making the connexion") 32,5. *cp. Fausbøll*, JRAS. '70, p. 8. *Feer*, JAs. '75. II p. 293.

anusaya, *m.* (*sa.* anu-çaya) inclination, attachment; *acc.* ~aṁ 96,12 (*v.* adhiṭṭhāna). — taṇhānusaya, *v.* taṇhā. — mānānusaya. *v.* mana. *cp.* SBE. X p. 81.

anusāsaka, *m.* (*sa.* anu-çāsaka) a counsellor. — attha-dhammā-°, *v.* attha[1] (7).

anusāsati, *vb.* (*sa.* anu-√çās) [1]) to admonish, to instruct (*acc.*); *inf.* ~ituṁ 81,18; *grd. m.* ~itabbo 79.15; *pot. 3. sg.* ~eyya Dh. 77, 158. — [2]) to give one (*gen.*) advice concerning (*acc.*); *aor. 3. sg.* ~i (rañño atthañ ca dhammañ ca) 58.26 (*cp.* attha[1] (7)). — [3]) to rule, to govern (*acc.*); *aor. 3. sg.* ~i (vinicchayaṁ „administered justice") 42,27.

anusikkhin, *mfn.* (*sa.* anu-çikshin) studying, learning; ahorattânusikkhinaṁ, *gen. pl.* Dh. 226 (studying day and night).

anussarati, *vb.* (*sa.* anu-√smṛ) to remember, to recollect; *aor.* ~i 28,26 (guṇe); *ger.* ~itvā 17,4 (attanā katakammaṁ) 28,15 (Buddha-guṇe); *part. m.* ~aṁ (dhammaṁ) Dh. 364; *m. pl.* ~antā. 28,16.

Anotatta, *m.* (*sa.* An-avatapta) *nom. pr.* of a lake in Himavanta; °-dahaṁ (*acc.*) 61,12.

anta[1], *m.* (*& n.*) (= *sa.*) [1]) end, term; *nom.* ~o (phalānaṁ) 1,15; *acc.* ~aṁ karissatha (dukkhassa) „make an end of" Dh. 275; *comp. loc.* vijayante, immediately after the victory, 60,35; maraṇanta, *mfn. q. v.* – [2]) limit, boundary, border, edge; *acc.* ~aṁ 83,21. *comp. loc.* velante 20,4 (*cp.* velā); vanante, Dh. 305, *v.* vana; accanta, santika, samanta, sāmanta, *q. v.* – [3]) side; *acc. adv.* ekamantaṁ, *q. v.* – [4]) extreme; *pl.* dve antā, 66,25; *acc. pl.* ubho ante, 66,28. 96,17; eko . . . dutiyo anto, 96,16-17. *cp.* ekantaṁ (*adv.*) Dh. 228, *q. v.* – [5]) nearly pleonastically at the end of certain comp., kammanta (*m.*), suttanta (*n.*) *q. v.*

anta[2], *n.* (*sa.* antra) the intestines; ~aṁ 82,4. 97,21. anta-guṇa, *q. v.*

Antaka, *m.* (*fr.* anta[1], = *sa.*) *nom. pr.* the king of death (Yama or Māra): *n.* ~o Dh. 48; *instr.* ~ena, Dh. 288.

anta-kara, *m(fn).* (= *sa.*) putting an end to (*gen.*); *m. pl.* ~ā 105,26 (dukkhasssa).

***anta-kiriyā**, *f.* (*sa.* *anta-kriyā) extinction; *dat.* ~āya 70,17.

***anta-guṇa**, *n.* (*sa.* *antra-guṇa) mesentery (*Sp. Hardy*, Man. of Buddh. p. 400: „lower intestines"): ~aṁ 82,4. 97,22.

***antamaso**, *adv.* (*sa.* *antama + ças) even; ~añjaliṁ paggahetvā ṭhite, even those who were standing with their joined hands raised, 22,7; ~biḷāra-nisakkana-mattaṁ (pākāra-vivaraṁ) even large enough that a cat can creep in, 90,35. (*cp.* antima).

antara, *n.* (= *sa.*) [1]) the interior part of a thing, interval; [a]) as the first part of *comp.* (= anto, *v. below*), [b]) at the end of *comp.*: kālantarena (*instr.*) „by progress of time" 99,28; buddhantaraṁ, a period between two Buddhas, 84,30; dant'antara-gato „having got in between the teeth" 13,29; *pl. loc.* lomantaresu, in the coat, 16,5 (*v.* loma). uddhanantaresu, 9,24 (*v.* uddhana); *pl. abl.* sākhantarehi, amongst the branches, 62,11, pupphantarehi, 62,12. For antaraṁ, antarā, antare *v.* separately. – [2]) difference (at the end of *comp.* = other): purisantaraṁ, another man, 48,11. (*cp.* antarikā, an-antara, santara).

antaraṁ, *indecl.* (= *sa.*) [1]) *adv.* within; ~katvā, having shut in (?) 23,10. – [2]) *prp. w. gen.* raṁsīnaṁ ~ pavisitvā, 87,33.

antaradhāna, *n.* (*sa.* antardhāna) disappearance; pariyatti-°, 102,2 (*q. v.*).

antaradhāyati, *vb.* (*sa.* antar-√dhā) to disappear; *aor. 3. sg.* ~āyi, 24,7. 72,25; (*impf.*) *3. sg. med.* ~āyatha, 104,18 (*cp. Kuhn*, Beitr. p. 110); *pp.* antarahita, *q. v.* – *caus.* antaradhāpeti, to cause to disappear (*acc.*); *pot. 1. pl.* ~eyyāma (lābhasakkāraṁ) 73,1.

***antarantarā**, *adv.* (antarā (*q. v.*) repeated) now and then, 35,1. 83,3.

***antara-vīthiyaṁ**, *adv.* (*fr.* antara + vīthi, *loc.*) in the very streets, 39,6.

antarahita, *mfn.* (*pp.* antar-√dhā, *cp.* antaradhāyati) disappeared, hidden; *f.* ~ā (pasādamattā) 94,23. – an-antarahita, *mfn.* (*q. v.*).

antarā, *adv. & prp.* (*abl. fr.* antara, = *sa.*) among, on the way, during; Dh. 237; *comp.* antarāmagge (*loc.*) on the way, 32,14. 85,2; repeated: antarantarā, *q. v.*

antarāya. *m.* (— *sa.*) [1]) obstacle; *acc.* ~aṁ akāsi, prevented, 68,3; *nom.* gaman'-antarāyo. 65,33 (*v.* gamana). — [2]) death; *acc.* ~aṁ. Dh. 286.

*antarikā. *f.* (*fr.* antara) interval; — sīmantarikā, *f.* a boundary territory, *loc.* ~āya (dvinnaṁ yakkhānaṁ) 40,32.

antare. *prp.* (*loc. fr.* antara. — *sa.*) within, among, between, *w. gen.* 10,31. 30,5. 43,6. 62,9, or at the end of *comp.* 73,20 (mālā-kacavara-⁰, „into the dust-heap") *cp.* antara.

antalikkha. *n.* (*sa.* antariksha) the sky, the air; *loc.* ~e, Dh. 127.

antavat, *mfn.* (— *sa.*) finite, limited; *m.* ~vā (loko) 89.28. — an-antavat, *mfn.* infinite, *ib.*

antika, *mfn.* (— *sa.*) near, bordering upon. — māraṇantika, *mfn. v.* māraṇa. (*cp.* santika).

antima, *mfn.* (= *sa.*) final, last; *m.* ~o (samussayo) 108.17 — Dh. 351. — *antima-sarira, *mfn.* one who has received his last body, *m. nom.* ~o, Dh. 352, *acc.* ~aṁ, Dh. 400.

antevāsika. *m.* (*fr.* ante — anto (*sa.* antar) + vāsika (√vas, to dwell)) a pupil; *acc.* ~aṁ, 32,32; *acc. pl.* ~e, 16,24; ācariyantevāsike (*acc. pl.*) a teacher and his pupil, 32.21; *gen. pl.* ~ānaṁ, 102,9.

anto, *prp.* (*sa.* antar, in some *comp.* ante, *cp.* last) in, within (*opp.* bahi); *w. gen.* tassa ~ 61,15; attano ñāṇajālassa ~ 86,28; *w. loc.* ~aṭaviyaṁ 30,30; in *comp.* anto-nagaraṁ 43,8 — anto-nagare „inside the town" 73,34 (*opp.* bahi-nagare); anto-gabbhe, within the chamber, 65,38; anto-jālaṁ, into the net, 88,35. (*cp.* antara).

*antogadha, *mfn.* (probably *fr.* anto + ogadha (*pp.* ava-√gāh) for ogāḷha) included, contained in. ⁰-hetu-attha, *mfn.* containing a causative meaning, 85,9 (*cp.* attha [1] (6)).

*anto-ḍāha, *m.* an internal flame; tassa ~o uppajji „he grew aflame within" 45,1.

antopura, *n.* (often written ante-pura, Tr. PM. 79,15, *sa.* antaḥ-pura) a king's harem; *loc.* ~e 38,17.

*antovalañjaka, *m. pl.* (*fr.* anto + valañja) in-door people; *gen.* ~ānaṁ, 43,6 (*opp.* bahivalañjaka).

andha, *mfn.* (— *sa.*) blind (also about mental blindness); *m.* ~o 25,15; *pl.* ~ā 88,27. — *andha-bāla, *mfn.* blinded by folly; *voc. m.* ~a 38,19; *voc. f.* ~e 59.21. — *andha-bhūta, *mfn.* mentally blinded; *m.* ~o 88,29 = paññācakkhuno abhāvena ~o, 88,31; *acc. pl. m.* ~e, Dh. 59. Andhabhūta-jātaka, a later reading for Aṇḍabhūta. 52,11 (*cp.* 50,12-15).

andhaka, *mfn.* (— *sa.*) blind. *andhaka-masakā, *m. pl.* gad-flies, 104,27.

andhakāra, *m.* (— *sa.*) darkness; *acc.* ~aṁ 19,17; *loc.* ~e 69,17; *instr.* ~ena, Dh. 146.

anna, *n.* (— *sa.*) food; *instr.* sā maṁ ~ena (*sc.* uddharī) 20,36.

annaya, *v.* dur-annaya (— anvaya, *cp.* anveti).

anvāya, *ger. fr.* anu-√i, *v.* anveti.

anvāhata, *pp.* (anu-ā-√han) struck, beaten, perplexed, *v.* an-anvāhata-cetasa.

anveti, *vb.* (*sa.* anu-√i) to follow, to reach, to affect or attack (*acc.*); *pr. 3. sg.* ~eti. 106,22 — Dh. 71, Dh. 1. 2. 124; *ger.* ~āya (vuddhiṁ, full-grown) 2,18. 18,2.

apakkamati, *vb.* (*sa.* apa-√kram), to go away, to retire from (*abl.*); *pot. 3. sg.* ~me (tamhā) 14.4; *aor. 3. sg.* ~mi (etto) 104,15.

apagacchati, *vb.* (*sa.* apa-√gam) to go away; *pp.* apagata, departed, gone off; as the first part of *adj. comp.*: ⁰-kāḷaka, ⁰-tacapapaṭika. ⁰-phegguka, ⁰-vattha. ⁰-sākhāpalāsa, *q. v.*; dvinnaṁ iṭṭhakānaṁ ⁰-ṭṭhānaṁ, the interval between two bricks, 91,29.

apacāyati, *vb.* (*sa.* apa-√cāy) to honour, to respect (*acc.*); *pr. 3. sg.* (metri causa ~āyatī) 30,9.

apacāyin, *mfn.* (*sa.* apa-cāyin, *fr. last*) rendering due respect; vaddhâpacāyin, *mfn.* „who reveres the aged", *m. pl.* ~ino. Dh. 109.

apaciti, *f.* (— *sa.*) honour, respect; *acc.* ~iṁ, 29,26. 30,4.

*apajita, *n.* (*pp.* apa-√ji), what is lost, defeat; *acc.* ~aṁ (*opp.* jitaṁ) Dh. 105.

Apaṇṇaka-jātaka, *n. nom. pr.*, the title of the first tale in the Jātaka-book, 102,20 [a-paṇṇaka, *mfn.* evident, certain, leading to salvation (*fr. sa.* a-parṇa, without leaves, *opp.* sa-paṇṇaka, but the semasiological process is unknown; *Weber,* Ind. Str. III. 150 and *Kuhn,* Beitr. p. 53 take it = *a-praçna-ka].

apattha, *mfn.* (*sa.* apāsta. *pp.* apa-√as[2]), thrown away; *n. pl.* ~āni (aṭṭhīni) Dh. 149.

apaneti, *vb.* (*sa.* apa-√nī) to take away, to remove (*acc.*); *pot. 1. sg.* ~eyyaṁ (aṭṭhiṁ) 13,14; *aor. 3. sg.* apānayi (putte) 13,4; *ger.* ~etvā, 44,12. 65,32; *pp.* apanīta, *n.* ~aṁ etaṁ Tathāgatassa, T. is free from this, 94,7; *grd.* ~etabba, to be removed, °-ākāra-ppattā (sāṭakā) „intolerable", 45,1.

*apabbūhati or apaviyūhati, *vb.* (*fr.* apa-vi-√ūh) to remove by digging up or scraping out (*acc.*); *aor. 3. sg.* apabbūhi (paṁsuṁ) 40,26. (*cp.* viyūhati).

apara, *pron.* (— *sa.*) another (by way of addition or progression in number, the original sense being „posterior, following", whilst para (*q. v.*) denotes what is opposite or distant, *cp.* añña); *acc.* ~aṁ (dīpaṁ) 23,21; aparaṁ pana ekadivasaṁ „and again on a certain day", 63,24-28; *n.* nâparaṁ, nothing more, 71,16; *instr.* ~ena samayena, afterwards, subsequently, 95,23. 101,16; *loc.* ~asmiṁ (kanakavimāne) 23,22; *m. pl.* ~e pi 'ssa tayo sahāyā ahesuṁ, further he had three friends, 14,9. — aparaṁ (*n.*) is often used adverbially, *esp.* aparam pi, besides that, also, too, 34,16. 54,21. — aparāparaṁ, *adv.* to and fro, from side to side, 2,27. 40,24. — pubbâ-para, *mfn.* (*q. v.*), aparajju, aparabhāge, *v. below.*

aparajju, *adv.* (*sa.* apare-dyus) on the following day; 101,27.

aparajjhati, *vb.* (*sa.* apa-√rādh) to offend against (*loc.*); *ger.* ~itvā (parassa vatthumhi) 58,13.

aparapaccaya, *v.* a- (p. 4).

aparādha, *m.* (— *sa.*) offence, fault; *acc.* ekâparādhaṁ, one such fault, 47,8. — nir-aparādha, *mfn.*, innocent, guiltless; *acc. m.* ~aṁ, 39,29.

*aparabhāge, *adv.* (*fr.* apara + bhāga, *loc.*) afterwards, later; 22,14. 24,13-16. 38,11.

*aparopita, *mfn.* (apa + ropita, *pp.*) consumed (?). This word is only due to my own conjecture (see Note p. 126); the Colombo Edition reads āropita (*fr.* āropeti. *q. v.*) 87,11.

apaviddha, *mfn.* (— *sa. pp.* apa-√vyadh) flung, thrown away; neglected; *acc. m.* ~aṁ, 34,15; *n.* ~aṁ (kiccaṁ) Dh. 292.

*apasādeti, *vb.* (*fr.* apa + sādeti, *caus.* √sad) to blame, to depreciate, disparage (*acc.*); *pr. 3. sg.* ~eti (maṁ) 74,29-30.

*apassena, *n.* (*fr.* apâ-√çri, *cp. sa.* apâçraya) a rest, a support; °-phalaka, *n.* a bolster-slab or head-rest; ~aṁ 84,16. [*cp. Morris,* JPTS. '84,71. — SBE, XX, 219.]

*apābhata, *mfn.* (*pp.* apā-√bhṛ) brought away, stolen; *n.* ~aṁ (rattibhattaṁ) 15,19.

apāya, *m.* (— *sa.*) [1]) going away, loss; piyâpāyo, loss of the beloved, Dh. 211. — [2]) state of suffering (*esp.* dwelling in hell, or in the world of animals, petas and asuras); *acc.* saggâpāyaṁ, heaven and hell, Dh. 423. — apāya-gāmin, *mfn.* going to an evil state; *m. pl.* ~ino 88,35 (*opp.* saggāya gacchati).

apāyin, *mfn.* (= *sa.*) going away. — an-apāyin, *mfn.* (*q. v.*).

apāruta, *mfn.* (*sa.* apāvṛta, *fr.*

apâ-√vṛ) open. °-dvāra. *mfn.* with open doors; *loc.* ~e (nivesane) 39,28.

api. *adv.* (= *sa.*) [1]) generally *enclit.* = pi (*q. v.*) or -âpi after *prec.* a, ā. — [2]) beginning a sentence (before a vowel sometimes app' or ap') [a]) even, Dh. 187. [b]) api ca .. vā .. vā, whether .. or, 96,31 (*w. foll.* api ca kho. nevertheless, 97,1); api ca, nevertheless, 101,13 (*cp.* kiñcâpi); api ca kho pana, but at all events, 32,25. [c]) app-eva nāma, perhaps (*w. foll. pot.*) 17,26. 69,5. [d]) particle of interrogation (*w. indic.* or *pot.*) 13,26. 69,1. 71,31. 104,14 (ap'); api nu, 73,4.

apekkhati. *vb.* (*sa.* apa-√īksh) to look for (*acc.*); *pr. 3. sg. med.* ~ate (kāme) 103,24.

apekkhā & apekhā. *f.* (*sa.* apekshā) desire, regard, care; Dh. 345 (-kh-, *w. loc.*).

apekkhin & apekhin. *mfn.* (*sa.* apekshin) looking for, regardful of. — an-apekkhin, *mfn.* (*q. v.*).

apeta, *mfn.* (= *sa.*; *pp. fr. next*) free from, deprived of (*w. instr.* or *comp.*); *m.* ~o (damasaccena) Dh. 9. — apeta-kaddama. *mfn.* without mud, *m.* ~o (rahado) Dh. 95. — °-viññāna, *mfn.* senseless, *m.* ~o (kāyo) 107,6 = Dh. 41.

apeti, *vb.* (*sa.* apa-√i) to go away; *pr. 3. sg.* ~eti, 50,1; *1. pl.* apema 104,16 (nibbijjâpema Gotamaṁ „being disgusted, we shall go away from Gotama", *Fausböll*, SBE. X[2], p. 71, who prefers the reading Gotamā, *cp.* SN. I, 124).

app', *v.* api.

appa. *mfn.* (*sa.* alpa) small, little; *m.* ~o 88,30 (only a few = kocid eva satto 89,1); *instr.* ~en' eva (trifling) 38,24; *n.* ~aṁ, a little, a small portion, Dh. 20. 259, *loc.* ~asmi yācito, asked for little, Dh. 224. — appa-kilamathena āgato si „you had no mishap?" 28,12 (*cp.* kilamatha).

appaka, *mfn.* (*fr. last, sa.* alpaka) small, little, trifling; *instr. n.* ~en' eva, at a trifle, 52,6; *m. pl.* ~ā (few) Dh. 85. — an-appaka. *mfn.* (*q. v.*).

*appaggha. *mfn.* (*sa.* *alpârgha. *cp.* aggha) of little value; °-bhaṇḍaṁ „wares of little value" 26,2.

*appabodhati. *vb.* (*fr.* appa (*sa.* alpa) + bodhati, a rare present formation of √budh, *cp.* bujjhati) to slight, disregard; *pr. 3. sg.* ~ati (nindaṁ) Dh. 143. (*Weber*, Ind. Str. I, 137; others (*Fausbøll & Max Müller*) have taken it = a (ɔ: na) + prabodhati (does not excite). or (*Childers & Subhûti*) = apa-bodhati (to ward off). *cp.* the readings ap(p)abodheti and *sa.* alpabuddhi. *mfn.*)

*appamaññati. *vb.* (*fr.* appa + √man. *cp. last*) to despise, underrate (*w. gen.*); *pot. 3. sg. med.* ~etha (pāpassa. puññassa) Dh. 121. 122.

appamatta. *mfn.* (*sa.* alpa-mātra) little, slight, mean; *m.* ~o (gandho) Dh. 56. (*cp.* a-ppamatta. p. 5.)

*appamattaka. *mfn.* (*fr. last*), of little importance; *m.* ~o (ārakkho) 17,16.

*appalābha, *mfn.* (*sa.* *alpa-lābha) receiving little; *m.* ~o (bhikkhu) Dh. 366.

*appasattha, *mfn.* (*sa.* *alpa-sārtha) having few companions; *m.* ~o (vāṇijo) Dh. 123 (*cp.* sattha).

*appassāda. *mfn.* (*sa.* *alpa-svāda) having a short taste; *m. pl.* ~ā (kāmā) Dh. 186.

*appassuta. *mfn.* (*sa.* *alpa-çruta) having learnt little; *m.* ~(o) (puriso) Dh. 152.

appiccha, *mfn.* (*sa.* alpeccha) who has but few desires; *acc. m.* ~aṁ. Dh. 404 (*cp.* icchā).

*appossukka, *mfn.* (*sa.* *alpa + autsukya. *cp.* ussuka) unconcerned, living at ease, with few wishes; *m.* ~o (viharatu) 74,21. Dh. 330.

abbahati. *vb.* (*sa.* ā-√vṛh) to pull out (*acc.*); *pot. 3. sg.* abbahe (sallaṁ) 108,9.

abbuda, *n.* (*sa.* arbuda) the foetus

in the first or second month after conception; *gen.* ~assa 99,10.

abbha, *n.* (*sa.* abhra) cloud; *abl.* ~ā (mutto candimā) Dh. 172.

abbhakkhāna, *n.* (*sa.* abhy-ākhyāna) false accusation, calumny; *acc.* ~aṁ, Dh. 139.

abbhantara, *n.* (*sa.* abhy-antara) the inner part, interior, interval; ~aṁ (*opp.* bāhiraṁ) 106,11 — Dh. 394. — *loc. prp. w. gen.* ~e, in, with, within, 3,25 (tuyhaṁ), 38,22 (rañño).

abbhuggacchati, *vb.* (*sa.* abhyud-√gam) to go out, to sally forth; *ger.* ~gantvā, 60,3.

abbhuta, *mfn.* (*sa.* adbhuta) wonderful, marvellous; *n.* ~aṁ 79,27. 98,32. — *n.* (*subst.*) one of the nine divisions of Buddha's doctrine (navaṅgaṁ Satthusāsanaṁ) 109,34 (jātak'-abbhuta-vedallaṁ).

abhi, *prp.* (— *sa.*) prefixed to verbs and nouns, expressing the direction „towards" or superiority; before vowels it takes the form abbh- (*v. above*).

abhikaṁkhati, *vb.* (*sa.* abhi-√kāṅksh) to desire, to wait for, to intend (*acc.*); *part. med. m.* ~māno (daḷha-ppahāraṁ) 30,13.

abhikīrati, *vb.* (*sa.* abhi-√kṛ, kir) to pour over, to overwhelm (*acc.*); *pr. 3. sg.* ~ati (ogho dīpaṁ) Dh. 25.

abhikkanta, *mfn.* (*sa.* abhikrānta, *pp.* abhi-√kram) advanced, excellent; *n.* ~aṁ, 69,14 — 95,26.

abhijānāti, *vb.* (*sa.* abhi-√jñā) to perceive, to know, to learn, to remember (*acc.*); *pr. 1. sg.* ~āmi, 27,33; *ger.* abhiññāya (attadatthaṁ) Dh. 166, sayaṁ ~, Dh. 353 (as I am intelligent myself); *pp.* abhiññāta, *v. below.*

abhiññā, *f.* (*sa.* abhijñā) supernatural faculty or intuitive knowledge; *dat.* ~āya saṁvattati, conduces to knowledge, 66,30. 93,8; *instr.* ~āya (sāvakānaṁ dhammaṁ desemi) from my intuitive knowledge, 90,16. — °-vosita, *mfn.* perfect in knowledge, *m.* ~o, Dh. 423 (*v.* vosita). — cha-ḷ-abhiñña, *mfn.* having the six supernatural faculties, *m. pl.* ~ā, 109,20 (*cp.* cha). — jñānâbhiññā, *f.* supernatural power attained by meditation (*v.* jhāna), *acc.* ~aṁ. 47,33.

abhiññāta, *mfn.* (*pp.* abhijānāti. *sa.* abhijñāta) known, distinguished; *m. pl.* bahu-abhiññātā, highly esteemed (sāvakā) 109,19.

abhittharati, *vb.* (probably an old error for abhi-tvarati or abhittarati. *sa.* abhi-√tvar) to make haste; *pot. 3. sg. med.* ~etha (kalyāṇe) „hasten towards the good", Dh. 116. (*cp.* tarati).

abhidhamma, *m.* (*sa.* abhi-dharma) the higher dhamma or transcendental doctrine. — Abhidhamma-piṭaka, *n.* name of the third of the three great collections („baskets", *cp.* piṭaka) of the Buddhist holy scriptures, comprising the following works: Dhammasaṅgaṇi, Vibhaṅga, Kathāvatthu, Puggala-paññatti, Dhātukathā, Yamaka, Paṭṭhāna; *loc.* ~e 102,13; *gen.* ~assa 113,15.

abhidhāvati, *vb.* (*sa.* abhi-√dhāv) to run up towards, to rush towards; *imp. 2. pl.* ~atha (*metri causa* ~athā) 30,19 („haste to the rescue"); *aor. 3. sg.* ~vi, 76,22.

abhinandati, *vb.* (*sa.* abhi-√nand) [1]) to rejoice at, to salute, to welcome (*acc.*); *pot. 3. sg.* ~eyya (sakkāraṁ) Dh. 75; *pr. 3. pl.* ~anti (purisaṁ sotthim āgataṁ) Dh. 219. — [2]) to applaud, to assent, to approve (*acc.*); *aor. 3. sg.* ~i (Bhagavato bhāsitaṁ) 93,18; *inf.* ~ituṁ (tad abhinanditun ti) 97,5.

abhinandin, *mfn.* (— *sa*) rejoicing at; *f.* tatra-tatrâbhinandinī (taṇhā) finding its delight here and there, 67,13.

abhinava, *mfn.* (— *sa.*) quite new, modern; *loc. pl.* ~esu potthakesu, in modern manuscripts, 52,12 (*opp.* porāṇa-).

abhinikkhamana, *n.* going

forth, *esp.* retiring from the household life. – mahā-⁰, *n.* „the great retirement" ɔ: Buddha's leaving his house in order to become a monk; ~aṁ nikkhamituṁ 65,13.

abhinimmināti, *vb.* (*sa.* abhi-nir-√mā) to create, to assume another appearance (*acc.*); *ger.* ~itvā (kassaka-vaṇṇaṁ, the appearance of a ploughman) 71,28.

abhinivesa, *m.* (*sa.* abhiniveça), adhering to, inclination to; upāyupādāna-⁰ 96,10 (*q. v.*); *comp. w. the synon.* adhiṭṭhāna (*v. h.*) 96,12.

***abhippakiṇṇa**. *pp.* (*sa.* *abhi-pra-√kir) strewn with (*instr.*); ⁰-sayana, *loc.* ~e (pupphānaṁ ammaṇamattena) 65,29.

***abhippahāraṇī**, *f.* (*adj. fr.* *abhi-pra-√hṛ, traced only in the foll. passage) ~ṇī (senā Kaṇhassa) the offensive (army of Kaṇha) 103,31.

abhibhavati, *vb.* (*sa.* abhi-√bhū) to overcome, to overpower (*acc.*); *pr. 3. sg.* ~ati (paccāmitte) 3,24; *ger.* ~bhuyya (sabbāni parissayāni) Dh. 328; *pp.* ~bhūta, *m.* khuppipāsâbhibhūto (peto), tormented by hunger and thirst, 84,32.

abhibhū, *mfn.* (— *sa.*) one who conquers or overcomes (at the end of *comp.*); sabbâbhibhū, *m.* having conquered all, Dh. 353; sabbalokâbhibhuṁ (vīraṁ, *acc. m.*) having conquered all the worlds, Dh. 418.

abhimatthati or **abhimanthati**, *vb.* (*sa.* abhi-√math, manth) to crush (*acc.*); *pr. 3. sg.* ~ati (dummedhaṁ) Dh. 161.

abhimukha, *mfn.* (— *sa.*) turned towards; *m. pl.* ~ā ahesuṁ, they met with one another, 43,19; most frequently at the end of *comp.*: *m.* varaṇarukkhâbhimukho, 5,4; nagarâbhimukho, 43,14; *f.* Jetavanâbhimukhī, 73,13; *acc. m.* devalokâbhimukhaṁ (rathaṁ akāsi) 60,19. – abhimukhaṁ, *adv.* 39,9–10 (matta-vāraṇe ~ āgacchante, *loc.* even if a furious elephant were going towards them).

abhirati, *f.* (— *sa.*) delighting in, pleasure; *acc.* tatra ~iṁ iccheyya Dh. 88. – an-abhirati, *f.* discontent (*q. v.*).

abhiramati, *vb.* (*sa.* abhi-√ram) to delight in, to take one's pleasure with; *pr. 3. sg.* ~ati (mayā saddhiṁ) 46,21; *3. pl.* ~anti (ubho) 50,6; *aor. 3. sg.* ~i (tena saddhiṁ) 20,11; *part. med. m.* ~māno (tāya saddhiṁ) 19,19. – *pp.* abhirata, *v.* an-abhirata; *abhiranta, only in *comp.* yathâbhirantaṁ, *adv.* as long as you like or think fit 70,30 (*v.* yathā, *cp.* yathākāmaṁ). dur-abhirama, *mfn.* (*q. v.*).

***abhiramāpeti**, *vb.* (*caus. II fr. last*) ¹) to cause one to take his pleasure with; *pot. 1. sg.* ~eyyaṁ (rājānaṁ mayā saddhiṁ) 46,25. – ²) to delight, to divert; *part. f. pl.* ~entiyo (itthiyo) 64,31.

abhirūpa, *mfn.* (— *sa.*) handsome, beautiful, lovely; *m.* ~o (mahāsamaṇo) 76,31; *acc.* ~aṁ (purisaṁ) 10,25; *f.* ~ā (haṁsapotikā) 10,4.

abhirūhati, *vb.* (*sa.* abhi-√ruh) to ascend, to mount (*acc.*); *pr. 3. sg.* ~ati (dantaṁ, *sc.* nāgaṁ) Dh. 321; *imp. 2. sg.* ~a (piṭṭhiṁ me) 1,19; *2. pl.* ~atha, 22,5; *aor. 3. sg.* 1,19. 25,19 (nāvaṁ); *3. pl.* ~iṁsu, 22,6; *ger.* ᵃ) ~ruyha, 20,13; ᵇ) ~rūhitvā. 21,10. 61,18 (pabbataṁ).

abhilakkhita, *mfn.* (*sa.* abhilakshita, *pp.* abhi-√laksh) fixed, determined for; *m.* ~o (mahā-uposatha-divaso) 22,19.

abhivaḍḍhati, *vb.* (*sa.* abhi-√vṛdh) to increase; *pr. 3. sg.* ~ati (yaso) Dh. 24. – *pp.* abhivaḍḍha, *n.* ~aṁ bīraṇaṁ „the abounding Bīraṇa grass", 107,32 — Dh. 335 (or have we to take this form as *part. pr.*? *Trenckner* takes it as *pp.* abhi-√vṛsh, *cp.* the readings ~vaṭṭaṁ & ~vuḍḍhaṁ, *Morris*, JPTS. '86, p. 143).

abhivādana. *n.* or ***abhivādanā**, *f.* (*sa.* abhivādana, *n.*) respectful salutation, reverence; ~ā (*w. loc.* ujjugatesu) Dh. 108. – *abhivādana-sīlin, *mfn.* (*cp. sa.* °-çila) respectful; *gen. m.* ~issa, Dh. 109.

abhivādeti, *vb.* (*caus.* abhivadati, *sa.* abhi-√vad) to salute respectfully (*acc.*); *ger.* ~etvā (Bhagavantaṁ) 68,17. 96,3.

abhisaṁkhata, *mfn.* (*pp.* abhisaṁkharoti, *sa.* abhi-saṁ-s-√kṛ) prepared, cooked; *gen.* ~assa (sappimadhu-sakkarā-°. pāyāsassa) 61,26.

abhisaṁkhāra, (*sa.* abhisaṁskāra) [1]) preparation. [2]) development, exercise, practise; *acc.* ~aṁ 68,36. 69,2. (iddhā-°, *v. next*).

*abhisaṁkhāreti, *vb.* (*caus.* abhi-saṁ-s-√kṛ) [1]) to prepare. [2]) to exercise, practise, effect (*acc.*); *pot. 1. sg.* ~eyyaṁ (iddhābhisaṁkhāraṁ, „an exercise of miraculous power“ (*v.* iddhi) 68,36; *aor. 3. sg.* ~esi (id.) 69,2.

abhisajati or abhisajjati, *vb.* (*sa.* abhi-√sañj) to offend; *pot. 3. sg.* ~saje (yāya na .. kañci, by words) Dh. 408.

*abhisambujjhati (*sa.* *abhi-sam-√budh) to gain perfect knowledge of; *pp.* ~buddha, *part.* ~budhāna. *v. below.*

*abhisambujjhana, *n.* (*fr. last*) enlightment, gaining the perfect knowledge (possessed of a Buddha); °-kāla, *m.* 63,7.

abhisambuddha, *mfn.* (*pp.* abhisambujjhati, *sa.* id.) having attained perfect knowledge; *m.* paṭhamābhisambuddho (Buddho) „having just attained the Buddhaship“, 66,3.

*abhisambudhāna, *mfn.* (*part. fr.* abhisambujjhati, *cp. sa. part. aor.* budhāna) who has learnt, understood; *m.* ~o (kāyaṁ marīcidhammaṁ) Dh. 46.

*abhisambhava, *m.* (*fr.* abhisambhavati, *sa.* abhi-sam-√bhū), reaching, attaining. – dur-abhisambhava, *mfn.* (*q. v.*).

abhiseka, *m.* (*sa.* abhisheka) anointing, inauguration of a king; *acc.* ~aṁ kāretvā „caused himself to be anointed king“ 36,29; etassa imasmiṁ rājābhisekakāle, now when he is being anointed king, 11,6.

abhisecana, *n.* (*sa.* abhishecana) = *prec.* ~aṁ (ulūkassa) 11,16.

amacca, *m.* (*sa.* amātya) a companion or minister of a king, courtier; ~o, 38,17; *pl.* ~ā, 40,9; *acc. pl.* ~e, 40,7; *instr. pl.* ~ehi, 39,31. – °-ādayo, the courtiers and others, 102,5 (*cp.* ādi). sesâmacce (*acc. pl.*), all his courtiers, 40,5 (*v.* sesa). mittāmaccā (*pl.*) friends and companions, 92,8. °-brāhmaṇa-gahapatike (*acc. pl.*) ɔ: all people of higher rank (*opp.* sabbaseṇiyo) 42,2 (*cp. Fick,* Soc. Glied. p. 93 & 164). °-sahassena (*instr.*) a thousand courtiers, 39,26. 62,8. °-parivuta, *mfn.* 40,30. °-gaṇa-parivuta, *mfn.* 39,28. °-parivārita, *mfn.* 112,26. sattâmacca-satânuga, *mfn. v.* anuga. sâmacca, *mfn.* (*q. v.*).

amuka, *mfn.* (*fr. the pron. base* amu-. — *sa. cp.* asu & asuka) this or that, such and such a person (or thing) referred to without name; *loc. m.* ~asmiṁ okāse, 75,6. (*cp.* ayaṁ, 4.)

amba, *m.* (*sa.* āmra) the mango tree (Mangifera Indica); ~o. 37,22; *gen.* ~assa, 37,1; *pl.* ~ā. 100,13; *acc. pl.* ~e. 100,14; *instr. pl.* ~ehi, 2,10. – °-pakka, *n.* (*sa.* *āmra-pakva) a mango fruit; ~aṁ. 36,31 = ambaphalaṁ, 36,34. °-panas'-âdīhi, 2,30 (*v.* panasa & ādi). °-piṇḍi, *f.* (*sa.* *āmra-piṇḍī) a bunch of mangos, *acc.* ~iṁ, 15,2. °-labujâdīnaṁ, 1,14 (*v.* labuja). °-vana, a mango grove, *loc.* ~e, 77,20; 45,14 (Makhādeva-°, *q. v.*) 45,7 (M~ uyyāne). °-sāmika, *m.* the owner of a mango tree, ~o, 100,12.

*ambho, *indecl.* (*fr.* ham + bhos, *cp.* hambho & bho) [1]) a voc. particle: Hallo! (*w. voc.*), ~sārathi, 43,21. [2]) exclamation expressive of anger or indignation (*w. voc.*), ~duṭṭha-brāhmaṇa. 33,16; ~purisa, 101,18.

amma, *indecl.* (used in addressing a woman), *v. next.*

ammā, *f.* (*sa.* ambā) a mother;

gen. ~āya. 46,8; *voc.* amme is usually shortened to amma: [1]) used by children addressing their mother, 9,19. 22,17; [2]) by any person addressing one (or more) women, 49,32 (a maid to her lady); 87,10 (a father to his daughter).

ammaṇa, *n.* (*sa.* armaṇa? *cp. Childers s. v.*) a certain measure of capacity, a trough, a canoe; °-mattena (*instr. v.* matta [2]) in a measure of an a-(pupphānaṁ ~ abhippakiṇṇa-sayana) 65,29.

amha, amhi, *v.* atthi.

amha(*n*), *n.* = asman (*sa.* açman) a stone; *instr.* ~anā. 104,6 (*cp. Windisch,* Māra, p. 8 & 12). – amha-maya, *mfn.* (*sa.* açma-maya) made of stone, hard; *acc.* ~aṁ (maṇiṁ) Dh. 161.

amhākaṁ, amhe, *etc.*, *v.* ahaṁ.

ayaṁ, *pron. m. & f.* (*sa.* ayam, *f.* iyam) *n.* idaṁ (*sa.* idam). The other forms are taken from the base ima- or a-: *nom. sg. m.* ayaṁ. 3,1. 6,3; by contraction with a preceeding a-sound: câyaṁ, 66,26; by elision: 'āyaṁ 17,28. 37,30; Dh. 56, or 'yaṁ, 108,17; before palatals: ayañ, 74,31. – *f.* ayaṁ, 21,17. 9,18 (ayañ ca). – *n.* idaṁ, 15,15; 'idaṁ, 67,3; imaṁ, 100,4. – *acc.* imaṁ 2,8 (*m.*); 3,25 (*f.*); 17,1; Dh. 196 (im') (*n.*). – *instr. m. n.* iminā. 3,22; 54,15. *f.* imāya, 42,18; 75,35. – *gen.* (*dat.*) *m.* (*n.*) imassa, 2,29; 4,31; assa. 1,5; 'ssa. 3,11; *f.* imissā. 3,3; 31,4; assā, 48,26; 73,23 (assa = assā?); 87,10. – *abl. m.* asmā, Dh. 220. – *loc. m.* (*n.*) imasmiṁ, 1,13; 3,23; asmiṁ, Dh. 242. – *pl. nom. m.* ime. 4,6; 66,25 ('me); 60,17 (mā-y-ime). – *acc. m.* ime. 41,22; *f.* imā, 2,9; *n.* imāni, 81,27. – *instr. m.* imehi, 55,25. – *gen. m.* imesaṁ, 2,6; 14,26. – *loc. m. n.* imesu, 31,16; 81,27. – [1]) this. this here (*referring to a person or thing present or in question*) *opp.* para, Dh. 220. 410. – [2]) *referring to the preceeding,* 67,5 (ayaṁ kho sā); 73,23 (ime divase. *acc. pl.* „the last few days"). – [3]) *referring to the following,* 67,3-10; 85,29. – [4]) — such, like that, 31,6 (imaṁ acchādanaṁ): 2,6 (imesaṁ sattānaṁ, like us), 54,33 (id.); repeated: ayañ ca ayañ ca, 43,33; idañ c'idañ ca, 44,13 (*cp.* asuka, amuka). – [5]) *combined w. pron. relat.*: y'āyaṁ (= yo ayaṁ) Dh. 56; yâyaṁ (*f.*) 67,12; yad idaṁ, 97,2. – [6]) ayaṁ is sometimes used as *pron. 3. pers.*, *esp.* the *gen. sg.* assa, assā, *enclit.* = tassa. tassā (*v.* ta-). *cp.* eta- (esa).

ayana, *n.* (= *sa. cp.* eti) walking, road. – ekāyana, *mfn.* (*q. v.*).

ayas, *m.* (*comp.* ayo. *nom.* ayo, *sa.* ayas, *n.*) iron; *instr.* ayasā (= ayato, Comm.) 106,19 = Dh. 240. (*cp.* āyasa. *mfn.*)

ayo-guḷa, *m.* (*sa.* ayo-guḍa) an iron-ball; ~o. 107,1 = Dh. 308.

ayya, *mfn.* (*sa.* ārya, *cp.* arya) honorable, worthy; *m.* ~o Devadatto, 75,4. – The *voc.* ayya is frequently used in respectfully addressing a person: 2,29. 4,3 etc. 33,1 (ayyā 'ti); *pl.* ayyā (by addressing more persons) 21,10. 73,4; and even the *nom. sg.* ayyo is used as voc. particle (in both genders and numbers): 18,8-21-25. (*cp.* ariya.)

ayya-putta, *m.* (*sa.* ārya-putra) the son of an honorable man, master; *nom.* ~o. 65,22; *voc.* ~a, 65,15 (designation of a master by his servant).

ayyikā, (*fr.* ayya. *sa.* āryikā, āryakā) grandmother; ~ā, 108,15.

ayyo. *v.* ayya.

arañña, *n.* (*sa.* araṇya) a forest; *acc.* ~aṁ, 6,7; *abl.* ~ato. 6,15; *loc.* ~e, 5,30; *pl.* ~āni. Dh. 99; *loc.* ~esu, 73,34. – *°-āyatana. *n.* a forest haunt; *loc.* ~e, 1,4. 3,30. – *°-ṭṭhāna, *n.* a place in a forest; *loc.* ~e, 32,14.

araha, *mfn.* (*sa.* arha) deserving, worthy; *m. pl.* ~ā („holy men") 109,3. – pūjāraha. *mfn.* (*sa.* pūjârha) deserving hommage; *acc. m. pl.* ~e, Dh. 195. – mahāraha, *mfn.* (*sa.* mahârha), very valuable, precious, splendid; *m.* ~o (manto) 32,10; *acc.* ~aṁ (uttamarathaṁ) 63,4; (sayanaṁ) 112,2; *n. pl.* ~āni (āsanāni) 61,25. (*cp. next.*)

arahat, *m.* (*sa.* arhat) a venerable person, a saint, an Arhat, who has reached the highest stage of sanctification from which he can enter Nirvāṇa; *nom. sg.* arahā (dasah' aṅgehi samannāgato) 82,14; *gen.* ~ato (Sammāsambuddhassa) 81,5; *acc.* ~antaṁ, Dh. 420; *pl.* ~anto (satta) the first seven Arhats, viz. Buddha himself, the pañcavaggiyā bhikkhū (*q.v.*), and Yasa, 70,18; *gen. pl.* ~ataṁ, Dh. 164. (*cp.* arahatta.)

arahati, *vb.* (*sa.* √arh) 1) to be worthy of (*acc.* or *inf.*); *pr. 3. sg.* ~ati (kāsāvaṁ, metrically — arhati) Dh. 9; *2. sg.* ~asi (mama vijite vasituṁ) 38,20; *part.* arahat (*v. h.*). — 2) to be obliged to, to be able to (*inf.*); ko taṁ ninditum ~ati, „who would dare to blame him?" Dh. 230.

arahatta, *n.* (*sa.* arhatva) Arhatship (*cp.* arahat); *acc.* ~aṁ. 89,16.

***Arahanta-vagga**, *m.* name of the seventh chapter of Dhammapada.

ariya, *mfn.* (*sa.* ārya, *cp.* ayya) honorable, noble; elect, holy; *m.* ~o, Dh. 270; *acc.* ~aṁ (= āryaṁ) Dh. 208; *gen. pl.* ~ānaṁ (= aryānaṁ) Dh. 22. 164. 206; *instr. pl.* ~ebhi, Dh. 162 bis; ~o aṭṭhaṅgiko maggo, 67,3. 108,14; *acc.* 107,20. — *⁰-ppavedita, *mfn.* preached by the elect; *loc.* ~e (arya-, dhamme) Dh. 79. — *⁰-bhūmi, *f.* the world of the elect; *acc.* ~iṁ, Dh. 236. — an-ariya, *mfn.* (*q. v.*).

ariya-sacca, (*sa.* ārya-satya) sublime truth; ~aṁ (dukkhaṁ) 67,8 (the sublime truth [concerning] the pain); 67,12 (dukkhasamudayaṁ, *q. v.*); *pl.* ~āni (cattāri) 82,10. 107,18.

***ariya-sāvaka**, *m.* an elect or holy disciple; ~o, 28,3. 71,5; *acc. pl.* ~e, 73,32.

aru, *n.* (*sa.* arus) a wound; *aru-kāya, *m.* a wounded body (or *mfn.* covered with wounds?) *acc.* ~aṁ, Dh. 147.

aruṇa, *m.* (— *sa.*) the dawn, the sun. — *aruṇuggamana, *n.* sunrise; *abl.* ~ā, 12,18. — *aruṇa-velā, *f.* (id.); *loc.* ~āya, in that very moment when the sun was rising. *ib.* (*cp.* velā).

arhati, *v.* arahati.

aḷa, *n.*(?) (*sa.* ala, *cp.* aḍa) the claw of a crab; *instr.* ~ena, 4,35; *instr. pl.* ~ehi (kammāra-saṇḍāsena viya) 5,3.

alaṁ, *indecl.* (— *sa.*) enough: 1) *w. voc.* ~ Devadatta, 74,24; ~āvuso, 75,31. — 2) *w. gen. pers.* ~mayhaṁ. I have had enough, 28,24. — 3) *w. instr.* ~ (vo ratanehi) 27,39; sometimes denoting what a person don't care for: ~etehi ambehi, 2,10. — 4) *w. dat. final.* ~hi te aññāṇāya ~sammohāya, no wonder that you feel ignorant and confused, 94,24.

alaṁkata, *mfn.* (*pp. fr. next.*, *sa.* alaṁ-kṛta) adorned, decorated; *m.* ~o, 45,30. Dh. 142; ⁰-sirigabbhe, 41,24 (*q. v.*); ⁰-paṭiyatta, *mfn.* splendidly dressed or decorated (*q. v.*).

alaṁkaroti, *vb.* (*sa.* alam-√kṛ) 1) to adorn; *ger.* ~itvā (*acc.*) 20,9. 58,19. 63,4. — 2) to adorn oneself; ~itvā, 19,13. — *pp.* alaṁkata, *v. above.* — *caus.* ~kārāpeti, *q. v.*

alaṁkāra, *m.* (— *sa.*) ornament, decoration; *instr.* sabbâlaṁkārena alaṁkaritvā, adorning it richly, 63,1; *instr. pl.* sabbâlaṁkārehi, 58,18. — sabbâlaṁkāra-paṭimaṇḍita, *mfn.* 64,29 (*q. v.*); ⁰-vibhūsita, *mfn.* 61,7 (*q. v.*).

***alaṁkārāpeti**, *vb.* (*caus.* II. alaṁkaroti) to cause to be decorated (*acc.*); *ger.* ~etvā (maggaṁ) 62,7.

alāpu, *n.* (*sa.* alābu) a gourd; *pl.* ~ūni, Dh. 149.

alika, *mfn.* (*sa.* alīka) false, displeasing. — *n.* falsehood, untruth; ~aṁ bhaṇaṁ, speaking a falsehood, Dh. 264; na tassa ~aṁ bhaṇitaṁ (*sc.* mayā) I did not tell him a lie, 108,30; ~aṁ bhāsasi. 97,31 (= musāvāda). — alika-vādin, *mfn.* lying, speaking a falsehood; *acc. m.* ~inaṁ 44,9.

allāpa, *m.* (*sa.* ālāpa) speaking to; °-sallāpa, *m.* conversation; ~aṁ katvā, 56,22. *cp.* ālapati.

*allika, *mfn.* (*probably fr.* ā-√lī. *ālayaka-*ālyaka) adhering, devoted to, *only comp. w.* sukha-, *v.* kāmasukhallika-.

allīyati, *vb.* (*sa.* ā-√lī) to adhere; *part. m.* an-allīyanto, careless of (*w. acc.* kilesaratiṁ) 46,19.

ava, *indecl.* (— *sa.*) prefix to verbs and nouns expressing „down, back, aside, away". This prefix is very frequently contracted to „o", both after another *prp.* (ajjh-o-harati) and before a single or double consonant (okāsa, okkamati); but after „vi" we find it sometimes uncontracted (vavatthāpita, *cp.* vohāra *etc.*) and in comp. like an-avakāsa, likewise before vowels (avekkhati). *cp.* ora, orima.

avakāsa, *v.* okāsa.

avaca, *mfn.* (— *sa.*) low (*opp.* ucca) *v.* uccāvaca.

avacara, *m.* (— *sa.*) only at the end of comp. = the sphere or dominion of, *v.* a-takkāvacara.

*avajalla, *v.* rajovajalla.

avajānāti. *vb.* (*sa.* ava-√jñā) to despise (*acc.*); *pr. 3. sg.* ~ati (metri causa) 103,30.

avajīyati, *vb.* (*sa. pass.* ava-√ji) to be conquered; *pr. 3. sg.* ~ati, Dh. 179.

avaṭṭhita, *mfn.* (*pp. fr.* avatiṭṭhati, *sa.* ava-√sthā) firm, steady. — an-avaṭṭhita-citta, *mfn.* (*q. v.*).

avattharaṇa, *n.* (*sa.* avastaraṇa) spreading; deploying an army; rañño °-bhāvaṁ ñatvā, „when he saw that the king had deployed his forces" 36,24 (*cp.* bhāva).

avattharati and ottharati, *vb.* (*sa.* ava-√stṛ) to spread, scatter about, overturn; to overspread, overwhelm (*acc.*); *ger.* ~itvā (bhattapātiṁ) 34,13; (turiyabhaṇḍāni) 65,5; ottharitvā (*sc.* jālaṁ, referred to the agens sākuṇikena) 88,34. — *pp.* otthaṭa, overwhelmed, caught; *loc. pl.* ~esu (Māra-jālena) when they have been caught in Māra's net, 88,35.

avadhāraṇa, *n.* (— *sa.*) ascertainment, emphasis; ~aṁ, the signification of the particle „kho", 85,34.

avasakkati, *v.* osakkati.

avasarati. *vb.* (*sa.* ava-√sṛ) to proceed towards, to come (down) to; *aor. 3. sg.* tad avasari. 77,19. 81,9.

avasāna, *n.* (— *sa.*) conclusion, termination, end; *loc. adv.* ~e, at last, 34,8; *comp.* bhattakiccâ-°, 86,15; gāthâ-°, 87,1; desanâ-°, 89,2. Contracted : osāna, °-gāthā, *f.* a final stanza, *acc.* ~aṁ, 27,21. *cp.* pariyosāna.

avasiṭṭha, *mfn.* (*sa.* avaçishṭa, *pp.* ava-√çish) left, remaining; *n.* ~aṁ (sūkaramaddavaṁ) 78,14; ~aṁ hoti (āyuṁ) 44,28; *m. pl.* ~ā ahesuṁ (dve janā) 33,21.

avasesa, *mfn.* (*sa.* avaçesha. *n.*) left, remaining; *m. pl.* ~ā. 7,14. 86,23 (*opp.* ekā); *gen.* (*dat.*) *pl.* ~ānaṁ. 7,15. — avasesa-sigālā (*m. pl.*) 40,21.

*avassuta, *mfn.* (*sa.* ava-sruta or *ava-ā-sruta. √sru) 'rotten, leaky'; *metaph.* lustful (*cp.* Jāt. IV 20,22 : anavassutā nāvā (watertight) and SBE. X,13). — an-avassuta-citta, *mfn.* (*q.v.*), *cp.* an-ussuta & āsava.

avaharati, *vb.* (*sa.* ava-√hṛ) to take away (*acc.*); *pr. 1. sg.* ~āmi (nāham ambe ~, I did not take away) 100,14; *pot. 3. sg.* ~eyya (ambaṁ) 100,12. — *pp.* avahaṭa. *m. pl.* ~ā, 100,13.

*avāpurāpeti. *vb.* (*caus.* II. avāpurati — *sa.* apā-√vṛ & apa-√vṛ) to cause to be opened; *ger.* ~etvā (nagaradvārāni) 39,25. *cp.* apāruta.

Avīci, *n.* (or *f.*) *nom. pr.* (— *sa. m.*) the last (lowest) of the eight great hells (*cp.* niraya); *loc.* ~imhi, 27,14.

avekkhati, *vb.* (*sa.* ava-√īksh) to look at, to look down upon (*acc.*); *pr. 3. sg.* ~ati (bāle) Dh. 28; *pot. 3. sg.* ~eyya (attano katāni) Dh. 50; *part. acc. m.* ~antaṁ (lokaṁ) Dh. 170.

avhaya, *m.* (*sa.* āhvaya) appellation, name; only at the end of *adj. comp.*, *v.* savhaya.

asani, *f.* (*sa.* açani) a thunderbolt, lightning; *nom. sg.* ~i (patitā) 17,22; *loc.* ~iyā (sīse patantiyā) 39,10; °-vegena (*instr.*) hastily like a flash of lightning (*cp.* vega) 12,22.

asi[1], *m.* (*sa.* asi) a sword; *acc.* ~iṁ, 111,25; *instr.* ~inā, 33,17; asi-satti-dhanu-ādīni (āvudhāni) 6,12; °-cammaṁ, *n.* sword and shield, 75,15.

asi[2], *pr. 2. sg.* atthi (*q. v.*).

asīti, *num.* (*f.*) (*sa.* açīti) eighty; caturāsīti — 84 (*sa.* catur-açīti), °-vassa-sahassāni, 44,20. — *asīti-koṭi-vibhava, *mfn.* very rich, *gen. m.* ~assa (seṭṭhino) 22,13. — °-sahassā, *m. pl.* (bhikkhū) 80,000, 97,4. *cp.* āsītika.

asu, *pron. mf.* (*sa.* asau) *n.* aduṁ (*sa.* adas) that; the other cases are formed on the base amu- (*cp.* amuka).

***asuka**, *mfn.* (*fr. last. cp. sa.* amuka) this or that, such and such a person (or thing); *loc. m.* ~asmiṁ (gāme) 92,14. — *comp.* °-kāle, 88,23; °-gehe, 58,3. *cp.* amuka and ayaṁ[4]).

asura, *m.* (— *sa.*) an evil spirit, demon; *pl.* the opponents of the gods; *nom. pl.* ~ā, 59,24; *acc.* ~e, 59,25; *gen.* ~ānaṁ, 60,14; *loc.* ~esu, 60,17. — *°-kaññā, *f.* daughter of the Asuras, *acc.* ~aṁ (Sujaṁ) 54,7. — *°-bhavanaṁ, *n.* the world of the A. 59,27.

astu, **asmi**, *v.* atthi.

assa[1], *m.* (*sa.* açva) a horse; *acc.* ~aṁ, 65,17; *pl.* ~ā, Dh. 94; *acc. pl.* ~e, 44,11; maṅgalasso, a horse of state (*v.* maṅgala) 24,29; valāhassa-, a flying horse (*v.* valāha) 21,34 (°-yoni); sīghasso „a racer" (*v.* sīgha) Dh. 29 (*opp.* abalassa „a hack", *v.* a-bala). — °-dūta, *m.* a messenger on horseback, 68,31. — *°-pota, *m.* a foal, 2,18 (°-ppamāṇa, *mfn.*); — *°-bhaṇḍaka, horse trappings (saddle and bridle) 65,17. — °-ratana, *n.* (*coll.*) valuable horses, 24,19. — °-rājan, *m.* 'king of horses' (Kanthaka) 65,19. — °-sālā, *f.* a stable for horses, 65,17. *cp.* assatara below.

assa[2], *pot. 3. sg. v.* atthi.

assa[3], **assā**, *pron. gen. v.* ayaṁ.

assatara, *m.* (*sa.* açvatara) a mule; *pl.* ~ā, Dh. 322.

assama, *m.* (*sa.* āçrama) the hut of an ascetic; *loc.* ~e, 36,6. — °-pada, *n.* a hermitage, a place where ascetics have made their huts; *acc.* ~aṁ, 36,6.

assava, *mfn.* (*sa.* āçrava) compliant, obedient; *f.* ~ā (gopī) 104,33; *n.* ~aṁ (cittaṁ) 105,2; *pl.* ~ā, 105,25.

assāda, *m.* (*sa.* āsvāda) enjoyment, delight; a delicacy; *acc.* ~aṁ 47,29 (*opp.* ādīnava) 104,15.

***assādanā**, *f.* (*cp. sa.* āsvādana, *n.*) a delicacy, 104,14.

assāsa, *m.* (*sa.* āçvāsa) breathing, inhaling; °-passāso, inhaling and breathing forth, 80,32.

assāseti, *vb.* (*sa. caus.* ā-√çvas) to cause to take breath, to comfort, to encourage (*acc.*); *ger.* ~etvā, 20,6. 40,29.

assu, *n.* (*sa.* açru) a tear or *coll.* tears; *nom. sg.* ~u, 82,5. 97,28; ~uṁ, 89,14; *instr.* ~unā (akkhīhi paggharantena) 5,14. — °-mukha, *mfn.* with a tearful face, *m.* ~o (rodaṁ) Dh. 67.

aha, *n.* (*sa.* ahar & ahan) a day. [1]) at the end of *comp.* ekāhen' (*instr.*) in the course of one day, 57,8; ekāha-dviha'-ccayena, in a day or two, 32,24 (*cp.* accaya); ekāhadvīhaṁ (*acc.*) one or two days, 50,6; katipāhaṁ (*q. v.*) a few days, 7,27 *etc.*; dvīha-tīhaṁ, two or three days, 36,8; sattāhaṁ, seven days, 23,16. 66,4. — In some few cases we find -aṇha (*fr.* the weak stem ahan) *v.* pubbaṇha, sāyaṇha. — [2]) as the first part of *comp.* 'aho' (*fr. sa.* ahar) *v.* aho-ratta, aho-ratti.

ahaṁ, *pron. 1. pers.* (*sa.* aham) 'I'; *nom.* ahaṁ (aham, ahan) 1,7. 2,2. 65,15; by contraction or elision: āhaṁ, 'haṁ, 1,21. 7,3. 104,21; after the verb: jāneyyâhaṁ, 94,31; labhāmi'haṁ, 108,25; patām' ahaṁ, 108,26. — *acc.* [1]) maṁ, 2,3. 13,15 (man'ti); [2]) mamaṁ, 16,2. 47,10 (mamañ ca). — *instr.* (*abl.*)

mayā, 3,14. 4,26. — *gen.* (*dat.*) 1) mayhaṁ, 2,11-29. 3,9. 4,12 *etc.* 2) mama, 1,17. 71,32 (mam') 72,20 (mama-y-idaṁ). 3) mamaṁ, 72,20. 4) me, 1,19. 2,2. 112,20 (m'); this form is also often substituted for other cases: — *instr.* 4,23. 45,5. 66,23. 90,25. — *abl.* 72,1. — *loc.* mayi. 19,29. — *pl. nom.* 1) mayaṁ, 1,8. 56,32 (= *sg.*). 2) amhe, 21,30. — *acc.* amhe, 4,19. 73,5. — *instr.* (*abl.*) amhehi, 6,15. 74,12. — *gen.* (*dat.*) 1) amhākaṁ, 1,24. 4,4. 2) no, 11,3. 12,3. 56,33 (= *sg.*); substituted for *instr.* 54,15. — *loc.* amhesu, 4,11. — *Combined w. pron. demonstr.* es'āhaṁ, 69,19; *acc.* taṁ maṁ, 103,2; *gen.* tassa me, 103,23; *w. pron. rel. pl.* ye mayaṁ, 105,23; *gen.* (*dat.*) yesan no, Dh. 200. — Constructions to be noticed: na te ahaṁ, I am not among those, 72,22; tumhe maṁ ... jānātha (*sc.* pesakārasālaṁ gacchamānaṁ) 88,13; mama rattindivam ... na jānāmi (*sc.* maraṇabhāvaṁ) 88,22. *cp. next.*

*ahiṁkāra, *m.* (*fr.* ahaṁ & √kṛ, *sa.* ahaṁkāra) the false view that there is an Ego, the first of the three anusayas (*q. v.*), explained in the comm. by 'diṭṭhi' (*q. v.*); 94,11: sabba-ahiṁkāra-mamiṁkāra-mānânusayānaṁ khayā. Some Mss. have here and in parallel passages the reading ahaṁkāra (= *sa. cp.* SN. III 32,1-2 (vol. I p. 132)), which generally means „selfishness, pride".

aho, *indecl.* (= *sa.*) an exclamation (*w. nom. or a full sentence*) expressive of satisfaction or enjoyment, 42,17 (aho vata bho), 58,12 (~ puññānaṁ phalaṁ), 86,24 (~ Buddhānaṁ kathā nāma acchariyā), or of reproach, 59,21 (~ andhabālâsi).

ahoratta, *m.* (*sa.* ahorātra) day and night; °-ânusikkhin, *mfn.* studying day and night, *gen. pl.* ~inaṁ, Dh. 226. *cp.* aha.

*ahoratti, *f.* (*sa.* *ahorātri) = *prec.*; *acc.* sabbaṁ ~iṁ. through the whole day and night, 107,25 = Dh. 387.

Ā.

ā. *prp.* (= *sa.*) near to, towards, until; generally prefixed to verbs and their derivatives, but shortened to 'a' before more consonants, *e. g.* acchādeti, assāseti, allāpa, *etc.*

ākaṁkhati, *vb.* (*sa.* ā-√kāṅksh) to wish, to desire (*acc.*); *pr. 3. sg.* ~ati (pacchāsamaṇaṁ) 82,26; *part. med. m.* ~amāno. 79,11 („if it should so wish"); *ger.* ākaṁkha (virāgaṁ) Dh. 343.

ākaḍḍhati, *vb.* (*sa.* ā-√kṛsh) to draw to or away with one's self; *ger.* ~itvā (hanukaṭṭhikena, by the jawbone) 40,18; 59,8.

ākappa. *m.* (*sa.* ākalpa) gestures, manners; *instr.* ~ena, 49,8.

ākara, *m.* (= *sa.*) plenty, multitude; a mine; ganthākara, *q. v.*

ākāra. *m.* (= *sa.*) form, appearance, condition; sign, token, hint; manner, way; anekākāra, *mfn.* multiform (*v.* an-eka); apanetabbākāra-ppatta, *mfn.* intolerable (*v.* apaneti); patanākāra-ppatta, *mfn.* being on the point of falling out, 12,21; sabbākāra-paripuṇṇa, *mfn.* altogether perfect, 10,26; sabbākāra-varūpeta. *mfn.* endowed with every grace, 81,4 (*cp.* vara); dvattiṁsākāra, *q. v.*; chātakākāra, sign of hunger, 41,8 (*v. h.*); olokitākārenêva (*instr.*), at the first sign of her being looked at (?) 87,25; āgamanākāra, 41,31 (how he had come back); aññenâkarena (*instr.*) in another way (ɔ: wrong) 91,32.

ākāsa, *m.* (*sa.* ākāça) the air, sky; space; *acc.* ~aṁ, 14,16; *instr.* ~ena, through the air, 19,17. 36,10; *abl.* ~ā. 33,6. ~ato, 32,11; *loc.* ~e, 11,19. 17,25. Dh. 254—5 (*cp.* bāhira & SBE. X, p. 64 Note). — °-cārika. *mfn.* going through the air, 35,35 (*m.* ~o). — °-ānañcāyatana, *n.* 80,5 (*v. h.*).

ākiñcañña, *n.* (*sa.* ākiṁcanya, *fr.* a-kiñcana. *q. v.*) want of any possession, nothingness. °-âyatana, *n.* the abode of nothingness, non-existence, *acc.* ~aṁ, 80,7; °- -samāpatti. 80,8 (*v. h.*).

ākirati, *vb.* (*sa.* ā-√kir) to scatter or sprinkle over (*acc.*); *ger.* ~itvā (paṁsuṁ, filled them up with earth) 40,6; (pādapaṁsūni upari muddhani, the dust at his feet over its head) 77,8; *pr. 3. sg. med.* ~ate (rajaṁ) Dh. 313.

***ākoṭeti**, *vb.* (*sa.* *ā-√kuṭ, *caus. cp.* koṭṭeti) to beat, to trample in (*acc.*); *ger.* ~etvā (paṁsuṁ) 40,6.

āgacchati, *vb.* (*sa.* ā-√gam & gā) to go, come, approach, arrive; to return, come back; *pr. 3. sg.* ~ati, 12,2; *1. sg.* ~āmi (pādena) 98,2; *1. pl.* ~āma, 23,19; — *imp. 3. sg.* ~atu, 4,23; *2. sg.* ~a, 75,7; *2. pl.* ~atha, 75,9. 76,25; — *pot. 3. pl.* ~eyyuṁ, 101,9; — *fut. 3. sg.* āgacchissati, 15,6, and āgamissati. 22,27. Dh. 121; *1. pl.* āgamissāma, 23,19; — *aor. 3. sg.* āgamā, 18,34. āgami, 57,14. āgā, 114,2; *2. pl.* āgamittha, 39,2; *3. pl.* āgamiṁsu, 73,31; — *part. m.* āgacchanto (maggaṁ) on the way, 28,12; 57,32; *acc.* ~antaṁ. 2,31; *acc. f.* ~antiṁ, 49,4; — *ger.* āgantvā. 6,30. 7,5. 9,24. 10,8. 31,23; āgamma (*sa.* āgamya) Dh. 87. 192 — 107,22. 61,19. 110,28; — *pp.* āgata. *q. v.*

āgata, *mfn.* (— *sa. pp. fr.* āgacchati) [1]) come, arrived, returned; *m.* ~o, 4,24. 16,12; *acc.* ~aṁ, 9,22; frequently used as finite tense : 9,27 (~o), 57,33 *etc.* āgato'smi, 98,3; āgat'amhi (*f.*) 73,18; — *comp.* maṁ tava santikaṁ āgata-kāle gaṇhāhi (when I have returned) 3,17; °-velāya (*loc.*) when he returned, 20,10; āgatâgatā (*m. pl.* raṭṭhavāsino) who from time to time came, 18,5; °-bhāva, *m.* coming, arriving. coming near, *acc.* ~aṁ, 40,17. 88,8; °-ṭṭhāna, *n.* — āgatabhāva (*cp.* ṭhāna) *acc.* ~aṁ, 19,18; °-matta, *mfn.* at one's arrival, *acc. m.* taṁ ~aṁ, 33,28; adhunāgata, *mfn.* a new-comer, 37,15 (*cp.* adhunā); cirāgata, *mfn.* long absent, *m.* ~o (na cirāgato — adhunāgato?) 9,27. — [2]) occurred, related (in quotations): Mahāpadāne °-nayena „in the manner related in M.“ 63,12. — [3]) known; āgatāgama, *mfn.* (= *sa.*) acquainted with the āgamas (*q. v.*), *m. pl.* ~ā, 109,26. — an-āgata, *q. v.*

āgama, *m.* (— *sa.*) [1]) arrival. [2]) knowledge, science, *esp.* a sacred work containing traditional doctrine, the five Nikāyas or Sutta-piṭaka thus called by the northern Buddhists (who, however, know only fragments thereof); °-piṭakaṁ (suttasammataṁ) 110,3 — Sutta-piṭaka. — āgatāgama, *mfn. v. above.*

āgamana, *n.* (— *sa.*) coming, arriving, returning; *acc.* ~aṁ, 22,28. 33,29. 87,6-26; °-bhāva, *m.* the having arrived, *acc.* ~aṁ, 9,14; °-ākāra, way of returning, 41,31 (*q. v.*).

āgāmin, *mfn.* (— *sa.*) coming, returning; *v.* sakad-āgāmin.

āgāra, *n.* (— *sa.*) a house, *v.* agāra, *cp.* an-āgāra.

āghāta, *m.* (— *sa.*) 'striking, killing'; ill-will, malice; ~o (Devadattassa Bhagavati) 74,32; °-matta. *n.* ~aṁ pi nâkāsi „not so much as an angry thought“, 40,1 (*cp.* matta [2]).

ācariya, *m.* (*sa.* ācārya) a teacher; ~o, 16,23 (disāpāmokkho, brāhmaṇo); °-antevāsike (*acc. pl.*) a teacher and his pupil, 32,21. — *acariya-bhāga, *m.* a teachers fee, 64,24 (~o). — *ācariya-vāda, *m. pl.* ~ā. the doctrines of old teachers. 113,27. — *cp.* aññathācariyaka.

ācāra, *m.* (= *sa.*) good conduct, morality; sīlâcaro. „virtues“, 43,33; sīla-guṇâcāro, a holy life, 28,34. — *ācara-kusala. *mfn.* perfect in behaviour, *m.* ~o, Dh. 376. — an-ācāra, *q. v.*

ācikkhati. *vb.* (*sa.* ā-√caksh) to tell, communicate, explain, point out (*acc.*); to instruct (*gen.*); *pot. 3. sg.* ~eyya (maggaṁ mūḷhassa) 69,16; — *aor. 3. sg.* ~i (atthaṁ) 13,14; — *fut. 1. sg.* ~issāmi (cittarucitaṁ tumhākaṁ) 55,27; — *imp. 2. sg.* ~a (maggaṁ no) 56,33; — *part. m.* ~anto (kāraṇaṁ) 37,33; — *ger.* ~itvā, 53,13. 56,34. 58,2 (*w. gen.* -bhariyāya); an-ācikkhitvā (tesaṁ) without telling them anything about it, 25,34.

ācinati & ācināti, *vb.* (*sa.* ā-√ci, -cinoti) to gather, accumulate; *part. m.* ācinaṁ (ācinanto) Dh. 121–22 (thokathokaṁ).

āchanna, *mfn.* (*sa.* ācchanna, *pp.* ā-√chad) — acchanna, *pp.* acchādeti (*q. v.*) covered; *m.* bhasmāchanno (pāvako) covered by ashes, 106,23 — Dh. 71.

*ājañña, *mfn.* (— ājānīya, *cp. sa.* ājāneya) of noble birth, *v.* purisājañña.

*ājāna, *mfn.* only in the *comp.* dur-ājāna, *q. v.*

ājānāti, *vb.* (*sa.* ā-√jñā) to understand, to perceive; *pr. 3. pl.* ~anti (atthaṁ) 90,30; *aor. 3. sg.* aññāsi, 57,3. 65,21. 87,25; 68,21 (*w. double acc.*); *ger.* aññāya, Dh. 275. 411; *caus.* āṇāpeti, *q. v.* — *cp.* aññā, *f.*, āṇā, *f.*, dur-ājāna, *mfn.*

ājānīya, *mfn.* (*sa.* ājāneya) of noble birth, of good breed (as a horse); *m. pl.* ~ā sindhavā „noble Sindhu horses", Dh. 322.

ājīva, *m.* (— *sa.*) livelihood; sammā-ājīvo, the right way of supporting life, 67,4. — suddhâjīva, *mfn.* & suddhâjīvin, *mfn.* (*q. v.*).

āṇā, *f.* (*sa.* ājñā) [1]) order, command; *acc.* ~aṁ, 39,35; — *°-sampanna, *mfn.* authoritative, *acc. m.* ~aṁ (purisaṁ) 10,26. — [2]) sentence of death, capital punishment; ~aṁ katvā, having passed sentence on (*gen.*) 42,7. — *cp.* aññā, *f.*

āṇāpeti, *vb.* (*denom. fr.* āṇā, *cp. sa.* ājñāpayati, *caus.* a-√jñā) to command, to give orders (*acc.*); *imp. 2. sg.* ~ehi (purise) 75,3; *aor. 3. sg.* ~esi (manusse) 75,4.

*ātappa, *n.* (*fr.* ā-√tap, *cp.* *ātāpa, *m.* exertion) perseverance; ~aṁ kiccaṁ „you must make an effort", Dh. 276. *cp.* ottappa, *n.*

ātāpin, *mfn.* (*fr.* ātāpa, *sa.* ātāpin) ardent, strenuous; used in connection with jhāyin (*q. v.*), *gen. m.* ~ino (brāhmaṇassa) 66,20; *m. pl.* ~ino, Dh. 143.

ātura, *mfn.* (— *sa.*) suffering, ailing; *acc. m.* ~aṁ (arukāyaṁ) Dh. 147; *loc. pl.* ~esu (manussesu) Dh. 198. — an-ātura, *q. v.*

ādāna, *n.* (— *sa.*) [1]) taking, seizing; ā-dinnâdānā (*abl.*) from taking what is not given to you ɔ: stealing, 81,22. — [2]) affection, greed; °-paṭinissagga, *m.* abandonment of affection, Dh. 89. *cp.* an-ādāna, sâdāna.

ādāya, *ger. v.* ādiyati.

ādi, *m.* (— *sa.*) [1]) beginning, starting-point; *nom.* tatrâyam ādi bhavati, Dh. 375; ādiṁkatvā (dovārike, *acc. pl.*) from (doorkeepers) and upwards, 58,21 (*cp.* karoti); *ādi-brahmacariyika, *mfn.* belonging to the principles or fundamentals of a religious life, *n.* ~aṁ, 93,7-11. — [2]) This word is very often used as the last part of *comp.* expressing „et-cetera, and so on, and the like". [a]) *subst. pl. n.* kasi-gorakkhâdīni, 21,3; naccâdīni, 65,1. *etc. instr.* °-ādīhi, 18,28; 61,28 (aññehi); *loc.* °-ādisu, 64,29; rattin-divam-pubbaṇhâdisu, whether at night, day, morning or at other times, 88,23; *m. pl.* °-ādayo, 6,11; amaccâdayo, 102,5; *f. gen. pl.* khattiyakaññâdīnaṁ, 47,15. Such *comp.* occur also as the first part of a greater *comp.*, 6,7 (muggarâdi-), 47,13 (nīluppalâdi-), 65,22 (uyyānakīḷâdi-), 88,32 (aniccâdi-vasena), 113,30 (Sāriputtâdi-). — [b]) *adj. n. sg.* taṇḍulâdi (nāvaṭṭhaṁ) 111,31; *n. pl.* °-ādīni (āvudhāni) 6,12; (puññāni) 17,33; *instr. m. pl.* °-ādīhi (phalarukkhehi) 2,20; *gen. n. pl.* °-ādīnaṁ (phalānaṁ) 1,14. — [3]) Similarly used, but uncompounded after „ti" (or ti evaṁ) 21,4. 73,30 (*n. pl.* ādīni). In this way it is to be found even as *adj.*, (taṁ yeva) „sassato loko" ti ādinā (*instr.*) nayena puṭṭhaṁ pañhaṁ, the question asked in that way by the words „sassato loko" *etc.*, 91,31.

ādicca. *m.* (*sa.* āditya) the sun; ~o, 107,23 — Dh. 387. — °-patha, *m.* the path of the sun, the sky, atmosphere; *loc.* ~e, Dh. 175. — °-bandhu, *m.* a member of the Ādicca-family, name of Gotama Buddha; *instr.* ~unā. Dh. p. 94, v. 3.

*ādiṇṇavat, *mfn.* (*sa.* *ā-dīrṇa-vat, *fr.* ā-√dṛ. to split) one who has torn asunder; *m.* ~vā (narindo) *w. acc.* (sīhaṁ), 112,31.

āditta, *mfn.* (*sa.* ādīpta, *pp.* ā-√dīp) set on fire, burning; *m.* ~o (cakkhusamphasso) 70,26; *n.* ~aṁ, *ib.*; *m. pl.* ~ā (rasā) 70,32. — °-geha-sadisa, *mfn.* like a burning house, 65,11. (*m. pl.* ~ā). — °-paṇṇa-sālaṁ (*acc.*) a burning hut of leaves, 44,29. — °-pariyāya, *n.* name of a chapter in Vinaya-Piṭaka, the Fire-Sermon, 71,18.

*ādiyati, *vb.* (*sa.* ā-√dā) to take, seize; to accept, choose; to take along with, carry off (*acc.*); *pr. 3. sg.* ~ati (adinnaṁ) 97,11. Dh. 246. 409 (ādiyate, *med.*); the formation ādiyati (ādeti is also to be found), which occurs only in *comp. w. prp.* ā, upā *etc.*, is possibly an old denominative form from *ger.* ādāya (or perhaps we have to suppose a weak form of the root; confusion *w. sa.* ādriyate may also be admitted in some instances) *cp.* dadāti & upādiyati. — *ger.* ādāya, often used almost like a *prp. w. acc.* = with, together with *etc.* 2,4. 6,7. 12,28-29. 32,13. 48,30. 101,3. 106,3 — Dh. 49. Dh. 287; varaṁ ~, choosing the best, Dh. 268. — *pp.* atta (*sa.* ātta) *q. v.* [The passive form is always -dīyati or -diyyati *etc.*]

ādīnava, *m.* (= *sa.*) distress, misery, evil result, disadvantage, danger; ~o. 67,31 (the evils of life); *acc.* ~aṁ, 47,23-29 (*opp.* assāda); 68,20 (kāmānaṁ); 86,8 (*opp.* ānisaṁsa). — *anekâdīnava, *mfn.* full of dangers, 23,7.

ādhipacca, *n.* (*sa.* ādhipatya, *fr.* adhipati) sovereignty, lordship; sabbalokâdhipaccena (*instr.*) „the lordship over all worlds", Dh. 178.

ānañca, *n.* (*sa.* ānantya, *fr.* an-anta, *q. v.*) infinity; ākāsânañca, the infinity of space, °-āyatana, *n.* the abode (state af mind) of the infinity of space, 80,5-6; viññāṇañca, the infinity of consciousness, 80,6-7. (contracted *fr.* viññāṇa + ānañca) *cp.* āyatana.

ānantarika or ānantariya, *mfn.* (or ānantariya, *n.* — *sa.* ānantarya, *n.*, immediate succession, *fr.* an-antara, *q. v.*) immediately following; *°-kamma, *n.* a deed which will bring retribution immediately (in this life) (= anantare yeva attabhāve vipaccanakaṁ kammaṁ, Ss.), ~aṁ (paṭhamaṁ Devadattena upacitaṁ) 76,5. — pañcânantariya-kamma, *n. sg.* (*coll.*) the five crimes that constitute „proximate karma", ~aṁ (*acc.*) 97,19; such crimes are killing one's father or mother, an Arhat or a Buddha; *cp.* SBE. XX, 246.

ānanda, *m.* (= *sa.*) [1]) joy, pleasure; ~o, Dh. 146. — [2]) Ānanda, *m. nom. pr.* the (younger) cousin of Gotama Buddha, his favorite disciple; ~o (āyasmā) 77,17. 90,28; (bahussutānaṁ [aggo]) 109,7; (bahussuto) 109,18; *voc.* ~a, *acc.* ~aṁ, 77,16; *gen.* ~assa, 90,23; °-savhaya, *m.* (*q. v.*) Ā. by name, *acc.* ~aṁ, 109,15. — [3]) *Ānanda, *m. nom. pr.* of a mythical fish, the king of the fishes; *acc.* ~aṁ nāma macchaṁ, 10,28; °-macchaṁ, 10,3.

*ānāpeti, *vb.* (*caus. II fr.* āneti, *q. v.*) to cause to be brought or fetched; *ger.* ~etvā (Bodhisattaṁ) 45,25.

*ānisaṁsa, *m.* (*fr.* *ā-ni-√çaṁs) blessings, profit, advantage; *acc.* ~aṁ (*w. loc.* nekkhamme) 68,20; (vacīsucaritapaṭisaṁyuttaṁ) 86,9 (*opp.* ādīnava). — sīlânisaṁsa-jātaka, the tale of the blessings of virtue, 28,1.

*ānubbhāva, *m.* (*fr.* anu-bhāva) power, extraordinary ability, *esp.* supernatural or magic power; *acc.*

~aṁ, 37,13; *instr.* ~ena. 16,3; m' [= me] ~ena, 112,20; iddhānubhāvena, 27,26 (*v.* iddhi); devatâ-°, 17,25; devâ-°, by the power of the gods, 63,32. — mahânubhāva. *mfn.* of great might, ~o (Bhagavā) 75,30; *gen.* ~assa (rañño) 62,14. — °-sampanna, *mfn.* possessed of magic power; ~aṁ (maṇikkhandhaṁ) 35,23.

āneti, *vb.* (*sa.* ā-√nī) to bring, to bring back (*acc.*); *pr. 3. sg.* ~eti, 6,19; *1. pl.* ~ema. 55,24; *imp. 2. sg.* ~ehi, 111,30; *2. pl.* ~etha, 16,26. 57,1; *pot. 1. sg.* ānaye (to recover) 31,35; *aor. 3. pl.* ~esuṁ, 24,21; ~ayiṁsu. 24,29; *1. pl.* ānāyimha (probably incorrect for ānayimha) 18,23; *inf.* ~etuṁ, 49,34; *ger.* ~etvā. 4,17. 6,15. 20,30; *pp.* ānīta. *m.* ~o. 18,22. 22,29; *f.* ~ā. 112,14; *n.* ~aṁ. 49,20; 113,26 (idhânītaṁ „extant here"); *caus.* ānāpeti, *q. v.*

āpajjati, *vb.* (*sa.* ā-√pad) to get in, to fall into (*acc.*); *pr. 3. sg.* ~ati (metri causa ~ī) Dh. 309; *aor. 2. sg.* mā āpajji (vissāsaṁ) „do not trust", 30,12; āpādi, Dh. 272 (vissāsa-mâpādi); *1. sg.* āpādiṁ. 94,21 (aññāṇaṁ „I am at a loss"); 94,22 (sammohaṁ „I have become greatly confused"); *ger.* ~itvā (saṁvegaṁ „in deep emotion").

āpaṇa. *m.* (= *sa.*) a shop; *abl.* ~ā, 49,5; *loc.* ~e, 30,10. — sabbagandhâpaṇa, *m.*, a perfumery shop, *acc.* ~aṁ, 48,31. — °-samīpena (*instr.*) near the shop, 49,3. — °-dvaraṁ (*acc.*) the entrance of the shop, 49,23.

āpatti, *f.* (= *sa.*) 1) misfortune. 2) fault, transgression, offence; °-sāmantā bhaṇamāno, *lit.* speaking from the neighbourhood of ~o: „when he is in danger of committing an offence by the words he says", 83,4 (*cp.* sāmanta).

āpāna, *n.* (= *sa.*) drinking, banquet. °-maṇḍala, *n.* a banqueting pavilion, 62,14.

āpucchati. *vb.* (*sa.* ā-√prach) 1) to ask, to offer (*cp.* pucchati). 2) to take leave, to bid farewell (*w. acc. pers.*); *ger.* ~itvā (rājānaṁ) 6,17; (brāhmaṇaṁ) 9,34.

ābadha, *m.* (= *sa.*) pain, sickness; ~o (kharo) 78,24; *acc.* ~aṁ, 78,30. Dh. 138.

ābharaṇa, *n.* (= *sa.*) decoration, ornament. — sabbâbharaṇa-bhūsitā. *f.* (*adj.*) decorated with every kind of ornaments, 112,1.

ābhassara, *mfn.* (*sa.* ābhāsvara) shining, bright; *m. pl.* ~ā devā, name of a class of gods, Dh. 200.

ābhāti. *vb.* (*sa.* ā-√bhā) to shine; *pr. 3. sg.* ~āti (rattiṁ candimā) 107,23 = Dh. 387.

***āma** 1, *indecl.* (*cp. sa.* ām) yes; ~ deva. yes sire! 31,8; ~ bhante. 99,18; āmâti, 44,5. — After a negative question : no, 31,30 (āma na sakkomi).

āma 2, *mfn.* raw, uncooked, unbaked, unripe; *n.* ~aṁ (pattaṁ) 104,6. — āmaka, *mfn. id.* (*v. next*).

***āmaka-susāna**, *n.* a cemetery where the dead bodies are left unburned; *nom.* ~aṁ 65,10; *acc.* ~aṁ. 39,32.

āmanteti, *vb.* (*sa.* ā-√mantr) 1) to address, to call, speak to, tell, command (*acc.*); *aor. 3. sg.* ~esi, 32,34. 44,22. 66,24. 80,1; *ger.* ~etvā, 9,11. 53,1. 63,3. — 2) to bid farewell, to take leave (*w. gen.*); *pr. 1. sg.* ~ayāmi (vo) 80,1.

āmisa, *n.* (*sa.* āmisha) 1) flesh, meat, food. — 2) carnal lust. lokāmisa, *n.* „the baits of the world"; vantalokāmisa. *mfn.* (*q. v.*).

āyatana, *n.* (= *sa.*) 1) dwelling-place, home, abode; araññâ-°, abode in a forest, *loc.* ~e. 1,4. 3,30. — 2) the six senses (*v.* saḷāyatana) each of which containing a) the organ of sense (*viz.* cakkhu. sota. ghāna. jivhā, kāya, mano) b) the contact with the object of sense (samphassa) c) the perception by means of the consciousness (viññāṇa); cakkhu-samphassa-viññāṇâyatanaṁ, the sense of sight, 72,1; sota-s. *etc.* 72,9. 12. 15. 16. 17, the sense of hearing *etc.* — 3) stage (state of mind) of ecstasy or religious meditation; ākāsânañcâ-⁰, the abode of infinity of space, 80,5; viññāṇañcâ-⁰, the abode of infinity of consciousness (*cp.* ānañca) 80,6; ākiñcaññâ-⁰ (*q. v.*), ~ of nothingness, 80,7; neva-saññā-nâsaññâ-⁰ (*q. v.*), ~ of neither perception nor non-perception, 80,8.

āyati, *f.* (— *sa.*) the future; *acc. adv.* ~iṁ, in the future, 75,26. 95,11.

āyasa. *mfn.* (— *sa.*) made of iron; *n.* ~aṁ (bandhanaṁ) Dh. 345. *cp.* ayas.

āyasmat, *m(fn).* (*sa.* āyushmat) 'possessed of long life', used in addressing or mentioning an older venerable person, *esp.* an Arhat or Thera (*q. v., cp.* 79,10); *m. nom.* ~mā, 77,17. 96,2-24; *voc.* ~mā, 79,10; *acc.* ~mantaṁ, 77,15-16; *instr.* ~atā, 96,25; *gen.* ~ato, 70,17 (tassa ~ato, without *nom. pr.*); *cp.* āyu.

āyāti. *vb.* (*sa.* ā-√yā) to come, to return; *imp. 1. pl.* āyāma, come! let us go (in summoning a single or more persons), 77,16 (āyām' Ānanda); *part.* āyanta: an-āyanta, *mfn.* not returning, *loc. pl.* ~esu, 111,15.

āyu, *n.* (*sa.* āyu & āyus) life, duration of life; *nom.* ~u, Dh. 109; ~uṁ avasiṭṭhaṁ, the rest of his lifetime, 44,28; *acc.* ~uṁ, Dh. 135. *cp.* āyasmat *& next.*

***āyuka**. *mfn.* (*fr.* āyu) living (at the end of *comp.*). yāvatāyukaṁ, *adv.* (*q. v.*).

āyudha, *n.* (— *sa., cp.* āvudha) a weapon. — naddha-pañcâyudha, *mfn.* „equipped with the 5 weapons of war", *m.* ~o, 111,16.

āyoga, *m.* (= *sa.*) employment, occupation (*w. loc.*); ~o (adhicitte) Dh. 185. (*cp. Fausböll*, Bem. p. 36.)

āragga, *v.* ārā¹.

ārakkha, *m.* (*sa.* āraksha) a guard, protection; ~o, 17,17; *acc.* ~aṁ (te gahetvā, protecting you) 17,15; ~aṁ (gāḷhaṁ) a close guard, 48,15; ~aṁ ṭhapesi, 60,26. — *ārakkhitthī, *f.* a woman on guard, *loc.* ~iyā, 49,36. — *⁰-manussa, *m.* a watchman, *instr. pl.* ~ehi (nirokāse ṭhāne) 41,29. — *gahitārakkha, *mfn.* carefully guarded, *loc. n.* ~e (bhavane) 41,28; *m. pl.* ~ā (mayā) 42,6.

āraddha, *mfn.* (*sa.* ārabdha, *pp.* ārabhati, *q. v.*) begun, undertaken. — *⁰-viriya, *mfn.* exerting one's strength, energetic; *acc. m.* ~aṁ, Dh. 8; *acc. pl. m.* ~e (sāvake) 108,19.

ārabbha, *ger.* (*fr.* ārabhati, *sa.* ārabhya) having begun; generally used as *prp. w. acc.* — about, concerning, 28,3. 84,28; santiṁ ~, keeping the tranquillity (of Nibbāṇa) in view.

ārabhati, *vb.* (*sa.* ā-√rabh) to begin, to undertake (*w. inf.*); *aor. 3. sg.* ~bhi, 10,15. 113,24; *3. pl.* ~iṁsu, 28,9; — *ger.* ārabbha (*q. v.*) — *pp.* āraddha, began, *m.* ~o, 17,21; *f.* ~ā, 51,19; — *part. gen. m.* ārabhato (viriyaṁ daḷhaṁ) Dh. 112 (*cp.* āraddha-viriya).

ārammaṇa, *n.* (probably another form for ālambana, *q. v.*) base, support; object of sense or thought. — *buddhārammaṇa, *mfn.* having its support in Buddha, *f.* ~ā pīti (*q. v.*), delightfully thinking on or putting confidence in B., 28,8; *acc.* ~aṁ pītiṁ, 28,6-9.

ārā¹, *f.* (= *sa.*) an awl, needle; āragga, *n.* (*sa.* ārâgra), the point of an awl or needle, *loc.* ~e, Dh. 401; *abl.* ~ā. Dh. 407. (*cp.* agga.)

ārā². *adv.* (*sa.* ārāt) far, far off; Dh. 253 (*w. abl.* āsavakkhayā).

ārādheti, *vb.* (*sa.* ā-√rādh, *caus.*) ¹) to conciliate, propitiate (*acc.*); *aor. 3. sg.* ~esi (rañño cittaṁ, „won the heart of the king") 96,27. — ²) to gain, achieve (*acc.*); *ellipt.* to be done for; *pot. 3. sg.* ~aye (maggaṁ) Dh. 281; ārādhe — ārādheyya (*w. abl.* kakkaṭakā) 5,22.

ārāma, *m.* (— *sa.*) a grove, a pleasure garden, a monastery; *loc.* ~e, (Anāthapiṇḍikassa) 71,21; ⁰-rukkha-cetyāni, „groves and sacred trees", Dh. 188 (*cp.* cetiya). — titthiyârāma, the heretics' grove, *acc.* ~aṁ, 73,3. – paribbājakâ-°, the grove of the mendicant friars. *abl.* ~ā, 29,23.

āriya. *mfn.* (Dh. 208) *v.* ariya.

āruyha, ārūḷha. *v.* ārohati.

ārogya, *n.* (= *sa. fr.* a-roga, *q. v.*) health; ārogya-paramā lābhā, health is the greatest profit, Dh. 204 (*cp.* lābha).

***āroceti**, *vb.* (*caus.* ā-√ruc) to tell, communicate, explain (*acc.*, *gen. pers.*); to speak to, say to (*gen.*); *aor. 3. sg.* ~esi, 6,23. 7,4. 62,4; *3. pl.* ~esuṁ, 8,2; ~ayiṁsu, 73,28; – *imp. 3. sg.* ~etu, 79,25; *2. sg.* ~ehi, 15,33. 98,3 (me rathaṁ); – *ger.* ~etvā, 58,18; – *pp.* ārocita; tumhehi °-saññāya, on account of your application to me, 25,18 (*cp.* saññā). – *caus. II.* *ārocāpeti, to cause to be told or announced, to make known, publish; *aor. 3. sg.* ~āpesi (manussānaṁ) 8,6; (Bhagavato kālaṁ, announced the hour (for the meal)) 78,3; – *ger.* ~āpetvā (rañño) 37,11.

āropeti, *vb.* (*caus. II.* ā-√ruh, *cp.* ārohati) [1]) to cause to ascend, to cause to be placed (*w. double acc.*), to put on board; *ger.* ~etvā (taṁ mama piṭṭhiṁ) 1,18; (taṁ [*sc.* nāvaṁ]) 19,27. 29,4. (mañcakaṁ [*sc.* naṁ]) 73,26 (having placed her on a handbarrow). – [2]) to cause to increase; *inf.* ~etuṁ, *comp.* ~etu-kāma, *mfn.*, *instr. pl.* ~ehi (avaṇṇaṁ Gotamassa, „wanting to bring disgrace upon G.") 74,12. – *pp.* āropita, undertaken, begun (?), *m.* ~o (sāṭako) *var. lect.* (Colombo Ed.) 87,11.

ārohati & ārūhati (āruhati), *vb.* (*sa.* ā-√ruh) to ascend, mount, to climb up on (*acc.*); *ger.* [a]) āruyha (rathaṁ) 7,5; (sayanaṁ) 53,33. [b]) ārohitvā (suvaṇṇa-pādukāyo „putting on his gilt slippers") 68,2. – *pp.* ārūḷha, [a]) having ascended, *pl.* ~a (manussā) 76,20; *acc. m. sg.* ~aṁ kathāmaggaṁ, the exposition of the doctrine contained in (*acc.* saṅgītittayaṁ) 113,29. [b]) ascended (*pass.*); tena °-nāvāya (*gen.*), a ship with him on board, 24,15. – *caus. II.* āropeti (*q. v.*).

ālapati, *vb.* (*sa.* ā-√lap) to address, to speak to (*acc.*); *pr. 3. sg.* ~ati (theraṁ) 85,28; *aor. 3. pl.* ~iṁsu, 73,3. *cp.* allāpa.

ālambati, *vb.* (*sa.* ā-√lamb) to cling to, to lean upon, to support one's self on; *ger.* ~iya (pāṇinā bhūmiṁ) 112,28.

ālambana, *n.* (= *sa.*, *cp.* ārammaṇa) depending on, supporting; object of sense. *ālambanī, *f.* (*adj.*), hanging down; rajju vâlambanī, like a rope for clinging to ɔ: a weak support, 47,27.

ālambara, *m.* (*sa.* āḍambara) a sort of drum; *acc.* ~aṁ, 67,29.

ālaya, *m.* (= *sa.*) [1]) house, dwelling. – [2]) longing, desire; *pl.* ~ā. Dh. 411. – an-ālaya, *m.* (*q. v.*). – [3]) dissimulation, pretence; *acc.* gilān'-ālayaṁ katvā, pretending to be ill, 49,22. – *cp.* allīyati.

Āḷavi, *f.* (*sa.* Āṭavī) *nom. pr.* of a town; *acc.* ~iṁ, 86,14. °-vāsino (*pl.*) the inhabitants of Ā. (*cp.* vāsin).

ālasiya, *n.* (*sa.* ālasya) sloth, want of energy; *acc.* ~aṁ, Dh. 280.

ālikhati, *vb.* (*sa.* ā-√likh) to delineate, to paint; *ger.* ~itvā (sasalakkhaṇaṁ) 16,17.

āliṅgati, *vb.* (*sa.* ā-√ling) to embrace; *ger.* ~itvā (aññamaññaṁ) 49,11.

āloka, *m.* (= *sa.*) light; *instr.* ~ena, 101,7; dīpālokena, by the lamplight, 41,27 (*cp.* dīpa [1])). – *āloka-sandhi, *m.* a window, casement; °-kaṇṇabhāgā, 84,19.

āloleti, *vb.* (*sa.* ā-√luḍ, *caus.*) to stir up, to agitate, shake (*acc.*); *ger.* ~etvā (ghaṭaṁ) 56,28.

***āḷhā**, *f.* (?) a rope or cord (?) *cp.* Mahratt. aḍhā (or āḍhā); this word is probably akin to āḷhaka (or āḷha) *m.* (= *sa.* āḍhaka), [1]) a post to which an animal is bound. [2]) a measure of capacity. – *āḷhā-baddha, *mfn.*

(or āḷha + ābaddha?) secured to a post by a cord, „spell-bound" (?), *m.* ~o (naro) 111,10.

ā v a j j a t i, *vb.* (*sa.* ā-√vṛj) [1]) to reflect, consider, to think about (*acc.*); *part. m. gen.* ~antassa, 44,32 (phalita-pātubhāvaṁ); *part. med. m.* ~amāno, 15,8. — [2]) to observe, maintain; *part.* ~anto (attano sīlaṁ) 15,1. *caus. v. next.*

ā v a j j e t i, *vb.* (*caus.* āvajjati) to turn over (*acc.*); *fut. 2. pl.* ~essatha (imaṁ (dadhighaṭaṁ)) 35,18.

ā v a t t a t i, *vb.* (*sa.* ā-√vṛt) to return; *ger.* ~itvā (hīnāyâ-[0]) returning to the world (*cp.* hīna) 69,27.

ā v a h a, *mfn.* (— *sa.*) bringing, producing; sukhāvaha, *mfn.* bringing happiness, *n.* ~aṁ (cittaṁ guttaṁ) Dh. 35; *hitāvaha, *mfn. id.*, *f.* sabbaloka-hitāvahā, 113,33.

*ā v ā ṭ a, *m.* (*cp. sa.* avaṭa) a hole in the ground; *acc. pl.* ~e (khaṇitvā) 39,32. [0]-mukha-vaṭṭiyaṁ, 40,28 (*v.* vaṭṭi).

ā v ā s a, *m.* (— *sa.*) [1]) dwelling, living; gharāvāsa, the household life, *acc.* ~aṁ. 64,33; *pl.* sattāvāsā (nava) the 9 forms of existence, 82,13 (*v.* satta [2]). — [2]) intercourse; manussâvāsa-kāraṇā „because I have had to do with men" 112,10. — [3]) a convent (vihāra), *loc. pl.* ~esu, Dh. 73. — dur-āvāsa (*q. v.*).

ā v ā h a, *m.* (— *sa.*) marriage, giving a son away in marriage (*opp.* vivāha, *q. v.*); *acc.* ~aṁ, 55,21. [0]-maṅgala, *n.* nuptial festival, *loc.* ~e, 112,15.

ā v i - k a r o t i, *vb.* (*sa.* āvish-√kṛ) to reveal, disclose; *part. m.* ~kubbaṁ (rahokammaṁ) 54,17.

ā v i j j h a t i, *vb.* (*sa.* ā-√vyadh) to encompass, to mark the boundary of (*acc.*); *ger.* (used adverbially *w. acc.* — all round) ~itvā (khettaṁ) 8,8.

ā v i l a, *mfn.* (— *sa.*) turbid, not clear; an-āvila, *mfn.* (*q. v.*).

ā v u ṇ ā t i, *vb.* (*sa.* ā-√ve. but confounded with ā-√vṛ) to string (as beads); *ger.* ~itvā (macche valliyā) 14,23.

ā v u d h a, *n.* (*sa.* āyudha) weapon; *nom.* ~aṁ, 112,20; *acc.* ~aṁ, 36,27; *pl.* ~āni, 6,12. — [0]-hattha, *mfn.* armed, *m. pl.* ~ā, 6,7. — paññāvudha, the weapon of knowledge, *instr.* ~ena, Dh. 40. A younger sanskritizised form is āyudha (*q. v.*).

*ā v u s o, *indecl.* a voc. particle used in addressing equals or inferiors: friend, brother! (also to more persons); 29,23. 75,6 (gacchâvuso). 80,12. 90,29. — *āvusa-vāda, *m.* addressing a person by the word āvuso, *instr.* ~ena, 79,7-9. — āvuso is perhaps an old *voc. fr. sa.* āyushmat (*āvusu *fr.* āyushman ? Tr.), *cp.* āyasmat.

ā s a, *m.* (*sa.* āça) food, eating; pātarāsa, sāyamāsa (*q. v.*) — an-āsakā, *f.* fasting (*q. v.*).

ā s a ṁ k a t i, *vb.* (*sa.* ā-√çaṅk) to doubt, fear, suspect; *aor. 2. pl.* ~ittha (mā aññaṁ kiñci, *cp.* añña) 7,11.

ā s a ṁ k ā, *f.* (*sa.* āçaṅkā) suspicion; kaham vo ~ā, where does your suspicion point to ? 73,22.

ā s a ṅ g a, *m.* (— *sa.*) clinging to, attachment; uttarāsaṅga, *m.* (*q. v.*).

ā s a j j a, *ger. v.* āsīdati.

ā s a d a, *m.* (— *sa.*) approaching, attack; nāga-m-āsado, approaching an elephant (with 'm' euphonically inserted) 77,3. *cp.* āsīdati.

ā s a n a, *n.* (— *sa.*) a seat; *acc.* ~aṁ, 22,28; *instr.* ~ena, 83,34; *abl.* ~ā (uṭṭhāyâ-) 70,12; *loc.* ~e (paññatte) 68,11; *pl.* ~āni, 61,25. — *cp.* ekāsana, pacchāsana, silāsana, senāsana (*q. v.*).

ā s a n n a, *mfn.* (— *sa. pp.* āsīdati, *q. v.*) near; *m.* ~o (kālo) 63,7. — accāsanna, *mfn.* too near (*opp.* atidūra, *v.* ati), *loc.* (*adv.*) ~e (gantabbaṁ) 83,2; nâtidūre nâccāsanne gacchanto, 12,29.

ā s a y a, *m.* (*sa.* āçraya or āçaya), [1]) refuge, shelter. [2]) meaning, intention. — nirāsaya, *mfn.* (*q. v.*).

ā s a v a, *m.* (*sa.* āsrava) probably

'foam, dirt'; sin, passion, desire (*synon.* kilesa); *pl.* ~ā, Dh. 93. 253. 292; *abl. pl.* ~ehi, 69,23. *⁰-kkhaya, *m.* destruction of passions, *acc.* ~aṁ, Dh. 272; *abl.* ~ā, Dh. 253. – khīṇāsava, *mfn.* having subdued the passions, *pl.* ~ā, 109,3. Dh. 89. – anāsava, *mfn.* (*q. v.*) *cp.* SBE. X p. 13—14.

āsā, *f.* (*sa.* āçā) [1]) wish, desire; *pl.* ~ā, Dh. 410. – vantāsa, *mfn.* having renounced desires, *m.* ~o, Dh. 97 (*cp.* vanta). – [2]) hope, expectation; ⁰-cchedaṁ a-katvā, without relinquishing all hope, 42,13 (*cp.* cheda).

āsāḷha, *m.* (*sa.* āshāḍha) name of a month (June—July). – uttarāsāḷha, *m.* one of the 27 lunar mansions (the 15th, *cp.* nakkhatta); ⁰-nakkhattena, at the moon's conjunction in the second half of the month Āsāḷha. *cp. next.*

āsāḷhi, *f.* (*sa.* āshāḍhi), the day of full moon in the month Āsāḷha. – ⁰-nakkhattaṁ, the midsummer festival (held on that day) 61,2.

āsiṁsati, *vb.* (*sa.* ā-√çaṁs) to hope, trust; to strive; *pot. 3. sg. med.* ~eth(a), 42,16 (*opp.* nibbindati).

*āsītika, *mfn.* (*fr.* asīti) being eighty years of age; *acc. f.* ~aṁ (nāriṁ) 47,21.

āsīdati, *vb.* (*sa.* ā-√sad) to approach; to attack, to lay hands on (*acc.*); *ger.* āsajja (selaṁ) 104,16. – *aor. 2. sg.* āsado (nāgaṁ) 77,3. – *pp.* āsanna (*q. v.*) *cp.* āsada.

āsīna, *mfn.* (= *sa.*, *part.* √ās, *cp.* acchati) sitting; *acc. m.* ~aṁ, Dh. 227. 386 („settled").

āsīvisa, *m.* (*sa.* āçīvisha) a venomous serpent; *acc.* ~aṁ, 86,18.

āha, *vb. defect.* (= *sa.*, *perf.* √ah) to say, speak (generally used in historical exposition with the signification of *pret.*); *3. sg.* āha, 75,5; *contracted*: 15,17 (evāha), 112,18 (āhâdissamāne); = *pr. 3. sg.* (says) 74,1; *w. acc.* gāthaṁ āha 3,25; *w. acc. pers.* 2,28. 14,17. – *3. pl.* āhu (panâhu, say) 64,3. Dh. 345; āhaṁsu, 4,19. 54,16 (bhastaṁ bālo'ti).

āharaṇa, *n.* (= *sa.*) fetching; dhanâharaṇatthāya, in order to fetch the money, 32,17 (*cp.* attha [1]).

āharati, *vb.* (*sa.* ā-√hṛ) [1]) to bring, fetch, take along with (*acc.*); *pr. 3. sg.* ~ati, 6,20; – *imp. 2. sg.* ~a, 36,12. 50,20 (te hatthaṁ); *2. pl.* ~atha, 41,16; – *pot. 2. sg.* ~eyyāsi, 87,12; – *aor. 3. sg.* ~i, 36,13; *1. sg.* ~iṁ, 29,1; *3. pl.* ~iṁsu, 25,2; – *fut. 3. sg.* ~issati, 35,6; *1. sg.* ~issāmi, 48,16. 92,9 (take out); *3. pl.* ~issanti, 53,25; – *ger.* ~itvā, 15,2. 32,19. 33,23. 41,3; – *pp.* āhaṭa; āhaṭāhaṭaṁ, *n.* (everything) brought, 57,6; āhaṭa-dhanaṁ, the money brought along from home, 57,36; – *pass. part.* āhariyamāna, *loc.* an-āhariyamāne (tasare) 87,15. – [2]) to tell, recite; *aor. 3. sg.* ~i (atītaṁ) 28,17; – *ger.* ~itvā (dhammadesanaṁ) 29,16; *grd.* āharitabba, *n.* ~aṁ (suttaṁ) 31,14.

āhāra, *m.* (= *sa.*) food; *acc.* ~aṁ, 15,11; *abl.* ~ato (tumhehi khāditabbâ-⁰) 14,19; *loc.* ~e, Dh. 93. – ⁰-atthāya, for food, 15,30 (*cp.* attha [1]). – an-āhāra, *mfn.* being without nutriment, ~o (aggi) 95,8. – āhāra-ṭṭhitika, *mfn.* living by food, *pl.* ~ā (sabbe sattā) 82,8.

*āhiṇḍati, *vb.* (*fr.* ā-√hiṇḍ, *cp. sa.* āhiṇḍaka) to wander, roam through (*acc.*) (to search for); *imp. 2. pl.* ~atha (nagaraṁ) 73,29. 74,11. – *part.* ~anta, *m.* ~o (pavādino, in search for disputants) 113,5.

āhita, *mfn.* (= *sa. pp.* ā-√dhā) put on, added; *m.* ~o (gini, „kindled") 104,22.

I.

*iṅgha, *indecl.*, a particle of invitation or permission: well! come! *etc.*; 12,5.

icc' = iti (*q. v.*).

icchati, *vb.* (*sa.* √ish) to wish, like, want; to seek for (*acc.*); *pr. 3. sg.* ~ati, 34,20; *2. sg.* ~asi, 31,16; *1. sg.* ~āmi, 50,11 (*w. inf.*). 62,4 (icchām'ahaṁ); — *pot. 3. sg.* ~e, Dh. 84; ~eyya, 79,14. Dh. 73; — *part. nom. m.* icchaṁ (vānaro) 107,30; *part. med.* icchamāna, *pl.* ~ā, 35,18; — *aor. 3. sg.* icchi, 18,30. 58,6 (na icchi, refused); *1. sg.* ~iṁ, 42,16; — *ger.* ~itvā, 34,25; — *pp.* ~ita, yathicchitaṁ, *adv.* according to one's desire, 111,28 (*cp.* yathā); icchiticchitaṁ, *acc. n.* „whatever she wants", 88,4.

icchā, *f.* (= *sa.*) wish, desire, lust; Dh. 74; *acc.* ~aṁ, 67,10. — °-lobha-samāpanna, *mfn.* Dh. 264. — °-dosa, *mfn.* „damaged by lust", *f.* ~ā (pajā) Dh. 359 (*cp.* dosa[1]). — vigaticcha, *mfn.* free from lust, *loc. pl.* ~esu, Dh. 359 (*cp.* vigata). — appiccha, *mfn.*, yenicchakaṁ, *adv.* (*q. v.*).

ijjhati, *vb.* (*sa.* √ṛdh) to prosper, succeed; *pr. 3. sg.* ~ati (paññavantānaṁ kiriyā) 57,6. *cp.* iddhi.

*iñjita, *n.* (*cp. sa.* iṅgita) motion, emotion; n'atthi Buddhānaṁ ~aṁ, Dh. 255.

iṭṭhakā, *f.* (*sa.* ishṭakā) a brick; *gen. pl.* ~ānaṁ, 91,29.

itara, *mfn.* (= *sa.*) [1]) the other (of two); *m.* ~o, 24,7. 43,22. 101,17; *f.* ~ā, (of two women) 46,10. 59,1; (not of two women, but of two persons mentioned) 47,3. 57,15. — [2]) second, next, following; *instr. m.* ~ena, 35,21; *pl. f. acc.* itarā (dve gāthā) 13,30. — [3]) other, *pl.* the rest; *m.* ~o ('taro jano, other people) 106,34 = Dh. 222; *f.* ~ā pajā, Dh. 85; *pl. m. acc.* itare (tayo) 14,17. — *cp.* añña & apara (para).

itarītara, *mfn.* (*sa.* itarêtara) whichsoever (whatsoever), the first comer; *instr. n.* (*adv.*?) ~ena (tuṭṭhī sukhā yā ~ „enjoyment is pleasant whatever be the cause") Dh. 331; it is questionable whether this word, in Pāli, can have the signification „mutual" or *adv.* „mutually", it seems everywhere to mean „whichsoever"; the *instr.* ~ena is probably governed by tuṭṭhi, *cp.* Sn. v. 42: santussamāno itarītarena.

iti, *indecl.* (= *sa.*) thus, in this manner (usually shortened to 'ti' by contraction or elision, and before vowels sometimes taking the form icc-) *v.* ti.

*Itivuttaka, *n.* (*fr.* iti + vutta, *q. v.*) *nom. pr.* of a canonical Pāli book, the fourth part of Khuddaka-Nikāya, thus named, because every chapter begins with the words 'vuttaṁ betaṁ Bhagavatā'; 109,33 (gāth'-udān'-itivuttakaṁ) a part of 'navaṅgaṁ Satthu-sāsanaṁ'.

ito, *adv.* (*sa.* itas) [1]) hence, from hence; 77,4 (~ paraṁ yato); 95,4 (~ katamaṁ disaṁ gato); ito c'ito ca „up and down", 36,2. — [2]) here, to this place, in this direction; 5,5. — [3]) from this time, 33,14. 87,7; ~ paṭṭhāya, henceforth, 6,16; ~ dāni paṭṭhāya, *id.* 39,2. — itoparaṁ, *adv.* later, afterwards (*opp.* ajja) 112,17. *cp.* tatoparaṁ.

ittara, *mfn.* (*sa.* itvara, but often confounded with itara, *q. v.*) hasty, inconstant; low, vile. *-dassana, *n.*, a hasty glance; *instr.* ~ena, at first sight, unconsiderately, 30,12.

*itthatta, *n.* (*sa.* ittham + *suff.* -tva) this condition, the speaker's own existence; *dat.* ~āya (nâparaṁ ~āyâti pajānâti, he understands that there is nothing more for him in this world, he has done with this world) 71,16.

itthī, *f.* (incidentally also 'thī', *sa.* strī) a woman; ~ī(ekā) 31,2; *acc.* ~iṁ, 31,22; *instr.* ~iyā, 48,25; *gen.* ~iyā, 31,9; *pl.* ~iyo, 46,9; *gen. pl.* ~īnaṁ, 46,9; thīnaṁ, 51,31. — ārakkhitthiyā, *loc.* a woman on guard, 49,36. — jānapaditthiṁ, *acc.* a countrywoman, 30,28. — duggatitthiṁ, a poor woman, 48,16. — sabbitthiyo, *pl.* all women, 48,7. — *°-kicca, *n.* (*cp. sa.* strī-kṛta) sexual intercourse, ∼aṁ (*acc.*) 111,28. — *°-kutta- (*q. v.*) women's wiles, 21,13. — *°-gabbha, *m.* a female child, 61,31. — °-lola, *mfn.* desirous of women, 50,16. — °-vesa, *m.* disguise of a woman, 58,31.

idaṁ, *pron. n.* (= *sa.*) *v.* ayaṁ.

idāni, *adv.* (*sa.* idānīm) now; 3,1. 5,3. 29,8. 47,24. 65,2. — When used without emphasis, this word usually is shortened to 'dāni'; 2,13. 3,11. 35,25. 74,22. 80,1. Dh. 235; — *with a negation* = no more, no longer; 41,34 (na dān'); 108,18 (n'atthi dāni); *cp.* ito dāni paṭṭhāya, 39,2 (*v.* ito).

iddhi, *f.* (*sa.* ṛddhi) magic or supernatural power; *instr.* ∼iyā, Dh. 175 (miraculously). — iddhânubhāva, *m. id.*, *instr.* ∼ena, 27,25. — iddhâbhisaṁkhāra, *m.* an exercise of miraculous power, *acc.* ∼aṁ, 68,35. *cp.* ijjhati.

*iddhika, *mfn.* (*fr.* iddhi) only in *comp. w.* mahā : mahiddhiko, *m.* of great miraculous power, 75,30; *pl.* ∼ā, 109,20.

iddhimat, *mfn.* (*sa.* ṛddhi-mat) possessed of magical power; *m nom.* ∼mā (viya, like a person endowed with magical power) 27,25.

idha, *adv.* (*sa.* iha, by contraction or elision : idhā-, -idha, idh', 'dha) ¹) here, in this place; 7,7. 35,35. 68,36. 85,22 (in the context); idh'eva, this very moment, 49,30. — ²) in this world; 107,26 = Dh. 18. (*opp.* pecca); 103,33 (idha jīvitaṁ); Dh. 402 (idh'eva, even in this existence). — ³) here, to this place; idhāgata, *mfn.* 21,8. 103,13. — ⁴) *unaccented* (sometimes without any pregnant meaning) 30,17 ('idha, voilà); 90,29 (idh'ekacce, 'occasionally'); 105,15; 106,6 = Dh. 267; tattha . . . idh'ānītā, brought thither 112,14; (tattha)idhâpi, accordingly (igitur), 112,15.

inda, *m.* (*sa.* indra) chief, lord, king; ∼o (devānam — Sakka) 80,26. — *comp.* : janinda, *m.*, a king, 55,1 (*voc.* ∼a, *cp.* jana). — devinda. *m.* the lord of Devas (Sakka) 110,24 (*voc.*). — narinda, *m.* a king, 7,15 (*voc. cp.* nara). — vānarinda, *m.* a king of monkeys (— kapirājan); *voc.* ∼a, 1,18; *gen.* ∼assa, 2,29 (*cp.* vānara). — Mahinda, *m. nom. pr.* (*q. v.*).

indakhīla, *m.* (*sa.* indrakīla) a threshold (ummāra); °-ûpama, *mfn.* like a threshold, *m.* ∼o, Dh. 95. (*cp.* upama.)

indanīla, *m.* (*sa.* indranīla) a sapphire; °-maṇi. (*q. v.*) 28,29.

indriya. *n.* (= *sa.*) sense, organ of sense; *pl.* ∼āni, Dh. 94; *loc. pl.* ∼esu, Dh. 7. °-gutti, *f.* „watchfulness over the senses", Dh. 375.

ima. base of the *pron. demonstr. v.* ayaṁ.

iva, *indecl.* (= *sa.*) like, as if, as it were; ᵃ) with an euphonical letter inserted : kakkaṭakā-m-iva, 5,22; usabho-r-iva, 105,19; *cp.* yad-iva, Dh. 195. ᵇ) contracted with a prec. a : macchassêva, 51,31 (°-êvodake); bahutiṇassêva, 51,33; amittenêva, Dh. 66. 207. ᶜ) shortened to va (*q. v.*). ᵈ) by metathesis — viya (*q. v.*).

isi, *m.* (*sa.* ṛshi) a saint or sage, an ascetic or hermit; °-pabbajjaṁ pabbajitvā, 34,32 (having left the world and become hermit, *v.* pabbajati); °-ppavedita, *mfn.* taught by the wises, *acc. m.* ∼aṁ (maggaṁ) Dh. 281. — mahesi (*q. v.*).

Isipatana, *n. nom. pr.* (*sa.* ṛshipatana) a forest near Benares; *nom.* ∼aṁ (migadāyo) 68,7; *loc.* ∼e, 66,24.

issara, *m.* (*sa.* īçvara) master, lord; ∼o, 11,10.

issariya, *n.* (*sa.* aiçvarya) lordship, sovereignty, empire; ∼aṁ (*acc.*) 60,13. Dh. 73.

*issukin, *mfn.* (*fr.* issā = *sa.* īrshā, īrshyā, by confusion *w.* ussuka (*q. v.*) *cp. sa.* īrshu, *mfn.*) envious; *nom. m.* ∼ī (naro) Dh. 262.

Ī.

īdisa, *mfn.* (*sa.* īdṛça) such; *m.* ~o pati) 64,15.

īsā, *f.* (*sa.* īshā) the pole of a chariot or plough; 98,4-7. °-mukhena, by means of the pole, 60,16 (*cp.* mukha).

U.

ukkaṁsati, *vb.* (*sa.* ut-√kṛsh) to raise, elevate; to praise; extol, exalt (*acc.*); *pr. 3. sg.* ~ati (*opp.* apasādeti) 74,30.

ukkaṇṭhati, *vb.* (*sa.* utkaṇṭhate) to be distressed, weary or disgusted (*sa.* 'to raise the neck' — to long for, sorrow for *etc.*); *part. med.* an-ukkaṇṭhamāna, *m.* ~o, 23,19; *pp.* ~ita, *m.* ~o, 46,18.

ukkamana, *n.* (*sa.* utkramaṇa) going out, getting out; rathassa °-ṭṭhānaṁ, *n.* room for a carriage to pass another; 43,19.

*ukkamāpeti, *vb.* (*caus. II. fr. sa.* ut-√kram) to let (a carriage) drive out of the way; *imp. 2. sg.* ~ehi (rathaṁ) 43,20; *ger.* ~etvā, 43,24.

ukkalāpa, *v.* uklāpa.

ukkāra, *m.* (*sa.* utkāra, *cp.* utkara. uccāra & avaskara) fæces, dung; °-bhūmi, *f.* a dunghill, *loc.* ~iyaṁ, 18,31.

*ukkujjati, *vb.* (probably *denom. fr. sa.* kubja (*cp.* √ubj, √kuc, kuñc)) to set up what has been overturned, or, to straighten what has been crooked (?); *pot. 3. sg.* ~eyya (nikkujjitaṁ, uparimukhaṁ kareyya, *Comm.*) 69,18. *cp.* nikkujjati.

ukkuṭika, *mfn.* (*sa.* utkuṭaka) sitting on the hams; °-ppadhāna, *n.* the sitting motionless (as a kind of ascetic exertion) ~aṁ, Dh. 141 (*cp.* padhāna).

ukkhitta, *mfn.* (*sa.* utkshipta, *pp.* ukkhipati) raised, removed; °-paligha, *mfn.* „who has destroyed all obstacles"; *acc. m.* ~aṁ, Dh. 398.

ukkhipati, *vb.* (*sa.* ut-√kship) to lift up, raise, reach out, draw up (*acc.*); *part.* ~anta, *m.* ~o, 42,3; *pl.* ~ā (jālaṁ) 36,32; — *inf.* ~itum (āvudhaṁ) 36,27; (hatthaṁ) 39,33; — *ger.* ~itvā, 5,6. 12,31. 17,20 (gīvaṁ). 23,30 (supporting, khura-cakkaṁ). 40,28. 50,21. 61,10. 111,25 (asiṁ). — *pp.* ukkhitta, *q. v.* — *caus. II.* *ukkhipāpeti, to cause to be lifted up (*acc.*); *ger.* ~etvā (deviṁ) 62,8; (Sundariṁ) 74,10.

*uklāpa, *mfn.* dirty; *m.* ~o (deso) 82,23; (sometimes written ukkalāpa).

uggacchati, *vb.* (*sa.* ud-√gam) to come forth, to rise; *pr. 3. sg.* ~ati, 27,2 (udakaṁ); — *pp.* uggata, uggatodakaṁ, *n.* the water that rises, 27,2-3; *loc. f.* ~āya (ūmiyā) 27,4; — paṭhamuggata, *mfn.* newly come out, in spring, *m.* ~o (kaḷīro) 47,9. *cp.* uggamana.

uggaṇhāti, *vb.* (*sa.* ud-√grah) to lift up; to acquire, to study, learn (*acc.*); *pr. 3. sg.* ~āti (sippaṁ) 32,12; — *aor. 3. sg.* ~i (Piṭakattayaṁ) 113,18; — *ger.* ~itvā (sabbasippāni) 45,27; uggahetvāna (Jinasāsanaṁ) 109,23. *cp.* uggahaṇa.

uggamana, *n.* (*sa.* udgamana) rising, sunrise; *abl.* aruṇ'-uggamanā, 12,18 (*v.* aruṇa); suriy'-uggamanakāle (*loc.*) at sunrise, 72,29.

uggahaṇa, *n.* (*sa.* udgrahaṇa) lifting up; *°-rajjuka, *m.* a rope or string for lifting, *acc.* ~aṁ, 14,32.

uggirati, *vb.* (*sa.* ud-√gṛ[2]) [1]) to spit out. [2]) to draw (a sword); *ger.* ~itvā (āvudhāni) 6,12.

ugghoseti, *vb.* (*sa.* ud-√ghush, *caus.*) to cry out, exclaim, declare aloud; *aor. 3. sg.* ~ayi, 114,23.

ucca, *mfn.* (— *sa.*) high, lofty, tall; *loc. n.* ~e (ṭhāne „to a high position") 76,11. — *compar.* uccatara, *mfn. m.* ~o, 3,1. — uccā, *adv.* as the first part of *comp. v. below.* — uccāvaca, *mfn. q. v.*

uccaya, *m.* (— *sa.*) gathering, accumulation; ~o (pāpassa) Dh. 117. *cp.* uccinati.

uccā, *indecl.* (— *sa.*) high, above, upwards; as the first part of *comp.*: uccā-sayana, *n.* a high or honorable seat or couch; ⁰-mahāsayanā veramaṇī, one of the ten precepts, 81,26.

uccāvaca, *mfn.* (— *sa.*, dvandva-*comp.* of ucca & avaca) high and low, various; *acc. n.* ~aṁ (na . . . dassayanti, „never appear elated or depressed") Dh. 83.

uccinati, *vb.* (*sa.* uc-√ci) to gather, collect; to choose, select; *ger.* ~itvā (varaṁ) 109,4. – uccaya, *m.* (*q. v.*).

ucchaṅga, *m.* (*sa.* utsaṅga) lap, bosom; embrace; *loc.* ~e (me putto) 31,34; *instr.* ~ena (paṇṇaṁ ādāya) 57,12.

ucchindati, *vb.* (*sa.* uc-√chid) to cut out or off; *imp. 2. sg.* ~a (sinehaṁ) Dh. 285.

ucchinna, *mfn.* (— *sa.*; *pp.* ucchindati) cut off, extirpated; *⁰-mūla, *mfn.* uprooted, *n.* ~aṁ (rūpaṁ Tathāgatassa) 95,11.

ucchu, *m.* (*sa.* ikshu) sugar-cane; *acc.* ~uṁ, 100,23.

uju, *mfn.* (*sa.* ṛju) straight, upright; right; *acc. n.* ~uṁ (karoti medhāvī) Dh. 33. – *ujuka, *mfn. id.*, *acc. m.* ~aṁ (matamanussaṁ ṭhapāpetvā) 41,17.

ujju, *mfn.* (— uju). – ujju-gata, *mfn.* righteous; *loc. pl.* ~esu, Dh. 108.

***ujjhāna**, *n.* (*fr.* ujjhāyati) complaining of, being offended; *⁰-saññin, *mfn.* inclined to be offended, *gen. m.* ~ino, Dh. 253.

***ujjhāyati**, *vb.* (*sa.* *ud-√dhyai) to be irritated or offended, to murmur, to complain of; *pr. 2. pl.* ~ath(a), 88,26; – *aor. 3. sg.* ~i, 88,2.

ujjhita, *mfn.* (— *sa.*; √ujjh) left, abandoned; *loc. n.* ~asmiṁ (saṁkāradhānasmiṁ) Dh. 58.

uṭṭhahati & **uṭṭhāti**, **uṭṭheti** (uttiṭṭhati), *vb.* (*sa.* ud-√sthā) to stand up, rise (from, *abl.*) to spring; to climb up (*acc.*); to rouse oneself, to make efforts; *aor. 3. sg.* uṭṭhāsi, 12,12; uṭṭhahi, 32,31. 50,20; *3. pl.* ~iṁsu (Sineruṁ), 60,2; – *pot. 3. sg.* uttiṭṭhe, Dh. 168 (*opp.* pamajjeyya); – *imp. 2. sg.* uṭṭhehi, 7,13. — *part. med.* uṭṭhahāna; an-uṭṭhahāno („who does not rouse himself") Dh. 280; – *ger.* uṭṭhāya, 7,23. 61,5. 70,12 (āsanā); tad-uṭṭhāya, because it springs from it, 106,19 — Dh. 240; uṭṭhahitvā (tato) 10,22. – *pp.* uṭṭhita, *pl.* ~ā (asurā) 60,3; *loc. sg. m.* ~e (suriye) 42,1. – *caus.* uṭṭhāpeti, to cause to stand up, awaken; to erect, raise, construct; *ger.* ~etvā (nāvaṁ) 23,4 (*var. lect.* for upaṭṭhapetvā, *cp.* corrections). *cp.* uṭṭhāna.

uṭṭhāna, *n.* (*sa.* utthāna) [1]) standing up, rising; *⁰-kāla, *m.* time to rise, *loc.* ~amhi, Dh. 280. – [2]) yield, revenues; sata-sahassuṭṭhāna, *mfn.* yielding 100,000, *acc. m.* ~aṁ (gāmavaraṁ) 45,3. – [3]) effort, exertion; *instr.* ~ena, Dh. 25; an-uṭṭhāna (*q. v.*).

uṭṭhānavat, *mfn.* (*sa.* utthānavat) possessed of effort, zealous; *gen. m.* ~ vato, Dh. 24.

***uṭṭhitatta**, *n.* (*fr.* uṭṭhita, *pp.* uṭṭhahati. *sa.* *utthita + tva, *cp.* utthita-tā) the state of having risen; *abl.* ~ā (vijayante) 60,25.

uṇha, *mfn.* (*sa.* ushṇa) hot, warm; *n. acc.* ~aṁ, 16,8. 83,26 (*sc.* udakaṁ); *instr.* ~ena, ib.; *loc.* ~e „in a hot place", 83,8-9; *loc. f.* ~āya (vālikāya) 97,35. — *⁰-kāra, *m.* signs of heat, *acc.* ~aṁ, 15,8.

utu, *m.* (*sa.* ṛtu) [1]) season. [2]) a woman's menstrual discharge, the mucus etc. secreted at a woman's delivery; *acc.* ~uṁ (gāhāpesuṁ) 62,32.

uttatta, *mfn.* (*sa.* ut-tapta) heated, glowing; shining; ⁰-kanaka-sannibha, *mfn.* like shining gold, *m.* ~o (kāyo) 85,7. *cp.* ottappa.

uttama, *mfn.* (— *sa.*) highest, extreme, principal; best, excellent; *m.* ~o, 25,15; *voc.* ~a, 108,11; *acc.*

m. n. ~aṁ (pucchaṁ) 91,15; (saraṇaṁ) 107,21 = Dh. 192; (dhammaṁ) Dh. 115; — *comp.* uttamatthaṁ (*acc.*) 54,29 (an excellent thing), Dh. 386 („the highest end"); uttama-porisa, *m.* the best or greatest man, ~o, Dh. 97 = purisuttama, Dh. 78 (*acc. pl.* ~e); °-yobbana-vilāsa-, 47,14; °-rathaṁ, 63,4; °-rūpa-dhara, *mfn.* 19,7; °-vedanaṁ, 103,23. — uttamaṅga, *n.* (= *sa.*) the head; ~aṁ, 47,7; ~ruha, *mfn.* (*v.* aṅga). — saṅgāmajuttama, *v.* saṅgāma. — Saññatuttama, *v.* saññata.

uttara, *mfn.* (= *sa.*) [1]) upper, higher, superior; uttaroṭṭha, *m.* (*sa.* uttaroshṭha) the upper lip or jaw, *loc.* ~e, 13,19. — [2]) later, last (*opp.* pubba); °-āsaḷha, *m.* (*sa.* uttarāshaḍhā, *f.*) a lunar mansion, the last half of the month āsaḷha (*q. v.*). — [3]) northern; *acc.* ~aṁ (disaṁ) 95,5; °-disato (*abl.* from the North) 61,18; °-dvāra, *n.* the northern door or gateway, *instr.* ~ena, 55,30; °-yavamajjhaka, *m. nom. pr.* of a village or a country district, *acc.* ~aṁ, 55,30. — an-uttara, *mfn.* (*q. v.*), *cp.* Aṅguttara & uttarāsaṅga.

uttarati, *vb.* (*sa.* ut-√tṛ) to step out (of the water), to disembark; *aor. 3. pl.* ~iṁsu (nagarasamīpe) 21,18; *ger.* ~itvā, 84,2; *pp.* uttiṇṇa, °-padaṁ (*acc.*) footsteps of those who had gone out of the water (? perhaps an error instead of otiṇṇa-padaṁ) 111,17.

uttarāsaṅga, *m.* (= *sa.*) the upper robe; *acc.* ~aṁ, 74,19, 82,18; *loc. pl.* ~esu, 33,7.

***uttariṁ**, *adv.* (*cp.* uttara) further, again; 88,12-17-21.

***uttari-bhāveti**, *vb.* (*fr.* uttara + *caus.* √bhū) to devote oneself especially to, or (perhaps better) to subdue completely, *pot. 3. sg.* vuttari-bhāvaye (pañca) „rise above" Dh. 370. *cp. Morris*, JPTS. '87,116.

uttaroṭṭha, *m. v.* uttara.

uttāna, *mfn.* (= *sa.*) lying on the back; °-seyyaka, *mfn.* id. (*cp. sa.* uttāna-çaya) *m.* ~o, 99,5.

uttiṇṇa, *mfn. pp.* uttarati, *q. v.*

uttiṭṭhati, *v.* uṭṭhahati.

***Uttiya**, *m. nom. pr.* of a wandering ascetic; ~o (paribbājako) 89,19; *voc.* ~a, 89,24; *acc.* ~aṁ, 90,28; *gen.* ~assa, 90,27.

utrasta, *mfn.* (a sanskritizised form for uttasita, *sa.* uttrasta, *fr.* ut-√tras) frightened, alarmed; *m.* ~o (puriso) 75,17; *acc.* ~aṁ, 75,19.

ud-°, (= *sa.*) prefix to verbs and nouns (= up, out) variously assimilated with a following consonant, but before h sometimes taking the form ū (*v.* ūhaññati). *cp.* uttama, uttara.

uda, *n.* (= *sa.*) water (only in *comp.*): °-kumbho, *m.* a water-pot, Dh. 121. — °-bindu, *m.* a water-drop, 108,2; °-bindu-nipātena (*instr.*) by the falling of water-drops, Dh. 121.

udaka, *n.* (= *sa.*) water; *nom. acc.* ~aṁ, 3,33, 5,18; *abl.* ~ā, 15,14; ~ato, 11,31, 89,14; *loc.* ~e, 1,20; 51,31 (macchassêvôdake); ~amhi, 28,6. — uggatodakaṁ „the water thus sucked away", 27,3. — khīrodakena (*instr.*) with milk-water, 36,35, 38,3 (khīrodaka-). — gandhodaka-, scented water, 38,3. — dārûdaka-, wood and water, 20,12. — pādodakaṁ, water for washing the feet, 83,5. — *mahôdaka, *mfn.* abounding with water, deep, *f.* ~ikā (Gaṅgā) 1,16. — mukhodakaṁ, water for rinsing the mouth, 82,18. — sakkharodaka-, sweet water, 38,3. — *°-kīḷā, *f.* 52,28 (*q. v.*). — °-dhārā, *f.* (= *sa.*) a gush or flow of water, *pl.* ~ā, 62,32. — *°-pariyanta, *m.* the edge of the water, *loc.* ~e, 4,2. — *°-ppamāṇa, *n.* the altitude of the water, ~aṁ, 3,2. — *°-sappa, *m.* a water-snake, *acc.* ~aṁ, 52,28. — *cp.* odaka, vodaka, sa-uduka.

udagga, *mfn.* (*sa.* udagra) [1]) high, elevated. [2]) joyful, elated; *m.* ~o, 68,16. — °-citta, *mfn.* elated, *acc. m.* ~aṁ, 68,22.

udapādi, *v.* uppajjati.

udaya, *m.* (= *sa.*) rising, origin;

°-vyayaṁ (*acc.*) origin and destruction, beginning and end, Dh. 113. 374. — *cp.* ñāṇodaya.

u d a r a, *n.* (— *sa.*) belly, stomach; *acc.* ~aṁ, 41,26; *loc.* ~e, 1,24.

u d a r i y a, *n.* (*sa.* udarya) the stomach; ~aṁ, 82,4 — 97,22. *cp.* sodariya.

u d ā n a, *n.* (— *sa. fr.* ud-√an) ¹) 'breathing upwards', heart's joy, a song of joy, a solemn utterance; *nom.* ~aṁ, 65,12; *acc.* ~aṁ, 42,18. 64,13. 66,19. — °-vasena. 42,14 (*v.* vasa). — ²) *nom. pr.* of a buddhist canonical work, a part of 'navaṅgaṁ Satthusāsanaṁ', 109,33 (gāth'-udān'-itivuttakaṁ).

u d ā n e t i, *vb.* (*sa.* udānayati, *denom. fr.* udāna) to disclose (the joy of one's heart); *aor. 3. sg.* ~esi (udānaṁ) 64,13. 66,19; — *ger.* ~etvā, 42,18.

u d ā h u, *adv. interr.* (*sa.* uta & utâho) or (latin 'an', at the beginning of the second part of a double interrogation), 59,12 (without interr. particle at the first part); 98,1 (kin nu . . . udāhu); 99,2 (so eva so. udāhu añño).

u d ī r e t i, *vb.* (*sa.* ud-√īr, *caus.*) to utter, speak; *pot. 3. sg.* ~aye (giraṁ saccaṁ) Dh. 408. *cp.* ereti.

u d u m b a r a, *m.* (*sa.* udumbara (uḍumbara)) name of a tree, Ficus Glomerata; ~o, 2,11; *acc.* ~aṁ, 1,26. — °-rukkha, *m. loc.* ~e, 2,5.

*U d u m b a r ā, *f. nom. pr.* name of a queen, the mother of Mahosadha (Bodhisatta), 55,20 (~devī).

u d d a, *m.* (*sa.* udra) a kind of aquatic animal, an otter; ~o, 14,10; *gen.* ~assa, 15,9.

u d d ā p a, *m.* (*sa.* udvāpa ?) the foundation of a wall; °-âdīni (*v.* ādi) 91,18. — daḷhuddāpa, *mfn. n.* ~aṁ (nagaraṁ) 90,31 — thira-pākāra-pādaṁ 91,20 (*cp.* daḷha).

u d d i s a t i, *vb.* (*sa.* ud-√diç) ¹) to show, point out, declare; *pot. 1. sg.* ~eyyaṁ (kaṁ . . . „whom should I indicate (as my teacher)") Dh. 353. ²) to explain, teach (*cp. next*).

*u d d i s ā p e t i. *vb.* (*caus. II.* uddisati) to cause to teach or give instruction; *ger.* ~etabba, who is to be called upon to give instruction, *m.* ~o, 84,6. — *fut.* ~etuṁ, *comp.* ~etukāma, *mfn.* wanting an occasion to give instruction, *m.* ~o, 84,6.

u d d e s a, *m.* (— *sa.*) ¹) illustration, enunciation. ²) region, place. — uddesika, *mfn.* (at the end of *comp.*, *cp. sa.* uddesaka) : soḷasa-vass'-uddesikā, *f.* about sixteen years of age, 86,23.

u d d h a ṁ, *adv.* (*sa.* ūrdhvam) upwards; ~ulloketvā, 76,2. — uddhaṁsota, *mfn.* (*sa.* ūrdhva-srotas) whose stream of life tends upwards, *m.* ~o, Dh. 218.

u d d h a t a, *mfn.* (— *sa. fr.* ud-√han) lifted up; *v.* an-uddhata.

u d d h a n a, *n.* (*sa.* uddhāna, uddhmāna) an oven, a fireplace; °-antaresu (*loc. pl.*) „into the oven", 9,24 (*cp.* antara).

u d d h a r a t i, *vb.* (*sa.* ud-√hṛ) to take out or up, to lift up, gather; pull out, draw out, take away, remove (*acc.*); *imp. 2. pl.* ~ath(a) (attānaṁ duggā) Dh. 327; — *aor. 3. sg.* uddhārī (maṁ aṁkena) 20,25; — *ger.* ~itva 14,23 (macche). 26,1. 34,6 (dārūni). 40,30. 44,26 (phalitaṁ); — *grd.* ~itabba, *n.* ~aṁ (āsanaṁ) 82,29. — *caus. v. next.*

u d d h a r ā p e t i, *vb.* (*caus. II.* uddharati) to raise, to cause to be pulled up (out); *ger.* ~etvā (mūlāni) 38,2.

u d d h u m ā y a t i, *vb.* (*sa.* ud-√dhmā) to swell; *aor. 3. sg.* ~āyi (galo) 13,11.

u n n a d a t i, *vb.* (*sa.* ud-√nad) to cry out, roar, make a noise; *aor. 3. pl.* ~iṁsu, 8,31. — *caus. v. next.*

*u n n ā d e t i, *vb.* (*caus.* unnadati) to cause to resound, echo, ring (*acc.*); *ger.* ~etvā (vanaṁ) 34,26; — *part. med.* ~ayamāna, *f.* ~ā (devatā vanaṁ) 5,20.

*u n n a ḷ a. *mfn.* evildoing, arrogant, insolent (?); *gen. pl.* ~ānaṁ (*opp.*

pamattānaṁ) Dh. 292 (*cp.* the expression „akiccaṁ pana kayirati", ib.).

u p a, *prp.* (= *sa.*) prefixed to verbs and nouns — near to, with (*opp.* apa).

u p a k a ḍ ḍ h a t i, *vb.* (*sa.* upa-√kṛsh) to draw towards; *pr. 3. sg.* ∼ati (nirayāya „leads to hell") Dh. 311.

u p a k a r a ṇ a, *n.* (= *sa.*) instrument, implement; *pl.* tunnavāya-upakaraṇāni, the implements of a tailor, 55,29.

u p a k ā r a, *m.* (= *sa.*) help, use; bahûpakāra, *mfn.* very useful, *m.* ∼o (sakuṇo) 18,13; — nir-upakāra, *mfn.* useless, *m.* ∼o (manusso) 35,29.

*u p a k ū ḷ i t a, *mfn.* (*fr. sa.* *upa-√kūḍ (*cp.* √kūṭ, kuṇḍ)) half-burnt, almost burnt up; *m.* ∼o, 9,32.

u p a k k a m a, *m.* (*sa.* upakrama) 1) beginning. 2) mode of proceeding. 3) treating, cure. 4) intervention, cooperation, influence, action. *v.* an-upakkamena, parûpakkamena.

u p a k k i l e s a, *m.* (*sa.* upakleça) a bad (depraving) quality, depravity; *acc. pl.* ∼e (cetaso) 91,7.

u p a g a, *mfn.* (= *sa.*) approaching; *m. pl.* jāti-jar'-ûpagā (narā) undergoing (again and again) birth and decay, Dh. 341.

u p a g a c c h a t i, *vb.* (*sa.* upa-√gam) to go near, to enter, approach (*acc.*); *aor. 3. sg.* ∼gañchi, 40,15. 62,18; upāgami, *v.* upâgacchati; — *inf.* ∼gantuṁ, 8,22; — *ger.* upagamma; an-upagamma, avoiding, 66,28 = 96,17; — *pp.* upagata, *m.* ∼o (niddaṁ, fell asleep) 65,2; an-upagato (diṭṭhigatāni) has not adopted them, 93,33. — *cp.* upâgacchati.

u p a g h ā t a, *m.* (= *sa.*) stroke, violation, injury, damage; an-upaghāta, *m.* (*q. v.*).

u p a g h ā t i n, *mfn.* (= *sa.*) injuring; parûpaghātin, *mfn.* who strikes others, *m.* ∼ī, Dh. 184.

u p a c ā r a, *m.* (= *sa.*) proceeding, practice, custom; *m.* ∼o (sippassa, „it is the way of the craft") 55,7; *acc.* ∼aṁ karohi, „go through the usual custom", 55,11.

u p a c i t a, *mfn.* (= *sa. pp.* upacinati, upa-√ci) heaped up, increased; *n.* ∼aṁ (kammaṁ) 76,6.

*u p a c c a g ā, *aor. 3. sg.* (upâtigacchati) (*sa.* *upa + ati-√gā) = to escape, to pass, overcome (*acc.*); khaṇo mā ∼ „no moment should escape" 108,6; saṅgaṁ ∼ („has overcome, subdued") Dh. 412.

u p a j j h ā y a, *m.* (*sa.* upâdhyāya) a teacher, preceptor; ∼o, 82,23. 97,16; *gen.* ∼assa, 83,1; *loc.* ∼amhi, 82,16.

u p a ṭ ṭ h a p e t i & ∼ ā p e t i, *vb. caus.* (*sa.* upa-√sthā) 1) to procure, provide (*acc.*); *pot. 3. pl.* ∼apeyyuṁ (bhisakkaṁ) 92,8; — *ger.* ∼apetvā (dhitiṁ) 41,27 („summoning his courage"); 23,1 *v.* corrections. — 2) to ordain (*acc.*); *inf.* ∼āpetuṁ, 81,17; — *grd.* ∼āpetabba, *m. pl.* ∼ā (sāmaṇerā) 81,14.

u p a ṭ ṭ h a h a t i & u p a ṭ ṭ h ā t i (-t i ṭ ṭ h a t i), *vb.* (*sa.* upa-√sthā) to appear, to come near, to wait upon (*acc.*); *part. m.* ∼ṭṭhahanto (Kosalarājānaṁ) 38,22; — *aor. 3. sg.* upaṭṭhāsi, appeared as, 23,28. 65,11; — *pp.* upaṭṭhitā, *m. pl.* (taṁ, have come near to thee) Dh. 235. *caus. v. above.*

*u p a ṭ ṭ h ā k a, *m.* (*cp. sa.* upasthātar) a servant; *acc. pl.* ∼e, 73,25. — 0-kula, *n.* ∼aṁ (Sāriputtassa „a family devoted to the service of S.") 81,11.

u p a ṭ ṭ h ā n a, *n.* (*sa.* upasthāna) attendance, waiting on, help, service; *acc.* ∼aṁ kurumānā, a waiting woman, 49,13; tesaṁ ∼aṁ gacchanto, in order to help them, 35,2; — *instr.* ∼ena (kiṁ me evarūpena rājû∼) „why should I serve such a king?" 25,11.

u p a ṭ ṭ h ā p e t i, *v.* upaṭṭhapeti.

u p a ḍ ḍ h a, *mfn.* (*sa.* upârdha, *n.*) half; *m.* ∼o (loko) 90,22. *cp.* aḍḍha.

u p a t i ṭ ṭ h a t i, *v.* upaṭṭhahati.

u p a t t a, *mfn.* (*sa.* upāsta, up-√as 2) cast down, thrown down; *v.* haritupatta.

upaddava, *m.* (*sa.* upadrava) attack; misfortune, calamity; *nom.* corupaddavo, attack from robbers, 42,5 (*cp.* cora). — an-upaddava, *mfn.* uninjured, Dh. 338 (*q. v.*). — nir-upaddava, *mfn.* without mishap, 25,20 (*q. v.*).

upadduta, *mfn.* (*sa.* upadruta, *pp.* upa-√dru) annoyed, oppressed; *m.* ~o (hatthīhi) 35,11; *n.* ~aṁ vata bho! „how oppressive is it all", 65,11. — an-upadduta, *mfn.* not oppressed, 68,14 (*q. v.*). — *cp.* upaddava.

upadhāna, *n.* (= *sa.*) the act of placing upon; para-dukkh'-ûpadhānena (*instr.*) „by causing pain to others", Dh. 291.

upadhāreti, *vb.* (*sa. caus.* upa-√dhṛ) to consider, regard; to reflect or meditate on; *pr. 1. sg.* ~emi, 55,35; *part. m.* ~ento, 86,29.

upadhi, *m.* (= *sa.*) 'adding, addition' (increase, substance?); *pl.* passions, affections (technically: the four upadhis, *viz.* khandhā, kāma, kilesa, kamma, cp. SBE, X 95, Note); *pl.* ~ī, 105,29 (narassa nandanā). — nir-ûpadhi, *mfn.* „free from all germs (of renewed life)", *acc. m.* ~iṁ. Dh. 418.

upanayhati, *vb.* (*sa.* upa-√nah) to tie or bind to, to put on; *pr. 3. pl.* upanay(i)hanti (ye taṁ ~) „who harbour such thoughts", Dh. 3—4.

upanāmeti, *vb.* (*sa. caus.* upa-√nam) to reach, hand to; to offer, present; *ger.* ~etvā (tassa bheriṁ) 35,13; — *part. gen. f.* ~entiyā (tassā) 89,5; — *grd.* ~etabba, *m.* ~o, 83,13.

upanikkhipati, *vb.* (*sa.* upa-nih-√kship) to throw, cast down; to place (down before), to procure; *grd.* ~khipitabba, *n.* ~aṁ, 83,6.

***upanibha**, *mfn.* (*sa.* *upa + nibha, *cp.* sannibha) almost like; *f.* veḷuriya-vaṇṇ'-ūpanibhā (gīvā) resembling the colour of lapis-lazuli, 10,19.

upanisā, *f.* (*sa.* upanishad) the secret art of doing or obtaining something; lābhūpanisa, *mfn.* (?) „leading to wealth", *f.* ~ā (*sc.* paṭipadā?) Dh. 75.

***upanissāya**, *prp.* (*ger. sa.* upa-ni-√çri) near to (*acc.*); Rājagahaṁ ~, 84,26.

upanīta-vaya, *mfn.* (*sa.* upanīta (brought near, upa-√nī) + vayas) whose life has come to an end; *m.* ~o, Dh. 237 (*cp.* vayas).

upapajjati, *vb.* (*sa.* upa-√pad) to approach, obtain; to appear; to be produced, *esp.* to be born again; *pr. 3. sg.* ~ati, 94,14; *3. pl.* ~anti (*w. acc.* gabbhaṁ, nirayaṁ), Dh. 126; *3. pl. med.* upapajjare (nirayaṁ) Dh. 307. — *pp.* upapanna, *q. v.*

upapatti, *f.* (= *sa.*) appearing, the being born again; *acc.* ~iṁ (sattānaṁ) Dh. 419.

upapanna, *mfn.* (= *sa.*, *pp.* upapajjati) having approached, reached, obtained; *acc. m.* jāti-mant'-ûpapannaṁ (brāhmaṇaṁ) possessed of high birth and holy wisdom, 30,9.

upama, *mfn.* (= *sa.*, at the end of *comp.*) like, resembling; aggi-sikh'-ûpama. *m.* ~o (ayoguḷo) „like flaring fire", 107,1 = Dh. 308; — indakhīl'-ûpama, Dh. 95; kumbh'-ûpama, Dh. 40; nagar'-ûpama, Dh. 40; pheṇ'-ûpama, Dh. 46; rājarath'-ûpama, Dh. 171 (*v. h.*), *cp. next.*

upamā, *f.* (= *sa.*) resemblance, comparison; a simile, example; *acc.* ~aṁ (te karissāmi) 90,29; attānaṁ ~aṁ katvā, supposing that it is your case, Dh. 129; — *loc.* ~āyaṁ (bhāsitassa atthaṁ) 90,29. — At the end of *comp.*: upama. *mfn.* (*q. v.*), *cp.* opamma.

uparava, *m.* (= *sa.*) noise (or bustle); ~o (rājaṅgaṇe aṭṭatthāya) 42,30.

uparājan, *m.* (= *sa.*) a viceroy; *nom.* ~ā, 45,27. *cp.* oparajja, *n.*

upari, *indecl.* (= *sa.*) [1]) *prp.* = above, over, upon, against; [a]) *w. gen.* aññassa ~, 7,9; coraraññō ~, 40,7; [b]) *w. loc.* ārakkhitthiyā ~, 50,1;

~muddhani, 77,8. — [2]) *adv.* = further, moreover; 47,17. — [3]) *comp.* °-pāsāda-vara-tala-gatā, *f.* „having ascended to the roof of the palace", 64,12; *cp. next* & uparima, *mfn.*

uparibhāga, *m.* (= *sa.*) the upper part or portion of something; *loc.* uparibhāge (*prp. w. gen.*) = above, 13,23 (tassa ~), *cp.* uparima.

*uparima, *mfn.* (*fr.* upari) uppermost, topmost; °-bhaga, *m.* — uparibhāga; *loc.* (*prp. w. gen.*) ~e (rañño) above, 40,25.

upaladdhi, *f.* (*sa.* upalabdhi) supposition, false opinion; sattûpaladdhi (*q. v.*) 91,13-32.

upalabhati, *vb.* (*sa.* upa-√labh) to find, to perceive; *pass.* upalabbhati, *pr. 3. sg.* „is to be found", 97,3. (u'ūpalabbhati) 97,7. — upaladdhi, *f.* (*q. v.*).

upalitta, *mfn.* (*sa.* upalipta, *pp.* upa-√lip) besmeared, anointed; anupalitta, *mfn.* (*q. v.*).

upavana, *n.* (— *sa.*) a small forest, a grove, garden; °-araññesu (*loc. pl. dvandva-comp.*) „in the parks and in the woods", 73,34.

upavisati, (or upâvisati) *vb.* (*sa.* upa-√viç) to sit down; *aor. 3. sg.* upāvisi (*w. acc.* rukkhamūlaṁ) 110,29.

*upasaṁvasati, *vb.* (*sa.* *upa-saṁ-√vas) to live together with, to keep company with (*acc.*); *pot. 2. sg.* ~vase (Sākhaṁ) 7,33.

upasaṁhita, *mfn.* (— *sa.*, *pp.* upa-saṁ-√dhā) connected with, accompanied by; sacc'-ûpasaṁhita, *mfn.* true, *n.* ~aṁ, 9,31.

upasagga, *m.*, *v.* upassagga.

upasaṁkamati, *vb.* (*sa.* upa-saṁ-√kram) to go to, come near, approach (*acc.*); *pr. 3. pl.* ~anti. 21,2; — *pot. 1. sg.* ~eyyaṁ, 71,27; — *aor.* ~i, 68,2; — *inf.* ~ituṁ, 8,19; — *ger.* ~itvā, 6,14. 19,25; — *pp. m.* ~kanto (idh') 75,25.

upasanta, *mfn.* (*sa.* upaçānta, *pp.* upa-√çam, *cp.* upa-sammati) calm, tranquil; *m.* ~o. Dh. 201. 378; *gen.* ~assa, Dh. 96.

upasama, *m.* (— *sa.*) becoming quiet, tranquillity of mind; *gen.* ~assa, Dh. 205; *dat.* ~āya (saṁvattati) 66,29. 93,8; dukkh'-ûpasama-, „quieting of pain", 107,20 = Dh. 191 (°-gāminaṁ maggaṁ); nekkhamm'-ûpasame, *loc.* „in the repose of retirement (from this world)", Dh. 181; vitakk'-ûpasame, *loc.* „in quieting doubts", Dh. 350; saṁkhār'-ûpasamaṁ, *acc.* cessation of existence, Dh. 368.

*upasampadā, *f.* (*fr.* upa-sam-√pad) [1]) taking, acquiring; Dh. 183. [2]) acquiring a priest's order, ordination of a priest; 70,17. 97,16; *acc.* ~aṁ, 70,15. — laddha-pabbajj'-ûpasampada, *mfn.* having obtained admission to the order and ordination, *m.* ~o, 89,16 (*cp.* pabbajjā).

upasammati, *vb.* (*sa.* upa-çāmyati, √çam) to become quiet; *pr. 3. sg.* ~ati, Dh. 4. (tes'ūpasammati — tesaṁ upa-°), Dh. 100; *pp.* upasanta (*q. v.*), *cp.* upasama.

upasussati, *vb.* (*sa.* upa-√çush) to dry up (by degress); *pot. 3. sg.* ~aye (n'ūpa-°) 103,19.

upasevati, *vb.* (*sa.* upa-√sev) to frequent, visit; to serve, worship; to have sexual intercourse with (*acc.*); *pr. 3. sg.* ~ati, (aññaṁ) 9,28.

upasevin, *mfn.* (— *sa.*) serving, worshipping; devoted to, coveting; *m.* para-dārûpasevī, „who covets his neighbours wife", Dh. 309.

upassagga, *m.* (— upasagga. *sa.* upasarga) an accident, misfortune; *acc.* ~aṁ (*var.* upasaggaṁ) Dh. 139.

upassaṭṭha, *mfn.* (*sa.* upasṛshṭa, *pp.* upa-√sṛj) afflicted, plagued; *n.* ~aṁ vata bho! „how stifling is it all!" 65,12. 68,12. — an-upassaṭṭha, *mfn.* (*q. v.*).

upahaññati, *vb. pass.* (*sa.* upa-√han, *pass.*) to be afflicted, oppressed; *pr. 3. sg.* ~ati (cittaṁ) 97,36; *pp. v. next.*

upahata, *mfn.* (*sa. pp.* upa-√han) struck, beaten; injured, afflicted, pained; *m.* ~o (kaṁso, „broken"), Dh. 134.

upahāra, *m.* (= *sa.*) ¹) receiving, acquiring. ²) offering; present, oblation; an-upahāra, *m.* (*q. v.*).

upāgacchati, *vb.* (*sa.* upâ-√gam) to come near, approach (*acc.*); to return; *aor. 3. sg.* ~gañchi, 112,1; ~gami, 103,4. 112,24. 114,32; — *pp.* upāgata, *m.* ~o, „rushed at her", 111,22.

upādāna, *n.* (= *sa.*) ¹) taking, grasping, clinging to existence, the 9th link of the paṭiccasamuppāda (*q. v.*), originating with taṇhā, 66,9 (taṇhāpaccayā ~aṁ) and causing bhava (~paccayā bhavo, *ib.*). — pañc' upādāna-kkhandhā (*m. pl.*) „the fivefold clinging to existence", 67,11 (*v.* khandha). — upādāna-nirodha, *m.* 66,18 (*cp.* corrections). — upāy'-upādāna, 96,10–11 (*q. v.*). — ²) fuel; tiṇa-kaṭṭh'-upādānaṁ (*acc.*), the fuel of grass and wood, 94,36. *cp. next.*

upādiyati, *vb.* (*sa.* upâ-√dā) ¹) to take with, include, comprise. ²) to grasp at, cling to the world; *pr. 3. sg.* ~diyati (upāyupādānaṁ, *q. v.*) 96,12; — *part. med.* upādiyāna, *m.* an-upādiyāno, „caring for nothing" Dh. 20 (*cp.* SBE. X, 8.); — *ger.* upādāya [often used as *prp.* = including, on account of, in comparison with, *etc.*]: an-upādāya, having become free from attachment, 69,23; Dh. 89 (ratā), 414 (nibbuto); anupādāya is sometimes shortened to anupādā (*adv.*) = absolutely, completely, 94,12 (vimutto). [The passive form is upādīyati or upādiyyati, *cp.* ādiyati.]

upāya, *m.* (= *sa.*) means, expedient, way; ~o 1,10. 43,26; *instr.* ~ena, by some means or other, 25,35. 26,16. 33,23 = eken' upāyena, 4,1; iminā (eten') upāyena, by these means, 55,8. 58,23; ten'eva (eten'eva) upāyena, in the same way, 2,24. 23,22; yena tena upāyena, anyhow, at any prize, 1,9; an-upāyena, „by misguided means", 34,17–20. — *upāya-kusala, *mfn.* skilful, clever; *m.* ~o, 25,14. 40,16. — *upāyupādāna, *n.* (*& m. pl.*) seems to denote the coveting and grasping of (wordly things), *acc.* ~aṁ (na upeti na upādiyati) 96,11; upāyupādānâbhinivesa-nibandho (*adj.* ayaṁ loko yebhuyyena) 96,10 ɔ: (upon the whole this existence is only) a chain of coveting, grasping, and clinging to (the world), *cp.* abhinivesa.

***upāyāsa**, *m.* (*cp. sa.* āyāsa) despair; *pl.* (*dvandva comp.*) ~ā, 66,11–17; *instr. pl.* ~ehi, 70,30. — sa-upāyāsa, *mfn.* coupled with despair, *n.* ~aṁ, 94,2.

Upāli, *m.* (= *sa.*) *nom. pr.* of a thera; ⁰-paṇḍito (aggo vinaye) 109,7; *acc.* ~iṁ, 109,15; ⁰-thero satimā, 109,18.

upāvisi, *v.* upa-visati.

upāsaka, *n.* (= *sa.*) a faithful layman, a lay disciple of Buddha; *voc.* ~a, 28,14; *acc.* ~aṁ, 28,3. 69,20; *pl.* ~ā, 28,15.

upāhanā, *f.* (*sa.* upānah) a shoe, sandal; *acc. pl.* ~ā, 82,17.

upeta, *mfn.* (= *sa.*; *pp. fr. next*) who has arrived at, entered into; possessed of, endowed with (*w. acc.* or *instr.* or at the end of *comp.*); *m.* ~o (ālasiyaṁ, „full of sloth") Dh. 280; (damasaccena) Dh. 10 (*opp.* apeto); — pāṇupeta, *mfn.* lifelong, *v.* pāṇa; vaṇṇa-gandha-ras'ūpeta, *mfn.* endowed with beauty, odour, and flavour, *m.* ~o (ambo) 37,30; sabbākāravar'ūpeta, *mfn.*, *v.* ākāra.

upeti, *vb.* (*sa.* upa-√i) to go to, approach, enter into (*acc.*); *abs.* to fit the case; *pr. 3. sg.* ~eti (nirayaṁ) 74,1; (upāyupādānaṁ) 96,12; (gabbhaṁ, to the born) Dh. 325; na upeti, 94,14 („it would not fit the case"); *pr. 1. pl.* ~ema (saraṇaṁ taṁ, take refuge in thee) 105,31; — *fut. 2. sg.* upehisi (jātijaraṁ) Dh. 238 = 348; *1. sg.* upessaṁ (gabbhaseyyaṁ) 105,20; — *ger.* upecca, 110,30; — *pp.* upeta, *q. v.* (*cp.* upāya).

uposatha, *m.* (*sa.* upavasatha) fast, fast-day; holy day, sabbath (occurring four times in the month), ~o,

14,17 — *⁰-divaso, 14,16; mahā-⁰, 22,20; puṇṇamuposathadivaso, 22,19 (the fullmoon-holiday); *acc.* ~aṁ, 22,20. *⁰-kamma, *n.* the fast-day service, *nom. acc.* ~aṁ, 14,13. 22,16. *⁰-aṅgāni (*pl.*) the holy day vows, 61,7 (*cp. Sp. Hardy,* Eastern Monachism).

*uposathika, *mfn.* (*fr.* uposatha) one who observes the sabbath, fasting; *m. pl.* ~ā, 14,19.

uppajjati, *vb.* (*sa.* ut-√pad) to arise, originate, begin, appear; to be be produced, to be found; *pr. 3. sg.* ~ati, 19,1 (yāva~, until he appeared); 25,32; 27,4 (saddo); 35,12 (me dukkhaṁ, I am annoyed); 53,10 (me bhayaṁ, I fear); 70,27 (-paccayā, from); 96,13; 99,2 (is born); *part. med.* ~māna, *n.* dukkhaṁ uppajjamānaṁ uppajjati, whenever something arises, then it is pain that arises, 96,13; *aor. 3. sg.* udapādi, 8,9. 68,26. 78,31; uppajji, 25,21. 45,1. 78,24. 89,10; — *ger.* ~itvā, having been produced, 80,29; — *pp.* uppanna, *q. v.*; — *caus.* uppādeti, *q. v.* (*cp.* upapajjati & *next*).

uppatati, *vb.* (*sa.* ut-√pat) to fly up, leap up; to rise, ascend; *aor. 3. sg.* uppati (ākāse) 11,19; — *ger.* ~itvā, 2,5-21. 21,36. 35,24; — *pp.* ~ita, *m.* ~o, 3,20; *acc.* ~aṁ (kodhaṁ) 106,33 — Dh. 222.

uppatti, *f.* (*sa.* utpatti; *fr.* uppajjati) arising, origin; ṭhānuppatti, *q. v.*

uppada, *m. v.* uppāda.

uppanna, *mfn.* (*pp.* uppajjati, *sa.* utpanna) arisen, produced, born; *m.* ~o, 1,23. 2,30 (dohaḷo); 42,5 (corupaddavo); 62,24 (putto); *loc. m.* ~e (lābhasakkāre) 72,28.

uppala, *n.* (*sa.* utpala) a lotus-flower, *esp.* the blue lotus; ~aṁ, Dh. 55; nīluppalâdi-kusuma-, 47,13.

*Uppalavaṇṇa, *m.* (*sa.* *Utpalavarṇa) *nom. pr.* of a deva in Sakka's heaven; *gen.* ~assa (devassa) 110,27.

uppāda, *m.* (*sa.* utpāda) arising, appearance, coming into existence, birth; ~o (Buddhānaṁ) Dh. 194; 182 (*metri causa*: uppado); *abl.* ~ā (phalitass') 44,31; — *uppāda-vaya-dhammin, *mfn.* subjected to genesis and destruction, *m. pl.* ~ino (saṁkhārā) 80,28. — anuppādadhamma, *mfn.* (*v.* an-uppāda. — Buddhuppāda. *m.* (*q. v.*).

uppādeti, *vb.* (*caus.* uppajjati. *sa.* utpādayati) to give rise to, to conceive, feel; to bring forward, produce, obtain, gain (*acc.*); *aor. 3. sg.* ~esi (ruciṁ tayi, „fixed her choice on you") 10,12; (vīsaṁ satasahassaṁ, „gained two millions") 23,3; 57,9; (ruhiraṁ, „made to bleed") 76,1; *2. sg.* ~esi (*id.*) 76,4; — *ger.* ~etvā (dohaḷaṁ, having conceived a longing for (*loc.*)) 1,6. 2,28; (kāruññaṁ, „felt compassion with" (*loc.*)) 16,31; (ruciṁ pabbajjāya) 64,2; (avaṇṇaṁ Gotamassa, „bringing reproach on G.") 72,32; — *pp.* uppādita, *n.* ~aṁ (ruhiraṁ) 76,7; ⁰-dhanaṁ (*acc.*), the money which he had earned, 57,35.

ubbigga, *mfn.* (*sa.* udvigna; *pp.* ubbijjati, *sa.* ud-√vij) frightened, anxious; *m.* ~o, 75,17; *acc.* ~aṁ, 75,18.

*ubbedha, *m.* (*cp. sa.* udviddha, *mfn.* & vedha, *m.* depth) height; yojana-sahass'-ubbedha, *mfn.* 1000 leagues high, *m.* ~o, 60,24.

ubbhata, *mfn.* (*sa.* udbhṛta, *pp.* ud-√bhṛ) carried away or out, drawn up; *m.* ~, (vārijo okamokata) Dh. 34; *pl.* ~ā (macchā udakā thalaṁ) 15,14 (*cp.* uddharitvā, 14,23).

ubbhijjati, *vb.* (*pass.* ubbhindati, *sa.* ud-√bhid) to break out, to sprout; *ger.* ubbhijja (tiṭṭhati „stands sprouting" (latā)) Dh. 340.

ubhaya, *mfn.* (= *sa.*) both; *instr. m.* ~ena (saññamena, on account of both sorts of abstinence ɔ: abstinence and non-abstinence) 85,19; *n.* ~aṁ, *adv.* both, Dh. 404 (c'ūbhayaṁ); *comp.* ubhaya-nagara-vāsinaṁ (*gen. pl.*) 62,9.

ubhayattha, *adv.* (*sa.* ubhayatra)

in both places, in both cases; 107,26 — Dh. 15—18.

ubho, *mfn. pl.* (*sa.* ubhau) both; *m.* ubho pi, 5,12. 43,18; ubho pi te, 74,2 — Dh. 306; ubho (gihī pabbajitā) Dh. 74; *n.* ubho „both sides", Dh. 269; *acc. m.* ubho (ante) 66,28 — 96,17; ubho saṅgaṁ (puññañ ca pāpañ ca) Dh. 412, *cp.* saṅga (Tr. P. M. p. 82); ubho (atthaṁ anatthañ ca) Dh. 256; *instr. m.* ubhobi (hatthehi) 27,19; *gen. mn.* ubhinnaṁ. 43,29. 58,9; *loc. mn.* ubhosu (passesu) 40,5.

ummāra, *m.* (*sa.* umbara, *cp. mahratt.* umbarā) a threshold (*cp.* indakhīla); *loc.* ~e, 65,15.

ummujjati, *vb.* (*sa.* ud-√majj) to emerge; *pr. 3. pl.* ~anti, 25,26. — ummujja-nimujja, *m*(?) emerging and diving; *acc.* ~aṁ karonti (udake) 25,23 (*cp. sa.* unmṛjāvamṛjā).

uyyāti, *vb.* (*sa.* ud-√yā) to go out (away); *imp. 2. sg.* ~yāhi (maggā, make way!) 44,3-10.

uyyāna, *n.* (*sa.* udyāna) a park, a (royal) garden; *acc.* ~aṁ, 6,17; *gen.* ~assa, 37,18; *loc.* ~e, 6,4. 36,35; Makhādev'-ambavan'-°, 45,7. — °-ābhimukha, *mfn.* turned towards the garden, *m.* ~o, 63,6. — *°-kīḷā & -kīḷikā, *q. v.* — °-pāla, *m.* a gardener, ~o, 37,11; *acc.* ~aṁ, 37,8-17; *gen.* ~assa, 37,14. — °-pālaka, *m.* id. *gen.* ~ass', 38,5. — *°-bhūmi, *f.* the garden-ground, *acc.* ~iṁ, 63,2.

uyyuñjati, *vb.* (*sa.* ud-√yuj) to go away, depart, leave one's house and family; *pr. 3. pl.* ~anti (traced only once) Dh. 91. — *caus.* uyyojeti (*q. v.*) *cp. next.*

uyyoga, *m.* (*sa.* udyoga) departure; °-mukhe, at the threshold of death, Dh. 235 (*cp.* mukha).

uyyojeti, *vb.* (*caus.* uyyuñjati, *sa.* udyojayati), to send away, to send out for some purpose, to take leave of (*acc.*); *aor. 3. sg.* ~esi, 19,22. 51,1. 59,22; — *ger.* ~etvā, 48,18.

ura & uras, *m.* (*sa.* uras, *n.*) the breast; *loc.* ~e, 23,31. 89,7. (*cp.* orasa.)

uracchada, *m.* (*sa.* uraçchada), a breastplate, armour; °-pasādhanaṁ (*q. v.*) a splendid armour, 23,32.

Uruvelā, *f.* (*sa.* Uruvitvā) *nom. pr.* of a town in the Magadha country, near the river Nerañjarā; *loc.* ~āyaṁ, 66,2.

uḷumpa, *m.* (*sa.* uḍupa) a raft, a float; *acc.* ~aṁ, 23,13.

ulūka, *m.* (= *sa.*) an owl; ~o, 11,19; *acc.* ~aṁ, 11,2; *gen.* ~assa, 11,16. — °-jātaka, *n.* 10,25 ff.

***ulloka**, *m.* (*fr. next*) perceiving, observing, sight; *abl.* ~ā paṭhamaṁ, as soon as it is seen, 84,18.

***ulloketi**, *vb.* (*sa.* *ut + √lok) to look at, look up; *aor. 3. sg.* ~esi (ākāsaṁ) 33,5; (Bhagavantaṁ) 69,33; — *ger.* ~etvā (uddhaṁ) 76,2; — *pp.* ~ita, *loc. abs.* ākāse ~e, 32,11.

usabha[1], *m.* (*sa.* ṛshabha) a bull; ~o, 105,12-19; *acc.* ~aṁ („the manly") Dh. 422.

***usabha**[2], *n.*, a certain measure of length = 20 yaṭṭhi (*q. v.*), about 70 meters; aṭṭhūsabha-matta, *mfn.*, *n.* ~aṁ ṭhānaṁ, a space of eight usabhas, 27,27. (*cp.* yojana.)

usīra, *n.* (*sa.* uçīra) the root of a fragrant grass (bīraṇa, *q. v.*); *°-attha, *mfn.* wanting usīra, *m.* ~o, 108,4 — Dh. 337. (*cp.* attha[1] (2)).

usu, *m*(& *f.*) (*sa.* ishu) an arrow. — usu-kāra, *m.* (*sa.* ishu-kāra) an arrow-maker, a fletcher; ~o, Dh. 33; *pl.* ~ā, 106,27 — Dh. 80. 145.

usuyyati, *vb. denom.* (*sa.* asūyati, *fr.* usūyā, usuyyā (— *sa.* asūyā) envy, jealousy) to envy, to be jealous; *part. m.* usuyyaṁ, 14,4 (an-usuyyaṁ, not envying).

***ussaṅkin**, *mfn.* (*fr. sa.* ut + √çaṅk) distrustful, anxious; *m.* ~ī, 75,17; *acc.* ~im, 75,18.

***ussada**, *m.* (probably *fr.* ut-√sad) [1]) abundance, swelling, tumor. [2]) name of a certain hell; °-nirayo, 23,26. (*cp. sa.* ud-√chad & *next*).

ussanna, *mfn.* (*sa.* utsanna, *pp.* ut-√sad) extensive, abundant; *n.* ~aṁ (suvaṇṇaṁ, „abundance of gold“) 26,9. (*cp. sa.* ucchanna).

ussava, *m.* (*sa.* utsava) feast, merriment; ~o mahā, 112,15.

ussahati, *vb.* (*sa.* ut-√sah) to be able to, to dare, venture (*w. inf.*); to bear, endure; *pr. 3. sg.* ~ati 50,3. 81,17. 83,31.

ussāpeti, *vb.* (*sa.* ucchrāpayati, *caus.* ud-√çri) to raise, to lift up (*acc.*); *ger.* ~etvā (soṇḍaṁ), 76,21.

ussāreti, *vb.* (*sa.* ut-sārayati, *caus.* ut-√sṛ) to cause to go away; *ger.* ~etvā (caturaṅgulaṁ kaṇṇaṁ ~etvā cīvaraṁ saṁharitabbaṁ, the robe ought to be folded up so that a corner of four inches more is hanging over) 83,10 (*cp.* SBE. XIII. p. 156).

ussīsaka, *n.* (*sa.* ucchirshaka) a head-pillow, a bed's head; *loc.* ~e, 41,16.

ussuka, *mfn.* (*sa.* utsuka) zealous, desirous, eager for, longing for, greedy; *loc. pl.* ~esu an-ussukā (*pl.*) „free from greed among the greedy“, Dh. 199; *n.* ~aṁ (na Tathāgatassa hoti, T. does not care about it, lays no stress upon that) 91,3. (*cp.* ossukka.)

***ussuta**, *mfn.* = avassuta (*q. v.*). — an-ussuta, *mfn.* (*q. v.*).

Ū.

ūkā, *f.* (*sa.* yūkā) a louse; *acc. pl.* ~ā (vicinanti, rañño sīse, being about to louse the king's head) 46,26.

ūna, *mfn.* (= *sa.*) wanting, deficient, less than, minus (*w. instr.*); *n.* ~aṁ (dvīhi ~aṁ purisa-sahassaṁ ɔ: 998 men = 500 + 250 + 125 + 62 + 31 + 16 + 8 + 4 + 2, who had successively been killed by their comrades) 34,9; *loc. pl.* ~esu (eken' ūnesu pañcasu attabhāva-satesu, in 500 existences but one) 17,7; *comp.* ekūnavīsati (*q. v.*).

ūmi, *f.* (*& m.*) (*sa.* ūrmi) a wave; *loc.* ~iyā uggatāya, when the wave rises, 27,3.

ūru, *m.* (— *sa.*) the thigh; *loc.* ~umhi. 29,27.

ūhaññati, *vb.* (*pass.* ūhanati, ūhanti, *sa.* ud-√han) to become destroyed, disordered, soiled; *aor. 3. sg.* mā vihāro rajena ūhaññi, „in order that the vihāra may not become dusty“, 84,23; — *pp.* ūhata, destroyed, *v.* anūhata (*cp.* (an-)uddhata).

E.

eka, *mfn.* (*num. & pron. indef.* — *sa.*) [1]) one; *n.* ~aṁ, 56,15. 82,8 (ekan); *gen.* ~assa, 56,16; *instr. m.* ~ena, 81,11; eken' ūnesu, 17,7 (*v.* ūna). — [2]) only, single, that one only; *m.* ~o (eḷako) 30,5; *acc.* ~aṁ (dhammaṁ) 106,14; (attānaṁ, oneself only) 107,4; *gen.* ~assa (eḷakassa) 17,6; *n. acc.* ~aṁ (palitaṁ) 46,27; — *comp.* ekâparādhaṁ, 47,8 (*v.* aparādha); eka-pāṇaṁ, 27,23; eka-puttako, 23,6; eka-purisikā, *f.* (*v. separately*); eka-macchaṁ pi na, not one single fish, 4,25; eka-vacanena (*instr.*), *lit.* at the word once spoken ɔ: directly, immediately, 57,31; — eka-ratti-vāsa, *mfn.* abiding for one night, *m.* ~o, 104,24; — eka-dvāra, *mfn.* having only one gateway, *n.* ~aṁ (nagaraṁ) 90,31. 91,22; — eka-saṁgahīta, *mfn.* unified, *m. pl.* ~ā, 99,16. — [3]) united continual; *comp.* eka-pallaṅkena (*instr.* *v.* pallaṅkā) 66,4; eka-ppahāren' eva, with one blow, with one voice, 27,14. 40,10. 74,8 (*cp.* pahāra); eka-phāliphullaṁ, 62,11 (*v. h.*); eka-viravaṁ, 60,11. — [4]) the same, one and the same; eka-divase (*loc.*) 45,24. — [5]) alone, solitary; *acc. m.* ~aṁ, 106,13 = Dh. 395; *gen.* ~assa, Dh. 330; ekacara (*q. v.*). — [6]) some (. . . or other), one or other, a certain; *pl.* some; *m.* ~o (upāyo) 1,10; (bako) 4,1; (Vijayo)

110,23; *acc.* ~aṁ (udumbaraṁ) 1,26; *instr.* ~ena (eken' upāyena) 46,24; *loc. m. n.* ~asmiṁ, 3,30. 8,20; ekasmiṁ samaye, once upon a time, 30,28 = ekaṁ samayaṁ, 66,23; *comp.* eka-divasaṁ (*acc.*), one day, 6,31. 13,22; eka-bhikkhussa (*gen.*), 79,17; — *pl. m.* eke, 77,12. 104,1. — [7]) *in the same sense used as an indefinite article* = a, an; *m.* ~o (suṁsumāro) 1,5; (dīpako) 2,19; *acc.* ~aṁ (assaṁ) 65,16; *gen. f.* ekissā, 6,32; *comp.* eka-palitaṁ, 46,23; eka-migaṁ (*acc.*) 6,19; eka-gandhakuṭiyaṁ (*loc.*) 73,11. — [8]) *repeated or corresponding w.* añña or dutiya = the one . . . the other; *m.* eko . . . eko, 33,24-25; *instr.* ekena . . . ekena. 83,17; *comp.* eka-divasaṁ . . . eka-divasaṁ, 6,25-26; *gen.* ekassa . . . aññassa, 7,2; eko . . . dutiyo (anto) 96,16. (*cp.* an-eka, ekaṁsa *etc.*)

ekaṁsa, [1]) *mfn.* (*sa.* ekāṁça) 'with one shoulder, belonging to one shoulder', only constructed with cīvara or uttarāsaṅga, *acc. m.* ~aṁ uttarāsaṅgaṁ karitvā, arranging the upper robe over one shoulder, 74,19. 82,18. — [2]) *m.* (*sa.* ekāṁsa) one part, totality (?); *nom.* ~o (tava jīvitaṁ „only one part of thee is life" (*Fsb.*), but perhaps we have to read ekaṁse (*adv.*)) 103,6; *instr.* ekaṁsena, *adv.* (*& loc.* ekaṁse, *adv.*) = in whole, upon the whole, entirely, totally, absolutely, undoubtedly, inevitably, 6,24. 86,3 (*cp.* aṁsa).

ekaka, *mfn.* (= *sa.*) single, alone, solitary; *m.* ~o va (quite alone) 33,31; *acc. m.* ~aṁ, 22,28; *acc. f.* ekikaṁ, 31,20.

*ekaghana, *mfn.* (*sa.* *eka + ghana) compact, solid, hard; *m.* ~o (selo) 106,29 = Dh. 81.

ekacara, *mfn.* (= *sa.*) wandering or living alone, solitary; *m.* ~o, 2,19; *acc.* ~aṁ. Dh. 37.

*ekacariyā, *f.* (*sa.* *eka + caryā) walking alone; *acc.* ~aṁ, Dh. 61 (metri causa read : ekacaryaṁ).

ekacca, *mfn.* (*fr. sa.* ekatara, *ekatra, *ekatya, *cp.* Tr. PM, p. 56) one of two, a single; *pl.* some (. . . others); *m. pl.* ~e, 18,4 (vāṇijā), 90,29 (viññū purisā); *repeated* : 22,5-6; *pl. f.* ~ā, 65,5-7.

ekato, *adv.* (*sa.* ekatas) [1]) on the one side (on the other side), 14,8. 27,4. — [2]) together; at once, simultaneously; ~vasantā, 14,10; ~sannipatati, 14,13. 72,29; tena saddhiṁ ~, 45,25; kena saddhiṁ ~ hutvā (by help of whom?) 72,32; — tīṇi pi ~ madditvā, 57,28; vācayiṁsu potthakattayaṁ ~, 114,19.

ekantaṁ (& ekantena), *adv.* (*sa.* ekāntaṁ) absolutely, exclusively, at any rate, always; ~ nindito, Dh. 228. (*cp.* ekaṁsena.)

*eka-purisikā, *f.* (*adj.*) (*fr.* eka + purisa) true to one man; *acc.* ~aṁ, 48,15; *instr.* ~āya (itthiyā), 48,25.

*ekamantaṁ, *adv.* (*fr.* eka + anta) on one side, apart, aside; by one's side, near; ~ nisīdi, 28,11. 35,3. 68,17; ~ ṭhatvā, 49,7; ~ aṭṭhāsi, 87,34; ~ karitvā (*acc.* laid aside) 75,20; ~ nikkhipitabbaṁ (cīvaraṁ) 83,29.

*ekarajja. *n.* (*sa.* *eka + rājya) sole sovereignty; *instr.* ~ena, Dh. 178.

*ekavāciya, *n.* (*sa.* *eka + vācya) a single remark or objection, private opinion; *acc.* ~aṁ, 11,11.

ekavāraṁ, *adv.* (= *sa.*) once; 50,16 (*cp.* vāra).

ekavīsaṁ & ekavīsati, *num.* (*sa.* eka-viṁçat[i]) twenty. — ekavīsatima, *mfn.* (*sa.* ekaviṁçatama) the 21th; *m.* ~o (vaggo) Dh. 305.

*ekasadisa, *mfn.* (*sa.* *eka + sadṛça) fully alike or resembling, identical; *pl.* ~ā (mātāputtā) 49,8.

*ekaseyyā, *f.* (*sa.* *eka + çayyā) lying, sleeping alone; *acc.* (*adv.*) ~aṁ (eko caraṁ) Dh. 305.

ekādasa, *num.* (*sa.* ekādaça) eleven. — ekādasama, *mfn.* (*sa.* ekādaçama) the eleventh; *m.* ~o (vaggo) Dh. 156.

ekāyana, *n.* (= *sa.*) a narrow

way, the only way to salvation; *mfn.* leading to salvation, *m.* ~o (maggo) 113,19.

***ekāsana**, *n.* (*sa.* *eka + āsana) sitting, living alone; *acc.* (*adv.*) ~aṁ (eko caraṁ) Dh. 305.

ekāha, *n.* (*sa.* ekāha[n]) one day, *v.* aha; *mfn.* lasting one day, *n.* ~aṁ (jīvitaṁ) Dh. 110.

ekikā, *f.* *v.* ekaka.

ekūnavīsati, *num.* (*sa.* ekonaviṁçati) nineteen. — ekūnavīsatima, *mfn.* the 19th, *m.* ~o (vaggo) Dh. 272.

ekeka, *mfn.* (*sa.* ekaika) one by one, several, each; *acc.* ~aṁ, 4,8-24; *w. loc.* ~aṁ (amhesu) 4,11.

ekekaso, *adv.* (*sa.* ekaikaças) one by one, severally, 111,14.

***ejā**, *f.* (*fr.* √ej) lust, desire, craving; an-eja, *mfn.* (*q. v.*).

etaṁ, *pron. demonstr. n. nom. acc.* (*sa.* etad), 8,27 *etc.*; etan, 1,31. 16,11; etad (the original form, used in some cases of Sandhi before a word beginning with a vowel) 3,3. 23,3. 64,19 (etad-ahosi), 68,13 (etad-avoca), 103,12 (etad-abravi). Dh. 390; — *m.* esa (*sa.* eshas) 1,8. 3,14; 5,1 *etc.* eso (with more emphasis) 59,2; 114,6; — *f.* esā (*sa.* eshā) 31,6. 87,28. 103,31; — *acc. m(f.)* etaṁ, 24,24 *etc.*; — *instr. m(n.)* etena, 4,24. 33,11 (eten'); — *gen.* (*dat.*) *m(n.)* etassa, 1,7. 11,5; *f.* etissā, 55,5; — *pl. n.* etāni, 2,1; *pl. m.* (*nom. acc.*) ete, 3,26. 5,9 *etc.*; *f.* etā, 21,31; — *gen.* (*dat.*) etesaṁ. 7,17. 60,13. 102,6; — *instr.* (*abl.*) etehi, 2,10. Otherwise the declension is that of taṁ (*q. v.*). — [1]) this, this here (what is nearest to the speaker) 33,11. — [2]) *referring to the preceeding*, 66,18. 103,31. 107,21. — [3]) *referring to the following*, 3,26. 23,3. — [4]) = such, like that, 31,5; no h'etaṁ „not so", 70,2. — [5]) *combined w. other pron.* (with an emphasis): es'āhaṁ. 69,19; sometimes plainly constructed with the *1. pers.* of the verb., esa te sīsaṁ chinditvā bhūmiyaṁ khipissāmi, 5,12; esa muñjaṁ parihare, 103,33; — ete te ubho ante, 96,17. — esā yā rati, 47,27. — *cp.* ayaṁ (idaṁ), enaṁ.

etarahi, *adv.* (*sa.* etarhi) now, at present; 29,30. 30,24. 56,11 (*opp.* atītânāgate, *cp.* Dh. 228), 94,23. 99,5. — *cp.* tarahi, carahi.

etādisa, *mfn.* (*sa.* etādṛça) such, of this kind; *m.* ~o, 44,3. 80,24. 85,20. *cp.* tādisa.

eti, *vb.* (*sa.* ā-√i) to go, to come, go to, reach (*acc.*); to come back, return; *pr. 3. sg.* eti (*w. acc.* catubhāgaṁ, is worth) Dh. 108; (paṭivātaṁ) Dh. 54; *1. sg.* emi, 108,28; *3. pl.* enti (return) 56,18; — *imp. 2. sg.* ehi. 1,19. 9,21. 57,31. 68,14. 108,28; *2. pl.* etha, 21,30. 73,21; Dh. 171; — *fut. 3. sg.* essati, 56,20; Dh. 369; ehiti, 12,6; *2. sg.* essasi, 56,20; ehisi, Dh. 236. 369; *1. sg.* essāmi, 56,20; *3. pl.* essanti, Dh. 86; — *part.* enta, *loc. abs.* ente (udake), 56,21; an-ente. *ib.* — *cp.* yāti.

etta, *mfn.* *v.* ettaka.

***ettaka**, *mfn.* (*fr.* *etāvataka, *cp. sa.* iyattaka, Tr. PM. p. 80) so great, so much; *pl.* so many; *acc. m.* ~aṁ (kālaṁ, all this time) 46,32; (allāpasallāpaṁ) 56,22; *n.* ettaṁ (contracted *fr.* ettakaṁ) Dh. 196 (im' ettaṁ puññaṁ); *instr. n.* ~enâpi. notwithstanding this, 39,4; *pl. m.* ~ā (tumhe, all of you) 88,25; (pāṇā) 90,35; *instr. n.* ~ehi (ratanehi) 27,29; *gen. m.* ~ānaṁ (all these) 10,12. 30,5. 54,14. *cp. next.*

***ettāvatā**, *adv.* (*fr.* etta — ettaka, *cp.* kittaka & kittāvatā) thus, so far, to that extent; ~ sammādiṭṭhi hoti. 96,15.

***etto**, *adv.* (*fr.* etaṁ, through *etato? *cp.* ito, tato) from thence, hence; over there; 104,15; 87,28; 5,5 (*opp.* ito).

ettha, *adv.* (*sa.* atra > *attha, phonetically influenced by etaṁ, *cp.* etta *etc. above*) [1]) here, in this place; 85,29. 88,29 — Dh. 174 (in this world); 104,1 (~ pagāḷhā ɔ: saṅgāme;

Fausbøll, SBE, X[2] p. 70 : plunged into this world ?); etth'eva = this very moment, 46,3. 56,25. — [2]) there, in that place; 3,5-12-32. 65,14. 112,24; ettha ce te mano atthi, 72,21 (ettha refers both to yaṁ vadanti and to ye vadanti : if your mind inclines to that about which people say „it is mine", or to those who say so, then you shall not escape me). — [3]) there, to that place; 2,3 (~ nehi maṁ). — [4]) in this case, in this matter, in that particular; 37,7. 73,7. 79,30. 91,1. 94,21. 96,15. — If attha = atra can be traced in the Pāli texts (it is found in Abhidhāna), then we could possibly take 'ttha in the phrase : kāya nu'ttha bhikkhave etarahi kathāya sannisinnā in the sense of „here"; but attha is more likely *pr. 2. pl.* of the verb atthi (*q. v.*) 29,30. 31,23.

etha, *imp. 2. pl. v.* eti.

edhati, *vb.* (*sa.* √edh) to prosper, to succeed in: *pr. 3. sg.* ~ati (sukhaṁ) Dh. 193; *w. instr.* (nikatyā sukhaṁ ~) 5,21.

enaṁ, *pron. demonstr.* (*sa.* ena, substituted for etaṁ, as naṁ (*q. v.*) for taṁ) this, that, it; *acc. m.* tam enaṁ („the same", that person in question) 100,12; *acc. f.* tam ena (metri causa for enaṁ) 47,21; *acc. n.* enaṁ, Dh. 118. 313.

enta, *mfn.* (*part.*) *v.* eti.

Erāvaṇa, *m. nom. pr.* (*sa.* Airāvaṇa) name of Sakka's elephant; °-paṭibhāga, *mfn.* equal to E., *gen.* ~assa, 45,30.

ereti, *vb.* (= īreti, *caus.* √īr, *sa.* īrayati) to move, to raise one's voice; *pr. 2. sg.* ~esi (sace n'eresi attānaṁ) Dh. 134 (*cp.* Tr. PM. p. 76; *Morris,* JPTS. '87. p. 146).

eḷaka, *m.* (*sa.* eḍaka) a ram, a goat; ~o, 16,27. 29,26; *voc.* ~a, 17,13; *acc.* ~aṁ, 16,24; *instr.* ~ena. 17,19; *gen. pl.* ~ānaṁ, 29,24 (*cp.* meṇḍa).

eva, *indecl.* (= *sa.*) just, even, only (mostly used to strengthen or limit the idea of a preceeding word and consequently to be rendered differently according to its different constructions). Besides eva we find also the forms yeva and ñeva, but their use in the texts is not strictly conformable to phonetical principles. [1]) eva : phalāphalaṁ tam eva (those fruits) 2,7; sarīram eva (it is true) 2,8; attano . . . eva (his own) 2,15; āgacchantam eva (as soon as) 2,31; ten'eva (the same) 2,24; eten'eva, 23,23; so eva (*id. opp.* añño) 99,2; tass'eva, 11,25 (*id.*); tass'eva (to him alone) 37,18; tath'eva (likewise) 2,25. 105,28; tatth'eva (on that very spot, that very moment) 3,6. 9,3 *etc.*; aham eva (just I) 29,19. 51,8; imam eva (*id.*) 65,20; 'ti . . . eva (just therefore) 47,4; ekam eva (only) 12,20; guṇakatham eva (*id.*) 43,7, *cp.* 49,1; ujjhāyath'eva (*id.*) 88,26; kocid-eva (only few) 88,34, but 99,17 („ganz beliebig"); yen'eva (by which verily) 96,27; ajj' eva (this very day) 65,13; aṭṭh' eva kahāpaṇe (again, as before) 24,33, *cp.* 86,25-27 (constantly); — but, on the contrary : 96,13-15; 74,30 (Sāriputta-Moggallānêva); eva . . . pana (*μέν—δέ*) 88,22-23. These examples, indiscriminately chosen, may easily be increased by others. — [2]) yeva, most frequently after words ending with palatal vowels (e, i, ī), but also often after ṁ and even after ā, o, u. [a]) after e : 1,14. 7,16. 9,3. 12,8 *etc.* [b]) after i (ī) : 31,26. 39,7. 86,2; 55,20. [c]) after ṁ : 10,21. 17,16-21. 23,20. 28,33. *etc.* [d]) after ā : 21,12. 43,25. 48,34. [e]) after o : 43,15 50,31. 88,17. 97,30. [f]) after u : 22,7. — [3]) ñeva, only after words ending with ṁ, which often, through assimilation, is altered to ñ : tvaṁ ñeva, 28,14. 54,32. 77,6; itthīnaṁ ñeva, 48,33; passantānaṁ ñeva, 54,14; tañ ñeva, 5,10; tasmiñ ñeva, 45,14; ahañ ñeva, 99,16. — [4]) After long vowels eva is very often (by elision of e) shortened to va (*v. h.*). — [5]) eva- as the first part of *comp.* °-rūpa, *mfn.* (*q. v.*), identical with evaṁ (*v. next*).

evaṁ, *adv.* (= *sa.*) thus, in this way; [a]) thus (as follows): 1,13. 3,15 (evam āha); 66,23. 93,21 (evaṁ me sutaṁ „thus I have heard"); — [b]) thus (as mentioned before): 3,28. 4,29. 6,28. 7,16 *etc.*; evaṁ hoti, 66,11; evaṁ passaṁ, 71,4; yadi evaṁ (if so) 5,15; evaṁ jānāhi („thus I declare thee") 72,33; evaṁ bhante (yes) 76,14; evam eva (even so) 91,3. 68,25 (*corresp. w.* seyyathā); na evaṁ (not so, *corresp. w.* yathā) 62,26; evam ete (only in this way and only those) 91,8; evaṁ = therefore, referring to a prec. *part.* denoting the cause (ādīnavaṁ sampassamāno. because you consider it dangerous) 93,32.

*evaṁ-gotta, *mfn.* (*sa.* *evaṁ + gotra) belonging to that family; *m.* ~o, 92,12.

evaṁ-nāma, *mfn.* (*sa.* evaṁ-nāman) having that name; *m.* ~, 92,12.

*evaṁ-diṭṭhi, *mfn.* (*sa.* *evaṁ + dṛshṭi) having that view; *m.* ~i, 93,27-31.

evarūpa, *mfn.* (*sa.* evaṁrūpa) [1]) such, like that; *n.* ~aṁ 51,28; mā ~aṁ karittha („do not do the like again") 39,2; (mukhaṁ) 11,6; (pāpakammaṁ) 51,7; *abl.* ~ā, 16,28; *loc. m.* ~e, 41,35; *instr. f.* ~āya rattiyā (in the dead of night) 41,28; *loc. f.* ~āyaṁ (parisāyaṁ) 87,23. — [2]) of such a form, beauty or virtue; *m.* ~o, (māṇavo) 19,11; *acc.* ~aṁ (mātugāmaṁ) 51,20; ~aṁ (attabhāvaṁ. „such a handsome figure") 64,16.

esa, *pron.* (*sa.* esha) this; *m.* esa & eso, *f.* esā, *v.* etaṁ.

esati, *vb.* (*sa.* ā-√ish) to seek, search, to strive to obtain; *part. m. med.* esāno (sukhaṁ) Dh. 131. 132. *cp.* gavesati, gavesaka *& next.*

esin, *mfn.* (*sa.* eshin) seeking, desiring; *v.* dhanesin. sukhesin; *cp.* gavesin *& prec.*

essati, *fut. v.* eti.

ehi, ehiti. *etc. v.* eti.

O.

o, *indecl.* = ava (*q. v.*).

oka[1], *n.* (*sa.* oka. *m.* & okas. *n.*) house, dwelling-place, home, asylum; *abl.* ~ā, Dh. 87; repeated: okamokaṁ (*acc.*) jahanti, „they leave their house and home", Dh. 91 (*cp. next*). — an-oka, *q. v.*

oka[2], *n.* (contracted *fr.* udaka or odaka, *q. v.*) water; okamokata ubbhato (vārijo) ɔ: oka-m-okato, with m inserted, *abl.* „from his watery house", Dh. 34 (*cp.* oka[1]).

*okāra, *m.* (*fr.* ava-√kṛ) *cp. sa.* apakāra) worthlessness; *acc.* ~aṁ (kāmānaṁ „the vanity of desires") 68,30. *cp.* vokāra.

okāsa (or avakāsa), *m.* (*sa.* avakāça) [1]) place, room; *acc.* ~aṁ (dehi, give place) 43,24; *loc.* ~e, (amukasmiṁ. at such and such a place) 75,8; yamh' okāse (. . . tattha) 108,28. — [2]) occassion, opportunity, permission; *acc.* ~aṁ (dento) 40,17; ~aṁ (labhati) 87,19; *loc. abs.* ~e laddhe, 87,30; — katokāsa, *mfn.* having got the opportunity or one's permission; *m. pl.* ~ā (mayā, „you have my leave") 49,34; — hatāvakāsa, *mfn.* (*q. v.*) *cp.* an-avakāsa, nir-okāsa.

okkamati, *vb.* (*sa.* ava-√kram) to go down, to descend, to enter into; *aor. 3. sg.* okkami (niddaṁ, fell asleep) 35,28; niddā okkami (Yasassa) *id.* 67,26; — *part. f. med.* ~mānā (niddaṁ) 61,9; — *ger.* ~itvā (*id.*) 22,25; — *pp.* okkanta: an-okkantamattaṁ, *acc. m. adj.* (before he has passed (the boundary of the kingdom, rajja-sīmaṁ)) 39,15.

ogadha, *mfn.* (= ogāḷha, *sa.* avagādha, *fr.* ava-√gāh, confounded with √gādh?) immersed, plunged into; antogadha (*q. v.*) & amatogadha (*v.* a-mata).

ogha, *m.* (= *sa.*) stream, torrent, flood; ~o, Dh. 25. *acc.* ~aṁ (vineyya „having overcome the torrent of passions") 104,30; — *o-tiṇṇa, *mfn.* „saved from the flood", *m.* ~o, Dh. 370; — mahogha, *m.* (*sa.* mahaugha, *mfn.*) a mighty flood, inundation; ~o, Dh. 47. 287; *acc.* ~aṁ, 35,19; °-sadisa, *mfn.* like a mighty flood, *loc. m.* ~e (lābhasakkāre) 72,27.

ojita, *mfn.* (*sa.* ava-jita, *pp.* ava-√ji) won, conquered, recovered; *ojitatta, *mfn.* (*fr.* attan) whose life is secured, *instr.* ~ena, 55,2. *cp.* avajīyati.

oṭṭha, *m.* (*sa.* oshṭha) a lip (or jaw); *loc.* adharoṭṭhe ca uttaroṭṭhe ca (between his lower and upper jaw) 13,19; — *vaṁkoṭṭha, *mfn.* (*cp. sa.* vakroshṭhi) „whose jaw is wrenched" *m.* ~o, 54,20 (*v.* vaṁka).

***oḍḍeti**, *vb.* (*fr.* ava- or ud- + √dā (to bind) or √dhā?) to set up, arrange (as snares *etc.*); *ger.* ~etvā (pāsaṁ) having laid a snare, 11,29.

oṇamati (or onamati), *vb.* (*sa.* ava-√naṁ) to bow down, bend down; *ger.* ~itvā, 62,18.

otata, *mfn.* (*sa.* avatata, *pp.* ava-√tan) overspread, covered; māluvā sālam iv'otataṁ (*acc. m.*) „as a creeper (does with) the tree which it surrounds" Dh. 162.

otarati, *vb.* (*sa.* ava-√tṛ) to descend (from: *abl.*, upon: *acc.* or *loc.*); *aor. 3. sg.* otari (rukkhā) 12,32; (ukkārabhūmiyaṁ, *loc.*) 18,31; (nadiṁ) 28,6; (pāsādatalato) 65,34; — *part. m.* ~anto, 62,27; — *ger.* ~itvā (saraṁ) 5,16; — *pp.* otiṇṇa, *m. pl.* ~ā (nāvāya bhūmiṁ) „landed", 112,27; — *caus.* otāreti (*q. v.*) *cp.* otāra.

otāpeti, *vb. caus.* (*sa.* ava-√tap) to dry, evaporate (as clothes); *grd.* ~etabba, *n.* ~aṁ (cīvaraṁ) 83,8.

otāra, *m.* (*sa.* avatāra) 'descent, point of attack (for temptations)', offence, fault; *acc.* ~aṁ, 104,12.

otāreti, *vb.* (*caus.* otarati) [1]) 'to cause to descend', take down, set down (*acc.*); *imp. 2. pl.* ~etha, 41,22; — *aor. 3. sg.* ~esi, 56,24; — *ger.* ~etvā, 8,17. 33,33. 40,6. — [2]) to lay down, expose, explain; *aor. 3. sg.* ~esi (sakaṁ mataṁ) 113,12; — *imp. 2. sg.* ~ehi (sakaṁ vādaṁ) 113,14.

***ottappa**, *n.* (*fr.* apa-√trap, *sa.* *āpatrapya > apatrapā (Tr.); this etymology must be preferred to that of *Childers*: *auttapya > uttāpa, ut + √tap) tact, decency (in behaviour), conscientiousness; ~aṁ (bahiddhāsamuṭṭhānaṁ, *q. v.*) 10,17. — hirottappa, *n.* & bhinnahirottappa, *mfn.* *v.* hiri; *cp.* SBE. XI. p. 8 & Dhamma-Saṅgaṇi, transl. by *Caroline Rhys Davids*, p. 20.

ottharati, *vb.*, & **otthaṭa**, *pp.* *v.* avattharati.

odaka, *n.* (= udaka, *sa.* audaka, odaka, *mfn.*) water; ~aṁ (sītaṁ) 15,25. — an-odaka, *mfn.* (*q. v.*). — khīrodaka, gandhodaka, *etc.* *v.* udaka.

odana, *m.* (*& n.*) (= *sa.*) rice, boiled rice; pakkodana, *mfn.* one who has his rice boiled, *m.* ~o, 104,21 (*cp.* pakka). Suddhodana, *nom. pr.* (*q. v.*).

onaddha, *mfn.* (*pp.* ava-√nah, *sa.* avanaddha) covered, enveloped, surrounded; *m. pl.* ~ā, 37,21 (sākhāhi sākhā), Dh. 146 (andhakārena).

opamma, *n.* (*fr.* upamā, *sa.* aupamya) a simile, an example; *acc.* ~aṁ (karohi „give an illustration") 99,3; paṇḍitabhāvassa °-atthaṁ, in order to give an example of prudence, 91,24.

oparajja, *n.* (*fr.* uparājan, *sa.* *auparajya) viceroyalty; *acc.* ~aṁ (katvā, ruling as viceroy) 44,21.

opāyika, *mfn.* *v.* tad-ūpika.

***opāteti**, *vb.* (*fr.* ava-√pat) 'to throw down', to interpose, insert; na ... bhaṇamānassa antarantarā kathā opātetabbā (*grd. f.*) let him not be interrupted, 83,4.

***opunāti**, *vb.* (= avāpurati, *fr. sa.* apā-√vṛ (?) but probably confounded with √pū) to uncover, lay bare (? *opp.* chādeti) or to scatter, disperse; *pr. 3. sg.* ~āti (paresaṁ vajjāni ~ yathā bhusaṁ, the faults of others like chaff) 106,17. — Dh. 252. *cp.* Tr. PM. p. 63; *Childers*, JRAS. 1871; *Morris*, JPTS. '87. p. 153; avāpurāpeti & āvuṇāti *above*.

obhagga, *mfn.* (*sa.* avabhagna, *pp.* ava-√bhañj) broken, bent down; °-sarīra, *mfn.* 63,9 (*acc. m.* ~aṁ).

obhāsa, *m.* (*sa.* avabhāsa) splendour, radiance; *acc.* ~aṁ (muñcanto) 26,4.

obhāsati, *vb.* (*sa.* ava-√bhās) 1) to shine forth, to gleam; *part. m. acc.* ~antaṁ, 26,12; *part. med.* ~mānaṁ (samuddaṁ) 26,18. — 2) to light up, illuminate (*acc.*); *pr. 3. sg. med.* ~ate (sabbā disā) 85,4 — *caus.* obhāseti, 85,8.

*obhoga, *m.* (*fr.* ava-√bhuj, *avabhoga) a curve or fold, the part of a cloth where it is folded (perhaps the inner side of the fold, *opp.* bhoga); *loc.* ~e. 83,11. *cp. Morris*, Academy 1882 (July 8. p. 33) and SBE. XIII, p. 156.

omasati, *vb.* (*sa.* ava-√mṛç) to touch; to prick, pierce; to gnaw off, gnaw all over (eating only a little); *pr. 3. sg.* ~anti (gāvo bahutiṇassa varaṁ varaṁ) 51,33; = khādanti, 52,3.

omuñcati, *vb.* (*sa.* ava-√muc) to loosen, take off (*acc.*); *ger.* ~itvā (muttāhāraṁ) 64,35; (upāhanā) 82,17.

ora-, (*sa.* avara, *fr.* ava) 'inferior', on this side; *v.* orapāraṁ, orima & *next*.

orato, *adv.* (*sa.* avaratas) on this side (turned towards the subject); 2,22 (*w. gen.* dīpakassa); 21,16 (*opp.* parato); 83,21 (*opp.* pārato).

*orapāraṁ, *adv.* (*fr. sa.* avara + pāra) from one side to the other; 108,26. This word is *acc.* of the *dvandva-comp.* ora-pāra, *n.* — this and the further shore, and consequently it means „to both shores" ɔ: to and fro (*cp.* aparāparaṁ, *v.* apara).

orasa, *mfn.* (*sa.* aurasa, *fr.* uras) own, produced by one's self, legitimate; *acc. m.* ~aṁ (puttaṁ) 20,25.

*orima, *mfn.* (*fr.* ora) being on this side (nearest to the subject); °-tīrato, *abl.* from this bank (of the river) 2,21 (*v.* tīra).

oruyha, *ger.* & oropeti, *caus. v. next*.

orohati, *vb.* (*sa.* ava-√ruh) to descend (from *abl.*); *pr. 3. sg.* ~ati (pāsādā) 67,24; *ger.* ~itvā (caṅkamā „left") 68,10; (suvaṇṇapādukāhi „put off") 68,16; oruyha (tato) 61,18. — *caus. II.* oropeti (*sa.* avaropayati) to let down, to put away; *ger.* ~etvā (soṇḍaṁ) 76,35.

olambati, *vb.* (*sa.* ava-√lamb) to hang down, to be suspended, to hang (on, *loc.*); *pr. 3. pl.* ~anti (udumbare) 2,2; *part. n.* ~antaṁ (*sc.* hadayaṁ) 2,4.

*oḷārika, *mfn.* (*fr.* uḷāra. *sa.* udāra, *audārika) large, gross; material, corporeal (of a rather considerable greatness?); *m. pl.* ~ā (pāṇā) 91,1.

*olubbha, *ger.* (*sa.* *avalabhya, √labh, but *pr.* olubbhati (a younger formation) agrees with ava-√lubh) clutching, taking hold of, leaning on (*w. acc.* or *loc.*): āvāṭa-mukhavaṭṭiyaṁ ~, 40,28. *cp. Morris*, JPTS. '87. p. 156.

oloketi, *vb.* (*sa.* ava-√lok) to look; to look at, regard, observe, watch; to look for, search for (*w. acc.*); *part. med.* ~ento, 6,18. 12,25. 87,26; 54,5. 86,28 (lokaṁ, observing the world); 33,29 (waiting for); 36,3 (olokento taṁ disvā); *f.* ~entī, 10,9; *pl. loc. m.* ~entesu (tumhesu) 50,12; *part. med. pl.* ~ayamānā, 11,3; — *pot. 2. pl.* ~eyyātha, 9,13; — *fut. 1. sg.* ~essāmi, 46,1; — *aor. 3. sg.* ~esi, 19,14. 87,24; — *ger.* ~etvā, 3,1. 14,16. 42,10. 65,31; — *pp.* ~ita. *m. pl.* ~itā, 11,7; °-ākārenĉva, 87,25 (*v.* ākāra); °-saññāṇenêva, 87,32 (*v.* saññāṇa).

ovadati, *vb.* (*sa.* ava-√vad) to exhort, admonish (*acc.*); *pr. 2. sg.* ~asi (maṁ) 9,23; — *part. m.* ~anto (attānaṁ) 46,31; *f.* ~antī (*cp.* corrections) 7,32; — *pot. 3. sg.* ~eyya, Dh. 77; — *aor. 3. sg.* ovadi. 40,8; — *inf.* ~ituṁ, 81,17; — *ger.* ~itvā, 8,11; — *grd. m.* ~itabbo, 79,15.

ovāda, *m.* (*sa.* avavāda) instruction, admonition; *nom.* ~o (Bodhisattato laddba-°) 8,11; *acc.* ~aṁ dadamāno, 12,33; ~aṁ datvā, 7,28. 44,13; ~aṁ dento, 85,24; — ovādavasena „by way of admonition", 14,13; — rājovāda-jātaka. 42,20.

osakkati, *vb.* (*sa.* apa-√srp) to draw back, give way; to go back — to be reduced; *pr. 3. sg.* ~ati (metri causa : avasakkatī, read : osakkatī) 30,13; — *part. acc. m.* ~antaṁ. 30,4; *part. med. acc. m.* ~mānaṁ (vaṁsaṁ) 45,17; — *aor. 3. sg.* osakki, 29,25. *cp.* Tr. PM. p. 60.

osāna, *n.* (*sa.* avasāna) end; *v.* avasāna.

osīdati, *vb.* (*sa.* ava-√sad) to sink (into, *loc.*); *aor. 3. pl.* ~iṁsu (uḋakamhi) 28,7; — *inf.* ~ituṁ. 28,8; — *ger.* ~itvā, 36,25. — *caus. II.* osīdāpeti, to cause to sink; *pr. 2. sg.* ~esi (udake maṁ). 1,21; *aor. 3. sg.* ~esi, 1,20; *fut. 3. pl.* ~essanti (nāvaṁ) 25,34.

ossukka. *n.* (*sa.* autsukya) eagerness, desire, longing for; appossukka, *mfn.* (*q. v.*) *cp.* ussuka.

***ohārin**, *mfn.* (*sa.* *ava-hārin, *fr.* ava-√hṛ) dragging down; *n.* ~inaṁ (bandhanaṁ) Dh. 346. *cp.* avaharati.

ohāreti, *vb.* (*caus.* avaharati) to cause to be taken away, remove; *grd. n.* ~etabbaṁ, 84,18.

ohita. *mfn.* (*sa.* avahita, *pp.* ava-√dhā) put down, placed into; turned downwards, downcast; *m.* ~o, Dh. 150. — *ohita-sota. *mfn.* „with attentive ears", *m. pl.* ~ā (bhikkhū dhammaṁ suṇanti) 71,24. — *ohitā-mukha, *mfn.* with downcast face, *m.* ~o, 54,20 (with ā metri causa, *cp.* Notes).

***ohīnaka**, *mfn.* (*fr.* ohīna, *sa.* avahīna, *pp.* ava-√hā) remaining, left; *acc. m. pl.* ~e, 22,10.

K.

ka-, base of *pron. interr. m.* ko, *f.* kā *etc. v.* kiṁ.

kaṁsa, *m*(& *n.*) (*sa.* kaṁsa & kāṁsya) a basin made of bell-metal and used like a drum or gong; ~o (upahato) Dh. 134.

kakkaṭaka, *m.* (*sa.* karkaṭaka) a crab; ~o, 4,25; *voc.* ~a, 4,26; *abl.* ~ā, 5,22.

kakkasa, *mfn.* (*sa.* karkaça) rough, harsh, cruel, violent; a-kakkasa, *mfn.* (*q. v.*).

***kakkāreti**, *vb.* (*caus. sa.* khāṭ-√kṛ, *cp.* kāt-√kṛ) to cough up, hawk up; *ger.* ~etvā (ambaphalaṁ) 37,25.

kakkhala. *mfn.* (also written ~aḷa, *sa.* kakkhaṭa & karkara) hard; fierce, cruel; *instr. m. pl.* ~ehi (yakkhehi) 41,34.

kaṁka, *m.* (= *sa.*) a certain bird, a heron (or a vulture, *Burnell:* Ind. Stud. XIII, 264); *gen.* ~assa, 92,30.

kaṁkhati, *vb.* (*sa.* √kāṅksh) to doubt; *pr. 3. sg.* ~ati, 96,14.

kaṁkhā, *f.* (*sa.* kāṅkshā) doubt; *nom. sg.* ~ā, 79,17; *nom. pl.* ~ā. 66,21.

***kacavara**. *m.* (*cp. sa.* kaccara & kavara. *mahratt.* kacarā) sweepings; *acc.* ~aṁ. 50,2. — °-chaḍḍana-pacchi. *f.* a basket for removing of sweepings, 48,34. — mālā-kacavara-, a dust-heap, 73,20 (°-antara).

Kaccāyana, *m.* (contracted : Kaccāna. *sa.* Kātyāyana) *nom. propr.* of a thera, one of Buddha's chief disciples; *voc.* ~a, 96,6; Kaccāno ([aggo] vibhajjanamhi) 109,10. — *Kaccāyana-gotta, *m.* (*sa.* °-gotra) 'member of the K.-family', name of the same person, also often called Mahā-Kaccāyana; ~o (ayasmā) 96,2.

kacci, *indecl.* (*sa.* kac-cid) a particle of interrogation (latin : *num*, *nonne*) 28,12; often combined with nu and sometimes so that the old form kacc*id* is preserved by sandhi : kaccinnu, 9,28; kacci nu kho (should it really be ?) 3,5. *cp.* kiṁ, kiñci *etc.*

kaccha[1], *mfn.* (*sa.* kāccha, *fr.* kaccha, or = *kākshya, *fr.* kaksha?) growing wild, or made of a plant that grows wild (Tr.), grown in the water, on marshy ground (?); *n.* ~aṁ (kaṇḍaṁ) 92,18 (*opp.* ropima, *q. v.*) *cp. next.*

kaccha[2], *m.* [1]) (*sa.* kaksha) armpit; *abl.* ~ā. 104,17; *loc.* ~e, 67,29. — [2]) (*sa.* kaccha) a meadow, swamp, fen, marshy ground; *loc.* ~e (rūḷhatiṇe „abounding with grass") 104,27.

kacchapa, *m.* (= *sa.*) a tortoise; ~o. 11,26; *acc.* ~aṁ. 11,32; *voc.* ~a, 12,5; *instr.* ~ena. 12,20; *gen.* ~assa, 12,26. *cp.* kaccha[2].

kañcana, *n.* (*sa.* kāñcana) gold; °-paṭṭa-sadisa, *mfn.* like a plate of gold, 46,31; — °-pallaṁke, *loc.* on a throne of gold, 42,9; — °-rūpaka-, a golden statue, 47,14.

kaññā, *f.* (*sa.* kanyā) a girl, virgin; daughter; asura-°, 54,7 (~aṁ, *acc.*); khattiya-°, 64,11. 47,15; deva-°, 64,30 (~ā, *pl.* „celestial nymphs").

kaṭa = kata (*q. v.*).

kaṭacchu, *n.*(?) (*sa.* kaṭacchu, *f.*?) a ladle, a spoon; suvaṇṇa-°, a golden spoon, *acc.* ~uṁ, 53,32.

kaṭuka, *mfn.* (= *sa.*) bitter, of a sharp, unpleasant taste; °-pphala, [1]) *n.* a bitter fruit (or perhaps name of a certain plant) 73,11 (-kaṭukapphalâdīni, *cp.* phala); [2]) *mfn.* with bitter fruit, 37,31 (*m.* ~o ambo); Dh. 66 (*n.* ~aṁ, kammaṁ). — *kaṭuka-pabhedana, *adj.* having pungent juice (flowing from the temples, as elephants), *m.* ~o (kuñjaro) Dh. 324.

kaṭṭha, *n.* (*sa.* kāshṭha) a piece of wood, stick; wood in general; — tiṇa-kaṭṭh'-upādānaṁ, 94,36. — danta-°, *n.* a small piece of wood for cleaning the teeth, a tooth-pick; ~aṁ, 82,18. — kaṭṭha-maya, *mfn.*, made of or consisting of wood, ~ā (vanā) 48,6, *cp.* vana, *n.*

kaṭṭhaka, *m.* (*sa.* kāshṭhaka, *m.* & *n.*) a kind of plant (probably a certain reed); *gen.* ~assa, Dh. 164.

kaṭhala, *n.* (*sa.* kaṭhalya & kaṭhalla) gravel; sakkhara-kaṭhala-vālikā, *pl.* 97,35.

kaṭhalikā (or kathalika), *v.* (pāda-)kathalika.

kaṭhina, *mfn.* (= *sa.*) hard, cruel; *f. pl.* ~ā, 51,34; (= thaddha-hadayā, hardhearted) 52,5.

kaḍḍhati, *vb.* (*sa.* √kṛsh, karshati) to draw, drag, pull (*acc.*); *part. m. pl.* ~antā (matamanussaṁ pāde gahetvā) 40,35; — *aor. 3. sg.* kaḍḍhi (vemaṁ) 89,7; *3. pl.* ~iṁsu, 59,9; — *inf.* ~ituṁ, 59,8; — *ger.* ~itvā (lekhaṁ) 59,7; kaḍḍhitvā kaḍḍhitvā, by constantly sucking up, 27,1. — *pass.* kaḍḍhiyati, *part. m.* ~iyamāno, 59,10. — *cp.* kasati, ā-kaḍḍhati, upa-kaḍḍhati & (sam)uk-kaṁsati.

kaṇikā, *f.* (= *sa.*) 'a small particle', meal or flour (of rice)? *instr. pl.* ~āhi (pūvaṁ pacitvā) 57,21. *cp.* taṇḍula.

kaṇṭaka, *m.* (= *sa.*) a thorn, a fish-bone; *instr.* maṇḍu-kaṇṭakena, 37,6 (*v.* maṇḍu); *acc. pl.* ~e, 4,22. — *°-rāsi, 5,8 (*v. h.*).

kaṇṭha, *m.* (= *sa.*) the neck; *loc.* ~e, 16,25; *abl.* ~to, 64,25. — kāsāva-°, *mfn.* Dh. 307 (*q. v.*).

kaṇḍa, *m.* & *n.* (*sa.* kāṇḍa & khaṇḍa) [1]) a part, portion (*esp.* of a book); *acc.* ~aṁ (Dhammasaṅgaṇiyā, Atthasālinim) 113,23. — [2]) an arrow or the shaft of an arrow; *acc.* ~aṁ, 92,18; *instr.* ~ena, 6,24.

kaṇṇa, *m.* (*sa.* karṇa) [1]) the ear; *acc.* ~aṁ, 22,24. — pahaṭṭha-kaṇṇavāla, *mfn.* 76,21 (*q. v.*). — [2]) a corner (of a room or of clothes); *acc.* ~aṁ (caturaṅgulaṁ) 83,10; gehassa kaṇṇakaṇṇehi (*abl. pl.*) „in the house from top to bottom", 49,35; -kaṇṇa-bhāgā (*m. pl.*) „the corner of the room", 84,19. — *cp.* kaṇṇikā, kālakaṇṇī.

kaṇṇakita, *mfn.* (*sa.* karṇakita, *fr.* karṇaka) dirty, musty (on account of mould or rust *etc.*); *f.* ~ā (bhitti)

84,20; (bhūmi) 84,21. *cp.* Vin. II, 115,1 fr. b. III, 198,5.

*Kaṇṇamuṇḍa, *m. nom. pr.* of a certain (mythical) lake; °-daha, *m. abl.* ~to, 36,31.

kaṇṇikā, *f.* (as first part of *comp.* also kaṇṇika-, *sa.* karṇikā) 'an ear-ring'; the pericarp of a lotus; *puppha-kaṇṇika-sadisa, *mfn.* „fair as the opening bud of a lotus", *acc. m.* ~aṁ (puttaṁ) 7,29.

kaṇha[1], *mfn.* (*sa.* kṛshṇa) black, dark; *metaph.* bad; *acc. m.* ~aṁ (dhammaṁ, *opp.* sukka) Dh. 87.

Kaṇha[2], *m.* (*sa.* Kṛshṇa) *nom. pr.* a name of Māra (*q. v.*) „the black one"; *gen.* ~assa, 103,31.

kata, *mfn.* (sometimes also written kaṭa, *pp.* karoti; *sa.* kṛta. √kṛ) done, made, performed, prepared *etc.*; [1]) Used as finite tense: *m.* ~o, 11,10; 25,3 (ratho); *n.* ~aṁ, 1,24. 3,23. 107,27 — Dh. 18; Dh. 74 (kata = kataṁ). — [2]) *adj.* as the first part of *comp.* (*w. instr.* of the agens): kata-kammaṁ, 17,4. 85,2; kata-parakkamena, 12,3; kata-pāpaṁ, 17,17; kata-pāpa-kammaṁ, 73,27 etc. — [3]) *subst. n. gen.* ~assa a-ppatikārakaṁ (*q. v.*) 14,1; katâkataṁ, *n.* what has been committed and omitted, Dh. 50. — [4]) as the last part of *adj.-comp.*: an-a-bhāva-kata. a-vatthu-kata, *q. v.*; kāla-kata, dead, 22,15 (*v.* kāla, *cp.* kālaṁ karoti); kāḷa-vaṇṇa-kata, blacked, 84,21 (*opp.* a-kata, not prepared, not blacked, 84,22); citta-kata. variegated, Dh. 147 (*cp.* citta[2]); parikamma-kata, prepared: lākhā-°, 5,28; geruka-°, 84,20; vatta-kata, open, 5,13; sayaṁ-kata. made by one's self, Dh. 347; *cp.* a-kata. dukkata (or dukkaṭa), sukata (or sukaṭa). — [5]) as the first part of *adj.-comp.*, *v.* kata-kicca *etc. below.*

kata-kicca, *mfn.* (*sa.* kṛta-kṛtya) one who has done his duty, dutiful; *acc. m.* ~aṁ, Dh. 386; *instr. pl.* ~ehi (therehi) 109,12.

kataññū, *mfn.* (*sa.* kṛta-jña) grateful; a-kataññuṁ (*acc. m.* [*sc.* na seveyya] niratthā tassa sevanā) ingrate, 14,1.

kataññutā, *f.* (*sa.* kṛtajñatā) gratitude; 14,2.

kata-puñña, *mfn.* (*sa.* kṛta-puṇya) one who has done good (meritorious) works, virtuous; *m.* ~o. 107,26 — Dh. 18; *acc.* ~aṁ, Dh. 220.

katama. *mfn. pron. interr.* (— *sa.*; *fr.* the base ka-. *v.* kiṁ) who, which (of two or many); *m.* ~o (ayaṁ samuddo) 25,27; ~o ettha Nāgaseno, 97,18; *acc.* ~aṁ (whom of three) 31,16; *m. pl.* ~e dve (antā) 66,25; — *f.* ~ā, 66,30; *acc.* ~aṁ disaṁ, in which direction, 95,4.

*kata-maṅgala-sakkāra, *mfn.* festively prepared; *f. loc. sg.* ~āya (bhūmiyā) 61,25. *cp.* maṅgala, sakkāra.

kata-viriya, *mfn.* (*sa.* kṛta-vīrya) energetic; *gen. m.* ~assa. 42,13.

kati, *pron. interr.* (— *sa.*; *nom. acc. mfn.* kati. *instr. abl.* ~īhi, *gen.* ~innaṁ) how many; ~ nu kho amhākaṁ sikkhāpadāni (*n. pl.*) 81,19. *cp. next.*

katipaya, *mfn.* (— *sa.*) so many, a certain number, some (latin *aliquot*); *instr. m. pl.* ~ehi (pahārehi) 55,7.

*katipāhaṁ, *adv.* (*fr.* katipaya + ahan. by elision of y) a few days, 7,27. 36,15. 112,24 (vasitvā); 57,17 (vasi). — katipāhaccayena, a few days later, 49,22 (*v.* accaya).

*katokāsa. *mfn.* [*sa.* *kṛta + avakāça] who has got opportunity or permission, *v.* okāsa.

kattabba, *grd.*, *v.* karoti.

kattar, *m.* (*sa.* kartṛ) [1]) a doer. maker; *nom.* kattā (kammānaṁ) 97,13. — [2]) a benefactor; *v.* a-kattar.

kattarikā (or kattarī), *f.* (*sa.* kartari, *f.*) scissors; *instr.* ~kāya. 5,17.

kattha. *adv. interr.* (by assimilation *fr.* kuttha, *sa.* kutra) where, where-in, where-to, wherefore? ~ amhehi sikkhitabbaṁ, 81,19 (in what

— kasmiṁ atthe); ~ gamissasi. 87,36 — kahaṁ gacchasi, 88,5. — *kattha-vāsika. *mfn.* living where? *m. pl.* tumhe ~ā. 21,8. — *cp.* kuto.

katthaci, *adv.* (*sa.* kutra-cid) somewhere; 52,12.

katvā, katvāna, *ger.*, *v.* karoti.

kathaṁ. *adv. interr.* (— *sa.*) how? 1,17. 4,28. 11,17 *etc.* kathaṁ nāma. how then? 41,30.

kathaṁkathā, *f.* (— *sa.*, *cp. sa.* kathaṁkathika, *fr.* kathaṁ) doubt, uncertainty. — vigata-kathaṁkatha, *mfn.* free from doubt; *m.* ~o, 69,18. — a-kathaṁkathin, *mfn. id.* (*v. h.*).

*kathalika, *n.* (= kaṭhalikā *f.*?) probably a foot-stool, or another implement, used by washing the feet (a towel? *Rh. Davids & Oldenberg*, SBE. XIII, 92); *nom.* pāda-kathalikaṁ, 83,6 (*cp.* the foll. quotation : imesaṁ yeva pādānaṁ candimasuriye pāda-kaṭhalikaṁ katvā nisīdiṁ, Ps. on MN. ch. 77; kaṭhalikam (*acc.*) *v.* Dhammapadatthakathā (Colombo '98) p. 161,5 fr. b.).

kathā, *f.* (— *sa.*) [1]) speech, talk, words; *nom.* ~ā, 24,33. 83,4. 86,24 (Buddhānaṁ acchariyā); *acc.* ~aṁ, 4,18. 33,4. 73,9. 89,20 (sammodaniyaṁ, *q. v.*); — guṇa-kathā, *f.* praise; *loc.* ~āya, 31,23; — sārambha-kathā, *f.* angry speech, Dh. 133. — [2]) speaking about, conversation; *acc.* ~aṁ (samuṭṭhāpesuṁ) 29,28; *loc.* ~āya, 29,31. 31,24; — *kathā-sallāpa. *m.* conversation, *instr.* ~ena, 94,22; — *°-samuṭṭhāpana, *n.* starting a conversation, 54,10 (°-atthaṁ). — [3]) exposition, explanation; dhammī kathā, a sermon, religious discourse, *instr.* dhammiyā ~āya. 71,22; — aṭṭha-kathā, anamatagga-kathā. anupubbi-kathā, dāna-°, sagga-°, sīla-° (*q.v.*); *cp.* Dhātu-kathā *& next.*

*kathā-magga, *m.* (*sa.* *kathā + mārga) way or method of exposition, explanation; *acc.* ~aṁ. 113,30.

*Kathā-vatthu, *n.* (*sa.* kathā + vastu) *nom. pr.*, name of a canonical Pāli-book, the 5th part of the Abhidhamma-piṭaka; 102,12.

kathika, *mfn.* (= *sa.*) a speaker, narrator; dhamma-kathika, *q. v.*

kathita, *mfn.* (*pp.* katheti) spoken, told, answered, pointed out; *m.* ~o (pucchitapañho) 88,24; *acc. f.* ~aṁ (gāthaṁ) 102,24; *n.* ~aṁ, 88,26; *m. pl.* ~ā (guṇā) 44,5; — tāya kathitamaggena. 56,34.

*kathin, *mfn.* (*fr.* kathā) at the end of *comp.* — kathika, *v.* vicitra-kathin.

katheti, *vb.* (*sa.* √kath, kathayati) to tell, say, speak of (*acc.*); to speak with (saddhiṁ); to mean, refer to (*acc.*); *pr. 3. sg.* ~eti, 24,37. 31,7. 88,4; *2. sg.* ~esi, 49,26; *1. sg.* ~emi, 85,28; *3. pl.* ~enti, 9,30; — *part. m.* ~ento, 3,6; *instr.* ~entena, 1,24; *gen.* ~entass(a), 20,36. 30,14; *part. med. f.* ~ayamānā (guṇaṁ, praising) 29,9; — *imp. 2. sg.* ~ehi, 54,33; — *pot. 2. sg.* ~eyyāsi, 49,28; — *fut. 1. sg.* ~essāmi, 25,33; — *aor. 3. sg.* ~esi. 12,19. 68,19 (anupubbikathaṁ); — *inf.* ~etum, 49,27. 55,17; — *ger.* ~etvā (rañño guṇe) 42,4; a-kathetvā, 49,27; — *pp.* kathita (*q. v.*).

kadariya, *mfn.* (*sa.* kad-arya) 'not liberal', mean, niggardly, avaricious; *acc. m.* ~aṁ (dānena jine) 44,9 — Dh. 223; *m. pl.* ~ā, Dh. 177.

kadali, *f.* (*sa.* kandalī & kadalī) [1]) a sort of deer; [2]) a flag, banner; [3]) the plantain or banana tree (Musa sapientum); °-puṇṇa-ghaṭa-, 62,6.

kadā. *adv. interr.* (— *sa.*) when? *cp. next.*

kadāci, *adv.* (*sa.* kadācid) [1]) sometimes, 6,19. [2]) perhaps, 55,24. *cp.* kudācanaṁ.

kaddama, *m.* (*sa.* kardama) mud, mire, dirt; °-makkhita, *mfn.* mud-stained (~ehi pādehi) 71,29; apeta-kaddama. *mfn.* Dh. 95.

kanaka, *n.* (— *sa.*) gold; *°-vimāna, *n.* a golden palace; ~aṁ, 61,15; *loc.* ~e, 23,23. — uttatta-kanaka-sannibha, *mfn.* 85,7.

kaniṭṭha, *mfn.* (*sa.* kanishṭha) the youngest, yonger born; *m.* a younger brother or the youngest son (*opp.* jeṭṭha(ka)); ~o, 35,21. 55,20; *gen.* ~assa, 35,15; — °-bhātā. 9,7; — jeṭṭhaka-kaniṭṭhe (*acc. pl.*) an elder and a younger brother, 32,21. — kaniṭṭha-bhaginī, *f.* a younger sister, *instr.* ~iyā, 56,36 (*cp.* bhaginī).

kantati, *vb.* (*sa.* √kṛt, kṛnatti) to spin; *part. f.* ~antī (tāpasī) 111,6.

kantāra, *n.* (*& m.*) (*sa.* kāntāra) a forest, wilderness; a difficult road; diṭṭhi-kantāraṁ, 94,1 (*q. v.*).

Kanthaka, *m.* (*sa.* Kanṭhaka) *nom. pr.* of the horse of Bodhisatta (Siddhattha); *acc.* ~aṁ, 65,19-20.

kandati. *vb.* (*sa.* √krand) to cry, weep; *pr. 3. sg.* ~ati, 30,19; *aor. 2. sg.* mā kandī. Dh. 371; *ger.* ~itvā, 49,10 (~ roditvā).

kapaṇa, *mfn.* (*sa.* kṛpaṇa), miserable, poor; °-addhika, 38,14 (*q. v.*).

kapāla, *n.* (— *sa.*) a shell, the skull; a bowl or pan; tatta-kapāle, *loc.* „on a hot plate". 11,7.

kapi, *m.* (= *sa.*) an ape, monkey; 108,24. — *°-yoni, *f.* 1,3. 2,17 (*v. h.*). — *°-rājan, *m.* 1,7 (*v. h.*).

kapila, *mfn.* (— *sa.*) brown, tawny, reddish; °-gāvi, 61,28.

Kapilavatthu, *n.* (*sa.* Kapilavastu) *nom. pr.* of a town in which Gotama Buddha was born (within the frontier of Nepal, *cp.* JRAS. 1897 & 1898); *abl.* ~uto, 62,5; *loc.* ~usmiṁ, 81,7; °-nagare, 61,2.

kappa. *m.* (*sa.* kalpa) [1]) age, any one of the ages of the world; *acc.* sakala-kappaṁ, throughout the whole kalpa, 16,15; *loc.* paṭhama-kappe, in remote antiquity, 10,2. — [2]) *mfn.* (at the end of *comp.*) almost like or equal to; *m. pl.* Satthu-kappā. similar to the Master, 109,27. — *cp.* kappaṭṭhiya, kappika.

kappaka, *m.* (*sa.* kalpaka) a barber; ~o, 44,23; *voc.* ~a, *acc.* ~aṁ, 44,22.

***kappaṭṭhiya** (& ~ika), *mfn.* (*sa.* *kalpa-stha, *w. suff.* -ka) lasting for a whole kalpa; °-rukkha, 59,29.

kappanā, *f.* (*sa.* kalpanā) 'preparing, arranging', *esp.* caparisoning of a horse or an elephant, tightening of the saddle-girth; ~ā (atigāḷhā) 65,21-22.

kappara, *n.* (*sa.* kūrpara) the elbow, the forearm; *instr.* ~ena (sīse pahari) 50,19. 51,1.

kappika, *mfn.* (*sa.* kalpaka, & ~ika) at the end of *comp.* = belonging to a certain kalpa: — paṭhamakappikā, *m. pl.* the first people of this kalpa (*q. v.*) 10,25; paṭhamakappikato, *abl. n.* (?) from the beginning of this world, 4,10.

kappūra, *m. & n.* (*sa.* karpūra) camphor; -kappūra-, 48,30. 73,11.

kappeti, *vb. caus.* (*sa.* √klp, kalpayati) [1]) to arrange, prepare; *imp. 2. sg.* ~ehi (assaṁ „saddle") 65,17; — *inf.* ~etuṁ (id.) 65,20; — *aor. 3. sg.* ~esi (id.) ib. (*cp.* kappanā); vāsaṁ ~ („lived") 1,4. 2,26 (*pr. 3. sg.* kappeti) 11,25. 35,37; *3. pl.* ~esuṁ, 34,33; jīvikaṁ ~esi („got livelihood") 8,15; — seyyaṁ ~eti, to lie, to sleep, 46,22 (ekako va); — *pass. part. m.* ~iyamāno (whilst he was being saddled) 65,21. — [2]) to trim, to cut off; *part. m.* ~ento (kattarikāya kumudanaḷaṁ) 5,18; — *ger.* ~etvā (gīvaṁ) ib. *cp.* kappaka, *m.*

kamati, *vb.* (*sa.* √kram) to walk, to go; *intens.* caṅkamati, *q. v.*

kabala, *m.* (*sa.* kavala) a mouthful, morsel; *acc.* ~aṁ (na bhuñjati, kuñjaro baddho) Dh. 324.

kampati, *vb.* (*sa.* √kamp) to tremble; *part. m.* ~amāno, 36,2.

kambala, *m. & n.* (— *sa.*) a woollen cloth or blanket; *°-ratana, *n.* „precious rug", 25,5 (*acc.* ~aṁ mahagghaṁ). — ratta-°, scarlet cloth, 5,27. — paṇḍu-°, 15,8 (°-silāsanaṁ) *q. v.*

kamma (& **kamman**) *n.* (*sa.* karman), *nom. acc. sg.* ~aṁ & ~a. [1]) what has been done, deed, act; *nom.*

~aṁ, Dh. 67; ~a, Dh. 96; *acc.* ~aṁ, 51,19. 73,30. — raho-kammaṁ, 54,17 (what is to be done in secret). — [2]) doing, action, work, labour; 6,15; — *kamma-cchedа, *m.* interruption of one's labour, 6,1; — karaṇa-kammaṁ, 9,13 (what she is doing); — pāṇa-vadha-°, 60,13 (killing of living beings); — pāpa-°, 9,18 (wickedness, *cp.* pāpa); — vicakkhu-kammāya, *dat.* in order to make (him) perplexed, 71,27; — mūlena ~aṁ n'atthi. 57,4 („gratis" or „there is no need of money"?); — duty, errand; Dh. 217; kena kammena (*instr.*) 21,8; uposatha-°, 14,13 (*q. v.*); — business, occupation, vocation; kasi-kamma, agriculture, tillage, 8,15 (*instr.* ~ena); — tunna-kamma, trade of a tailor, 57,8; — niyyāmaka-kamma, a mariner's vocation, 24,14. — [3]) (in the dogmatics) good or bad deed, past deeds, *esp.* the influence of past deeds on one's future destiny — merit, deserts, karma; ~aṁ, 24,1. 100,5; *instr.* ~ena, 100,6; *gen.* ~assa (vipākavasena) 84,32; *abl. pl.* ~ehi (pāpakehi) 100,8; *gen. pl.* ~ānaṁ, 97,13; attano pubba-kammaṁ. 16,27 = attanā kata-kammaṁ, 17,4 (his own past deeds); pāpakammā (*abl.*) Dh. 127; saka-kammāni (*n. pl.*) one's own deeds, 106,20 = Dh. 240; ānantarika-°, 76,5 (*q. v.*); yathā-kammaṁ, *adv.* (*q. v.*); — *kamma-kiliṭṭha, *n.* evil karma, *opp.* *kamma-visuddhi, *f.* good karma, Dh. 15. 16; — kamma-patha. *m.* way of action, *acc. pl.* ~e (tayo) Dh. 281. — [4]) *mfn.* at the end of *comp.* nihīnakamma, suci-kamma (*q. v.*). — daṇḍakamma, parikammakata *& next.*

kamma-kara, *m.* (*sa.* karmakara) a labourer, a servant; ~o (nāvikānaṁ) „a sailor's drudge", 35,30.

*kamma-karaṇā, *f.* (*cp. sa.* kāraṇā) punishment, pain, torture; °-anubhavanaṭṭhānaṁ, 23,27 (*v. h.*).

kammaja, *mfn.* (*sa.* karma-ja) 'caused by karma', inborn. — *°-vātā, *m. pl.* pains, birth-throes; assā ~ calimsu (came upon her) 62,19. (*cp.* vāta).

kammanta, *m.* (*sa.* karmānta) action, work, business; sammā-kammanto, right conduct, 67,4.

kammāra, *m.* (*sa.* karmāra) a smith (blacksmith or goldsmith); ~o, Dh. 239; *gen.* ~assa, 78,29. — *°-putta, *m.* by family a smith, ~o, 77,20. — *°-saṇḍāsa, *m.* a smith's tongs; *instr.* ~ena, 5,2.

kammin, *mfn.* (*sa.* karmin) acting (only at the end of *comp.*); *m. pl.* pāpa-kammino, evil-doers (upapajjanti nirayaṁ) Dh. 126.

kayirati, kayirā (kayrā) *etc.* *v.* karoti.

kara, *mfn.* (= *sa.*) doing, making; *v.* anta-kara, takkara, dukkara, pabhaṁ-kara, vacana-kara, su-kara.

karaṇa[1], *mf(ī)n.* (= *sa.*) making, effecting, causing; cakkhu- ~ī (paṭipadā) leading to insight, 66,29; ñāṇa- ~ī (id.) leading to wisdom, ib.

karaṇa[2], *n.* (= *sa.*) the act of making; *°-kammaṁ, 9,13 (*v. h.*); a-karaṇa, *n.* avoiding (*q. v.*); *cp.* dvidhā-°, vāk-°, vohāra-°.

karaṇā, *f.* (*cp. sa.* kāraṇā), *v.* kamma-karaṇā.

karaṇīya, *n.* (*grd.* karoti, = *sa.*) 'to be done', duty, business; katam ~aṁ, „the duty is fulfilled", 71,16; *instr.* kenacid-eva ~īyena „on some business", 32,13.

karaṇḍaka, *m.* (= *sa.*) a basket of hurdle-work; *jāla-karaṇḍaka, *m.* probably a fence or enclosure of network, used as a sort of bathing-house in the river (Tr.), *loc.* ~e kīḷantassa, 36,30 („casting nets and weels in the river for sport"? *Fausbøll*, Five Jāt. p. 27).

karavīra, *m.* (= *sa.*) name of a fragrant plant, Oleander; *°-patta, *n.* name of a sort of arrow, ~aṁ, 92,24 (*cp.* patta[1]).

karīsa, *n.* (*sa.* karīsha) feces; ~aṁ, 82,4 = 97,22.

karuṇa, *mfn.* (= *sa.*) [1]) miserable,

pitiable, *v.* ati-karuṇa. — [2]) compassionate; *acc. f.* ~aṁ (vācaṁ), 103,4. *cp.* kāruñña, nikkaruṇatā & *next.*

karuṇā, *f.* (= *sa.*) pity, compassion, mercy; *instr.* ~āya, 22,2.

karoti, *vb.* (*sa.* √kṛ) [1]) *w. acc.* to do, make, perform, accomplish, finish, *esp.* kālaṁ ~, to die (*q. v.*); to execute (vacanaṁ); to effect, produce, 6,3. 47,4. 89,6. *etc.*, very often periphrastically: kopaṁ ~. 40,7 (to become angry); satiṁ ~, 63,18 (to think of); saññaṁ ~, 5,7 (to imagine) *etc.*; to put, place, direct, 6,10. 15,32. 60,19. 65,15. 71,28, 83,11-21; to treat, 57,26. — [2]) *w. double acc.* to make (*adj.*) 73,6; to elect (*subst.*) 10,2. — [3]) *w. adv.* to act, behave, 58,5; to manage, arrange, 12,2. — The usual present formation is karoti, but besides this we find kubbati (*1. sg.* also kummi), and even *karati must be supposed as base for certain forms of *part.*, *imper.*, *pot.* (kayirati is found at the grammarians): *3. sg.* ~oti (tath' eva) 2,25; *2. sg.* ~osi (saññaṁ) 5,7. (pāpakammaṁ) 9,30; *1. sg.* ~omi (evarūpaṁ, = *fut.*) 51,28; na ~, 74,1 (I did not do it); *1. pl.* ~oma, 4,7. 60,13 (= *fut.*); — *pr. med. 3. sg.* kurute (vasaṁ, subdues) Dh. 48. (piyaṁ) Dh. 217. — *part.* [a]) *m.* karonto (vohāraṁ) 8,16. (sotthiṁ) 54,31; *loc.* ~e, 19,29. (viriyaṁ akaronte) 42,11; *acc. pl.* ~e, 21,3; *gen. sg.* karoto, Dh. 116; *acc. f.* ~iṁ (anācāraṁ) 52,31; *pl.* ~iyo (kalahaṁ) 59,3. [b]) *gen. sg. m.* kubbato, 13,28. Dh. 51—52; *med.* [1]) kubbāna, *acc. m.* ~aṁ, Dh. 217. [2]) kurumāna, *f.* ~ā. 49,13. 89,6; *pl. f.* ~ā, 51,28. [c]) *m.* karaṁ, Dh. 136. — *imp.* [a]) *2. sg.* karohi. 19,28. 73,9. 86,1; *2. pl.* ~otha (mama vacanaṁ) 32,25. 75,5. 108,6; *3. pl.* ~ontu, 8,7. [b]) *2. sg.* kara, 22,16. — *pot.* [a]) *3. sg.* kareyya (kālaṁ) 92,8; *2. sg.* ~eyyāsi, 15,34. 35,8 (aggiṁ). 86,3 (pāpaṁ); *1. sg.* ~eyyaṁ, 15,12; *3. pl.* ~eyyuṁ, 17,26; *2. pl.* ~eyyātha, 4,8. [b]) *3. sg.* kare, Dh. 42—43; *3. pl.* (?) 48,7 (perhaps we have here an old form of *pr. 3. pl. med.*, *cp. Kuhn*, Beitr. p. 94; but kare is also *pr. 1. sg. med.* = karomi, Jāt. II 138,13.). [c]) *3. sg.* kayirā (*fr.* *karyāt), Dh. 42. 53. 105. 117. 159 (kayrā); *3. sg. med.* kayirātha, Dh. 25. 117. 313 (kayrātha). [d]) *2. pl.* kubbetha, 29,12. — *fut.* [a]) *3. sg.* karissati (mukhaṁ) 11,17. (satiṁ) 63,18; *2. sg.* ~issasi. 15,31 (= *imper.*), 77,6 (id.), 54,32 (*cp.* the use of *fut.* bhavissati. *v.* bhavati); *1. sg.* ~issāmi, 9,21. 12,2. 47,4 (lobhaṁ imassa); *3. pl.* ~issanti. 4,6. 7,15; *2. pl.* ~issatha, Dh. 275. [b-c]) kāhāmi & kassāmi *etc.*; *2. sg.* kāhasi, 103,7 (puññāni), Dh. 154 (gehaṁ). — *aor.* [a]) *3—2. sg.* akāsi, 19,32. 57,26. 60,19. 86,1; *1. sg.* akās' ahaṁ, 108,30: *3. pl.* akaṁsu (sīhaṁ rājānaṁ) 10,3. 13,2. 21,22. 109,5. [b]) *3. sg.* akarī, 80,33. 85,5 (= akāsi. 85,13); *2. sg.* mā kari. 53,8; *1. sg.* kariṁ, 47,4 (karin ti); *3. pl.* kariṁsu. 10,27. 24,12 (nāmaṁ assa). 58,5; *2. pl.* mā evarūpaṁ karittha, 39,2. [c]) *3. sg.* akā (Visuddhimaggaṁ nāma, composed) 114,12; *1. pl. med.* akaraṁhase, 13,25. — *inf.* kātuṁ, 11,8. 27,16. 51,14 *etc.* — *ger.* [a]) katvā, 4,36 (gīvaṁ sugahitaṁ). 6,2-10. 40,21 (daḷhaṁ ~, with a strong grasp). 58,12 (kusalaṁ ~, *sc.* tayā). 65,15 (ummāre sīsaṁ). 82,21 (nīcaṁ ~, holding down); a-katvā, 24,17. 34,3. 40,7. 42,13; ādiṁ-katvā, *v.* ādi. [b]) katvāna. 112,5. [c]) karitvā, 42,18. 71,28 (naṅgalaṁ khandhe, „having shouldered"). 73,6. 74,19; vasiṁ ~. *q. v.* (*cp.* sakkaccaṁ). — *pass.* kayirati, Dh. 292 (= kayrati). — *pp.* kata, *mfn.* (*q. v.*). — *grd.* [a]) kattabba, *mfn.* what is to be done; *n.* ~aṁ (sahāyassa, „a friend's part") 12,34. (viriyaṁ) 42,13. 54,13. Dh. 53; °-kicca (*v. h.*); °-yutta. *mfn.* what ought to be done, *n.* ~aṁ. 54,32. [b]) kātabba. *mfn.*; *m.* ~o (saṁsaggo) 29,7; *n.* ~aṁ (kin nu kho ~) 11,32; *m.* ~o (brahmadaṇḍo, to be imposed) 79,13; °-yuttakaṁ (etesaṁ karissanti, shall do for them) 39,34. e) kicca, *mfn.* (*v.* separately). d) kāriya, *mfn.*; a-kāriyaṁ, *n.* 106,15 — Dh. 176. e) kayira, *mfn.* (= kāriya. *fr. sa.* kārya); *n.* ~ añ ce, Dh. 313. f) karaṇiya, *mfn.* (*v.* separately). — *caus.* kāreti (*q. v.*). — aṭṭhi-°, alaṁ-°, āvi-°, manasi-°, sacchi-karoti (*v. h.*), *cp.* kattar, kamma, kara, karaṇa, kāra(ka), kārana, kārin, kiriyā.

*Kalandaka-nivāpa, *m. nom. pr.* of a garden at Veḷuvana near Rājagaha (*lit.* 'an offering to the squirrels', Sp. H. Man.[2] 198); *loc.* ~e, 84,27.

kalala, *n.* (= *sa.*) [1]) the embryo a short time after conception; *gen.* ~assa, 99,10. — [2]) mud, mire; *acc.* ~aṁ, 46,33; *loc.* kāma-kalale, „in the mud of desire", ib.; gūtha-kalale (nimugga-gāmasūkaro) in the dung-hill-pool, *ib.*

kalaha, *m.* (= *sa.*) strife, quarrel; *acc.* ~aṁ (karontiyo) 59,3; ~aṁ (aññamaññaṁ karonti) 74,5.—*°-sadda, *m.* brawl, *acc.* ~aṁ, 59,4.

kalā, *f.* (= *sa.*) [1]) a part, portion (*esp.* the sixteenth part of the moon's diameter), *acc.* ~aṁ (soḷasiṁ, a sixteenth part) Dh. 70. — [2]) any mechanical or fine art, 113,3 (vijjā-sippa-kalā-vedī).

kalāpa, *m.* (= *sa.*) [1]) a bundle; *acc.* dāru-kalāpaṁ (sīsena ādāya) a bundle of fire-wood, 57,12. — [2]) a quiver; *acc.* dhanu-kalāpaṁ, bow and quiver, 75,15.

kali, *m.* (= *sa.*) the unlucky die, loss at game, misfortune; sin, vice; n'atthi dosasamo ~, Dh. 202 (= sin? *cp.* SBE. X, 55); *acc.* ~iṁ (the bad die), 106,18 — Dh. 252 [kali, *opp.* kaṭa (*sa.* kṛta) *v.* Jāt. VI, 228,19. 282,17. 357,5].

*kaliṅgara, *m. & n.* (also spelt with ḷ, Burm. read. kaliṅkara) [1]) a log of wood (explained by comm. by kaṭṭhakhaṇḍa, khāṇu); *n.* ~aṁ (niratthaṁ) Dh. 41 (*cp.* Thī. 468, MN. I, 449,16). — [2]) (*sa.* kaḍaṅgara & kaḍaṅkara) straw, chaff (Abidh. 453).

kaḷīra, *m.* (*sa.* karīra) the top-sprout of a plant; ~o (paṭhamuggato) 47,9.

kalyāṇa, *mfn.* (= *sa.*) beautiful, good; *loc. n.* ~e, Dh. 116 (*opp.* pāpa); *acc. m. pl.* ~e (mitte, *opp.* pāpake mitte) Dh. 78. 375. — *°-rūpa, *mfn.* beautiful, *m.* ~o (catuppado) 30,8.

Kalyāṇī, *f.* (= *sa.*) *nom. pr.* of a river in Ceylon; *acc.* ~im, 21,16.

kalla, *mfn.* (*sa.* kalya) healthy, salutary; able, clever; ready, prepared, perfect; *n.* ~aṁ (kallan nu kho tad abhinanditum) 97,5; *m.* kallo si bhante, 99,35. — *°-citta, *mfn.* whose mind is prepared, *acc. m.* ~aṁ, 68,31.

kavāṭa, *n.* (*sa.* id. & kapāṭa) a door (not the aperture, dvāra, *q. v.*, but that by which the aperture could be closed, *cp.* SBE. XX, 160). — *°-piṭṭha, *n.* the backside of the door („door & doorpost", SBE. XIII, 159), *acc.* ~aṁ, 84,12 (*cp.* piṭṭha & Vin. I, 368,9; SBE. XX, 105).

kasaṭa, *mfn.* (probably by metathesis *fr. sa.* sakaṭa, which also is found in the mss., *cp. sa.* çata & kashṭa) bad, vile, nasty; a certain taste: sour, bitter, acrid, or: insipid, tasteless = niroja, niyyūsa; *subst. m.* fault, vice; bitter juice, sediment, dregs (?); — kasaṭa-phalāni (*n. pl.*) 1,13; — nimba-kasaṭaṁ (*acc.*) bitter nimba-juice, 37,25.

kasati, *vb.* (*sa.* √kṛsh, kṛshati, *cp.* kaḍḍhati & (sam)ukkaṁsati) to plough; *pr. 3. sg.* ~ati, 56,16; *3. pl.* ~anti, 30,29. *cp.* kasi, kassaka & *next.*

*kasana, *n.* (*fr.* kasati, *sa.* karshaṇa) the act of ploughing; ~aṁ, 56,16. °-ṭṭhānaṁ, *n.* the place where one is ploughing, 56,1.

kasā, *f.* (*sa.* kaçā) a whip; *acc.* kasām-iva (= kasaṁ viya) Dh. 143; *acc. pl.* ~ā, 55,14; *instr. pl.* ~āhi, 77,12. — *°-niviṭṭha, *mfn.* touched by the whip, *m.* ~o (asso) Dh. 143[b].

kasāva, *m. & n.* (*sa.* kashāya) dirt, impurity; fault, sin. — vantakasāva, *mfn.* one who has thrown away sin, *m.* ~[o] Dh. 10. — a-nik-kasāva (*q. v.*), *cp.* kāsāva.

kasi, *f.* (*sa.* kṛshi) ploughing, agriculture; °-kamma, *n.* id; *instr.* ~ena, 8,15. — °-gorakkhādīni, 21,3 (ploughing, tending cattle &).

kasmā, *adv.* why? (*pron. interr. abl.*) *v.* kiṁ.

kassaka, *m.* (*sa.* karshaka & kṛshaka) a ploughman, farmer; *pl.* ~ā, 31,1. — *°-kula, *n.* the family of a farmer, *loc.* ~e, 8,14. — *°-vaṇṇa, *m.* the appearance of a ploughman, *acc.* ~aṁ, 71,27.

Kassapa, *m.* (*sa.* Kāçyapa) [1]) *nom. pr.* of the Buddha before Gotama; *gen.* ~assa (Bhagavato) 84,28. °-dasabala, *gen.* ~assa, 22,12. °-sammāsambuddha, 28,18. — [2]) *nom. pr.* of a thera, one of Buddha's great disciples, president of the first council; ~o (dhutavādānaṁ aggo) 109,6; = Mahākassapathero, 109,17. — [3]) Kumāra-kassapa, *q. v.*

***kahaṁ**, *adv. interr.* (*cp.* kattha, kuhiṁ & *sa.* kuha) where? whereto? 1,25 (~ ṭhapetha), 21,8 (gacchissatha), 34,10 (kahan nu kho), 49,6 (~ gatâsi), 73,13 (gacchasi), 88,5 (id. = kattha gamissasi, 87,36).

kahāpaṇa, *m.* (& *n.*) (*sa.* kārshāpaṇa) a certain weight of gold, silver or copper, a coin, a piece of money, money in general; *instr.* ~ena, 18,10; *acc. pl.* ~e (aṭṭha) 24,28; dhuttānaṁ ~e datvā, hiring some villains, 73,19; *instr. pl.* ~ehi (suraṁ pivantā) 74,4. — *°-vassa, *n.* a shower of money, *instr.* ~ena. Dh. 186. — °-sataṁ, *n.* 100 k.s, 18,13. — °-sahassena (*instr. n.*) 1000 k.s, 57,32.

kā, *pron. interr. f.*, *v.* kiṁ.

kāka, *m.* (= *sa.*) a crow; ~o. 11,5. 18,16; *acc.* ~aṁ, 18,8. — *°-sīsa, *mfn.* having a head like a crow, *m.* ~o, 21,34. — *°-sūra, *m.* „a crow hero", designation of a cowardly or impudent fellow, *instr.* ~ena, Dh. 244. — disā-kāka, *m. q. v.*

***kākacchati**, *vb. onomat.*, to snore; *part. f. pl.* ~antiyo, 65,6. This word is said to be akin to √kās, to cough, *cp. Fausbøll*, Bem. 1888, p. 38 (44), but *Kern* and *Trenckner* derive it from √krath, *v.* Mil. 85,32 Note.

kākā, *indecl.* (= *sa.*), „caw, caw", *onomat. fr.* the cawing of a crow, 18,30.

kāja, *m.* (*sa.* kāca) a yoke to support burdens; *v.* khāri-kāja.

kāṇa, *mfn.* (= *sa.*) one-eyed, blind of one eye; °-mahā-macchaṁ, *acc. m.* 4,15.

kātabba, *grd.* & **kātuṁ**, *inf.*, *v.* karoti.

kāpotaka, *mfn.* (*sa.* kāpota & kapotaka) pigeon-coloured, grey, white; *n. pl.* ~āni (aṭṭhīni) Dh. 149.

kāma, *m.* (= *sa.*) [1]) wish, desire; most frequently *pl.* = desires, (sensual) pleasures, (sensual) love; *acc.* (*adv.*) ~aṁ, *q. v.*; *abl.* ~ato (jāyatī soko) Dh. 215; *pl.* ~ā, 20,17. 45,5 (mānusakā, *opp.* dibba-kāme, *acc.* (ib.)); 103,25 (te [Mārassa] paṭhamā senā); *acc. pl.* ~e, 46,18. 69,27. 103,24. Dh. 88. 383. 415; *instr.* sabba-kāmehi, 61,29; *gen.* ~ānaṁ, 68,20; *loc.* ~esu, 47,29. 52,24 (atittaṁ), Dh. 48 (id); 65,9 (viratto); 97,11 (micchā carati, „commits immorality"); Dh. 186 (titti) 218. 401. — *°-kalala (*v. h.*). — *°-taṇhā, thirst for pleasure, 67,14 (in the series: kāma-, bhava-, vibhava-). — *kāma-rati (*dvandva comp.*), love and lust; °-santhava, *m.* familiarity with ~, *acc.* ~aṁ, Dh. 27. — yattha-kāma(ṁ), *q. v.* — kāma-kāma, *etc. v. below.* — [2]) *mfn.* (at the end of *comp.*) desiring, longing for, intending; a-kāma, *mfn.* (*q. v.*); sukha-kāma, *mfn.* longing for happiness, *n. pl.* ~āni (bhūtāni) Dh. 131; very frequently *comp. w. inf.* in tu-: āropetu-°, 74,12. uddisāpetu-°, 84,6. khādāpetu-°, 1,23. khāditu-°, 1,7. 4,11. gaṇhitu-°, 55,16. gantu-°, 4,18. 22,2. 50,9 (brāhmaṇaṁ paharitvā ~o, kāma- is here logically to be combined with paharitvā). caritu-°, 36,10. jīvitu-°, Dh. 123. daṭṭhu-°, 19,12. (dātu-°, v. a-dātu-kāmatā). nahāyitu-°, 83,24. nikkhamitu-°, 65,16. paripucchitu-°, 84,7. pavisitu-°, 82,24. 83,27. paharitu-°, 29,25. bhuñjitu-°, 83,12. māretu-°, 9,20. vañcetu-°, 5,1. 51,16. sotu-°, 87,13.

kāmaṁ, *adv.* (*acc. sg. fr.* kāma, = *sa.*) willingly, readily, with pleasure; ~ cajāma asuresu pāṇaṁ, 60,17.

kāma-kāma, *mfn.* (— *sa.*) desirous of lust, having desires; *m. pl.* na ~ā (lapayanti santo) Dh. 83.

*kāma-gavesin, *mfn.* looking for pleasures; *m. pl.* ~ino, Dh. 99.

kāma-guṇa, *m.* (= *sa.*) passion, affection; object of sense, *pl.* the passions, taken as five different kinds, according to the five external senses; *acc. pl.* ~e, Dh. 371; *instr. pl.* ~ehi (pañcahi samappitassa) 67,25.

*kāmatā, *f.* (*cp.* kāma, [2])) inclination to; *comp. w. inf.* in tu-: kīḷitu-° (sālavana-kīḷaṁ, deviyā udapādi) 62,15. *cp.* a-dātu-kāmatā, 16,14.

*kāma-bhava, *m.*, *v.* kāmābhava.

*kāma-sukha, *n.* sensual pleasure, the pleasure of love; *acc.* ~aṁ (pahāya) 47,28 = Dh. 346—47. — *kāmasukh'allika, *mfn.* (?), °-anuyoga, *mfn.* 66,26 (*v. h.*).

*kāmābhava, *m.* (— kāma-bhava, with a lengthened metri causa) [1]) sensual existence in one of the eleven Kāmalokas. [2]) rise or origin of lust; °-parikkhīṇa, *mfn.* one in whom lust can rise no more, *acc. m.* ~aṁ, Dh. 415 („in whom all concupiscence is extinct"). *cp.* taṇhā-bhava, nandībhava.

kāya, *m.* (— *sa.*) the body; ~o, 70,32. 107,5 = Dh. 41; *gen.* ~assa, 7,26; *instr.* ~ena (saññato) 84,29; (saṁvuto) Dh. 231—234 (in the series: kāyena, vācāya, manasā); ~ena dhammaṁ passati, „sees the law bodily", Dh. 259 (*cp.* SBE. X, 65); *loc.* ~asmiṁ, 71,10; *acc. pl.* ~e, 112,20. — aru-kāya. *m.* or *mfn.* (?) *v. h.* — santa-kāya. *mfn.* whose body is quieted, *m.* ~o, Dh. 378. — *°-gatā, *adj. f.* directed to the body (sati, *q. v.*) Dh. 293. — *°-duccarita, *n.* the bad deeds of the body, *acc.* ~aṁ, Dh. 231. — *°-ppakopa, *m.* bodily anger, *acc.* ~aṁ, Dh. 231. — °-bandhana, *n.* a girdle, ~aṁ, 82,25. — *°-viññāṇa, *n.* body-consciousness, the sense of touch, ~aṁ (dukkha-sahagataṁ, a painful perception) 98,1. — *°-samphassa-viññāṇâyatana. *n.* the sense of touch, ~aṁ, 72,16 (*cp.* āyatana).

kāyika, *mfn.* (— *sa.*) belonging to or concerning the body; *instr. m.* ~ena (saññamena, saṁvarena) 85,17-18.

kāra, *mfn.* (— *sa.*) doing, making (at the end of *comp.*), *v.* andha-°, ahiṁ-°, uṇha-°, usu-°, mamiṁ-°, sādhu-°, *cp.* purekkhāra, sakkāra.

kāraka, *m(fn).* doing, making; a maker, doer (at the end of *comp.*), *v.* kūṭaṭṭa-°, gaha-°, pesuñña-°, bhatta-°, sassa-°, sāsana-°.

kāraṇa, *n.* (— *sa.*) [1]) cause, reason, motive (means); *nom.* ~aṁ, 3,1. 7,4. 29,1 (taṁ ~aṁ, that is why). 37,7. pabbajjā-° (tumhākaṁ), 45,9; *acc.* ~aṁ (imaṁ, the cause of that) 15,9. ~aṁ katvā, giving as cause, 85,24; *instr.* kena ~ena, for what reason? 16,33. 100,17; kin te mama hasita-kāraṇena, „what is that to you why I laugh", 53,34; a-kāraṇena, *q. v.*; *abl.* ~ā, often in *comp. w.* kiṁ-°, why? 9,20. 28,34. 53,34; manussâvāsa-kāraṇā, „because I have had to do with men", 112,10. — [2]) event, affair, the state of the case, circumstance, fact; *acc.* ~aṁ (asallakkhetvā) 3,18; (sutvā) 24,28; (ñatvā) 35,1; kiñci ~aṁ ajānanto, unsuspecting, 50,17. — [3]) doing, making (at the end of *comp.*; sometimes written -kārana); asanta-paggaha-°, 29,27 (*v.* a-santa).

kāraṇā, *f.* (— *sa.*) punishment, pain, torture (in *comp.* often shortened to kāraṇa-); *kāraṇa-ghara, *n.* & *m.* house of torment, *loc.* ~e, 21,15. *cp.* (kamma-) karaṇā.

kārin, *mfn.* (= *sa.*) doing, making (at the end of *comp.*), *v.* nisamma-°, pāpa-°, sātacca-°.

kāriya, *mfn.* (*sa.* kārya) *grd.* *v.* karoti & a-kāriya.

kāruñña, *n.* (*fr.* karuṇa, *sa.* kāruṇya) compassion; *acc.* ~aṁ (*w. loc.* brāhmaṇe) 16,31; *instr.* ~ena (tayi) 17,13. 58,14. *cp.* karuṇā.

kāretar, *m.* (*sa.* kārayitṛ) one who causes something to be done; *nom. sg.* ~tā (kammānaṁ) 97,13. *cp.* kattar.

kāreti, *vb.* (*caus.* karoti, *sa.* kārayati) to cause to do or to be done (*acc.*), to cause another (*acc.*) to be (*acc.*), to cause another (*acc.*) to perform (*acc.*); periphrastically : rajjaṁ ~, to reign, to be king (*cp.* karoti : rajjaṁ karotha, 42,6); *part. loc. m.* ~ente (rajjaṁ) 1,2; *part. med. loc. m.* kārayamāne (id.) 5,24; — *imp. 2. sg.* ~ehi (id.) 47,10; — *aor. 3. sg.* ~esi (rajjaṁ) 19,6; (maṅgalaṁ) 58,20; a-kārayi (yakkhiṁ sapathaṁ) 111,29; — *ger.* ~etvā (dānasālā) 38,13; (purohitaṁ rājānaṁ) 46,16; (abhisekaṁ, *q. v.*) 36,29. — *subst.* kāretar, *m.* (*v. h.*); *cp.* kakkāreti.

kāla, *m.* (= *sa.*) time, space or point of time, right or proper time; death (in the phrase : kālaṁ karoti, to die); *nom.* ~o bhante! the time has come, sir! 78,3; abhisambujjhana-kālo, 63,7; nekkhamma-kālo, 45,6; *acc.* ~aṁ (ārocāpesi) 78,3; ~aṁ (akari, died) 80,33; ~aṁ (katvā) 34,33. 84,30 (*cp.* kāla-kata, kāla-kiriyā); *gen.* ~assa (ass'eva, betimes) 82,17; *abl.* ~ato, *comp.* tass' āgata-kālato paṭṭhāya, „from the day of his coming", 18,29; Gotamassa uppanna-kālato paṭṭhāya, 72,30; tassa nikkhanta-°, 9,15; *loc.* kāle (or kālamhi) in time, seasonably (*opp.* vikāle) 9,12; kāle gacchante, in the course of time, 14,15. 102,4; tasmin kāle, 2,26; pacchime kāle, in the hour of death, 86,18; hemantike kāle, in the winter-time, 100,24; very frequently in *comp.* *w.* verbal nouns or *pp.* : rājābhiseka-°, 11,6; suriyuggamana-°, 72,29; mahā-janassa nagaraṁ pavisana-kāle, 73,12; dhītu maraṇa-kāle, 89,13; tava santikaṁ āgata-kāle (mam gaṇhāhi) 3,17; asuka-kāle, 88,23 (*v. h.*); uṭṭhāna-kālamhi (time to rise) Dh. 280. — kālantarena (— *sa.*), *v.* antara. — kālika, *mfn.* (*q. v.*). — a-kāla, *m.* (= *sa.*) wrong time; *°-pupphāni (*n. pl.*) flowers out of season, 37,16; *°-vātaṁ, *n.* unseasonable wind (contrary wind?) 25,21.

kāḷa (or kāla), *mfn.* (*sa.* kāla) black; *m.* ~o (puriso) 92,13; *n. pl.* ~āni (kesāni) 47,1. — °-pāsāṇa-, a black rock, 24,21. — *°-vaṇṇa-kata, *mfn.* blacked, *f.* ~ā (bhūmi) 84,21. *cp. next* & kāla-kaṇṇī.

kāḷaka, *mfn.* (*sa.* kālaka) black; *subst. n.* (?) dirt, speck, stain : *apagata-kāḷaka, *mfn.* free from dirt or black specks. *n.* ~aṁ (vatthaṁ suddhaṁ) 68,25.

kāla-kaṇṇī, *f.* (*sa.* kāla-karṇī) ill luck, misfortune; a fatal or ill-boding person or thing, a fury; — *~i-sakuṇa, *m.* a bird of ill omen, *instr.* ~ena. 12,10; — *~i-salākā, *f.* the lot which points out the guilty or fatal person, 23,12.

***kāla-kata**, *mfn.* (— kata-kāla. *sa.* *kāla-kṛta, *cp.* kāla-gata) dead; *acc. m.* ~aṁ, a dead person, 63,25; *loc.* ~e (pitari) 22,15.

kāla-kiriyā, *f.* (*sa.* kāla-kriyā) death; puthujjana-kālakiriyaṁ (*acc.*) katvā, having died like common people, 87,29.

kāḷā, *f.* (*sa.* kālā) name of a certain plant, a climbing or creeping plant (= kāḷa-valli, Comm.); *°-pavāḷā, *f.* a tender stalk (said of a tender maiden), 47,20.

kālika, *mfn.* (— *sa.*) 'depending

on time', future ɔ: which will not come before long (*opp.* sandiṭṭhika, MN. I 474,6. SN. I 117,26); *n.* mā ~aṁ anudhāvi. 47,10 (*cp.* bhavitabbam ev'etaṁ kathesi, 47,11).

kāsāva, *mfn.* (*sa.* kāshāya, *cp.* kasāva) yellow, dark-yellow; *n.* the yellow robe of the Buddhist monks; *acc.* ~aṁ (vatthaṁ). Dh. 9—10. — *°-kaṇṭha, *mfn.* 'yellow-necked', wearing the yellow robe; *m. pl.* ~ā, Dh. 307. (*cp.* SBE. X. 6 Note.)

Kāsi, *m.* (*pl.*) (*sa.* Kāçi) *nom. pr.* of a country and its people, whose capital was Benares (Bārāṇasī, *q. v.*); °-raṭṭha, *n.* the kingdom of K., *acc.* ~aṁ, 38,21; *loc.* ~e, 34,31; °-raṭṭha-vāsi-manusso. *m.* a man from K. 35,28.

Kāsika, *mfn.* (*sa.* Kāçika) coming from Kāsi or Benares; °-vattha, *n.* Benares-cloth, a sort of fine cotton cloth; *loc.* ~e, 62,29 (*cp. Fick,* Soc. Glied. p. 176).

kiṁ[1], *pron. interr. n.* (= *sa.*) what? *mf.* ko, kā, who? which? — kiṁ, a) *nom. n.* 13,13 (~dukkhaṁ); 16,11 (kiṁ nām' etaṁ); 93,9 (kiñ ca, and what?); constructed *w. gen. pers. & instr. rei* = what is one (*gen.*) to do with (*instr.*): 31,31 (kin te bhātarā); 32,32 (kim me dukkhena); 49,14. 53,34. 59,25. 79,31. 106,10 *etc.*, or only *w. instr.* 20,29. 111,20; — *comp.* *kiṁsaddo nām'esa, „what sort of noise is this", 60,9; kiṁsaddo iti (apucchi) 112,8; kiṁkāraṇā (*abl.*) why? 9,20; kinnāma, *mfn.* (*q. v.*); kimatthaṁ & kimatthāya, *v.* attha[4]); — b) *acc. n.* kiṁ (cintento) 4,3; (karissanti) 7,16; (karomi) 55,6; (maññasi) 69,34; kin'ti vyākareyyāsi. 95,6; — c) kiṁ (*adv.*) *v. below.* — *m. nom.* ko (si tvaṁ) 3,12; (jānati) 13,17; (ettha) 65,14; (pan' ettha Nāgaseno) 97,31; (~ nu dīpo) 110,31; (~ nu hāso) Dh. 146; — *acc.* kaṁ, 25,13. Dh. 353. — *f. nom.* kā (nāma tvaṁ) 56,10. — *instr.* a) (*m.*) *n.* kena, 16,33. 35,3. 70,28; b) *adv.* why? 22,29. 54,27. — *instr.* (*etc.*) *f.* kāya, 29,30 (kathāya). — *gen. m.* a) kassa, 98,13; b) kissa, 36,33 (phalaṁ, *scil.* rukkhassa). — *gen. n.* (*adv.*) kissa, why? 101,6. — *abl. n.* (*adv.*) kasmā, why? 7,7. 87,28. — As to the rest the declension is that of taṁ and other pronouns, *e. g. instr. pl. m.* kehi, 74,9. An old neuter form kad- has been preserved in kac-ci & kad-ariya (*q. v.*). — kiñ carahi, ko carahi, *v.* carahi. — *cp.* kiñca, kiñcana, kiñcāpi, kiñci, koci *etc.*

kiṁ[2], *adv. interr.* (= *prec.*; in its different meanings often combined with other particles). — 1) = how? 1,8 (kin ti); 70,24 (kiñ ca sabbaṁ ādittaṁ); 74,28 (kim pana, „how much less"); 86,29 (kin nu kho bhavissati, how is she now, I wonder?); 87,13 (kin nu kho); Dh. 146 (kim ānando). — 2) = why? 1,14. 3,8. 85,32. 88,4 (kiṁ nāma, why then?). — 3) *interr. particle* (introductory of a full sentence): a) = latin *-ne, num*; kiṁ jānāsi, do you know? 113,11; kiṁ so sabbarattiṁ dīpeyya (*pot.*) 99,18; kiṁ bhavissati, Dh. 264; kin nu kho. 38,27 (*w. pot.* siyā, should he possibly be?); 89,22. 97,18; kiṁ pana (by putting forth a second question) 89,25. 97,26; kiṁ pana (expressive of astonishment) 44,4. — b) = latin *nonne* (*w. foll.* 'na'); kin te . . . na vaṭṭati, had you not better. . .? 1,15; kiṁ na passasi, 111,19; kiñ ca lohitaṁ n'ūpasussaye (*pot.*) 103,19. — c) kiṁ . . . na . . . (disjunctive, = *utrum* . . *an*), 9,24 (kiṁ mātā vo anācāraṁ karoti na karotīti). — 4) used as a mere interjection, by calling one's attention to a question (without full sentence) = now! look here! halloh! 3,11 (kiṁ bho vānarinda!); 73,16 (kiṁ Sundari, kahaṁ gatāsi).

kicca, 1) *mfn.* (*grd.* karoti, *sa.* kṛtya) to be done or made; *n.* ~aṁ (ātappaṁ) Dh. 276; kiccaṁ, a-kiccaṁ, Dh. 292; kiccākicca, *loc. pl.* ~esu, Dh. 74. — 2) *n.* duty, service, kindness; business, purpose, cause, motive, use, need; *nom.* tumhākaṁ vināsena ~aṁ n'atthi, „there is no need for" (*instr.*)

55,7; *acc.* ~aṁ, 13,25 (service); sakicca-ppasuta, *mfn.* intent upon one's own business, *m. pl.* ~ā. 86,23; kattabba-kicca, *n. pl.* „the objects of one's mission", *loc.* ~esu, 114,31. — itthi-°, kata-°, kilamana-°, bhatta-°, *q. v.*

kiccha, *mfn.* (*sa.* kṛcchra) painful, attended with pain or labour; *m.* ~o (Buddhānaṁ uppado) Dh. 182; *n.* ~aṁ (saddhammasavanaṁ) *ib.*

kiñca, *n. pron. indef.* (— *sa. cp.* kiñci) anything; aññaṁ kiñca yathicchitaṁ, whatever else you might wish, 111,28.

kiñcana(ṁ), *n. pron. indef.* (*sa.* kiṁ-cana) anything; na ~aṁ, nothing, Dh. 200. 421. — a-kiñcana, *mfn.* (*q. v.*). — *cp.* ākiñcañña, *n.* & sakiñcana, *mfn.*

kiñcâpi, *indecl.* (— *sa.*) certainly, although, in spite of; ~ na jānāti (*w. foll.* pana) 63,31; ~ so evaṁ vadeyya, 100,17 („in spite of what he might say").

kiñci, 1) *n. pron. indef.* (*sa.* kiṁcid) something, anything (whatever); *w. foll. negation* = nothing; *nom.* yaṁ kiñci . . . sabbaṁ taṁ (whatsoever) 68,27; *adj.* ~ diṭṭhigataṁ, 94,6; *acc.* api kiñci labhāmase (any reward) 13,26; aññaṁ ~ (*v. h.*) 7,11; mā kiñci vadetha, 55,26; ~ vattuṁ na visahati, 87,21; *adj.* na kiñci pāpaṁ, 104,34; na . . . aṇumattaṁ ~ dubbhāsitaṁ padaṁ (not even the smallest) 110,12; *instr.* kenaci, 73,4; kenacid-eva (karaṇīyena) 32,13; *loc.* kismici, Dh. 74. — 2) *adv.* altogether, *w. foll. negation* = not at all; sace kiñci āhāraṁ labheyyaṁ, 15,11; na kiñci abhavissa, 42,11; ~ kāraṇaṁ a-jānanto, 50,17. — koci, *m.* (*v. h.*) *cp.* kacci & kiñca above.

kiṇāti, *vb.* (*sa.* √krī) to buy; *pr. 1. sg.* ~āmi (dadhiṁ tava hatthato) 101,29 (= I did not buy); *ger.* kiṇitvā, 101,26.

kitava, *m.* (= *sa.*) a gamester, gambler; kitavāsaṭho, a fraudulent gambler, 106,18 — Dh. 252, which probably ought to be written kitavā saṭho, kitavā being *nom.* (= *sa.* kitavaḥ) after the analogy of words ending with -vat (Tr. *cp.* Jāt. VI, 228,19: kitavā sikkhito yathā, in both instances before 's'; *gen.* ~assa, SN. I, 24,4 = Vin. III, 90.) The Comm. takes kitavā = kitavāya, but *Weber* (Ind. Str. I, 158) and *Max Müller* (SBE. X, 63) take it for an *abl.* = vor dem Spielgegner, from the player.

***kittaka**, *mfn.* (formed after the analogy of ettaka *etc.* Tr. PM. p. 80, *cp. sa.* kiyat), how much? how many? *n.* ~aṁ pacāmi, how much have I to cook? 57,10. *cp. next.*

***kittāvatā**, *adv.* (*cp.* ettāvatā & *prec.*), how far? to what extent? 96,5.

kinnara, *m.* (= *sa.*) a kind of mythical being, a male fairy, *f.* ~ī; the kinnaras are of extraordinary beauty, celebrated dancers and musicians (*cp.* Jāt. IV, 252 & 438). — *°-līḷhā, *f.* the grace of a kinnara, *instr.* ~āya. 49,12.

kinnāma, *mfn.* (*sa.* kiṁ-nāman) having what name; *m.* ~o si bhante, what is your name? 96,29.

kipillika, *m.* (*sa.* pipīlika. *cp.* pipīlikā) an ant; *pl.* ~ā, 60,1.

kimatthaṁ & **kimatthāya**, *v.* kiṁ & attha 1).

kira, *adv.* (*enclit.* — *sa.* kila) indeed, really, probably; namely, often to be rendered by „you know", „you see"; „we hear", „it is said"; or indicating what the subject concludes from facts mentioned or imagined; — 87,6; evaṁ kir', 40,3. 51,26; saccaṁ kir' evam, 54,16; na kir', 31,6; expressive of astonishment: 54,13; in interrogative sentences: 51,7. 68,15. 69,7 (kirâhaṁ); after a question: 32,17. 87,28; — 3,2. 18,5. 23,26. 29,22. 32,9; — 8,8. 11,10. 31,8. 39,14. 54,12. 60,2. 61,2-9. 72,27; — ayam pi kira rājā yeva, 43,25.

kiriyā, *f.* (*sa.* kriyā) doing; work, undertaking; *nom.* ~ā (paññavantānaṁ ijjhati) 57,6. — anta-°. kāla-°, sacca-°, *q. v.*

kilanta, *pp. v. next.*

kilamati, *vb.* (*sa.* √klam) to grow weary, to become tired, to be troubled or exhausted; *pr. 3. pl.* ~anti. 6,21; *1. pl.* kimatthaṁ ~āma (why weary ourselves) 65,2; *imper. 3. pl.* ~antu, 60,12. — *pp.* kilanta, *m. pl.* ~ā, 112,28. *cp. next.*

kilamatha, *m.* (*sa.* klamatha) fatigue, exhaustion, suffering; *instr.* appa-kilamathena, 28,12 (*v. h.*). — *atta-° (*v. h.*)

***kilamana**, *n.* — *prec.* — °-kiccaṁ (n'atthi aññesaṁ. „none shall suffer") 39,16 (*cp.* kicca).

kiliṭṭha, *mfn.* (*pp.* √kliç, *sa.* klishṭa). impure, dirty; *n.* impurity; *kamma-kiliṭṭhaṁ, evil karma (*opp.* °-visuddhi) Dh. 15. *cp.* kilissati & kilesa.

kilinna, *mfn.* (*pp.* √klid, *sa.* klinna), moistened, wet; lālā-kilinnagatta, *adj.* 65,5.

kilissati, *vb.* (*sa.* √kliç) [1]) to be tormented, feel pain, suffer; *pot. 3. sg.* ~eyya, Dh. 158. — [2]) to be impure (through sin); *pp.* kiliṭṭha (*q. v.*) *cp. next.*

kilesa, *m.* (*sa.* kleça) pain; depravity, passion; *acc. pl.* ~e (jahituṁ) 44,31; *loc. pl.* ~esu (virattamānasassa) 64,19-32; sabba-kilesa-darathesu (*loc. pl.*) „all passions and torments", 64,21; kilesa-vasena, „under the influence of passion", passionately, 20,11; *°-rati, *f.* sensual pleasure, love, *acc.* ~iṁ, 46,18; *instr.* ~iyā, 53,24. 73,18. — *citta-klesa, *m.* (— °-kilesa), depravity of mind, *abl. pl.* ~ehi, Dh. 88.

kiloma & **kilomaka**, *n.* (*sa.* kloma & kloman) any kind of membranaceous tissue, *esp.* the peritoneum, abdomen or paunch; *nom.* ~kaṁ, 82,3 — 97,21 (*cp.* Jāt. IV, 292,13. III, 49,23-25).

kisa, *mfn.* (*sa.* kṛça) lean, emaciated; *m.* ~o (tvam asi) 103,5; *acc.* ~aṁ, 106,12 — Dh. 395.

***Kisāgotamī**, *f. nom. pr.* of a therī, a relative of Gotama; *nom.* ~ī (khattiyakaññā) 64,11; *gen.* (*dat.*) ~iyā, 64,25.

kismici, *loc. sg. n.*, *v.* kiñci.

kissa, [1]) *gen. pron. interr.* [2]) *adv.* — why, 101,6. *v.* kiṁ [1].

kīdisa, *mfn.* (*sa.* kīdṛça) of what kind? what like? *m.* ~o (sīlācāro) 43,33; *n.* ~aṁ (kammaṁ) 85,12.

kīḷati, *vb.* (*sa.* √krīḍ) to play, to sport, to amuse one's self in or by (*w. loc.* or *acc.* of the name of the play, very often a *comp.* ending with -kīḷā, *q. v.*); *pr. 3. sg.* ~ati (jūtaṁ Tambarājena saddhiṁ, plays at dice) 19,10. 48,5; (nakkhattaṁ, enjoys the festival) 61,3; *1. pl.* ~āma, 48,22; — *part. m.* ~anto, 48,5; *gen.* ~antassa (*w. loc.* jāla-karaṇḍake, *q. v.*) 36,30; *part. med. m.* ~ amāno, 7,29; — *aor. 3. sg.* kīḷi (raññā saddhiṁ) 48,21; (pokkharaṇiyaṁ udaka-kīḷaṁ, amused himself in the lotus tank) 52,28; — *inf.* ~ituṁ (jūtaṁ) 20,4; *comp.* kīḷitukāmatā, *f.* 62,15. — *caus.* kīḷāpeti (*q. v.*); *cp. next* & kīḷā, kīḷikā.

kīḷana, *n.* (*sa.* krīḍana) playing; °-kāle (ambākaṁ pokkharaṇiyaṁ) 53,6; jūta-kīḷana-, playing at dice, 20,14.

kīḷā, *f.* (*sa.* krīḍā), play, sport, amusement; frequently last part of *comp.* (object of the verb kīḷati): udaka-kīḷaṁ kīḷi (amused himself by bathing) 52,28; uyyāna-kīḷādi-gamana, *n.* riding in the park *etc.* 65,29; kumāra-kīḷaṁ [*sc.* kīḷitvā] 44,20 (*v. h.*); nakkhatta-kīḷaṁ (anubhavamānā, the festivities) 61,5; sālavana-°, 62,15.

kīḷāpeti, *vb.* (*caus. II.* kīḷati) to cause to play, to play with (*acc.*); *ger.* ~etvā (taṁ. *sc.* dārakaṁ) 58,33.

***kīḷikā**, *f.* (*dimin. fr.* kīḷā) pleasure, excursion; *acc.* uyyāna-kīḷikaṁ gacchanto (taking a walk in the park) 52,18.

***kīva**, *indecl.* (*correl.* of yāva, *cp. sa.* kiyat & *ved.* kīvat) how much? (quanto), *w. foll.* pi — how much soever (quamvis); — °-mahanta, *mfn.* how great, *acc. n.* ~am pi (pāpakammaṁ) 51,27.

k u -, *indecl.* (— *sa.*) prefix, implying deterioration, contempt *etc.* (originally pron. base, *cp.* kuto). — ku-samudda, *m.* the dreadful or fatal sea, ~o, 20,16. (*cp.* kiṁ, kiṁsadda).

k u k k u ṭ a, *m.* (— *sa.*) a cock; pañjare pakkhitta-kukkuṭo, a cock in a cage, 46,20.

k u c c h i, *m.* & *f.* (*sa.* kukshi, *m.*) the belly, womb, uterus; *acc.* ~iṁ, 61,21; — *abl.* mātu-kucchito, 62,26; *abl. m.* ~imhā, 42,23; — *loc. m.* ~ismiṁ, 38,9; ~imhi, 61,31; — *instr. f.* ~iyā (pariharitvā) 62,2; — *loc. f.* ~iyaṁ (pakkhipitvā, „even if you had her inside you") 50,34.

k u j j h a t i, *vb.* (*sa.* √krudh) to become angry; *pot. 3. sg.* na kujjheyya, Dh. 224; *aor. 2. pl.* mā mayhaṁ ~ittha, 19,31; *ger.* ~itvā, 33,16; a-kujjhitvā, 57,25. — *pp.* kuddha (*q. v.*), *cp.* kujjhana, kodha.

*k u j j h a n a, *n.* becoming angry. — °-sīla, *mfn.* prone to anger, irascible; *f. pl.* ~ā, 52,6.

k u ñ j a r a, *m.* (— *sa.*) an elephant; *voc.* ~a, 77,3-4; *pl.* ~ā, Dh. 322.

k u ṭ i (& kuṭī), *f.* (*sa.* kuṭī) a hut, a house; *nom.* ~i (channā) 104,22-25; *loc.* ~iyaṁ, 14,29; (eka-)gandha-kuṭiyaṁ (*q. v.*) 73,17.

k u ṭ u m b a, *n.* (= *sa.*) household, family; *acc.* ~aṁ (vicārentī) 22,15; (saṇṭhapetuṁ) 56,6.

k u ṭ u m b i k a, *m.* (— *sa. cp.* kuṭumbin) a householder, paterfamilias (*esp.* of the middle class, *cp. Fick,* Soc. Gl. 166); *nahāpita-°, *m.* 28,19 (*v. h.*).

k u ṇ a p a, *n.* (— *sa.*) a corpse, a dead body; vippaviddha-nānā-kuṇapa-bharita, *mfn.* 65,10.

k u ṇ ḍ a l a, *n.* (— *sa.*) a ring, ear-ring or bracelet; *loc. pl.* maṇi-kuṇḍalesu, precious stones and rings, Dh. 345.

k u ṇ ḍ i k ā, *f.* (— *sa.*) the water-pot of an ascetic; *loc.* ~āyaṁ, 110,33.

k u t o, *adv. interr.* (*sa.* kutas, *cp.* ku-) [1]) whence? from where? 21,8. 55,3. 59,2. 87,35. — [2]) how much less? (*latin* nedum): na soko kuto bhayaṁ (neither — — nor) Dh. 212. — a-kuto-bhaya, *mfn.* (*q. v.*).

*k u t t a, *n.* (?) at the end of *comp.* — acting or performing the part of (?). — itthi-kutta- „women's wiles", 21,13. (kutta is explained in the commentaries by -kataṁ or kiriyā, and is *synon. w.* kutti, *f.* (*sa.* kṛti?); accordingly it is possibly derived from *sa. suff.* kṛt).

k u d ā c a n a ṁ, *adv.* (*sa.* kadā cana) ever, at any time; *w. negation* — never at any time; na ~, 106,23 — Dh. 5; mā ~, 106,35 = Dh. 210. *cp.* kadāci.

k u d d h a, *mfn.* (*sa.* kruddha, *pp.* √krudh, *v.* kujjhati) angry; *m.* ~o, 57,28; *instr.* ~ena, 11,7; *gen.* ~assa, 11,6. — a-kuddha, *mfn.* (*q. v.*); *cp.* kodha.

k u p i t a, *mfn.* (= *sa.*; *pp.* kuppati, √kup) offended; angry; *m.* ~o, 74,30. *cp.* kopa.

k u b b a t o, k u b b ā n a ṁ, k u b b e t h a, *v.* karoti.

k u m ā r a, *m.* (— *sa.*) a son, a young man, prince; *°-kīḷaṁ [katvā] (having amused himself as prince, *cp.* kīḷā) 44,20; *°-pañha, *n.* the novice's questions, 82,14; deva-kumāra, a son of a god, ~ vaṇṇin, *mfn.* 45,26 (*v. h.*). — kumāra is often used as last part of a *nom. pr.* — younger, junior, *v.* Ajatasattu-, Brahmadatta-, Siddhattha-, Sīlava-, Suppāraka-, Susīma-. *cp.* kumārī.

*K u m a r a - k a s s a p a, *m. nom. pr.* of a thera; ~o (vicitrakathī) 109,9.

k u m ā r ī, *f.* (= *sa.*) a young girl; *acc.* ~iṁ (dahariṁ) 47,19. *cp.* kumāra. — *dimin.* kumārikā, *f.* (= *sa.*) *id.* ~ā, 86,26. 112,14; *voc.* ~e, 87,35; *acc.* ~aṁ, 48,19; *instr.* ~āya, 86,30.

k u m u d a, *n.* (— *sa.*) the white lotus; *acc.* ~aṁ (sāradikaṁ) Dh. 285. — *°-naḷa, *m.* a lotus-stalk, *acc.* ~aṁ,

5,18. — *°-patta-vaṇṇa, *mfn.* having the colour of the petals of the white lotus, *acc. pl.* ~e (maṅgala-sindhave) 63,4.

kumbha, *m.* (= *sa.*) [1]) a jar, pitcher; *°-'ūpama, *mfn.* like a jar (fragile), *acc.* ~aṁ (kāyaṁ) Dh. 40; — uda-°, *m.* a water-pot, ~o, Dh. 121. [2]) one of the frontal globes of an elephant; *acc.* ~aṁ (hatthissa) 77,1.

kumbhīla, *m.* (*sa.* kumbhīra) a crocodile (of the Ganges); ~o, 2,26. 108,27 (ruddadassano); *gen. pl.* ~ānaṁ, 3,17. — *°-rāja, *m.* 1,16 (*voc.*) *cp.* rājan.

kuruṅga, *m.* (*sa.* kuraṅga) a kind of antelope; *°-miga, *m.* the k.-deer, ~o, 11,24; ~jātaka, p. 11—13.

kurute, kurumāna, *v.* karoti.

kula, *n.* (= *sa.*) a family, household; class or caste in general (*v. Fick,* Soc. Gl. 22, *cp.* jāti), and more especially designation of a family of the numerous castes of the middle class (merchants and tradesmen, *v.* kuladhītar & °-putta below); *nom.* taṁ kulaṁ. Dh. 193; jāti-gotta-kula-padesa, *m.* 43,30 (*v. h.*); para-kulesu (*loc. pl.*) „among other people", Dh. 73; rāja-kula. *n.* the king's palace, *acc.* ~aṁ (pavisitvā) 58,17; *abl.* ~ato, 48,15; *loc.* ~e, 53,30. — kassaka-°, 8,15; vāṇija-°, 30,3; purāṇa-seṭṭhi-°, 55,31 (*v. h.*). *cp.* upaṭṭhāka-°, 81,11. kulin, *mfn.* (*q. v.*).

kula-dhītar, *f.* (*sa.* kula-duhitṛ) the daughter of a respectable family (*esp.* of the middle class); *acc.* ~araṁ, 87,18. *cp. next.*

kula-putta, *m.* (*sa.* kula-putra) a young man of respectable family (*esp.* of the middle class, *cp. Fick,* Soc. Gl. 164); ~o (seṭṭhi-putto) 67,21; *acc.* ~aṁ, 68,10; *gen.* ~assa, 67,25.

***kula-santaka**, *mfn.* belonging to one's family; *acc. m.* ~aṁ (nagaraṁ), 62,4.

***kulala**, *m.* (*cp. sa.* kurara & krura) a hawk or falcon; *gen.* ~assa, 92,20.

kulāvaka, *n.* (*sa.* kulāya, *m.* + -ka) a nest; ~kā, *f.* (or *pl.*?) brood of birds (= supaṇṇa-potakā, Comm.) 60,16 (*cp.* SN. I, p. 8,1 ff.) — vikulāva, *mfn.* (*q. v.*).

kulin, *mfn.* (= *sa.*) belonging to a noble family; *a-kulin, of base extraction, 102,4 (*q. v.*).

***Kuveṇī**, *f. nom. pr.* of a female yakkha; ~ī nāma yakkhinī, 111,5.

kusa, *m.* (*sa.* kuça) the Kusa-grass (Poa Cynosuroides); ~o, 26,20; Dh. 311 (duggahīto hatthaṁ anukantati); nīla-kusa-tiṇa. *n.* dark K.-grass, ~aṁ, 26,18.

kusagga, *n.* (*sa.* kuçāgra) the sharp point of a blade of Kusa-grass; *instr.* ~ena (bhuñjetha bhojanaṁ, like an ascetic) Dh. 70.

***Kusamāla**, *m.* (?) *nom. pr.* of an ocean; *acc.* ~aṁ (nāma samuddaṁ) 26,19. = Kusamālin, *m.* (?), 26,23 (~ māliti vuccati). *cp.* Aggimāla.

kusamudda, *m. v.* ku-.

kusala, *mfn.* (*sa.* kuçala) good, right; clever, skilful; *m.* ~o, Dh. 44; *n.* ~aṁ, 4,32 (sace..., icc-etaṁ kusalaṁ); ācāra-kusala, *mfn.* perfect in behaviour, *m.* ~o, Dh. 376; parappavāda-°, skilled in disputation, *m.* ~o, 110,9; *gen. pl.* kusalâ-kusalānaṁ kammānaṁ, good and bad deeds, 97,13. — *subst. n.* a good thing, good things, good deeds, merit; *nom.* ~aṁ, 97,12; ~aṁ bahuṁ, Dh. 53; *acc.* ~aṁ katvā, 58,12; *instr.* ~ena, Dh. 173; *gen.* ~assa, Dh. 183. — a-kusala, *mfn.* (*q. v.*).

Kusinārā, *f.* (*sa.* Kuçinagara) *nom. pr.* of a town in Northern India, the capital of the Mallas, where Buddha died; ~ā, 78,27; *acc.* ~aṁ nagaraṁ, 78,32.

kusīta, *mfn.* (*sa.* kusīda) idle, lazy; *m.* ~o (*synon.* hīnavīriyo) Dh. 112. 280; *acc.* ~aṁ, Dh. 7. *cp.* kosajja.

kusuma, *n.* (= *sa.*) a flower; nīluppalâdi-kusuma-dāma-, 47,13.

***kuhiṁ**, *adv. interr.* (*cp.* kahaṁ

& *sa*. kuha) [1]) whereto? ~ me puttaṁ nesi, 59,1; ~ gantvā, 72,1. – [2]) where? 46,5 (~ me mātā); 94,18 (~ upapajjati).

***kuhiñci**. *adv*. (*fr*. last, *cp*. *sa*. kuhacid) to any place; na ~. nowhere, Dh. 180.

kūṭa[1], *mfn*. (= *sa*.) false, deceitful. – *kūṭaṭṭa, *m*. false suit (*cp*. aṭṭa[2]); ⁰-kāraka. *m*. a false suitor, *pl*. ~ā, 42,29.

kūṭa[2], *m*. & *n*. (= *sa*.) summit, peak; kāḷa-pāsāṇa-kūṭa-vaṇṇa, *mfn*. 24,21; gaha-kūṭaṁ, *n*. Dh. 154; pabbata-kūṭā, *m*. *pl*. 75,36. *cp*. Gijjhakūṭa.

kūpa[1], *m*. (= *sa*.) a hole. – lomakūpa, *m*. a pore of the shin; ⁰-mattam pi, 16,10 (*v*. matta[2]).

kūpa[2] & **kūpaka**, *m*. (= *sa*.) the mast of a ship; kūpagge, on the top of the mast, 18,6 (*v*. agga); *pl*. kūpakā (tayo) 28,29.

kūla, *n*. (= *sa*.) the bank of a river; *loc*. nadī-kūle, 108,24; parakūle, on the opposite bank, 108,29. – paṁsu-kūla, *n*. (*v*. *h*.).

kedāra, *m*. (= *sa*.) a field; *instr*. *pl*. ~ehi, 56,30.

kevala, *mfn*. (= *sa*.) [1]) alone, only. [2]) whole, entire, all; *acc*. *m*. ~aṁ (dhammaṁ) 109,25; *gen*. ~assa (dukkhakkhandassa) 66,11-17.

kevalaṁ, *adv*. (= *sa*.) only, merely; if only; 88,26; 11,13.

kesa, *m*. & *n*. (*sa*. keça *m*.) the hair of the head; *acc*. ~aṁ (ekaṁ) 46,28; *pl*. *m*. ~ā, 63,11. 82,2. 97,18; *pl*. *n*. ~āni (kāḷāni) 47,1; *gen*. ~ānaṁ, 44,24; *loc*. ~esu (gahetvā, by the hair) 111,24. – palita-kesa, *mfn*. 63,9; muñja-kesa, *mfn*. 21,35; haṭahaṭa-kesa, *mfn*. 71,29 (*q*. *v*.) *cp*. vikesika.

ko, *pron*. *interr*. *m*., *v*. kiṁ.

koci(d), *pron*. *indef*. *m*. (*subst*. or *adj*. — *sa*. kaç-cid) [*n*. kiñci, *q*. *v*.] some, any, anybody; *w*. *negation* = nobody; koci (aguṇavādī) 43,5; kocid eva, only some few, 88,34; kocid eva satto, id. 89,1; kocid eva puriso, some man or other, 99,17. 100,11; koci (puriso) few persons = nobody, Dh. 143; – na koci, nobody, 8,3. 72,31; koci na, 18,29; mā koci, 68,8; koci kiñci vattuṁ na visahati. 87,21; – *acc*. kañci (a-passitvā, a-disvā) 13,5. 42,31. 43,6; mā ~, Dh. 133; – *instr*. kenaci (asucinā) a-makkhito, 62,29; ~ (na sakkā puññaṁ saṁkhātuṁ) Dh. 196; – *gen*. kassaci (pi na) 17,18; ~ an-āgamanabhāvaṁ, 40,11; na ~, 65,25. 105,8; – *combined w. other pron*.: na añño koci, nobody else, 51,8. yo koci (samaṇo) whichsoever, 110,8; *pl*. ye keci pāṇā . . . te sabbe, 91,1; ye keci paṭhaviṭṭhitā. „any earthly being", 110,11.

***koñca**[1], *m*. or *n*. (?) name of a certain sound, a cry, roar, *esp*. the roaring or trumpeting of an elephant (also written kunca (& kuñja) *cp*. √kuc & √kūj & kuñjara; Jāt. VI, 581,18. V, 49,15. VI, 538,8); koñcanāda, *m*. the trumpeting of an elephant, *acc*. ~aṁ naditvā, 61,19.

koñca[2], *m*. (*sa*. krauñca) a kind of heron; *pl*. jiṇṇa-koñcā, old herons, Dh. 155.

koṭi, *f*. (= *sa*.) [1]) end, top, point; *loc*. ~iyaṁ ṭhito, last, 17,8. – *aṭṭhi-koṭi, the end of a bone, *acc*. ~iṁ, 13,20. – vema-⁰, the part of a loom that is moved, *loc*. ~iyaṁ, 89,6. – [2]) the highest number (10 millions); asīti-koṭi-vibhava, *mfn*. (*q*. *v*.).

koṭṭeti, *vb*. (*sa*. √kuṭṭ) to crush, pound, grind; *ger*. ~etvā (taṇḍule) 57,20. (*cp*. ākoṭeti).

***koṭṭha(ka)**[1], *m*. (Birm. read. koṭṭaka, which is probably the true spelling, *cp*. koṭṭeti) a certain bird, a woodpecker, *v*. rukkha-koṭṭhaka (*cp*. Jāt. VI, 539,9; Ind. Stud. III, 128; Five Jāt. p. 36).

koṭṭhaka[2], *m*. *n*. (*sa*. koshṭa(ka)) a surrounding wall, any enclosed space, reservoir, receptacle for, store-room; dvāra-koṭṭhaka, 48,32 (*v*. *h*.).

***koṭṭhāsa**, *m*. a part, portion;

acc. ~aṁ (ekaṁ, one half part) 58,23; *pl.* ~ā (dve, two companies) 33,20; *ib.* 30 (= two portions); *acc. pl.* ~e, 41,18.

*Koṭṭhita, *m. nom. pr.* of a thera; ~o (paṭisambhidā [aggo]) 109,10.

kodaṇḍa, *m.* (= *sa.*) a kind of bow; ~o, 92,15.

kodha, *m.* (*sa.* krodha) anger; *acc.* ~aṁ, 44,8. 106,33 = Dh. 222. — a-kkodha, *m.* mildness (*q. v.*). — kodha-vagga, *m.* the XVIIth chapter of Dh. *cp.* kujjhati.

kodhana, *mfn.* (*sa.* krodhana) angry. — a-kkodhana, *mfn.* free from anger (*q. v.*).

kopa, *m.* (= *sa.*) anger; *acc.* ~aṁ akatvā, without getting angry (*opp.* mettā) 40,7. *cp.* kupita.

kolāhala, *m.* (= *sa.*) uproar, turmoil; *acc.* ~aṁ (katvā) 73,22.

kovida, *mfn.* (= *sa.*) skilled, learned in (*gen.* or *comp.*); *acc. m.* ~aṁ (maggāmaggassa) Dh. 403; Sambuddha-mata-⁰ (saṁghaṁ) experienced in the doctrines of Buddha, 114,18; nirutti-pada-kovida, Dh. 352. (*q. v.*).

kosajja, *n.* (*sa.* kausīdya; *cp.* kusīta) indolence, sloth; ~aṁ, Dh. 241.

Kosala, *m.* (= *sa.*) *nom. pr.* of a people and its country (north of the Ganges). — ⁰-raṭṭha, *n.* the kingdom of K. *loc.* ~e, 30,29. — ⁰-rājā, *m.* the king of K. 43,15; *gen.* -rañño, 31,1. — ⁰-rajja-sāmiko, id. 43,23.

kosiya, *m.* (*sa.* kauçika) an owl (= ulūka); ~o, 11,10.

klesa, *v.* kilesa.

Kh.

khagga, *m.* (*sa.* khaḍga) a sword; *acc.* ~aṁ (gahetvā) 33,24; ⁰-talena, with the flat of the sword, 41,26. — maṅgala-⁰, a sword of state, *acc.* ~aṁ, 41,16.

*khajjopanaka, *m.* (akin to *sa.* khajyotis, khadyota *etc.*) a firefly; ⁰-sadisā, *m. pl.* like fireflies, 72,29.

khaṇa, *m.* (*sa.* kshaṇa) [1]) an instant, moment, the right moment, ~o, 108,6 (mā upaccagā); *acc.* taṁ khaṇaṁ yeva, just at that moment, instantly, 17,21. 32,30. 53,13; *loc.* tasmiṁ khaṇe, by this time, 12,20; khaṇe khaṇe, from time to time, Dh. 239; *comp. w. vb. nouns* or *part.*: vanditvā ṭhita-kkhaṇe, 87,35; khaṇâtīta, *mfn.* who allows the right moment to pass, *pl.* ~ā, 108,7. — [2]) leisure, state of rest; *acc.* ~aṁ paraṁ, 110,18 (*synon.* santi).

khaṇati, *vb.* (*sa.* √khan) to dig, dig up; *pr. 3. sg.* ~ati (mūlaṁ) Dh. 247; *imp. 2. pl.* ~atha (do.) 108,4; *ger.* ~itvā (āvāṭe) 39,32. This verb is sometimes written khanati, *cp. Oldenberg,* KZ. XXV (1881) p. 326.

khaṇḍa, [1]) *m. n.* (= *sa.*) a piece, fragment, section of a book; *n.* pūva-khaṇḍaṁ, a morsel of cake, 53,18. — [2]) *mfn.* broken; *⁰-danta, *mfn.* „broken-toothed", *acc. m.* ~aṁ, 63,8.

khaṇḍeti, *vb.* (*denom. fr. prec.*, *sa.* khaṇḍayati) to break, to interrupt; — to renounce, to remit (*acc.*); *ger.* vetanaṁ ~etvā (in stead of), 19,25.

khattiya, *m. f.* (*subst. & adj.*, *sa.* kshatriya) one who belongs to the warrior (or royal) caste; ~o, 92,10. 107,24 = Dh. 387; rājāno khattiye (*acc. pl.*), „valiant kings", Dh. 294. — *⁰-kaññā, *f.* a maid of that caste, 64,11; ~âdīnaṁ, 47,15. — *⁰-sukhumāla, *m.* „a delicate prince", 97,33.

khattuṁ, *indecl.* (*sa.* kṛtvas) a suffix of numeral adverbs, implying multiplication („times"); *v.* ti-kkhattuṁ.

khanati, *vb.*, *v.* khaṇati.

khanti, *f.* (*sa.* kshānti) [1]) patience, forbearance, forgiveness; ⁰-mettânuddaya-sampanno, 7,12. 38,15; *nom.* khantī, Dh. 184. — *⁰-bala, *mfn.* whose strength is patience, *acc. m.* ~aṁ, Dh. 399. *cp.* khamati. — [2])

acquiescing in, belief, faith, *v.* añña-khantika, *mfn.*

khandha, *m.* (*sa.* skandha) [1]) the shoulder; *loc.* ~e (karitvā) 71,28; (-vāraṇassa) 45,31; hatthi-⁰, on the back of an elephant, 102,23. — [2]) a stem, a mass, multitude; *v.* aggi-kkhandha, maṇi-kkhandha. — [3]) in the dogmatics: [a]) aggregation; dukkha-kkhandha, aggregation of misery, *acc.* ~aṁ, 108,22; *gen.* ~assa (samudayo, nirodho) 66,11-18; — [b]) *pl.* ~ā, the five constituent elements of a human being, viz. rūpa, vedanā, saññā, saṁkhārā, viññāṇa (*q. v.*) 94,8-10. 95,9. 15. 18. 19; 99,27 (in one *comp.*); pañc' upādānakkhandhā, „the fivefold clinging to existence", 67,11. 82,10; *loc.* ~esu, 98,31 (santesu, *q. v.*); *gen.* ~ānaṁ, Dh. 374 (udayavyayaṁ); — *khandhā-disa, *mfn.* like the elements of the body, *pl.* ~ā (dukkhā, *q. v.*) Dh. 202.

khamati, *vb.* (*sa.* √ksham) [1]) to be patient, endure; to forgive anything (*acc.*); *imp. 2. sg.* khama (ekāparādhaṁ) 47,8. — [2]) to be fit, to seem good to (*gen.*); yathā te khameyya (*pot. 3. sg.* „as may seem good to you") 94,28. — *caus. v. next.* (*cp.* khanti, *f.*)

khamāpeti, *vb.* (*caus. II.* khamati) to propitiate, conciliate; to ask one's (*gen.*) pardon; *ger.* ~etvā (rājānaṁ) 41,36.

khaya, *n.* (*sa.* kshaya) loss, destruction, extinction; *acc.* ~aṁ (taṇhānaṁ) Dh. 154; *abl.* ~ā (sabbamaññitānaṁ *etc.*) 94,12. — āsavakkhaya, jāti-⁰, jīvita-⁰ (*v. h.*); taṇhakkhaya (*v.* taṇhā) *cp.* khīyati.

khara[1], *mfn.* (= *sa.*) hard, rough, sharp, painful; *m.* ~o (ābādho) 78,24; *f. pl.* ~ā (vedanā) 13,12; (sakkhara-kaṭhala-vālikā) 97,35.

khara[2], *m.* (= *sa.*) a donkey (= gadrabha), a mule. — *⁰-putta, *m.* a derisive name of a sindhava (*q. v.*), 54,19 (*voc.*); Khara-putta-jātaka, *n.* p. 52 ff.

khalu, *indecl.* (= *sa.*, generally contracted to kho, *q. v.*) indeed, surely; 111,18.

khāṇu(ka), *v.* khānuka.

khādaka, *m.* (= *sa.*) an eater, eating (at the end of *comp.*); *instr. pl.* lohita-maṁsa-khādakehi, 41,34.

khādati, *vb.* (*sa.* √khād) [1]) to eat. [2]) to chew (*e. g.* tambūlaṁ), to gnaw (asunder), to grind one's teeth (dante). [3]) to destroy. — *pr. 3. sg.* ~ati, 13,23 (vana-mahisaṁ); 106,19 = Dh. 240 (destroys); *1. sg.* ~āmi, 13,16 (= *fut.*); *3. pl.* ~anti (sassāni) 7,36; — *imp. 2. sg.* khāda (pūvaṁ) 57,26; *2. pl.* ~atha, 6,16 (maṁsaṁ), 21,5 (khādaniyaṁ); — *part. gen. m.* ~antassa, 53,18; *f. pl.* ~antiyo (dante) 65,6; — *pot. 3. sg.* ciraṁ khādeyya (might long have eaten) 9,1; *2. sg.* ~eyyāsi, 13,15; *2. pl.* ~eyyātha, 14,20; — *fut. 1. sg.* ~issāmi, 4,2-12; *3. pl.* ~issanti, 21,30; — *aor. 3. pl.* ~iṁsu, 22,11; — *inf.* ~ituṁ, 1,16. 12,7 (camma-varattaṁ); — *ger.* ~itvā, 2,24 (phalāni); 41,14 (tambūlaṁ). — *grd.* [a]) khāditabba; tumhehi khāditabbâhārato datvā, „giving food from your own table", 14,19; [b]) khādaniya (*q. v.*); — *pp.* khādita (*q. v.*); — *caus.* khādāpeti (*q. v.*) *cp.* khādaka, *m.*

khādaniya, *n.* (*sa.* khādanīya, *grd. fr.* khādati) hard or solid food (*opp.* bhojaniya, *q. v.*); *acc.* ~aṁ (khādantassa) 53,17; 78,1; khādaniya-bhojaniyaṁ, 18,30.

khādita, *mfn.* (*pp.* khādati) eaten, gnawed asunder; *m. pl.* ~ā (macchā) 5,8; *f. pl.* ~ā (varattā) 12,20. — *⁰-ṭṭhāna, *n.* eating-place, *acc.* ~aṁ. 52,2.

***khānuka**, *m.* (often written khāṇuka, *fr.* khāṇu or khānu (√kshan?) *cp.* Prākr. khāṇu, *sa.* sthāṇu, Tr. PM. 58. Note 6, *Pischel.* Gr. § 309.) a stump or trunk; *loc.* ~e, 12,25.

khāyati, *vb.* (*pass.* √khyā. *sa.* khyāyate) to seem to be (*nom.*), to have the aspect of, to appear as (viya); *pr. 3. sg.* ~ati (uccataro) 3,1; *part.*

med. ~māna, *acc. m.* ~aṁ (veḷuvanaṁ viya) 26,25; *aor. 3. pl.* ~iṁsu (āditta-geha-sadisā viya) 65,11.

khāri, *f.* (= *sa.*) a certain measure of capacity (of grain *etc.*); the provisions of an ascetic, worn by means of a yoke (*khāri-kāja, *m.* (or -kāca, *cp. sa.* kāca)) = *khāri-bhāra, *m.* 30,17 (vaṭṭito ~o) *cp.* SBE. XIII, 132.

khitta, *mfn.* (*pp.* khipati, *sa.* kshipta) thrown, cast; *m.* ~o (rajo paṭivātaṁ) Dh. 125. ratti-khitta, shot by night, *m. pl.* ~ā (sarā) Dh. 304.

khipati, *vb.* (*sa.* √kship) to throw, cast; *pr. 3. sg.* ~ati (pāsake) 48,8; (daḷhaṁ daḷhassa, to repel force by force) 44,1; — *fut. 1. sg.* ~issāmi (bhūmiyaṁ sīsaṁ te) 5,12; — *aor. 3. sg.* khipi (khuracakkam tassa sīse) 24,4; 111,13-14; *3. pl.* ~iṁsu (taṁ samudde) 23,14; — *ger.* ~itvā, 59,32; — *pp.* khitta (*q. v.*); — *caus.* khepeti & khipāpeti (*q. v.*) *cp.* khipana, khepa.

***khipana**, *n.* (*fr.* khipati) the act of throwing or the state of being thrown; raññā (*instr.*) pāsaka-khipana-kāle, when the king was throwing the dice, 48,23.

***khipāpeti**, *vb.* (*caus. II.* khipati) to cause to be thrown or cast; *aor. 3. sg.* ~esi (asure Sineru-papāte) 59,26; *ger.* ~etvā (jālaṁ, „lowered a net") 26,1.

khippaṁ, *adv.* (*sa.* kshipram) quickly; 27,17. Dh. 137.

khila, *m.* (= *sa.*) stubbornness, obduracy; vigata-khila, *mfn.* free from stubbornness, *m.* ~o, 104,24.

khīṇa, *mfn.* (*sa.* kshīṇa; *pp.* khīyati) destroyed; exhausted, subdued; *n.* ~aṁ (mayhaṁ kammaṁ) 24,1; *f.* ~ā (jāti) 71,16. — khīṇāsava, *mfn.* having subdued the passions (*v.* āsava). — *⁰-maccha, *mfn.* without fishes, *loc. n.* ~e (pallale) Dh. 155.

khīyati, *vb.* (*pass.* √kshi, *sa.* kshīyate) to perish, to waste away; *part. med.* ~māna, *loc. pl. n.* ~esu (maṁsesu) 103,21; *fut. 3. sg.* ~issati (dhanaṁ) 48,11. — *pp.* khīṇa, *v. above. subst. m.* khaya, *q. v.* (*cp.* khepeti).

khīra, *n.* (*sa.* kshīra) milk; *nom. acc.* ~aṁ, 26,11-13; (mātu ~) 24,32; (duyhamānaṁ) 99,28; 106,21 = Dh. 71; — *duddha-khīra, *mfn.* one who has milked, 104,21 (*m.* ~o). — khīrodaka, *n.* milk-water (*v.* udaka). — *⁰-ghaṭa, *m.* a pot of milk, *acc.* ~aṁ, 101,26. — *⁰-paka, *mfn.* drinking milk, sucking, *m.* ~o (vaccho mātari) Dh. 284 (*var.* khīra-pāno). ⁰-**paṇṇin**, *m.* (*sa.* kshīra-parṇin) name of a tree whose leaves contain a milky sap, Calotropis gigantea, *gen.* ~ino, 92,17.

khīla, *m.* (*sa.* kīla & khīla) a pin, stake, post; *pl.* ~ā (nikhātā) 105,17. inda-khīla, *q. v.*

khudā, *f.* (*sa.* kshudh & kshudhā) hunger; *v.* khuppipāsā.

khudda & khuddaka, *mfn.* (*sa.* kshudra(ka)) small, little, low; trifling, insignificant; *gen. masc.* ~kassa (mātā, mother of the little child) 99,11. — *comp.* ⁰-mañcaka, *m.* a small or low bed, *loc.* ~e, 42,1; repeated in a *dvandva-comp. w.* anu inserted : khuddānukhuddakāni (*n. pl.*) sikkhāpadāni samūhantu (saṁgho), the order may in the course of time abolish some precepts or other that are of minor consequence, 79,12.

***Khudda(ka)-Nikāya**, *m.* name of a collection of canonical books (the fifth of the five Nikāyas) comprising the foll. books : Khuddaka-Pāṭha, Dhammapada, (Udāna), (Itivuttaka), Sutta-Nipāta, (Vimāna-Vatthu), (Peta-Vatthu) Thera-Gāthā, Therī-Gāthā, Jātaka, (Niddesa), (Paṭisambhidā-Magga), (Apadāna), (Buddha-Vaṁsa), Cariyā-Piṭaka. Specimens of these books are found in the Reader, except those put within parentheses. The name Khuddaka-Nikāya is probably due to the title of its first section, viz. Khuddaka-Pāṭha; *nom.* Khuddanikāyo, 102,16.

***Khuddaka-Pāṭha**, *m.* name

of the first section of Khuddaka-Nikāya; specimens thereof p. 82,2-14.

khuppipāsā, *f.* (*sa.* kshut-pipāsā. *cp.* khudā) hunger and thirst; ~ā (tatiyā senā Mārassa) 103,26. *°-âbhibhūta, *mfn.*, *v.* abhibhavati.

khura, *m.* (*sa.* khura & kshura) [1]) the hoof of an animal. [2]) a razor; *°-cakka, *n.* a wheel sharp as a razor, *nom. acc.* ~aṁ, 23,30-36; — *khuranāsa, *mfn.* (*cp. sa.* khura-ṇasa) having a nose like a razor, *m. pl.* ~ā (macchā) 25,28; °-nāsika, *mfn.* id. *pl.* ~ā (manussā) 25,26. *cp. next.*

khurappa, *m.* (*sa.* khurapra & kshurapra) a kind of arrow; *acc.* ~aṁ, 92,28.

***Khuramāla**, *m.* (?) name of an ocean; °-samudda, *m.* 25,22 (*acc.* ~aṁ). — *Khuramāli(n), *m.* (?) id. 25,31 (*cp.* Aggimāla).

khetta, *n.* (*sa.* kshetra) a field; ~aṁ, 100,27 (daḍḍhaṁ); *acc.* ~aṁ, 8,7; 100,26 (ḍaheyya); *pl.* ~āni (tiṇadosāni) Dh. 356; *loc.* ~esu, 8,9; sāli-yava-khettesu, 8,18. — *khetta-gopaka, *m.* a field-watcher; *gen.* ~assa, 14,29. — khetta-pāla, *m.* id. *gen.* ~assa, 15,19. — °-rakkhaka, *m.* (*sa.* kshetra-raksha) id. *pl.* ~ā, 8,18. — *°-sāmika, *m.* the owner of the field. ~o, 100,26.

khepa, *m.* (*sa.* kshepa, *cp.* khipati) 'throwing, casting'; loss; *citta-kkhepa, *m.* (*cp. sa.* manaḥ-kshepa) loss of mind, perplexity; *acc.* ~aṁ, Dh. 138.

khepeti, *vb.* (*caus.* khipati, √kship) [1]) to throw away, to do away with (*acc.*). [2]) to pass or while away (kālaṁ, āyuṁ *etc.*); *ger.* ~etvā (dīghaṁ addhānaṁ), having grown old (?) or long time after, 44,21-23. In this sense *Trenckner* takes it = *sa.* kshāpayati, √kshi, PM. 76,28. (*cp.* khīyati.)

khema, *mfn.* (*sa.* kshema) safe, giving tranquillity, security & happiness; *n.* ~aṁ (saraṇaṁ) 107,21 = Dh. 189—92. — *subst. n.*, safety, tranquillity, happiness (of Nibbāna); yoga-kkhema, *n.* (*v. h.*).

khemin, *mfn.* (*sa.* kshemin) enjoying security or peace; *m.* ~ī, Dh. 258.

kheḷa (or khela), *m.* (*sa.* kheṭa, *cp.* kshveḍa) phlegm, saliva; ~o. 82,5 = 97,23; *instr.* ~ena, 57,24. — paggharita-°, *mfn.* „with trickling phlegm", *f. pl.* ~ā, 65,5. — *°-mallaka, *m.* a spitting-box, ~o, 84,15. — vi-kkheḷika, *mfn.* (*q. v.*) *cp.* lālā & *next.*

***kheḷāpaka**, *m.* (*var.* kheḷāsika. *fr.* kheḷa + √āp or ā-√pā) *lit.* 'whose teeth water', or 'eating spittle' ɔ: a covetous person or a lick-spittle (?), used as a term of abuse of Devadatta; *gen.* ~assa, 74,28. °-vāda, *m.* use of the abusive term kheḷāpaka, calling one by that name; *instr.* ~ vādena, 74,29. (*cp.* SBE. XX, 239; Dbp. (1855) p. 143.)

kho, *adv.* (before vowels sometimes khv'-, *sa.* khalu) an enclitic particle of ascertainment or emphasis: indeed, verily, truly; kho 'ti avadhāraṇaṁ, 85,34; abhabbo ~, 69,27; pasādā ~, 79,29; avyākataṁ ~, 89,23; — *after pron.*: mayhaṁ ~, 2,29; ete ~, 66,28; idaṁ ~, 67,8; so ca ~, 61,31 (et quidem); yo ~ evaṁ vadeyya, 92,2; — *after a negation*: na ~, 28,14; no ca khv'assa, 90,35; mā ~, 32,26; mā h'evaṁ ~, 90,24; — *combined w. foll.* pana: na sakkā kho pana, 7,8; na ~ pana, 9,31. 79,4; api ca kho pana. 32,35; yathā ~ pana, 79,6; siyā ~ pana, 79,2; — *following other particles* (atha, pi *etc.*) *esp.* in historical exposition = now, now further: atha kho, 66,3. 76,9. 89,19; tatra kho, 66,24; tâpi kho. 22,10; te pi kho, 74,4; Bodhisatto pi kho, 34,1; api ca kho, 97,1; evaṁ bhante ti kho, 76,14; — *in interr. sentences* (after nu): kin nu kho, 1,21. 89,22; kacci nu ~, 3,5; atthi nu ~. 14,26; kahan nu ~, 34,11. (*cp.* khalu.)

G.

g a, *mfn.* (= *sa.*, only at the end of *comp.*) going; *v.* atiga, anuga, dugga, pāraga.

G a ñ g ā, *f.* (= *sa.*) *nom. pr.*, the river Ganges; 1,16; *acc.* ~aṁ (adho ~, *q. v.*) 14,24; *loc.* ~āya, 1,5; pāra-Gañgāya, on the other side of the G., 1,14; — *⁰-nivattane, *loc.* in a curve of the river, 1,4.

g a c c h a t i, *vb.* (*sa.* √gam) to go, to move, start, go away; to go to (*w. acc.* or *adv.* (tattha *etc.* or santikam *w. gen.*); gahetvā ~, to go away with; — *pr. 3. sg.* ~ati, 6,2 (migavaṁ); 6,31 (gahetvā); 7,30 (santikaṁ); 47,20 etc.; *2. sg.* ~asi, 1,17 (= *fut.*); 88,14 (gacchasîti jānātha, you know where I am going); *1. sg.* ~āmi, 1,23. 9,12. 69,19 (Bhagavantaṁ saraṇaṁ); 78,32 (~ām'ahaṁ); *3. pl.* ~anti, 19,34; 104,2 (yena, *sc.* maggena); *1. pl.* ~āma (let us go) 39,14; — *part. m.* ~anto, 9,11. 34,4 (on his way); *acc.* ~antaṁ, 2,27; *loc.* ~ante (kāle) 14,15. 102,4; *f.* ~antī, 49,3; *m. pl.* ~antā, 6,14; *gen. m. pl.* ~antānaṁ, 9,16; *part. med. f.* ~amānā, 87,33; *f. pl.* (id.) 23,18; — *imp. 2. sg.* a) gaccha, 2,13. 7,1 (~tvaṁ); 75,6 (gacchâvuso); b) gacchāhi, 4,19. 6,35; *2. pl.* ~atha, 4,15. 8,3; — *pot. 3. sg.* ~eyya (nagaraṁ pattharitvā („would spread through the town") 65,24; pariṇāmaṁ ~ (yassa), could be digested (by) 78,17; *2. sg.* ~eyyāsi, 7,32; — *fut.* a) *3. sg.* gamissati, 58,14; *2. sg.* ~asi, 7,26. 77,6. 87,36; *1. sg.* ~āmi, 1,17. 4,36. 23,7 (~ām'eva); 101,27 (sve gahetvā ~ „I will come to-morrow and take it"); *3. pl.* ~anti, 104,10; *1. pl.* ~āma, 6,33. 22,4; — b) *2. pl.* gacchissatha, 21,8; — *aor.* a) *3. sg.* a-gamā (nabhasâ-) 111,1; — b) *3. sg.* a-gamāsi, 2,4. 87,24; *3. pl.* a-gamaṁsu, 8,30. 23,20; — c) *2. sg.* mā gami, 23,7; *2. pl.* mā gamittha, 39,17; — d) *3. sg.* a-gañchi (nâgañchi, 20,30, probably from ā-gacchati, *q. v.*) *cp.* Tr. PM. p. 71—74; — *inf.* gantuṁ, 35,36. 62,5; *comp.* gantu-kāma, *mfn.* desiring to go; *m.* ~o, 50,9 (*cp.* kāma); *pl.* ~ā, 4,18; — *ger.* gantvā, 1,13. 89,7 (moving); 104,10; a-gantvā (not going) 39,6. 42,27; — *grd.* gantabba, *mfn.* ~aṁ (*n.*) 83,2; — *pp.* gata (*v. h.*) *cp.* ga, gati, gama, gamana, gāmika, gāmin.

g a ṇ a, *m.* (= *sa.*) a flock, company, multitude, number, (herd, swarm); mostly at the end of *comp.* amacca-⁰, 39,28; go-gaṇe (*acc. pl.*) 21,4; dāsi-⁰, 21,1; deva-gaṇena (*instr.*) 60,23; dvija-gaṇā (*nom. pl.*) 7,20; — bhamara-gaṇā (*do.*) 62,12; miga-gaṇaṁ (*acc.*) 6,11; sakuṇa-gaṇā (*pl.*) 10,7. *cp. next.*

g a ṇ i n, *mfn.* (= *sa.*) one who has attendants; *m.* mahā-gaṇī, a great teacher, 109,17 (Anuruddho); *m. pl.* gaṇī (therā), teachers, 109,31.

g a ṇ e t i, *vb.* (*sa.* √gaṇ) to count, number, reckon; *part. m. sg.* gaṇayaṁ (gāvo) Dh. 19.

*g a ṇ ṭ h i k ā, *f.* (*fr. sa.* granthi, *m.*) a knot, tie; *acc.* ~aṁ (paṭimuñcitvā) 82,28. *cp.* gaṇḍikā.

g a ṇ ḍ a, *m.* (= *sa.*) 1) the cheek. 2) a boil, pimple; a bump; ~o (uṭṭhahi) 50,20.

*g a ṇ ḍ i k ā, *f.* (or gaṇḍi, also written gaṇṭhi & gaṇṭhikā. *cp. sa.* gaṇḍi(kā)) a block; dhamma-gaṇḍikā, *f.* a block for execution, shambles; *loc.* ~āya (sīsaṁ ṭhapetvā) 6,27; ⁰-ṭṭhāna, *n.* the place of execution, *loc.* ~e, 6,25.

g a ṇ h a t i (& gaṇhāti), (*sa.* √grah) to take, seize (*acc.*); to catch, capture, 14,24. 32,20. 39,15; to acquire, obtain, get, 33,25. 52,17. 55,16; to take possession of, to conquer, win, 35,19. 39,8. 59,32; to keep, retain, 33,32. 49,21; to receive, adopt, 113,19; to assume, put on, 58,16; to follow, obey, 9,19. 52,33; to choose, 10,8-26; to take upon one's self, 7,10. 17,16. — *pr. 2. pl.* gaṇhatha, 33,9; *1. pl.* ~āma (let us capture) 39,15; — *part. m.* gaṇhanto (macche) 14,24; (gocaraṁ, seeking food) 52,17; *acc. f.* ~antiṁ (attano vacanaṁ a-gaṇhantiṁ, disobeying)

52,33; — *imp.* *2. sg.* gaṇha, 1,9; gaṇhāhi, 3,17; *3. sg.* ~atu, 10,8. 102,35; *2. pl.* ~atha (mūlena. buy it) 18,10; *3. pl.* ~antu. 39,17; — *pot.* *3. sg.* gaṇheyya, 12,35; *1. sg.* ~eyyaṁ, 33,32; — *fut.* a) *1. sg.* gahessāmi, 39,8; b) *3. sg.* gaṇhissati. 55,8; *2. sg.* ~issasi, 4,28. 22,32; *1. sg.* ~issāmi, 2,31. 29,4. 39,14. 65,32; *1. pl.* ~issāma, 6,8. 36,22; — *aor.* a) *3. sg.* aggahi, 113,19; *3. pl.* aggahuṁ, 114,30; b) *3. sg.* aggahesi, 62,19; c) *3. sg.* gaṇhi (paṭisandhiṁ. was born) 5,25; (māṇavikaṁ hatthe) 51,31; 40,19. 59,2; *2. sg.* gaṇhi, 59,20; *3. pl.* ~iṁsu, 18,26. 22,6. 33,8; *2. pl.* ~ittha. 18,23. 33,1; — *inf.* a) gahetuṁ (*sa.* grahītum) 4,34. 36,8; b) gaṇhituṁ, 1,9. 13,11 (gocaraṁ, to eat); — *ger.* a) gahetvā (*sa.* gṛhītvā) 1,22. 4,8. 15. 28. 7,10 (tassā santakaṁ maraṇaṁ); 8,20 (nivāsaṁ); 12,8; 17,18 (ārakkhaṁ (te, *gen.*) to guard); 22,32; 24,27 (hatthiṁ ~ āgate, those who had brought the elephant); b) gaṇhitvā, 4,19; — *pass.* (gayhati), *part.* gayhamāna; ~ka, *mfn.* being captured, *loc. pl.* ~esu (vaṭṭakesu) 88,34; — *pp.* gahita & gahīta (*v. h.*). — *caus.* *v.* gaṇhāpeti & gāhāpeti. *cp.* gaha[2], gahaṇa. gāha, gāhin.

g a ṇ h ā p e t i, *vb.* (*caus. II.* gaṇhati) to cause to be taken or seized; to procure (*acc.*); *part. m.* ~ento (akālaphalāni) 37,16; *ger.* ~etvā, 39,30. *cp.* gāhāpeti.

g a t a, *mfn.* (*pp.* gacchati) gone (away), arrived at, directed towards, fallen into (*acc.* or *comp.*), often used as finite tense = went, has gone; *m.* gato, 2,15. 3,28; *f.* ~ā (kahaṁ gatāsi) 49,6; upari-pāsāda-vara-tala-gatā, ascended on, 64,12; *n.* ~aṁ (patitvā ~, fell away) 13,20; *subst. n.* gataṁ = gamanaṁ, 51,31. 52,1; *instr.* ~ena (kin te aññattha ~ „why go elsewhere for that?") 49,15; *loc. m.* ~e (suriye atthaṁ) 32,29; *m. pl.* ~ā, 26,3. 109,3 (guṇaggataṁ, *q. v.*); *loc. pl.* ~esu (parinitthitiṁ. fullfilled) 114,31; — gata-ṭṭhāna, *n.* = gatabhāva, 19,18 (*v.* ṭhāna); gata-gata-ṭṭhāne (*loc.*) wherever he went, 8,17; gata-gata-kāle, whenever he went, 20,4. — *comp.* *v.* addha-gata, 74,21 (*cp.* gataddhin below); ujju-°, Dh. 108; kāya-°, Dh. 293; diṭṭhi-°, 90,25; niṭṭhaṅ-gata. Dh. 351 (*v.* niṭṭhā, *f.*); pāra-°, 104,30; pāramī-°. 109,21; Buddha-°, Dh. 296; visaṁkhāra-°, Dh. 154. — a-gata, *mfn.* not gone to. not yet frequented; *acc. f.* ~aṁ disaṁ (Nibbāna) Dh. 323; purisantaraṁ a-gataṁ mātugāmaṁ „a maid that has not seen another man", 48,11. *cp.* duggata. -saha-gata, su-gata, sugatin.

***g a t a d d h i n**, *mfn.* (*cp. sa.* gatādhvan) one who has finished his journey (= addha-gata. *v.* addhan); *gen. m.* ~ino, Dh. 90.

g a t i, *f.* (= *sa.*) going, moving; course, way, *esp.* the course of fate (the five gatis are the several modes of receiving existence after death, *viz.* in hell, among animals, petas, men, or devas, *cp. next*); *nom.* ~i (sakuntānaṁ ākāse) Dh. 92; attā hi attano gati, Dh. 380 (refuge); gatī pāpikā. the evil way (hell) Dh. 310; *acc.* ~iṁ, Dh. 420. — a-gati, *f.* not admission; ~ tava tattha, there you cannot come, 72,8. — vaṁka-gatī. *adj. f.* 48,6 (*v. h.*). *cp.* duggati, sugati (suggati).

g a t i k a, *mfn.* (*sa.* gatika, *n.*) at the end of *comp.* = having a certain gati (*q. v.*); niyata-°, *mfn.* whose path is certain, *f.* ~ā, 87,30; a-niyata-°, 87,29 (*v. h.*).

g a t t a, *n.* (*sa.* gātra) the body; *acc.* ~aṁ, 84,2; *abl.* ~ato, 84,3. — lālā-kilinna-°, *mfn.* 65,6 (*v. h.*).

g a d r a b h a, *m.* (*sa.* gardabha) an ass, donkey; ~o. 8,24; *acc.* ~aṁ. 8,17; *gen.* ~assa. *ib.*; *gen. pl.* ~ānaṁ, 113,11; — *°-bhāraka, *m.* goods carried by a donkey; *instr.* ~ena. 8,16. — *°-bhāva, *m.* the being an ass (*cp.* bhāva), *acc.* ~aṁ, 8,25. — *°-rava (or -rāva) *m.* the braying of an ass; *acc.* ~aṁ. 8,25; *instr.* -rāvena. 113,10.

gantabba, gantu-, gantuṁ, gantvā, *v.* gacchati.

gantha, *m.* (*sa.* grantha) 1) a band, fetter; *pl.* ~ā, fetters (ɔ: desires) Dh. 211; sabba-gantha-ppahīna, *mfn.* „who has thrown off all fetters", *gen. m.* ~assa, Dh. 90. — 2) composition, text, book; often *opp.* to attha: *abl.* ~ato atthato, 114,30 (*cp.* attha[5]).

***Ganthākāra**, *m.* (*sa.* *grantha + ākāra, *lit.* a mine of books) *nom. pr.* of a vihāra at Anurādhapura in Ceylon; *loc.* ~e, 114,26.

gandha, *m.* (= *sa.*) odour, scent, perfume; ~o. 20,16; Dh. 56; *pl.* ~ā, 70,31; *acc. pl.* ~e, 41,5. 53,25; *instr.* ~ehi. 33,3; *loc.* ~esu, 71,9; — maccha-gandhaṁ (*acc.*) scent of fish, 14,25; catu-jāti-°, the four kinds of scent, 41,5; °-dhūpa-, 48,30; °-mālâdīni, 49,14; °-cuṇṇaṁ, 53,26; māla-°, 61,4. 73,11; vaṇṇa-°, 106,2. 37,30; — *(sabba-)gandh'āpaṇa, *m.* a perfumery shop, 48,31; — gandhôdaka, *n.* scented water, *instr.* ~ena, 20,8 (dibba-); 38,3; — °-kuṭi, *f. v. separately*; — °-jāta, *n.* a sort of perfume; *gen. pl.* ~ānaṁ, Dh. 55; — °-tela, *n.* scented oil; *instr.* ~ena, 37,2; °-tela-ppadīpā, 65,3. — *°-pañcaṅgulika (*v. h.*); — dibba-gandha-puppha, *n.* a flower of heavenly perfume; *instr. pl.* ~ehi. 20,9. — puppha-°, sīla-°, suci-° (*q. v.*) *cp.* su-gandha, a-gandhaka, sa-gandhaka & gandhin.

gandha-kuṭi, *f.* (*sa.* °-kuṭī) 'a perfumed house or room', name of a room or house occupied by Buddha, *esp.* that made for him by Anāthapiṇḍika in Jetavana; Gotamassa ~-samīpe, 73,20; Gotamena saddhiṁ eka-gandha-kuṭiyaṁ (*loc.*) vasitvā, dwelling in private with G., 73,14-17 (*cp.* eka[4-5]). (*cp.* Jāt. I, 92,23. Ind. Ant. XIV, 140. ZDMG. XL, 65.)

gandhabba, *m.* (*sa.* gandharva) 1) a Gandharva or heavenly musician; ~o, Dh. 105; °-mānusā, *pl.* Gandharvas & men, Dh. 420. — 2) a singer or musician in general; ~o, 19,20; *acc.* ~aṁ, 19,21. — 3) *n.* (?) (*sa.* gāndharva) music, song; *acc.* ~aṁ (karoti) 19,26-28.

gandhin, *mfn.* (= *sa.*) fragrant, odoriferous; *f.* candana-gandhinī. having a scent of sandal wood, 20,34.

gabbha, *m.* (*sa.* garbha) 1) embryo, foetus, child; ~o (kucchimhi patiṭṭhito) 61,31; itthi-gabbho, a female child, *ib.*; purisa-gabbho, a male child, *ib.*; paripuṇṇa-gabbhā, *adj. f.* ready to be delivered, 62,3; — *gabbha-parihāra, *m.* 'protection of the embryo', a certain ceremony performed when a woman became pregnant; laddha-°, *mfn.* duly protected while being in the womb, *m.* ~o, 42,22 (*cp.* pariharati); — *gabbha-vuṭṭhāna, *n.* delivery; ~aṁ. 62,21. — 2) the womb (*cp.* kucchi); *acc.* ~aṁ (upeti, to be born) Dh. 325; (upapajjanti, are born again) Dh. 126; *abl.* ~ato (paṭṭhāya) 48,13. 50,32; — gabbha-seyyā, *f.* the womb, *acc.* ~aṁ (upessaṁ) 105,20. — 3) the interior of anything; *loc.* gabbhe, at the end of *comp.*: aṅgāra-°, amid the flame, 15,33. — 4) a bed-chamber, any interior chamber; *acc.* ~aṁ, 53,3; *loc.* anto-gabbhe, 65,28; gabbha-dvāra, *n.* the door of the bed-chamber, ~aṁ, 65,27; — sayana-°, siri-° (*v. h.*) *cp. next.*

gabbhinī, *f.* (*adj. sa.* garbhiṇī) pregnant; *acc.* ~iṁ (duggatitthiṁ) 48,17; °-migī, *f.* 6,32.

gama, (at the end of *comp.* = *sa.*) 1) *mfn.* going, able to go; *v.* dūraṅgama, mano-pubbaṅgama, vehāsaṅgama. 2) *m.* going, course; *v.* atthagama, atthaṅgama.

gamana, *n.* (= *sa.*) going (to or away); ~aṁ (= gataṁ) 52,1; *acc.* ~aṁ (na labhāmi) 108,25; *instr.* ~ena (saggassa) Dh. 178; *loc.* uyyānakīḷâdi-gamane. 65,22; nibbāna-gamana, *mfn.* leading to Nibbāna, *acc. m.* ~aṁ (maggaṁ) Dh. 289; — *°-antarāya, *m.* ~o (me, hindrance to my departure) 65,33; — *°-bhāva, *m.* the having departed, going away, *acc.* ~aṁ (aññassa purisassa) 9,13; — *°-magga, *m.* way; añño me ~o n'atthi, 3,14; *loc.* tassa ~e, along his way, 60,6.

gami, gamittha, gamissati, *etc. v.* gacchati.

gambhīra, *mfn.* (*sa.* gabhīra & gambhīra) deep, profound; difficult to be perceived; *m.* ~o (dhammo) 94,24; (Tathāgato) 95,12; — *°-ghosatta, *n.* (*sa.* *°-ghoshatva) 'the having a deep voice', the being profound in predication; *abl.* ~ā, on account of his profundity (eloquence?) in preaching the law, 113,20; — *°-pañña, *mfn.* one whose knowledge is deep, *acc. m.* ~aṁ, Dh. 403.

gamma, *mfn.* (*sa.* grāmya, *cp.* gāma) 'relating to villages', relating to common people or to sensual pleasures, mean, sensual; *m.* ~o (anto) 66,26.

Gayā, *f.* (= *sa.*) *nom. pr.* of a city in Behar; *loc.* ~āyaṁ (viharati) 70,28.

Gayāsīsa, *n.* (*sa.* Gayāçīrsha) *nom. pr.* of a mountain near Gayā; *nom.* ~aṁ, 70,21; *loc.* ~e, 70,23.

*gayhamānaka, *mfn. v.* gaṇhati, *pass.*

garahati, *vb.* (*sa.* √garh) to reproach, blame; *pp.* garahita, *m.* ~o (pamādo, is blamed) Dh. 30 (garhito).

garu, *mfn.* (*sa.* guru) heavy; valuable; reverend; *m. pl.* ~ū, 109,27. *cp.* gārava & *next.*

garuka, *mfn.* (*sa.* guruka) heavy, hard, serious; *acc. m.* ~aṁ (ābādhaṁ) Dh. 138; (daṇḍaṁ) Dh. 310.

garhita, *v.* garahati.

gala, *m.* (= *sa.*) the throat, neck; ~o, 13,11; *abl.* ~ato (paṭṭhāya) 85,30; *loc.* ~e, 13,11; — *°-pariyosāna, *mfn.* forming the end of the throat, *n.* ~aṁ (mukhatuṇḍakaṁ) 18.7; — *°-ppamāṇa, *mfn.* going up to the neck, *acc. m. pl.* ~e (āvāṭe) 39,32.

galati, *vb.* (*sa.* √gal) to drip; *part.* galanta, *mfn.* dripping, *n.* ~aṁ (lohitaṁ) 23,32.

gava-, base of the subst. *m. f.* go, a bull, cow; sometimes used in *comp.* (*v. below*).

gavampati, *m.* (*fr.* go, *gen. pl.* + pati, *sa.* gavāmpati) 'lord of cows', a bull; 105,12 (usabho ~patī).

*gavesaka, *mfn.* (*fr. next*) seeking, searching; a-guṇa-°, *mfn.* 43,16 (*v. h.*).

gavesati, *vb.* (*sa.* gaveshate) to seek, search for (*acc.*); *part. m.* ~anto (nibbānaṁ) 64,23; Dh. 153; *fut. 2. pl.* ~essatha, Dh. 146; *inf.* ~ituṁ, 64,34; *adj.* gavesaka, gavesi*n* (*q. v.*).

gavesi*n*, *mfn.* (*sa.* gaveshin) seeking, looking for (at the end of *comp.*); kāma-°, Dh. 99; pāra-°, Dh. 355; suci-°, Dh. 245.

gaha[1], *n.* (*sa.* gṛha, *cp.* geha & ghara) a house; *loc.* ~e („the layman's life") 47,26. — gaha-kāraka *etc. v. below*; *cp.* gihi*n*.

gaha[2], *mfn.* (*sa.* graha) seizing, holding (at the end of *comp.*), *v.* aṁkusa-ggaha.

gaha-kāraka, *m.* (*sa.* gṛha-kāraka) 'a house builder', *metaph.* the cause of existence; *acc.* ~aṁ. Dh. 153 (Comm. imassa attabhāva-gehassa kārakaṁ taṇhāvaḍḍhakiṁ); *voc.* ~a, ib. 154. (*cp.* SBE. X. p. 43.)

*gaha-kūṭa, *n.* (*sa.* *gṛha-kūṭa) the peak of a house, roof, ridge; ~aṁ, Dh. 154 („ridge-pole", SBE. X, 42).

gahaṭṭha, *m.* (*sa.* gṛha-stha) a householder, one who leads a layman's life; *instr. pl.* ~ehi, Dh. 404 (*opp.* an-āgāra).

gahaṇa, *n.* (*sa.* grahaṇa) seizing, catching, getting; grip, hold; ~aṁ (ambākaṁ su-gahaṇaṁ, „we have got a very tight grip") 4,35; °-atthāya, 3,5 (*v.* attha[1]); ajjhāsaya-gahaṇatthaṁ, 11,4 (*v. h.*); — dārūdaka-°, 20,12; — nāma-gahaṇa-divase, 38,9; — maccha-°, 25,35; — hattha-°, 51,14.

gahana, *n.* (= *sa.*) an impervious wood or thicket, abyss; *metaph.* impurities; ~aṁ (abbhantaran te) 106,11 = Dh. 394; diṭṭhi-°, a jungle of theories or heresy, 94,1; — *⁰-ṭṭhāna, *n.* a place or lair in the jungle, *abl.* ~ato, 6,12; *loc.* ~e, 33,24.

gahapati, *m.* (& gahapatika. *sa.* gṛhapati) a householder, *esp.* designation of a man of higher rank within the third caste (*cp.* kuṭumbika); seṭṭhi ~, 68,31; *gen.* ~issa, 69,9; brāhmaṇa-gahapatikesu (*loc. pl. dvandva comp.*) 7,25; amacca-brāhmaṇa-gahapatike (*acc. pl. v.* amacca) 42,2. *cp. Fick,* Soc. Gl. p. 165.

gahita & **gahīta**, *mfn.* (*pp.* gaṇhati, *sa.* gṛhīta) seized, taken, captured; *m.* ~o (hatthe) 23,9; *pl.* ~ā (-ī-) 111,18; *n. pl.* gahita-gahitāni turiyāni, the various instruments which they held in their hands, 65,2; — *⁰-ārakkha, *mfn.* carefully guarded (*v. h.*); — *n.* a grasp, tug; *⁰-nimittena, by a tug (*v.* nimitta) 89,7; — daḷha-⁰, duggahita, su-gahita (*q. v.*).

gahetuṁ, **gahetvā**, **gahessāmi**, *v.* gaṇhati.

gāthā, *f.* (= *sa.*) a verse, stanza; ~ā (catuppādikā) 102,22; *acc.* ~aṁ, 3,25; osāna-⁰, the final stanza, 27,21; *instr.* ~āya, 42,18; anantara-gāthāya, in the stanza next following, 26,7; *pl.* ~ā (sataṁ) Dh. 102; *acc. pl.* ~ā, 2,9. 103,11; ~āyo, 80,30; *instr. pl.* ~āhi, 77,2; — *comp.* (also shortened to gātha-): *⁰-âvasāne, after the stanza has been ended, 87,1; — *⁰-pada, *n.* a word of a gātha, ~aṁ (ekaṁ) Dh. 101; — gāth'-udān'-itivuttakaṁ (parts of navaṅgaṁ Satthu-sāsanam) 109,33; — *gātha-dvayaṁ, two gāthās, 47,23-29; 114,9 (gāthā-); — catuppādika-gātha-jānanaka, *m.* 102,27. — Thera-⁰, Therī-gāthā (*q. v.*).

gāma (& gāmaka), *m.* (*sa.* grāma(ka)) a village; *acc.* ~aṁ, 82,23; luddassa vasana-⁰, 12,8; *gen.* ~assa, 95,31; *loc.* ~e, 57,7 (sakala-); 32,8 (gāmake); ~amhi, 111,4; — *⁰-jana, *m.* the people of the v., 101,5 (~o); — purāṇa-gāma-ṭṭhāna, *n.* a ruined v., 35,23 (*loc.* ~e); — *⁰-dārakā (*m. pl.*) the village boys, 52,17; — *⁰-dvāre (*loc.*) before a v., 8,20; — *⁰-vara, *m.* the best of villages, an excellent v., *acc.* ~aṁ datvā, 45,8; — ⁰-vāsin, *m.* the inhabitant of a v., *pl.* ~ino, 8,23-29; — *⁰-samīpe, near a v. 33,23; — ⁰-sūkara, *m.* a village pig, ~o, 46,33 (gūtha-kalale nimugga-). — dvāra-⁰, paccanta-⁰, mātu-⁰ (*v. h.*) *cp.* gamma, nigama.

gāmika, *mfn.* (*e. c.* = *sa.*) going, wandering, travelling; *m.* a traveller; *pl.* ~ā, (Jambudīpa-, „passengers for India") 28,31.

gāmin, *mfn.* (*e. c.* = *sa.*) going, leading to; *acc. m.* ~inaṁ (dukkh'-ūpasama-⁰, maggaṁ) 107,20 = Dh. 191; *f.* ~inī (dukkha-nirodha-⁰, paṭipadā) 67,17. — apāya-⁰, nibbāna-⁰, pāra-⁰ (*q. v.*).

gāyati, *vb.* (*sa.* √gai) to sing; recite; *pr. 3. pl.* ~anti, 77,11; *part. m.* ~anto, 48,8; *ger.* ~itvā, 48,23; *pp.* gīta (*q. v.*) *cp.* gāthā, geyya.

gārava, *m.* & *n.* (*fr.* garu, *sa.* gaurava, *n.*) venerableness; reverence, respect; Satthu-gāravena (*instr.*) out of respect to the teacher, 79,24.

gāḷha, *mfn.* (*sa.* gāḍha, *pp.* √gāh, as to the signification confounded with √gādh) tight, close, fast; *acc. m.* ~aṁ (ārakkhaṁ) 48,15; *⁰-palepana, *mfn.* thickly smeared, 92,7 (~ena sallena); — *⁰-bandhana, *mfn.* firmly tied down, *acc. m.* ~aṁ (bandhitvā) 39,31; — ati-gāḷha, *mfn.* (*q. v.*) — gāḷhaṁ, gāḷhakaṁ, *adv.* tightly, 49,6; 40,19.

***gāvi**, *f.* (a younger form of go, *pl.* gāvo) a cow; kapila-gāvi-dāna, *n.* a gift of tawny cows (to Brahmans), 61,28.

gāvuta, *n.* (*sa.* gavyūta) a measure of length, a quarter of a yojana (*q. v.*) = 80 usabhas (about 5,6 Kilomètres); ti-gāvuta-ppamāṇa, *mfn.* having an extent of three gāvutas, *loc.* ~e (padese) 63,23.

gāvo, *v.* go.

gāha, *mfn.* (*e. s. sa.* grāha) seizing, holding; *v.* rasmi-ggāha, *m.* 106,34.

gāhāpeti, *vb.* (*caus. II.* gaṇhati) to cause to take; to cause to be taken, seized or fetched; to remove (*acc.*); *aor. 3. pl.* ~esuṁ (utuṁ sarīre) 62,32; *ger.* ~etvā, 16,24. 21,1. 55,14; 59,8 (dārakaṁ mātarā pādesu); *w. double acc.* mahājanaṁ tava kathaṁ ~etvā (having caused people to believe your words) 73,9. *cp.* gaṇhāpeti.

gāhin, *mfn.* (*e. c. sa.* grāhin) grasping after; *m.* piya-ggāhī, Dh. 209.

gijjha, *m.* (*sa.* gṛdhra, *cp.* gṛdhya) a vulture; *gen.* ~assa, 92,19.

Gijjhakūṭa, *m.* (*sa.* Gṛdhra-kūṭa) 'the Vulture's Peak', *nom. pr.* of a mountain near Rājagaha; *acc.* ~aṁ (pabbataṁ) 75,34; *gen.* ~assa, 75,33; *loc.* ~e (Rājagaha-samīpe) 84,31.

gini, *m.* (= aggi, *sa.* agni) fire; *nom.* ~i (āhito, nibbuto) 104,22-25.

gimha, (*m.*) (*sa.* grīshma) the hot season, summer; *loc. pl.* hemanta-gimhisu (metri causa for -gimhesu?) in winter and summer; Dh. 286. *cp. next.*

***gimhika**, *mfn.* (*fr. prec.*) relating to the summer, made for the summer; *m.* ~o (pāsādo) 67,23.

gira, *n.* & **girā**. *f.* (*sa.* gīr. *f.*) speech, words; *nom.* ~aṁ (subhaṇaṁ) 9,31; *acc. f.* ~aṁ (saccaṁ ... yāya) Dh. 408.

giri, *m.* (= *sa.*) a mountain; *v.* Nālagiri.

gilati, *vb.* (*sa.* √gṝ) to swallow, devour; *aor. 2. sg.* (mā) gilī (lohaguḷaṁ) Dh. 371.

gilāna, *mfn.* (*sa.* glāna) sick, ill; *f.* ~ā, 46,5; *m. pl.* ~ā, 6,22; – *⁰-ālaya, *m.* (*v. h.*); – ⁰-paccaya-bhesajja-, medicine for the help of the sick, 97,8.

gihin, *m.* (*sa.* gṛhin) a householder, one who leads a domestic life; *nom. pl.* gihī (laymen, *opp.* pabbajitā) Dh. 74. *cp.* gaha, geha.

gīta, *mfn.* (= *sa.*, *pp.* gāyati, √gai) sung, recited; *acc. m.* ~aṁ (kathāmaggaṁ, Sāriputtâdi-⁰, propounded by S. and others) 113,30. – *n.* singing, song; *⁰-rava, *m.* sound of song, *acc.* ~aṁ, 112,7; – *⁰-sadda, *m.* id. ~o (madhura-) 23,33; – *⁰-ssara. *m.* id. *acc.* ~aṁ. 19,32; – *dvandva-comp.* nacca-gīta-, 64,29. 81,24. – jūta-⁰, 48.8 (*q. v.*).

gīvā, *f.* (*sa.* grīvā) the neck, throat; 10,19; *acc.* ~aṁ, 4,33; (ukkhipitvā) 40,17. 87,24; *loc.* ~āya. 14,32. 40,18. 111,28; 17,23 (pasārita-⁰); – maṇi-vaṇṇa-⁰, *mfn.* „with a neck of jewelled sheen", *acc. m.* ~aṁ (moraṁ) 10,9.

guṇa, *m.* (= *sa.*) kind, quality; good quality, advantage; virtue, merit; ~o. 16,15; *acc.* ~aṁ. 29,9. 30,6. 41,33; *abl.* ~ato, („as though they were virtues") 43,34; *pl.* ~ā, 41,34; *acc. pl.* ~e, 42,4; pabbajita-guṇe, 63,32; Buddha~, 28,15; *loc. pl.* ~esu (vattissāmi, to live a good life) 43,4; – sīla-guṇâcāro. 28,34 (*q. v.*). – *⁰-kathā, *f.* praise, 31,23 (*loc.* ~āya); 43,6 (*acc.* ~aṁ); – anta-⁰, kāma-⁰, mālā- (*q. v.*) *cp.* a-guṇa, sa-guṇa.

***guṇaggatā**, *f.* (*sa.* *guṇāgratā) the state of having the best qualities, perfection; *acc.* ~aṁ (gatā) 109,3.

gutta, *mfn.* (*sa.* gupta) guarded, protected; *m.* ~o (dhammassa = dhamma-gutto, law-protected, one who is well-guarded with respect to the law) Dh. 257 (*cp.* ūratthikassa bhinno, Jāt. I 317,21 and the curious reading udarassa phāletvā, Jāt. III 297,27, ɔ: udaraṁ assa (?). Otherwise *Fausbøll* & *M. Müller* who take gutta = *sa.* goptṛ („guardian of the law")). *n.* ~aṁ (cittaṁ) Dh. 36; (nagaraṁ) Dh. 315. – atta-⁰ (*q. v.*) *cp.* gopeti & *next.*

gutti, *f.* (*sa.* gupti) guarding, protecting, protection; *nom.* indriyaguttī, Dh. 375 (*v. h.*).

gumba, *m.* (*sa.* gulma) a bush; a thicket, jungle; the lair of an animal in a thicket; rukkha-gumbâdayo (*pl. v.* ādi) 6,11; *loc.* ~e, 11,24. 15,4; pāsāṇapiṭṭhaṁ nissāya jāta-⁰, 17,20; nivāsa-⁰, vasana-⁰, sayana-⁰, the thicket where one is dwelling, 14,15-27-33; vana-°, 16,18.

guḷa, *m.* (*sa.* guḍa) a globe, ball; ayo-guḷo, 107,1 (*q. v.*) = loha-°, Dh. 371; maṇi-°, a jewel, pearl, 5,26. 18,7.

guhā, *f.* (= *sa.*) a hiding-place, cave; the heart; °-saya, *mfn.* being hiding in the heart, *n.* ~aṁ (cittaṁ) Dh. 37. *cp.* Sattapaṇṇa-guha, 109,31.

gū, *mfn.* (*e. c.* = *sa.*) going; *v.* addha-gū, pāra-gū.

gūtha, *m. n.* (= *sa.*) fæces, dung; *°-kalala, *n.* 46,33 (*q. v.*).

geyya, *n.* (*sa.* geya) a certain kind of the holy scriptures (navaṅgaṁ Satthu-sāsanaṁ) mixed prose and verse; ~aṁ, 109,33.

geruka, *n.* & gerukā, *f.* (*sa.* gairika, ~kā) red chalk; °~a-parikammakata, *mfn.* „coated with red chalk“, *f.* ~ā (bhitti) 84,18.

geha, *n.* (= *sa.*) a house; *nom.* ~aṁ, 48,31; *acc.* ~aṁ (home) 8,29. 13,6; *abl.* ~ā, 35,29; ~ato (pesakāra-°) 88,5; *loc.* ~e, 41,33; asuka-°, 58,3; °-patana-, falling of the house, 19,16; āditta-geha-sadisa, *mfn.* 65,11 (*q. v.*) *cp.* gaha, gihin.

go, *m. f.* (= *sa.*) an ox, cow; *pl.* cattle; *gen.* gavassa, 92,21; *nom. pl.* gāvo, 51,33. 104,27; *instr.* gohi, 105,28; *gen.* gavaṁ, *v.* gavampati. *cp.* gavesati. gāvī *&* *next.*

gogaṇa, *m.* (= *sa.*) a herd of cattle; *acc. pl.* ~e. 21,4.

gocara, *m.* (= *sa.*) [1]) pasture-ground, hunting-ground; pasture, food; *nom.* ~o (mando) 4,5; *acc.* ~aṁ, 13,11; Dh. 135; — *°-ṭṭhāna, *n. id.* 14,11 (*loc.* ~e); — *°-pasuta, *mfn.* intent on seeking food, *m.* ~o. 13,13; — jala-°, *mfn.* 1,8 & thala-°, *mfn. ib.* (*q. v.*). — [2]) sphere of perception, object of sense; ~o, Dh. 92; *loc.* ~e (ariyānaṁ) Dh. 22; — ananta-°, *mfn.* Dh. 179 (*v.* an-anta); — micchā-saṁkappa-°, *mfn.* & sammā-saṁkappa-°, *mfn.* Dh. 11—12 (*v. h.*).

Gotama, *m.* (*sa.* Gautama) *nom. pr.* of Gotama Buddha, by non-Buddhists mentioned as samaṇo Gotamo, 71,25. 93,30 *etc.*, and adressed as bhavaṁ Gotamo (*nom.* in stead of the *pron.* of the second person) 93,27, or bho Gotama! (*voc.*) 89,22; *instr.* bhotā Gotamena, 90,15. His mother was Māyā: Māyā janayi Gotamaṁ, 108,21, his father Suddhodana (64,5), and his son Rāhula (64,7). — mahā-Gotama-buddho, 87,7. — *Gotama-sāvakā, *m. pl.* the disciples of G. Dh. 296; *gen.* ~ānaṁ, 74,13. *cp.* Bhagavat, Satthar. Sugata.

Gotamī, *f.* (*sa.* Gautamī) *nom. pr.*, *v.* Mahāpajāpatī.

gotta, *n.* (*sa.* gotra) family, race (more comprehensive than ‘kula’, but not so extensive as ‘jāti’); *instr.* ~ena, by family, 106,8 = Dh. 393; 79,9 (by the family name); — evaṁ-gotta, *mfn.* 92,12 (*q. v.*); — jāti-gotta-kula-, 43,30. — *cp.* Kaccāyana-gotta, Vacchagotta.

*godharaṇī, *f.* (*adj.*) being able to be paired (said of a young cow) or: being with calf (?); *pl.* ~iyo (paveniyo) 105,11-14.

godhā, *f.* (= *sa.*) a kind of great lizard (which is eaten by poor people); *nom. sg.* ~ā, 15,20; *acc.* ~aṁ, 14,30-32.

gopa, *m.* (= *sa.*) a cowherd, herdsman; ~o, 104,20; Dh. 19. *cp.* gopī, *f.*

gopaka, *m.* (*e. c.* = *sa.*) a guardian; *v.* khetta-gopaka.

gopānasī, *f.* (= *sa.*) the wood of a thatch; *°-bhogga-sama, *mfn.* „bent like rafter-tree“, *acc. f.* ~aṁ (nāriṁ) 47,22.

gopāla(ka), *m.* (= *sa.*) a cowherd; ~lo, Dh. 135; *gen.* ~lakassa, 101,25.

gopī, *f.* (= *sa.*) a herdsman's wife; 104,33. 105,25. *cp.* gopa, *m.*

gopeti, *vb.* (*sa.* gopayati) to guard, protect; *pot. 3. sg.* (*med.* or *imp. 2. pl.*) ~etha (attānaṁ) Dh. 315; *pp.* gopita, *mfn.* 58,13 (rakkhita-gopita-vatthu). *cp.* gutta.

*gomika, *m.* (*cp. sa.* gomin) the owner of cows; ~o, 105,28.

gorakkhā, *f.* (*sa.* gorakshā) cow-keeping, tending cattle; kasi-gorakkhâdīni, 21,3.

Gh.

ghacca (*grd.* = *sa.* ghātya?) to be killed or destructed; mūla-ghaccaṁ, *adv.* (*q. v.*) *cp.* ghāteti.

*ghañña, *n.* (*fr. sa.* ghana, *cp.* hatya & ghānya) killing, destruction; atta-ghañña (*q. v.*).

ghaṭa, *m.* (= *sa.*) a jar, pot; *acc.* ~aṁ, 16,29; kadali-puṇṇa-ghaṭa-, plantaintrees set in pots, 62,6; *⁰-ppamāṇa, *mfn.* as large as a waterpot; *n.* ~aṁ (ambapakkaṁ) 36,33; khīra-⁰, dadhi-⁰, yāgu-⁰, *q. v.*

ghaṭeti, *vb.* (*sa.* ghaṭayati, √ghaṭ) to connect, unite; *ger.* ~etvā (anusandhiṁ, *q. v.*) 32,5; ~etvā (vaṁsaṁ osakkamānaṁ, to restore) 45,17.

ghata, *n.* (*sa.* ghṛta) clarified butter; *acc.* ~aṁ, 99,29.

ghana, [1]) *mfn.* (= *sa.*) compact, hard, firm, dense, thick; *acc.* ~aṁ (paṁsuṁ ākoṭetvā) 40,6; ⁰-sāṭaka, *m.* a thick cloth; *acc.* ~aṁ, 50,13; ekaghana, *mfn.* (*q. v.*). — [2]) *m.* (= *sa.*) the foetus at a certain stage (the last before birth?); *gen.* ~assa, 99,11.

ghara, *n.* (*sa.* gṛha; *cp.* gaha & geha) a house; *nom.* ~aṁ, 101,5; *acc.* ~aṁ, 55,28; *abl.* ~ato, 48,30; *loc.* ~e, 23,6. 48,12 (~e karissāmi, „to keep under lock in the house"); *pl.* ~ā (= gharāni) Dh. 241. 302; — ⁰-dvāra, *n.* a house-door; *loc.* ~e, 27,27; — *⁰-āvāsa, *m.* (*v. h.*). — kāraṇa-⁰ (*v.* kāraṇā); — ñāti-⁰, *q. v.* — *cp.* jantāghara, sayanighara; Mahāpadhāna-ghara.

ghasa, *m.* (= *sa.*) an eater; *v.* mahagghasa.

ghāṇa, *v.* ghāna.

ghāta, *m.* (= *sa.*) killing, murder; pantha-ghāta, *m.* 32,15 (*q. v.*).

ghātaka, *mfn.* (= *sa.*) killing, murderer; manussa-⁰, 76,9 (*q. v.*).

*ghātitatta, *n.* (*fr.* ghātita, *pp.* ghāteti; *sa.* *ghātitatva) the having killed; *abl.* ~ā (because I had killed) 17,7.

ghātin, *mfn.* (= *sa.*) killing, murderer; pāṇa-ghātī, *m.* 17,29 (*q. v.*).

ghāteti, *vb.* (*caus.* √han, ghātayati; *cp.* hanti) to cause to be killed; to slay, kill, slaughter (*acc.*); *pr. 3. sg.* ~eti, Dh. 405; *imp. 2. sg.* ~ehi (yakkhe) 112,17; ghātaya, 112,19; *pot. 3. sg.* ~aye, Dh. 129; *1. sg.* ~eyyaṁ, 33,28; *fut. 1. sg.* ~essāmi, 112,18; *3. pl.* ~essanti, 112,10; *aor. 3. sg.* aghātayi, 112,21; *3. pl.* ghātayiṁsu (aññamaññaṁ) 33,22; *ger.* ~etvā, 16,30; ghātiya (sabbe yakkhe ca ~) 112,9, is probably a modern formation (*cp.* cintiya, *fr.* cinteti) which however more likely ought to be corrected thus: sabbe yakkhā ca ghātiyā (*m. pl. grd.*, *sa.* ghātya). *cp.* ghacca, ghāta *etc.*

ghāna, *n.* (*sa.* ghrāṇa) smelling, the nose (as the organ of smelling, *cp.* nāsā); ~aṁ, 70,31; *instr.* ~ena (spelt ghāṇena) Dh. 360; *loc.* ~asmiṁ, 71,8. — ⁰-samphassa-viññāṇâyatanaṁ, the sense of smelling, 72,12 (*v.* āyatana).

ghāyati, *vb.* (*sa.* √ghrā) to smell, scent; *ger.* ~itvā (maccha-gandhaṁ) 14,25. ghāna, *n.* (*q. v.*).

ghuṭṭha, *mfn.* (*sa.* ghushṭa, *pp.* √ghush; *cp.* ghoseti) proclaimed; *n.* ~aṁ (āsāḷhi-nakkhattaṁ ~ ahosi) 61,2.

ghosa, *m.* (*sa.* ghosha) sound (of speech etc.) *v.* Buddha-ghosa.

*ghosatta, *n.* (*fr. prec.*; *sa.* *ghoshatva; only *e. c.*) the having a certain sound; gambhīra-⁰, 113,30 (*v. h.*).

ghosavat, *mfn.* (*sa.* ghoshavat) sounding, roaring; *m.* ~vā (kusamuddo) 20,16.

ghoseti, *vb.* (*sa.* ghoshayati, *caus.* √ghush) to cry aloud, proclaim; *aor. 3. sg.* ~esi, 28,31; *ger.* ~etvā (tikkhattuṁ) 14,26. *cp.* ghuṭṭha, ghosa, *etc.*

C.

c', 1) = ti (after *prec.* -i and before a vowel; *sa.* -ty-) 74,1; — 2) by elision = ca or ce (*v. h.*).

ca, *ind. enclit.* (= *sa.*), by elision and contraction before vowels: c' or câ-. 1) and; also (connecting two words, whole sentences, or parts of sentences): atthaṁ anatthañ ca, Dh. 256; after a *dvandva-comp.* pubbāparāni ca, Dh. 352; c'ettha, 3,32; c'assa, 5,26; only after the third or fourth word of a series: 2,10; 114,21; after the third and second word: 4,5; tato . . . ca (also) 102,5; in historical exposition: tadā ca, now at that time, 19,24. — 2) ca . . . ca, both . . . and, 3,2. 7,13 etc.; c'eva . . . ca, 16,32. 18,14. 30,8. 63,10; 107,17 (thrice); connecting whole sentences (or parts of sentences): 'ti sampaṭicchitvā . . . 'ti ca vutte, 1,19; 42,12 etc.; yo câyaṁ . . . yo cāyaṁ, 66,26; hoti ca na ca hoti, 89,30; api ca . . . api ca kho, 96,31 (*v.* api); anacoluthic ca . . . ca. 112,9 (but see corrections). — 3) = but, 9,2. 18,34. 108,1 (yo c'etaṁ); often after a negation: 2,12. Dh. 54. 190. 256. — 4) sometimes = ce, if (*q. v.*): 96,11 (tañ c'āyaṁ). *cp.* kiñca.

cakka, *n.* (*sa.* cakra) a wheel; *pl.* ~āni, 98,5. — khura-°, *n.* (*v. h.*).

cakkavattin, *m.* (*sa.* cakra-vartin) a sovereign of the world, universal monarch; *nom. sg.* ~ī (rājā) 61,32.

cakkavāla. *m.* (*sa.* cakra-vāla & -vāḍa) a mythical range of mountains supposed to encircle the world; *pl.* worlds or spheres (thus encircled) of which an infinite number is supposed to exist through the space; *abl. pl.* ~ehi (aññehi, from other worlds) 60,30.

cakkhu, *n.* (*sa.* cakshus) the eye; sight, insight (*esp. e. c.*); *nom. sg.* ~uṁ, 70,35. 71,32; *instr.* ~unā, Dh. 360; *loc.* ~usmiṁ, 71,5; *pl.* ~ūni, 24,16; — dibba-°, *n.* supernatural vision, *loc.* ~umhi, 109,8; — dhamma-°, *n.* knowledge of the truth, *nom.* ~uṁ, 68,26; — paññā-°, *n.* intellectual faculty, *nom.* ~uṁ, 88,27; *gen.* ~uno, 88,31; — *°-karaṇī, *adj. f. v.* karaṇa 1; — *°-viññāṇa, *n.* & *°-samphassa, *m.* (*v. h.*); *°-samphassa-viññāṇâyatanaṁ, the sense of sight, 72,1 (*cp.* āyatana). vicakkhu-kamma, *q. v.*

cakkhumat, *mfn.* (*sa.* cakshushmat) having eyes, seeing, clear-sighted; *m. sg.* ~mā, Dh. 273; *voc.* ~ma (Buddha) 105,24; *pl.* ~anto, 69,17. 88,28.

caṅkama, *m.* (*sa.* caṅkrama, *m.* & ~ā, *f.*) walking about; the place where one is walking, *esp.* a covered walk or portico; *abl.* ~ā (orohitvā) 68,10.

caṅkamati, *vb.* (*intens.* √kram, *sa.* caṅkramyate) to walk about, walk up and down; *pr. 3. sg.* ~ati, 68,9. 75,33.

*caṁgoṭa(ka), *m.* a casket, box; suvaṇṇa-caṁgoṭake, *loc.* in a golden casket, 102,24.

cajati, *vb.* (*sa.* √tyaj) to leave, abandon, give up, offer; *pr. 1. pl.* ~āma (asuresu pāṇaṁ) 60,17; *pot. 3. sg.* caje (mattāsukhaṁ) Dh. 290. *cp.* cāga.

caṇḍa, *mfn.* (= *sa.*) fierce, violent, passionate; *m.* ~o (hatthī) 76,8.

catasso, *f. pl. v.* catu.

catu (in *comp.* also catur) base of the numeral *pl. m.* cattāro, caturo, *f.* catasso, *n.* cattāri (*sa.* catvāras (*acc.* caturas), catasras, catvāri) = four; *nom. m.* cattāro, 14,10; Dh. 109; caturo, 3,26; Dh. 273; *acc.* cattāro, 25,31. 45,15; *instr.* ~ūhi, 3,23; *gen.* ~unnaṁ, 89,14; — *f.* catasso, 38,13 (dānasālā); — *n.* cattāri, 61,6. 82,9; *loc.* ~ūsu, 38,12. 86,32. 91,7. The *instr. & loc.* ~ūhi, ~ūsu are very frequently spelt ~uhi, ~usu; the base catur is catur- in *comp. w. foll. vowel*, before *cons.* the r drops through assimilation, *e. g.* catuddasa (*sa.* catur-daça) which generally (through elision of t) is shortened to cuddasa (*q. v.*). — catu-jāti-gandha-, the four kinds of scent, 41,5 (*cp.* corrections). — catuttha, *mfn.* (*v. h. etc.*).

catuttha, *mfn.* (*sa.* caturtha) the fourth; *m. loc.* ~e (vāre) 58,7; *f.* ~ā & ~ī; *nom. f.* ~ī (senā) 103,36; *acc.* ~aṁ (gāthaṁ) 15,35; *n.* ~aṁ (*adv.* = the fourth time) 88,35. — °-jjhāna, 80,4 (*v.* jhāna).

catuddisā, *adv.* (*abl. loc. sg.* = āya, or *acc. pl.* ? *cp. sa.* catur-diçaṁ) in or towards the four quarters (of the horizon); 68,31 (assadūte uyyojetvā). *cp.* disā.

catu-dvāra, *mfn.* (*sa.* catur-dvāra) having 4 doors or gates; *n.* ~aṁ (nagaraṁ) 23,26; °-jātaka, p. 22.

*catu-parisā, *f.* (*sa.* *catush-parishad) the fourfold assembly, *sc.* of male and female bhikkhus and upāsakas; catuparisa-majjhe, amidst of an assembly (thus compounded) 86,6.

catuppada, *m.* (*sa.* catushpada) a quadruped; ~o, 30,8; *pl.* ~ā, 7,18.

catuppādaka, *mfn.* (*sa.* catush-pādaka) consisting of four parts; *f.* ~ikā gāthā, a four-line stanza, 102,22; catuppādika-gātha-jānanaka, *m.* one who remembers one single four-line stanza (of the holy scriptures), *acc.* ~aṁ, 102,27.

catu-bhāga, *m.* (*sa.* caturbhāga), the fourth part, quarter; *acc.* ~aṁ eti, is worth a quarter, Dh. 108.

catur-aṅgin, *mfn.* (= *sa.*) 'having four limbs', comprising four parts; *f.* ~inī (senā) an army consisting of elephants, chariots, cavalry, and infantry, 36,23; *instr.* ~iniyā senāya, 35,14. (*cp.* Jāt. VI, 275,25.)

catur-aṅgula, *mfn.* (= *sa.*) four fingers or four inches broad; *n.* ~aṁ kaṇṇaṁ (ussāretvā, *v.* ussāreti) 83,10.

caturāsīti, *num. f.* (*sa.* catur-açīti) = 84; °-vassa-sahassāni, 84,000 years, 44,20. (*cp.* asīti.)

catu-vīsati, *num. f.* (*sa.* catur-viṁçati) = 24. — catu-vīsatima, *mfn.* the 24th; *m.* ~o (vaggo) Dh. XXIV.

catu-saṭṭhi, *num. f.* (*sa.* catuḥ-shashṭi) = 64; °-matta, *mfn.* (*sa.* °-mātra) being 64 in number; *acc. m. pl.* ~e, 61,28.

cattāri, cattāro, *v.* catu.

cana & canaṁ, *indecl.* (*sa.* cana) a suffix added to interrogatives, making them indefinite; *v.* kiñcana, kudācanaṁ; shortened to ca, *v.* kiñca.

canda, *m.* (*sa.* candra) the moon; *acc.* ~aṁ, 14,16; — °-maṇḍala, *n.* the moon-disc; ~aṁ, 32,31; *loc.* ~e, 16,16; — puṇṇa-°, *m.* the full-moon; *acc.* ~aṁ, 42,3; °-mukha, *mfn.* with a face like the full-moon, *m.* ~o (Gotamabuddho) 87,6. *cp.* candimā.

candana, *m. & n.* (= *sa.*) sandal-tree or -wood; *n.* ~aṁ, Dh. 54—55; — *°-gandhin, *mfn.* having a scent of sandal wood; *f.* ~inī, 20,24; — *°-vilepana, *n.* perfumed powder of sandal wood, ~aṁ, 23,23. — tagara-candanin, *mfn.* (*q. v.*).

candimā, *f.* (?) or candimas, *m.* (*sa.* candramas, *m.* & candrimā, *f. cp.* pūrṇimā) the moon; *nom.* ~mā, 107,23. Dh. 172. 208. 382. 387. *cp.* canda.

capala, *mfn.* (= *sa.*) trembling, unsteady; *n.* ~aṁ (cittaṁ) Dh. 33.

camara, *m.* (= *sa.*) a kind of ox, the Yak; *gen.* ~assa (vāladhi) 5,28.

camma, *n.* (*sa.* carman) [1]) skin, leather; *nom.* ~aṁ, 29,22; sīha-°, a lion's skin, 8,30; *instr.* ~ena, 8,13; °-jātaka, p. 8; — *°-varattā, *f.* a leather-thong, *acc.* ~aṁ, 12,7; — *°-sāṭaka, *m.* an ascetic wearing clothes of skin; *acc.* ~aṁ (nāma paribbājakaṁ) 29,22; °-jātaka, ib. — [2]) a shield; asi-cammaṁ, sword and shield, 75,15.

cara, *mfn.* (= *sa.*) going, wandering; *v.* eka-cara, saddhiṁ-cara. (*cp.* gocara.)

c a r a ṇ a, *n.* (= *sa.*) acting, behaviour; good conduct, virtue; sampanna-vijjā-caraṇa, *mfn.* Dh. 144 (*v. h.*).

c a r a t i, *vb.* (*sa.* √car) [1]) to go, walk, wander about (*w. acc.* cārikaṁ) travel; dwell, live. [2]) to behave, conduct one's self; to practise, exercise, commit (*acc.* dhammaṁ, anācāraṁ *etc.*). — *pr. 3. sg.* ~ati (gocaraṁ gaṇhanto) 52,17; (viravantī) 53,21; (kāmesu micchā ~, commits immorality) 97,11; *2. sg.* ~asi, 1,14; *1. sg.* ~āmi (sabbaloke) 105,8; (gavesanto ~, I am looking for) 64,33; *3. pl.* ~anti, 104,27; *1. pl. med.* carāmase, 105,35; — *part. m.* [a]) caraṁ (*nom.*) travelling, Dh. 61 (carañ ce); Dh. 305 (eko ~); *gen. m.* carato, 103,8; [b]) ~anto (dhammaṁ, walking in righteousness) 7,25; (samaṁ, *q. v.*) 7,26; (bhikkhāya ~, wandering about for alms) 29,24; *f. acc.* ~antiṁ, 47,22; *gen. pl.* ~antānaṁ (amhākaṁ) 1,25; *part. med. m.* caramāno (cārikaṁ, wandering) 81,8; — *imp. 2. sg.* cara (dhammaṁ) 7,24; 47,2 (carā, with ā metri causa); (brahmacariyaṁ, lead a holy life) 70,16; — *pot. 3. sg.* [a]) care (gāme, dwell) 106,3 = Dh. 49; (eko ~) Dh. 329; (nâññesaṁ pihayaṁ ~, let him not envy others) Dh. 365; (dhammaṁ sucaritaṁ ~, practise virtue) Dh. 168; (kāyena sucaritaṁ ~) Dh. 231; [b]) careyya (samaṁ) Dh. 142; Dh. 328; — *fut. 1. sg.* carissāmi, 92,3; — *aor. 3. sg.* [a]) a-cāri (cārikaṁ) Dh. 326; [b]) cari (anācāraṁ) 9,15; — *inf.* carituṁ; *comp.* ~itu-kāma, *mfn.* wanting to go (*m.* ~o, ākāsena, through the air) 36,10; — *ger.* ~itvā, 2,32. 61,18. 86,5 (piṇḍāya); a-caritvā, Dh. 155; — *pp. v.* carita & ciṇṇa; — *caus. II.* carāpeti (*q. v.*) *cp.* cara, caraṇa, cariyā; cāraka, cārikā, cārin.

c a r a h i, *indecl.* = tarahi (*sa.* tarhi) combined *esp. w.* interrogatives, and also other *pron.* & *adv.* = then, in that case; kiñ ~, 90,15; ko ~, 97,7. The change of t into c is probably due to the frequent combination with interrogatives (analogy of kiñca, kiñci, koci *etc.*) *cp.* etarahi.

c a r ā p e t i, *vb.* (*caus. II.* carati) to cause to move; bheriṁ ~, to beat the drum; *ger.* ~etvā, 42,2. 102,26.

c a r i t a, *n.* (= *sa.*; *fr.* carati) acting, behaviour, conduct; living; ekassa caritaṁ, living alone, Dh. 330. — duccarita, sucarita (*q. v.*).

c a r i m a, *mfn.* (*sa.* carama) subsequent, last (*opp.* pubba); a-carimā, *mfn.* (*q. v.*) *cp.* a-pubba.

c a r i y a, *n.* & c a r i y ā, *f.* (mostly *e. c.*; *sa.* carya & caryā) wandering; conduct; — eka-°, *f.* (*v. h.*); — kapirāja-°, *n.* a chapter of Cariyā-piṭaka (*q. v.*) 108,23; — nagga-°, *f.* nakedness, Dh. 141; — brahma-°, *n.* (*v. h.*), — sama-°, *n.* (*v. h.*).

C a r i y ā - p i ṭ a k a, *n. nom. pr.* name of the last book of Khuddaka-nikāya; specimen thereof 108,23 ff.

c a l a, *mfn.* (= *sa.*) moving, trembling, unsteady; a-cala, nic-cala (*v. h.*).

c a l a t i, *vb.* (*sa.* √cal) to be moved; to tremble, to be agitated, excited, confused, or frightened; *fut. 3. pl.* ~issanti (macchā) 19,29; *aor. 3. pl.* ~iṁsu, 19,33; assā kammajavātā ~, 62,19 (came upon her). — cala, calana, cāla (*q. v.*).

c a l a n a, *n.* (= *sa.*) trembling, excitement; ~aṁ (macchānaṁ) 19,31.

c a v a t i, *vb.* (*sa.* √cyu) to fall, fall away, disappear; to die, *esp.* to pass (through re-birth) from any existence into another; *ger.* ~itvā (tato) 84,31; *pp.* cuta (*q. v.*); *caus.* cāveti (*q. v.*) *cp.* cuti.

c ā g a, *m.* (*fr.* cajati; *sa.* tyāga) leaving, abandoning, giving up; resigning, devotedness, self-sacrifice; ~o (taṇhāya) 67,16; *abl.* ~ā, 94,12; *gen.* ~assa, 29,10.

*c ā ṭ i, *f.*, a vessel, jar, waterpot;

madhu-°, a honey-jar, 53,20. *cp.* Hindī cāṭā.

cāpa, *m. & n.* (= *sa.*) a particular kind of bow (dhanu); *nom. m.* ~o, 92,15; *abl.* ~ato, Dh. 320 (metri causa cāpāto); *pl.* cāpā (atikhīṇā, *q. v.*) Dh. 156.

cāra(ka) & cārika, *mfn.* (*e. c.* = *sa.*) wandering about; *v.* vanacāraka, ākāsa-cārika.

*cārikā, *f.* (*fr.* √car) wandering; *acc.* ~aṁ carati, to wander about (said of the mendicant friars) 81,8. Dh. 326; ~aṁ pakkāmi (yena Gayāsisaṁ tena, went forth to G.; otherwise *w. acc.* Vin. I, 80,2) 70,21.

cārin, *mfn.* (*e. c.* = *sa.*) wandering, living; *v.* atidhona-°, anudhamma-°, dhamma-°, bāla-saṅgata-°, brahma-°, pamatta-°, saññata-°.

cāla, *m.* (= *sa.*) moving, trembling; *v.* bhūmi-°.

cāveti, *vb.* (*caus.* cavati; *sa.* cyāvayati) to cause to fall (*acc.*); to drive away from (*abl.*); *aor. 3. sg.* a-cāvayi (mā maṁ ṭhānā ~, that he may not drive me away from my place) 104,4.

ci, *ind.* (*sa.* cid) suffix to interrogatives, rendering them indefinite; *v.* kacci, kadāci, kiñci, koci; *cp.* ca, cana(ṁ).

ciṇṇa, [1]) *mfn.* (*pp.* carati; *sa.* cīrṇa) that has been wandered over; practised, performed; ciṇṇa-ṭṭhāne yeva, „in this old familiar place", 1,14. — [2]) *n.* deed, good deed; *v.* sammukha-°.

citaka, *m.* & citakā, *f.* (*sa.* citā, citikā) a heap, pile; a funeral pile, pyre; *acc.* ~aṁ, 34,6. *cp.* cetiya, cīyati (√ci).

citta[1], *n.* (= *sa.*) thinking, thought, intention; mind, heart; *nom.* ~aṁ (pabbajjāya nami) 65,13; *acc.* ~aṁ, 96,27; *instr.* ~ena (mettena) 76,34; 80,34; *pl.* ~āni, 71,18. Very often used at the end of *adj. comp.*, *v.* an-avaṭṭhita-°, an-avassuta-°, udagga-°, kalla-°, ṭhita-°, tuṭṭha-°, duṭṭha-°, namita-°, nānā-°, paṭibaddha-°, pamudita-°, pasanna-°, mudu-°, metta-°, vadhaka-°, vinīvaraṇa-°, vimutta-°, viratta-°, santa-°, supatiṭṭhita-°, suddha-°; — sacitta, *n.* (*sa.* sva-citta) one's own thought or mind, *acc.* ~aṁ, Dh. 327; °-pariyodapana, Dh. 183 (*v. h.*) *cp.* sa-[3]. — citta-k(i)lesa *etc.* (*q. v.*) *cp.* cinteti, cetas.

citta[2] & citra, *mfn.* (*sa.* citra) variegated, manifold; bright, brilliant, excellent; *acc. m.* ~aṁ (imaṁ lokaṁ) Dh. 171; su-citta, *mfn.* very brilliant; *m. pl.* ~ā (rājarathā) Dh. 151: — *citra-pekkhuṇa, *mfn.* having a variegated tail; *acc. m.* ~aṁ (moraṁ) 10,10. *cp.* ati-citra, vi-citra; cittakata *etc.*

*cittakata, *mfn.* (*fr.* citta[2] + kata) adorned, decorated, dressed up; *acc.* ~aṁ (bimbaṁ) Dh. 147.

*cittak(i)lesa, *m.* (*fr.* citta[1]) *v.* kilesa.

*cittakkhepa, *m.* (*fr.* citta[1]) *v.* khepa.

*Cittapāṭalī, *f.* (*fr.* citta[2] + pāṭali) *nom. pr.* 'the pied trumpet-flower', name of a tree (kappaṭṭhiyarukkha) in the world of Asuras, 59,29; *loc.* ~iyā, ib.

*cittarucita, *mfn.* (*fr.* citta[1] + rucita) being after one's heart; *acc. m.* ~aṁ (sāmikaṁ) 10,5.

*Cittalatā, *f.* (*fr.* citta[2] + latā) *nom. pr.* of Sakka's garden; °-vanasadisa, *mfn.* equal to the C.-grove in Sakka's heaven, 62,14.

*cittavagga, *m.* (*fr.* citta[1] + vagga) name of the third chapter in Dhammapada.

citra, *mfn.* (= *sa.*), *v.* citta[2].

cintana, *n.* (= *sa.*) thinking, reflecting; care. — *cintanaka, *mfn.* thinking for, taking care of; macchānaṁ °-bako, 4,10.

cinteti, *vb.* (*sa.* √cint.) to think, reflect; to care for (*gen.*); *pr. 2. sg.* ~esi (amhākaṁ) 4,4; *part. m.* ~ento (nisīdi) 4,2; (tumhākaṁ) 4,4; *aor.*

3. sg. ~esi, 3,2; *2. sg.* mā cintayi (etaṁ nissāya) „don't worry yourself", 49,31; 61,30 (be not anxious); *3. pl.* ~esuṁ, 6,3; *ger.* a) ~etvā, 3,11; b) cintiya, 111,18. 112,11. — cintana (*q. v.*) *cp.* citta[1], cetas.

cira, *mfn.* (= *sa.*) long, lasting a long time; *acc. m.* ~aṁ (addhānaṁ) 110,5; — *n. adv.* ciraṁ, long, for a long time; 9,1; 23,34 (long enough); 59,23 (~jīva); Dh. 248; — *dat. adv.* cirāya, id. Dh. 342; — *cirāgata, *mfn. v.* āgata; — cira-ppavāsin, *mfn.* long absent; *acc. m.* ~vāsiṁ (purisaṁ), Dh. 219; — a-cira, *mfn.* (*q. v.*) *cp. next.*

cirassaṁ, *adv.* (*sa.* cirasya, *gen.*) after a long time, at last; ~ vata bho nāgo nāgena saṁgāmessati, at last we shall see an elephant (*sc.* of men) that can fight a fight with (this) elephant! 76,33; na cirass'eva or nacirass'eva, shortly after, until in no long time, 23,3. 89,16.

cīyati, *vb.* (*pass.* cināti, *sa.* √ci) to be gathered, heaped up, acquired, constructed; *præs. 3. sg.* cīyate (= *sa.*) 103,9 (pahūtaṁ (te) ~ puññaṁ).

cīvara, *n.* (= *sa.*) the robe of a Buddhist monk; *nom.* ~aṁ, 83,8; *acc.* 83,20; patta-cīvaraṁ, bowl and robe, 76,16; cīvara-⁰ 97,8; — *⁰-rajju, *f.* a rope for hanging up a robe, *acc.* ~uṁ, 83,21; — *⁰-vaṁsa, *m.* a bamboo peg for hanging up a robe, *acc.* ~aṁ, 83,20.

cuṇṇa, 1) *mfn.* (*sa.* cūrṇa) pulverised, grinded, crushed; cuṇṇa-vicuṇṇa, *mfn.* severely hurted or injured, *n.* ~aṁ (hadayaṁ) 1,25. — 2) *n.* aromatic powder; ~aṁ, 83,27; gandha-⁰, id. 53,26; gandha-dhūpa-cuṇṇa-, 48,30.

cuta, *mfn.* (*pp.* cavati; *sa.* cyuta) fallen; having died or passed from one existence into another; *m.* ~o (tato) 45,16. — a-ccuto. *mfn.* (*q. v.*).

cuti, *f.* (*sa.* cyuti) falling down; destruction; *acc.* ~iṁ (sattānaṁ) Dh. 419 (*opp.* upapatti).

cuddasa, *num.* (contracted *fr.* catuddassa (*v.* catu); *sa.* catur-daça) = 14; — cuddasama, *mfn.* the 14th, *m.* ~o (vaggo) Dh. XIV.

*Cunda, *m. nom. pr.* of a smith (kammāraputta) in Pāvā, whom Buddha visited before his death; *nom.* ~o, 77,20; *acc.* ~aṁ, 77,24; *gen.* ~assa, 77,20.

ce, *ind.* (*sa.* ced) if; most frequently combined with other particles (*v.* sace, noce, yañce) and never found at the beginning of a sentence; ettha ce te mano atthi, 72,31; tañ c'āyaṁ, 96,11 (*cp.* ca); attha ce patthayasī, 104,32 *sq.*; puññañ ce puriso kayirā, Dh. 118; passe ce vipulaṁ sukhaṁ, Dh. 290; yañ ce viññū pasaṁsanti . . . ko taṁ *etc.* (si quem . . ., quis eum . . .) Dh. 229; yañ ce = than if, 107,2. Dh. 106, *v.* yañce; — api ce or pi ce, even if; sakalo pi ce . . . (n'eva) 16,13; alaṁkato ce pi, Dh. 142 = alaṁkato pi ce or: sace alaṁkato pi; — ti ce (in commentaries = if you ask so) 85,33 (kiṁ idan ti ce ti āha = viz. with the following words; *cp.* corrections).

ceṭa & ceṭaka, *m.* (= *sa.*) a servant, slave; *acc. pl.* ~ke, 56,13.

cetas, *m. n.* (?) (= *sa.*) mind, thought; *instr.* ~asā (vippasannena) Dh. 79; *gen.* ~aso, 80,35. 91,6. 96,12; sabba-cetaso, *gen. adv.* with all one's mind, 71,23 (~samannāharitvā dhammaṁ suṇanti). — an-anvāhata-cetasa, *mfn.* (*q. v.*).

Cetā, *m. pl.* (*sa.* Cedi) *nom. pr.* of a people and its country, south of the Ganges; ~ā, 34,21. *cp. next.*

Cetiya[1]-raṭṭha, *n.* (*cp. sa.* Cedika) = *prec.*; *acc.* ~aṁ, 32,14.

cetiya[2], *n.* (*sa.* caitya) a sepulchral monument, sanctuary, temple, place of worship; *loc.* ~e (Aggāḷave) 86,12; *pl.* ~āni, Dh. 188 (ārāma-rukkha-⁰).

codeti, *vb.* (*sa.* codayati, *caus.* √cud) to exhort, correct, punish, reprove; to request, ask; *imp. 2. sg.* codaya, Dh. 379 (coday' attānaṁ, *synon.* paṭimāse, *ib.* & saññāmaya, 380); *pp. m.* codito, 113,14.

cora, *m.* (*sa.* cora & caura) a thief, robber; *acc.* ~aṁ, 36,22; *pl.* ~ā, 30,30; *acc. pl.* ~e, ib.; — payuttaka-°, pesanaka-° (*v. h.*). — corarājan, *m. gen.* ~rañño („the ruffianly king") 39,35; — corupaddava, *m.* attack from robbers, ~o, 42,5.

corī, *f.* (*sa.* corī & caurī) a female thief; as *adj.* — thievish, deceitful; *pl.* ~iyo, 51,34. 52,4 (= prodigal, extravagant ?); *gen. pl.* ~inaṁ (thīnaṁ) 51,30; — dāraka-°, *f.* a female kidnapper, *acc.* ~iṁ, 59,16.

coḷaka, *m.* (*sa.* coḍa(ka) & cola(ka)) cloth, rag, *esp.* a rubbing-cloth or mop; *acc.* ~aṁ, 84,20.

Ch.

cha, *mfn.* (*nom. acc. pl.*) *num.* (*sa.* shash (shaṭ)) = 6; 38,13. 82,11; the declination is: *instr. abl.* chahi, *gen. dat.* channaṁ; *loc.* chasu or chassu. *cp. next* & chattiṁsati, chabbaṇṇa, chabbīsati, chaḷabhiñña, saṭṭhi, soḷasa.

chaṭṭha, *mfn.* (*sa.* shashṭha) the sixth; *f.* ~ā (senā) 103,27.

chaṭṭhama, *mfn.* (*sa.* shashṭhama) = *prec.*; *acc. f.* ~aṁ (gāthaṁ) 54,35.

chaḍḍana, *n.* (*sa.* chardana) throwing away, ejecting; kacavara-°, *v. h.*

chaḍḍāpeti, *vb.* (*caus. II.* √chṛd) to cause to be thrown away; *aor. 3. sg.* ~esi (appagghabhaṇḍaṁ) cast overboard, 26,2.

chaḍḍeti, *vb.* (*sa.* chardayati, *caus.* √chṛd) to fling, throw away, eject, vomit; to leave, quit, expose, reject (*acc.*); *pr. 3. sg.* ~eti (kacavaraṁ, tassā upari) 50,2; *part. m. pl.* ~entā (matamanussaṁ āmakasusāne) 40,31; *aor. 3. sg.* ~esi, 50,1; *3. pl.* ~esuṁ. 40,33; *ger.* ~etvā (brāhmaṇaṁ magge) 33,18; (sirivi bhavaṁ) 47,32; 52,2-4 (rejecting); 64,23 (gharāvāsaṁ); 86,21 (āsīvisaṁ daṇḍakena); *grd.* ~etabba, *n.* ~aṁ (saṁkāraṁ) 84,24; °-bhāvaṁ pāpuṇi, 42,32 („was deserted", *cp.* bhāva). — *caus. II.* chaḍḍāpeti (*q. v.*) *cp.* chaḍḍana, *n.*

chatta, *n.* (*sa.* chattra) a parasol, umbrella, canopy (ensign of royal power); *gen.* seta-cchattassa heṭṭhā, under a white canopy, 42,8. *cp.* chādeti (√chad) *etc.*

chattiṁsati, *f. num.* (*sa.* shaṭtriṁçat) thirty-six; Dh. 339 (~ti sotā).

chadana, *n.* (= *sa.*) a thatch, roof; *loc. pl.* ~esu (ārūḷhā) 76,29.

chadda, *n.* (*sa.* chadman ?) a thatch, roof (Abhidhāna.); only in the *comp.* vivatta-cchadda (*q. v.*).

chanda, *m.* (= *sa.*) delight, wish, will, desire; *acc.* ~aṁ (na tamhi ~ kayirātha, let him not delight in it) Dh. 117; chandâdi-vasena, according to one's will etc. (by chandâdi is probably meant chanda, dosa, moha, bhaya, or the four wrong courses (modes of proceeding, agati)) 42,27 (*v.* vasa); — *chanda-jāta, *mfn.* in whom desire has sprung up, *m.* ~o (anakkhāte) Dh. 218.

channa[1], *mfn.* (= *sa.*, *pp.* √chad, *cp.* chādeti) covered, thatched; *f.* ~ā (kuṭi) 104,22 (*opp.* vivaṭa). — ducchanna, *mfn.* & succhanna, *mfn.* (*q. v.*).

*Channa[2], *m.* [1]) *nom. pr.* of Buddha's servant; ~o, 65,15; *acc.* ~aṁ, 65,26. — [2]) *nom. pr.* of a certain bhikkhu; ~o. 79,14; *gen.* ~assa, 79,12.

*chabbaṇṇa, *mfn.* (*fr.* cha + vaṇṇa; *sa.* *shaḍ-varṇa) six-coloured; *gen. pl.* ~ānaṁ (raṁsīnaṁ, the six-coloured rays of light emitted from Buddha's body) 87,33.

chabbīsati, *f. num.* (*sa.* shaḍviṁçati) = 26; ~tī vaggā, Dh. p. 94, v. 3. — chabbīsatima, *mfn.* the 26th; ~o (vaggo) Dh. XXVI.

chaḷabhiñña, *mfn.* (*fr.* cha +

abhiññā, *sa.* shaḍ-abhijña) possessed of the six abhijñas, *v.* abhiññā.

chava, [1]) *m. n.* (*sa.* çava) a corpse, dead body. — [2]) *mfn.* low, vile, contemptible; *gen. m.* ~assa (kheḷāpakassa) 74,28.

chavi, *f.* (= *sa.*) skin, colour, splendour; *chavi-vaṇṇa, *m.* beauty; *acc.* ~aṁ, 18,6; — *chavi-saṇṭhāna, *n.* the appearance of the skin; *loc.* ~e, 85,23 (vaṇṇasaddo idha ~ va daṭṭhabbo, the word vaṇṇa is here to be understood as complexion); — maṅgura-cchavi, *mfn.* (*q. v.*) *cp.* anucchavika, *mfn.*

chāta, *mfn.* (= *sa.*, *cp. sa.* psāta) emaciated, hungry; *m. pl.* ~ā, 111,31 (*cp. Pischel,* Gr. d. Prakr. Spr. § 328 & *next.*)

*chātaka, *n.* (*fr. prec.*) hunger; °-ākāra, *m.* sign of hunger; *acc.* ~aṁ (dassesi, gave them to understand that he was hungry) 41,8.

chādeti, *vb.* (*sa.* chādayati, *caus.* √chad) to cover, hide (*acc.*); *pr. 3. sg.* ~eti (attano vajjāni) 106,18 = Dh. 252; *aor. 3. pl.* ~esuṁ (devatā poṭṭhakaṁ, rendered the book invisible) 114,16. *cp.* chatta, chadana, channa.

chāyā, *f.* (= *sa.*) shade, shadow; *nom.* ~ā (anapāyinī) Dh. 2; *gen.* ~āya (abhāvena, on account of the absence of shadow (sign of being a Yakkha) 59,18; — *sīta-cchāya, *mfn.* (*q. v.*).

chijjati, *vb.* (*pass.* chindati, √chid) to be cut off, to be split, torn, destroyed; *pr. 3. sg.* ~ati (vanatho) Dh. 284; *3. pl.* ~anti (hatthapādā) 99,13; *ger.* ~itvā 17,23; repeated: 60,7 (being mowed down everywhere); *pp.* chinna (*q. v.*).

chidda, *n.* (*sa.* chidra) a hole, leak; fault, defect; acchiddavutti, *v.* a-cchidda, *mfn.*

chindati (& a-cchindati), *vb.* (*sa.* √chid & ā-√cchid) to cut off; to tear, split, cleave, destroy (*acc.*); *imp. 2. sg.* chinda (pāsaṁ) 12,1; *2. pl.* ~atha, Dh. 283; — *pot. 3. sg.* chinde, Dh. 370; — *fut. 3. sg.* checchati, Dh. 350 (esa-cchecchati, probably *fr.* a-cchindati); — *aor. 3. sg.* acchidda (= acchidā, B. acchindi, *fr.* chindati or a-cchindati) Dh. 351; — *inf.* chettuṁ, 105,18; — *ger.* [a]) chinditvā (gīvaṁ) 4,33; (sīsaṁ) 5,12; (dvidhā ~. to cut in two) 33,18; a-chinditvā (vissāsaṁ, „in unbroken amity") 13,7; — [b]) chetvā, 33,34. 105,19; Dh. 283. 369: — [c]) chetvāna, 47,28; Dh. 346; — *caus. II.* chindāpeti, *pass.* chijjati, *pp.* chinna (*q. v.*) *cp.* chidda, cheda.

*chindāpeti, *vb.* (*caus. II.* chindati) to cause to be cut off, to let be removed (*acc.*); *ger.* ~etvā, 36,19. 38,1.

chinna, *mfn.* (= *sa.*, *pp.* √chid) cut down, torn, split; *m.* ~o (rukkho) Dh. 338; *acc.* ~aṁ, 34,5; *n.* ~aṁ (mūsika-cchinnaṁ ṭhānaṁ) 25,7; chinna-pasibbaka, 13,5; chinna-taṭa-, a sheer precipice, 27,3; chinna-ṭṭhāna, *n.* a crack, fissure, 91,30; vāta-cchinna, *mfn.* driven away by the wind, °-valāhaka, *m.* 40,28 (*v. h.*).

chuddha, *mfn.* (*sa.* kshubdha, √kshubh) thrown away, rejected; *m.* ~o (kāyo) Dh. 41 (Comm. = apaviddho; *cp.* Jāt. V, 302,4. 303,4 = chaḍḍita). *Fausbøll* (Rem. p. 19) & *Trenckner* (Mil. p. 422—23) refer it to √kshiv = √shṭhiv; *cp. Pischel*, Gr. d. Prakr. Spr. § 66 & 120. *v.* niṭṭhubhati & nuṭṭhubhati *below.*

cheka, *mfn.* (= *sa.*) clever, shrewd; skilful, skilled in (*loc.*); *instr. m.* ~ena (sākuṇikena) 88,33; *nom.* ~o (aṅga-vijjāya) 48,16.

checchati, chetvā, chetvāna, chettuṁ, *v.* chindati.

cheda, *m.* (= *sa.*) cutting off; interruption, abandonment; āsā-ccheda, *m.*, kamma-°, *m.*, sandhi-°, *mfn.*, sīsa-°, *m.* (*v. h.*).

J.

ja, *mfn.* (*e. c.* = *sa.*) born; *v.* atta-ja, dāru-°, dvija (dija), pabba-°, yoni-°, vāri-°, Sīhabāhu-narinda-°. *cp.* jāyati.

jagatī, *f.* (= *sa.*) the earth, world; *jagati-ppadesa, *m.* a spot in the world, ∼o, Dh. 127.

jaccā, *instr.* = jātiyā, *v.* jāti.

jaggati, *vb.* = jāgarati (*q. v.*).

jajjara, *mfn.* (*sa.* jarjara) infirm from age, decayed, old; jarā-°, *mfn.* (*v. h.*) *cp.* jara *etc.*

jañña, *mfn.* (*sa.* janya) 'to be born or produced', charming, excellent (? *cp.* MN. I p. 528, ad p. 29,19); *v.* a-jañña & purisājañña.

jaññā, *pot. v.* jānāti.

jaṭā, *f.* (= *sa.*) the platted or matted hair (of an ascetic); Dh. 141; *instr. pl.* ∼āhi, 106,8 = Dh. 393. *cp. next.*

jaṭila, *m.* (= *sa.*) an ascetic (wearing matted hair); *instr. pl.* purāṇa-jaṭilehi (who had been Jaṭilas before) 70,23.

jana, *m.* (= *sa.*) people (*coll.* sometimes constructed *w. pl.* of the verb), *pl.* men, persons; *nom.* ∼o, 106,34 = Dh. 222; Dh. 249 (*w. pl.* dadanti); bahu-jano, many people, a multitude of people, the vulgar, 88,32; bahujjano. id. Dh. 320; mahājano. id. 17,23; mahājana-majjhe, before all the people, 51,16; loka-mahājano = loko (*q. v.*) 88,31; *acc.* janaṁ (aññaṁ bahukaṁ) 108,12; mahā-janaṁ, 88,6; *gen.* janassa. 110,16; mahā-janassa, 73,12. 87,3; *loc.* mahā-jane (among men) 114,15; – *pl.* dve janā, 6,33. 37,15; *gen. pl.* tiṇṇaṁ janānaṁ, 14,13; – gama-jana, puthujjana (*v. h.*) *cp.* janapada, janinda.

janana, *mfn.* (*e. c.* — *sa.*) producing, causing; bhaya-°, *mfn.* terrific; *m.* ∼o (saddo) 27,4.

janapada, *m.* (= *sa.*) [1]) an inhabited country, the country (*opp.* the town), the continent; *acc.* ∼aṁ, 22,3 (*opp.* Tambapaṇṇadīpa); 43,10 (*opp.* nagara); raṭṭha-janapada-vāsino, *m. pl.* „the country people of the kingdom", 102,5. — [2]) a nation, tribe; subjects. *cp.* jānapada.

janinda, *m.* (*fr.* jana + inda; *sa.* janendra) a sovereign, king; *voc.* ∼a, 47,10 (janindā'ti); 55,1.

janeti, *vb.* (*caus.* √jan, *sa.* janayati, *cp.* jāyati) to bear, bring forth (*acc.*); *aor. 3. sg.* janayi (Māyā Gotamaṁ). 108,21. *cp.* jana, janana.

*jantāghara, *n.* a bathing place for hot sitting baths; *nom. acc.* ∼aṁ. 83,27-31; *abl.* ∼ā, 83,35; *loc.* ∼e, 83,34; °-pīṭha, *n.* the chair belonging to the jantāghara, *acc.* ∼aṁ, 83,28. The etymology of this word is not clear; *Bühler* (& *Oldenberg*) take it = *sa.* yantra-gṛha (an oil-mill) KZ. XXV (1881) p. 325, but the prakritizising of ya (into ja) is upon the whole very questionable and *esp.* in this case, because yanta (*sa.* yantra) frequently occurs in Pāli-texts. *E. Hardy*, (Deutsche Litt. Zeit. 1902 p. 339) refers to *sa.* jentāka (a dry hot bath) the etymology of which is likewise unknown. *cp.* SBE. XIII p. 157.

jantu, *m.* (= *sa.*) a creature, man, person; *nom.* ∼u, Dh. 107; *acc.* ∼uṁ, 106,12 = Dh. 395; *gen.* ∼uno, 106,14 = Dh. 176; Dh. 105. 341.

jambu, *f. n.* (= *sa.*) [1]) *f.* the rose apple tree (Eugenia). [2]) *n.* the fruit of the Jambu tree; *instr. pl.* ∼ūhi, 2,10.

Jambudīpa, *m.* (*sa.* Jambudvīpa, the central one of the seven continents = the known world) *nom. pr.* of India (*sa.* Bharata-varsha); *acc.* ∼aṁ, 114,32; *loc.* sakala-Jambudīpe, 39,11. 98,13; *°-gāmika, *mfn.* (*v. h.*).

jambonada, *n.* (*sa.* jāmbūnada) a kind of gold (from the Jambū river); *gen.* ∼assa (nekkhaṁ) Dh. 230.

jamma, *mfn.* (*sa.* jālma) [1]) contemptible, poor, miserable; *m.* ∼o (gadrabho) 8,28. [2]) cruel, fierce; *f.* ∼ī (taṇhā) 107,31; *acc.* ∼iṁ, 108,1.

jaya, *m.* (= *sa.*) victory; jaya-parājaya, *m.* victory and defeat, *acc.*

~aṁ, Dh. 201. — jayaṁ (Dh. 201) *part. m.*, *v.* (jināti &) jeti.

jara, *mfn.* (only as first part of *comp.* = *sa.* jarat) old (an epithet implying contempt or vexation); jara-Sakko, 59,31. *cp.* jīrati, jiṇṇa *& next.*

jarā, *f.* (= *sa.*) old age, decrepitude, decay; *nom.* ~ā, 63,13. 67,8; *instr.* ~āya, 70,29; — *°-jajjara, *m.* a decrepit old man; *acc.* ~aṁ, 63,8; — *jarappatta (*sa.* *jarā-prāpta) *mfn.* decrepit, decayed; *gen. f. pl.* ~ānaṁ. 47,15; — °-maraṇaṁ, *n.* old age and death, 66,10-16; — jāti-jarā, *f.*, jāti-jarūpaga, *mfn.*, yāva-jarā, *adv.* (*v. h.*). — Jarā-vagga, *m.* the 11th chapter of Dh.

jala, *n.* (= *sa.*) water; *instr.* ~ena, 110,33; *loc.* ~e (samattho. *q. v.*) 4,11; — *°-gocara, *mfn.* living in the water; *m. pl.* ~ā, 1,8; — thala-jala-, 19,22, loṇa-jala-, 24,16 (*v. h.*).

jalati, *vb.* (*sa.* √jval) to burn, shine; *pr. 3. sg.* ~ati (aggi) 94,30; *part. loc. pl.* ~antesu (padīpesu), 65,18; *pot. 3. sg.* ~eyya, 94,29; *aor. 3. sg.* a-jali, 95,7; *caus.* jaleti & jāleti (*q. v.*).

jaleti, *vb.* (*caus. fr. prec.*) to set on fire, light, kindle (*acc.*); *ger.* ~etvā (aggiṁ) 100,24. *cp.* jāleti.

java, *mfn.* (= *sa.*) quick; Java-sakuṇa-jātaka, *n.* (the tale of the dexterous bird) 13,8 (if not java is the name of a bird; *Trenckner* refers to *sa.* cavyā = vacā, but this seems not to agree with rukkha-koṭṭhaka, 13,10, which is = *sa.* çatapattra, Jātakamālā p. 235,20). — *m.* speed; *instr.* ~ena, quickly, 23,14.

jaha, *mfn.* (*e. c.* = *sa.*) leaving, abandoning; *v.* sabbañjaha. *cp. next.*

jahāti (& jahati), *vb.* (= *sa.* √hā) to leave, abandon (*acc.*); *pr. 3. pl.* ~anti (okamokaṁ) Dh. 91; *pot. 3. sg.* jahe, Dh. 221. 370 (*cp.* vippa-jaheyya); *1. sg.* jaheyyaṁ (rajjaṁ) 8,8; *fut. 3. sg.* jahissati (attānaṁ, will loose his life) 54,30; *inf.* jahituṁ, 44,31. 46,34; *ger.* hitvā (abalassaṁ, leaving behind) Dh. 29; (kāme) Dh. 88; Dh. 91. 231. 417; *pp.* hīna (*v. h.*); *caus.* hāpeti, *pass.* hāyati (*q. v.*) *cp.* jaha, *mfn.*

jāgarati (& jaggati), *vb.* (*sa.* √jāgṛ) to be awake; *part. gen. m.* ~ato, 107,9 = Dh. 60; *part. med.* jāgaramāna, *gen. pl.* ~ānaṁ (sadā ~, ever watchful) Dh. 226. *cp.* paṭi-jaggati & bahujāgara.

jāta, [1]) *mfn.* (= *sa. pp.* √jan, *cp.* jāyati & janeti) born, grown, produced; become (in this sense often used as finite tense); *m.* ~o, 18,28. 34,24. 45,24. 113,2; *instr.* ~ena (maccena) Dh. 53; *gen.* ~assa („every one that is born") 63,13; *loc.* ~e (varaṇarukkhe) 4,21; ~amhi (atthamhi) Dh. 331; *f.* ~ā, 28,8; *acc.* ~aṁ, Dh. 340; Yakkhinī jatāsi (you have been born a Yakkhinī) 59,21; *n.* ~aṁ, 31,21. 49,24; *m. pl.* ~ā (dantā) 12,31; *n. pl.* ~āni (kesāni, sīsamhi) 47,1; *comp.* pīti-somanassa-jātā, *adj. f.* filled with pleasure and satisfaction, 64,13; pāsāṇapiṭṭhaṁ nissāya jāta-(gumbe) 17,30; — *jāta-divasa, *m.* birthday, *loc.* ~e, 24,31. 45,21; — chanda-°, *mfn.*, sayaṁ-°, *mfn.* (*q. v.*). — [2]) *n.* a kind, sort; gandha-° (*v. h.*) *cp.* jātarūpa & *next.*

jātaka, [1]) *mfn.* (= *sa.*) born; *m.* a child; nahāpitassa ~o, 25,10 (a bastard). — [2]) *n.* [a]) *nom. pr.* name of a Pāli work, the 10th section of the Khuddaka-nikāya; *acc.* ~aṁ, 102,16; *loc.* ~e, 102,20; *comp.* jātak'-abbhuta-vedallaṁ (parts of the navaṅgaṁ Satthusāsanaṁ) 109,34. The Jātaka is the Book of Birth-Stories, containing 547 tales of the anterior existences of Gotama Buddha (jātakāni) and an introduction (nidāna-kathā) about the legendary history of the Buddhas; *cp.* *L. Feer*, Étude sur les Jātakas, JAs. (1875) sér. 7. vol. V—VI; a useful bibliography is given by *H. Wenzel*, JRAS. 1893, p. 351. Specimens are found p. 1—60, 72—74; of Nidāna-kathā p. 61—65. — [b]) a tale of the

Jātaka-book, consisting of two chief parts, viz. paccuppanna-vatthu (story of the present) generally in prose only, and atīta-vatthu (story of the past) in mixed prose and verses (gāthā) together with a verbal commentary (aṭṭhavaṇṇanā or aṭṭhakathā); the tale concludes in a short summary (samodhāna, identification of the actors in the atīta-vatthu). Jātaka-tales are also found in Cariyā-piṭaka, Buddha-vaṁsa and passim in other holy scriptures (*cp. Rhys Davids*, Buddhist Birth Stories, Introd.), with the northern Buddhists in Mahā-vastu, Jātaka-mālā, Divyāvadāna, Avadāna-çataka *etc.*; numerous scenes of Jātaka-tales are figured on the Bharhut-Stūpa, Boro-Boedoer, and Mangala Cheti Dagāba (*cp.* the notes of Part I). Specimens of Jātakas in their whole extent (without commentary) are found p. 28—32, a little proof of the verbal commentary p. 52,1-7. ∼aṁ samodhānesi („identified the birth") 29,16. 30,24. 32,5.

jātarūpa, *n.* (= *sa.*) gold; jātarūpa-rajata-paṭiggahaṇa, *n.* accepting gold and silver, *abl.* ∼ā, 81,26.

jāti, *f.* (= *sa.*) 1) birth, re-birth, (former) existence; *nom.* ∼i, 66,10. 67,8; *instr.* ∼iyā (or jaccā, *v. below*) 70,29; *gen.* ∼iyā, 63,13; *loc.* ∼iyaṁ (atīta-°) 85,12; — *°-kkhaya, *m.* end of births, *acc.* ∼aṁ, Dh. 423; — *°-jarā, *f.* birth and decay, *acc.* ∼aṁ, Dh. 238. 348; °-jar'-ūpaga, *mfn.* (*v.* upaga); — *°-nirodha, *m.* cessation of births, ∼o, 66,16; *abl.* ∼ā, ib.; — *°-paccayā (*v. h.*); — *°-maraṇa, *n.* birth and death, *gen.* ∼assa, 105,26; — *°-saṁsāra, *m.* the revolution of being, 108,18; — *°-sambhava, *m.* existence, 17,28; — °-ssara- (*sa.* jātismara), remembering one's former existences; *°-ñāṇa, *n.* the power of remembering one's former existences, *instr.* ∼ena, 17,4; — pañca-jāti-satāni (*acc.* through 500 births = 500 times) 17,10. — 2) age; *instr.* jaccā = jātiyā, by age, 47,21. — 3) caste; *acc.* ∼iṁ, 111,21 (mama jātin ti, my royal lineage); *instr.* jaccā, by caste, 106,8 — Dh. 393; — °-gotta-kula-padesa, *m.* position with regard to caste, race and family, *acc.* ∼aṁ, 43,30; — °-mant'-ūpapanna, *mfn.* (*v.* upapanna). *cp. Fick*, Soc. Glied. p. 22. — 4) kind, sort; catu-jāti-gandha, *m.* (*v.* catu, *cp.* jāta, *n.*).

jātu, *adv.* (— *sa.*) at all, ever (generally explained by ekaṁse(na) or kadāci); tāsu ko ∼ vissase, 51,4.

*jānana, *n.* (*nom. act. fr.* jānāti) knowing, knowledge; °-manta, *m.* a spell of knowledge, *acc.* ∼aṁ, 53,36; sabba-ruta-jānana-manta, *m.* 53,14 (*v.* ruta).

*jānanaka, *mfn.* (*fr. prec.*) knowing, a knower; catuppādika-gātha-°, *v.* catuppādaka, 102,27.

jānapada, *mfn.* (— *sa.*) living in in the country; *m. pl.* country-people; *acc. pl.* ∼e, 6,2 (negama-°); — *jānapaditthī, *f.* a country-woman, *acc.* ∼iṁ, 30,28.

jānāti, *vb.* (*sa.* √jñā) to know, understand, learn (*acc.*); perceive, observe; recognize; be aware, find (find out); experience (suffer); *pr.* *3. sg.* ∼āti (ko ∼ kiṁ karissati) 13,17; 30,6. 32,9. 72,24. 102,25; *2. sg.* ∼āsi, 5,11; *1. sg.* ∼āmi, 41,33. 51,10. 87,26. 92,10; *1. sg. med.* jāne, 113,12; *2. pl.* ∼ātha, 59,15; *3. pl.* ∼anti, 51,35. 59,30. 104,2; — *part.* a) (jānaṁ) *gen.* *m.* jānato, Dh. 384; a-jānato (te) 101,30; b) *m.* jānanto, 57,3; *pl.* ∼ā (nāma nâhesuṁ, no one knew) 19,19; a-jānanto, not knowing, unaware, unsuspecting, 5,1. 50,17; *pl.* ∼ā, 21,6; *f.* ∼antī, 57,24; c) *med. pl. m.* jānamānā, 17,26; — *imp.* *2. sg.* jānāhi, 46,8. 72,23 (evaṁ); Dh. 248; *2. pl.* ∼ātha (find out) 74,3; — *pot.* a) *2. sg.* jāneyyāsi, 94,29; *1. sg.* jāneyya (∼âhaṁ) 94,31; *3. pl.* ∼eyyuṁ, 17,28; *2. pl.* ∼eyyātha, 9,14; b) *3. sg.* jaññā, Dh. 157. 352; — *fut.* *3. sg.* ∼issati, 56,8; *2. sg.* ∼issasi (tuyhaṁ pattaṁ, suffer) 6,35; *1. sg.* ~issāmi (pacchā, see to it afterwards) 15,16; – *aor.* [a]) *3. sg.* aññāsi, *v.* ājānāti; [b]) *3. pl.* jāniṁsu (taṁ kāraṇaṁ) 37,8; – *ger.* [a]) ñatvā, 3,20. 8,25. 12,9-26. 33,5. 34,14 (sabbaṁ). Dh. 12. 22 etc.; [b]) jānitvā, 50,31; a-jānitvā, 53,1; – *pass.* ñāyati, *pp.* ñāta, *caus.* ñāpeti & jānāpeti (*q. v.*) *cp.* ñāṇa, ñātaka, ñāti, -ññū, & jānana(ka).

jānāpeti, *vb.* (*caus. II.* jānāti) to let know, to inform any one (*acc.*); *imp. 2. sg.* ~ehi (naṁ) 55,23; *ger.* ~etvā (taṁ) ib. *cp.* ñāpeti.

jāni, *f.* (*sa.* jyāni; *fr.* jāpeti, √jyā) [1]) loss (of property), amercement. [2]) growing old, infirmity; *acc.* ~iṁ, Dh. 138.

jāyati, *vb.* (— *sa.* √jan) to be born; *pr. 3. sg.* ~ati, Dh. 193; ~atī, Dh. 212 foll. Dh. 282 foll. (birm. read. ~te); *pot. 3. sg. med.* ~etha, Dh. 58; *aor. 3. sg.* jāyi, 45,22; *pp.* jāta, *grd.* jañña (*v. h.*); *caus.* janeti (*q. v.*) *cp.* jātaka, jāti, jana *etc.*

jāra, *m.* (— *sa.*) a paramour, lover; *acc.* ~aṁ, 51,1.

jāla, *n.* (— *sa.*) a net, snare; cob-web; wire-net, lattice; *acc.* ~aṁ (khipāpetvā) 26,1; Dh. 347 (cob-web); antojālam, 88,35 (*v.* anto); suvaṇṇa-[0], a golden net, 62,22; *instr.* ~ena, 88,34; 62,23 (suvaṇṇa-[0]); 88,35 (Māra-[0]); *abl.* ~ato (muccati) 88,34; [0]-mutto (sakunto) 88,30; – *ñāṇa-jāla, *n.* the limits of one's perception; *gen.* ~assa (anto paviṭṭhaṁ disvā, calling her into his mind) 86,28; – *[0]-karaṇḍaka, *m.* (*v. h.*).

jālin, *mfn.* (— *sa.*) 'having a net', ensnaring, deceptive, fascinating; *f.* ~inī (taṇhā) Dh. 180.

jāleti, *vb.* (*caus.* jalati) to cause to burn or shine (*acc.*); *pr. 3. pl.* ~enti (dīpaṁ) 37,2 (*cp.* jaleti).

ji, *mfn.* (*e. c.* — *sa.* jit) winning, victorious; *v.* saṅgāmaji (*cp.* jināti).

jigacchā, *f.* (*sa.* jighatsā) hunger; Dh. 203 (var. B. digacchā).

jiṇṇa, *mfn.* (*pp.* jīrati; *sa.* jīrṇa) old, decayed; *m.* ~o, 74,20; *acc.* ~aṁ (purisaṁ) 63,15; — [0]-koñcā, *m. pl.* Dh. 155. — mogha-[0], *m.* Dh. 260 (*v. h.*) *cp.* parijiṇṇa.

jiṇṇaka, *mfn.* (*sa.* jīrṇaka) old, worn out; *n. pl.* ~āni (pilotikāni) 57,5.

jita, *mfn.* (*pp.* jeti & jināti; = *sa.*) conquered; attā jitaṁ seyyo („one's own self conquered is better") Dh. 104 (where jitaṁ is an old nasalized form instead of *m.* jito, *cp.* Dhpd. (1855) p. 287; *Kuhn,* Beitr. p. 59); *acc. m.* ~aṁ (Māraṁ) Dh. 40; — *subst. n.* victory; Dh. 179; *acc.* ~aṁ, Dh. 105 (*opp.* apajitaṁ).

Jina, *m.* (= *sa.*) 'victor', epithet of the Buddha; [0]-sāsana, *n.* the doctrine of Buddha; *acc.* ~aṁ (navaṅgaṁ) 109,22 (= Satthu-sāsanaṁ, 109,32); *loc.* ~e, 109,6.

jināti (& jeti, *q. v.*) *vb.* (*sa.* √jyā & √ji) to win; to conquer, overcome (*acc.*); *pr. 3. sg.* ~nāti (niccaṁ) 48,9; Dh. 354 (sabbadānaṁ, exceeds); 103,32 (naṁ); — *pot. 3. sg.* jine (kodhaṁ) 44,8; 107,3 = Dh. 103; *aor. 3. sg.* a-jini, Dh. 3; *pass.* jīyati, *v.* parājīyati.

jiyā, *f.* (*sa.* jyā) a bow-string; *acc.* ~aṁ, 92,16.

jivhā, *f.* (*sa.* jihvā) the tongue; 70,31. Dh. 65; *instr.* ~āya, Dh. 360; *loc.* ~āya, 71,9; — [0]-samphassa-viññāṇâyatanaṁ, 72,15, the sense of taste (*cp.* āyatana).

jīyati, *vb.* [1]) = jīrati (*q. v.*) – [2]) *pass.* jināti & jeti, *v.* parājīyati.

jīrati, *vb.* (*sa.* √jṝ, jīryati) to grow old, become decrepit; *pr. 3. sg.* ~ati, Dh. 152; *3. pl.* ~anti, Dh. 151 (are destroyed); *pp.* jiṇṇa (*q. v.*) *cp.* jara, jarā, jajjara.

jīva, *m. n.* (= *sa.*) [1]) *n.* life, soul; *nom.* ~aṁ, 89,28-29 (*opp.* sarīraṁ); *acc.* ~aṁ, 103,17; – yāvajīvaṁ, *adv.* all the life long, 13,7. Dh. 64; – dujjīva, sujīva, *mfn.* (*q. v.*). — [2]) *m.* a living being; [0]-loka, *m.* living beings; ~o, 47,17.

jīvati, *vb.* (*sa.* √jīv) to live; to live by, subsist on (nissāya); *pr. 2. sg.* ~asi, 13,29; *1. sg. med.* (or *pot.*) jīve, 103,34; *1. pl.* ~āma, Dh. 197; *part. m.* jīvaṁ, 103,7; *f. med.* jīvamānā, 31,17; *pot. 3. sg.* jīve, Dh. 110 (*1. sg.* 103,34 ?); *imp. 2. sg.* jīva (ciraṁ) 59,23; jīva bho, 103,7; *fut. 1. sg.* ~issāmi (rājānaṁ nissāya „in the king's service") 24,18; *inf.* ~ituṁ (asakkonta) 39,1; jīvitu-kāma, *mfn.* loving life, *m.* ~o, Dh. 123. *cp.* jīva, jīvikā, jīvita, jīvin.

jīvikā, *f.* (= *sa.*) livelihood; *acc.* ~aṁ (kappesi, kasikammena) 8,15.

jīvita, *n.* (= *sa.*) life; *nom.* ~aṁ, 86,15; *acc.* ~aṁ, 4,33; *abl.* ~ā, 75,3; – °-kkhaya, *m.*, death; *acc.* ~aṁ, 4,22; – *°-dāna, *n.* saving one's life; *acc.* ~aṁ (dassāmi) 12,26; 42,12. – *°-paṭilābha, *m.* rescue, escape, ~o, 42,10; – *°-pariyosāna, *n.* the end of life, *loc.* ~e, 34,29; – *°-saṁkhaya, *m.* = jīvita-kkhaya; *loc.* ~ambhi, Dh. 331.

jīvin, *mfn.* (*e. c.* = *sa.*) living, *v.* dhamma-jīvin.

juti, *f.* (*sa.* dyuti) splendour; – *jutin-dhara, *mfn.* bright, splendid; *m. pl.* ~ā (pakkhi) or *voc.* ~a (?) 11,14; – jutimat, *mfn.* (= *sa.*) id., *m. pl.* ~manto, Dh. 89. *cp.* jotati.

juhati & jūhati, *vb.* (*sa.* √hu, juhoti) to offer; to sacrifice to, worship (*acc.*); *part. gen. m.* jūhato (aggihuttaṁ) 103,8; *pp.* huta (*q. v.*).

jūta, *n.* (& *m.* ?) (*sa.* dyūta) game at dice; *acc.* ~aṁ kīḷati, plays at dice, 19,10. 48,5; – *°-gīta, *n.* a verse sung for luck in game; *acc.* ~aṁ (gāyanto) 48,8; 50,29; – °-maṇḍala, *n.* a game-chamber or dicing-table; *acc.* ~aṁ, 19,13; 50,28.

jūhati, *vb.* = juhati (*q. v.*).

jeṭṭha, *mf(n).* (*sa.* jyeshṭha) first, chief; first born, elder brother or sister; *m. gen.* (*dat.*) ~assa (yakkhassa) 112,13; niyyāmaka-°, 24,10; °-putta, *m. acc.* ~aṁ, 45,3; °-bhātā, 34,33; °-yakkhinī, *f.* 21,21; °-vāṇija, *m. acc.* ~aṁ, ib.

*jeṭṭhaka, *mf(n).* = *prec.*; *m.* niyyāmaka-jeṭṭhako, 24,14; °-kaniṭṭhe, *acc. pl. m.* two brothers, 32,21 (*cp.* kaniṭṭha); °-tāpasa, *m. acc.* ~aṁ, 35,2; °-bhātika, *m. acc.* ~aṁ, 32,31.

Jetavana, *n. nom. pr.* of a garden near Sāvatthī, bought from prince Jeta (a son of Pasenadi) by Anāthapiṇḍika, who built a monastery there and presented it to Buddha (Jāt. I p. 92. II, 216); *acc.* ~aṁ, 86,26; *abl.* ~ā, 87,3; *loc.* ~e, 28,2; – °-âbhimukhī, *f.* 73,13 (*v.* abhimukha); – °-magga, *m.* the road from J., *acc.* ~aṁ, 73,15.

jeti, *vb.* (*sa.* jayati, √ji; *cp.* jināti) to win; to conquer, overcome, exceed (*acc.*); *pr. 3. sg.* jeti (sādhuṁ sādhunā) „pays good with goodness", 44,2; *part. m.* jayaṁ (the victor) Dh. 201; *pot. 3. sg.* jeyya (jeyya-m-attānaṁ, conquers himself) 107,4 = Dh. 103; *ger.* jetvā, 103,32; *pp.* jita (*v. h.*) *cp.* jaya. *m.* ji, *mfn.* & Jina, *m.*

jotati, *vb.* (*sa.* dyotate, √dyut) to shine; *part. m.* ~anto (maṇiratanaṁ viya) 62,30. *cp.* juti, *f.*

Jh.

jhāna, *n.* (*sa.* dhyāna) abstract religious meditation, ecstasy, divided into four stages, through which the mind comes into a state of complete indifference; *nom.* ~aṁ, Dh. 372; *acc.* paṭhama-, dutiya-, tatiya-, catuttha-jjhānaṁ, 80,3-5; *abl.* ~ā, ib.; *loc.* a-parihīna-jjhāne, 45,15; – *jhānâbhiññā, *f.* (*v.* abhiññā); – *°-pasuta, *mfn.* given to meditation, *m. pl.* ~ā, Dh. 181; – *samādhi-jhāna, *n.* the ecstasy of self-concentration, *acc.* ~aṁ, 109,21.

jhāpeti, *vb.* (*caus.* jhāyati[1]) to burn, set on fire (*acc.*); *pr. 2. sg.* ~esi (gāmaṁ) 101,6; *1. sg.* ~emi (nâham khettaṁ ~, I did not set the field on fire) 100,28; *pot. 3. sg.* ~eyya, 101,4; *aor. 3. sg.* ~esi (ayaṁ aggi mā maṁ ~) 51,18; *ger.* ~etvā, 34,6; *pp.* jhāpita, *m.* ~o (gāmo) 101,8.

jhāyati[1], *vb.* (*sa.* kshāyati, √kshai) [1]) to burn (intr.); *pr. 3. sg.* ~ati, 65,28; *3. pl.* ~anti, 65,8; *part. med.* ~māna, *m.* ~o, *n.* ~aṁ, 101,4. — [2]) to waste away, dry up, to be emaciated, perish; *pr. 3. pl.* ~anti, Dh. 155. *cp. Bollensen,* ZDMG, XVIII, 834; *Weber,* Ind. Str. I, 143; *Pischel,* Gramm. § 326. *Fausbøll,* Dhpd. (1855) p. 323 refers to √jyā. *Trenckner* to √dah (*cp.* PM. p. 65,25), but jhāma, *mfn.* (burnt, scorched) must be identical with *sa.* kshāma. — *caus.* jhāpeti (*sa.* kshāpayati) *v. h.*

jhāyati[2], *vb.* (*sa.* dhyāyati, √dhyai) to contemplate, meditate; *part. m.* [a]) *acc.* ~antaṁ, 103,3; 106,13 = Dh. 395; *gen.* ~ato, 66,20; a-jhāyato, Dh. 372; — [b]) *nom.* ~anto, Dh. 27; — *imp. 2. sg.* jhāya, Dh. 371. jhāna, *n.* (*q. v.*) *cp. next.*

jhāyin, *mfn.* (*sa.* dhyāyin) reflecting, thoughtful, absorbed in meditation; *nom. m.* ~ī (brāhmaṇo) 107,24 = Dh. 387; *acc.* ~iṁ, Dh. 386; *gen.* ~ino, Dh. 110; *m. pl.* ~ino, Dh. 23. 276.

Ñ.

ñatta, *n.* (*sa.* jñātra) the intellectual faculty; *nom.* ~aṁ (bālassa jāyati) Dh. 72. (*cp.* Dhpd. (1855) p. 262 = jānanabhāva; it can hardly be *sa.* jñapta, *Max Müller,* SBE. X, p. 22; ñatte (*loc.*) Jāt. V, 26,6 & 486,13 (= santike, near) stands for ñante. *sa.* ny-ante).

ñatva, *ger. v.* jānāti.

ñāṇa, *n.* (*sa.* jñāna) understanding, knowledge, intelligence; *nom.* ~aṁ. 71,15; 79,30 (*opp.* pasāda); 90,35 (assa evaṁ ~ hoti, he reasons that); 96,14; *instr.* ~ena (sekhena) 69,34; jātissara-°, 17,4; — *°-karaṇa, *mfn.*, *°-jāla. *n.* (*q. v.*); — *°-sampanna, *mfn.* full of intelligence, *m.* ~o, 24,14; — a-ññāṇa, *n.* (*v. h.*).

*Ñāṇodaya, *m.* (**sa.* jñāna + udaya) *nom. pr.* of a work by Buddhaghosa; *acc.* ~aṁ (nāma pakaraṇaṁ) 113,22.

ñāta, *mfn* (*pp.* jānāti; *sa.* jñāta) known; *pl. m.* ~ā (guṇā) 41,34; *gen.* ~ānaṁ, 90,33. a-ññāta & a-ññātaka, *mfn.* (*v. h.*).

*ñātaka, *m.* (*fr.* *ñātika, *cp. sa.* jñāti & *next*) a relative, kinsman; *pl.* ~ā, Dh. 43; rāja-°, 76,11. (*cp.* Tr. PM. p. 76,1.)

ñāti, *m.* (*sa.* jñāti) a relative, kinsman; *pl. nom.* ~ī, Dh. 204; *instr.* ~īhi, 11,10; *gen.* ~īnaṁ, Dh. 139. 207; *loc.* ~īsu, Dh. 288; ñāti-mitta-*etc.* 47,31; ñāti-mittā, *m. pl.* kinsmen and friends, Dh. 219; — *°-gharaṁ, „home to her relatives", 62,3; — °-sālohitā, *m. pl.* 92,8 (*v. h.*).

ñāpeti, *vb.* (*caus.* jānāti, *sa.* jñāpayati) to make known, explain; *part. m.* ~ento (iti ~) 9,30. *cp.* jānāpeti.

ñāya, *m.* (*sa.* nyāya) [1]) method; [2]) right manner, fitness; the right path (= ariyo aṭṭhaṅgiko maggo. 67,3); *gen.* ~assa (adhigamāya) 90,18 (*cp.* Tr. PM. 58,15).

ñāyati, *vb.* (*pass.* jānāti) to be called, named; *pr. 3. sg.* ~ati (kathaṁ bhadanto ~) 96,29; *1. sg.* ~āmi, (Ñāgaseno ti ~) 96,30.

ñeva, *indecl.* (after a nasal → yeva), *v.* eva[3]).

°-ññū, *mfn.* (*e. c.*, *sa.* jña) knowing; *v.* a-kataññū, mattaññū; *cp.* viññū.

Ṭh.

ṭhatvā, *ger.*, *v.* tiṭṭhati.

ṭhapāpeti, *vb.* (*caus. II.* tiṭṭhati) to cause to stand, to cause to be placed; *ger.* ~etvā (matamanussaṁ ujukaṁ, setting the dead body upright) 41,17; 102,34.

ṭhapita, *mfn.* (*pp.* ṭhapeti; *cp. sa.* sthāpita) placed; left at one's disposal, prepared for; mukhe ṭhapita-mattā (yāgu, as soon as it had come into her mouth) 57,22 (*cp.* matta[2]); °-vāsita-udakaṁ, 41,2; like ṭhita this word is often combined with a preceeding *ger.* : saṁharitvā ṭhapite (sāṭake, *acc. m. pl.*, the clothes that were lying folded up) 41,4.

ṭhapeti, *vb.* (*caus.* tiṭṭhati; *sa.* sthāpayati) 'to cause to stand', to place, set, lay (*acc. & loc.*); to fix, make firm (*acc.*); to appoint (to any office, *loc.*); to place aside, save, except (*acc.*); *pr. 2. sg.* kiṁ ṭhapesi (why do you except her?) 50,31; *2. pl.* ~etha, 1,26; — *imp. 2. sg.* ~ehi, 44,26; — *aor. 3. sg.* ~esi, 5,17. 75,8; *3. pl.* ~esuṁ, 16,27; — *inf.* ~etuṁ (nīca-ṭhāniyaṁ ucce ṭhāne) 76,11; — *ger.* ~etvā, [1]) 6,27. 9,10 (te putta-ṭṭhāne); 13,19; (pitu yāguṁ ~, having saved a portion for her father) 56,31; 57,33. 65,30-31; 87,27 (laid aside); (cittam idaṁ ~, making firm) Dh. 40; a-ṭhapetvā (hatthe) 56,27; — [2]) used like a *prp. w. acc.* (before or after) = except, but; ekam eva vaddhaṁ ~, 12,20; ~ maṁ (except me) 27,15; ~ mama māṇavikaṁ, 48,24; tumhe ~, 51,9; Sāvatthi-vāsino ~, 73,32; — *grd.* [a]) ṭhapetabba, °-yuttakaṁ (*acc. m.*, rāja-ṭṭhāne) 11,1; — [b]) ṭhapanīyaṁ (pañhaṁ, *acc. m.*, a question not to be asked) 91,31; — *pp.* ṭhapita (*q. v.*) *cp.* thapāpeti.

ṭhassati, *fut.*, *v.* tiṭṭhati.

ṭhahati & ṭhāti, *vb.* = tiṭṭhati; *v.* uṭṭhahati, adhiṭṭhāti.

ṭhāna, *n.* (*sa.* sthāna) [1]) place, spot, locality, dwelling-place; *nom.* ~aṁ, 25,7; *abl.* ~ā, 104,4; *loc.* ~e, 17,24; cinna-ṭṭhāne, 1,14 (*v. h.*); phāsuka-°, 35,26; a-vijjamāna-°, 18,15 (*v.* vijjati) *loc. pl.* saka-saka-ṭṭhānesu. 22,9; pañcasu ~esu, 60,26; — apagata-°, 91,29 (*q. v.*); — arañña-°, 32,14; — gata-°, gata-gata-°, gahana-° (*q. v.*) — chinna-° (= vivara) 91,30; — dhamma-gaṇḍika-°, 6,25 (*v.* gaṇḍikā); — nivesana-°, 2,15; — purāṇa-gāma-°, 35,23 (*v.* gāma); — yujjhana-°, 29,24; — vasana-°, 2,24. 6,10. — [2]) place or room for; rathassa ukkamana-ṭṭhānaṁ, 43,19. — [3]) space, extent; *acc.* ~aṁ (yojanamattaṁ) 6,9; (aṭṭhū-sabhamattaṁ) 27,27. — [4]) case, circumstance, point, occasion; *loc. pl.* catūsu ~esu, 86,32. — [5]) state, condition (*e. c.* = bhāva); *acc.* ~aṁ, Dh. 137; *acc. pl.* ~āni (cattāri) Dh. 309; — āgata-ṭṭhānaṁ vā gata-ṭṭhānam vā (her coming or going) 19,18; — *loc.* (*e. c.*) = instead of : putta-ṭṭhāne, 9,9. — [6]) position, office, rank; *loc.* rāja-ṭṭhāne, 11,1; ucce ṭhāne, 76,11 (*cp.* nīca-ṭhāniya, *mfn.*). — [7]) cause, object, thing, means (*e. c.* = things that serve to or cause); *instr. pl.* tīhi ṭhānehi, Dh. 224. 391; °-pamāda-ṭṭhānā, *abl.* (veramaṇī, which cause indifference) 81,23; °-vibhūsana-ṭṭhānā (*id.* which serve to decoration *etc.*) 81,25. — a-ṭṭhāna, *n.* (*q. v.*) *cp. next.*

ṭhāniya (or ṭhānīya) *mfn.* (*sa.* sthānika & sthānīya) *e. c.* = having a certain position; *v.* nīca-ṭhāniya.

*ṭhānuppatti(ka), *mfn.* (*fr.* ṭhāna + uppatti) 'arisen on the spot', immediate; (or : resulting from one's office (ɔ: practice or competence?)); *instr. f.* ~iyā (medhāya samannāgato, comm. on 'medhāvī') 91,27. *cp.* Jāt. VI, 304,16 & 308,23.

ṭhita, *mfn.* (*pp.* tiṭṭhati; *sa.* sthita) standing; *m.* ~o (dīpake) 2,32; (koṭiyaṁ, *q. v.*) 17,8; kimatthaṁ ~o'si, why do you stand there? 15,11; *acc.* ~aṁ, 65,19; *loc.* ~e (saraṁ nissāya) 3,31; *acc. m. pl.* ~e (mige) 6,8; often combined with a preceeding *ger.* (*cp.* ṭhapita) : nahātvā ~assa, *gen. m. sg.* (when he had finished his bathing) 41,8; nivāsetvā ~, 41,4 *etc.*; also *comp. w.* kāle, khaṇe : 41,7-14; 87,35; dārakaṁ gahetvā ~ā, *f.* (she who has taken the child) 59,14; ~puriso, 86,21 (like a man who, having seen a snake from afar, has cast it away by means of a stick). — *°-citta, *mfn.* whose mind is firm or constant, *gen. m.* ~assa, 80,32; — paṭhavi-°, yattha-°, *mfn.* (*q. v.*).

*ṭhitaka, *mfn.* (= *prec.*) standing; *m.* ~o (pāde pasāretvā) 62,28; 65,31.

ṭhiti, *f.* (*sa.* sthiti), 'standing, remaining'; continuance, steadfastness; Dh. 147.

*ṭhitika, *mfn.* (*e. c.*, *fr. prec.*) standing, remaining, lasting; existing or living by, depending on; *v.* āhāra-°.

°-ṭṭha, *mfn.* (*e. c.* = *sa.* stha) standing; *v.* gahaṭṭha, dhamma-°, nāva-°, pabbata-°, bhaya-°, samīpa-°. *cp.* kappaṭṭhiya.

Ḍ.

ḍayhati, *vb.*, *pass.* ḍahati (*q. v.*).

ḍasati, *vb.* (*sa.* daçati, √daṁç) to bite; *part. acc. m.* (*med.*) ~mānaṁ (gīvāya) 40,18; *inf.* ~ituṁ, 40,17; *ger.* ~itvā, 4,28; 14,27 (valliyaṁ); 35,24 (maṇikkhandhaṁ mukhena). *cp.* saṇḍāsa.

ḍahati, *vb.* (*sa.* dahati, √dah) to burn (*trans.*); *pr. 3. sg.* ~ati (agārāni) Dh. 140; *part. nom. m.* ḍahaṁ, Dh. 31; *nom. n.* ~antaṁ (pāpaṁ kammaṁ) 106,22 = Dh. 71; *pot. 3. sg.* ~eyya (khettaṁ) 100,26; *pp.* daḍḍha (always spelt with initial 'd', which occurs also in the other forms) *v.* aggi-daḍḍha; *pass.* ḍayhati (*sa.* dahyate & ~ti); *part. m.* ~māno, Dh. 371. *cp. next.* (*Pischel*, Gr. § 222.)

ḍāha, *m.* (*sa.* dāha) burning, heat; *v.* anto-ḍāha.

T.

taṁ[1], *pron. demonstr.* (*sa.* tad). *n.* taṁ, 13,29. 22,31 *etc.*; by sandhi: tam, 26,16 (tam pi); 97,29 (tam ahaṁ); tan t'āhaṁ, 85,25; taṅ ñeva, 5,10; the older form tad is also to be found before vowels: tad avasari, 81,9; tad eva, 91,10; tad abhinandituṁ, 97,5; tad ajj'ahaṁ (cittaṁ) Dh. 326, and in some *comp.* (*v. below*; *cp.* takkara); — *m.* so or sa: 1,18. 2,4. 7,9 (sv-āhaṁ = so ahaṁ); 106,7. 107,4. 114,8 *etc.*; — *f.* sā: 2,27 *etc.*; — except the *nom. sg.* the declension is a regular pron. inflexion of the base ta-: *acc. m.* taṁ, 1,8. 5,1; *f.* taṁ, 58,17; — *instr. m. n.* tena, 1,9. 2,24 (ten'eva); 50,1; *f.* tāya, 19,19; — *gen.* (*dat.*) *m. n.* tassa, 1,6-11 *etc.*; *f.* tassā, 2,19. 7,10 *etc.*; — *abl. m. n.* tasmā, 17,11; tamhā, 14,4. 108,2; — *loc. m. n.* tasmiṁ, 2,22 *etc.*; tamhi, Dh. 117; — *plur. m. nom. acc.* te, 3,24. 21,30 *etc.*; *f. nom. acc.* tā, 20,33. 59,3-4; — *instr. m. n.* tehi, 25,28; *f.* tāhi, 21,6; — *gen. m. n.* tesaṁ, 4,17 *etc.* Dh. 4 (tes'); *f.* tāsaṁ, 21,17; — *loc. m. n.* tesu, 14,21; *f.* tāsu, 51,4. — [1]) = it, that, this; *m.* he; *f.* she; (*subst.* & *adj.*): 25,27. 29,27. 58,17 *etc.* — [2]) *corresponding w. prec. pron. rel.* (*cp.* yaṁ): 68,23 (yā . . . taṁ); 84,7-8 (yasmiṁ . . . so); 99,30; 107,4; and sometimes *combined w. pron. rel.* in the sense of a *pron. indef.* = whichsoever, whatsoever; *n.* yan taṁ, Dh. 42 (quicquid); *instr.* yena tena upāyena, 1,9; *pl. m.* ye te manussā, 76,30. — [3]) *repeated*: *acc. m.* taṁ taṁ (bhaccaṁ, each) 112,23; *loc. m. pl.* tesu tesu (kathentesu, all of them constantly) 49,9; taṁ jīvaṁ taṁ sarīraṁ (= the same, *opp.* aññaṁ . . . aññaṁ) 89,28. — [4]) emphatically, [a]) *before subst. or nom. pr.*: tassa sā bhariyā, 2,27; ayaṁ kho sā majjhimā paṭipadā, 67,5; so Kassapo, 109,6; — [b]) *before pron. 1. pers.*: sv'āhaṁ, 7,9; *acc.* taṁ maṁ, 103,2; *gen.* tassa me, 103,23; — [c]) *before pron. 2. pers.*: tassa te, 97,34; *cp.* so karohi, Dh. 236. — [5]) *pleonastically*: *m. pl.* te (pamattā) 77,5 (*or corr. w. a prec.* ye that has dropped). — [6]) *several cases are used adverbially*: taṁ (*acc. n.*), tena (*instr. n.*), tasmā (*abl. n.*) *v. separately.* — [7]) *comp. v.* tad-, takkara, taṁ-nāmaka.

taṁ [2], *adv.* (by sandhi tad = taṁ [1], *acc. n.*) [1]) = there, to that place: tad avasari (*corr. w.* yena = where) 77,19. 81,9. — [2]) = now, then, in that case; thereafter; tad eva (*corr. w.* yad eva) 91,10; taṁ kiṁ maññasi, 94,29. 99,4; tam ahaṁ, 97,29. 98,10; tam enaṁ, 47,21. 100,13. — [3]) therefore; tañ c'āyaṁ, 96,11.

taṁ [3], *pron. 2. pers. acc.*; *v.* tvaṁ.

takka, *m.* (*sa.* tarka) reasoning, speculation; *v.* a-takkāvacara, *mfn.*

takkara, *mfn.* (*sa.* tat-kara) doing that; *m.* ~o (naro) Dh. 19.

Takkasilā, *f.* (*sa.* Takshaçilā) *nom. pr.* of a city in the Gandhāra-country (*Τάξιλα* in Panjab); *acc.* ~aṁ. 42,25; *loc.* ~āya, 45,26.

takkola(ka), *n.* (*sa.* kakkola, *cp.* takkola) a sort of perfume, Bdellium; tambūla-takkolakâdīni, 49,16.

tagara, *n.* (= *sa.*) a kind of tree and a sort of perfume or fragrant powder prepared from it; ~aṁ, Dh. 55; — *⁰-candanin, *mfn.* prepared from Tagara and Candana (*q. v.*); *m.* ~ī (gandho) Dh. 56; — *⁰-mallikā, Tagara and Mallikā (*q. v.*) Dh. 54 (*cp.* SBE. X p. 18).

taca & tacas, *m. & n.* (*sa.* tvac. tvacā, *f.* & tvaca (*comp.* -tvacas) *n.*) [1]) skin; *nom.* ~o, 82,2 = 97,20. [2]) bark; *⁰-papaṭikā, *pl. f.* „loose shreds of bark", 95,22; apagata-⁰, *mfn.* free from that, *m.* ~o (sālarukkho) 95,23-24.

tacchaka, *m.* (*sa.* takshaka) a carpenter; *pl.* ~ā, 106,28 — Dh. 80.

tajjita, *mfn.* (*sa.* tarjita, *pp.* tajjeti) frightened; *m. pl.* ~ā (maraṇa-bhayena, struck with horror of death) 6,21; maraṇa-bhaya-tajjito, *m.* 5,11; bhaya-tajjitā, *m. pl.* („driven by fear") Dh. 188.

tajjeti, *vb.* (*sa.* tarjayati, √tarj) to threaten, frighten, scare; *ger.* ~etvā (niraya-bhayena) 17,30.

taṭa, *m.* (= *sa.*) a shore, bank, slope; precipice; chinna-⁰, a sheer precipice; 27,8.

taṇḍula, *m.* (= *sa.*) rice-grain; *acc.* ~aṁ, 57,18; *pl.* ~ā, 16,1; *acc. pl.* ~e, 33,25. 57,20; *instr. pl.* mūla-taṇḍulehi, the most coarse-grained rice, 57,20; majjhima-⁰, the middle-sort of the rice, ib., *opp.* kaṇikā, the finest grains or flour, 57,21; — taṇḍulâdi, *adj. n.* (nāvaṭṭhaṁ) consisting of rice *etc.* 111,31; tila-taṇḍulâdayo, 15,6.

taṇhā, *f.* (rarely tasiṇā, *sa.* tṛshṇā) 'thirst', desire, craving; ~ā (vedanā-paccayā, originating from vedanā and causing upādāna, *q. v.*) 67,13; 107,29; Dh. 180; catutthī (senā Mārassa) 103,26; *acc.* ~aṁ, 108,1; *gen.* ~āya, 67,15. 108,4; *abl.* ~āya, Dh. 216; *gen. pl.* ~ānaṁ (khayaṁ) desires, Dh. 154; — *⁰-ânusaya, *m.* the attachment to desires, *loc.* ~e, Dh. 338; — taṇhakkhaya, *m.* (taṇhā + khaya) destruction of desire, *loc.* ~e, Dh. 353; ~rata, *mfn.* delighting in that, *m.* ~o, Dh. 187; — *⁰-bhava-, Dh. 416 (*cp.* kāmā-bhava); — *⁰-vasika, *mfn.* being in the power of desires, enslaved by desire, *m.* ~o, 23,20; — *⁰-vagga, *m.* the XXIVth chapter of Dh.; — kāma-⁰, bhava-⁰, vibhava-taṇhā, *f.* 67,14; hetu-⁰, *f.* 108,13 (*v. h.*); — vīta-taṇha, *mfn.* who is without desire, Dh. 351–52 (*m.* ~o). *cp.* pipāsā.

tatiya, *mfn.* (*sa.* tṛtīya) the third; *acc. f.* ~aṁ, 11,15; Dh. 309 (tatīyaṁ); *loc. m.* ~e (vāre, for the third time) 114,17; *acc. n. adv.* ~aṁ, thirdly, for the third time, 74,25. 79,22 (~am pi kho); yāva-tatiyaṁ, up to the third time, 3,7 (*cp.* 102,26); — ⁰-jjhāna, *n.* 80,4 (*v.* jhāna); — ⁰-sāvanā, *f.* (*v. h.*) *cp.* aḍḍhatiya, aḍḍhateyya, & ti [2] (tayo, tīṇi).

tato, *adv.* (*sa.* tatas) [1]) thence, from that place; 2,23. 3,21; ~ yeva, from the same source, 101,13. — [2]) thereupon, then, afterwards, further; 6,18 (~ paṭṭhāya, *q. v.*); 63,14 (~ va);

101,16. 103,16; Dh. 42 (pāpiyo ~); tato tato (*corr. w.* yato yato, as soon as, the more . . . the more) Dh. 390. — [3]) for that reason; 112,30 (*corr. w.* yato).

tatoparaṁ, *adv.* (*sa.* tataḥparaṁ & tato 'paraṁ) then, afterwards, immediately after; 55,15 (*cp.* itoparaṁ, para & apara).

tatta, *mfn.* (*sa.* tapta; *pp.* tapati) heated, hot, red-hot; *m.* ~o (ayoguḷo) 107,1 — Dh. 308; *loc. f.* ~āya (bhūmiyā) 97,34; — °-kapāla, *n.* (*v. h.*).

tattato, *adv.* (*sa.* tattvatas, *fr.* tattva) according to the truth, really, accurately; ~ ajānitvā, „not knowing the truth", 53,1.

tattha (& tatra, *v. next*) *adv.* (*sa.* tatra) [1]) there, on that (this) place; 2,23-25, *etc.*; 108,27 (tatth'); tatth'eva, [a]) on the same place, 3,6. 12,24, [b]) on that very spot, straightway, 72,25. 104,18; — tattha tattha, here and there, 21,3; yattha . . . tattha. 72,7-8; tattha idhâpi, both there and here, 112,15; — very frequently used at the begin of commentaries: 85,6-17-27. — [2]) there, to that place; 1,15 (~ gantvā) 1,17. 2,1; 111,14; tatth'-eva, to the same place, 58,15; tattha tatth'eva (bhijjissāma, in all directions) 11,8. — [3]) then, therefore, thence; Dh. 249; 112,16 (tattha saddo'yaṁ).

tatra, *adv.* (— *prec.*) 110,21; tatr'assa, 73,23. 90,32; tatrâpi, 43,8-9; tatrâyaṁ, 82,17; tatra kho, 66,21. 70,23; — tatra-tatrâbhinandin, *mfn.* 67,13 (*v.* abhinandin).

tathā, *adv.* (— *sa.*) so, thus; tath'eva, in the same way, likewise, 2,25. 39,5. 105,28; 44,20 (id. without eva); tathā . . . c'eva . . . ca, 10,30; tathā . . . ca . . . na, nor, 113,27; often *corr. w.* yathā. so . . . that, 12,2-6; Dh. 282; yathā . . . tath'eva. as . . . so also, 5,8; *corr. w.* yena, so . . . that, 77,6. *comp.*, *v. next.*

Tathā-gata, *m.* (— *sa.*) 'who comes and goes in the same way' [as the Buddhas], probably orig. a designation of an Arhat, afterwards *esp.* of Gotama Buddha (as Sammāsambuddha, while still living as a human being, preaching the truth), used in the holy scriptures when Buddha is represented as speaking of himself in the third person; hence *pl.* ~ā appellatively = the Buddhas (*cp.* the most important note by *Rhys Davids & Oldenberg*, SBE. XIII, p. 82; *E. Sénart*, JRAS. 1898 p. 865; *R. Chalmers*, ib. p. 103; *Böhtlingk*, Ber. d. Sächs. Ges. 1898 p. 78; Dhammasaṅgaṇi, transl. p. 294). — *nom.* ~o, 80,25. 94,10; hoti ~o parammaraṇā, does T. exist after death? 89,29; rūpasaṁkhāvimutto T-o, gambhīro appameyyo duppariyogāho seyyathā pi mahāsamuddo, 95,12; *acc.* ~aṁ, 76,27; *instr.* ~ena, 66,29. 94,8; *gen:* ~assa, 76,4. 94,7. 110,26; *pl.* ~ā (anupakkamena ~ parinibbāyanti) 76,28; aggadhammā ~ā, 109,28 (*v. h.*, otherwise *Geiger*, Dīpavaṁsa u. Mahāvaṁsa, 1905, p. 5); akkhātāro ~ā, Dh. 276 (the T.s are only preachers); nippapañcā ~ā, Dh. 254 („free from vanity").

tathā-bhāva, *m.* (= *sa.*) the being so; *acc.* ~aṁ (ñatvā) 3,20.

tathā-rūpa, *mfn.* (= *sa.*) such, like that; pregnantly = so great, important, *etc.*; *acc. m.* ~aṁ, 68,35 (*w. foll.* yathā); *gen. m.* ~assa, Dh. 105; *gen. f.* ~āya (parisāya) 87,31. (*cp.* eva-rūpa).

tad-, *pron. demonstr. n.*, used by sandhi instead of taṁ (*v.* taṁ [1-2]) & *comp.* (*v.* tad-anurūpa, tad-uṭṭhāya, tad-ūpika).

***tad-anurūpa**, *mfn.* conformable, suitable to that; *acc. n.* ~aṁ (vyañjanaṁ) 57,21.

tadā, *adv.* (= *sa.*) at that time, then; 1,5; 29,18. 30,24 (*cp.* tena samayena. 32,6); tadāsi, 81,3 (= tadā āsi).

tad-uṭṭhāya, (*fr. ger.* uṭṭhahati) = having sprung from that, 106,19 = Dh. 240; tad- stands possibly for tat' (Comm. tato uṭṭhahitvā, Dhpd. (1855) p. 370).

*tad-ūpika (or °-ūpiya) *mfn.* (*fr.* tad- + opāyika = *sa.* aupāyika) conformable, suitable to that, answering; *f.* ~ā (paññā) 2,12. (*Trenckner*, PM. p. 78, takes it = *sa.* *tadopya, *fr.* ā + √vap).

tanaya, *m.* (= *sa.*) a son; *nom.* rāja-tanayo, 112,4 (a prince).

tanu, *mfn.* (= *sa.*) thin, little, small; *°-bhūta, *mfn.* id.; °-soka, *mfn.* whose mind has been relieved, light-hearted, comforted, *m.* ~o, 89,15. *cp.* su-tanu.

tanuka, *mfn.* (= *sa.*) = *prec.*; *m.* ~o (tanuk' ettha vipassati, few only) 88,29 = Dh. 174; 88,32 (= na bahujano).

tanti, *f.* (= *sa.*) a string (of a lute); *°-ssara, *m.* the sound of the strings; *instr.* ~ena, 19,32 (*cp.* sara[3]).

tantu(ka), *m.* (= *sa.*) a thread; tasara-° (*q. v.*, *cp.* corrections).

tandita, *mfn.* (*sa.* tandrita; *fr.* tandi, drowsiness, lassitude, sloth, = *sa.* tandrā & tandrī) only *comp. w.* the negative prefix a- (*v. h.*) *cp.* dandha.

taṁ-nāmika, *mfn.* (*sa.* tan-nāmika) named thus; *f.* ~ikā, 56,11.

tapa, *m.* & tapas, *n.* (*sa.* tapas, *n.*) [1]) religious austerities, penance, devotion; *nom.* ~o (sukho) Dh. 194; ~o (paramaṁ) Dh. 184. – [2]) virtue, chastity; ~o (bhinno, māṇavikāya) 50,32; *gen.* ~assa, 50,29. *cp.* tāpasa, tāpasī.

tapati, *vb.* (*sa.* √tap) [1]) to shine (as the sun), to be bright; *pr. 3. sg.* ~ati. 107,23-24 = Dh. 387. — [2]) to burn = to cause pain or repentance; pacchā tapati dukkataṁ, Dh. 314. – *pp.* tatta, *pass.* tappati (*q. v.*) *cp.* tapa *etc.*

tappati, *vb.* [1]) (*pass.* tapati; *sa.* tapyate) to be burnt, tormented; to suffer; *pr. 3. sg.* ~ati, Dh. 17. 136 (sehi kammehi dummedho). – [2]) (*sa.* √tṛp) to be satisfied or weary; *pp.* titta (*v. h.*, *cp.* titti.)

tamba, *mfn.* (*sa.* tāmra) red, copper-coloured; °-bhūmi-, 112,29; — tamba-paṇṇī, 112,29, is probably a pun (= tamba-pāṇayo, *adj. m. pl.* with red hands, *cp.* pāṇi) in order to make the etymology of the *nom. pr.* Tambapaṇṇī to agree with the tale.

Tamba, *m. nom. pr.* of a king; *voc.* ~a, 20,17; ~rājā, 19,6; *instr.* ~rājena, 19,10.

Tambapaṇṇī, *f.* (*sa.* Tāmraparṇī) *nom. pr.* of a city in Ceylon and of the island itself, 112,30; *acc.* ~iṁ = °-nagaraṁ, 112,24-25; — °i-dīpa, *m.* the island C., *loc.* ~e. 20,32; — °i-sara, *m. n.* a lake in C., *loc.* ~e, 21,36. *cp.* Laṅkā.

tambūla, *n.* (*sa.* tāmbūla) betel or betel-leaves (to chew after the meal); *acc.* ~aṁ, 41,14; °-takkolakâdīni, 49,16; – *°-pasibbaka, *m.* a betel-sack; *loc.* ~e, 57,33.

taya, *n.* (*sa.* traya) a triad; *e. c.* -ttaya, *v.* Piṭaka-°, potthaka-°, Saṅgīti-°.

tayo, *num. mf.* (*sa.* trayas) *v.* ti[2].

tarati, *vb.* [1]) (*sa.* √tṝ, tarati) to cross over (*acc.*); *aor. 2. sg.* atari (samuddaṁ) 20,19; *pp.* tiṇṇa (*q. v.*) *cp.* su-duttara, *mfn.* — [2]) (*sa.* √tvar) to make haste; *v.* abhi-ttharati.

tarahi, *adv.* (*sa.* tarhi) then, at that time; 74,31; *cp.* carahi & etarahi.

taruṇa, *mfn.* (= *sa.*) young, tender; new, fresh; *m.* ~o, 46,32. 99,4; *f.* ~ī (dārikā) 101,19; taruṇakāle yeva, while (they were) yet quite young, 9,8; °-dabba-tiṇa, *n.* young Kusa-grass, 16,17.

'taro, *v.* itara.

tala, *n.* (= *sa.*) level, surface, bottom; side, end, flat, roof *etc.*; *loc.* imasmiṁ ~e, on this side, 35,13; paṭhavī-°, 28,7; pāsāṇa-°, 10,7; bheri-°, 35,21; Manosilā-°, 61,11; mahī-°, 113,21; heṭṭhima-°, on the lowest level, 59,27; — *instr.* khagga-talena, with the flat of the sword, 41,26; —

abl. pāsāda-talato, down from the palace, 65,34; — pāsādavara-tala-, the roof of the palace, 64,12; — mahā-tala. *n.* (*v. h.*).

tasa, *mfn.* (*sa.* trasa) moving, trembling; feeble; *loc. pl.* ~esu (bhūtesu) Dh. 405 (*opp.* thāvara).

tasati, *vb.* (*sa.* √tras) to tremble, to be afraid of (*gen.*); *pr. 3. sg.* ~anti (daṇḍassa) Dh. 129; tasa, *mfn.* (*q.v.*).

tasara, *m.* (*sa. id.* & trasara) a shuttle; *acc.* ~aṁ (vaḍḍhetvā) 87,12; — *⁰-tantuka, *m.* 87,11 (*v.* corrections); — *⁰-pacchi, *f.* a basket or box with a shuttle, 89,5; *acc.* ~iṁ, 87,27. 89,3.

tasiṇā, *f.* (= taṇhā, *q. v.*; *sa.* tṛshṇā) *acc.* ~aṁ, Dh. 343; *instr.* ~āya, ib.

tasita, *mfn.* (*pp.* tasati; *sa.* trasta) trembling, frightened; *m. pl.* bhīta-tasitā, 27,5.

tasmā, *adv.* (*abl. n. pron.* taṁ; *sa.* tasmāt) on that account, therefore; 12,35. 86,22. 110,25. Dh. 211 *etc.*; ~hi, Dh. 356; — tasmā ti ha, 'therefore just so', accordingly (pointing to the following) 93,2.

***tahiṁ** (or *tahaṁ), *adv.* (formed after the analogy of kuhiṁ, kahaṁ) = there, thither; 112,25 (~ vasi); 114,18 (~ saṇṭhapesuṁ).

tāṇa, *n.* (*sa.* trāṇa) protection; *dat.* ~āya (na santi puttā, „are no help") Dh. 288.

***tāṇatā**, *f.* (*fr.* tāṇa *w. suff.* -tā) protection; Dh. 288.

tāta, *m.* (= *sa.*) a father; *voc.* tāta & *pl.* tātā is very frequently used as a term of affection to one or more persons (*esp.* to younger or inferior persons) — friend, my dear *etc.*; tāta, 9,21. 15,32. 69,31 (tāta Yasa); to two persons: 9,12; — tātā, 16,24. 25,18. 38,33.

tādi, *adj. m.* (*sa.* tādṛç) such, like that; often pregnantly said of Buddha's holy disciples ('like him') and even of the Buddha himself; *gen. m.* ~ino, Dh. 94. 95. 96; 80,32.

tādisa, *mfn.* (*sa.* tādṛça) such, like that; *m.* ~o, 7,12. 55,1; 85,16 (vaṇṇo); *acc.* ~aṁ, Dh. 76. 208; *acc. m. pl.* ~e, Dh. 196. *cp.* etādisa.

tāpasa, *m.* (= *sa.*) a hermit, ascetic; ~o, 35,6; paṇḍuroga-⁰, 35,4 (*v. h.*); *acc.* jeṭṭhaka-tāpasaṁ, 35,2; *gen.* ~assa, 36,7.

tāpasī, *f.* (= *sa.*) a female ascetic; 111,6; *acc.* ~iṁ, 111,7.

tāla, *m.* (= *sa.*) the Palmyra or fan-palm; ⁰-vaṇṭa, *n.* (*sa.* ⁰-vṛṇta), the leaf of P. used as a fan; *loc. pl.* ~esu (maṇi-, „upon jewelled fans") 41,6; — ⁰-vana, *n.* (= *sa.*) a grove of P.-trees; *acc.* ~aṁ, 60,7; — *tālā-vatthukata, *mfn.* (= tāla + a-vatthu-kata) „pulled out of the ground like a P.", *n.* ~aṁ (rūpaṁ Tathāgatassa) 95,11.

tāḷeti, *vb.* (*sa.* tāḍayati, √taḍ) to beat, strike (*acc.*); *ger.* ~etvā, 61,21.

tāva, *adv.* (before vowels sometimes tāvad-; *sa.* tāvat) ¹) so much (before *adj.*); ~ mahato, 10,14. — ²· ᵃ) so long, until; pāto va ~, until to-morrow, 15,16; ajjâpi ~ na, never before to-day, 10,13; often *corr. w.* yāva: 33,21; 102,3. Dh. 284; na ~, . . . yāva na, not . . . until, 92,2. — ᵇ) meanwhile, 37,22. — ᶜ) now, first (*w. fut.*): vīmaṁsissāmi ~, 3,6. 38,31; 41,2. 65,26; likewise *w. pr. 1. sg.* 55,25. — ᵈ) tāvad-eva, at once, immediately, straightway; 7,5. 23,14. 33,6. 62,19. 64,29. 105,21. — ³) well, indeed, really; well and good, be it then (often *w. imp.* or *fut.*) 7,18-21. 44,6; *w. foll.* paṇa: ahaṁ ~ . . . ayam pana (*quidem*, μέν) 17,10; — yasmā tayā ~ diṭṭhaṁ, tasmā . . 85,31; yakkhinī ~ jānāti, 111,21. — ⁴) *emphatically* in exhortations (*w. imp.*): ehi ~, 9,22; tiṭṭha ~, 11,5; gaccha ~, 19,21; taṁ tāva me detha, 22,31; adhivāsehi ~, 53,25; kathehi ~, 54,32. *cp. next.*

***tāvataka**, *mfn.* (*fr. prec.*) so much; *pl.* so many; *acc. pl. m.* ~e (*corr. w.* yāvatake) 81,18.

tāvatā, *adv.* (= *sa.* tāvatā, *instr.*) ¹) so long; 110,5 (*corr. w.* yāva). —

[2]) on that account, for that reason; 106,5 (na tāvatā, *scil.* yāvatā bhikkhate pare = Dh. 266).

tāvatiṁsa-°, [1]) *num.* (*sa.* trayastriṁçat) 33, only at the beginning of *comp.* = the 33 gods, whose chief is Sakka (while the *num.* 33 always is tettiṁsa); *°-bhavana, *n.* Sakka's devaloka on the mount Sineru (Meru), *loc.* ~e, 59,24; — *°-devaloka-ppamāṇa, *mfn.* „equal in extent to the realm of the Thirty-tree", *n.* ~aṁ, 59,23. — [2]) *mfn.* *id.*, frequently *m. pl.* ~ā (devā). *cp.* *Pischel,* Gr. § 254 & tiṁsa *below.*

ti[1], *indecl.* (*sa.* iti) thus, so; besides ti we also meet with the full form iti which is contracted to -īti with a *prec.* i, 1,16-17, and before a vowel is changed into icc', 4,32; but generally the first i drops by elision, and a *prec.* short vowel (a, u) is lengthened, 1,9-18-19 *etc.*, while *prec.* ṁ is changed into n, 1,8-21. 3,1 *etc.*; instead of the final i we find also y : ty'āha, 111,30 (= c' after *prec.* i : na karomi c'āha, 74,1 = Dh. 306) and even v : tv'eva, 42,24. 60,25, or the i drops before e : t'eva, 32,18. — [1]) The full form iti is used [a]) at the beginning of a sentence = thus, in this manner (as told before) 30,33. 47,23. 88,2. 110,33. 112,11. Dh. 62. 74. 186. 286; diṭṭhaṁ h'etam Tathāgatena : iti rūpaṁ etc., thus (is) form = this is the nature of form, 94,8. — [b]) after evaṁ, 47,26, *cp.* evaṁgotto iti, 92,13. — [c]) after another (i)ti : moghaṁ aññan ti iti puṭṭho (iti perhaps = etc., *cp.* [5]) *below*) 90,4. — [d]) in the apodosis : sace .... icc'etaṁ kusalaṁ, 4,32. — [e]) metri causa like the ordinary ti : 98,30. 111,3. 112,31 (*v. below*). — [2]) ti (iti) is most frequently used by quoting in oratio directa one's words uttered or the contents of one's thoughts, emotions, or judgements, preceeded or followed by a verbum sentiendi et declarandi : 1,8-16 (after āha); 3,5 (after ten'assa etad ahosi); 1,18 (ti sampaṭicchitvā); 1,19 (ti vutte); 1,21 (ti āha); 3,1 (ti cintesi), but also without a such word preceeding or following : 3,6-9-12. 35,29. *etc. etc.* Of such quotations we find often one included within another : ti saññī ahosi, 2,6 *etc.* Verses quoted end always with ti which stands without the metre : 2,13. 3,27 *etc.*, but in poetic style it is often omitted, 103,10 (followed by imā gāthā bhaṇaṁ); 104,16 *etc.* (*cp.* 111,4. 113,17, where iti forms the half of the last foot), and even in prose ti may be omitted by very short sentences (questions and answers) and generally before maññe (*q. v.*) 3,26. 5,7. 35,35 (*cp.* 50,33. Dh. 74). Useful examples illustrative of the use of ti are also found on p. 88. — [3]) ti after single words or names (in *nom.*) : mātā ti, such a thing as a mother, 99,7; pitā ti, 99,8; diṭṭhigatan ti. 94,7; saddo ratho iti. the sound (word) 'ratha', 98,30; satto ti sammuti, the phrase 'a living being' 98,31; Nāgaseno ti, 96,29 *etc.*; bālo ti vuccati, Dh. 63. *cp.* Dh. 218. 257. 367. 370. 388; likewise by glosses in commentaries : 'me' ti mayhaṁ, 85,20; 'tan' ti tasmā, 85,27 *etc.*; *cp.* above under iti [1]). — [4]) ti is sometimes used to connect two sentences (coordinate) = in this way, by means of, for this reason, *etc.* : atth' eko upāyo ti khādāpessāmi taṁ ..., 1,10; abhirūpā ahosīti so tassā varaṁ adāsi, 10,4; puññam me katan ti nandati, 107,27 = Dh. 18; so sīham ādiṇṇavā iti Sīhalo, for that reason (he was called) Sīhala, 112,31. — [5]) = and, and so on (*w. foll.* ādi) : 73,30 (*cp.* ādi [3])); ti anukkamena, and so on by degrees, 34,8; ti iti, 90,1. *v. above* [1, c]). — [6]) ti is sometimes strengthened by a *foll.* eva or evaṁ : 32,18. 42,24. 60,25; 86,17. — [7]) *emphatically* after other *adv.* : kin ti. how? 1,8 (= kiṁ[2]); tasmā ti ha, accordingly, 92,2 (*v.* tasmā). *cp.* *Franke,* ZDMG, vol. 48, p. 87.

ti[2], *num.* (*sa.* tri) three; *n.* tīṇi, *nom.* 21,11. 82,9; *acc.* 28,25 (saraṇāni); 57,28. 86,26; — *m.* tayo. *nom.* 14,9 (sahāyā); 65,11 (bhavā); *acc.* 6,21 (pahāre); — *f.* tisso, *nom.* 82,9 (vedanā); *acc.* 20,31 (gāthā); — *instr.* tīhi, Dh. 224. 391; — *gen.* tiṇṇaṁ, 14,13. 28,26 (ratanānaṁ); Dh. 157; — *loc.* tīsu, 31,16. 114,22. — *comp. v.* ti-kkhattuṁ *etc.*, tīha, te-piṭaka, *etc.*, *cp.* tatiya, taya, tāvatiṁsa (tettiṁsa), tiṁsa, terasa.

tiṁsa (& **tiṁsati**), *num.* (*nom.* tiṁsaṁ or tiṁsā; *sa.* triṁçat) thirty; tiṁsa-yojana-maggaṁ, *acc.* (āgato) 87,19. *cp.* tāvatiṁsa (tettiṁsa), dvattiṁsa & chattiṁsati.

ti-kkhattuṁ, *adv.* (*sa.* tri-kṛtvas) three times; 11,4.

tikhiṇa, *mfn.*, *v.* tiṇha.

ti-gāvuta, *v.* gāvuta.

tiṭṭhati (& ṭhāti, *comp. w. prp.* also ṭhahati; *sa.* tishṭhati, √sthā), to stand; to stay, remain, stop; to be present, be alive; to abide by, acquiesce in, *etc.*; *pr. 3. sg.* ~ati, 102,3 (pāli, is extant); 103,22 (bhiyyo ~, "gets more steadfast"); 110,5. Dh. 340; *2. sg.* ~asi, Dh. 235; *3. pl.* ~anti, 110,4; — *part. med. gen. f.* tiṭṭhamānāya (sākhaṁ gahetvā) 62,20; — *imp. 2. sg.* tiṭṭha, 11,5. 16,13. 111,10; — *pot. 3. sg.* tiṭṭheyya, 98,33; — *fut. 2. pl.* ṭhassatha (mama vinicchaye) 59,6; *1. pl.* ~āma, ib.; — *aor. 3. sg.* [a]) aṭṭhā, 103,11, [b]) aṭṭhāsi, 3,32. 15,10. 26,4. 41,20; pharitvā ~, pervaded, 57,23; *3. pl.* ~aṁsu, 22,7. 87,18; — *ger.* ṭhatvā. 3,6. 8,13 (Bodhisattassa ovāde); 17,33 (id.) 34,29 (yāvatāyukaṁ); 36,20. 46,1. 108,26; — *pp.* ṭhita; *caus.* ṭhapeti & ṭhapāpeti (*v. h.*) *cp.* -ṭṭha, *mfn.*, ṭhāna, *n.*, ṭhiti, *f. etc.*

tiṇa, *n.* (*sa.* tṛṇa) grass, straw (of a thatch); herb, weed; *acc.* ~aṁ (the thatch) 101,4; *gen.* bahu-tiṇassa, 51,33. 52,3; *pl.* ~āni, 15,5; *comp.* tiṇa-⁰, 94,36; tiṇa-dosa, *mfn.* "damaged by weeds", *n. pl.* ~āni (khettāni) Dh. 356; dabba-⁰, nivāpa-⁰, nīlakusa-⁰, rūḷha-⁰ (*v. h.*).

tiṇṇa, *mfn.* (*pp.* tarati, *sa.* tīrṇa) who has crossed, gone through, passed over to, overcome; *m.* ~o ("I have passed over to Nibbāna") 104,30; *⁰-vicikiccha, *mfn.* having overcome uncertainty, *m.* ~o, 69,13; *⁰-soka-pariddava, *mfn.* "who has crossed the flood of sorrow", *acc. m. pl.* ~e, Dh. 195; ogha-⁰ (*q. v.*).

tiṇṇaṁ, *gen. pl.*, *v.* ti[2].

tiṇha, *mfn.* (generally tikhiṇa, *sa.* tīkshṇa) sharp; *instr. m.* ~ena (asinā) 33,17.

titikkhati, *vb.* (*sa.* titikshate, *desid.* √tij) to bear, endure (*acc.*); *pr. 3. sg.* ~ati (ativākyaṁ, akkosaṁ) Dh. 321. 399; *cond. 1. sg.* ~issaṁ (I had to endure) Dh. 320 (*cp.* adhigacchissaṁ, sandhāvissaṁ *etc.*).

titikkhā, *f.* (*sa.* titikshā) endurance, forgiveness, long-suffering; Dh. 184 (*synon.* khanti).

titta, *mfn.* (*pp.* tappati[2]; *sa.* tṛpta) satisfied; *v.* a-titta, *cp.* titti.

tittaka, *mfn.* (*sa.* tiktaka) bitter; *⁰-bhāva. *m.* a bitter flavour, *acc.* ~aṁ, 37,9.

titti, *f.* (*sa.* tṛpti) satisfaction; Dh. 186 (kāmesu).

tittha, *n.* (& rarely *m.*) (*sa.* tīrtha) a landing-place (on the shore of a river), a bathing-place; a ferry or harbour, *metaph.* religious persuasion; *loc.* ~e, on the shore, 28,5. — *pānīya-⁰, a watering-place; *loc.* ~e, 11,28. *cp. next.*

titthiya, *m.* (*sa.* tīrthya & tīrthika) an adherent of another sect, a heretic; *pl.* ~ā, 73,31; *gen.* ~ānaṁ, 19,4. — *añña-⁰, *v. h.* — *titthiyārāma, *m.*, *v.* ārāma.

ti-piṭaka, *n.* (*sa.* tri-piṭaka) 'the three baskets', the three collections of the Buddhist sacred books (*cp.* piṭaka *etc.*). — tepiṭaka, *mfn.* (*v. h.*).

tibba, *mfn.* (*sa.* tīvra) sharp, strong, violent; *⁰-rāga, *mfn.* full of strong passions, *gen. m.* ~assa, Dh. 349.

ti-bhāga, *m.* (*sa.* tri-bhāga) the third part; ~o, 90,28.

***ti-maṇḍala**, *n.* (*sa.* *tri-maṇḍala) 'the three circles', *viz.* the navel and the two knees; *acc.* ~aṁ, 82,27 (*cp.* SBE. XIII, 155).

timīra. *m.* (= *sa.*) name of a tree; *gen. pl.* ~ānaṁ (gandho) 20,16.

***ti-yojana-satika**, *mfn.* (*sa.* *tri-yojana-çataka) 300 yojanas long (*cp.* yojana); *gen. n.* ~assa (rajjassa) 43,31.

tila, *m.* (= *sa.*) sesame, sesame seed; *pl.* ~ā (tatta-kapāle pakkhitta-°) 11,7; °-taṇḍulâdayo, 15,6. *cp.* tela.

tisso, **tīṇi**, *v.* ti[2].

tīra, *n.* (= *sa.*) a shore, bank; *acc.* ~aṁ, Dh. 85 (anudhāvati, "runs up and down the shore", *i. e.* without reaching the other shore (Nibbāna)); 4,20 (sara-°); 21,17 (samudda-°); 28,4 (Aciravatī-°); *loc.* ~e, 66,8; 1,12 (Gaṅgā-°); 2,19 (nadī-°); 3,21 (para-°, on the opposite bank); *abl.* orimatīrato (*v. h.*) *cp.* anutīre.

tīha, *n.* (*sa.* tryaha) three days; dvīha-tīhaṁ, two or three days, 36,6 (*cp.* aha).

tīhi, *instr.*, *v.* ti[2].

tuccha, *mfn.* (= *sa.*) empty; °-pātim (*acc.*) the empty bowl, 56,27.

tuṭṭha, *mfn.* (*pp.* tussati; *sa.* tushṭa) pleased, satisfied; *m.* ~o, 24,28; *°-citta, *mfn.* id.; *m.* ~o, 32,1; *pl.* ~ā, 41,21; — *°-mānasa, *mfn.* id.; *m.* ~o, 65,23; *f.* ~ā, 87,7; — *°-haṭṭha, *mfn.* pleased and rejoicing, *m.* ~o (saṁgho), 114,23.

tuṭṭhi, *f.* (*sa.* tushṭi) joy, enjoyment; *nom.* tuṭṭhī, Dh. 331; *acc.* ~iṁ ("the glad news") 64,6; *instr.* ati-tuṭṭhiyā ("by his extreme joy") 10,13.

tuṇḍa, *n.* (= *sa.*) a beak; *instr.* ~ena, 4,21. — *tuṇḍaka, *n.* (?) id.; mukha-°, 4,8. 18,7.

tuṇhī, *indecl.* (*sa.* tūshṇīm) silently; ~ ahosi (Bhagavā, remained silent) 90,23; ~ ahesuṁ, 79,21; by sandhi: tuṇhīm āsīnaṁ, Dh. 227; — *comp.* tuṇhī-bhāva, *m.* the being silent; *instr.* ~ena (adhivāsesi Bhagavā) 70,11 = 77,29; — tuṇhī-bhūta, *mfn.* silent; *m.* ~o (nisīdi) 87,20; *acc.* ~aṁ, 87,21.

tudati, *vb.* (*sa.* √tud) to strike, torment; *pr. 3. pl.* ~anti (maṁ, kāmā) 20,17; *pp. v. next.*

tunna, *mfn.* (*pp.* tudati) struck, hurt; *gen. pl.* vyādhi-maraṇa-tunnānaṁ, suffering from disease and death, 108,22.

***tunna-kamma**, *n.* the trade of a tailor; *acc.* ~aṁ, 57,8.

tunna-vāya, *m.* (= *sa.*) a tailor; ~o, 57,3; °-upakaraṇāni, *n. pl.* 55,29 (*v.* upakaraṇa); °-vesaṁ gahetvā, in the disguise of a tailor, 58,16.

tumhe, *pron. pl.* & **tuyhaṁ**, *gen. sg.*, *v.* tvaṁ.

turiya, *n.* (*sa.* tūrya) any musical instrument; *pl.* ~āni (gahita-gahitāni) 65,2; nānā-°, all kinds of musical instruments, 64,30; *instr.* ~ehi (nippurisehi) 67,23; *°-bhaṇḍāni, *n. pl.* musical instruments or implements, 65,4; *°-sadda, *m.* sound of music, *acc.* ~aṁ, 112,7.

tulā, *f.* (= *sa.*) a balance; *acc.* ~aṁ va paggayha ("as with a balance") Dh. 268; a-tula, *mfn.* (*v. h.*).

tuvaṁ, *pron.* in the gāthās = tvaṁ, 47,9. 54,19. 105,24.

Tusita, *m. nom. pr.* (*sa.* Tushita) *pl.* ~ā (devā) a class of celestial beings; °-vimāna, *n.* the residence of the T.-angels (the fourth devaloka), *loc.* ~e, 87,31.

tussati, *vb.* (*sa.* √tush) to be satisfied or pleased; *ger.* ~itvā, 24,33. 55,3; *pp.* tuṭṭha (*v. h.*) *cp.* tuṭṭhi, *f.*

te, *pron.* 1) *gen. sg.*, *v.* tvaṁ; 2) *m. pl.*, *v.* taṁ[1].

teja & **tejas**, *m(n).* (*sa.* tejas) splendour; power, efficacy; *instr.* ~asā (tapati Buddho) 107,25 = Dh. 387; ~ena, 15,7 (sīla-°); 111,11 (paritta-sutta-°).

tejana, *n.* (= *sa.*) an arrow; *acc.* ~aṁ, 106,27 = Dh. 80. 145.

tena, *adv.* (*instr. fr.* taṁ¹; = *sa.*) ¹) in that direction, there (*corr. w.* yena) : 68,3 (yena nivesanadvāraṁ ten' upasaṁkami); 68,5 *etc.* 74,20. ²) for that reason, therefore, now then (in this sense often *comb. w.* hi) : 3,8. 7,13. 54,20. 106,4; tena hi : 1,10-19. 2,3. 19,31. 22,30. 41,21. 113,14.

***tepiṭaka**, *mfn.* (*fr.* tipiṭaka) belonging to 'the three baskets' (*cp.* piṭaka); *n. loc.* ~e Buddhavacane, the word of the Buddha contained in the holy scriptures, 102,3.

***temeti**, *vb.* (*caus.* √tim) to wet, moisten; *grd.* temetabba, *f.* ~ā (mattikā) 83,28.

terasa, *num.* (*sa.* trayodaça) 13; terasama, *mfn.* the 13th; *m.* ~o (vaggo) Dh. XIII.

tela, *n.* (*sa.* taila) oil (prepared from the seeds of the sesame plant); *acc.* ~aṁ, 50,24; *instr.* ~ena (gandha-°, with scented oil) 37,2; — °-ppadīpa, *m.* an oil-lamp; ~o, 67,27; *pl.* ~ā (gandha-°) 65,3; — °-pajjota, *m.* id. *acc.* ~aṁ, 69,17. *cp.* tila.

***tevācika**, *mfn.* (*sa.* *traivācika, *cp.* trivācika) effected by the three words or the triple formula, *viz.* Buddhaṁ saraṇaṁ gacchāmi *etc.* (*v.* saraṇa); *m.* ~o (upāsako, a lay-discipel by the triple formula) 69,21.

tevīsati, *num.* (*sa.* trayoviṁçati) 23; ~ima, *mfn.* the 23th; *m.* ~o (vaggo) Dh. XXIII.

toraṇa, *n.* (= *sa.*) an arch, portal, gateway; daḷha-pākāra-°, *mfn.* 90,31 (*n.* ~aṁ, nagaraṁ); 91,21 (daḷhatoraṇaṁ = thira-piṭṭhasaṁghāṭakaṁ).

ty', ¹) = ti¹ (iti), 111,20; *cp.* c', 74,1. — ²) = te (*gen.* tvaṁ) 13,26.

tv', = ti¹ (iti); 42,24. 60,25. 64,9.

tvaṁ, *pron. 2. pers.* (= *sa.*) thou; *nom.* a) tvaṁ (taṁ) 1,14. 3,12 (tvan ti); b) tuvaṁ, 47,9. 54,19. 105,24; — *acc.* taṁ (tvaṁ) 1,11-17-21. 2,3. 4,27 (tam pi); 5,10 (tañ ñeva); 94,27 (taṁ yev'); 94,32. 105,24; — *instr.* (*abl.*) tayā, 4,29. 5,9; — *gen. dat.* a) tuyhaṁ, 3,16. 3,25 (~ abbhantare); 7,13; b) tava, 1,22. 3,16 (~ santikaṁ); 12,1. 55,4; c) te, 1,15 (vaṭṭati); 2,3 (dassāmi); 2,8 (atthi); 7,13 (pasanno); 13,26 (ty' atthu); 78,13. 85,4 *etc.*; te may also be used for *instr.* (and *acc.*) : kathentena te sundaraṁ kataṁ, 1,24; 78,7 (?); *cp.* t'āhaṁ = te ahaṁ (*acc.*?) 85,27 [*Pischel*, GGA. 1877, p. 1066; ZDMG. 35, p. 714]. — *loc.* tayi, 10,12. 17,14; — *pl. nom.* tumhe, 1,26; to a single person : 25,17. 35,18; — *acc.* tumhe, 4,11. 12,33; 97,15; — *instr.* tumhehi, 12,33; — *gen. dat.* a) tumhākaṁ, 4,4. 6,15. 35,13. 97,7; b) vo, 9,25. 108,3; *dat. ethicus* : 42,16; 47,19 (id. or *gen. partitivus*); vo may also be used for *acc.* 4,8. 108,5; — *loc.* tumhesu (= *sg.*) 50,10.

Th.

thaṇḍila, *n.* (*sa.* sthaṇḍila) an open place, bare ground; °-sāyikā, *f.* the act of lying on the bare ground (as a penance), Dh. 141.

thaddha, *mfn.* (*sa.* stabdha) firm, hard; *m.* ~o (pahāro) 50,22 (*opp.* muduko); — *°-hadaya, *mfn.* hard-hearted; *f. pl.* ~ā (*comm.* on kaṭhinā) 52,5.

thambha, *m.* (*sa.* stambha) a post, pillar; *metaph.* insensibility, stupor; ~o, 103,28; *acc.* ~aṁ, 60,2.

tharaṇa, *n.* (*sa.* staraṇa) the act of spreading, *v.* bhumma-ttharaṇa, which is probably °-attharaṇa (*sa.* āstaraṇa, ā + √stṛ) = a carpet, 84,17.

thala, *n.* (*sa.* sthala) the land, dry land, firm earth; *acc.* ~aṁ, 15,14. 105,21 (*opp.* ninnaṁ); *loc.* ~e (*opp.* jale) 4,14; 27,27. 52,16; Dh. 98 (*opp.* ninne); *°-gocara, *mfn.* living on land, *m.* ~o, 1,8; — °-patha, *m.* a road by land; *acc.* °-jala-pathaṁ, everywhere by land and water, 19,22.

*thavikā, *f.* a purse; *acc.* sahassa-thavikaṁ, a purse containing a 1000 pieces of money, 102,24.

thavira, *v.* thera.

thāma, *m.* (*sa.* sthāman, *n.*) strength, power; *⁰-sampanna, *mfn.* strong; *m.* ~o, 1,3. 40,27.

thāvara, *mfn.* (*sa.* sthāvara) immoveable, firm, strong; *loc. pl.* ~esu (bhūtesu) Dh. 405 (*opp.* tasa).

thira, *mfn.* (*sa.* sthira) firm, hard, solid, strong; *n. pl.* ~āni (uddāpâdīni) 91,18 (*opp.* dubbalāni); *thira-pākāra- *etc. mfn.* 91,20-21 (*comm.* on daḷha-⁰).

thī, *f.* (*sa.* strī) = itthī, a woman (*v. h.*); *gen. pl.* thīnaṁ, 51,31.

thīna, *n.* (*sa.* styāna) sloth, indifference; *⁰-middha, *n.* "sloth and drowsiness" (pañcamī senā Mārassa), 103,27.

thūla (& thulla), *mfn.* (*sa.* sthūla) large, thick, coarse; *v.* aṇuṁthūla.

thera, *m.* & (~ī) *f.* (*sa.* sthavira) old, venerable; an 'Elder' (said of venerable bhikkhus); *m. nom.* ~o, 81,12. Dh. 260; Dh. 261 (to be scanned thaviro); mahā-thero, 113,8; *instr.* ~ena, 85,15; *pl.* ~ā, 109,22; mahā-⁰, 109,11; *acc.* ~e (bhikkhū) 83,33; *instr.* ~ehi, 109,12; *gen.* ~ānaṁ, 109,5; added to a *nom. pr.*: Upāli-⁰, 109,18; Mahākassapa-⁰, 109,17; — dhamma-kathika-⁰, *m.* (*v. h.*) — *compar.* theratara, *m.* ~o (bhikkhu) 79,10; *instr.* ~ena, 79,8. *cp. next.*

Thera-gāthā, *f. pl.* name of a canonical book, a section of the Khuddaka-Nikāya; specimen thereof: 107,28 *seqv.*

*thera-vāda, *m.* the doctrine of the Theras, the orthodoxe Buddhist doctrine; ~o, 109,14 (therehi katasaṁgaho); = aggavādo, 109,30; *acc.* ~aṁ, 114,5; *instr. pl.* ~ehi. 114,31.

*theriya, *mfn.* (*fr.* thera) belonging to the theras; *m. pl.* ⁰-ācariyā, the old teachers or, the propounders of the thera-vāda, 114,30.

Therī-gāthā, *f. pl.* name of a canonical book, a section of the Khuddaka-Nikāya; specimen thereof: 108,10 *seqv.*

thoka, *mfn.* (*sa.* stoka) little, small, short; *acc.* ~aṁ (*adv.*) a little: ~ netvā, 1,20; ~ gantvā, 36,11; ~ sayitvā, 12,11; ~ kīḷāpetvā, 58,33; *f.* ~ā (yāgu) 57,1; — *thoka-thokaṁ, *adv.* little by little, Dh. 121—22 (~am pi); Dh. 239.

*thokaka, *mfn.* (*fr. prec.*) small, short; *f.* ~ikā (ratī, a short pleasure) Dh. 310.

thometi, *vb.* (*denom. fr.* *thoma, *sa.* stoma, stomayati) to praise (*acc.*); *ger.* ~etvā (paṇḍitaṁ) 59,23.

D.

-d-, sandhi-consonant, inserted in attadattha, sadattha-pasuta (*q. v.*); likewise in samma-d-eva *etc.* (*v.* sammā). On account of sandhi an old 'd' is often preserved in some *pron.*: tad-, yad- (*v.* taṁ, yaṁ). kocid- (= koci) *etc.* [*Kuhn*, Beitr. p. 62—63; Tr. PM. p. 82; *Windisch*, Ber. d. sächs. Ges. 1893. p. 228 *seqv.*]

*dakkhati & dakkhiti, *vb.* (√dṛç) to see, perceive; *pr.* (*fut.*) *2. sg.* ~asi (na me maggaṁ ~, "the path I tread you never can find") 72,23; *3. pl.* ~inti, 69,18 (cakkhumanto rūpāni ~); — *aor.* addakkhi, *3. sg.* 77,8; *2. sg.* 20,19. Formally dakkhati & dakkhiti look like *fut. fr.* √dṛç (*sa.* drakshyati), but really these forms may have sprung either from *aor.* addakkhi (*sa.* adrākshīt) or from an old base *dṛksh-⁰ [*Kuhn*, Beitr. p. 116; Tr. PM. p. 61; *Pischel*, Gr. § 554] *cp.* dissati.

dakkhiṇa, *mfn.* (*sa.* dakshiṇa) 1) right, on the right hand; *instr. m.* ~ena (hatthena) 77,1. 111,24 (*opp.* vāma-hatthena); ⁰-passaṁ, the right side, 61,21. — 2) southern; *acc. f.* ~aṁ (disaṁ) 95,5; ⁰-samudda, *m.*

the southern sea, *gen.* ~assa, 60,4. *cp.* padakkhiṇa.

dajjā, *pot.*, *v.* dadāti.

daṭṭhabba, *grd.* & daṭṭhuṁ, *inf.*, *v.* dissati.

daḍḍha, *mfn.* (*pp.* ḍahati, *q. v.*) burnt; *n.* ~aṁ (khettaṁ) 100,27; aggi-°, *mfn.* (*v. h.*).

daṇḍa, *m.* (= *sa.*) 1) a stick, staff; a handle; *acc.* ~aṁ (gahetvā, "staff in hand") 47,22; *instr.* ~ena, 77,12; *loc.* ~e (the handle) 35,5; — °-hattha, *mfn.* leaning on a staff; *acc. m.* ~aṁ, 63,9; — a-daṇḍa, atta-daṇḍa (*q. v.*). — 2) punishment; *acc.* ~aṁ, Dh. 310. 405; *instr.* ~ena, Dh. 131; purisa-vadha-°, punishment for murder, 74,14; *gen.* ~assa, Dh. 129; — °-kamma, *n.* fine, mulct, penalty; idam me ~aṁ, "in this way I make amends", 53,13; — *°-ppatta, *mfn.* liable to punishment; *m.* ~o, 100,15; — paṭidaṇḍa, brahma-daṇḍa (*q. v.*). — Daṇḍa-vagga, *m.* the 10th chapter of Dh.

daṇḍaka, *m.* (= *sa.*) a stick, staff; *acc.* ~aṁ, 13,19; 36,1 (a twig from a tree); *instr.* ~ena, 86,21; — *ratha-°, *m.* (*q. v.*).

datta, *mfn.* (*e. c.* = *sa.*; *pp.* dadāti, *cp.* dinna) *v.* Devadatta, Brahmadatta. *cp.* atta[1].

datvā, *ger.*, *v. next.*

dadāti, *vb.* (*sa.* √dā) 1) to give (*w. gen. pers. & acc. rei*) 29,3. 31,16 *etc.*; to hand, deliver, give in charge, pay (do.) 82,18; 31,2; 39,20. 111,12; 37,18; 102,8; to offer (an oblation, *acc.*) 17,6 (eḷakaṁ); — 2) variously constructed *w. acc.* : okāsaṁ ~, to give an opportunity to (*inf.*) 40,17; ovādaṁ, to admonish, 85,24; dānaṁ, to make gifts, give alms, 14,12. 86,14; jīvita-dānaṁ, to spare one's life, 12,26; paṭivacanaṁ, to answer, 3,9; phalaṁ, to bear fruit, 36,36; maggaṁ, to give place to, 44,12; matakabhattaṁ, to offer an oblation to the dead, 16,23; saññaṁ, to make a sign, communicate, 55,29; sādhukāraṁ, to applaud, 5,19; — 3) to permit, allow (*acc. & inf.*) 5,10. 12,17. 17,19. 39,24. 48,19. 52,30; — 4) constructed *w. ger.* of another verb = to do that to any one : dārūni āharitvā . . . dassati, 35,9; rajjaṁ gahetvā dātuṁ. 35,19; āharitvā adaṁsu, 41,4; vibhajitvā adāsi. 41,19. — a) *pr. 1. sg.* dadāmi, 10,20; *3. pl.* dadanti, Dh. 249; *part. gen. m.* dadato, Dh. 242; *part. med. m.* dadamāno, 12,33; *f.* ~ā, 5,20; *pot. 3. sg.* 1) dadeyya, 98,34; *2. sg.* ~āsi, 53,15; *1. sg.* ~aṁ, 33,13. 41,1; 2) *3. sg.* dajjā, Dh. 224; — b) *pr. 1. sg.* dammi, 7,14. 15,24. 29,3; — c) *pr. 3. sg.* deti, 12,17. 28,24. 98,8; *2. sg.* desi, 3,9; *1. sg.* demi. 31,16; *3. pl.* denti, 37,2; *2. pl.* detha, 18,11. 52,20; *1. pl.* dema, 18,11. 39,24. 114,10 (demā'ti); *imp. 3. sg.* detu. 36,21. 39,20; *2. sg.* dehi, 5,15. 69,32. 101,28. 111,27 (read : jīvitaṁ dehi); *2. pl.* detha. 18,9. 31,3. 114,8; *part. m.* dento, 40,17. 85,24; — [d) rare or ficticious present-formations are : dajjati (*cp. pot.* dajjā) & dāti]; — *fut. 3. sg.* dassati, 3,8. 30,13; *2. sg.* ~asi, 2,2; *1. sg.* 2,4. 5,10; 15,12 *etc.*; *1. pl.* ~āma, 17,19. 60,14; — *aor. 3. sg.* a) adāsi, 3,11. 6,18. 36,36; dāsi, 114,9; *1. sg.* adāsiṁ, 17,6. 42,13; *3. pl.* adaṁsu, 4,15. 31,3. 41,4 *etc.*; b) adā (*3. sg.*) 111,12 (nâdā), 114,25; — *inf.* dātuṁ, 15,5. 31,30. 102,8; a-dātu-kāmatā. *f.* (*q. v.*); — *ger.* datvā. 7,28. 16,26; a-datvā. 48,19. 55,29; — *grd.* a) dātabba, *n.* ~aṁ. 14,12. 82,18; b) deyya. *n.* ~aṁ. 112,9; — *pp.* dinna (& datta, *e. c.*) *v. h.*; — [*pass.* dīyati, *cp.* ā-diyati]; — *caus.* dāpeti (*v. h.*) *cp.* dāna, dāya, dāyaka.

dadhi, *n.* (= *sa.*) sour milk, curd; *nom.* dadhi, 99,28-30. 101,27; dadhiṁ, 26,13; *acc.* ~iṁ, 26,11. 35,22. 101,28; *instr.* ~inā, 35,17; *loc.* ~imhi, 36,25; — *°-ghaṭa, *m.* a milkbowl, *acc.* ~aṁ, 35,17; — *°-māla, *m. n. pr.* of an ocean; *acc.* ~aṁ, 26,12; °-mālin, id. 26,15 (°-māliti) *cp.* Aggimāla; — *°-vāraka, *m.* a pot of milk-curd, *acc.* ~aṁ, 14,30; *gen.* ~assa, 14,31; —

°-vāhana, *m. n. pr.* of a king; ~o nāma rājā, 36,29; °-jātaka, *n.* 34,30.

danta[1], *m.* (= *sa.*) a tooth; *nom. pl.* ~ā, 12,1. 82,2 = 97,20; *acc. pl.* ~e, 65,6; *instr. pl.* ~ehi, 12,5; khaṇḍa-°, *mfn.* (*q. v.*); dantantara-gata, *v.* antara; – °-kaṭṭha, *n.* (*v. h.*).

danta[2], *mfn.* (*pp.* √dam, *sa.* dānta) tamed, subdued; tame, mild, patient; *m.* ~o, 77,10-13; Dh. 321; *acc. m.* ~aṁ, ib.; *n.* ~aṁ (cittaṁ) Dh. 35; *pl. m.* ~ā, Dh. 322; – *atta-danta, *mfn.* & sudanta, *mfn.* (*v. h.*) *cp.* dameti.

***dandha**, *mfn.* slow, slothful, indocible; ~aṁ, *adv.* slothfully, Dh. 116. The etymology of this word is doubtful; *Fausbøll* & *Weber*, ZDMG. 14. p. 48 refer to *sa.* *tandra (*cp.* a-tandra); *Trenckner*, PM. p. 65 to dṛḍha (& dhandha), but *cp.* tandita & daḷha. According to *Müller*, PGr. p. 22 we ought to look for something like *dardhra or dṛdhra (*cp. Lüders*, ZDMG. 58 p. 700).

dabba (& dabbha), *m.* (*sa.* darbha) the Kuça-grass; – *°-tiṇa, *n.* id., *pl.* ~āni, 15,4; °-sayana, *n.* a lair of K.-grass, *abl.* ~to, 16,4.

dabbi & **dabbī**, *f.* (*sa.* darvi & ~ī) a ladle, spoon; *nom.* ~ī, Dh. 64.

dama, *m.* (= *sa.*) moderation, self-command (*synon.* saññama); ~o, Dh. 261; *instr.* ~ena, Dh. 25; °-sacca, *n.* temperance and truth, *instr.* ~ena, Dh. 9; duddama, *mfn.* (*q. v.*).

damatha, *m.* (= *sa.*) self-command; ~o (cittassa) Dh. 35.

dameti (& damayati), *vb.* (*sa.* damayati, *caus.* √dam) to tame, subdue; to convert (*acc.*); *pr. 3. pl.* damayanti (daṇḍena) 77,12; (attānaṁ paṇḍitā) 106,28 = Dh. 80; *part. nom. m.* damayaṁ (attānaṁ) Dh. 305; *inf.* dametuṁ (vaṭṭati, *q. v.*) to convert, 113,9; *cp.* danta & *prec.*

dammi, *pr. 1. sg.*, *v.* dadāti.

dara, *m.* (= *sa.*) fear; *v.* niddara & vīta-ddara.

daratha, *m.* (= *sa.*) pain, suffering; *loc. pl.* sabba-kilesa-darathesu, 64,21.

darī, *f.* (= *sa.*) a cave, hole, cleft; *°-saya, *m.* a lair in a hole or cleft, *loc.* ~e, 108,24 (if not to be corrected into darīsayo (*mfn.*) 'having my lair in a hole on the bank of a river', *cp.* Jāt. I. p. 18. v. 106, & darīcara, *mfn.* Jāt. V. p. 70,15).

daḷha, *mfn.* (*sa.* dṛḍha) firm, hard, strong, fast; *f.* ~ā (bhūmi) 110,7; *n.* ~aṁ (vīriyaṁ) Dh. 112; ~aṁ daḷhassa khipati (*v. h.*) 44,1; °-ppahāra, *m.* a violent stroke, *acc.* ~aṁ, 30,13; — *°-parakkama, *mfn.* undaunted, firm, energetic; *m. pl.* ~ā, Dh. 23; *acc.* ~e, 108,19; — *°-pākāra-toraṇa, *mfn.* having strong walls *etc.*, strongly fortified; *n.* ~aṁ (nagaraṁ). 90,31. 91,21; — *°-uddāpa, *mfn.* having a strong foundation; *n.* ~aṁ, 90,31. 91,20. — daḷhaṁ, *adv.* firmly, strongly; Dh. 61. 313; ~aṁ katvā (gahita-sigāle) with a fast hold, 40,24; daḷha-gahita-, 40,20. (*cp.* dandha).

dasa[1], *num.* (*sa.* daça) ten; 31,13 (bhātaro); 81,21 (sikkhāpadāni); °-māse (*acc.*) 62,2; *instr.* dasahi, 18,16. 82,14; *gen.* dasannaṁ, Dh. 137 (dasann'). At the end of *comp. num.* 'd' is often changed into 'r' (or ḷ) *cp.* aṭṭhārasa, ekādasa, cuddasa, terasa, pannarasa, soḷasa.

dasa[2], *mfn.* (*e. c.*, *sa.* dṛça), *v.* duddasa, sududdasa. (*cp.* dassa).

dasabala, *m.* (*sa.* daça-bala) 'possessing 10 powers' = Buddha; Kassapa-° (*q. v.*).

dasama, *mfn.* (*sa.* daçama) the 10th; ~o (vaggo) Dh. X.

dassa, *mfn.* (*e. c.*, *sa.* darça), *v.* sudassa. (*cp.* dasa[2]).

dassati, *fut.*, *v.* dadāti.

dassana, *n.* (*sa.* darçana) seeing, looking; perception, intelligence, insight; religious persuasion; ~aṁ (appiyānaṁ, to see what is unpleasant) 106,26 = Dh. 210; (ariyānaṁ, "the sight of the elect") Db. 206; *instr.* ~ena (sekhena) insight, 69,35; ittara-°, 30,12 (*v. h.*); *abl.* ~ā (°-visūka-, seeing spectacles *etc.*) 81,24; *gen.* ~assa (visuddhi) Db. 274; — sīla-dassana-sampanna, *mfn.* (*q. v.*); *cp.* a-dassana.

dassanīya, *mfn.* (*sa.* darçanīya) visible, fair to see, beautiful; *m.* ~o (rājā) 47,9.

dassayati, *vb.*, *v.* dasseti.

dassin, *mfn.* (*e. c.*, *sa.* darçin) seeing, finding; *v.* bhaya-°, vajja-°.

dassivas, *mfn.* (*e. c.*, *sa.* darçivas) seeing; *v.* bhaya-°.

dasseti, *vb.* (*caus.* √dṛç, *cp.* dissati) to cause to be seen or to appear, to show, point out, produce, manifest, give to understand (*acc.*); to show to, present to, to bring before (*acc.* & *gen.*); *pr. 3. sg.* ~eti (mayhaṁ apacitiṁ) 29,26; *3. pl.* ~enti, 21,4; dassayanti (uccāvacaṁ, *q. v.*) Dh. 83; *part. m.* dassento, 2,1; *imp. 2. sg.* ~ehi, 114,10; *2. pl.* ~etha, 24,21; *pot. 3. sg.* ~eyya, 100,12; *fut. 1. pl.* ~essāma (pubbanimittaṁ) 63,8; *aor. 3. sg.* a) ~esi (attānaṁ) 12,27; (uṇhakāraṁ) 15,8; (chātakākāraṁ) 41,8; (pahāraṁ, *q. v.*) 52,33; (soṇirūpena, *scil.* attānaṁ, presented herself) 111,2; b) dassayi, 113,13. *3. pl.* ~esuṁ, (core rañño) 38,33. 74,8; 63,10; *inf.* dassetuṁ, 91,25; *ger.* ~etvā. 4,16. 36,9.

daha, *m.* (*sa.* draha, by metathesis = hrada) a lake, pond; *acc.* Anotatta-dahaṁ, 61,13; *abl.* Kaṇṇamuṇḍa-dahato, 36,31.

dahati, *vb.* 1) (*sa.* dadhāti, √dhā) to put, hold, consider; *pp.* hita (*q. v.*) *cp.* dheyya; antaradhāyati, pidahati, saṁvidahati, saddahati, sandahati. — 2) = ḍahati (*q. v.*).

dahara, *mfn.* (= *sa.*) young; *m.* ~o, 46,22. 99,4; (bhikkhu) Dh. 382; *pl.* ~ā (pakkhī) 11,14; *f.* ~ī (dārikā) 101,19; *acc.* ~iṁ, 101,15; 47,19 (kumāriṁ); — daharitthī, a young wife, *gen.* ~iyā, 49,13; — *compar.* daharatara, *mfn.* the younger of two, *gen. m.* ~assa, 43,26.

dātabba, **dātuṁ**, *v.* dadāti.

dāna, *n.* (= *sa.*) giving, gift, *esp.* alms, almsgiving, liberality; *nom.* ~aṁ (dātabbaṁ) 14,12; Dh. 177; dinna-°, almsgiving, 14,18; *acc.* ~aṁ. 86,14 (Satthari Āḷaviṁ anuppatte nimantetvā ~ adaṁsu); mahā-°, 61,6; *instr.* ~ena, 16,13. *loc.* ~e (attanā dinna-°) 29,2; — dānâdīni puññāni, 17,33; dānâdīhi, 22,17; — *dāna-kathā, *f.* talking about (the duty and profits of) almsgiving, *acc.* ~aṁ (pakāsesi) 68,19; — °-sālā, *f.*, a hall for almsgiving, *pl.* ~ā, 38,13; — jīvita-°, dhamma-° (*v. h.*).

dāni, *adv.* = idāni (*q. v.*).

dāpeti, *vb.* (*caus.* dadāti, *sa.* dāpayati) to cause or order to be given (*acc.* & *gen.*); *aor. 3. sg.* ~esi (tassa aṭṭha kahāpaṇe) 24,28; *fut. 1. sg.* ~essāmi, 43,27; *pp.* dāpita, *n.* ~aṁ (aggaṁ) 111,35.

dāma, *n.* & *m.* (*sa.* dāman, *n.*) a rope, cord; a chain, wreath; *m. pl.* ~ā (muñjamayā) 105,17; *n. pl.* ~āni (mālā-°) 37,2; kusuma-dāma-sadisa-, *mfn.* 47,13; rajata-dāma-vaṇṇa, *mfn.* 61,19 (*v. h.*).

dāya[1], *m.* (= *sa.*) a gift, donation; ~o, 25,10; nahāpita-°, ib. (a barber's fee).

dāya[2], *m.* (*sa.* dāva) a forest, grove; *v.* miga-dāya.

dāyaka, *mfn.* (= *sa.*) giving; *v.* paccaya-dāyaka.

dāra, *m. sg.* (*sa.* dāra, *m. pl.*) a wife; *loc. pl.* ~esu, Dh. 345; para-°, another man's wife, *acc.* ~aṁ, Dh. 246; paradārûpasevin, *mfn.* one who covets another man's wife, *nom. m.* ~ī, Dh. 309; puttadāra, *m. sg.* wife and children, *acc.* ~aṁ, 38,20.

dāraka, *m.* (= *sa.*) a child, son, boy; ~o, 58,32; *acc.* ~aṁ, 58,30. 81,11; *loc.* ~e, 59,12; *pl.* ~ā (gāma-°) 52,17; *acc. pl.* ~e, 21,1; *°-corī, *f.* (*q. v.*); °-mātar. *f. nom.* ~ā, the child's mother, 59,22.

dārikā, *f.* (= *sa.*) a daughter, girl, young maid; ~ā, 101,19; *acc.* ~aṁ, 55,27. 101,15.

dāru, *n.* (= *sa.*) wood, timber; a stick, log of wood, *pl.* fire-wood; *acc.* ~uṁ, 106,28 = Dh. 80; *pl. acc.* ~ūni, 15,32. 35,6. 57,13; *instr.* ~ūhi, 35,7; *⁰-kalāpa, *m.* (*q. v.*); *⁰-rāsi, *m.* (*q. v.*); dārūdaka-, 20,12 (fire-wood and water).

dāruja, *mfn.* (= *sa.*) made of wood; *n.* ~aṁ (bandhanaṁ) Dh. 345.

dāruṇa, *mfn.* (= *sa.*) horrible, dreadful; *acc. n.* ~aṁ (abbhakkhānaṁ) Dh. 139.

dāleti, *vb.* (*sa.* dālayati, √dal) to cause to burst, to break through (*acc.*); *ger.* dālayitvā (pūtilataṁ), 105,19.

dāsa, *m.* (= *sa.*) a slave, servant; ~o, 5,7.

dāsī, *f.* (= *sa.*) a female servant or slave; *voc.* ~i (term of abuse) 111,25; dāsi-gaṇa-, 21,1 (a troop of ~).

di-⁰, at the beginning of *comp.* = dvi (two, double), *v.* dija, dipada, diyaḍḍha.

digacchā = jigacchā (*q. v.*).

dija, *m.* (*sa.* dvija) a bird; *pl.* ~ā, 60,17. *cp.* dvija.

diṭṭha¹, *mfn.* (*pp.* dissati, √dṛç; *sa.* dṛshṭa) ¹) seen, perceived; *m.* ~o, 12,14. 108,17; *n.* ~aṁ, 85,25; *instr.* ~ena (iminā, what we have seen here) 54,15; ⁰-pubba, *mfn.*; yathā-⁰, *mfn.* (*v. h.*); — ²) known, understood; *n.* ~aṁ (h'etaṁ Tathāgatena) 94,8; — ³) belonging to this world (*cp.* diṭṭha-dhamma below); *loc.* ~e va dhamme, in the present life, 92,32. dud-diṭṭha. *mfn.* (*v. h.*).

diṭṭha², *m.* (*sa.* dvishṭa, *mfn.*) an ennemy; *acc.* ~aṁ, 3,27.

diṭṭha-dhamma, (*sa.* dṛshṭa-dharma) ¹) *mfn.* having seen the truth; *m.* ~o, 69,12. — ²) *m.* this world, the present life; ⁰-sukhavihāraṁ anuyutto, "in the enjoyment of happiness reached even in this world", 74,22; *cp.* dhamma & diṭṭha¹ above.

diṭṭhi, *f.* (*sa.* dṛshṭi) view, belief, doctrine, theory, *esp.* false theory; *acc.* ~iṁ (pāpikaṁ) 91,16. Dh. 164; *loc.* (i)ti diṭṭhiyā sati, even if we suppose that, 92,27; — ⁰-gata, *n.* (false) theory or doctrine; ~aṁ (pāpakaṁ) 90,24; (sassato loko ti) 93,33; (uppanna-⁰) 91,17; 94,7 (apanītam etaṁ Tathāgatassa); *pl.* ~āni, 93,33; — *⁰-gahana, -kantāra, -visūka. -vipphandita, -saṁyojana (*v. h.*) 94,1-2; — sammā-⁰, *f.* right belief, right views, 67,4. 96,5; — micchā-⁰, *f.* false doctrine, *acc.* ~iṁ, Dh. 167; ⁰-samādāna, *mfn.* (*q. v.*) Dh. 316. — *cp.* evaṁ-diṭṭhi, *mfn.* & añña-diṭṭhika, *mfn.*

*dinna, *mfn.* (*pp.* dadāti) given, presented; *n.* ~aṁ. 21,6 (tāhi); 49,21 (mūlaṁ); Dh. 356 (vītarāgesu, a gift bestowed on . . .); as finite tense: *m.* ~o, 8,2; *f.* ~ā, 57,1; *n.* ~aṁ, 7,7; — ⁰-dāna, *n.* almsgiving, 14,18; ⁰-suṅkā, *f.* (mayā) 101,21 (*v.* suṅkā). *cp.* a-dinna.

dipada, *m.* (*sa.* dvipada) a biped, a man; *gen. pl.* ~ānaṁ, Dh. 273.

dibba, *mfn.* (*sa.* divya) heavenly, divine; charming, beautiful; *acc. m.* ~aṁ (yogaṁ) Dh. 417; *f.* ~aṁ (ariyabhūmiṁ) Dh. 236; *loc. pl. m.* ~esu (kāmesu) Dh. 187; *comp.* dibbakāme (*acc. pl. m.*) 45,5; ⁰-gandha-, 20,8-9; -cakkhumhi (*loc.*) 109,8; -pānaṁ, 59,25; -pupphāni, 61,14; -bhojanaṁ, 20,7; -vattha, *n.* 20,8. 61,13; -sampatti, 23,17; -sayana, *n.* 20,9. 61,16.

diyaḍḍha, *mfn.* (*sa.* dvyardha) $1^1/_2$; ⁰-yojana-satika, *mfn.* 150 yojanas long, *instr. m.* ~ena, 60,4. *cp.* aḍḍha.

divasa, *m.* & *n.* (= *sa.*) a day; *nom. m.* ~o (uposatha-⁰, fastday) 14,16; *acc.* ~aṁ, by day, in the course of the day, 2,32; taṁ ~aṁ, on that day, 87,31; ~am pi, 'all day long', 42,30; ~am pi sapathaṁ kurumānā nānācittā va honti, even on that same day they will change their minds and take their oath . . ., 51,28; eka-⁰, one day, 13,22. 63,2; *instr.* ~ena (eka-⁰, on one and the same day) 64,8; *abl.* ~ato (sattama-⁰ paṭṭhāya) 61,3; (dhammadesanaṁ suta-⁰, from the day on which she had heard) 86,30; *loc.* ~e (puna-⁰, next day) 2,25; (jāta-⁰, on his birthday) 24,31. 45,21; (eka-⁰, on the same day) 45,24; *acc. pl. m.* ime ~e, "the last few days", 73,23; *n.* ~āni. 25,20; *loc.* ~esu (aññesu, *q. v.*) 3,10. 65,21. *cp.* devasikaṁ, *adv.* & *next.*

divā. *adv.* (= *sa.*) by day; ~ tapati ādicco, 107,23 = Dh. 387; rattim pi divâpi, night and day, 9,16; ~ vā rattiṁ vā, Dh. 249; ~ ca ratto ca, Dh. 296. *cp.* rattindivaṁ, *adv.* 86,25.

disa¹, *mfn.* (*e. c.*; *sa.* dṛça) like that; *v.* īdisa, etā-⁰, kī-⁰, tā-⁰, sa-⁰; khandhā-disa, *v.* khandha. *cp.* dasa².

disa², *m.* (*sa.* dvisha) an enemy; ~o, Dh. 162; *acc.* ~aṁ, Dh. 42.

disā, *f.* (*sa.* diç & diçā) quarter, direction; region, country; *acc.* ~aṁ (katamaṁ, in which direction) 95,5; (agataṁ ~, "the untrodden country" = Nibbāna) Dh. 323; *abl.* ~ato (uttara-⁰, *q. v.*) 61,18; *acc. pl.* ~ā (sabbā) 85,4. Dh. 54; *loc. pl.* ~āsu (sabba-⁰, in each direction) 63,19. *cp.* catuddisā & *next.*

*disā-kāka, *m.* a crow kept on board ships in order to search for land; *acc.* ~aṁ, 18,4. (*cp. Fick,* Soc. Gl. p. 173; *E. Hardy,* Buddha, p. 18.)

*disā-pāmokkha, *mfn.* world-famed, very celebrated; *m.* ~o (ācariyo) 16,23.

*disvā, *disvāna, *ger., v. next.*

dissati, *vb.* (*sa.* √dṛç, *pass.* dṛçyate) ¹) *pass.* to be seen, appear; *pr. 3. sg.* ~ati, 44,25. 52,11; na ~ati (has disappeared) 68,30; *3. pl.* ~anti (na, are not seen, *opp.* pakāsenti) Dh. 304; 104,1 (ettha [*scil.* saṅgāme] na ~, don't devote themselves to this battle, *cp. Windisch,* Māra, p. 27; the 'na' is perhaps interpolated); *part.* dissamāna, *acc. pl. m.* ~e (= a-dissamāne, invisible) 112,18; *pp.* diṭṭha, seen (*v. h.*); *grd.* daṭṭhabba, *mfn.* to be regarded or understood, *m.* ~o (attho) 85,10-23, *n.* ~aṁ, 79,4. — ²) *act.* to see, regard, understand (*acc.*) (the suppletive verb is passati, *q. v.*); *aor. 3. sg.* ᵃ) addasa, 4,25 (nâddasa); 23,16; addasā, 75,18. 76,20 (~ā kho); *2. sg.* addasa or addasā, 71,31 (addasā ti); *3. pl.* addasāsuṁ, 76,18; *1. pl.* addasāma, 105,23; ᵇ) addakkhi, *v.* dakkhati; *fut. v.* dakkhati; *inf.* daṭṭhuṁ, 48,19. 87,9; *comp.* daṭṭhu-kāma, *mfn.* wishing to see, *f.* ~ā (taṁ) 19,12; *ger.* ᵃ) disvā, 1,6 *etc.*; ᵇ) disvāna, 67,31. 68,10. 76,19 (at the beginning of a sentence). *cp.* dasa², dassa *etc.*; diṭṭhi, disa¹.

dīgha, *mfn.* (*sa.* dīrgha) long; *m.* ~o (puriso, tall) 92,13 (*opp.* rasso); *f.* ~ā, 107,9 = Dh. 60; *n.* ~aṁ, Dh. 409; *acc.* ~aṁ (addhānaṁ) 44,21; (pācanayaṭṭhiṁ) 71,29.

*Dīgha-nikāya, *m.* name of a Pāli work, the first of the 5 Nikāyas (*q. v.*); ~o, 102,15. Specimens thereof: p. 77,14—81,4.

*Dīgha-bhāṇaka, *m.* a repeater (expounder or follower) of Dīgha-nikāya; *pl.* ~ā, 64,2.

dīgha-rattaṁ, *adv.* (*sa.* dīrgha-rātram) for a long time; 90,27. 104,33.

dīpa¹, *m.* (= *sa.*) a lamp; *acc.* ~aṁ, 37,2; dīpālokena, 41,27 (*v.* āloka). *cp.* padīpa.

dīpa², *m.* (& *n.*) (*sa.* dvīpa) ¹) an island; land, continent; ~o, 110,31. 112,30; *acc.* ~aṁ, 114,2; *loc.* ~e, 19,9; sabba-dīpamhi (over all Jambudīpa) 113,5. — ²) *metaph.* a support, refuge; karohi dīpam attano, Dh. 236. *cp.* Jambu-dīpa, Nāga-⁰, Laṅkā-⁰, Seruma-⁰, *n. pr.*

*dīpaka, *m.* (*fr. prec.*) a little island; ~o, 2,20; *gen.* ~assa, 2,22; *abl.* ~ā, 3,20; ~ato, 2,31; *loc.* ~e, 2,28.

dīpana, *mf(~ī)n.* (= *sa.*) explaining, illustrating; *v.* Paramattha-dīpanī.

*Dīpavaṁsa, *m.* (*fr.* dīpa²)

name of a Pāli work, the oldest chronicle of Ceylon; Specimen thereof: p. 109–110,16.

dīpin, *m.* (*sa.* dvīpin) a panther or leopard; *gen.* ~ino, 8,27.

dīpeti, *vb.* (*caus.* √dīp) [1]) to illustrate, explain, teach (*acc.*); *pr. 3. sg.* ~eti (atthaṁ dhammañ ca) Dh. 363; — [2]) *intr.* to emit light, shine; *pot. 3. sg.* ~eyya (sabbarattiṁ) 99,18.

du-, *indecl.* (*sa.* dus-) prefix to nouns (*subst.* & *adj.*) implying 'evil, bad, difficult' (*opp.* su-). Before vowels the old form dur- is preserved, *e. g.* dur-accaya, *etc.*, before consonants du- with the *foll. cons.* doubled, *e. g.* dukkata, ducchanna, dummana, *etc.* (v becomes bb: dubbaca, dubbaṇṇa), except before r, where the u is lengthened, *e. g.* dū-rakkha. By vṛddhi we have do-[0], *e. g.* domanassa (*cp.* dohaḷa).

dukkaṭa & **dukkata**, *n.* (*sa.* dush-kṛta), evil deed, sin, offending; ~aṁ (akataṁ) Dh. 314; (-t-, manasā) Dh. 391; sukaṭa-dukkaṭa, *mfn.* good and evil, *gen. pl.* ~ānaṁ (kammānaṁ) 97,14.

dukkara, *mfn.* (*sa.* dush-kara) difficult to do, difficult; *m.* ~o (maggo padhānāya) 103,10; *n.* parama-dukkaraṁ, very d. Dh. 163.

dukkha, [1]) *mfn.* (*sa.* duḥkha) unpleasant, painful (*opp.* sukha); *m.* ~o, 66,27. 67,10. Dh. 117; *f.* ~ā, 67,8; *n.* ~aṁ, 67,9; 70,27; a-dukkham-asukhaṁ, neither pleasant nor painful, 70,27; — dukkhaṁ, *adv.* Dh. 201 (~ seti, "is unhappy"). — [2]) *n.* (sometimes written dukha metri causa, Dh. 83. 203) pain, misery; grief, suffering; *nom.* ~aṁ, 35,12. 77,3; kin te ~, "what ails you?" 13,13; dukkh', 17,28; ~ ariyasaccaṁ (*q. v.*) 67,8; sabba-[0], 108,15; *acc.* ~aṁ, 16,30. 23,16. 107,19; (maraṇa-[0]) 7,9; (sīsaccheda-[0]) 17,12; *instr.* ~ena (-kh-) Dh. 83; *dat.* ~āya, Dh. 248; *gen.* ~assa, 70,17. 107,19; *abl.* [a]) ~ā, 16,28. 107,22 = Dh. 192 (sabba-[0]); [b]) ~ato, 31,20; *loc.* ~e. 107,12 — Dh. 277; *pl.* ~ā (— ~āni, *cp. Kuhn,* Beitr. p. 72) Dh. 202. 203 (-kh-). 221; *instr. pl.* ~ehi, 70,30; — *comp.* *dukkhânupatita, *mfn.* "beset with pain", Dh. 302; — *[0]-ânubhavana-, 23,18 (*v.* anubhavana); — *[0]-ûpadhāna, *n.* causing pain; Dh. 291 (para-[0], *v.* upadhāna); — *[0]-ûpasama-gāmin, *mfn.* leading to quieting of pain, *acc. m.* ~inaṁ (maggaṁ) 107,20 — Dh. 191 (*v.* upasama); — *[0]-kkhandha, *m.* (*v.* khandha); — [0]-domanassa, *n. pl.* (*dvandva comp.*) 90,18; — *[0]-nirodha, *m.* cessation or destruction of misery; ~aṁ (ariyasaccaṁ [*q. v.*] *adj. n.*, a scholastic expression — concerning the cessation of misery) 67,15; [0]-nirodha-gāminī (*adj. f.* leading to that) 67,17; — *[0]-ppatta, *mfn.* afflicted by pain, *m.* ~o, 59,10; — *[0]-samudaya, *m.* (*v. h.*); ~aṁ (*adj. n. cp.* dukkha-nirodha above) 67,12; — *[0]-samuppāda, *m.* 107,18 (*v. h.*) *cp.* sa-dukkha, *mfn.* & *next.*

dukkhin, *mfn.* (*sa.* duḥkhin) pained, afflicted, sorrowful; *m.* ~ī. 2,14. 72,25.

dukha, *n.* — dukkha.

dugga, *mfn.* (*sa.* dur-ga) difficult, impassable; painful, evil; *m.* ~o (maggo) 103,10; *acc.* ~aṁ (saṁsāraṁ), Dh. 414; *abl. n.* ~ā ("out of the evil way") Dh. 327.

duggata, *mfn.* (*sa.* dur-gata) unfortunate, miserable, poor; [0]-itthī, *f.* a poor woman, *acc.* ~iṁ, 48,16; — *[0]-bhāva, *m.* poverty; *acc.* ~aṁ, 57,2.

duggati, *f.* (*sa.* dur-gati) 'evil path', hell, unfortunate existence; *acc.* ~iṁ. Dh. 17; 106,20 — Dh. 240. (*cp.* suggati).

***duggahīta**, *mfn.* badly grasped; *m.* ~o (kuso) Dh. 311.

duccarita, [1]) *mfn.* (*sa.* duç-carita) evil; *acc. m.* ~aṁ (dhammaṁ, — sin) Dh. 169; — [2]) *n.* ill-conduct, sin; kāya-[0], mano-[0], vacī-[0] (*v. h.*).

*ducchana, *mfn.* ill-thatched; *n.* ~aṁ (agāraṁ) Dh. 13.

*dujjāna, *mfn.* (*cp. sa.* dur-jñāna & jānana above) difficult to be understood; *m.* ~o (dhammo, tayā) 94,26.

dujjīva, *mfn.* (*sa.* dur-jīva) difficult to live; *n.* ~aṁ (jīvitaṁ) Dh. 245 (*w. instr.*).

duṭṭha, *mfn.* (*sa.* dushṭa) bad, evil, malignant; *f. pl.* ~ā, 52,6; °-brāhmaṇa, *voc.* 33,16; *°-citta, *mfn.* evil-minded, with evil intention; *m.* ~o, 75,24. *cp.* a-duṭṭha, paduṭṭha & dussati.

dutiya, *mfn.* (*sa.* dvitiya) the second (*cp.* añña, itara) *acc. m.* ~aṁ, 35,10; *f.* ~aṁ (gāthaṁ) 8,31; °-jjhāna, *n.* (*v.* jhāna); — dutiyaṁ, *adv.* for the second time, ~aṁ pi (kho) 74,25. 79,21. 88,17; yāva ~aṁ pi, up to the second time, 102,26. *cp.* dvi (dva).

duttara, *mfn.* (*sa.* dus-tara) difficult to be passed; *v.* su-duttara.

duddama, *mfn.* (*sa.* dur-dama) difficult to be subdued; *m.* ~o (attā) Dh. 159.

duddasa, *mfn.* (*sa.* dur-dṛça) difficult to be seen; *m.* ~o (dhammo) 94,25; *n.* ~aṁ, 106,16 — Dh. 252 (*opp.* su-dassa); su-duddasaṁ, Dh. 36.

duddiṭṭha, *mfn.* (*sa.* dur-dṛshṭa) confused, misguided; *acc. m.* ~aṁ, Dh. 339.

duddha, *mfn.* (*pp.* dohati, duhati (-ū-); *sa.* dugdha, √duh) milked; *°-khira, *mfn.* (*v. h.*) *cp.* duyhati, *pass.*

dundubhi, *m.* (= *sa.*) a kettle-drum; deva-°, *m.* & *f.* thunder, *pl.* ~iyo (*f.*) 80,20.

dunniggaha, *mfn.* (*sa.* dur-nigraha) difficult to be restrained; *gen. n.* ~assa (cittassa), Dh. 35.

dunnivāraya, *mfn.* (*sa.* dur-nivārya) difficult to be kept back or restrained; *n.* ~aṁ (cittaṁ) Dh. 33; *m.* ~o (kuñjaro) Dh. 324. *cp.* nivāreti.

duppañña, *mfn.* (*sa.* dush-prajña) stupid, foolish, ignorant; *m.* ~o, Dh. 111. 140.

*duppabbajja, *n.* the painful life of a pabbajita (*q. v.*); *nom.* ~aṁ (durabhiramaṁ) Dh. 302 (differently *Max Müller*, SBE. X. 73). *cp.* pabbajjā, *f.*

*duppamuñca, *mfn.* difficult to be loosened; *n.* ~aṁ (bandhanaṁ) Dh. 346. (*cp.* pamuñcati).

*dupparāmaṭṭha, *mfn.* badly practised; *n.* ~aṁ (sāmaññaṁ) Dh. 311. (*cp.* parāmasati).

*duppariyogāha, *mfn.* difficult to get at the bottom of, unfathomable; *m.* ~o (Tathāgato) 95,13. (*cp.* pariyogāha).

dubbaca, *mfn.* (*sa.* dur-vacas) abusive, unruly; difficult to reason with, self-willed; *°-bhāva, *m.* self-will, *instr.* ~ena, 34,16. (*cp.* vacas).

dubbaṇṇa, *mfn.* (*sa.* dur-varṇa) of a bad colour, ill-favoured; *m.* ~o, 103,5.

dubbala, *mfn.* (*sa.* dur-bala) weak, feeble; *m.* ~o, 12,27; *acc.* ~aṁ, Dh. 7; *n. pl.* ~āni (uddāpādīni) 91,19.

*dubbalatta, *n.* (*sa.* *dur-balatva) weakness; *abl.* ~ā, 12,21.

*dubbalī-karaṇa, *mfn.* who causes weakness; *acc. pl. n.* ~e (*w. gen.* paññāya, *scil.* pañca nīvaraṇe) 91,7.

dubbuddhin, *mfn.* (*sa.* dur-buddhi) foolish, without insight; *m. pl.* ~ino, 76,30.

dubbhati, *vb.* (*sa.* √druh, druhyati) to be hostile to, plot against (*loc.*); *fut. 1. sg.* ~issāmi (tayi) 41,35. *cp.* dūbha.

dubbhāsita, *mfn.* (*sa.* dur-bhāshita) badly spoken; *n.* ~aṁ (padaṁ) 110,12.

duma, *m.* (*sa.* druma) a tree; dumagga, *n.* the top of a tree, *abl.* ~amhā, 13,4 (*cp.* agga[4]).

dummati, *m.* (*sa.* dur-mati) a fool; *nom.* ~i (ahaṁ) 30,22.

dummana, *mfn.* (*sa.* dur-manas)

dejected, in bad spirits; *m.* ~o, 2,14. 72,25. 104,18.

dummedha, *m.* (*sa.* dur-medha) a fool; *nom.* ~o, Dh. 136; *voc.* ~a, 106,10 = Dh. 394. *cp. next.*

***dummedhin**. *mfn.* foolish, stupid; *m. pl.* ~ino (janā) Dh. 26.

duyhati, *vb.* (*pass.* dohati, √duh) to be milked; *part. n.* ~ mānaṁ (khīraṁ) new milk, 99,28; *pp.* duddha (*q. v.*).

duraccaya, *mfn.* (*sa.* dur-atyaya) difficult to be conquered; *acc. f.* ~aṁ (taṇhaṁ) 108,1 = Dh. 336.

duranubodha, *mfn.* (= *sa.*) difficult to be comprehended; *m.* ~o (dhammo) 94,25.

durannaya, *mfn.* (*sa.* dur-anvaya) difficult to be fathomed; *f.* ~ā (gati) Dh. 92.

***durabhirama**, *mfn.* difficult to be enjoyed; *n.* ~aṁ (duppabbajjaṁ) Dh. 302.

durabhisambhava, *mfn.* (= *sa.*) difficult to reach or enter upon; *m.* ~o (maggo) 103,10.

***durājāna**, *mfn.* difficult to be understood; *m.* ~o (bhāvo thīnaṁ) 51,31.

***durāvāsa**, *mfn.* difficult to dwell in, d. to be lived or led; *pl.* (*n.*) ~ā (gharā, the household life) Dh. 302.

dullabha, *mfn.* (*sa.* dur-labha) difficult to be found or obtained; *m.* ~o, 31,18. Dh. 193; *acc.* ~aṁ, Dh. 160; *n.* su-dullabhaṁ (saccaṁ) 51,30; — °-manussattaṁ, *n.* the state of man which is one difficult to obtain, 22,15.

dussa, 15,19, according to the Comm. *gen. pron. demonstr.* = amussa (*cp.* asu, amuka), but this can hardly be correct; the reading dussaṁ which, in spite of the Comm., has been maintained by the Cingalese Mss., ought no doubt to be preferred; dussa, *n.* (*sa.* dūshya, dūçya or dūrça) a kind of woven stuff, occurs frequently in the Pāli texts; hence *dussika, *m.* a manufacturer of that stuff, or a cloth-seller (Jāt. VI, 276,25. Mil. 262,14. 333,12); but I think that in this case dussa must be *adj.* = *sa.* dūshya, corruptible, easily to be spoiled or damaged, *n.* ~aṁ (khettapālassa rattibhattaṁ). *Francis & Neil*, Jāt. III. p. 16, translate "wrongfully" (dussaṁ, *adv.*, *cp.* dussati below) and it is perhaps in order to avoid this interpretation (which does not agree with the tendency of the prose tale) that the Comm. has taken it for *gen. pron. Trenckner* accepts the *gen.* dussa (= amussa) although that form is not found elsewhere. *Henry* (Précis de gramm. Pālie, p. 94) corrects dussa into amussa.

dussati, *vb.* (*sa.* dushyati, √dush) to sin, offend (against, *gen.* or *loc. pers.*); *pr. 3. sg.* ~ati (appaduṭṭhassa) Dh. 125; (appaduṭṭhesu) Dh. 137; *pp.* duṭṭha (*v. h.*); *caus.* dūseti (*q. v.*) *cp.* dussa above.

dussīla, *mfn.* (*sa.* duḥ-çīla) ill-natured, bad, wicked, vicious; *m.* ~o, 107,3 = Dh. 308; Dh. 110. 320; *f.* ~ā, 9,11; *instr. f.* ~āya, 20,29.

***dussīlya**, *n.* (*fr. prec.*) wickedness; *nom.* ~aṁ (accanta-°) Dh. 162.

duhati, *vb., v.* dohati (dūhati).

dūta, *n.* (= *sa.*) a messenger; *pl.* ~ā (deva-°) 45,12; *acc. pl.* ~e (assa-°) 68,31.

***dūbha**, *m.* (*fr.* dubbhati, √druh; base of dūbhati, *vb.* = dubbhati; *cp. sa.* droha) malice, perfidy, treachery; only in *comp.* a-dūbha (*q. v.*) *cp.* a-dūbhāya (*dat.*) Jāt. I, 180,22; a-drūbhāya, Vin. I, 347,2 fr. b.

dūra, *mfn.* (= *sa.*) distant, far (*opp.* vidūra); — dūraṁ, *adv.* far away, 12,29; dūrañ-gama, *mfn.* going far away, *acc. m.* ~aṁ, Dh. 37; — dūrato (*abl.*) *adv.* from afar, 68,10. 76,20. 86,20. Dh. 219; — dūre (*loc.*) *adv.* & *prp. w. abl.*, far, far away; ~ ṭhito, 56,8; ~ pakāsenti. Dh. 304; dumaggamhā ~, 13,4; ~ito, 20,17; *cp.* atidūra.

dūrakkha, *mfn.* (*sa.* dū-rakshya) difficult to be guarded; *n.* ~aṁ (cittaṁ) Dh. 33.

dūrañgama, *mfn.* (= *sa.*) *v.* dūra.

*dūrama, *mfn.* difficult to be enjoyed; yattha ~aṁ (*n.*), where enjoyment is difficult.

dūseti, *vb.* (*caus.* dussati, *sa.* dūshayati) to spoil, destroy, infest (*acc.*); *aor. 3. sg.* dūsayi, 9,2 (without *obj.* = spoiled the game; = attānaṁ dūsayi, Comm.).

deti, *vb.* & deyya, *grd.*, *v.* dadāti.

deva, *m.* (= *sa.*) [1]) a god, deity; mostly *pl.* the gods, *esp.* the Devas (*opp.* Asuras) or inhabitants of the Devaloka, whose chief is Sakka; *nom.* ~o. 110,11; Dh. 105; *gen.* ~assa, 110,27; *pl.* ~ā, Dh. 94. 181. 230. 366. 420; ~ā ābhassarā (*v. h.*) Dh. 200; *gen. pl.* ~ānaṁ, 59,28. 80,26; Dh. 30. 224 (devāna); *loc.* ~esu, Dh. 56; — *comp.* (often implying the sense of 'celestial, superhuman', *etc.*) : *devānubhāvena (*instr.*) by the power of the gods, 63,32 (*v.* ānubhāva); devinda, *m.* the lord of the Devas (Sakka), 110,24-26; ⁰-kaññā, *f.* a celestial nymph, *pl.* ~ā, 64,30; *⁰-kumāra, *m.* a son of a god, ⁰-vaṇṇin, *mfn.* beautiful like that, *pl. m.* ~ino, 45,26 (*cp.* ⁰-putta); ⁰-gaṇa, *m.* a class or troop of gods, *instr.* ~ena, 60,23; ⁰-ṭṭhāna, *n.* place or seat in heaven, 16,18; *⁰-nagara, *n.* = ⁰-pura, *n.* the city of the Devas, 17,34. 59,33; 27,31; ⁰-putta, *m.* (= ⁰-kumāra) *acc.* ~aṁ. 63,8 (*cp.* putta); ⁰-rājan, *m.* (= devinda), *nom.* ~ā, 45,30; ⁰-loka, *m.* the world of the Devas or any superior world, heaven, *nom.* ~o, 59,30; *acc.* ~aṁ, Dh. 177; *loc.* ~asmiṁ, 59,30; *loc. pl.* ~esu (dvīsu, *viz.* Sakka's and Brahma's worlds) 60,23; ⁰-âbhimukha, *mfn.* (*v.* abhimukha); tāvatiṁsa-⁰, 59,28 (*v. h.*); — *⁰-vimāna, *n.* the palace of the gods, ⁰-sadisa, *mfn.* like that, *acc. m.* ~aṁ (rathaṁ) 63,6; — *⁰-saṁkhalikā, *f.* a magic chain, *instr.* ~āya, 21,14. — [2]) the sky, atmosphere; the rain-god; ~o (na vassati) 102,6; *voc.* ~a, 104,22; *gen.* ~assa (vassato) 105,22; ⁰-dundubhi (*v. h.*). — [3]) the god of death; deva-dūta, *m.* a messenger of death; *pl.* ~ā (uttamañgarubā) 45,12. — [4]) a lord, *voc.* deva frequently used in addressing a king ('sire, your majesty') 6,14. 31,9-19. 65,17; Makhādeva, *m.* *nom. pr.* (*q. v.*). *cp.* dibba, *mfn.*, devī, *f.*, sadevaka, *mfn.* & *next*.

devatā, *f.* (& *m.*), (= *sa.*) a god, deity; a spirit, ghost; in *sg.* often used instead of deva (*cp.* deva-putta); *nom.* ~ā (varaṇarukkhe adhivatthā) 5,19; *pl.* ~ā, 63,7. 65,24. 114,15; *instr.* ~āhi, 63,20; *loc.* ~āsu, 34,26; — rukkha-⁰, a dryad, 3,31; — samudda-⁰, a spirit of the sea, 28,28; — devatânubhāvena, *instr.* 17,25 (*v.* ānubhāva); — *⁰-paribhoga, *mfn.* fit to be enjoyed by the gods, *n.* ~aṁ (ambapakkaṁ) 36,31; — *⁰-sannipāta, *m.* an assembly of gods, *loc.* ~amhi, 110,30.

Devadatta, *m.* (= *sa.*) *nom. pr.* of a relative (cousin) and enemy of Gotama Buddha; ~o, 74,19, *seqv.*

*Devadaha, *n. nom. pr.* of a town, near the Lumbini-Grove, belonging to the family of Gotama Buddha's mother; ⁰-nagaraṁ, 62,5-6. [*cp. Lassen*, IA. II. p. 66 & XXXIII.]

*devasikaṁ, *adv.* (*fr.* divasa, *cp. sa.* daivasaka, *mfn.*) daily, every day; 6,2.

devī, *f.* (= *sa.*) [1]) a goddess; *pl.* ~iyo, 61,12. — [2]) a queen; *nom.* ~ī, 61,22; *voc.* devi, 55,26; *acc.* ~iṁ, 19,14; *gen.* ~iyā, 19,21. 61,30; *comp. w. nom. pr.* Amarā-⁰, the wife of Mahosadha, 55,32. 56,23; = Amarā, 56,12; — Udumbarā-⁰ (*q. v.*).

desa, *m.* (*sa.* deça) region, place, country; part, portion; *nom.* ~o, 82,33. 112,30; *acc.* ~aṁ, 31,35; *loc.* ~e (majjhima-⁰) 91,18. *cp.* padesa, videsa.

desanā, *f.* (*sa.* deçanā) a sermon, discourse, lesson; *nom.* ~ā, 86,9. 87,2; *acc.* ~aṁ, 30,24; ⁰-âvasāne, at the end of the discourse, 89,2; — dhamma-⁰, *f.* id.; instruction in the sacred doctrine; 68,23 (buddhānaṁ); *acc.*

~aṁ, 17,31. 29,16; — saddhamma-⁰, *f.* id. Dh. 194.

desita, *mfn.* (*pp.* deseti, *sa.* deçita) shown, set forth, taught; *m.* ~o (dhammo) 79,5; *n.* ~aṁ (nibbānaṁ) Dh. 285; *acc. m.* ~aṁ (Buddha-⁰, taught by the B.) 109,25; (Sammāsambuddha-⁰, kathāmaggaṁ) 113,29; *m. pl.* ~ā (vaggā) Dh. p. 94. v. 3. su-desita, *mfn.* (*q. v.*).

deseti, *vb.* (*sa.* deçayati, *caus.* √diç) to show, set forth, teach, preach (*acc.*); *pr. 1. sg.* ~emi (dhammaṁ) 90,17; *part. m.* ~ento (dhammaṁ) 17,27. 47,18. 74,18; *aor. 3. sg.* ~esi, 17,30; *fut. 1. sg.* ~essāmi, 68,15; *ger.* ~etvā, 7,27; *part. pass.* desiyamāna, *loc. m.* ~e (dhamme) 69,22; *pp.* desita (*q. v.*), *cp.* desanā.

deha, *m.* (= *sa.*) the body; *nom.* ~o, 85,6 (*comm.* on kāya).

domanassa, *n.* (*sa.* daurmanasya) dejectedness, despair; grief; *instr. pl.* ~ehi, 70,30; *gen. pl.* ~ānaṁ (dukkha-⁰ *dvandva-comp.*) 90,18; 66,10-17 (do.); ⁰-ppatta, *mfn.* sorrowful, *m.* ~o, 13,6. *cp.* dummana, *mfn.*

dovārika, *m.* (*sa.* dauvārika) a door-keeper, porter; ~o, 90,32; *acc.* ~aṁ, 91,25; *gen.* ~assa, 58,1; *acc. pl.* ~e, 58,21 (*cp. Fick,* Soc. Gl. p. 102); *instr. pl.* ~ehi (paṇḍita-⁰) 91,23. *cp.* dvāra.

dosa[1], *m.* (*sa.* dosha) fault, guilt; ~o, 74,13; *e. c. mfn.* (damaged by) *v.* icchā, tiṇa, dosa[2], moha, rāga.

dosa[2], *m.* (*sa.* dvesha) hatred; *acc.* ~aṁ. Dh. 20 (in the series: rāga, dosa, moha); *⁰-aggi, *m.* the fire of hatred, 64,20 (do.); *⁰-dosa, *mfn.* (*sa.* *dvesha-dosha) damaged by hatred, *f.* ~ā (ayaṁ pajā) Dh. 357; *⁰-sama, *mfn.* like hatred, *m.* ~o (kali) Dh. 202; vanta-⁰, vīta-⁰, *mfn.* free from hatred, Dh. 263. 357. (*cp. Pischel,* Gr. § 129).

dohati (& duhati) *vb.* (*sa.* √duh) to milk; *pass.* duyhati, *pp.* duddha (*q. v.*).

dohaḷa, *m.* (*sa.* dohada, *m.*, *cp. sa.* daurhṛda, *m.*) wish, desire, *esp.* the morbid longing of pregnant women (*w. loc.*); *nom.* ~o, 1,23; *acc.* ~aṁ, 1,6 (hadayamaṁse); hence the frequently occurring *adj. f.* dohaḷinī, [1]) pregnant, [2]) desiring, longing for (*w. loc.* or *comp.*): Jāt. IV, 334,21. VI, 484,16; III, 27,22. VI, 326,15 *etc.* The sanskritic etymology dohada = daurhṛda has been called in question by *Lüders* (Gött. Nachr. 1898,1: *fr.* *dvihṛd); likewise *Jolly,* Idg. Forsch. X, 213 and *Pischel,* Gr. § 436; but *Böhtlingk,* ZDMG. Vol. 55,98 takes it = doha-da ("das Verlangen nach dem. was Milch erzeugt", *scil.* kāma?)

dva-, dvā-, in *comp.* = 2; *v. next* (*cp.* dvi (dve)).

dvattiṁsa, *num.* (*sa.* dvātriṁçat) 32; 23,23 (petiyo); *⁰-ākāra, *n.* name of a chapter of Khuddakapāṭha (the 32 parts of the body) 82,6.

*dvattikkhattuṁ, *adv.* (*sa.* *dvā-tri-kṛtvas) for a second and third time; 114,16. *cp.* khattuṁ & tikkhattuṁ.

dvaya, [1]) *mfn.* (= *sa.*) twofold, double; *loc. pl.* ~esu (dhammesu) Dh. 384. — [2]) *n.* a pair, couple; two (opposite) things; *acc.* ~aṁ (nissito loko) 96,6; gātha-dvayaṁ, two gāthās, 47,23. 114,9; potthaka-⁰, 114,18 (two copies).

dvādasa, *num.* (*sa.* dvādaça) twelve; dvādasama, *mfn.* the twelfth, *m.* ~o, Dh. XII.

dvāra, *n.* (= *sa.*) door, gate, entrance; *nom.* ~aṁ (nivesana-⁰, nagara-⁰) 68,2-5; *acc.* ~aṁ, 6,5. 68,3; *instr.* ~ena, by the door or gateway, 12,10 (pure-⁰, the front door); 12,13. 57,13 (pacchima-⁰, the back door); 55,30 (uttara-⁰, the northern gateway); 59,3 (sāla-⁰, *q. v.*); *loc.* ~e, 57,13 (pure-⁰); often *e. c.* = at, before: gāma-⁰, 8,20; ghara-⁰, 27,27; *acc. pl.* ~āni (nagara-⁰) 39,25; *loc. pl.* ~esu, 38,12. 43,9; *comp.* gabbha-⁰ (*q. v.*); ⁰-samīpaṁ (*v. h.*); — dvāra-koṭṭhaka, *m.* a gateway; *loc. pl.* ~esu, 48,32;

satta-dvāra-koṭṭhaka, *mfn.* having 7 gateways, *acc.* ~aṁ (gehaṁ) ib.; — *dvāra-gāma, *m.* a suburb; *abl.* ~ato, 19,23; ⁰-gāmaka, *m.* id., *acc. pl.* ~e, 43,9; — apāruta-dvāra, *mfn.* (*v. h.*); eka-dvāra, *mfn.* (*v.* eka[2]); catu-⁰, pihita-⁰, bahu-⁰, *mfn.* (*q. v.*) *cp.* dovārika.

dvāvīsati, *num.* (*sa.* dvāviṁçati) 22; dvāvīsatima, *mfn.* the 22th; *m.* ~o (vaggo) Dh. XXII.

dvi-, (= *sa.*) base of the *num.* dve (*nom. acc. mfn.*) = two; *nom.* 6,33 (janā); dve pi, both, 19,14; 24,16 (cakkhūni); *acc.* 6,16 (mige); 62,28 (hatthe); ekaṁ dve karoti (= kasati) 56,16; *instr.* dvīhi, 7,14; 12,2; *gen.* dvinnaṁ. 12,33; 40,31; *loc.* dvīsu, 60,22. *cp.* di- (dija, dipada, diyaḍḍha); dutiya, *mfn.*; dva-, dvā-; dvaya, *mfn.* & *next.*

dvija, *m.* (= *sa.*; *cp.* dija) a bird; *⁰-gaṇa, *m.* a flock of birds; *pl.* ~ā. 7,20.

dvidhā, *adv.* (= *sa.*) twofold, divided in two; 33,18 (chinditvā); 58,22 (bhinditvā); — ⁰-karaṇa, *n.* the dividing in two (= kasana), 56,16. *cp.* dvedhā.

dviha, *n.* (*sa.* dvy-aha, *m.*) a period of two days; *v.* aha, *cp.* tīha.

dve, *num. nom. acc.*, *v.* dvi-.

dvedhā, *adv.* (= *sa.*; *cp.* dvidhā) twofold, divided in two; *⁰-patha, *m.* a double path, cross-way; doubt: *acc.* ~aṁ, Dh. 282.

Dh.

dhaṁsin, *mfn.* (rather = *sa.* dharshin than *sa.* dhvaṁsin (Tr.); *cp.* Dhpd. (1855) p. 372–3) audacious, obtrusive, importunate; *instr. m.* ~inā, Dh. 244 (*cp.* MN. I p. 236,1).

dhaja, *m.* (*sa.* dhvaja) a banner, flag or standard; ⁰-patākâdīhi, 62,7.

dhajinī, *f.* (*sa.* dhvajinī) an army (arrayed); *acc.* ~iṁ, 104,3.

dhana, *n.* (= *sa.*) wealth, property; money; *nom.* ~aṁ, 23,6. 48,11; *acc.* ~aṁ, 29,6. 38,20. 48,18; *gen.* ~assa, 52,5; — ⁰âharaṇatthāya, 32,17 (*v.* āharaṇa); dhanatthāya, 32,29 (*v.* attha[1]); ⁰-lobha, *m.* desire of money; *instr.* ~ena, 22,23; *⁰-vassa, *n.* & *⁰-vasāpanaka, *mfn.* (*v. h.*); ⁰-santike, 33,26 (*q. v.*); — mahad-dhana, *mfn.* (*q. v.*); *cp.* nid-dhana, sa-dhana & dhanesin.

*Dhanapālaka, *m. nom. pr.* of an elephant (said to be identical with Nālāgiri, *q. v.*); *nom.* ~o nāma kuñjaro, Dh. 324 (*cp.* Jāt. V, 337,1).

*Dhaniya, *m. nom. pr.* of a herdsman; ~o (gopo) 104,20.

dhanu, *n.* (& *m.* ?) (*sa.* dhanus & dhanu, *m.*) a bow; *acc.* ~uṁ, 61,20. 92,15; asi-satti-dhanu-ādīni (āvudhāni) 6,12; dhanu-kalāpa, (*m.* ?) bow and quiver, 75,15.

dhanesin, *mfn.* (*sa.* dhanaishin) longing for riches; *gen. pl.* ~inaṁ (vāṇijānaṁ) 20,22 = 25,30.

dhamani, *f.* (= *sa.*) a vein, nerve; ⁰-santhata, *mfn.* (*q. v.*) covered with veins (said of an emaciated person); *n.* ~aṁ (jantuṁ kisaṁ) 106,12 — Dh. 395 (*cp.* Weber, Bhag. II. 289,2-3).

dhameti, *vb.* (*caus.* dhamati, to blow; *sa.* √dhmā) to blow (any instrument, *acc.*); *part. m. pl.* ~entā (saṁkhe) 8,23.

dhamma[1], *m.* (rarely *n.*) (*sa.* dharma) [1]) ordinance, law; right, duty; *nom.* ~o (sanantano) 106,24 — Dh. 5; *acc.* ~aṁ (ekaṁ) 106,14 — Dh. 176; (vissaṁ, the whole law) 106,3 — Dh. 266; *gen.* ~assa (anudhammacārī, *q. v.*) Dh. 20; *n. pl.* ~āni, Dh. 82; samaṇa-⁰, priestly duties, 15,12; often *opp.* attha (*v. h.*). — [2]) righteousness, morality; virtue, good quality; ~o, 106,9 — Dh. 393; 3,27; Dh. 261; ~aṁ (cara) 7,24, *cp.* Dh. 169; *instr.* ~ena, righteously, 36,29. 42,26. Dh. 257; ~assa (gutto, *q. v.*) Dh. 257; *loc.* ~e (with honourable intentions) 1,31; *pl.* ~ā (caturo)

3,26; (cattāro) Dh. 109; (pāpakā, sins) Dh. 242; *instr.* ~ehi, 3,24; *gen.* ~ānaṁ, Dh. 273. *cp.* a-dhamma, *m.* — 3) "the truth"; a) any religious doctrine or philosophical system, *esp.* that taught by Buddha (the Four Truths *etc.*); preaching of that doctrine; ~o, 94,25; ~aṁ (suṇāhi) 22,17; (sossāmi) 87,16; (deseti) 7,27. 51,5; (uttamaṁ) Dh. 115; (kaṇhaṁ, *q. v.*) Dh. 87; vara-°, 87,9; Satthu ~aṁ, 87,13; *loc.* ~e (desiyamāne) 69,22; — b) the second great collection of the Buddhist sacred books (tipiṭaka, also named sutta-piṭaka) *opp.* vinaya (*q. v.*, *cp.* abhidhamma) : ~o ca vinayo ca, 79,5; ~aṁ, 109,15; °-vinaya-saṁgaha, *m.* 109,13; — c) *in the triple formula*: Buddha, dhamma, saṁgha, 69,19. 107,17 = Dh. 190 (*cp.* tevācika & saraṇa). — *cp.* sad-dhamma, a-sad-dhamma (*v.* a-sat); at the end of *adj. comp. v.* agga-dhamma, diṭṭha-°, patta-°, pariyogāḷha-°, vidita-°, saṁkhata-°. — 4) *In the psychology* = nature, character; condition of being, condition of life; thing; in *pl.* dhammā is often = mental objects in general, phenomena (just as rūpā are the objects of sense to the eye, 70,25), sometimes taken as identical with saṁkhārā (*q. v.*); *loc.* diṭṭhe va dhamme, in this world, in the present life, 92,32 (*cp.* diṭṭha-dhamma); sahetu-dhamma, *m.* the effect together with its cause, *acc.* ~aṁ, 66,21; *pl.* ~ā, 66,20; 70,32; sabbe ~ā anattā, 107,15 = Dh. 279; manopubbaṅgamā ~ā, the states of mind are the result of thought (?) Dh. 1 (*cp.* manas); *loc. pl.* ~esu (sabbesu) Dh. 353; dvayesu ~esu (in two things; *i. e.* samatha & vipassanā, *Comm.*) Dh. 384. — The denotion of "nature, state, condition" may be seen in many *comp.* (*subst.* & *adj.*): mitta-dhamma, *m.* friendship, 14,3; methuna-°, *m.* love, 54,11; more frequently at the end of *adj. comp.* = having the nature of, being subject to : a-nivattana-dhamma, a-vinipāta-°, an-uppāda-°, nirodha-°, pāpa-°, marīci-°, vaya-°, samudaya-°, *mfn.* (*v. h.*). As to the different explanations of the meaning of the word dhamma *cp. Max Müller,* SBE. X. p. 3—4; *Caroline Rhys Davids,* Transl. of Dhamma-Saṅgaṇi, Introd. p. XXXII seqv., p. XLI. *cp. next. etc.*

dhamma 2, *mf(ī)n.* (*sa.* dhārma) belonging to dhamma 3; *instr. f.* ~iyā (kathāya, by a sermon or religious discourse) 71,22 = 77,25.

dhamma-kathika, *m.* (*sa.* dharma-kathaka) a preacher or propounder of the dhamma; ~o, 22,29. 62,27; *instr.* ~ena, 22,30; *gen. pl.* ~ānaṁ. 109,9; *°-thera, *m.* the elder who preaches the dhamma, *acc.* ~aṁ, 22,27.

***dhamma-gaṇḍikā**, *f.* a block for execution; 6,25-27 (*v.* gaṇḍikā).

***dhamma-gata**, *mfn.* directed to the law; *f.* ~ā (sati) Dh. 297.

dhamma-cakkhu, *n.* (*sa.* dharma-cakshus) the eye of the truth; *nom.* ~uṁ (udapādi, Yasassa) 68,26.

dhamma-cārin, *mfn.* (*sa.* dharma-cārin) observing the law, virtuous, dutiful; *nom. m.* ~ī, Dh. 168 (*cp.* anudhammacārin).

***dhamma-jīvin**, *mfn.* virtuous, dutiful; *gen. m.* ~ino, Dh. 24; *gen. pl.* ~inaṁ, Dh. 164.

dhamma-ṭṭha, *mfn.* (*sa.* dharma-stha) just; *m.* ~o, Dh. 256. 257; *acc. m.* ~aṁ, Dh. 217. — °-vagga, *m.* Dh. ch. XIX.

dhammatā, *f.* (*sa.* dharmatā) inherent nature; manners, practice, habit; 21,17. *cp.* su-dhammatā, *f.*

dhamma-dāna, *n.* (*sa.* dharma-dāna) the gift of the law (or the truth); Dh. 354.

dhamma-desanā, *f.* (*sa.* dharma-deçanā) instruction in the truth (or in the four truths); a sermon, religious discourse; ~ā (Buddhānaṁ) 68,23; *acc.* ~aṁ, 17,31.

dhamma-dhara, *m.* (*sa.* dharma-dhara) 'a supporter of the dhamma', one who knows the sacred doctrine; ~o, Dh. 259; *pl.* ~ā, 109,26.

*dhamma-pada, *n.* a word or verse of the sacred doctrine, also *nom. pr.* of a canonical book, being a collection of moral sentences; *nom. & acc.* ~aṁ, Dh. 102; 44. 45 (sudesitaṁ); ekaṁ pi ~aṁ, one single word of the sacred doctrine, 22,28. *cp. Max Müller,* SBE. X, Introd. p. LIII; *Weber,* Ind. Str. I, 125; *Franke,* ZDMG. XLVI, 734. Specimens thereof p. 106–107. – Dhammapadaṭṭhakathā, *f.* the Commentary on Dh.; specimen p. 86,12–89,17.

*dhamma-pītin, *mfn.* drinking in the law; *m.* ~ī, Dh. 79. — °-rasa, *m.* the sweetness of drinking in the law: *acc.* ~aṁ, Dh. 205.

dhamma-rata, *mfn.* (*sa.* dharma-rata) delighting in the dhamma, virtuous; *m.* ~o, Dh. 364.

dhamma-rati, *f.* (*sa.* dharma-rati) delight in the dhamma; *nom.* ~ī, Dh. 354.

*dhamma-rasa, *m.* the sweetness of the dhamma; ~o, Dh. 354.

dhamma-rāja(*n*), *m.* (*sa.* dharma-rāja) a righteously ruling king; 'the king of truth' (epithet of Buddha); *nom.* ~ā, 38,12; Buddho ~ā, 19,1.

*dhamma-vinicchaya, *m.* investigation of what is right, righteous decision; *instr.* ~ena, Dh. 144.

dhamma-saṁgaha, *m.* (*sa.* dharma-saṁgraha) the collection of sacred books, called Dhamma-, or Sutta-piṭaka; *acc.* ~aṁ, 109,16. – dhamma-vinaya-saṁgaho, the collection of Dhamma & Vinaya, 109,13. *cp.* dhamma[3].

*Dhamma-saṅgaṇi, *f. nom. pr.* of a canonical Pālibook, the first part of the Abhidhamma-piṭaka, being a compendium of psychology; 102,12; *gen.* ~iyā, 113,33 (commentary thereon : Atthasālinī, *q. v.*).

*dhamma-santati, *f.*, the continuity or serial succession of the living beings, 99,25 (~ sandahati).

dhamma-sabhā, *f.* (*sa.* dharma-sabhā) a place or hall of religious meeting; *loc.* ~āyaṁ, 29,26.

dhamma-savana, *n.* (*sa.* dharma-çravana) the hearing of a sermon, attending divine service; °-atthāya (gate), in order to attend service, 28,5.

dhammassāmi(*n*), *m.* (*sa.* dharma-svāmin) 'lord of Dhamma', *i. e.* Buddha; *gen.* ~issa, 114,6.

*dhammānuvattin, *mfn.*, following the law (*cp.* anuvattin); *m. pl.* ~ino, Dh. 86.

*dhammārāma, *mfn.* 'one who has Dhamma for his pleasure garden', dwelling in the law; *m.* ~o, Dh. 364 (*cp.* ārāma).

dhammāsana, *n.* (*sa.* dharmāsana) a cathedra, preaching-seat; *abl.* ~ato, 62,27.

dhammika, *mfn.* (*sa.* dhārmika) righteous, pious, religious; *m.* ~o (dhammarājā) 38,12; 39,8. *cp.* a-dhammika, a-dhammikatā.

°dhammin, *mfn.* (*sa.* dharmin) having the nature of, subject to; uppāda-vaya-° (*v.* uppāda, *cp.* dhamma[1]), 80,28.

dhammī, *adj. f.*, *v.* dhamma[2].

°dhara, *mfn.* (*e. c.* = *sa.*) holding, wearing; possessing; jutin-° (*v.* juti); dhamma-°, paṁsukūla-°, vinaya-° (*q. v.*); uttama-rūpa-° (*v.* rūpa) *cp.* dhāreti.

dharaṇī, *f.* (= *sa.*) earth, land, kingdom (*orig. adj. f.* bearing, supporting); godharaṇī, *f.* (*v. h.*).

dhāti, *f.* (*sa.* dhātrī) a nurse; *acc. pl.* ~iyo, 45,25.

dhātu, *f.* (*& m.*), (= *sa.* dhātu, *m.*) a primary element (*e. g.* a verbal root); the property of a primary element (colour, *etc.*); any constituent part (*esp.* of the body); a sacred relic; *pācīna-loka-°, the eastern quarter (or horizon), *abl.* ~to, 32,30.

°dhātuka, *mfn.* (*e. c.* = *sa.*) having the qualities of, affected with; paṇḍuroga-°, having jaundice, m. ~o.

35,16; — vāmanaka-⁰, "having the qualities of one that is deformed", *m.* ~o (pacchā-⁰) 24,24.

Dhātukathā, *f. nom. pr.* of a canonical book, the third part of the Abhidhamma-Piṭaka; 102,12.

dhāna, *n.* (= *sa.*), only *e. c.* = a receptacle for, a heap of, *v.* saṁkāra-⁰.

dhāraṇa, *n.* (= *sa.*) holding, wearing (of ornaments); mālā-gandha-vilepana-⁰, 81,25.

dhārā, *f.* (= *sa.*) stream, current; udaka-⁰, 62,32 (*q. v.*).

dhāreti, *vb.* (*caus.* √dhṛ; *sa.* dhārayati) [1]) to hold, bear, wear; carry, bring (*acc.*); *pot. 3. sg.* ~eyya (andhakāre telapajjotaṁ) 69,17; *pp.* ~ita, *n.* ~aṁ (padumaṁ) 23,35. — [2]) to hold back, restrain (*acc.*); *pot. 3. sg.* dhāraye (kodhaṁ) 106,33 = Dh. 222. — [3]) to bear in mind, remember (by tradition); to hold, consider, understand (*acc.* or *acc.* & *abl.*); *aor. 3. pl.* ~esuṁ (Jinasāsanaṁ) 109,23; *fut. 3. pl.* ~ayissanti (Jātakaṁ) 102,17–21; *inf.* ~ayituṁ, 102,18; — *imp. 2. pl.* ~etha (vyākataṁ me vyākatato, consider only that elucidated what has been elucidated by me) 93,2–8. — [4]) to admit, receive, take up, sustain (a cause, *acc.*); *imp. 3. sg.* ~etu (upāsakaṁ maṁ) 69,20; *pot. 2. sg.* ~eyyāsi (kassa atthaṁ) 101,9. *cp.* dhara, dhāraṇa, *etc.*; dhiti.

dhāvati, *vb.* (*sa.* √dhāv) to run; *pr. 3. sg.* ~ati (vanaṁ, *q. v.*) Dh. 344; *part. gen. f.* dhāvantiyā (pathe) 31,34; *ger.* ~itvā, 59,1.

dhi (or dhī), *indecl.* (*sa.* dhik) *interj.* of reproach or displeasure: fie! shame on, woe upon (commonly *w. acc.* or *gen.*); dhī (brāhmaṇassa hantāraṁ) Dh. 389; dhī (y'assa muñcati) *ib.*; very often combined with *imp.* atthu before which an euphonic 'r' is inserted: dhi-r-atthu (idha jīvitaṁ) 103,33; ~ (jātiyā) 63,13.

dhiti, *f.* (*sa.* dhṛti) firmness, fortitude, courage; *nom.* ~i, 3,37; *acc.* ~iṁ (upaṭṭhapetvā) 41,27.

dhir- & dhī, *v.* dhi.

dhītar, *f.* (*sa.* duhitṛ) a daughter; *nom.* dhītā, 10,4; 10,11 (rāja-⁰); 86,24 (pesakāra-⁰); *acc.* ~araṁ, 10,9; 86,13; *gen.* dhītu (later dhītāya, *v. below.*) 57,1; *pl.* ~aro, 32,30 (mātu-⁰, *i. e.* mother and daughter). Besides dhītar we find also the base dhītā (*esp.* in younger texts & at the end of *comp.*): *gen.* ~āya (pesakāra-⁰) 89,17; *loc. pl.* ~āsu (putta-⁰, *dvandva-comp.*) 7,25. — kula-dhītar, *f.* (*v. h.*).

dhīra, *mfn.* (= *sa.*) constant, firm, energetic; wise, thoughtful; *m.* ~o (*i. e.* Buddha) 78,30; Dh. 28 *etc.* *m. pl.* ~ā, 47,28. 109,20; Dh. 23 *etc.*

dhuta, *mfn.* (*sa.* dhuta & dhūta, 'shaken') 'one who has shaken off his sins', dutiful (?) *cp.* Vin. II. 197,1; dhuta, *n.* = dhutaṅga, *n.* is a designation of certain priestly duties; hence dhutavāda, *m.*, [1]) the doctrine of Dhutaṅga, the Dhutaṅga precepts, *cp.* Dh. (1855) p. 259,7; [2]) a teacher or propounder of those precepts (= dhutavādi(*n*), Jāt. I. 130,22). *gen. pl.* ~ānaṁ (aggo, Kassapo) 109,6, *cp.* AN. I. p. 23; [3]) *adj.* = dhuta (Mil. 380,20, "pure in speech") *cp.* dhona *below.*

dhutta, *m.* (*sa.* dhūrta) a fraudulent fellow, gamester; scoundrel, villain; scamp, rogue; ~o, 49,22; *acc.* ~aṁ. 48,27; *gen.* ~assa, 49,3; *pl.* ~ā, 74,4; *acc.* ~e, 74,7; *gen.* ~ānaṁ, 73,19.

dhura, *m.* (= *sa.*) the foremost or chief part of anything, a yoke, the fore end of a ship; *loc.* ~e (nāvāya), 18,19. 27,19. *cp.* dhorayha.

dhuva, [1]) *mfn.* (*sa.* dhruva) fixed, permanent, certain; *n.* ~aṁ (maraṇaṁ), 86,16. a-ddhuva, *mfn.* (*v. h.*). [2]) *n.* permanence, durability; ~aṁ. Dh. 147.

dhūpa, *m.* (= *sa.*) incense; gandha-dhūpa-⁰ *etc.* (*dvandva comp.*) 48,30.

dhenu, *f.* (= *sa.*) a milk-cow; *miga-°, a female deer, hind, doe; 7,29.

*dhenupa, *m.* a calf; *pl.* ~ā, 105,11.

°dheyya, *n.* (*sa.* dheya) realm, region; *v.* Maccu-°, Māra-°.

*dhona, *mfn.* (probably = dhota, *pp.* dhovati, to wash; *sa.* dhauta, √dhāv [2]) pure, purified from sin. The commentators agree in explaining this word by dhuta-pāpa (*v.* dhuta, √dhu, dhunāti) or by dhuta-kilesa = buddha (Pj. ad Sn. v. 834 & Ps. ad MN. ch. 56). *Fausbøll*, Gloss. Sn. p. 203 refers it to √dhu, to shake, which after all may be closely related to dhovati; but it is questionable whether this word is contained in the *comp.* ati-dhona-cārin (*q. v.* Dh. 240). I think it better to take atidhona = *sa.* atidhāvana *fr. vb.* atidhāvati, to transgress. A *subst. n.* dhona is mentioned in the Comm. on Dh. v. 240 (= the 4 paccayas, *v. Childers*) and on MN. ch. 56 (= ñāna; hence dhona, *mfn.* 'tena samāgato').

*dhorayha, *m.* (*fr.* *dhorvayha, *sa.* *dhaurvahya, *abstr. fr.* dhūrvaha) a beast of burden. — °-sīla, *mfn.* having the virtue of a (good) draught-cattle, "much enduring"; *acc. m.* ~aṁ, Dh. 208.

dhovati, *vb.* (*sa.* dhāvati, √dhāv [2]) to wash, to clean by rinsing or rubbing (*acc.*); *aor. 3. sg.* dhovi (pāde) 57,16; *ger.* ~itvā, 22,25 (mukhaṁ); 41,19 (khaggaṁ); 82,21 (bhājanaṁ); a-dhovitvā (pātiṁ) 56,25; *pp.* dhota or (more rarely) dhovita : hatthe dhovita-kāle ("when he was washing his hands") 41,13. *cp.* dhona & *next.*

dhovana, *n.* (*sa.* dhāvana) washing; mukha-dhovanatthāya gantvā ("when he went to wash his face") 21,28; hattha-°, 56,23 (washing the hands, or : water for washing?).

N.

na, *adv.* (= *sa.*) not; before vowels 'a' may be dropped (n'atthi, 1,15; n'etaṁ, 8,27) or contracted with a *foll.* 'a' (nâhaṁ, 1,21); before 'i' we find sometimes 'y' inserted (na-y-idaṁ, 23,35). — [1]) na is the usual negation before verbs : 1,9. 16. *etc.*, but it occurs also often before other words : na Sākhaṁ upasaṁvase, 7,33 (*cp.* mā); na gahe rame, 47,26; nâtidūre, 83,2; na tāvatā, 106,5, and especially at the beginning of a sentence : nâhaṁ, 1,21; na koci, 8,3 *etc.* — [2]) *in questions,* used like the English 'not' : [a]) kiṁ na passasi (have you not seen?) 111,19; kaccin nu . . . na, 9,28; [b]) *in disjunctive questions :* kiṁ . . . karoti na karoti (= or not) 9,25. — [3]) *repeated :* [a]) n' . . . na . . . na (neither . . . nor . . . nor) 8,27. 94,3. Dh. 127; n'eva . . . na, 3,3. 10,16. 74,13 (id.); n'eva upapajjati na na upapajjati, 89,31. 94,18; *cp.* neva-saññā-nâsaññāyatana; na ca . . . na ca (id.) 99,3; [b]) na kiñci na (all, every) 51,35, *cp.* na . . . akiñci ("not a little") Dh. 390. — [4]) *comb. w. other particles :* [a]) n'eva, not for all that (after 'pi ce') 16,14; n'eva . . . na (*v. above*); [b]) na kho (pana), verily not, 9,31. 93,27; [c]) na ca = than, 8,3 (rajjaṁ jaheyyaṁ na ca taṁ paṭiññaṁ); ca na ca (both . . . and not) 89,30. 94,16; na ca . . . na ca (neither . . . nor, *v. above*); [d]) na hi (non enim) Dh. 5; in answers = no, nay verily, 97,19. — [5]) *negative prefix in comp.* = a- (*cp.* nir-, vi-) *v.* na-cira, na-nikāma-seyyā (natthitā, *f.* (*q. v.*) is *abstr. fr.* the phrase n'atthi). *cp.* nanu, nūna, no & mā.

*naṁ, *pron. demonstr.* (in several cases besides *nom.* substituted (enclitically) for taṁ, *cp.* enaṁ & the base ana-, *sa. instr.* anena *etc.*) him, her, it; *acc. mfn.* naṁ : *m.* 4,33. 7,30. 16,15 etc. 103,32. 113,20; nan (ti) 3,6. 12,28; *f.* 55,16. 88,3; nan, 9,18; *n.* 94,28; — *acc. pl.* ne, 74,8; *gen. pl.* nesaṁ,

8,10. 73,1. — naṁ is also sometimes pleonastically inserted, *e. g.* 73,18 (*cp.* taṁ, 9,1; Cinghalese reading: naṁ). In such cases the commentaries explain it as a particle (nipāta) or as a shortened form of nāma (?); *cp.* *Pischel,* Gr. § 150. (431).

nakkhatta, *n.* (*sa.* nakshatra) [1]) an asterism or constellation, a conjunction of stars (*esp.* that of the moon with any constellation, a lunar mansion); *acc.* ~aṁ (oloketi, to read the stars) 32,31; — °-yoga, *m.* id., *loc.* ~e laddhe, ("at a certain conjunction of the planets") 32,10. — [2]) a festival; ~aṁ (kīḷati, to enjoy the festival) 61,8; — *°-kīḷā, *f.* "the festivities" (*v. h.*) 61,5; °-patha, *m.* 'star-path', the starry sky, *acc.* ~aṁ, Dh. 208. — āsāḷhi-°, 61,2 (*v. h.*) *cp.* āsāḷha.

nakha, *m.* (= *sa.*) a nail; *pl.* ~ā, 82,2 — 97,20.

nagara, *n.* (= *sa.*) a town, city; a fortress; *nom.* ~aṁ (yakkha-°) 20,32; (aṭṭhīnaṁ, "a stronghold of the bones") Dh. 150; *acc.* ~aṁ, 58,24 (the inhabitants of the city); anto-° (*v. h.*); saka-°, to his own city, 44,16; *loc.* ~e, 19,15; 61,2 (Kapilavatthu-°); 77,15 (Bhoga-°); *comp.* °-âbhimukha, *mfn.* (*v.* abhimukha); nagarûpama, *mfn.* like a fortress, *n.* ~aṁ, Dh. 40 (*cp.* upama). °-dvāra (*v. h.*); °-samīpe, 21,18; °-vīthisu, 73,29; °-vāsin. *mfn.* (*v. h.*); — *deva-° = deva-pura, *n.* (*q. v.*); anto-nagare & bahi-nagare (inside & outside the town) *q. v.* *cp.* nāgara.

nagga, *mfn.* (*sa.* nagna) naked; *f.* ~ā, 31,10-13; *n.* ~aṁ, 31,12. — °-cariyā, *f.* going naked; Dh. 141.

naṅgala, *n.* (*sa.* lāṅgala) a plough; *acc.* ~aṁ (mahantaṁ) 71,28.

nacira, *mfn.* (= *sa.*) not of long duration; nacirass'eva (*adv.*) *v.* cirassaṁ.

nacca, *n.* (*sa.* nṛtya) dancing; *instr.* ~ena, 10,20; °-jātaka, *n.* 10,1; *dvandva-comp.* ~âdīni, ~âdisu, 65,1. 64,32; °-gīta-, 64,29. 81,24.

naccati, *vb.* (*sa.* nṛtyati, √nṛt) to dance; *pr. 3. sg.* ~ati, 18,18; *part. m.* ~anto, 10,15; *imp. 2. sg.* ~assu, 50,11; *fut. 1. sg.* ~issāmi, 50,13; *aor. 3. sg.* nacci, 18,20; *inf.* ~ituṁ, 10,15; *comp.* naccitu-kāma, *mfn.* wishing to dance, 50,35 (°-kām'amhi, I (*f.*) wish to dance). *cp.* nacca & nāṭaka.

naṭṭha, *mfn.* (*pp.* nassati; *sa.* nashṭa) lost, perished; *acc. m.* ~aṁ (yasaṁ) 42,12.

nattar, *m.* (*sa.* naptṛ) a grandson; *gen.* nattu, 64,9.

natthitā, *f.* (*sa.* nāstitā; *fr.* n'atthi) non-existence, non-reality; *acc.* ~aṁ, 96,7 (*cp.* atthitā).

nadati, *vb.* (*sa.* √nad) to cry, roar; to make a noise (*acc.*); *pr. 3. sg.* ~ati, 8,28; *part. m. pl.* ~antā (mahānādaṁ) 6,13; *aor. 3. sg.* nadi (sīhanādaṁ) 16,14; *ger.* ~itvā (koñcanādaṁ) 61,20; *pp.* nadita (*v. next*); *cp.* nāda.

nadita, *n.* (*pp. fr. prec.*; *cp. sa.* nādita) roar, noise; ~aṁ (sīhassa) 8,27.

nadī, *f.* (= *sa.*) a river; *nom.* ~ī, 14,9; 35,18 (mahā-°); *acc.* ~iṁ, 16,25. 103,2; *instr.* ~iyā ("upstream") 29,5; *gen.* ~iyā, 2,19-21; tassā nadiyā vasati, 2,26 (tassā must here be taken as *loc. f.*, *cp.* Jāt. I. 170,11; MN. I. 385,9); *loc.* ~iyaṁ (mahā-°) 36,30; *gen. pl.* ~īnaṁ, 103,18; 72,27 (mahā-°); — °-kūla, *n.* = °-tīra, *n.* the bank of a river, *loc.* ~e, 2,19. 108,24; — °-pāre, on the opposite side of the river, 56,21; — °-majjhe, in the middle of the river, 2,22.

naddha, *mfn.* (*pp.* nayhati (nandhati); *sa.* naddha, √nah) tied, bound, put on; °-pañcāyudha, *mfn.* 111,16 (*v.* āyudha). *cp.* onaddha, sannaddha.

***nanikāma**, *mfn.* (*fr.* nikāma, *m.*) disagreeable; °-seyyā, *f.* "an uncomfortable bed", Dh. 309 (*acc.* ~aṁ).

nanu, *indecl.* (= *sa.*) [1]) particle of interrogation (*latin*: nonne); ~

mayā tuyhaṁ abhayaṁ dinnaṁ, 7,6; ~ brahmacariyassa te kālo, 46,34; ~ so mutto bhavissati, 100,7. — [2]) particle of affirmation : surely, certainly; ~ na sakkā, 91,16.

nandati, *vb.* (*sa.* √nand) to rejoice; to delight in, to be glad of (*instr.*); *pr. 3. sg.* ~ati (puttehi) 105,28; 107,26 = Dh. 18. *cp. next.*

nandanā, *f.* (= *sa.*) delight; 105,29. — rāja-nandana, *m.* a prince (poetically); *acc.* ~aṁ, 112,11.

nandi[1], *m.* & nandī, *f.* (*sa.* nandi, *m.*) joy, pleasure; °-rāga-, pleasure and lust, 67,13 (-sahagata); *nandībhava, *m.* rise of pleasure; °-parikkhīṇa, *mfn.* "in whom all gaiety is extinct", Dh. 413 (*acc. m.* ~aṁ) *cp.* kāmābhava. — nandi[2], *f.*, *v. next.*

nandhi, *f.* (*sa.* naddhrī) a leathern strap or thong (often spelt nandi); *acc.* ~iṁ (chetvā) Dh. 398.

nabha(s), *n.* (*sa.* nabhas) sky, atmosphere; *instr.* ~asā (°-āgamā, "departed through the air") 111,1.

namati, *vb.* (*sa.* √nam) to bend or bow to (*intr.*); *aor. 3. sg.* nami (cittaṁ, pabbajjāya) 65,13; *pp.* namita, bent; °-citta, *mfn.* 46,18 (*m.* ~o, pabbajjāya, one whose mind has turned to retiring from the world). — *caus.* namayati (& nāmeti), to bend (*acc.*); *pr. 3. pl.* ~ayanti, 106,27 = Dh. 80. *cp.* an-amatagga.

namassati, *vb.* (*denom. fr.* namas (*v.* namo below); *sa.* namasyati) to pay honour to (*acc.*); *pr. 3. sg.* ~ati (apujjaṁ) 30,21; *pot. 3. sg.* ~eyya, Dh. 392.

namita, *mfn.* (*pp.* namati, *q. v.*).

Namuci, *m.* (= *sa.*) *nom. pr.* of a demon (identical with Māra, *q. v.*); *nom.* ~ī, 103,4; *voc.* ~i, 103,31.

namo, *indecl.* (*sa.* namas, *n.*) an exclamation of adoration or homage (*w. gen. pers.*; also often combined with verbs, as karoti, dadāti); ~ ty'atthu ("homage to thee") 13,26. 108,11; ~ tassa Bhagavato Arahato Sammāsambuddhassa, 81,5 (the usual formula at the beginning of a Pāli book).

naya, *m.* (= *sa.*) 'leading', instruction, plan, method; way, manner; *instr.* ~ena (Mahāpadāne āgata-°, "in the manner related in M.") 63,12; 'ti ādinā ~, 91,31 (*v.* ādi[3]); purimanayen'eva, in the same manner as before, 26,10. 63,21; heṭṭhāvutta-°, id. 63,22.

nayati, *vb.* (*sa.* √nī) *v.* neti.

nayhati (or nandhati), *vb.* (*sa.* √nah) to bind, tie; only *comp. w. prep.*, *v.* upa-nayhati, pilandhati; *pp.* naddha (*q. v.*) *cp.* nandhi (nandi) *f.*

nara, *m.* (= *sa.*) a man; *nom.* ~o, 111,10; *acc.* ~aṁ, Dh. 47; *gen.* ~assa, 105,29; *loc. pl.* ~esu, 47,20. — *f.* nārī (*v. h.*) — narinda, *m.* (*sa.* narendra) 'man-lord', king; ~o, 112,31; *voc.* ~a, 7,15; Sīhabāhu-narinda-ja, *m.* son of S. (Vijaya) 110,22 (*nom.* ~jo).

nala or **naḷa**, *m.* (*sa.* id. & naḍa) name of a species of reed; a reed or stalk in general; *nom.* ~o, 26,27; *acc.* ~aṁ (-ḷ-) 108,5 = Dh. 337; 5,18 (kumuda-°); — °-vana, *n.* a thicket of reeds, 26,25. *cp.* nāḷikā, *f.*

Nalamāla, *m.* (*sa.* Naḷamālin) 'reed-garlanded', *nom. pr.* of an ocean; *acc.* ~aṁ, 26,25. — Nalamāli(*n*), *m.* id. 26,30.

nalāṭa, *n.* (*sa.* lalāta) the forehead; *loc.* ~e (sedā muccimsu) 46,31.

nava[1], *num.* (= *sa.*) nine; 82,13. — *navaṅga, *mfn.* ninefold (*v.* aṅga). navama, *mfn.* the ninth, *m.* ~o (vaggo) Dh. IX. *cp.* navuti, nāvutika.

nava[2], *mfn.* (= *sa.*) new, young; *m. pl.* ~ā (dāmā) 105,17; (bhikkhū) 83,33. *cp.* abhinava & *next.*

navaka, *mfn.* (= *sa.*) new, young; *compar.* ~tara, younger (*opp.* theratara), *m.* ~o (bhikkhu) 79,8; *instr.* ~ena, 79,9.

navanīta, *n.* (= *sa.*) fresh butter; *nom.* ~aṁ, 99,29; *abl.* ~ato, *ib.*

navuti, *num.* (*sa.* navati) 90; *v.* nāvutika, *mfn.*

nassati. *vb.* (*sa.* naçyati. √naç) to perish, to be destroyed; *pr. 3. sg.* ~anti, 6,24; *aor. 3. pl.* ~iṁsu (tassa cakkhūni ~, "lost their sight") 24,16; *cond. 3. sg.* nassissa, 29,8 (he would have perished); *pp.* naṭṭha & *caus.* nāseti (*q. v.*) *cp.* nāsa, *m.*

nahāta, *mfn.* (*pp.* nahāyati, *q. v.*).

nahātaka, *m.* (*sa.* snātaka) 'one who has bathed', a Brahman who has finished his studies; *acc.* ~aṁ (metrically = nhātakaṁ) Dh. 422 ("accomplished", SBE. X, 96). *cp.* MN. I, 280,19 & Sn. v. 521 (who has washed away all sins).

nahāna, *n.* (*sa.* snāna) bathing, bath; ~aṁ, 83,25; °-atthāya (rañño, for the king's bath) 41,3.

nahāpita, *m.* (*sa.* nāpita) a barber; *gen.* ~assa (jātako, "a barber's brat", *i. e.* bastard) 25,10; — *°-kuṭumbika, *m.* & *°-dāya, *m.* (*v. h.*). — In the ancient times the barbers belonged to the lowest castes (*cp. Fick,* Soc. Gl. p. 211); there cannot in my opinion be doubt about the identity of *sa.* nāpita and nahāpita, but if the latter is not a mere literary form (it is not rarely spelt nhāpita and even nāpita), then it must be derived from nahāpeti (*v. next*) through *nahāpitar (as salla-katta from çalya-kartṛ). *cp. Pischel,* Gr. § 210.

nahāpeti, *vb.* (*caus.* nahāyati; *sa.* snāpayati) to cause to bathe, to wash; *ger.* ~etvā (eḷakaṁ) 16,25.

nahāyati (or nhāyati), *vb.* (*sa.* snāyati, √snā) to bathe; *imp. 2. sg.* nahāya, 111,20; *fut. 1. sg.* ~issāmi, 41,1; *inf.* ~ituṁ, 58,30; nahāyitukāma, *mfn.* wishing to bathe, *m.* ~o, 83,24; *ger.* nahātvā, 41,3. 53,23. 111,8; nahāyitvā, 57,34. 61,6; *pp.* nahāta, one who has bathed, *instr. m.* ~ena, 84,1; *dvandva-comp.* °-ânulitto, 41,9 (bathed and scented); *caus. v.* nahāpeti, *cp.* nahātaka, nahāna & nahāpita.

nahāru, *m.* (& *n. coll.?*) (*sa.* snāyu, *f. n. Pischel,* Gr. § 255) a sinew, tendon; ~u, 82,2 = 97,20; *instr.* ~unā, 92,21; *gen.* ~ussa, 92,17.

nāga, *m.* (= *sa.*) [1]) a Nāga or serpent-demon; *°-bhavana, *n.* (*sa.* nāgaloka) the world of serpents; *abl.* ~ā, 52,16; — *°-māṇavaka, *m.*, a young Nāga; *pl.* ~ā, 53,10; *acc. pl.* ~e, 53,1; — *°-māṇavikā, *f.*, a Nāga girl; 52,27 *etc.*; — °-rāja(*n*), *m.*, a serpent-king; *nom.* ~ā, 28,27. 52,10; *instr.* ~ena, 52,15. — [2]) an elephant (with the Buddhists the emblem of endurance); *metaph.* a preeminent man; *nom.* ~o, Dh. 320; 105,19; *acc.* ~aṁ, 77,5; *instr.* ~ena, 76,31; — *nāga-m-āsada, *m.* attacking an elephant, 77,3 (*v.* āsada); — °-bala, *mfn.*, strong as an elephant; *m.* ~o, 1,5; *instr.* ~ena (raññā) 40,19; — *°-vagga, *m.* the 23th chapter of Dhpd.; — °-vana, *n.* the elephant grove, *gen.* ~assa, Dh. 324; — nāga-hata, *m.* "he who strikes the elephant (of men, *i. e.* Buddha)" = *hata-nāga; *gen.* ~assa, 77,4. *cp.* mahā-nāga, hatthi-nāga. (*Rhys Davids,* Buddhist India, p. 220).

Nāgadīpa, *m.* (*sa.* Nāgadvīpa) *nom. pr.* of an island (*i. e.* the northwestern part of Ceylon?); ~o, 19,8 (formerly called Seruma-dīpa. *q. v.*) *cp. Lassen,* IA. I.[2] p. 241; *Tennent,* Ceylon I. p. 331.

nāgara, *m.* (*fr.* nagara; = *sa.*) a citizen; *acc. pl.* ~e, 6,7.

Nāgasena, *m.* (= *sa.*) *nom. pr.* of a Buddhist sage (thera), in the philosophical work Milinda-pañha disputing with King Milinda (*q. v.*); *nom.* ~o (āyasmā) 96,24; *voc.* ~a, 98,32. *etc. cp.* SBE. vol. XXXV. p. xxv.

nāṭaka, *n.* (= *sa.*) a play or drama; *acc. pl.* ~āni, 63,17.

nātha, *m.* (= *sa.*) refuge; protector, lord; ~o, (attā hi attano ~) Dh. 160. 380.

nāda, *m.* (= *sa.*) roaring, crying,

noise; *acc.* ~aṁ (mahā-⁰) 6,13; — koñca-⁰, *m.* (*v. h.*).

nānā, *indecl.* (= *sa.*) separately, differently, variously; this word is mostly used at the beginning of *subst.* or *adj. comp.*, where it may be translated by 'different, divers, various, many' *etc.*; before double *cons.* the final ā is shortened: *nānaggarasa, *m.* (or *mfn.*) (= nānā + agga-rasa) all the choicest delicacies (of food): *acc. pl.* ~e, 57,14; ⁰-bhojanaṁ, 41,10; — nānappakāra, *mfn.* various, of all kinds (*cp.* pakāra); *m. pl.* ~ā (sakuṇa-saṁghā) 62,12; *n. pl.* ~āni (phalāni) 2,23; *instr. pl.* ~ehi (phalarukkhehi) 2,20; — *nānā-kuṇapa, *n.* (*v. h.*); *nānācitta, *mfn.* of different mind, falsehearted; *pl. f.* ~ā (itthiyo) 51,29, — *nānā-turiyāni, *n. pl.* 64,30 (*v.* turiya); — *nānā-pupphāni, *n. pl.* flowers of divers kinds, 41,6. 49,16; — *nānāvudha, *n.* 6,7 (muggarâdi-⁰) *v.* āvudha.

nāma¹, *indecl.* (*fr. next*; = *sa.*) ¹) by name (after *nom. pr.* or in interrogative sentences): Tambarājā ~, 19,6; *cp.* 44,13. 102,2; nāmena N. nāma, 5,30; kissa phalaṁ ~, 36,34; kā ~ tvaṁ (what is your name?) 56,10; kiṁsaddo nām' esa, 60,9; ko nām' esa puriso, 63,11 (who is this man?). — ²) particle of affirmation or emphasis after *subst.* (*adj.*) *pron. etc.* = just, indeed, certainly; 2,6. 4,10. 9,29. 88,23 *etc.*; tvaṁ ~, 9,21; ekan ~, 82,8; — app'eva nāma (perhaps, *v.* api) 17,26. 69,5; seyyathā pi ~ (just as) 68,24. — ³) *in exclamations*: aho puññānaṁ phalaṁ ~, 58,12; 86,24. *cp.* 63,13. — ⁴) after *interr.* = 'then'; kathaṁ ~ (how then?) 41,30; kiṁ ~, 4,6. 16,11. 88,4. — ⁵) *in answers*: imāya ~, 29,31. 31,24. — ⁶) *with negation* = not at all; ... nāma n'atthi, 4,32. 8,10. 10,31. 18,5 (*cp.* 18,24). 19,31 (*cp.* 19,19). 87,32.

nāma², *n.* (*sa.* nāman) name, appellation; *nom.* ~aṁ. 9,7. 98,34; *acc.* ~aṁ (akaṁsu, called) 38,10. 60,25; 96,31; (the old *acc.* nāma is used adverbially, *v. above*); *instr.* nāmena, by name (often combined with nāma, before the *nom. pr.* or after nāma, 5,30) 112,13; — nāma is often *opp.* to rūpa (*q. v.*) *cp.* nāmarūpa *below*; — *comp.*: ⁰-gahaṇa-divasa, *m.* nameday, *loc.* ~e, 38,9; ⁰-matta, *n.* a mere name (*cp.* matta²) ~aṁ, 97,2; — evaṁ-nāma, kin-nāma, taṁ-nāmika, *mfn.* (*q. v.*); sa-nāma, *n.* (his name) 111,32, *v.* sa⁴. *cp. next.*

nāmaka, *mfn.* (= *sa.*) named, called (*e. c.*); anupariyāya-⁰ (*q. v.*) 91,28 (~aṁ maggaṁ). *cp.* taṁ-nāmika.

nāma-rūpa, *n.* (= *sa.*) 'name and form' = individual being; *nom.* ~aṁ, 66,7 (viññāṇa-paccayā, originating from viññāṇa and causing saḷāyatanaṁ); 100,3; *loc.* ~asmiṁ, Dh. 367 ("mind and body", *cp.* SBE. X. p. 87); ⁰-nirodha, *m.* 66,13 (*v. h.*).

nāyaka, *m.* (= *sa.*) a leader, chief, lord; loka-⁰, *m.* 'lord of the world', *i. e.* Buddha, ~o, 110,19.

Nārada, *m.* (= *sa.*) *nom. pr.* of several persons; *nom.* ~o (āyasmā, a thera living at Gijjhakūṭa) 84,34; *voc.* ~a. 85,16.

nārāca, *m.* (= *sa.*) a kind of arrow, an iron arrow; *acc.* ~aṁ, 92,31; — *⁰-valaya, *m. n.* an iron ring or collar, *instr.* ~ena, 111,33.

nārī, *f.* (= *sa.*) a woman; *nom.* ~ī, 64,15; *acc.* ~iṁ, 47,21; *loc. pl.* ~isu, Dh. 284. *cp.* nara.

Nālāgiri, *m.* (= *sa.*) *nom. pr.* of an elephant; *nom.* ~i (nāma hatthī) 76,8; *acc.* ~iṁ, 76,13; *gen.* ~issa, 77,1. *cp.* Dhanapālaka.

nāḷikā, *f.* (*sa.* nālikā & nāḍikā) ¹) a small tube or pipe, a hollow stalk or stick; ²) a small measure (of capacity): aḍḍha-nāḷika-matta, *mfn.* containing as much as a half nāḷikā, *acc. m.* ~aṁ (taṇḍulaṁ) 57,18.

*nāvaṭṭha, *n.* (*sa.* *nāva-stha) "articles from ships", ~aṁ, 111,32. (*cp.* Vin. III 49,11.)

nāvā, *f.* (*sa.* nau & nāvā) a ship,

boat; *nom.* ~ā, 23,10; *acc.* ~aṁ, 19,27; Dh. 369 (*metaph.* = the human body); *instr. gen. abl. loc.* ~āya, 18,4; 19,25-27; 23,5; 112,27; 20,1; 25,19; 24,15 (ārūḷha-°, *v.* ārohati); — bhinna-nāva, *mfn.* shipwrecked (*v. h.*) *cp. next* & nāvaṭṭha.

nāvika, *m.* (= *sa.*) [1]) a mariner, sailor; *gen.* ~assa, 27,27; *gen. pl.* ~ānaṁ, 35,30. — [2]) a ferryman; *loc.* ~e, 28,5.

*nāvutika, *mfn.* (*fr.* navuti) 90 years old; *acc. f.* ~aṁ (nāriṁ) 47,21.

nāsa, *m.* (*sa.* nāça) destruction, ruin, death; *acc.* ~aṁ (mahā-° pāpuṇissanti) 34,18.

nāsā, *f.* (= *sa.*) the nose; *°-vāta, *m.* the breath from the nostrils, *instr.* ~ena, 53,2; — khura-nāsa, *mfn.* & °-nāsika, *mfn.* (*v.* khura).

nāseti, *vb.* (*caus.* nassati. *sa.* nāçayati) to destroy, spoil; to kill (*acc.*); *pr. 2. sg.* ~esi (mama taṇḍule) 57,24; *2. pl.* ~etha (amhākaṁ kammaṁ) 6,15; 63,17; *ger.* ~etvā, 37,9; *inf.* ~etuṁ (attānaṁ) 54,34.

ni-, *indecl.* [1]) (= *sa.*) prefix to verbs and nouns, implying 'in, into; down', sometimes confounded with next. — [2]) before double *cons.* = nir-, nī- (*sa.* nis (nir-)) prefix implying 'out, away', *v. below.*

nikati, *f.* (*sa.* nikṛti) wickedness, fraud; *instr.* ~iyā (metri causa : nikatyā) 5,21; — °-ppañña, *mfn.* versed in fraud; *m.* ~o, 5,21.

nikāma, *m.* (= *sa.*) desire, pleasure; *v.* nanikāma, *mfn.*

nikāya, *m.* (= *sa.*) a collection of Buddhist Suttas, name of the 5 sections of the Sutta or Suttanta Piṭaka, *viz.* Dīgha-°, Majjhima-°, Saṁyutta-°, Aṅguttara-°, Khudda(ka)-°, 102,14-16 (*q. v.*).

niketa, *m.* (= *sa.*) a house, abode; *loc.* ~e, Dh. 91.

nikkaḍḍhati, *vb.* (*sa.* nish-√kṛsh) to drive out, expel; *pp.* ~ito, *m.* (gehā) 35,29.

nikkaruṇatā, *f.* (*sa.* nish-karuṇatā) unmercifulness, hardheartedness; *instr.* ~āya, 59,18.

nikkasāva, *mfn.* (*sa.* nish-kashāya) free from dirt or sin; *v.* a-nikkasāva.

*nikkujjati, *vb.* (*fr.* ni + kubja? *opp.* ukkujjati, *q. v.*) to overturn; *pp. n.* ~itaṁ, 53,20. 69,15 (Comm. adhomukha-ṭṭhapitaṁ heṭṭhāmukha-jātaṁ).

nikkhanta, *mfn.* (*pp.* nikkhamati, *q. v.*).

nikkhamati, *vb.* (*sa.* nish-√kram) to go out, go away, depart, get out, issue (*w. abl.*); *pr. 3. pl.* ~anti (mātukucchito) 62,26; 90,36 (nagaraṁ pavisanti vā ~ vā); *part. m.* ~anto (mukhato) 13,21; *acc.* ~antaṁ (puredvārena) 12,10; *instr.* ~antena, 12,14. 83,35; *pl. m.* ~antā, 62,25; — *aor. 3. sg.* nikkhami, 12,8. 36,23; *3. pl.* ~iṁsu, 19,16; — *fut. 1. sg.* ~issāmi, 12,15; *3. sg.* ~issati, 12,13; — *ger.* [a]) nikkhamma (agārā, leave the household life) 61,33. 64,23; [b]) nikkhamitvā, 13,21. 40,29. 45,2 (to retire from the world); 86,26 (tato). 114,1 (id.); — *inf.* ~ituṁ, 12,17. 36,25; 65,13 (mahābhinikkhamanaṁ, *v.* abhinikkhamana); *comp.* °~itu-kāma, *mfn.* 65,16 (*m.* ~o, id.) — *grd.* ~itabbaṁ, *n.* 83,36; — *pp.* nikkhanta, *m.* ~o, 5,25. 12,12; °-kālato, 9,15 (*v.* kāla); — *caus.* nikkhameti (& ~āmeti, *v. h.*) *cp. next* & nekkhamma.

nikkhamana, *n.* (*sa.* nish-kramaṇa) going out, departing; °-bhāva, *m.* 12,9 (*v. h.*).

nikkhameti (& nikkhāmeti), *vb.* (*caus.* nikkhamati; *sa.* nish-krāmayati) to cause to go out, to bring forth or away (*acc.*); *aor. 3. pl.* ~āmesuṁ, 39,36; *ger.* ~etvā (ubho pi jane samuddā, "conveyed them oversea") 29,4.

*nikkhittaka, *m(fn).* (*fr.* nikkhitta, *pp.* nikkhipati, *q. v.*) one to whose charge anything has been committed; *m. pl.* agga-nikkhittakā (therā) 109,11 (*v.* agga).

nikkhipati, *vb.* (*sa.* ni-√kship)

to throw, lay down or away, loose, drop (*acc.*); to give in charge of (*acc. loc.*); *part. instr. m.* ~antena, 83,17; — *aor. 3. sg.* nikkhipi (nahāpitaṁ upāsakassa hatthe) 28,21; 36,27; *3. pl.* ~iṁsu, 73,28; — *fut. 3. pl.* ~issanti (samussayaṁ) 80,23; — *ger.* ~itvā, 57,13. 73,20. 75,21. 101,26; — *grd.* ~itabbaṁ, *n.* 83,16; ~o, *m.* 83,18; — *pp.* nikkhitta, *acc. m.* ~aṁ (maṅgalakhaggaṁ, ussīsake, lying) 41,15; *comp.* °-maṇiratanaṁ (Kāsikavatthe) 62,29. *cp.* nikkhittaka & *next.*

nikkhepa, *m.* (*sa.* ni-kshepa) 1) throwing away, laying down; 2) mark, footprint; *acc.* ~aṁ (suvaṇṇapādukānaṁ) 68,33.

nikhaṇati, *vb.* (*sa.* ni-√khan) to dig into, bury (*acc.*); *imp. 2. sg.* ~āhi (taṁ sobbhe) 78,14; *2. pl.* ~atha, 39,33; *ger.* ~itvā, 78,19; *pp.* nikhāta, rammed down, *m. pl.* ~ā (khīlā) 105,17.

nigacchati, *vb.* (*sa.* ni-√gam) to enter, undergo, come to (*acc.*); *pr. 3. sg.* ~ati (dukkhaṁ, suffers) Dh. 69; (dasann' aññataraṁ ṭhānaṁ) Dh. 137.

nigama, *m.* (= *sa.*) a little town, or market-place; *gen.* ~assa, 95,21; *loc.* ~e, 92,14. *cp.* negama. (*Fick*, Soc. Gl. p. 104.)

nigaḷa, *m. n.* (*sa.* nigaḍa) an (iron) chain for the feet; loha-nigaḷasadisa, *mfn.* 11,29 (*v. h.*).

nigūhati, *vb.* (*sa.* ni-√guh) to hide, conceal (*acc.*); *pr. 3. pl.* ~anti (itthiyo rahassaṁ na ~) 46,9.

niggaṇhati, *vb.* (*sa.* ni-√grah) to hold back, restrain; *fut. 1. sg.* ~gahessāmi (cittaṁ) Dh. 326; *grd.* niggayha (*sa.* ni-gṛhya) *v. next*; *cp.* dunnigaha, *mfn.*

***niggayha-vādi(n)**, *mfn.* (*fr. sa.* nigṛhya, *grd.* ni-√grah) 'resenting what is to be blamed', censuring, reproving; *acc. m.* ~iṁ, Dh. 76.

nigrodha, *m.* (*sa.* nyagrodha) the Banian-tree, Ficus Indica; °-rukkha, *m.* 20,2 (*gen.* ~assa). — Nigrodha, *m. nom. pr.* of a deer; *acc.* ~aṁ, 7,33; *loc.* ~asmiṁ, 7,34; = °-migarājā, 5,30.

nighāta, *m.* (= *sa.*) striking down, suppression, destroying, extinction; *acc.* ~aṁ (yes[aṁ] *i. e.* jāti, jarā, maraṇaṁ, *etc.*) 92,32.

niccaṁ, *adv.* (*sa.* nityam) always, constantly; ~ luddāni kubbato, 13,28; ~ candanagandhinī, 20,34; ~ jināti, 48,9. a-nicca, *mfn.* & a-niccatā, *f.* (*q. v.*).

***niccamma**, *mfn.* (*sa.* *niç-carma) excoriated, scourged; *acc. f.* ~aṁ (piṭṭhiṁ kāretvā, "flogging the skin of her back") 55,17.

niccala, *mfn.* (*sa.* niç-cala) immovable; *f.* ~ā (nāvā aṭṭhāsi) 23,11.

nicchāreti, *vb.* (*caus.* niccharati; *sa.* niç-√car) to cause to issue or come forth; *ger.* ~etvā (madhurassaraṁ) 18,20.

[**nicchinati**], *vb.* (*sa.* niç-√ci) to decide, fix upon; to discriminate (*acc.*); to persuade oneself, be convinced, consider (*w. prec.* 'ti'); *pot. 3. sg.* niccheyya (atthaṁ anatthañ ca) Dh. 256; *ger.* nicchiya (ti ~) convinced, 114,6; *pp.* nicchita, do. 111,21 (*m.* ~o).

niṭṭhā, *f.* (*sa.* nishṭhā) firm persuasion; completion, perfection; conclusion, end; niṭṭhaṅgata, *mfn.* (*sa.* nishṭhā-gata) who has reached perfection, *m.* ~o, Dh. 351.

***niṭṭhāpeti**, *vb.* (*caus.* niṭṭhāti, niṭṭhāyati, *sa.* ni-√sthā) to accomplish, complete, finish, make ready; *imp. 2. sg.* ~ehi, 48,29; *aor. 3. sg.* ~esi (āhatāhataṁ) 57,6; *fut. 1. sg.* ~essāmi, 87,11-12. *cp. next.*

niṭṭhita, *mfn.* (*sa.* nishṭhita, *pp.* ni-√sthā, *cp. prec.*) finished, come at an end; completed, ready, prepared; *n.* ~aṁ (jātakaṁ *etc.*) 52,11. 71,18; (bhattaṁ) 78,3; *loc.* ~e (bhatte) 33,32. a-niṭṭhita, *mfn.* (*q. v.*) *cp.* pari-niṭṭhiti, *f.*

niṭṭhubhati & nuṭṭhubhati, *vb.* (*sa.* *nih + √stubh, but as to the signification equal to *sa.* ni*h*-shṭhiv⁰) to spit out; *aor. 3. sg.* nuṭṭhubhi (kakkāretvā ~) 37,35; *ger.* niṭṭhubhitvā (yāguṁ) 57,25. [*Pischel,* Gr. § 120.] *cp.* chuddha.

niḍḍa (& other varr. niḍḍha, niḍha, niḍa = nīḷa, *sa.* nīḍa) *n.*, a nest; place, seat; roga-niḍḍaṁ (idaṁ rūpaṁ, "full of sickness") 107,7 = Dh. 148.

nidahati, *vb.* (*sa.* ni-√dhā) to lay down, deposit; to lay aside; *grd.* ~itabbaṁ, *n.* (cīvaraṁ, unhe) 83,9; *ger.* nidhāya (daṇḍaṁ (*q. v.*) sabbesu bhūtesu, "without hurting any creatures") Dh. 142. 405. *cp.* nidhi.

nidāgha, *m.* (= *sa.*) heat; ~o (mahanto) 4,5. *⁰-samaya, *m.* the hot season, *loc.* ~e, 3,32.

niddara, *mfn.* (*sa.* nir-dara) free from fear; *m.* ~o, Dh. 205. *cp.* dara & vīta-ddara.

niddā, *f.* (*sa.* nidrā) sleep; ~ā (Yasassa okkami) 67,26; *acc.* ~aṁ (gate, being asleep) 21,23; (okkamitvā (okkami) fell asleep) 22,24. 64,32; (upagato, id.) 65,2. *cp. next.*

niddāyati, *vb.* (*sa.* ni-drāyate, √drā) to sleep; *pr. 3. sg.* ~ati, 41,25. 65,30; *part. m. acc.* ~antaṁ, 35,32; *gen.* ~antassa, 41,26; *f. pl.* ~antiyo (itthiyo) 65,5; *aor. 3. sg.* niddāyi, 89,4.

*niddāyitar, *m.* (*fr. prec.*) a sleepy person; *nom.* ~tā, Dh. 325.

niddhana, *mfn.* (*sa.* nir-dhana) without property, poor; *acc. m.* ~aṁ, 52,4.

niddhanta, *mfn.* (*pp.* niddhamati, *q. v.*) blown off, driven out; *⁰-mala, *mfn.* one whose impurities are blown away, free from sin; *m.* ~o, Dh. 236. 238 (*synon.* an-aṅgana).

niddhamati, *vb.* (*sa.* nir-√dhmā) to blow off; to drive out, expel, remove (*acc.*); *pot. 3. sg.* niddhame (malaṁ) Dh. 239; *pp.* niddhanta (*v. h.*).

nidhāya, *ger.* nidahati (*q. v.*).

nidhi, *m.* (= *sa.*) a treasure; *gen. pl.* ~īnaṁ, Dh. 76.

nindati, *vb.* (= *sa.* √nind) to blame (*acc.*); *pr. 3. pl.* ~anti (bahubhāṇinaṁ) Dh. 227; *inf.* ~ituṁ, Dh. 230; *pp.* ~ita, *mfn.* blamed, *m.* ~o (poso) Dh. 228; a-nindita, *mfn.* Dh. 227; *cp. next.*

nindā, *f.* (= *sa.*) blame, reproach, reproof; *acc.* ~aṁ, Dh. 143. 309; ⁰-pasaṁsāsu (*loc. pl.*) blame and praise, 106,30 = Dh. 81.

ninna, *mfn.* (*sa.* nimna) deep; *loc. m.* ~e (sakaṭa-magge, a sunken road, defile) 43,18. – *n.* low ground, depth (of the sea); *acc.* ~aṁ (*opp.* thala) 105,21; *loc.* ~e (do., "on sea") Dh. 98.

*nipaka, *mfn.* (*sa.* *nipaka) intelligent, prudent; *acc. m.* ~aṁ (sahāyaṁ) Dh. 328.

nipajjati, *vb.* (*sa.* ni-√pad) to lie down; *pr. 3. sg.* ~ati, 6,30; *imp. 3. sg.* ~atu, 6,28; *aor. 3. sg.* nipajji, 2,31. 3,19. 12,24. 30,16; *3. pl.* ᵃ) ~iṁsu, 65,3; ᵇ) ~isuṁ, 112,6; *ger.* ~itvā, 42,1; *pp.* nipanna (*q. v.*); *caus. v. next.*

*nipajjāpeti, *vb.* (*caus.* nipajjati) to cause to lie down, lay down, deposit (*acc.*); *aor. 3. pl.* ~esuṁ, 32,30. 61,16; *ger.* ~etvā, 13,17. 16,18. 20,7. 41,36. 59,7.

nipatati, *vb.* (*sa.* ni-√pat) to fly down, descend on, fall down on (*loc.*); *pr. 3. sg.* ~ati, 2,32; *ger.* ~itvā (Bhagavato pādesu sirasā, "falling at his feet") 75,22. *cp.* nipāta *etc.*

nipanna, *mfn.* (*pp.* nipajjati) lying; *m.* ~o, 3,5-13. 7,4. 35,31 (phalake, floating on a plank); 65,15 (sleeping); 110,19; *comp.* tassa ~ṭṭhānaṁ (where he was lying) 49,24; ⁰-kāle (while he was sleeping) 53,3.

*nipannaka, *mfn.* (*fr. prec.*) lying; *acc. m.* ~aṁ, 6,31.

nipāta, *m.* (= *sa.*) ¹) falling; *instr.* udabindu-nipātena, "by falling of waterdrops", Dh. 121. – ²) a particle or indeclinable word; *nom.* ~o ('mā'ti) 85,33. – ³) a section of a book (*esp.* of Jātaka or Aṅguttara

Nik., whose single books are arranged according to their length or number of stanzas); Sutta-°, *m. nom. pr.* (*v. h.*) *cp. next.*

***nipātaka**, *mfn.* (*fr.* nipāta[3]) divided into nipātas (as Aṅguttara-Nikāya); *acc. m.* ~aṁ (saddhammaṁ pavibhajja) 110,2.

nipātin, *mfn.* (= *sa.*) flying or falling down; yattha-kāma-°, *mfn.* "rushing wherever it listeth", *acc. n.* ~inaṁ (cittaṁ), Dh. 36; *gen.* ~ino (cittassa) Dh. 35.

nipuṇa, *mfn.* (= *sa.*) clever, skilful; fine, subtile; *m.* ~o (dhammo) 94,25; su-nipuṇa, *mfn.* (*q. v.*) *cp.* nepuñña.

nippapañca, *mfn.* (*sa.* nish-prapañca) free from diffuseness, calm, undisturbed; *m. pl.* ~ā (Tathāgatā) Dh. 254.

nippabha, *mfn.* (*sa.* nish-prabha) without splendour; *m. pl.* ~ā (aññatitthiyā) 72,29; *cp.* pabhā, *f.*

nippāpa, *mfn.* (*sa.* nish-pāpa) free from sin; *m.* ~o, Dh. 205.

nippīḷeti, *vb.* (*sa.* nish-pīḍayati, √pīḍ) to press, squeeze (*acc.*); *aor. 3. sg.* ~esi (tassa gīvaṁ) 5,13.

nippurisa, *mfn.* (*sa.* nish-purusha) without men, female; *instr. n. pl.* ~ehi (turiyehi, "a female orchestra") 67,23 (*cp. Speyer,* Rem. on Divyāvadāna, Wien. Zeitschr. XVI p. 105.)

nipphatti, *f.* (*sa.* nishpatti) completion, perfection; *acc.* ~iṁ (niyyāmakasippe) "complete mastery", 24,13.

nibaddha, *mfn.* (*pp.* nibandhati; = *sa.*) 1) bound (on or to), fixed; *~aṁ, *adv.* constantly, 6,14. — 2) asked, pressed; *m.* ~o (punappuna, "being asked again and again") 53,35.

nibandha, *m.* (= *sa.*) binding, chain, attachment to; continuance, continuity; upāyupādānābhinivesa-°, 96,10 (*q. v.*).

nibandhati, *vb.* (*sa.* ni-√bandh) 1) to bind on; 2) to press, urge, importune; *aor. 3. sg.* nibandhi, 54,1; *pp.* nibaddha (*q. v.*) *cp.* nibandha.

nibbattati, *vb.* (*sa.* nir-√vṛt) to become, come forth, be born (again), sprout up; *pr. 3. sg.* ~ati (dukkhaṁ) Dh. 338; *fut. 3. sg.* ~issati (Tusitavimāne) 87,31; *2. sg.* ~issasi, 88,15; *1. sg.* ~issāmi, 88,16; *aor. 3. sg.* nibbatti (rukkhadevatā hutvā) 3,31; *ger.* ~itvā (kapiyoniyaṁ) 1,3; (rukkho) 36,36; *pp.* nibbatta, *m.* ~o, 17,24. 28,27. 84,30 (niraye). 101,11 (aggi); nibbatt'amhi, 88,10; *f.* nibbattâsi, 88,9. *caus.* nibbatteti (*q. v.*).

nibbattana, *n.* (*sa.* nirvartana) the coming forth, being born, growing, sprouting; rukkha-nibbattana-bhayena, for fear that a tree would grow up, 37,5; aṁkura-°-ṭṭhāna, *n.* (*q. v.*).

nibbatteti, *vb.* (*caus.* nibbattati) to bring forth, produce, complete, perform; *ger.* ~etvā (jhānābhiññaṁ) 47,33.

nibbana, *mfn.* (*sa.* nir-vana) 1) without forest, woodless (Jāt. II, 358,8). — 2) free from desires; *m. pl.* ~ā, Dh. 283 (*cp.* vana[2]).

***nibbanatha**, *mfn.* (*fr.* nir + vanatha, *q. v.*) free from lust; *m.* ~o (*synon.* vana-mutto) Dh. 344.

nibbāna, *n.* (*sa.* nirvāṇa) 1) extinction, the being extinguished (as a fire or a lamp); ~aṁ (pajjotassa) 80,35 (*cp.* Jāt. I, 212,8). — 2) the Buddhist Nirvāṇa: a) absolute extinction of all desires and passions, complete sanctification or Arhatship (*cp.* arahat); b) absolute annihilation of individual existence (*i. e.* in the Saṁsāra), release from every conceivable attribute of being (*cp.* an-abhāvakata), the eternal happiness attained after death by an Arhat or a Buddha (tathāgata), whereafter he shall not be born or die again; ~aṁ (Sugatena desitaṁ) Dh. 285; *acc.* ~aṁ, 64,33. 89,2. Dh. 23. 134. 184. 203. 226. 369; *dat.* ~āya (saṁvattati) 66,30; *gen.* ~assa (sacchikiriyāya) 90,18; ~ass'-eva santike, near to N., Dh. 32 = °-santike. Dh. 372; — *°-gamana, *mfn.* leading to N., *acc. m.* ~aṁ (maggaṁ) Dh. 289; *⁰-gāmin, *mfn.* id., *f.* ~inī (*scil.* paṭipadā) Dh. 75; *⁰-paṭisaṁyutta, *mfn.* 71,22 (*v. h.*); — magga-phala-nibbānāni (*n. pl.*, *dvandva-comp.*) "the paths, the fruits, and the N.", 97,10; — The transition into N. is described as vimokho cetaso, 80,35, which is compared with the extinction of a lamp (pajjotassêva nibbānaṁ, *cp.* AN. I, p. 236; epithets of N. are a-kata, a-mata, pāra *etc.* *cp.* nibbāyati, nibbuta, parinibbāna. [*D'Alwis*, Buddhist Nirvāna; a review of Max Müller's Dhammapada. Colombo 1871; *Childers*, Dictionary (sub voce) 1875; *Dahlmann*, Nirvāṇa. Berlin 1896; *Eklund*, Nirvāṇa. Upsala 1899; *Pfungst*, Was ist das buddhistische Nirvāna in Wirklichkeit? (Aus der indischen Kulturwelt. Stuttgart 1904, p. 56); *Oldenberg*, Buddha, 3. Aufl. p. 310; *Trenckner*, Mil. p. 424.]

nibbāpeti, *vb.* (*caus. fr. next*; *sa.* nir-vāpayati) to extinguish, annihilate; to cool, refresh; *imp. 2. pl.* ~etha (sokaṁ me) 89,12; *inf.* ~etuṁ (do.) 89,10.

nibbāyati, *vb.* (*sa.* nir-√vā) to be blown out or extinguished; to be refreshed, to feel happy, attain the Nirvāṇa; *pr. 3. sg.* ~ati (mātuhadayaṁ) 64,17; *pot. 3. sg.* ~eyya (aggi) 95,1; *caus.* nibbāpeti (*q. v.*); *pp. v.* nibbuta, *cp.* nibbāna.

nibbijja, *ger.* (*fr.* nibbindati; *sa.* nir-vidya) having become despondent, depressed, or disgusted with (*abl.* or *acc.*); *ger.* nibbijjâpema (Gotamaṁ, *cp.* apeti, *vb.*) 104,16 [or have we to take nibbijjāpema as *pr. 1. pl.* from *nibbijjāpeti, to give up (on account of despondency)? *cp.* *nibbejaniyā, *f. pl.* or *gen. sg.* nirvij⁰?) SN. I, p. 124,3].

nibbiṭṭha, *mfn.* (*pp.* nibbisati; *sa.* nir-vishṭa) gained, earned; *instr. n.* ~ena (carāmi, "with what I have gained I wander about") 105,8.

nibbida, *m.* (or nibbidā, *f.* (?); *sa.* nirvid, *f.* & nirveda, *m.*, *cp.* Jāt. IV, 471,25. 473,3) aversion, disgust, weariness; *dat.* ~āya (cittaṁ saṇṭhāsi, "his mind became weary") 67,31; ~āya (saṁvattati) 93,7 (*cp. Kuhn*, Beitr. p. 70).

nibbindati, *vb.* (*sa.* nir-√vid, nirvindati & *pass.* nirvidyate) to be indifferent, to become weary of or disgusted with (*loc.*); *pr. 3. sg.* ~ati (rūpesu) 71,5-13; (dukkhe) 107,12 = Dh. 277 (metri causa ~atī); *part. m.* ~aṁ. 71,14; *pot. 3. sg.* ~eyya (*opp.* āsiṁsetha) 42,16; *ger.* nibbijja (*v. h.*); *cp.* nibbida.

nibbisati, *vb.* (*sa.* nir-√viç) *lit.* 'to enter into'; to earn, gain; *part. m.* nibbisaṁ, *v.* a-nibbisaṁ.

nibbuta, *mfn.* (*sa.* nir-vṛta) ¹) happy, content, free from passions; ²) extinguished (through false etymology combined with nibbāyati, nibbāna); *m.* ~o (pitā) 64,14; (gini, *i. e.* the fire of passions) 104,25; (anupādāya) Dh. 414; *acc.* ~aṁ (*opp.* attadaṇḍa; "mild") Dh. 406; *acc. pl.* ~e. Dh. 196; *f.* ~ā (mātā) 64,14; *loc. n.* kasmiṁ nu kho ~e hadayaṁ ~aṁ nāma hoti, after what having become extinguished does the heart feel happy? 64,18.

nimanteti, *vb.* (*sa.* ni-√mantr) to invite; *aor. 3. sg.* ~esi, 56,23; *3. pl.* ~ayiṁsu, 87,5; *ger.* ~etvā (dānam adaṁsu) 86,14.

Nimi, *m. nom. pr.* of a king (= *sa.*); ~ nāma rājā (Mithilāyaṁ) 45,16.

nimitta, *n.* (= *sa.*) ¹) sign, omen; *pl.* ~āni (cattāri) 64,3; pubba-⁰, id. *acc.* ~aṁ, 63,7; *pl.* ~āni, 63,1. — ²) cause, reason; gahita-nimittena, *instr.* 'on account of his having taken hold of it', *i. e.* by a tug, 89,7; a-nimitta, *mfn.* (*v. h.*).

nimisa, *m.* (*sa.* nimisha) winking or twinkling of the eye; a-nimisa, *mfn.* not winking; *subst. f.* a-nimisatā (*v. h.*).

nimīlati, *vb.* (*sa.* ni-√mīl) *intr.*

to shut, close (as the eyes); *pr. 3. pl.* ~anti (akkhīni, kumbhilānaṁ mukhavivaṭe) 3,18; *caus.* nimīleti. to close (the eyes, *acc.*); *ger.* ~etvā (akkhīni) 3,19.

nimugga, *mfn.* (*pp.* nimujjati; *sa.* ni-magna) sunk or plunged in (*loc.*); gūthakalale °-gāmasūkaro, 46,33.

nimujjati, *vb.* (*sa.* ni-√majj) to sink, dive in (*loc.*); *pr. 3. pl.* ~anti, 25,26; *ger.* ~itvā (kāmakalale) 46,33; *pp.* nimugga (*q. v.*); *caus. II.* nimujjāpeti, to cause to sink (*acc.*); *ger.* ~etvā (nāvaṁ) 27,12; ummujja-nimujja, *m.* (*v.* ummujjati).

nimba, *m.* (= *sa.*) the Nimb tree, Azadirachta Indica (with bitter fruits); *pl.* ~ā, 37,20; *acc. pl.* ~e, 38,19 = pucimanda, 37,33. 38,1. — *°-kasaṭa, *n.* (*v. h.*). — °-paṇṇa-sadisa-rasa, *mfn.* having a (bitter) taste like the leaves of a Nimb tree, *m.* ~o, 37,32.

nimmakkhika, *mfn.* (*sa.* nirmakshika) free from flies; °-madhupaṭala-°, 38,23 (*v. h.*).

nimmala, *mfn.* (*sa.* nir-mala) spotless, taintless, sinless; *m. pl.* ~ā (bhikkhavo) Dh. 243.

nimmita, *mfn.* (*sa.* nir-mita, √mā) constructed, built, fashioned, created; *acc. n.* ~aṁ (uyyānaṁ devatāhi) 63,20.

niyata, *mfn.* (= *sa.*; √yam) [1]) held back, restrained; *m.* ~o (*synon.* danto) Dh. 142; — [2]) fixed, certain; sure, insured; limited; *m.* ~o (bhikkhu) 79,34; *n.* ~aṁ (maraṇaṁ) 86,17; *°-gatika, *mfn.* (*q. v.*); a-niyata, *mfn.* uncertain, unlimited (*v. h.*).

niyāma, *m.* (*sa.* niyama & niyāma) [1]) restraining, determination *etc.* — [2]) practice, way, method; *instr.* ~ena (iminā) 2,25; maccha-gahaṇa-° („as if to catch fish") 25,35.

niyyāti, *vb.* (*sa.* nir-√yā) to go out, depart; to get out (*esp.* from the saṁsāra); *pr. 3. pl.* ~anti (lokamhā) 91,6; *aor. 3. sg.* ~āsi, 39,9; *3. pl.* ~iṁsu, 91,5; *fut. 3. sg.* ~issati, 90,32; *3. pl.* ~issanti, 91,6.

niyyādeti, *vb.* (also niyyāteti; *sa.* nir-√yat, *caus.* niryātayati) to deliver, to give anything (*acc.*) into one's charge (*gen.*); *pr. 1. pl.* ~ema (-mige rañño) 6,5; *ger.* ~etvā (brāhmaṇiṁ amhākaṁ) 9,18; 38,5.

niyyānika, *mfn.* (*sa.* nir-yāṇika) conducing to blessing, salutary, profitable; *a-°, *mfn.* (*q. v.*).

niyyāma(ka), *m.* (*sa.* nir-yāma(ka)) a navigator, master, mate; ~ko, 25,16; *acc.* ~kaṁ, 25,18; *niyyāmakakamma, *n.* "the mariner's calling", *acc.* ~aṁ, 24,14; *°-jeṭṭha, *m.* "master mariner", *gen.* ~assa. 24,10; *°-jeṭṭhaka, *m.* id., ~ko, 24,14; *°-sippa, *n.* "the art of seamanship", *loc.* ~e, 24,13; *°-sutta, *n.* "mariner's lore", *instr.* ~ena, 25,26.

nir- (before vowels) *indecl. prefix* (*sa.* nis) to verbs or nouns, implying "out, away", or "without, free from" (*cp.* a-, an-, na-, vi-); before *cons.* it is always shortened to ni- (*v. h.*) and the *foll. cons.* is doubled (nikkaḍḍhati *etc.*; nuṭṭhubhati), but before r, h it is lengthened to nī- (nīroga, nīharati, *cp.* nibbana, nīvaraṇa).

niraṁkaroti (or nirākaroti) *vb.* (*sa.* nir-ā-√kṛ) to throw away, repudiate; to ruin, destroy; *ger.* ~atvā (attaṁ) 55,1.

nirattha, *mfn.* (*sa.* nir-artha) useless, vain; *f.* ~ā (tassa sevanā) 14,2; *n.* ~aṁ (kaliṅgaraṁ) 107,6 = Dh. 41. — niratthaka, *mfn.* id. (*sa.* nir-arthaka); °-lapana, *n.* 52,6 (*v. h.*).

niraparādha, *mfn.* (= *sa.*) unoffending, guiltless; *acc. m.* ~aṁ, 39,29.

niraya, *m.* (= *sa.*) hell; *acc.* ~aṁ, 58,14. 74,1; *dat.* ~āya (upakaḍḍhati) Dh. 311; *loc.* ~e (nibbatto) 84,30; ~amhi, 108,7; ussada-°, 23,26 (*q. v.*); — *°-bhaya, *n.* fear for hell, *instr.* ~ena, 17,30; °-bhaya-bhīta, *mfn.* fearing hell, *m. pl.* ~ā, 17,31;

*°-vagga, *m.* name of the ch. XXII of Dh. (*cp.* nerayika).

*nirāsaṁkatā, *f.* (*cp. sa.* nir-āçaṅka, *mfn.*) the not hesitating; *instr.* ~āya, 59,18 (*cp.* āsaṅkā, *f.*).

nirāsaya, *mfn.* (*sa.* nir-āçraya) standing alone, supportless, who has no inclinations; *acc. m.* ~aṁ, Dh. 410 (*cp.* āsaya).

nirujjhati, *vb.* (*pass.*, *sa.* ni-√rudh) to cease, end, to be dissolved; *pr. 3. pl.* ~anti, 66,17. 80,29; *part.* ~māna, *n.* ~aṁ (dukkhaṁ nirujjhati, *opp.* uppajjati, (*q. v.*)) 96,13. (*cp.* nirodha).

nirutti, *f.* (*sa.* nirukti) grammatical analysis, etymology; pronunciation, diction, dialect; *instr.* (or *abl.*?) ~iyā (Māgadhānaṁ) 113,33; (Māgadhāya) 114,38; °-pada-kovida, *mfn.* skilled in the [interpretation of] words of the nirutti, *i. e.* the old dialect or the original language of the holy scriptures, *m.* ~o, Dh. 352. (*cp.* SBE. X. p. 84.)

*nirupakāra, *mfn.* (*cp. sa.* nir-upakārin) useless; *m.* ~o, 35,28.

nirupaddava, *mfn.* (*sa.* nir-upadrava) without affliction or mishap, happy, secure; *f.* ~ā (nāvā) 25,20.

nirumbhati, *vb.* (*sa.* ni-√rudh) to stop, suppress; to hush, silence (*acc.*); *ger.* ~itvā (saddaṁ) 65,25. (*cp.* Tr. PM. p. 59.)

nirūpadhi, *mfn.* (*sa.* nir-upadhi, with u lenghtened metri causa (?), *cp.* *Fausbøll*, Dhpd. (1855) p. 433 & Tr. PM. p. 78) free from passions; 105,29. Dh. 418 (*v.* upadhi).

nirokāsa, *mfn.* (*sa.* nir-avakāça) inaccessible, impossible, inconvenient; *loc. n.* ~e (ṭhāne) 41,29 (*cp.* an-avakāsa & okāsa).

nirodha, *m.* (= *sa.*) cessation, destruction; *nom.* ~o, 66,18. 108,14 (*scil.* sabba-dukkhassa); saṁkhāra-° *etc.* 96,12 *etc.* (*v. h.*); a-sesa-virāga-°, 67,15 (*v. h.*); *acc.* ~aṁ (saññā-vedayita-°) 80,10; *dat.* ~āya, 93,8; *abl.* ~ā, 94,12; *-dukkha-°, *mfn.* (*q. v.*); — *°-dhamma, *mfn.* subject to destruction, *n.* ~aṁ, 68,27 (*cp.* dhamma [4])).

nilīna, *mfn.* (*pp.* nilīyati; = *sa.*) sitting on (*loc.*); hidden, concealed; *m.* ~o (sākhāya) 13,13; *loc.* ~e, 50,23.

nilīyati, *vb.* (*sa.* ni-√lī) to sit down (*esp.* in order to hide one's self); *pr. 3. sg.* ~ati, 50,7; *aor. 3. sg.* nilīyi (sākhagge, *loc.*) 13,22; 50,23; *ger.* ~itvā (rukkhe) 4,21; — *caus. II.* *nilīyāpeti, to cause one to hide one's self, to conceal (*acc.*); *ger.* ~etvā (dhuttaṁ) 50,9.

nivattana, *n.* (*sa.* nivartana) turning back, fleeing; a bend or curve of a river; *loc.* ~e (Gaṅgā-°) 1,4. — a-nivattana, *mfn.* (*q. v.*).

nivattati, *vb.* (*sa.* ni-√vṛt) to turn back, return; to flee, disappear, vanish; *pr. 3. sg.* ~ati (hiṁsa-mano) Dh. 390; *part. instr. m.* ~antena, 83,5; *imp. 3. sg.* ~atu (sotthiṁ nāvā, "return to safety") 27,24; *aor. 3. sg.* nivatti (nagarābhimukho) 43,15; *inf.* ~ituṁ, 27,11; *ger.* ~itvā, 5,16. 12,11; *pp.* nivatta, *m.* ~o (bhavissati) 60,21. — *caus.* nivatteti & nivattayati, to turn, lead back; *part. acc. m.* ~ayamānaṁ. 60,19; *imp. 2. sg.* ~aya (nivattay'etaṁ rathaṁ) 60,14; *ger.* ~etvā, 60,18.

nivattha, *mfn.* (*pp.* nivasati; *sa.* nivasita) [1]) dwelling, living, inhabiting; [2]) clothed, dressed in, wearing (*acc.* or *e. c.*); *f.* ~ā (sāṭakaṁ) 31,10; *m.* ~o (sāṇa-sāṭī-°) 71,29; su-nivattha, *mfn.* carefully dressed; *acc. m.* ~aṁ (pabbajitaṁ) 63,30.

nivāta, *mfn.* (= *sa.*) sheltered from the wind, low (*opp.* pavāta. *sa.* pravāta); — *nivāta(ka), *n.* a place sheltered from the wind, calm, stillness; *loc.* ~e (labbhamāne) 48,7 must be understood in the sense of "opportunity", if we have not here an old error for nimantaka, *m.* (*sa.* nimantraka, *cp.* nimanteti) an inviter, *i. e.* a wooer or seducer, *cp.* the comm. Jāt. V, 437,18 (raho nimantake paribhedake) & Mil. p. 205.

nivāpa, *m.* (= *sa.*) seed; food, a portion of food, gift of food; *acc.* ~aṁ (vapitvā, migānaṁ) 6,4; — *°-tiṇa, *n.* "grass to eat", *acc.* ~aṁ (ropetvā) 6,6; *°-puṭṭha, *mfn.* "fed on grains", *m.* ~o (mahā-varāho), Dh. 325.

***nivāretar**, *m.* (*sa.* *nivārayitṛ) one who holds back, who refuses to admit any person; *nom.* ~ā (a-ññātānaṁ) 90,32 (*opp.* pavesetar).

nivāreti, *vb.* (*caus.* ni-√vṛ, *sa.* nivārayati) to keep back or away from (*abl.*); to prohibit, forbid; *pot. 3. sg.* ~āraye (asabbhā) Dh. 77; (pāpā cittaṁ) Dh. 116; *aor. 3. sg.* ~esi, 39,17-19; *grd.* ~etabba, *m.* ~o, 83,4; nivāretar, *m.* (*q. v.*) *cp.* dun-nivāraya.

nivāsa, *m.* (= *sa.*) dwelling, abode; *acc.* ~aṁ (gahetvā, "stopped") 8,30. — pubbe-°, *m.* (*v. h.*).

nivāsana, *n.* (= *sa.*) an under-garment; *nom.* ~aṁ (*opp.* pārupanaṁ) 29,23; 82,24 (*cp.* paṭinivāsana).

***nivāsāpeti**, *vb.* (*caus. II.* ni-√vas, *cp. next*) to cause to be dressed (with double *acc.*); *ger.* ~etvā (maṁ ahatavatthāni) 27,18; (deviṁ dibbavatthaṁ) 61,13.

nivāseti, *vb.* (*caus.* ni-√vas, *sa.* nivāsayati) to put on (clothes, *acc.*), to dress one's self; *ger.* ~etvā (te, *scil.* sāṭake) 41,4; 76,16. 78,4 (having dressed himself); parimaṇḍalaṁ ~, 82,27 (*q. v.*) *cp.* nivāsana & *prec.*

niviṭṭha, *mfn.* (*pp.* nivisati, *sa.* ni-√viç, niviṣhṭa) entered, settled down, founded, situated; married; kasā-°, *mfn.* touched by the whip, *m.* ~o (asso) Dh. 143[b] (lit. "married to the whip"?).

nivedeti, *vb.* (*caus.* ni-√vid, *sa.* nivedayati) to communicate, report, announce, proclaim (*acc.*); *imp. 2. pl.* ~etha (tuṭṭhiṁ) 64,6; *aor. 3. pl.* ~ayiṁsu, 31,6.

nivesana, *n.* (*sa.* niveçana) [1]) 'entering', dwelling, mansion, house, home; *nom.* ~aṁ, 78,5; *acc.* ~aṁ (gantvā, "went home") 51,6; *loc.* ~e (sake) 78,1; — *°-ṭṭhāna, *n.* id. 2,15; — °-dvāra, *n.* the entrance or gate of a house, 68,2. 73,31; *loc.* ~e, 38,18; — rāja-°, the king's palace, *abl.* ~ā, 19,16. — [2]) *metaph.* attachment of mind or false opinion (Comm. = diṭṭhi), *v.* a-nivesana, *mfn.* Dh. 40.

niveseti, *vb.* (*caus.* ni-√viç, *sa.* niveçayati) to cause to enter; attānaṁ ~, to place or direct one's self; *pot. 3. sg.* ~aye, Dh. 158; ~eyya, Dh. 282. *cp.* niviṭṭha, nivesana.

nisamma, *indecl.* (*ger.* nisāmeti, to observe, attend to; *sa.* ni-çamya, √çam) carefully, considerately; *°-kārin, *mfn.* acting considerately; *gen. m.* ~ino, Dh. 24.

nisiñcati, *vb.* (ni-√sic, *sa.* niṣhiñcati) to sprinkle, besprinkle (*acc.*); *ger.* ~iya (te jalena) 110,33.

nisinna, *mfn.* (*pp.* nisīdati; *sa.* niṣhaṇṇa) seated, sitting; *m.* ~o (dhanasantike) 33,26; *acc.* ~aṁ (kūpagge) 18,6; *gen.* ~assa, 86,6; *pl.* ~ā (assembled) 109,32; *gen. pl.* ~ānaṁ, 61,25; *comp.* °-kāle, while sitting, 1,12; °-pallaṁkato, 65,27 (*q. v.*); rukkhe °-puriso, 36,3; as finite tense: nisinno'si (cintento), 4,3. *cp.* sannisinna. — nisinnaka, *mfn.* (*sa.* niṣhaṇṇaka) id., *m.* ~o (va niddāyi) 89,4.

nisīdati, *vb.* (ni-√sad, *sa.* niṣhīdati) to sit, be seated, sit down; to dwell; *part. m.* ~anto (ekato), 45,28; *imp. 2. sg.* nisīda (dvāre) 57,29; *aor. 3. sg.* nisīdi, 11,26 (rukkhagge); 12,13. 66,4; *3. pl.* [a]) ~iṁsu (tassā guṇakathāya, were lauding) 31,23; [b])~isuṁ, 112,28; *ger.* [a]) nisīditvā (rukkhe) 2,5; 42,31. 87,34; [b]) nisajja, 78,6; *pp.* nisinna (*q. v.*); *grd.* nisīditabba, *n.* ~aṁ, 83,33; *caus.* nisīdāpeti (*q. v.*) *cp. next.*

***nisīdana**, *n.*, a mat to sit on; °-paccattharaṇaṁ, 84,10 (*v. h.*).

***nisīdāpeti**, *vb.* (*caus. II.* nisīdati) to cause to sit down or take place, to cause to remain, leave; *ger.* ~etvā (Bodhisattaṁ hatthipiṭṭhe) 45,32; 58,2-19.

nisedha, *m.* (*sa.* nishedha) keeping off, holding back, restraining, prohibition; ~o (manaso piyehi, "holding the mind back from the pleasures of life") Dh. 390; — *hirī-°, *mfn.* restrained by shame, *m.* ~o (puriso) Dh. 143.

nisedheti, *vb.* (*caus.* ni-√sidh, *sa.* nishedhayati) to keep off, restrain, prohibit, warn (*acc.*); *part. m.* ~ento (paribbājakaṁ) 30,10.

nisevati, *vb.* (*sa.* ni-√sev, nishevate) to attend, follow, practise, cultivate; (*acc.*) *pr. 3. pl. med.* nisevare (sākhā sākhā, wind round one another) 37,34.

nissaṁsayaṁ, *adv.* (*sa.* niḥsaṁçayam) undoubtedly, surely; 114,24. (*cp.* saṁsaya).

***nissakkana**, *n.* (*fr.* nissakkati, *sa.* niḥ-√sṛp) creeping out; biḷāra-nissakkana-matta, *mfn.* 90,35 (*v. h.*).

nissajjati, *vb.* (*sa.* niḥ-√sṛj) to let loose; give up, give over (*acc.*); *imp. 3. sg.* ~atu (mama bhikkhusaṁghaṁ) 74,23; *pot. 1. sg.* ~eyyaṁ, 74,27.

nissadda, *mfn.* (*sa.* niḥ-çabda) noiseless, silent; *acc. m.* ~aṁ (mahājanaṁ) 88,6.

***nissāya**, *prp. w. acc.* (*ger.* nissayati, *sa.* *niçrāya, √çri, lit. 'leaning on') 1) near to; padumasaraṁ ~, 3,31; pāsāṇapiṭṭhaṁ, 17,20; — 2) by means of, by one's support; tumhe ~, 12,33; rājānaṁ ~ ("in the king's service") 24,18; taṁ ekikaṁ ~, 31,20; taṁ ~, 87,2; imaṁ kāyaṁ ~, "through connection with", 99,16; — 3) because of, by the reason of, for sake of; Mittavindakaṁ ~, 23,11-13; dhanaṁ ~, 33,36; maṁ ~, 39,16; etaṁ ~, 49,31; amhe ~, 60,12; issariyaṁ ~, 60,13; diṭṭhiṁ ~ pāpikaṁ, Dh. 164. *cp. next.*

***nissita**, *mfn.* (*pp.* ni-√çri; *cp. sa.* ā-çrita) depending on, devoted to (*acc.* or *comp.*); *m.* ~o (dvayaṁ, ayaṁ loko) 96,6; rāga-°, *mfn.* devoted to passions, *m. pl.* ~ā (saṁkappā) Dh. 339. *cp.* a-nissita, san-nissita.

nisseṇi (or ~ī), *f.* (*sa.* niḥ-çreṇī) a ladder, stairs; *abl.* ~ito (otaranto) 62,27.

nihata, *mfn.* (= *sa.*, *pp.* ni-√han) 'slain', dejected; humiliated, humble; *m.* ~o (seti) 30,21; *°-māna, *mfn.* whose pride is defeated, humble; ~māna-bhāva, *m.* humility, *acc.* ~aṁ, 57,30.

nihīna, *mfn.* (= *sa.*, *pp.* ni-√hā) low, vile, mean; *°-kamma, *mfn.*, *pl. m.* ~ā (manujā) "men of evil deeds", 74,2.

***nīgha** (or nigha), *m.* (*cp. sa.* nigha, sin) suffering, pain; *a-nīgha, *mfn.* (*q. v.*).

nīca, *mfn.* (= *sa.*) low (*opp.* ucca); *acc. m. n.* ~aṁ (katvā, "holding it down, turning it downwards") 82,21. 84,11; *°-ṭhāniya, *mfn.* occupying a low position, *acc. m.* ~aṁ (ucce ṭhāne ṭhapetuṁ) 76,11.

nīta, *mfn.* (= *sa.*; *pp.* neti) led, brought; *acc. pl. m.* ~e (attano santikaṁ) 38,30.

nīyati, **nīyamāna**, *pass. v.* neti.

nīroga, *mfn.* (= *sa.*) free from sickness; *m.* ~o (sīho) 13,23.

nīḷa, *n.* (*sa.* nīḍa) a nest; *v.* niḍḍa.

nīla, *mfn.* (= *sa.*) dark, blue, green; °-vaṇṇa, *mfn.* id. *acc. m.* ~aṁ (samuddaṁ) 26,18; — nīl'uppala-, 47,13 (*v.* uppala); — °-kusa-tiṇa, *n.* 26,18 (*v.* kusa); — °-maṇi & inda-nīla (*v. h.*).

nīvaraṇa, *n.* (& *m.*?) (*sa.* nivaraṇa & nivāraṇa, *n.*) an obstacle, hindrance; *acc. pl.* pañca ~e, 91,6 (the five obstacles to a religious life, *i. e.* lust, malice, sloth, pride, and doubt, *v. Childers*, Dict.); vi-nīvaraṇa-citta, *mfn.* (*q. v.*) *cp.* nivāraṇa, *n. fr.* nivāreti (*q. v.*).

nīharati, *vb.* (*sa.* nir-√hṛ) to take out, to pull or drive out (*acc.*); *aor. 3. sg.* nīhari (kacchapaṁ) 12,32;

50,25; *ger.* ~itvā (migagaṇaṁ gahanaṭṭhānato) 6,13; 14,26; 37,17. 57,33. 84,9.

nu, *indecl.* (= *sa.*) [1]) a particle combined with interrogatives, very frequently followed by kho (*q. v.*); kin nu kho, 1,21. 86,29 *etc.* (*v.* kiṁ [2]); kin nu kāraṇaṁ, 3,1; kacci ~ kho, 3,5; kaccin nu, 9,28; kāya nu . . . kathāya. 29,30; ko nu dīpo, 110,31; kahan ~ kho, 34,11; kathaṁ ~ kho, 81,15; kati ~ kho, 81,19; api nu, 73,4. — [2]) particle of interrogation (generally = *ne*, *num*); atthi nu kho, 14,36; bhabbo nu kho, 70,1; saddo yeva nu kho Nāgaseno ("is N. anything but a mere sound") (= *nonne*) 97,30; sometimes pleonastically inserted after a relative before the following interrogative sentence: yan nu ahaṁ bālo, atha kena . . . 54,26; yo nu kho evaṁ vadeyya . . ., sammā nu kho so vadeyya, 99,29–31. — [3]) particle of asseveration; at the end of a sentence: nū 'ti cintiya (certainly, surely) 111,18. *cp.* nanu & nūna.

nuṭṭhubhati, *vb.* = niṭṭhubhati (*q. v.*).

nudati, *vb.* (*sa.* √nud) to push, drive away (*acc.*); *pr. 3. sg.* ~ati (pamādaṁ) Dh. 28.

nūna, *indecl.* (*sa.* nūnam) [1]) *interrogative* (*comb. w.* yaṁ): yan nūna, "what if?" (*w. pot.*) 6,4. 33,27. 46,23. 68,35. — [2]) *affirmative*: certainly, surely; na nūna visahati, 90,26; nibbutā nūna sā mātā, 64,14. *cp.* nu.

nekkha, *m.* (or nikkha; *sa.* nishka) a golden ornament; a certain coin of gold; *acc.* ~aṁ (jambonadassa) Dh. 230.

nekkhamma, *n.* (*sa.* naishkramya, *fr.* nish-√kram, *cp.* nikkhamati) renunciation of the world, abandonment of desires; *loc.* ~e, 68,20; °-kālo, 45,8; °-sukhaṁ, Dh. 272, "the happiness of release", *cp.* SBE. X, 67; °-ūpasama, *m.* (*v.* upasama) Dh. 181. As nekkhamma frequently occurs in the phrase ~aṁ nikkhamati and the Burmese often write nikkhamma, it seems to be advisable to derive it from *sa.* naishkramya. The northern Buddhists write generally naishkarmya (*fr.* karman), but this is surely due to false etymology; nekkhamma is often *opp.* to kāma, wherefore *Rhys Davids & Oldenberg* (SBE. XIII, 104) have preferred to derive it from *sa.* *naish-kāmya. *cp.* abhinikkhamana.

negama, *m.* (= *sa.*) a citizen, townsman (*opp.* jānapada); °-jānapadā, *m. pl.* "townsmen and country-folk", *acc.* ~e, 6,3; *loc.* ~esu, 7,25. *cp.* nigama.

neti (& nayati), *vb.* (*sa.* √nī) [1]) to lead, guide; to bring, carry off, take, take with (*acc.*); *pr. 2. sg.* nesi, 5,5; 101,18 (tava bhariyaṁ); *1. sg.* nemi, 101,19; *3. sg.* ~ati (metri causa: ~atī) Dh. 257; *3. pl.* ~anti, 106,20-27 = Dh. 240; 80; *imp. 2. sg.* nehi (maṁ) 2,3; *2. pl.* netha, 19,26. 58,15; *pot. 3. sg.* naye (atthaṁ sahasā, "to carry a matter with violence") Dh. 256; *fut. 1. sg.* nessāmi, 1,18; *2. pl.* nessatha, Dh. 179–80; *aor. 3. sg.* nayi (sā nayi, perhaps = sânayi, *fr.* āneti) 111,30; *3. pl.* nayiṁsu, 24,23; *inf.* netave (= netuṁ) Dh. 180; — *pass.* nīyati, *3. pl.* ~anti (lokamhā, *abl.*) Dh. 175; *part. loc. pl.* nīyamānesu, 40,2; *pp.* nīta (*q. v.*) *cp.* naya, nāyaka *& next.*

*nettika, *m.* (*fr. sa.* netra) one who makes conducts for watering; *pl.* ~ā (udakaṁ nayanti) 106,27 = Dh. 80.

nepuñña, *n.* (*sa.* naipuṇya, *fr.* nipuṇa) experience, skill, wisdom; *acc.* ~aṁ, 114,15.

Nerañjarā, *f.* (*sa.* Nairañjanā) *nom. pr.* of a river in Magadha, near Uruvelā; *acc.* ~aṁ, 103,3; *gen.* ~āya, 66,2.

nerayika, *mfn.* (*sa.* nairayika, *fr.* niraya) belonging to hell, suffering in hell; *°-satta, *m.* an inhabitant of hell or condemned to hell; *nom.* ~o, 24,1; *gen. pl.* ~ānaṁ, 23,27.

neva, *indecl.* (*sa.* naiva, *fr.* na + eva) *v.* na[3-4].

neva-saññā-nâsaññā, *f.* (*sa.* naiva-saṁjñā-nâsaṁjñā) neither perception nor not perception, only *comp.* °-āyatana, *n.* 80,8-9 (*v. h.*).

no[1], *gen. pl. pron.*, *v.* ahaṁ.

no[2], *adv.* (= *sa.*) a negative particle, equal to 'na', but with more emphasis : [1]) not (*non*) 10,20. Dh. 95; no h'etaṁ, "certainly not so", 70,2 (*cp.* h'); no ca kho, "and certainly not", 90,35 (followed by atha kho); 'ti evaṁ no, "in this way you cannot reason", 92,28; 'ti evam pi no, "nor so", 92,29; no yāti koci, Dh. 179 (Comm. = na uyyāti?); — [2]) and not (*neque*) : saṁsādeti no vissajjeti, 90,26. *cp. next.*

noce, *adv.* (*fr.* no + ce. *q. v.*; *sa.* no ced) if not (*opp.* sace); 4,33. 56,20 (*w. foll. fut.*); no ce pāragavesino (*v. h.*) Dh. 355.

P.

*pa[1], *indecl.*, a syllable indicating abbreviation = etc., sometimes used instead of pe (*q. v.*); 102,19 (*cp.* ḷa).

pa-[2], *indecl.* (*sa.* pra) prefix to nouns and verbs, sometimes implying 'on, forth, away', otherwise giving the verbs a certain perfective meaning or making them inchoative (*cp.* parodati) or intensive (*cp.* pamodati); in *comp.* after vowels the p is sometimes doubled, *e. g.* a-ppamāda *etc.*

-pa[3], *mfn.* (= *sa.*) only *e. c.* [1]) drinking; *v.* dhenu-pa; [2]) guarding, protecting; *v.* gopa.

paṁsu, *m.* & *n.* (*sa.* pāṁsu, *m.*) soil, dust, earth; *nom. m.* ~u (sithilo) 40,24; *acc.* ~uṁ (madhuraṁ) 38,2-3; *gen.* ~uno, 40,26; *n. pl.* ~ūni (*acc.* pāda-°, "the dust at his feet") 77,7. — °-kūla, *n.* 'a dust-heap', a certain ascetic dress made of rags; *°-kūladhara, *mfn.* "wearing dirty raiments", *acc. m.* ~aṁ, 106,12 = Dh. 395.

pakati, *f.* (*sa.* prakṛti) nature, natural state; at the beginning of *comp.* = natural, real; usual, ordinary; what has been hitherto, former; *°-samudda, *m.* (*opp.* the mythical or supernatural ocean) 25,21; *°-uyyānapālaka, *m.* ("his former gardener") *gen.* ~assa, 38,5.

pakaraṇa, *n.* (*sa.* prakaraṇa) 'production', a literary work, book, treatise; Ñāṇodayaṁ nāma ~aṁ, 113,22; Mahā-°, (*v. h.*).

pakāra, *m.* (*sa.* prakāra) kind, sort; nāna-ppakāra, *mfn.* (*v.* nānā).

pakāseti, *vb.* (*caus.* pra-√kāç, *sa.* prakāçayati) [1]) to illustrate, explain, declare, preach, make known (*acc.*); *part. m.* ~ento (imam atthaṁ) 2,9; 30,16. 43,35. 47,24; *aor. 3. sg.* ~esi (saccāni) 52,9; (ānisaṁsaṁ) 68,21; *inf.* ~etuṁ, 11,9. 114,15; *ger.* ~etvā, 29,16. 47,30; *pp.* pakāsita, *m.* ~o (dhammo) 69,18. — [2]) *intr.* to shine; *pr. 3. pl.* ~enti (dūre santo, *opp.* na dissanti) Dh. 304.

pakiṇṇaka, *mfn.* (*sa.* prakīrṇaka) mixed, miscellaneous; °-vagga, *m.* the XXIth chapter of Dh.

pakopa, *m.* (*sa.* prakopa) anger, rage; *kāya-ppakopa, *mano-°, *vacī-°, Dh. 231–33 (*v. h.*).

pakka, *mfn.* (*sa.* pakva) [1]) boiled, roasted; *acc. m.* ~aṁ (agginā) 16,2; *loc. n.* ~e (sarīre) 15,33; *pakkodana, *mfn.* (*v.* odana). — [2]) ripe, mature; pakka-phala-, 2,1; *n.* ~aṁ, fruit (= phala); amba-°, mango fruit, 15,25 (ambapakk'); 36,31. *cp.* paripakka.

pakkamati, *vb.* (*sa.* pra-√kram) to go forth, go away; *pr. 3. pl.* ~anti, 42,32; *pot. 3. sg.* ~eyya, 100,25; *aor. 3. sg.* pakkāmi, 9,4. 59,23; cārikaṁ ~, 70,31 (*v.* cārikā); *3. pl.* pakkamiṁsu, 6,17; *pp.* pakkanta, *f.* ~ā, went away, 73,10; *loc. m.* acira-ppakkante, 70,13 (*v.* a-cira).

pakkosati, *vb.* (*sa.* pra-√kruç) to call, call upon, invite (*acc.*); *aor. 3. sg.* pakkosi (nahāpitaṁ) 28,33; *ger.* ~itvā, 9,22. 19,38. — *caus. II.*

*pakkosāpeti, to send for (*acc.*); *aor. 3. sg.* ~esi (dhītaraṁ) 10,9; *ger.* ~etvā, 6,23; *pp. m.* ~ito (tena), 37,12.

pakkha, *m.* (*sa.* paksha) a wing; *acc. pl.* ~e (pasāretvā) 10,14; (vidhūnitvā) 18,19. *cp.* pakkhin & pekkhuṇa.

pakkhandati, *vb.* (*sa.* pra-√skand) to make off, spring forth (out) or over (*acc.*); *aor. 3. sg.* pakkhandi (nāvāya samuddaṁ, went to sea) 23,10; (nāvā samuddaṁ ~) 23,14; *3. pl.* ~iṁsu, 25,20; *ger.* ~itvā (ṭhānaṁ) 27,27; *pp.* pakkhanta, *m.* ~o (Simbalivanaṁ) 60,6; *f.* ~ā (videsaṁ) 27,25. *cp. next.*

pakkhandikā, *f.* (*sa.* praskandikā) diarrhoea; *v.* lohita-°.

pakkhandin, *mfn.* (*sa.* praskandin) 'springing forth', attacking, insulting; *instr. m.* ~inā, Dh. 244.

pakkhitta, *mfn.* (*pp.* pakkhipati; *sa.* prakshipta) thrown, cast or put on (into); *comp.* °-tilā (tattakapāle) 11,7; °-kukkuṭo (pañjare) 46,20.

pakkhin, *m.* (*sa.* pakshin; *fr.* pakkha) a bird; *nom. pl.* ~ī, 11,14.

pakkhipati, *vb.* (*sa.* pra-√kship) to throw, cast, place (*acc.*) on or into (*loc.*); *pr. 3. pl.* ~anti (te kāraṇaghare) 21,15; *aor. 3. sg.* pakkhipi, 9,34; *inf.* ~ituṁ (maraṇadukkhaṁ aññassa upari) 7,9; *ger.* ~itvā, 4,21. 18,18. 39,33 (paṁsuṁ); 40,18. 50,34. – *caus. II.* *pakkhipāpeti, to cause to put into; *aor. 3. sg.* ~esi (taṁ nāvāya) 26,17; *ger.* ~etvā, 38,3.

pagabbha, *mfn.* (*sa.* pragalbha) bold, arrogant; *m. instr.* ~ena, Dh. 244. – a-ppagabbha, *mfn.* (*v. h.*).

pagāḷha, *mfn.* (*pp.* pra-√gāh; *sa.* pragāḍha) sunk or plunged into, devoted to; *m. pl.* ~ā (ettha, *v. h.*) 104,1.

paggaṇhati (or ~āti), *vb.* (*sa.* pra-√grah) to stretch out, raise, lift up; to take, seize *etc.* (*acc.*); *ger.* [a]) paggayha (añjaliṁ) 22,4; (bāhā) 30,19; (tulaṁ) Dh. 268; – [b]) paggahetvā (añjaliṁ) 22,6; – [c]) paggaṇhitvā (añjaliṁ) 30,6. *cp.* paggaha.

paggayha, *ger.*; *v. prec.*

*paggava, *m.* a kind of creeping (bitter) plant (probably = phaggava, "a sort of pot herb", Abhidhānap., *cp.* Vin. I 201,14 & 381,17 (pakkavan ti latājāti)); *acc. pl.* ~e, 38,1. – °-vallī, *f.* id.; *acc. pl.* ~iyo, 37,19.

paggaha, *m.* (*sa.* pragraha) 'stretching forth, seizing', assuming, accepting, friendly reception; *asanta-°, *v.* a-santa.

paggahetvā, *ger.*, *v.* paggaṇhati.

paggharati, *vb.* (*sa.* pra-√ghṛ) to flow, trickle or ooze forth; *part. instr. n.* ~antena (assunā) 5,14; *pp.* ~ita, *n.* ~aṁ (assuṁ) 89,13; °-kheḷa, *mfn.* 65,5 (*v. h.*).

paṁka, *m*(*& n*). (= *sa.*) mud, clay; dirt, sin; *loc.* ~e (sanno) Dh. 327; °-piṭṭhe, on the mud (*v.* piṭṭha) 5,17; *pl.* ~ā (dirt) Dh. 141.

pacati, *vb.* (*sa.* √pac) [1]) to cook (*acc.*); *pr. 1. sg.* ~āmi (kittakaṁ) 57,10; *imp. 2. sg.* ~āhi, 57,19; *aor. 3. sg.* paci, 57,11; *inf.* ~ituṁ, 57,24; *ger.* ~itvā, 28,23. – [2]) *intr.* to burn, to be tormented (in hell); *ger.* ~itvā (*cp. pass.* paccati, *q. v.*) 84,30. – *caus. II.* *pacāpeti, to cause to be cooked (*acc.*); *part. m.* ~ento (pātarāsaṁ) 8,20; *inf.* ~etuṁ (bhattaṁ) 33,25. *cp.* pakka.

pacināti, *vb.* (*sa.* pra-√ci) to collect, pluck (*acc.*); *part. acc. m.* ~antaṁ (pupphāni) Dh. 47–48; *fut. 3. sg.* pacessati (pupphaṁ iva-ppacessati) Dh. 44.

paccakkhato, *adv.* (*abl. fr.* paccakkha, *mfn.* visible, perceptible; *sa.* pratyakshatas) before the eyes, visibly; attanā ~ ñatvā, 38,18; ~ passasi, 85,21.

paccakkhāti, *vb.* (*sa.* praty-ā-√khyā) to refuse, deny, abandon (*acc.*); *ger.* ~āya (purimaṁ ambaṁ a-paccakkhāya, not being able to deny the first mango) 100,18.

paccati, *vb.* (*pass.* pacati); [1]) to be cooked, ripen (*metaph.* of actions which are ripe for retribution); *pr. 3.*

sg. ~ati (pāpaṁ) Dh. 69. 119. — 2) to burn, be tormented (in hell); *part.* paccamāna, *acc. m.* ~aṁ (nerayika-sattaṁ) 23,30; *m. pl.* ~ā (sattā, Avīcimhi) 27,14.

paccattaṁ, *adv.* (*sa.* praty-ātmam) singly, by one's self; suddhī asuddhī ~, "one is pure or impure by himself", Dh. 165.

***paccattharaṇa**, *n.* (*fr.* praty-ā-√stṛ, *cp. sa.* āstaraṇa) a carpet or sheet (to lay on a bed); nisīdana-° ~aṁ, 84,10 ("the mat and the sheet").

paccanta, *mfn.* (*sa.* pratyanta) bordering on; *n.* ~aṁ (nagaraṁ, "frontier fort") Dh. 315; *comp.* °-gāma, *m.* & °-gāmaka, *m.* a border-village, 38,29. 14,9; °-bhūmi, *f.* a bordering country, *acc.* ~iṁ, 43,13; °-sīmato, *abl.* from the frontier, 43,14. (*cp.* sīmā, *f.*)

paccantima, *mfn.* (*sa.* pratyantima) = *prec.*; *n.* ~aṁ (nagaraṁ) 90,31.

paccaya, *m.* (*sa.* pratyaya) 1) belief, trust, confidence; 2) requisite, means, help, reliance; *acc. pl.* ~e, 102,8; gilāna-° -bhesajja, 97,8 (*v. h.*); °-dāyaka, *m.* "one who gives the reliances (to the priests)", *pl.* ~ā, 102,8; 3) cause or concurrent occasion (*cp.* hetu); vināsa-°, 34,21 (*q. v.*); *abl.* paccayā (*e. c.*) = depending on, on account of, avijjā-° [*etc.*] 66,6 *etc.*, cakkhu-samphassa-°, 70,27 (*q. v.*); a-para-ppaccaya, *mfn.* (*v. h.*) *cp.* paṭicca; *Waddell*, Lamaism, p. 118.

paccavekkhati, *vb.* (*sa.* praty-ava-√īksh) to look at, consider, contemplate; *part. gen. m.* ~antassa (yathāviditaṁ bhūmiṁ) 69,23.

paccassosuṁ, *aor. 3. pl.*, *v.* paṭisuṇāti.

paccāgacchati, *vb.* (*sa.* praty-ā-√gam) to come back again, return; *aor. 3. sg.* ~āgami, 25,12; *3. pl.* ~āgamiṁsu, 40,12. 45,27. *cp. next.*

paccāgamana, *n.* (*sa.* pratyāgamana) coming back; na °-ṭṭhānaṁ, the place from where one does not return, 56,18.

paccāmitta, *m.* (*sa.* praty-amitra) an enemy, adversary; *pl.* ~ā, 35,14; *acc. pl.* ~e, 3,24. On account of false etymology the 'a' has been lengthened, as it were derived from paccā (*sa.* praty-ā) + mitta (*sa.* mitra), *cp.* mitta & a-mitta.

paccāsiṁsati, *vb.* (*sa.* praty-ā-√çaṁs) to expect (*acc.*); *pr. 3. sg.* ~ati (mamâgamanaṁ) 87,26-27.

paccuggacchati, *vb.* (*sa.* praty-ud-√gam) to go out (towards), go to meet; *pr. 1. sg.* ~āmi (*w. dat.* yuddhāya, to battle) 104,4; *ger.* ~gantvā, 83,6.

paccuṭṭheti [or paccuṭṭhāti], *vb.* (*sa.* praty-ut-√sthā) to rise, arise; *ger.* ~ṭṭhāya, 68,9.

paccūsa, *m.* (*sa.* pratyūsha) dawn, daybreak; °-kāle (*loc.*) at dawn, 12,8; °-samayaṁ (*acc.*) & °-samaye (*loc.*) id. 68,8. 86,27.

pacceti, *vb.* (*sa.* praty-(ā-)√i) to go back, return; to fall back (upon, *acc.*); *pr. 3. sg.* ~eti (pāpaṁ; to be scanned: paṭi-eti) Dh. 125.

***pacchato**, *adv.* (& *prp. w. gen.*) (*abl. fr. sa.* paçca); behind; 83,32 (*opp.* purato); Dh. 348 (*opp.* pure); tesaṁ ~ agamāsi, 33,7; ~ nisinnaṁ, 46,2; ~ kassaci anāgamanabhāvaṁ ñatvā, "having observed that nobody pursued them", 40,11. *cp. next.*

pacchā, *adv.* (*sa.* paçcāt) 1) behind; Dh. 421 (*opp.* pure); *cp.* pacchā-bāhaṁ. *etc.*; — 2) afterwards; ~ jānissāmi, 15,27; ~ pivissāmi, 22,32; 35,36; 55,2; 113,19; pacchā-bhattaṁ (*v. h.*), *cp.* pacchima.

***pacchā-bāhaṁ**, *adv.* (*fr.* bāhā or = pacchā-baddhaṁ?) with the hands tied behind the back; ~ bandhitvā, 39,31.

***pacchā-bhattaṁ**, *adv.*, after the meal, in the afternoon; 86,5.

***pacchā-vāmanaka-dhātuka**, *mfn.* deformed behind; *m.* ~o, 24,24 (*cp.* dhātu & dhātuka).

***pacchā-vippaṭisārin**, *mfn.*

feeling regret or remorse afterwards; *m. pl.* ~ino, 79,18.

paccḥāyā, *f.* (*sa.* pracchāya, *n.*? *cp.* chāyā) a shadowy place; *loc.* ~āyaṁ, 75,33.

*pacchāsana, *n.* a back seat (on an elephant); *loc.* ~e (hatthipiṭṭhe) 45,32.

pacchā-samaṇa, *m.* (*sa.* paçcāc-chramaṇa) a junior Buddhist monk who accompanies a senior monk, walking behind him at some distance; an attendant priest; *acc.* ~aṁ, 82,28; *instr.* ~ena, 70,10. 83,1.

*pacchi, *f.* (*cp. sa.* praçna, *m.* (?) & pastya (Tr.); Prākr. pacchi. *cp. Pischel,* Gr. § 293) a basket; *loc.* ~iyaṁ, 50,25; puppha-⁰, flower-basket, *instr.* ~iyā, 49,36; *loc.* 50,4. — kacavara-chaḍḍana-⁰, 48,34 (*v.* kacavara). — tasara-⁰, 87,27 (*v. h.*).

pacchindati, *vb.* (*sa.* pra-√chid) to cut off, break off, discontinue, leave (*acc.*); *ger.* ~itvā (āhāraṁ) 46,4. — *pass.* pacchijjati, to cease; *aor. 3. sg.* pacchijji, 42,30.

pacchima, *mfn.* (*sa.* paçcima, *cp.* pacchā) [1]) being behind or at the back of; ⁰-gehe (*loc.*) behind the house, 12,13; ⁰-dvārena (*instr.*), by the back-door, ib.; ⁰-pādehi (*instr. pl.*) "in his hind feet", 24,26. — [2]) last, latest; *f.* ~ā (vācā Tathāgatassa) 80,3; *loc. m.* ~e (kāle) 86,18; (yāme) 99,23; ⁰-viññāṇa-saṁgaha (*q. v.*) 99,28. — [3]) western; *acc. f.* ~aṁ (disaṁ) 95,5.

*pacchimaka, *mfn.* (*fr. prec.*) back, last; *m.* ~o (bhikkhu) 79,33.

pajahāti, *vb.* (*sa.* pra-√hā) to leave, abandon, give up, eschew (*acc.*); *fut. 2. pl.* pahassatha (metri causa ~ā, B. jahissatha) to get rid of, overcome (dukkhaṁ) Dh. 144; *inf.* [a]) pahātuṁ (yasaṁ) 54,35; [b]) pahātave (in order to escape, māradheyyaṁ) Dh. 34; *ger.* [a]) pahāya, 9,4 (taṁ); 43,4; 91,6 (pañca nīvaraṇe); Dh. 329; [b]) pahatvāna, Dh. 243. 415; *pp.* pahīna (*v. h.*) *cp.* pahāna.

pajā, *f.* (*sa.* prajā) offspring, race; creatures, men, people; *nom.* ~ā, Dh. 85. 254. 342; *acc.* ~aṁ, Dh. 28; *loc.* ~āya, 78,16. *cp.* pajāpati.

*pajāna, *mfn.* (*nom. ag. fr. next*) possessed of knowledge; sampajāna, *mfn.* Dh. 20 (*v. h.*) *cp.* pañña.

pajānāti, *vb.* (*sa.* pra-√jñā) to know, understand, perceive (*acc.*); *pr. 3. sg.* ~āti (sahetudhammaṁ) 66,21; 71,16; Dh. 402 (dukkhassa khayaṁ); *pass.* paññāyati, *caus.* paññāpeti (*q. v.*) *cp.* pajāna, pañña, paññā *etc.*

pajāpati, *m.* (*f.* ~ī) (*sa.* prajāpati) lord, husband (*f.* lady, wife); ~ī-hadayaṁ, the heart of a wife, 64,18; — sa-pajāpatika, *mfn.* being together with one's wife or husband; *m.* ~o (kumbhīlo) 2,26. — Pajāpatī, *f. nom. pr.*, *v.* Mahāpajāpatī Gotamī.

pajjalita, *mfn.* (*pp.* pajjalati, pra-√jval, *sa.* prajvalita) flaming, blazing, burning; *loc.* ~e sati (niccaṁ, "as [this world] is always burning") Dh. 146; ⁰-aggikkhandha, *m.* 26,3 (*v. h.*).

pajjota, *m.* (*sa.* pradyota) light, flame, fire; *gen.* ~assêva nibbānaṁ, 80,35 ("even as a flame dies away"); tela-⁰, *m.* (*v. h.*).

pajjhāyati, *vb.* (*sa.* pra-√dhyai, *cp.* jhāyati[2]) to muse, mourn, to be afflicted; *part. m.* ~anto (parājito viya dukkhī dummano) 2,14.

pañca, *num.* (= *sa.*) five; *nom. acc.* ~a, 82,10; 67,11 (pañc' upādānakkhandhā); 91,6 (~ nīvaraṇe); ~ (*scil.* saṅge) Dh. 370 (*cp.* pañcasaṅgâtiga); *instr.* (*abl.*) ~ahi (kāmaguṇehi) 67,35; *gen.* (*dat.*) ~annaṁ (mahānadīnaṁ) 72,27; (bhikkhu-satānaṁ, *cp.* pañcasata) 79,33; *loc.* ~asu (sīlesu, *q. v.*) 7,24; (ṭhānesu) 60,36; — *comp.* pañca-vaṇṇa-, of five colours, 4,9. 62,12; ⁰-sugandhika-parivāra, *mfn.* 41,13 (*v. h.*) *cp. next etc.*, paññāsa, paṇṇarasa & pannarasa.

pañcaṅgika, *mfn.* (= *sa.*) having five parts, five-fold; ⁰-bandhana, *n.* 23,31.

*pañcaṅgulika (or pañcaṅgula,

~li), *n.* (*cp. sa.* pañcāngula & ~li) 'a mark of five fingers', a) an ornament in the shape of a spread hand used as a symbol to avert misfortune; gandha-pañcaṅgulikaṁ (*acc.*) "perfumed garlands with five sprays", 37,1 (*cp.* Jāt. III 303,21; III 23,20 & 160,3; IV 153,27; Vin. II 123,18); — b) an inaugural mark (consisting of perfumed garlands) to be placed on the neck of the victim; *acc.* ~aṁ, 16,25 (*cp.* Jāt. I 192,3). [*Morris*, JPTS. 1884 p. 84; Jāt. transl. by *Rouse*, II p. 72; SBE. XX p. 116.]

pañcama, *mfn.* (= *sa.*) the fifth; *acc. f.* ~aṁ (gāthaṁ) 54,28; *nom. f.* ~ī (senā) 103,27; *loc.* ~e (*i. e.* in the fifth chapter of Upāsaka-vagga of the AN) 91,13; veyyaggha-°, Dh. 295 (*v. h.*).

*pañca-vaggiya, *mfn.* (*cp. sa.* pañca-varga) belonging to a group of five; *acc. m. pl.* ~e (bhikkhū) the five monks (*i. e.* Kondañña, Vappa, Bhaddiya, Mahānāma & Assaji, Vin. I 12–13; Jāt. I p. 82) 66,24.

pañca-vīsati, *num.* (*sa.* pañca-viṁçati) 25; °-vīsatima, *mfn.* the 25th, *m.* ~o (vaggo) Dh. XXV.

*pañca-saṅgâtiga, *mfn.*, "escaped from the five fetters", *m.* ~o, Dh. 370; *v.* saṅga & atiga.

pañca-sata, *num.*, *mfn. pl.* (*sa.* pañca-çata) 500; *m. pl.* ~ā, 21,18. 32,15; *acc.* ~e, 21,22; *f.* ~ā, 21,21; *instr.* ~ehi (therehi) 109,12; *gen.* ~ānaṁ, 109,5; *comp.* °-miga-parivāra, *mfn.* 5,29; sata is often separated from pañca, forming the last part of a *subst. comp.*, pañca-jāti-satāni (*n. pl.*) 17,10; pañcasu attabhāva-satesu (*loc.*) 17,7; pañcannaṁ bhikkhu-satānaṁ (*gen.*) 79,33. — pañca-satima, *mfn.* the 500th; *m.* ~o, 17,8.

*pañcânantariya-kamma, *n.*, *v.* ānantariya.

pañcâyudha, *n.* (= *sa.*) five sorts of weapon; naddha-°, *mfn.*, *v.* āyudha.

pañjara, *n.* (& *m.*) (= *sa.*) a cage; *loc.* ~e, 18,26. 46,20; 18,14 (suvaṇṇa-°); — *ratha-°, *n.* the body of a chariot, ~aṁ, 98,5; — *sīha-°, *n.* a window, *loc.* ~e, 46,1.

pañña, *mfn.* (*sa.* prajña) wise, prudent, intelligent; *acc. m.* ~aṁ, Dh. 208; nikati-°, *mfn.* (*q. v.*) *cp.* a-pañña, duppañña & paññā, *f.*

paññatta, *mfn.* (*pp.* paññāpeti, *sa.* prajñapta, *caus.* pra-√jñā) made known, ordered, appointed; prepared, arranged, laid down; *m.* ~o (dhammo ca vinayo ca desito ~) 79,5; *n.* ~aṁ (sikkhāpadaṁ) 81,13; *loc.* ~e (āsane) 68,11; yathāpaññattaṁ (bhummattharaṇaṁ) 84,17 ("how it was spread out").

paññatti, *f.* (*sa.* prajñapti) 1) declaration, ordinance; 2) name, designation; *nom.* ~i (*synon.* vohāro) 97,3. — puggala-° (*v. h.*).

paññapeti, *vb.* = paññāpeti (*q. v.*).

paññavat & paññavanta, *mfn.* *v.* paññāvat.

paññā, *f.* (*sa.* prajñā) wisdom, intelligence, knowledge, understanding; *nom.* ~ā, 2,8. 103,16; Dh. 372; *instr.* ~āya, 91,24. 104,6. 107,11 = Dh. 277; *gen.* ~āya, 91,7. Dh. 280 (maggaṁ, "the way to knowledge"); — °-cakkhu, *n.* (*q. v.*). — *°-pāsāda, *m.* 'palace of wisdom', *acc.* ~aṁ (āruyha, "climbing the terraced heights of wisdom") Dh. 28; — *°-āvudha, *n.* (*v.* āvudha); — °-sīla-samāhita, *mfn.* rich in knowledge and virtue, *acc. m.* ~aṁ, Dh. 229; — *°-saṁkhāta, *mfn.* named paññā, *instr. f.* ~āya (medhāya) 91,27. — gambhīra-pañña, *mfn.*, mahā-pañña, *mfn.* (*q. v.*), sammappaññā, *f.* (*v.* sammā) *cp.* pañña, *mfn. etc.*

paññāpeti (& paññapeti) *vb.* (*caus.* pajānāti, pra-√jñā, *sa.* prajñāpayati & prajñapayati) to make known, declare, prescribe; designate, predicate; to prepare, arrange, lay down (*acc.* as a seat, carpet *etc.*); *pr. 1. sg.* ~apemi (nighātaṁ, *q. v.*) 92,32; yena rūpena Tathāgataṁ ~āpayamāno (*part. med. m.*) paññāpeyya (*pot. 3. sg.*) "all form by which one could predicate the existence of the saint", 95,10; *ger.* ~etvā (āsanaṁ) 22,28; (dibbasayanaṁ) 61,16; *grd. n.* ~etabbaṁ (āsanaṁ) 82,19; *pp.* paññatta (*q. v.*).

paññāyati, *vb.* (*pass.* pajānāti) 1) to be known or seen, to be visible, appear, look like; *pr. 3. sg.* ~ati (mahā hutvā) 3,4; (mahāsobbho viya) 27,3; *3. pl.* ~anti (sīse me palitāni) 46,23; — 2) to be, exist, be found; *pr. 3. sg.* ~ati (rājā) 10,30; *fut. 3. sg.* ~issati (jarā, "old age must come") 63,13.

paññāvat (or paññavat) & paññāvanta (or paññavanta). *mfn.* (*sa.* prajñāvat) wise, intelligent; *nom. m.* ~vā (-a-) 99,9; *pl. m.* ~anto (pakkhī) 11,14; — *gen. m.* ~antassa, Dh. 111; *gen. pl.* ~antānaṁ, 57,6.

paññāsa(ṁ), *num.* (*sa.* pañcāçat) 50; *n.* a collection of 50 suttas in the Majjhima-Nikāya; paññāsaka, *mfn.* (*sa.* pañcāçaka) divided into paññāsas (as M. N.); vagga-paññāsakaṁ (saddhammaṁ, *acc.*) according to vaggas and paññāsas, 110,2.

pañha, *m. & n.* (*sa.* praçna, *m.*) a question; *nom.* ~o (mayā pucchita-⁰) 88,11; *acc.* ~aṁ (puṭṭho) 90,26; *acc. pl.* ~e (cattāro) 86,32; *n.* kumara-⁰ (*v. h.*); *⁰-paṭibhāna. *n.* (*q. v.*) *cp.* Milinda-⁰.

paṭa, *m. & n.* (= *sa.*) a sort of cloth, dress; *⁰-sāṇi, *f.* a curtain, veil or screen of fine cloth, *instr.* ~iyā (parikkhepo pan'assa ~ ahosi) 37,3. *cp.* paṭṭa.

paṭala, *n.* (= *sa.*) a layer, cover, membrane; a heap, mass; madhu-⁰, a honey-comb, 38,24 (nimmakkhikamadhupaṭala-sadisaṁ).

paṭi, *indecl.* (= pati, *q. v.*; *sa.* prati) *prp.* (*w. acc.*, *cp.* paṭi-lomaṁ, paṭi-vātaṁ) & prefix to verbs and nouns implying 'towards, near to, against, back, in return' *etc.*; it is also used distributively, *esp.* inserted in *dvandva comp.* like vatta-paṭivatta (*q. v. cp.* anu). Before the vowels a, u, e, o it is always contracted to pacc- (*v. above*), which still sometimes may be metrically equivalent to paṭi, Dh. 125 : pacceti = pati-eti.

*paṭikujjeti, *vb.* (*denom. fr.* *paṭikujja, *mfn.* (*sa.* *prati-kubja) lying flat with the face downwards, Jāt. I 456,26; V 145,27) to cover (*acc.*, as a bowl or a dish); *ger.* ~etvā (-pātiyo) 61,37; *cp.* ukkujjati, nikkujjati; *Pischel*, Gr. § 206.

*paṭikuṭati, *vb.* (*sa.* *prati + √kuṭ) to bow, bend (towards or back); *pp.* ~ita, bowing, *m.* ~o (paṭisakki) 77,8; (*cp.* Mil. 297,15 : patikuṭati).

paṭikkamati, *vb.* (*sa.* prati-√kraṁ) to retire, turn back; *imp. 3. sg.* ~atu, 76,25; *aor. 3. sg.* ~ami, 29,26. 62,20; *ger.* a-paṭikkamitvā, 30,5; *pp. m.* paṭikkanto (piṇḍapāta-⁰, *q. v.*) 86,6.

paṭikkūla (& paṭikūla) *mfn.* (*sa.* pratikūla) 'against the bank', contrary, disagreeable; *instr. n.* ~ena (a-sucinā) 62,25. The form with 'kk' relates to *sa.* *pratī-kūla, *cp. Kuhn*, Beitr. p. 19, d.

*paṭikkosati, *vb.* (*sa.* prati-√kruç) to contradict, reject (*acc.*); *pr. 3. sg.* ~ati (sāsanaṁ arahataṁ) Dh. 164.

paṭikkhipati, *vb.* (*sa.* prati-√kship) to refuse, reject, repulse; *ger.* ~itvā, 46,15; *pp.* paṭikkhitta, *f.* ~ā (pi puna nibandhi) 54,1. *cp. next.*

*paṭikkhipana, *n.* (*cp. sa.* pratikshepana) refusing, rejection; *nom.* ~aṁ, 56,23.

*paṭigacca, *indecl.*, only in the phrase paṭigacc'eva, previously, 67,26 (*i. e.* "sooner than usual"); paṭigacca (*ger.*) derives from *sa.* pratikaroti (√kṛ; the Birman spelling is often paṭikacc'eva) = 'to provide against future events', Tr. Mil. p. 421–22.

paṭigaṇhāti (& -gaṇhati), *vb.* (*sa.* prati-√grah) to take, receive, accept (*acc.*); *pr. 3. pl.* ~anti (pati-⁰,

C; paṭi-° B.) Dh. 220; *imp. 3. sg.* ~ātu (accayaṁ accayato, *v.* accaya) 75,25; *pot. 3. sg.* ~eyya (rajanaṁ) 68,25; *ger.* paṭiggahetvā (with the 'g' doubled before the weak form of the root) 82,21. 109,24; *grd. n.* ~ggahetabbaṁ, 82,24. *cp. next.*

paṭiggahaṇa, *n.* (*sa.* pratigrahaṇa) accepting; *abl.* ~ā (jātarūpa-rajata-°) 81,26.

paṭicodeti, *vb.* (*sa.* prati-√cud, *caus.* ~codayati) to exhort, admonish, reprove (*acc.*); *imp. 2. pl.* ~etha (manusse) 73,36.

paṭicca, *prp.* (*orig. ger.* from prati-√i) resulting from, depending on, on account of (*w. acc.*); kiṁ ~, 94,33; isaṁ [etc.] . . paṭicca . . ratho ti . . nāmaṁ pavattati, "the word 'ratha' is but a name for pole" [etc.] 98,32. — °-samuppāda, *m.* 'origination by dependence', the Buddhist chain of causation, or the formula explaining the twelve causes of existence, beginning with a-vijjā (*v.* 66,8 *etc.*); *acc.* ~aṁ, 66,5. *cp.* paccaya.

paṭicchati, *vb.* (*sa.* prati-√ish) to take, receive (*acc.*); *inf.* ~ituṁ (etaṁ, aṁsena, *v.* aṁsa) 24,25; *caus. v.* paṭicchāpeti.

paṭicchanna, *mfn.* (*pp.* paṭicchādeti; *sa.* praticchanna) covered, hidden, concealed; protected; *n.* ~aṁ, what has been hidden, 69,16; *loc.* ~e (ṭhāne, a secluded or private place) 33,34; paṭicchanna-ṭṭhāne, 36,14. 54,13; a-ppaṭicchanna, su-paṭicchanna, *mfn.* (*v. h.*).

paṭicchādeti, *vb.* (*sa.* prati-√chad, ~cchādayati) to cover, conceal (*acc.*), to hid or cover one's self; *part. instr. m.* ~entena (timaṇḍalaṁ) 82,27; *fut. 1. pl.* ~essāma (-pāpakammaṁ) 73,27; *ger.* ~etvā (rohitamacche vālikāya) 14,24; 20,10. 83,32.

***paṭicchāpeti**, *vb.* (*caus. II.* paṭicchati) to deliver over, to charge with, intrust to (*w. double acc.*); *ger.* ~etvā (brāhmaṇiṁ sukapotake, "leaving his wife in charge of the young parrots") 9,14; (rājānaṁ rajjaṁ) 42,5. 47,21; (amacce rajjaṁ) 43,11.

paṭijaggati, *vb.* (*sa.* prati-√jāgṛ) to watch over, take care of, look after; to feed (*acc.*); *intr.* to be awake, be watchful; *pr. 3. pl.* ~anti (uyyānaṁ) 37,15; *part. med. f.* ~mānā. 20,10; *pot. 3. sg.* ~eyya, Dh. 157 (*intr.*); *aor. 3. sg.* paṭijaggi, 9,10; *3. pl.* ~iṁsu (taṁ, phalāphalena) 18,15. — *caus. II.* *paṭijaggāpeti, to cause to be carefully tended (or fed; *acc.*); *aor. 3. sg.* ~esi (gandhodakehi ambaṁ) 38,4. *cp. next.*

paṭijaggana, *n.* (*sa.* pratijāgaraṇa) watching over, attending to; *sarīra-°, *n.* care of the body (washing one's self, etc., *cp. sa.* çarīra-cintā) *acc.* ~aṁ (katvā) 85,1.

***paṭijānāpeti**, *vb.* (*caus.* paṭijānāti, *sa.* prati-√jñā) to cause to consent (promise or believe, *acc.*); *ger.* ~etvā (rājānaṁ, "make him believe it") 46,24 (*cp.* Dhpd. (1855) p. 164,2 fr. b.).

paṭiññā, *f.* (*sa.* pratijñā) promise, agreement; *acc.* ~aṁ, 8,3.

paṭidaṇḍa, *m.* (*sa.* prati-daṇḍa, *mfn.*) retribution; *pl.* ~ā ("blows for blows") Dh. 133.

paṭinivattati, *vb.* (*sa.* prati-ni-√vṛt) to return; *aor. 3. sg.* ~vatti, 63,15; *ger.* ~itvā, 63,14.

paṭinivāsana, *n.* (*sa.* pratinivāsana) a kind of garment, a second under-garment (used only as a house-dress); *acc.* ~aṁ, 82,24 (*cp.* SBE. XIII, p. 155).

paṭinissagga, *m.* (*sa.* prati-niḥsarga) giving up, abandonment, doing away with; *nom.* ~o (taṇhāya) 67,16; *abl.* ~ā, 94,12; ādāna-°, *m.* (*q. v.*).

paṭipajjati, *vb.* (*sa.* prati-√pad, ~padyate) 1) to go to, arrive at, reach; to walk on a path (*acc.*); *aor. 3. sg.* ~pajji (tam eva maggaṁ) 56,3; 76,17; *imp. 2. pl.* ~atha (etaṁ maggaṁ) Dh. 274; *pp. m.* paṭipanno (imaṁ racchaṁ) 76,13; *m. pl.* ~ā, Dh. 275. — 2) to undertake, take upon one's self (*acc.*); *imp. 2. sg.* paṭipajja (rajjaṁ) 45,6. —

³) to proceed or deal with (*loc.*); to behave; *ger.* ~itvā (bhatte pi tath'eva) 57,27; *grd. n.* ~itabbaṁ (kathaṁ nu kho mayā ~, "now what am I to do?") 81,15. – *caus.* paṭipādeti (*q. v.*) *cp. next.*

paṭipadā, *f.* (*sa.* pratipadā) the path to be walked; *nom.* ~ā (majjhimā, the middle path) 66,29; (dukkhanirodhagāminī, *q. v.*) 67,17; *loc.* ~āya, 79,18 (the right path, the right course of conduct, *synon. w.* magga (?) or = the first steps on the right path (?)).

paṭipanna, *mfn.* (*pp.* prati-√pad) *v.* paṭipajjati.

***paṭipāṭi**, *f.* (*sa.* *prati-pāṭi, *cp.* paripāṭi) order, row; *instr.* (or *loc.*) ~iyā, "in a row", 34,32.

***paṭipāda(ka)**, *m.* (*sa.* *pratipāda) that which supports the bedstead; mañca-paṭipādakā. *pl.* ("supporters of the bed") 84,14.

paṭipādeti. *vb.* (*caus.* paṭipajjati, *sa.* pratipādayati) to cause one (*acc.*) to go on a road or in a certain direction (*acc.*); *imp. 2. pl.* ~etha (hatthiṁ, imaṁ racchaṁ) 76,14; *aor. 3. pl.* ~esuṁ, 76,19.

***paṭipuggala**, *m.* (*sa.* *pratipudgala) one who is equal to another, a rival; a-ppaṭipuggala, *mfn.* unequalled, 80,24.

paṭipucchati, *vb.* (*sa.* prati-√prach) to inquire, ask in return (*acc.*); *fut. 1. sg.* ~issāmi (taṁ yeva) 94,28; *inf.* ~ituṁ (Bhagavantaṁ) 79,20.

***paṭippassambhati**, *vb.* (*sa.* *prati-pra-√çrambh) to cease, to be dissolved or dispersed; *caus.* ~eti, to cause to cease, put an end to (*acc.*); *pot. 1. sg.* ~eyyaṁ (iddhābhisaṁkhāraṁ) 69,29; *aor. 3. sg.* ~esi, 69,30.

paṭibaddha. *mfn.* (*sa.* pratibaddha, *pp.* prati-√bandh) bound to; ⁰-citta, *mfn.* whose mind is turned to, fallen in love (with *loc.*), *m.* ~o (mayi) 64,26; *pl.* ~ā (aññamaññaṁ) 19,14; – *⁰-mana, *mfn.* whose mind is bound, *m.* ~o, Dh. 284.

paṭibala, *mfn.* (*sa.* pratibala) able to (*inf.*), competent; *m. pl.* ~ā, 76,11; *m. instr.* ~ena (bhikkhunā) 81,16.

***paṭibāheti**, *vb.* (*caus.* *paṭibāhati; *sa.* prati-√vṛh, *cp.* prati-√bādh) to repel, dislodge (*acc.*); *grd. m. pl.* ~etabbā (navā bhikkhū; āsanena, with regard to their seats) 83,34.

paṭibujjhati, *vb.* (*sa.* prati-√budh) to awake; *ger.* ~itvā, 67,28.

***paṭibhāga**, *mfn.* (*sa.* *pratibhāga) like, equal to; *m.* pendant, counterpart; Erāvaṇa-⁰, *mfn.* equal to E., *gen. m.* ~assa, 45,31; kañcanarūpaka-⁰, *mfn.* like a golden statue, *gen. pl.* ~ānaṁ, 47,14.

paṭibhāna, *n.* (*sa.* pratibhāna) intelligence, sagacity, presence of mind, readiness of speech; *pañha-⁰, *n.* a difficult or intricate question, *pl.* ~āni, 98,33.

paṭibhānavat, *mfn.* (*sa.* pratibhānavat) endowed with intelligence & presence of mind, quick-witted; *m.* ~vā (Vaṅgiso) 109,8.

paṭimaṇḍita, *mfn.* (*sa.* pratimaṇḍita) decorated, adorned; *f. pl.* ~ā (sabbālaṁkāra-⁰) 64,29.

***paṭimasati**, *vb.* (*sa.* *prati-√mṛç, *cp.* pari-√mṛç) to examine, explore; *pot. 2. (3.) sg.* (?) paṭimāse (*sa.* *prati-marçes > ⁰mṛçes) Dh. 379; *cp. Pischel*, Gr. § 486 (saṁphāse); Dhpd. (1855) p. 424; *Childers & Ed. Müller* take it for *imp. 2. sg.* from *caus.* *paṭimāseti (not yet traced in Pāli).

paṭimuñcati, *vb.* (*sa.* prati-√muc) to put on (clothes, *acc.*); to tie; *ger.* ~itvā (gaṇṭhikaṁ) 83,1.

paṭiyatta, *mfn.* (*pp.* prati-√yat, *cp. next*) made ready, prepared; adorned, decorated; *n.* ~aṁ (sūkaramaddavaṁ) 78,8; alaṁkata-⁰, *mfn.* splendidly dressed (or decorated), *acc. m. & n.* ~aṁ, 39,29. 61,8. 65,9; *f. pl.* ~ā. 21,1.

paṭiyādeti, *vb.* (*caus.* prati-√yat. pratiyātayati) to prepare, make ready (*acc.*); *ger.* ~etvā (bhojaniyaṁ) 22,28; *grd. n.* ~etabbaṁ (nahānaṁ) 83,25; – *caus. II.* *paṭiyādāpeti, to cause to be prepared (*acc.*); *ger.* ~etvā, 78,2.

paṭilabhati, *vb.* (*sa.* prati-√labh) [1]) to receive back, recover (*acc.*); *aor. 1. sg.* ~labhiṁ (naṭṭhaṁ yasaṁ) 42,12; – [2]) to take, form (as a dislike, or a resolution); *pr. 3. sg.* ~ati (pāpakaṁ diṭṭhigataṁ) 90,25. *cp. next.*

paṭilābha, *m.* (*sa.* pratilābha) recovering, obtaining, attainment; *nom.* ~o (paññāya) Dh. 333; jīvita-⁰, 42,10; manussa-⁰ (the conception of men) Dh. 182.

paṭilomaṁ, *adv.* (*sa.* prati-loma) 'against the hairs', contrarily, obstinately; in reverse order, backwards; anuloma-⁰, 66,6 (*v. h.*).

paṭivacana, *n.* (*sa.* prativacana) answer; *acc.* ~aṁ (alabhanto) 3,7; 73,4.

paṭivatta, *v.* vatta [1].

paṭivatteti, *vb.* (*caus.* prati-√vṛt) to overturn, subvert; *inf.* ~etuṁ, 110,10; *grd.* paṭivattiya, *v.* a-ppaṭivattiya, *mfn.*

paṭivadati, *vb.* (*sa.* prati-√vad) to answer, reply; *pot. 3. pl.* ~eyyu (taṁ, 'will answer thee in the same way') Dh. 133.

paṭivasati, *vb.* (*sa.* prati-√vas) to live, dwell; *pr. 3. pl.* ~anti, 59,24.

paṭivātaṁ, *adv.* (*sa.* prativātam) against the wind; ~aṁ (khitto) Dh. 125; ~am (eti) Dh. 54.

paṭivedeti, *vb.* (*caus.* prati-√vid) to make known, announce; *aor. 3. sg.* ~esi (Bodhisattassa) 63,5.

paṭisaṁyutta, *mfn.* (*sa.* prati-saṁ-yukta) connected with, concerning; resulting from; *instr. f.* ~āya (nibbāna-⁰) 71,22; *acc. m.* ~aṁ (vacīsucarita-⁰) 86,8

paṭisaṁvedin, *mfn.* (*sa.* pratisaṁvedin) feeling, experiencing; *nom. m.* ~ī (vimutti-sukha-⁰, "experiencing the bliss of emancipation") 66,4.

paṭisakkati, *vb.* (*sa.* prati-√sṛp) to go back, retire; *aor. 3. sg.* paṭisakki, 77,8.

paṭisattu, *m.* (*sa.* prati-çatru) an enemy, adversary; *acc.* ~uṁ, 39,27.

*paṭisanthāra, *m.* (*sa.* *pratisaṁstāra, √stṛ) friendly greeting, conversation; *acc.* ~aṁ (karonti) 21,7; 28,11. – ⁰-vutti, *mfn.* (*sa.* *⁰-vṛtti) friendly, kind; ⁰-vutt'assa (*varr.* ⁰-vuttyassa, -vuttissa) "let him live in charity", Dh. 376.

paṭisandahati, *vb.* (*sa.* prati-saṁ-√dhā) to be re-born (into a new existence); *pr. 3. sg.* ~ati, 100,2-5; *pot. 3. sg.* ~eyya, 100,9. *cp.* sandahati *& next.*

paṭisandhi, *m. & f.* (*sa.* pratisaṁdhi, *m.*) re-birth, transmigration; *acc.* ~iṁ (gaṇhi) 5,25; 42,22; *loc.* ~ismiṁ, 101,12.

*paṭisambhidā, *f.* (*cp. sa.* pratisaṁvid, *f.*) analytical science; *loc.* ~ā (*i. e.* ~āya) 109,10; patta-⁰, *adj. pl. m.*, possessed of analytical knowledge, 109,20. The four paṭisambhidās are: attha-⁰, dhamma-⁰, nirutti-⁰, paṭibhāna-⁰, *i. e.* expertness in the Buddhist theory and practice, etymology, and dialectics, Mil. 339,7-8; *cp. Childers* sub voce.

paṭisammodati, *vb.* (*sa.* prati-sam-√mud) to exchange friendly greetings, to return one's greeting; *aor. 3. sg.* ~modi, 96,27.

paṭisāmeti, *vb.* (*caus.* prati-√çam) to arrange, put in order; to put by, keep safe, lay away (*acc.*); *grd. n.* ~etabbaṁ, 82,22.

paṭisuṇāti, *vb.* (*sa.* prati-√çru) to promise, assent (*gen.*); *aor. 3. sg.* paccassosi (Bhagavato), 77,18; *3. pl.* ~osuṁ (Devadattassa) 76,15; *ger.* [a]) paṭissutvā, 78,10-18; [b]) paṭisuṇitvā (sādhū'ti) 16,26. 63,3; *pp. n.* paṭisutaṁ (tumhehi mayhaṁ sahassaṁ) 22,31.

paṭisedha, *m.* (*sa.* pratishedha) prohibition, denial; *loc.* ~e (nipāto, "mā"ti, a particle implying prohibition) 85,33.

paṭisedhana, *n.* (*sa.* pratishedhana) warding off, warning against; phala-paṭisedhana-mukhena pi hetum eva paṭisedheti, by warning against the results he even warns against the cause. 86,4.

paṭisedheti, *vb.* (*caus.* prati-√sidh) to prevent, prohibit, warn against (*acc.*); *pr. 3. sg.* ~eti (hetuṁ) 86,4. *cp.* paṭisedha, ~sedhana.

paṭisevati (& **patisevati**, *q. v.*) *vb.* (*sa.* prati-√sev) to practise, pursue; feel, undergo, suffer (*acc.*); *pr. 3. sg.* ~ati (vipākaṁ) Dh. 67.

paṭissutvā, *ger.*, *v.* paṭisuṇāti.

paṭihaññati, *vb.* (*pass.* paṭihanti, *sa.* prati-√han) to knock together, strike against (*loc.*); *ger.* ~itvā (vemakoṭiyaṁ), 89,6.

paṭṭa, *m.* (= *sa.*) [1]) a tablet or plate (of gold *etc.* for writing or painting upon); kañcana-paṭṭa-sadisa, *mfn.* 46,31 (*q. v.*) — [2]) a strip or slip of cloth (*cp.* paṭa); sumana-paṭṭa-vitāna, *mn.* 65,18 (*q. v.*).

paṭṭana, *n.* (*sa.* paṭṭana & pattana) a port, seaport; *acc.* ~aṁ (Bharukaccha-°) 25,13; *°-gāma, *m.* a seaport-town, ~o, 24,10.

paṭṭhāna, *n.* (*sa.* prasthāna) [1]) origin, cause; *sati-paṭṭhāna, *n.* (*v. h.*) — [2]) *nom. pr.* name of the seventh (last) book (pakaraṇa) of Abhidhammapiṭaka, also called Mahāpakaraṇa, 102,11.

paṭṭhāya, *prp.* (*ger.* patiṭṭhati, *sa.* prasthāya) beginning from, from (*w. abl.*); [a]) dvāra-gāmato p., 19,33; sīsato p., 57,29; mūlato p., 62,10; galato p., 85,30; — [b]) paṭhamakappikato p., 4,10; tassa nikkhanta-kālato p., 9,15; dhammadesanaṁ suta-divasato p., 86,30; ito p., henceforth, 6,16; ito dāni p., id. 39,3; tato p., thenceforth, 6,18.

paṭhama, *mfn.* (*sa.* prathama) [1]) foremost, first, former (*cp.* purima); *f.* ~ā (senā) 103,25; *acc. f.* ~aṁ (gāthaṁ) 8,26; paṭhama-jjhāna, *n.* 80,3 (*opp.* dutiya *etc.*); paṭhama-kappa & -kappika (*v. h.*); paṭhama-gahitā (*m. pl.*) "others already caught", 21,14-19; — *acc. n.* ~aṁ (*adv.*) at first, for the first time, 4,19. 12,12. 15,9. 18,33. 69,21. 102,14. Dh. 158; ~am eva (*opp.* pacchā) 35,36; 102,11 (first of all). — [2]) *comp.* = just, newly; *paṭhamâbhisambuddha, *mfn.* having just attained Buddhaship, *m.* ~o, 66,3; *paṭhamuggata, *mfn.*, newly-blown, *m.* ~o (kaḷīro) 47,9.

paṭhamaka, *mfn.* (*sa.* prathamaka) = *prec.*; °-bhāṇavāra, *n.* (*v. h.*) Dh. I–XIV.

paṭhamataraṁ, *adv.* (*sa.* prathamataram) before, first (of two) 83,5 = 84,1-4.

paṭhavī (or pathavī [puthuvī, ~avī]), *f.* (*sa.* pṛthivī) the earth; *acc.* ~iṁ (maddanto) 28,14; ~iṁ (adhisessati) 107,5 = Dh. 41; *gen.* (or *loc.*) ~iyā, Dh. 178 (pathavyā); paṭhavī-tale (on dry land) 28,7; *paṭhavi-ṭṭhita, *mfn.* living on the earth, *m. pl.* ~ā (earthly beings) 110,11; *paṭhavī-sama, *mfn.* like the earth, *m.* ~o, Dh. 95.

paṇāmeti, *vb.* (*caus.* pra-√nam) to bend forwards, stretch out (*acc.*); *ger.* ~etvā (añjaliṁ) 74,30.

paṇihita, *mfn.* (*sa.* pra-ṇihita, *pp.* pra-ṇi-√dhā) laid on, applied; micchā-°, *mfn.* wrongly directed, *n.* ~aṁ (cittaṁ), Dh. 42; sammā-°, *mfn.* well-directed, Dh. 43.

paṇīta, *mfn.* (*pp.* paṇeti, *sa.* praṇīta) 'performed, finished'; excellent; *m.* ~o (dhammo) 94,25; *n.* ~aṁ (khādaniyaṁ) 78,1.

paṇeti (& paneti), *vb.* (*sa.* pra-√nī) 'to lead to', perform, execute, apply (*acc.*); *pr. 3. sg.* ~eti (daṇḍaṁ garukaṁ) Dh. 310; *pp.* paṇīta (*v. h.*).

paṇḍara, *mfn.* (*sa.* pāṇḍara) white, pale; *instr. pl. n.* ~ehi (-kesehi) 47,13.

paṇḍicca, *n.* (*sa.* pāṇḍitya) erudition; cleverness, skill; *instr.* ~ena, 91,26.

paṇḍita, *mfn.* (= *sa.*) wise, intelligent, clever; *m.* ~o, 57,35; *gen.* ~assa, 24,22; *m. pl.* ~ā, 9,29; (*w. loc.* appamādamhi) Dh. 22; *f.* ~ā, 56,8; often *e. c.* : sasa-paṇḍito, 14,12; Suppāraka-°, 25,14; Upāli-°, 109,7; – °-dovārika, *m.* 91,23 (*q. v.*); *°-bhāva, *m.* cleverness, skill, *gen.* ~assa, 91,24; °-mānin, *mfn.* one who thinks himself wise, *m.* ~ī (bālo) Dh. 63; *°-vagga, *m.* the sixth chapter of Dh.; *°-vedaniya, *mfn.* "intelligible only to the wise", *m.* ~o (dhammo) 94,26; *°-saṁsagga, *m.* company or intercourse with wise men, *gen.* ~assa, 29,8.

paṇḍu, *mfn.* (*sa.* pāṇḍu) yellow, pale, white; °-kambala, *m.* a white woollen blanket : °-silāsanaṁ, 15,8 (*v. h.*); °-palāsa, *m.* a withered leaf, *nom.* ~o, Dh. 235; °-roga, *m.* jaundice : °-tāpaso, *m.* 35,4, *°-dhātuka, *mfn.* suffering from jaundice, 35,16.

paṇṇa, *n.* (*sa.* parṇa) [1]) a leaf (*esp.* betel leaf); *acc. pl.* ~āni, 17,21; nimba-paṇṇa-°, 37,22 (*q. v.*); *°-saññā, *f.* a mark of leaves (tied up in order to indicate the boundary of a field), *acc.* ~aṁ, 8,8; *paṇṇa-bandhana-saññā, *n.* (= paṇṇa-saññā-bandhana?) tying up leaves, *nom.* ~aṁ, 8,9; paṇṇa-sālā, *f.* a hut of leaves and grass, hermitage, *acc.* ~aṁ (āditta-°) 44,30; *loc.* ~āya (by the hut) 35,11; *acc. pl.* ~ā, 34,33. Satta-°, *nom. pr.* (*v. h.*). – [2]) a leaf for writing upon, a letter; a bond, deed of gift, donation; *acc.* ~aṁ (pāhesi) 36,22 (*cp. next*). – [3]) a feather, wing (only *e. c.*) *v.* supaṇṇa.

*paṇṇākāra, *m.*, a present, donation; *acc.* ~aṁ, 58,21-24; *acc. pl.* ~e, 58,22. *cp.* paṇṇa [2]) & ākāra.

Patañjali, *m.* (= *sa.*) *nom. pr.* of a philosopher (propounder of the Yoga philosophy); *v.* Pātañjali-.

patati, *vb.* (*sa.* √pat) to fly, jump, fall; to fall down (upon, *loc.* or *acc.*); *pr. 3. sg.* ~ati (dīpake) 2,23; *1. sg.* ~āmi (yamh'okāse ṭhatvā orapāraṁ patām'ahaṁ, standing where I use to jump over, *cp.* orapāraṁ) 108,26; *part. m.* ~anto (nāvāya) 20,1; *loc. f.* ~antiyā (asaniyā) 39,10; *part. med.* ~māna, *loc. n.* ~e (piṭṭhiyaṁ pahārasate) 55,12; – *fut. 3. sg.* ~issati, 53,26; 112,20 (tesaṁ kāye, *acc. pl.*); *1. sg.* ~issāmi (aṅgāragabbhe) 15,33; – *aor. 3. sg.* pati, 16,7. 89,8; (tassa hatthe, fell to his share) 23,12; *3. pl.* ~iṁsu (poured down) 33,6; – *perf. 3. sg.* papāta (kālaṁ katvā) 89,8 [but here the reading of the Colombo edition : papatā, *aor. 3. sg.* (from papatati, *q. v.*) undoubtedly ought to be preferred, because this formation is generally found elsewhere, *e. g.* Jāt. VI, 566,8 (= patitā); Vin. III, 17,23 (*cp.* II. 126,3)]; – *ger.* ~itvā, 13,20. 49,5. 89,9; – *pp.* ~ita, *f.* ~ā (asani), 17,32; *acc. m.* ~aṁ (cāpāto saraṁ, "sent from the bow") Dh. 320; – *caus.* pāteti (*q. v.*) *cp.* patana, pāta.

patana, *n.* (= *sa.*) falling, ruin; *°-ākāra-ppatta, *mfn.* being on the point of falling out, *m. pl.* ~ā (dantā) 12,21; *n. pl.* ~āni (akkhīni) 50,19; – geha-°, 19,16 (*q. v.*).

patākā (& paṭākā), *f.* (= *sa.*) a flag, banner; dhaja-patākâdīhi, 62,7 (*cp.* ādi).

pati[1], *m.* (= *sa.*) husband; lord, master; *nom.* ~i, 31,34. 64,15; *comp. v.* gavampati, gahapati, Sahampati.

pati[2], *indecl.* (*sa.* prati) [1]) *prp. w. acc.*, near to, towards; nadiṁ Nerañjaram ~, 103,2; [2]) prefix to verbs & nouns, generally spelt paṭi- (*q. v.*) *cp. next etc.*

patikāra, *m.* (*sa.* pratikāra) reward, return, retribution; *a-ppatikāraka, *mfn.* (*q. v.*).

patiṭṭhati, *vb.* (*sa.* pra-√sthā) to depart from, originate; *ger.* paṭṭhāya (*prp. w. abl.*) *v. h.*; *caus.* paṭṭhapeti, to set forth, propound, explain; *cp.* paṭṭhāna, *n.*

patiṭṭhahati & patiṭṭhāti, *vb.* (*sa.* prati-√sthā) to stand firm, to be established; *aor. 3. sg.* ~ṭṭhahi (sotāpattiphale) 89,3; (sakadāgāmiphale) 29,17; *1. sg.* ~ṭṭhahiṁ (parakūle) 108,29; – *fut. 3. sg.* a) ~ṭṭhahissati, 87,2; b) ~ṭṭhissati (Laṅkāyaṁ mama sāsanaṁ) 110,24; – *ger.* ~ṭṭhāya (sīle, "standing fast in moral practice") 14,18; (rajje, "became king") 42,26; – *pp.* ~ṭṭhita, *m.* ~o, 38,11 (rajje), 61,31 (gabbho kucchimhi), 95,34 (sāre, "standing in its strength"); su-patiṭṭhita, *mfn.* (*q. v.*) – *caus.* patiṭṭhāpeti, to set or lay down, establish (*acc.*); *aor. 3. sg.* ~esi (phalitaṁ rañño pāṇimhi) 44,27; *ger.* ~etvā, 22,9. 29,6; (rājānaṁ pañcasu sīlesu) 7,24; 17,32. 59,32.

patiṭṭhā, *f.* (*sa.* pratishṭhā) 1) resting-place, support; *acc.* ~aṁ (labhitvā, to get footing) 28,13-16; – 2) security, refuge; *nom.* ~ā, 28,25.

patidissati, *vb.* (*pass.* patipassati; *sa.* prati-√dṛç) to appear (as), to look like; *pr. 3. sg.* ~ati (yathā aggīva suriyo va) 26,5 *etc.*

patimāneti, *vb.* (*sa.* prati-√man, *caus.*) to honour; to await, wait for (*acc.*); *part. f.* ~entī (tassāgamanaṁ) 22,28.

patirūpa, *mfn.* (*sa.* pratirūpa) like, similar; suitable, fit; *loc. n.* ~e ("what is proper") Dh. 158.

patisevati (& **paṭisevati**, *q. v.*) *vb.* (*sa.* prati-√sev) to practise, pursue (*acc.*); *part. m.* ~anto (methunadhammaṁ, making love) 54,11; *aor. 3. sg.* ~sevi (asaddhammaṁ, id.) 52,29.

***patissata**, *mfn.* (*sa.* *pratismṛta) recollecting, thoughtful; *m. pl.* ~ā, Dh. 144.

patissaya, *m.* 1) (*sa.* pratiçraya) refuge, house; *2) (*sa.* praçraya) obedience, respect; *v. next.*

patissava, *m.* (*sa.* pratiçrava, √çru) obedience, respect; *a-ppatisava, *mfn.* (also spelt a-ppatissaya and sometimes shortened to a-ppatissa) disrespectful; hence *a-ppatissavāsa, *m.* anarchy, 10,31.

patīta, *mfn.* (*sa.* pratīta, *pp.* prati-√i) pleased, glad; *m.* ~o (*synon.* sumano) Dh. 68.

patoda, *m.* (*sa.* pratoda) a goad; *cp.* °-patodaṁ (*n.*, "pole, axle [*etc.*] and goad unitedly") 98,7; °-laṭṭhi, *f.* (*sa.* pratoda-yashṭi) "the goading-stick", 98,6.

patta1, *n.* (*sa.* pattra) a wing, feather; a leaf; karavīra-°, *n.* (*q. v.*), *instr. pl.* ~ehi (vājitaṁ, kaṇḍaṁ) 92,19; kumuda-patta-vaṇṇa, *mfn.* (*v. h.*); pokkhara-°, *n.* a lotus leaf, *loc.* ~e, Dh. 401.

patta2, *m.* (*sa.* pātra. *n.*) a vessel, pot, bowl, *esp.* the alms-bowl of a Buddhist monk; *nom.* ~o, 82,26; *acc.* ~aṁ, 87,18; (āmaṁ) 104,6; *instr.* ~ena, 62,2; – *°-cīvara, *n.* bowl and robe, 76,16. 83,7; – *°-pariyāpanna, *n.* (*v. h.*).

patta3, *mfn.* (*pp.* pāpuṇāti; *sa.* prāpta) 1) *pass.* attained, reached, acquired; 2) *act.* one who has attained to, reached, *etc.* (*w. acc.* or *e. c.*, also used as finite tense); *m.* ~o (jātikkhayaṁ) Dh. 423; patto si nibbānaṁ, Dh. 134; *f.* ~ā (Khuramāla-samuddaṁ) 25,28; *n.* ~aṁ (vināsaṁ) 34,9; tuyhaṁ pattaṁ (*pass.* "the consequences of your own fortune") 6,35; *gen. m.* ~ass' (uttamavedanaṁ) 103,23; *acc. pl. m.* patte (jīvitakkhayaṁ) 34,8; – *comp.* (*mfn.*) apanetabbākāra-ppatta, 45,1; jara-°, 47,15 (*v.* jarā); daṇḍa-°, 100,15; dukkha-°, 59,10; domanassa-°, 13,6; patanākāra-°, 12,31; bala-°, 80,25; rūpa-°, 64,30; rūpagga-°, 49,12; lābhaggayasagga-°, 18,16; vajjha-°, 40,14; vaya-°, 8,15; vāra-°, 6,27; vesārajja-°, 69,13; vyasana-°, 8,30; saṁvega-°, 53,11; santāsa-°, 86,19; somanassa-°, 15,29; hattha-°, 67,30; – *patta-dhamma, *mfn.* "having mastered the truth", *m.* ~o, 69,18; *°-paṭisambhidā, 109,20 (*v. h.*); a-ppatta, *mfn.* (*q. v.*).

patti, *f.* (*sa.* prāpti) acquiring, gain; share, part, portion; *acc.* ~iṁ (attanā ... bhāvita-bhāvanāya, etassa dammi) 29,3; *dat.* ~iyā (yogakkhemassa, "for the sake of acquiring") 103,3.

patthaddha, *mfn.* (*sa.* prastabdha) stark, stiff (as a pillar); *instr. m.* ~ena (kāyena) 75,17.

patthayati, *vb.* (*sa.* prārthayate) to wish, desire (*acc.*); *pr. 2. sg.* ~asi (atha ce ~asi, if you like) 104,22 *etc.*; *part. med. m.* ~māno (tava hadayamaṁsaṁ) 3,13; *pl.* ~mānā (vaḍḍhiṁ) "seeking gain", 34,18.

pattharati, *vb.* (*sa.* pra-√stṛ) to spread, extend (*trans. & intr.*, *w. acc.*); *ger.* ~itvā (sakalanagaraṁ, "through the whole town") 65,24.

patvā, *ger.*, *v.* pāpuṇāti.

patha (or pantha, *q. v.*), *m.* (= *sa.*) road, path, way; *loc.* ~e, 31,34; mahā-⁰ ("on the highway") Dh. 58; *comp. v.* *anupariyāya-⁰, ādicca-⁰, kamma-⁰, thala-jala-⁰. *dvedhā-⁰, nakkhatta-⁰, sagga-⁰, *hattha-⁰. *cp.* pada, paḷipatha, pātheyya.

pathavī, *f.* (= paṭhavī, *q. v.*) the earth; *gen.* ~vyā, Dh. 178.

pada, *m. & n.* (= *sa.*, *cp.* pāda) ¹) foot; *v.* catuppada, *m.*, dipada, *m.* — ²) step, footstep, trace, track; *acc.* ~aṁ (vañceti, *q. v.*) 12,30; uttiṇṇa-⁰, 111,17 (*v. h.*); padā padaṁ (*abl. & acc.*) "step by step", 104,11; *instr.* ~ena (kena, "by what track") Dh. 179; *⁰-valañja, *m.* footprint, *acc.* ~aṁ, 11,28. — ³) way, path; position, standpoint; place, abode, home; *nom.* (*n.*) ~aṁ (maccuno) Dh. 21; Dh. 93. 254; *acc.* ~aṁ (santaṁ = Nibbāna) Dh. 368 = amataṁ padaṁ, Dh. 114, *cp.* amata-pada (*v.* a-mata) & a-pada, *mfn.*; assama-⁰, *n.*, jana-⁰, *m.*, sagga-⁰, *n.* (*cp.* sagga-patha) *q. v.* — ⁴) a word, verse (or quarter of a verse), sentence; *n.* idaṁ ~aṁ, 85,9; *acc.* ~aṁ (dubbhāsitaṁ) 110,12; *m. pl.* ~ā (caturo, saccānaṁ *i. e.* cattāri ariyasaccāni) Dh. 273; attha-⁰, *n.* (*v. h.*); *gātha-⁰, *n.* (*v.* gāthā); *dhamma-⁰, *n.*, nirutti-pada-kovida, *mfn.*, *sampuṇṇa-⁰, *mfn.*, sikkhā-⁰, *n.* (*v. h.*).

padakkhiṇa, *mfn.* (*sa.* pradakshiṇa) 'moving to the right'; clever, good, auspicious; ~aṁ, *indecl.* (*constr. w.* karoti, to walk round persons or objects, keeping the right side towards them as token of respect, to salute respectfully (*acc.*); to go round (a city, *acc.*) in procession; ~aṁ katvā (mātu sayanaṁ) 61,21; (Bhagavantaṁ abhivādetvā) 70,12; ~aṁ kurumānassa (nagaraṁ) 64,12; ~aṁ akāsi (do.) 45,32.

padadāti, *v.* padeti.

padara, *mn.* (*sa.* pradara) ¹) *m.* 'splitting', a cleft (in the earth); — ²) *n.* a piece of wood, a plank; *nom. pl.* ~āni, 28,30.

padeti (padāti & padadāti) *vb.* (*sa.* pra-√dā) to give away (*acc.*); *fut. 3. sg.* padassati (uttamatthaṁ bhariyā) 54,29.

padīpa, *m.* (*sa.* pradīpa) a lamp, light; *nom.* ~o, 99,22; 101,8; *acc.* ~aṁ, 99,18; ⁰-aggi, *m.* & tela-⁰, *m.* (*v. h.*).

padīpeti, *vb.* (*caus. sa.* pra-dīpayati) to light, kindle (*acc.*); *pot. 3. sg.* ~eyya (padīpaṁ) 99,18; *pp.* padīpita, *mfn.* burning, shining; *m.* ~o (sabbarattiṁ) 99,24.

paduṭṭha, *mfn.* (*sa.* pradushṭa) corrupt, wicked, malignant; *instr.* ~ena (manasā) Dh. 1 (*opp.* pasanna); a-ppaduṭṭha, *mfn.* (*q. v.*) *cp.* dussati.

*padubbhati, *vb.* (*sa.* *pra-√druh) to do wrong, offend, commit treachery; *ger.* ~itvā (antopure) 38,17 (*cp.* dubbhati).

paduma, *n.* (& *m.*) (*sa.* padma) a lotus; *nom.* ~aṁ (hutvā) like a lotus, 23,31; 23,34; *acc.* ~aṁ (seta-⁰, a white lotus) 61,19; pañca-vaṇṇa-⁰ (of five different colours) 4,9; *⁰-puñja, *m.* a cluster of lotuses, *loc.* ~e, 16,6; ⁰-sara, *mn.* a lotus-lake, *acc.* ~aṁ, 3,30.

padesa, *m.* (*sa.* pradeça) ¹) spot, place, region, district; *nom.* ~o (jagati-ppadeso) Dh. 127; *acc.* ~aṁ, 43,18. Dh. 303; *loc.* ~e, 22,24; (Himavanta-⁰) 1,3. 13,9; — ²) extent, distance; *loc.* ~e (tigāvuta-ppamāṇe, yojana-ppamāṇe) 63,23-28; yathā-padese, *adv.* (*cp. sa.* yathā-pradeçaṁ) all over, at all sides, 47,1; — [3]) position, rank, order (?); *acc.* ~aṁ (jāti-gotta-kula-⁰, *q. v.*) 43,30; samāna-bal(âdi)-⁰, *mfn.* having equal position with regard to military force *etc.*, *m. pl.* ~ā, 43,31. *cp. next.*

*padesika, *mfn.* (*fr. prec.*) 'being in the region', in the neighbourhood of (only *e. c.*); soḷasa-vassa-⁰, *mfn.* about 16 years old, *m.* ~o, 38,10. *cp.* uddesika.

padhāna, *n.* (*sa.* pradhāna, as to the meaning = *sa.* pra-ṇi-dhāna, *cp.* also *buddh. sa.* prahāṇa) exertion, profound religious meditation; *instr.* ~ena (kiṁ kāhasi, "what do you want with exertion?") 103,9; *dat.* ~āya, 103,10; *ukkuṭika-ppadhāna, *n.* Dh. 141 (*v. h.*); *⁰-pahitatta, *mfn.* whose mind is intent upon meditation, *acc. m.* ~aṁ, 103,2; *⁰-sutta, *n. nom. pr.* of a chapter of Sutta-nipāta, p. 103 –04; *cp.* Mahāpadhāna-ghara.

pana, *indecl.* (the enclit. form of 'puna', *q. v.*; *sa.* punar) [1]) now! well! (in the continuation of a tale): 2,19; 2,26 (tasmiṁ ~ kāle, "now, at that time"); 10,3 *etc.* — [2]) but (adversative, often combined with other particles): 1,22. 4,12. 8,8 (the preceeding sentence negative); 5,5. 50,23. 65,25 *etc.* Dh. 252. 292; ca pana (but) 7,35. 71,17; atha ca ~ (nevertheless) 3,4; na kho pana (but certainly not) 7,8. 9,31; eva pana (on the contrary) 5,10; corresponding with a preceeding eva (it is true, no doubt . . . but, *cp.* greek μέν . . . δέ) : maraṇabhāvam eva jānāmi [maraṇadivasam] pana na jānāmi, 88,22-23; sometimes repeated in both sentences : eva pana . . . pana na, 2,8; — vā pana (or else) 81,17; *cp.* Dh. 42 (verivā pana = verī vā pana?); — [3]) then! (in interrogative sentences, often expressive of surprise): kahaṁ ~, 1,26; kiṁ ~, 44,4; aguṇā pana kīdisā, 44,5; katamo ~, 79,13; in a second question : kiṁ ~, 89,25; ko ~ ettha N., 97,31; after a negative sentence : kiṁ ~ (how much less) 74,28. *cp. Pischel,* Gr. § 342.

panasa, *m.* (= *sa.*) the bread-fruit tree; *instr. pl.* ~ehi, 2,10; amba-panasâdīhi, 2,20.

panudati, *vb.* (*sa.* pra-√nud) to drive away (*acc.*); *imp. 2. sg.* panuda (kāme) Dh. 383.

paneti, *vb.*, *var. lect.* for paṇeti, Dh. 310 (*v. h.*).

panta, *mfn.* (*sa.* prānta) distant, secluded, solitary; *n.* ~aṁ (sayanā-sanaṁ, "sleeping and sitting alone") Dh. 185.

pantha, *m.* (= patha; *cp. sa.* panthan) way, road; *⁰-ghāta, *m.* murder and robbery of highwaymen, brigandage; *acc.* ~aṁ (karonti) 32,15.

panna, *mfn.* (= *sa.*, *pp.* ⁰-pajjati, √pad) fallen, gone; *⁰-bhāra, *mfn.* "who has put down his burden", *acc. m.* ~aṁ, Dh. 402.

pannarasa, *num.* (sometimes written paṇṇarasa = pañcadasa, *sa.* pañcadaça) fifteen; ~ma, *mfn.* the fifteenth, Dh. XV.

papañca, *m.* (*sa.* prapañca) abundance, diffuseness, error, vanity; this word may also often be translated by 'detriment, decay; delay, omission, waste of time' *etc.*; it is generally explained in the commentaries by taṇhā-diṭṭhi-māna-⁰; *⁰-âbhirata, *mfn.* "delighting in vanity", *m. pl.* ~ā, Dh. 254; *⁰-samatikkanta, *mfn.* "who has overcome the host of evils", *acc. pl. m.* ~e, Dh. 195. — *Papañca-sūdanī, *f. nom. pr.* of a commentary on Majjhima-nikāya by Buddhaghosa; specimen p. 61.

*papaṭikā, *f.* (rarely papatikā) [1]) a splinter, piece, fragment; *nom.* ~ā (-t-) 76,1; — [2]) the outer dry bark of a tree, falling off in loose shreds; taca-⁰, 95,22-23 (*v. h.*).

papatati, *vb.* (*sa.* pra-√pat) to fall off; *pr. 3. pl.* ~anti (sokā tamhā)

108,3; *aor. 3. sg.* papatā (Ed. papāta) 89,8 (*v.* patati).

*p a p a t i k ā, *f.*, *v.* papaṭikā.

p a p ā t a[1], *pf.* (*fr.* patati, to be corrected to papatā, 89,8) *v.* papatati.

p a p ā t a[2], *m.* (*sa.* prapāta) a steep rock, precipice; ~o, 27,7; *loc.* ~e (Sineru-°) 59,26; °-sadisa, *mfn.* like a wall, *n.* ~aṁ, 27,4.

*p a p u p p h a k a, *n.* (*sa.* *pra-push-paka) 'flower-pointed', *pl.* the flower-arrows of Māra; *pl. acc.* ~āni, Dh. 46 (ἁπαξ λεγ.).

p a p p o ṭ h e t i (or papphoṭeti). *vb.* (*caus.* pra-√sphuṭ) to beat, slap, shake (as clothes, in order to dust them, *acc.*); to flap the wings (*acc.*); *ger.* ~etvā (pakkhe) 12,9.

p a p p o t i, *vb.*, *v.* pāpuṇāti.

p a p p h ā s a, *n.* (*sa.* pupphusa, *m.* & phupphusa, *n.*) the lungs; *nom.* ~aṁ, 82,4. 97,21.

*p a b ā ḷ h a, *mfn.* (*cp. sa.* bāḍha, √baṁh) strong, sharp; *f.* ~ā (vyādhi) 78,31; *pl.* ~ā (vedanā) 78,24; *acc. m.* ~aṁ (ābādhaṁ) 78,30.

p a b u j j h a t i, *vb.* (*sa.* pra-√budh) to wake up, awake (*intr.*); *pr. 3. pl.* ~anti, Dh. 296; *fut. 3. sg.* ~issati, 65,32; *ger.* ~itvā, 36,1. 65,4. 89,6; *pp.* pabuddha, *f.* ~ā (devī, awoke) 61,23. *cp.* su-pabuddhaṁ. *adv.*

p a b b a j a, *m.* (= babbaja, *sa.* balbaja) a sort of coarse grass; *pab-baja, *mfn.* (= pabbaja-maya) made of grass (hemp), *n.* ~aṁ (bandhanaṁ) Dh. 345. *cp. Weber,* Ind. Str. III, 394.

p a b b a j a t i, *vb.* (*sa.* pra-√vraj) 'to go forth', *esp.* to leave the world in order to become a hermit, or to enter the order of Buddhist monks; *fut. 3. sg.* ~issati (agārā nikkhamma) 61,33; 63,16; *inf.* ~ituṁ, 45,3; *comp.* ~itu-kāma, *mfn.* "bent on retiring from the world", *acc. m.* ~aṁ, 45,8; *ger.* [a]) pabbajja, 113,17; [b]) pabbajitvā (*w. acc.* isi-pabbajjaṁ) 34,32. 45,13; 64,21 (nikkhamma); 113,18; – *pp.* pabbajita (*m.*) *q. v.* – *caus.* pabbājeti (*q. v.*) *cp. next* & *duppabbaja.

p a b b a j a n a, *n.* (*sa.* pravrajana) passing over to a religious life; a-pabbajanatthāya, 47,5 (*v.* a-pabba-jana).

p a b b a j i t a, *m.* (*pp.* pabbajati) a monk (or hermit); ~o, 63,32; Dh. 184; *acc.* ~aṁ, 63,30; *instr.* ~ena, 66,25; *pl.* ~ā, Dh. 74; °-guṇa, *m.* (*q. v.*).

p a b b a j j ā, *f.* (*sa.* pravrajyā) re-tiring from the world, the ordination of a layman wishing to become a Buddhist monk; *acc.* ~aṁ (labheyyâ-haṁ) 70,15; (yācitvā) 89,15; (isi-°, *q. v.*) 34,32. 45,13; *gen.* (*dat.* & *abl.*) ~āya (namitacitto) 46,18; (satiṁ na karissati) 63,18; (cittaṁ nami) 65,13; (antarāyaṁ, agārasmā ana-gāriyaṁ) 68,4; – °-kāraṇa, *n.* & °-samaya, *m.* 45,9-12 (*v. h.*); laddha-pabbajjûpasampada, *mfn.* (*v.* upa-sampadā).

p a b b a t a, *m.* (*sa.* parvata) a mountain, hill, rock; *nom.* ~o (Hi-mavanto) Dh. 304; *acc.* ~aṁ, 16,16; *gen.* ~assa, 75,33; *pl.* ~āni (with neuter termination by attraction to the foll. vanāni (?) or *adj. n.* = *sa.* pār-vatāni (?)) Dh. 188; *gen. pl.* ~ānaṁ, Dh. 127; – *°-kūṭa, *m.* a mountain-peak, *pl.* ~ā, 75,36; – *°-pāda, *m.* the foot of a mountain, ~o, 14,9; *loc.* ~e, 84,31; – *°-rasa, *m.* "the essence of the mountain", *acc.* ~aṁ, 16,16; Rajata-°, Suvaṇṇa-°, *m. nom. pr.* (*q. v.*).

p a b b a t a - ṭ ṭ h a, *mfn.* (*sa.* par-vata-stha) standing on a mountain; *m.* ~o, Dh. 28 (*opp.* bhumaṭṭha).

p a b b ā j e t i, *vb.* (*caus.* pabbajati; *sa.* pravrājayati) [1]) to send or drive away (*acc.*) (from, *abl.*); *part. nom. m.* ~ājayaṁ (attano malaṁ) Dh. 388; *aor. 3. sg.* ~esi (raṭṭhā). – [2]) to or-dain (*acc.*), admit to the Buddhist monastic order (through the pabbajjā, *q. v.*); *imp. 3. sg.* ~etu (imaṁ dā-rakaṁ) 81,12.

p a b h a ṁ k a r a, *m.*, *v.* pabbhā.

p a b h a ṅ g u ṇ a (& pabhaṅgu), *mfn.*

(*sa.* prabhañgura?) fragile, brittle; frail; *n.* ~aṁ (idaṁ rūpaṁ, *var.* ~guraṁ) 107,7 = Dh. 148; – *pabhañguṇa, *n. subst.* fragility; destroying, destruction, ~aṁ (bhogānaṁ) Dh. 139.

pabhā, *f.* (*sa.* prabhā) light, splendour; *instr.* ~āya, 85,7; – pabhaṁkara, *m.* (*sa.* prabhākara) 'lightmaker', the sun; epithet of Buddha; ~o (Buddho dhammarājā) 19,1; – nippabha, *mfn.* (*q. v.*).

pabhāta, *mfn.* (*sa.* prabhāta) begun to become light, *loc. f.* ~āya (rattiyā) "at daybreak", 42,1. – *subst. n.* = daybreak, morning.

pabhāseti, *vb.* (*caus.*, *sa.* pra-√bhās) to illuminate, enlighten (*acc.*); *pr. 3. sg.* ~eti (sabbā disā; tassa pabhāya = attano pabhāya ?) 85,8; (imaṁ lokaṁ) Dh. 172.

pabhinna, *mfn.* (*sa.* prabhinna, *pp.* pra-√bhid) 'burst open', flowing with juice, *esp. m.* said of an elephant in rut; *hatthi-prabhinna, *m.* a furious elephant, *acc.* ~aṁ, Dh. 326. *cp. next.*

pabhedana, *n.* (*sa.* prabhedana, *cp.* prabheda) the flowing of juice from the temples of an elephant; *kaṭuka-pp°, *mfn.* Dh. 324 (*v. h.*).

pamajjati[1], *vb.* (*sa.* pra-√mad) to be careless, negligent, or idle; *trans.* to neglect (*acc.*); *pr. 3. sg.* ~ati (na-pp°) Dh. 172. 259; *pot. 3. sg.* ~eyya (do.) Dh. 168; *ger.* ~itvā, Dh. 172; *aor. 2. sg.* pāmado (mā ~) 77,5 (*cp.* Notes); Dh. 371; *pp.* pamatta (*q. v.*) *cp.* pamāda, *m.*

pamajjati[2], *vb.* (*sa.* pra-√mṛj) to sweep, rub, scour, wipe off (*acc.*); to stroke (along with the hand); *ger.* ~itvā (hatthena cīvaravaṁsaṁ) 83,21; *grd. n.* ~itabbaṁ (udakaṁ gattato) 84,3; *f.* ~ā (bhitti) 84,20; *m. pl.* ~ā (-kaṇṇabhāgā) 84,19.

pamatta, *mfn.* (*pp.* pamajjati[1]; *sa.* pramatta) careless, inattentive, negligent, thoughtless, indolent; *m.* ~o, Dh. 19. 309; *gen.* ~assa, 41,25; *pl.* ~ā, 77,5. Dh. 21; *gen. pl.* ~ānaṁ, Dh. 292; *°-bandhu, *m.* "friend of the indolent" (*i. e.* Māra) 103,13 (*voc.*). – *°-cārin, *mfn.* (*cp. sa.* pramādacārin) acting in a careless manner, *gen. m.* ~ino, 107,29 = Dh. 334. – a-ppamatta, *mfn.* (*q. v.*).

pamathita, *mfn.* (*pp.* pra-√math) agitated; *vitakka-°, *mfn.* (*q. v.*).

pamāṇa, *n.* (*sa.* pramāṇa) measure, size, extent, length, *etc.*; *e. c.* (*mfn.*): equal in extent to; *nom.* ~aṁ (n'atthi gacchantānaṁ, "there was no end to them") 9,16; *acc.* ~aṁ (attano, na jānāsi, "you don't know your measure") 9,28; *instr.* ~ena (tesaṁ, in proportion to them) 57,11; *comp.* udaka-ppamāṇa, *n.* 3,3; pāsāṇa-°, *n.* ib.; – assa-potaka-°, *mfn.*, gala-°, *mfn.*, ghaṭa-°, *mfn.*, tāvatiṁsa-devaloka-°, *mfn.*, ti-gāvuta-°, *mfn.* & yojana-°, *mfn.* (*v. h.*).

pamāda, *m.* (*sa.* pramāda) negligence, carelessness, indolence; *nom.* ~o (maccuno padaṁ) Dh. 21; ~o rajo sabbadā, ~ânupatito rajo, indolence is always dirt (*i. e.* moral defilement), dirt is the result of it (*v.* anupatati), 108,8; *instr.* ~ena, Dh. 167; °-pamāda-ṭṭhānā (*abl.*) 81,23 (*v.* ṭhāna [7])).

pamāreti, *vb.* (*sa.* pra-mārayati, *caus.* pra-√mṛ) to strike one dead, to maltreat, hurt severely (*acc.*); *pot. 3. sg.* ~eyya (maṁ) 87,15.

pamukha, *mfn.* (*sa.* pramukha) being at the head of, chief (*e. c.*); Vijaya-ppamukhā, *m. pl.* "with V. at their head", 110,30. 112,27. *cp.* pāmokkha.

pamuccati, *vb.* (*pass.* pamuñcati, *q. v.*).

pamuñcati, *vb.* (*sa.* pra-√muc) to liberate, send away, shake off (*acc.*); *pr. 3. sg.* ~ati (pupphāni, "sheds the flowers") Dh. 377; – *pass.* pamuccati, to be delivered (from, *abl.*), Dh. 189. 192 = 107,22 (sabbadukkhā); *fut.* pamokkhati, *3. pl.* ~anti (Mārabandhanā) Dh. 276; – *caus.* pamoceti, to deliver (*acc.*) from (*abl.*); *aor.*

2. & *3. sg.* ~esi (maṁ dukkhā) 108,12. – *cp.* duppamuñca, *mfn.*

pamudita, *mfn.* (*pp.* pamodati; *sa.* pramudita) greatly delighted, pleased; *°-citta, *mfn.* greatly delighted in his mind, *m.* ~o, 16,7.

pameyya, *mfn.* (*sa.* prameya) measurable; *v.* a-ppameyya, *mfn.*

pamokkhati, *fut. pass.*, *v.* pamuñcati.

pamoceti, *vb.* (*caus.* pamuñcati, *q. v.*).

pamodati, *vb.* (*sa.* pra-√mud) to be delighted, to rejoice greatly; *pr. 3. sg.* ~ati, Dh. 16; *pp.* pamudita (*q. v.*); *cp.* pāmojja.

pamohana, *n.* (*sa.* pramohana, *mfn.*) bewilderment, delusion; *nom.* ~aṁ (Mārassa) Dh. 274.

payāti, *vb.* (*sa.* pra-√yā) to go forth, set out, advance, proceed; *aor. 3. sg.* pāyāsi (*w. augm.*) 5,4. 34,4. 54,4; *3. pl.* pāyiṁsu (do.) 33,7; *pp.* payāta, *loc. fem.* ~āya (sukha-°, navāya, "when the ship was fairly off") 19,27; *gen. pl. m.* ~ānaṁ (vāṇijānaṁ, Bharukacchā, who have come from Bh.) 25,30; Bharukacchapayātānaṁ (do.) 20,22.

payirupāsati, *vb.* (*sa.* pary-upa-√ās) to sit beside, attend on (*acc.*); *pr. 3. sg.* ~ati (metrically = payrupāsati) Dh. 64–65 (paṇḍitaṁ).

*payuttaka, *mfn.* (*fr. sa.* prayukta, *cp. next*) hired, bribed, suborned; *m.* ~o, 38,28; °-coro, 38,27; °-dhuttā, *m. pl.* 49,7.

payojeti, *vb.* (*caus.* payuñjati; *sa.* pra-yojayati, √yuj) to use, employ; direct; practise (*acc.*); *pr. 1. pl.* payojayāma (naccādīni) 65,1; *aor. 3. sg.* ~esi (purise, "directed some men") 74,4; *3. pl.* ~ayiṁsu (naccagītavāditāni) 64,31.

para, *mfn.* (= *sa.*) ¹) other, different (*opp.* attan, *cp.* añña, apara); *m.* ko . . . paro ("who else?") Dh. 160; *acc.* ~aṁ, Dh. 184; (lokaṁ) Dh. 220; *gen.* ~assa, 58,13; parassahetu, "for the sake of others", Dh. 84 (*opp.* attahetu); *loc.* ~amhi (loke, *opp.* asmiṁ) Dh. 168; – *instr. n.* (*adv.*) parena (= aparena samayena) afterwards, later on, 47,21; – *m. pl. nom.* pare (others, other people; sometimes pregnantly = bad or impious people) Dh. 6; *acc.* pare, 103,30. 106,4. Dh. 257; *gen.* paresaṁ, 8,5; 34,25 (*opp.* attanā, *cp.* aññesaṁ, 34,24); 41,33 (paresaṁ (= *instr.*) tava guṇā ñātā); – *comp.* °-santaka, *mfn.* (*q. v.*, *cp.* corrections); – °-kula, *n.* (*v. h.*); °-kūla, *n.* = °-tīra, *n.* (*q. v.*); *°-dukkh'ūpadhāna, *v.* upadhāna; °-loka, *m.* another world, 106,15 (vitiṇṇa-°, *q. v.*); *°-vajjânupassin, *v.* anupassin (*cp.* vajja); para-paccaya, *v.* a-para-paccaya; *para-ppavāda *etc.*, *v.* below; in *comp.* with words beginning with u the final a drops and the u is lengthened, *v.* parūpakkama, parūpaghātin. – ²) higher, superior; highest, supreme; *acc. m.* ~aṁ (khaṇaṁ) 110,18; santipara, *mfn.* "higher than rest", *n.* ~aṁ (sukhaṁ) Dh. 202. – paraṁ, *indecl.* (*v. next*). – *superl.* parama (*q. v.*). – *cp.* parato, parattha, pāra, pārato *etc.*

paraṁ, *indecl.* (= *sa.*) afterwards, after (*w. abl.*); ito-paraṁ, tato-paraṁ (*v. h.*); paraṁ-maraṇā, after death, 89,20.

parakkama, *m.* (*sa.* parākrama) exertion, effort; *acc.* ~aṁ (karonto) 34,23; *instr.* ~ena (kata-°, "when we do our best") 12,5; *daḷha-°, *mfn.* (*v. h.*).

parakkamati, *vb.* (*sa.* parā-√kram) to advance, attack (*acc.*); to show courage *etc.*; *pot. 3. sg.* parakkame (daḷham enaṁ) Dh. 313; *ger.* ~kamma, "valiantly", Dh. 383.

parato, *adv.* (*sa.* paratas) ¹) afterwards, further; 26,3. 34,7 (gacchanto). – ²) on the other side; 21,16 (*opp.* orato) *cp.* pārato.

parattha¹, *adv.* (*sa.* paratra) in another place, in the other world; 74,2 (~ā'ti); Dh. 177.

parattha², *m.* (*sa.* parārtha) the

advantage or interest of others; *instr.* (for the sake of) ~ena, Dh. 166 (*opp.* attadattha, *q. v.*).

***parappavāda**, *m.* (*cp. sa.* parapravādin) disputation; °-kusala, *mfn.* 110,9 (*q. v.*) *cp.* pavādin, *mfn.*

parama, *mfn.* (= *sa.*) highest, best (or worst); *f.* ~ā (rogā) Dh. 203; *n.* ~aṁ (sukhaṁ). ib. & 184; *n. pl.* ~ā (dukhā, *v.* dukkha) ib.; *abl. n.* paramā va seyyo (better than the best) 55,3; — *comp.* *ārogya-parama, *mfn.* having health for its best, *f.* ~ā (lābhā, *v.* ārogya) Dh. 204; *vissāsa-°, *mfn.* ib. (*q. v.*). — *°-dukkara, *mfn.* (*q. v.*); °-attha, *m.* the best sense, the whole truth (*v. next*); *abl.* paramatthato (*adv.*) *v.* attha 6).

***Paramattha-dīpanī**, *f. nom. pr.* of a commentary, by Dhammapāla, on several books of the Khuddaka-Nikāya; specimen of the comm. on Petavatthu p. 84,25–86,10.

parājaya, *m.* (= *sa.*) defeat; jaya-°, *m.* victory and defeat, *acc.* ~aṁ, Dh. 201.

parājita, *mfn.* (= *sa.*; *pp.* parā-√ji [& jyā]) defeated, conquered; one who has lost (in game, *w. acc.*); *m.* ~o (sahassaṁ) 2,14; 50,31 (as finite tense, "he lost"); 60,4 (tehi ~o).

parājīyati, *vb.* (*pass.* parājeti [& -jināti]; *sa.* parā-√ji [& jyā]) to be overcome, defeated; to lose (in game); *pr. 3. sg.* ~ati (*opp.* jināti) 48,9.

parāmasati, *vb.* (*sa.* parā-√mṛç) to touch, feel, stroke (*acc.*); *part. m.* ~anto (hatthissa kumbhaṁ) 77,1; *ger.* ~itvā ([taṁ] hatthena) 24,30. 25,2; *pp.* parāmaṭṭha, *v.* dupparāmaṭṭha.

parāyana, *n.* (*sa.* parāyaṇa) aim; refuge, resort; *e. c. mfn.* = destined for, resorting to; *Brahmaloka-°, *mfn.* 47,33; *sambodhi-°, *mfn.* 79,34 (*q. v.*).

pari-, *indecl.* (= *sa.*) prefix to verbs and nouns, implying 'round, around; richly, fully, completely' *etc.*; before vowels it takes the form pariy- (*v. below*), but before u also payir- (metathesis, *v.* payirupāsati); it is sometimes changed into paḷi- (*q. v.*).

parikamma, *n.* (*sa.* parikarman) 1) attendance, waiting upon; ~aṁ (kātabbaṁ, *w. gen.*) 84,1. — 2) preparation, treatment (as painting, cleansing, dressing *etc.*); *°-kata, *mfn.* prepared, treated (*e. c.*): geruka-°, 84,19; lākhā-°, 5,28 (*v. h.*).

parikkhaya, *m.* (*sa.* parikshaya) destruction, ruin, loss; *acc.* ~aṁ (gacchati, to be lost) 48,10; (ñātīnaṁ *etc.*) Dh. 139. *cp.* parikkhīṇa.

parikkhāra, *m.* (*sa.* parishkāra) provisions, utensils, *esp.* the priestly requisites (cīvara *etc.*); *acc.* (*e. c.*) ~aṁ, 97,8.

parikkhipati, *vb.* (*sa.* pari-√kship) to put, hang, or wind around, to surround (*acc.*); *pr. 3. pl.* ~anti (mālādāmāni) 37,2; *aor. 3. pl.* ~iṁsu, 6,10; *ger.* a) ~itvā (ṭhānaṁ) 6,9; (mālaṁ kaṇṭhe) 16,25; (assā sāṇiṁ) 62,20; b) ~itvāna, 112,6; — *pp.* parikkhitta, *m.* ~o (rajjuyā, tied with ropes) 54,20; *n.* ~aṁ (nahārunā, kaṇḍaṁ, "wound round with sinews") 92,21; pākāra-°, 23,26 (*v. h.*); su-parikkhittaṁ (sayanaṁ) 112,3 (sāṇiyā). *cp.* parikkhepa.

parikkhīṇa, *mfn.* (*pp.* parikkhīyati; *sa.* parikshīṇa, pari-√kshi) vanished, disappeared, extinct; *m. pl.* ~ā (āsavā) Dh. 93; *kāmābhava-°, *taṇhābhava-°, *nandībhava-°, *mfn.* (*v. h.*) *cp.* parikkhaya.

parikkhepa, *m.* (*sa.* parikshepa) throwing about, surrounding, that by which anything is surrounded; ~o, 37,3.

pariganhati, *vb.* (*sa.* pari-√grah) 1) to embrace (*acc.*); *part. m.* ~anto, 21,26; *ger.* pariggahetvā (bāhāhi) 20,6; — 2) to examine, search (through); to try, test (*acc.*); *part. m.* ~anto (bahivalañjanake) 43,8; 43,5-28; 38,18; 57,16 (taṁ, in order to test her); *part. med. m.* ~amāno, 43,12; *aor. 3. sg.* ~i (antonagaraṁ) 43,9; *fut.*

1. sg. ~issāmi (janapadaṁ) 43,11; *ger.* ~ggahetvā (do.) 44,15. – *caus. II.* pariganhāpeti, to cause to be examined; *part. m.* ~ento, 48,26. *cp. next.*

pariggaha, *m.* (*sa.* parigraha) 'belonging to, dependent', family, wife, property, *etc.*; a-pariggaha, *mfn.* (unmarried) *v. h.*, *opp.* sa-pariggaha, *mfn.* 56,4-7.

pariggahetvā, *ger.*, *v.* pariganhati.

parighaṁsati, *vb.* (*sa.* pari-√ghṛsh) to rub, scrub; *part. instr. m.* a-parighaṁsantena (*sc.* bhājanaṁ, without rubbing) 82,21.

paricarati, *vb.* (*sa.* pari-√car) 'to go round', to attend, wait on; to serve, worship (*acc.*); *pot. 3. sg.* ~care (aggiṁ) Dh. 107. – *caus.* paricāreti (*v. h.*) *cp. next.*

paricārikā, *f.* (= *sa.*) a female attendant, waiting woman; *nom.* ~ā (itthī) 49,3; *gen. pl.* ~ānaṁ, 19,13; pāda-⁰, *f.* id. & wife, *instr.* ~āya, 56,11; *pl.* ~ā, 21,12; *⁰~ika-yakkhinī, *f.* a menial Y., 111,3.

paricāreti, *vb.* (*caus.* paricarati; *sa.* paricārayati) to surround (*acc.*); *pass. part. m.* paricāriyamāno (nippurisehi turiyehi, "surrounded by") 67,24.

pariccajati, *vb.* (*sa.* pari-√tyaj) to abandon, give up, sacrifice (*acc.*); *fut. 1. sg.* ~issāmi (attānaṁ tuyhaṁ) 3,16; *ger.* ~itvā (attānaṁ) 15,33; (jīvitaṁ) 60,14. *cp. next.*

pariccāga, *m.* (*sa.* parityāga) leaving, abandoning, giving up; *abl.* ~ā (mattāsukha-⁰) "by leaving (a small pleasure)" Dh. 290.

parijana, *m.* (= *sa.*) surrounding or attending people, servants; *acc.* ~aṁ, 67,28; *gen.* ~assa, 67,26.

parijiṇṇa, *mfn.* (*pp.* parijīyati; *sa.* parijirṇa, √jṝ) worn out, decayed, exhausted; *n.* ~aṁ (purāṇaseṭṭhikulaṁ, impoverished, reduced) 55,31; (idaṁ rūpaṁ) 107,7 = Dh. 148.

pariññāta, *mfn.* (*pp.* parijānāti; *sa.* parijñāta, √jñā) thoroughly known; *n.* ~aṁ (sabbadukkhaṁ, *sc.* mayā) 108,13; *⁰-bhojana, *mfn.* "living on recognized food", *i. e.* one who has the right view of the food he eats (who exactly knows the substance of which it consists, that it is only vile and impure matter, and that there is no pleasure in eating it) *m. pl.* ~ā, Dh. 92 (*cp.* Dh. (1855) p. 281; *Childers* Dict. pariññā).

pariṇamati, *vb.* (*sa.* pari-√nam) to bend, change (*intr.*); to develop, ripen, become old, be digested (as food); *part. loc.* ~ante (vaye, "as age ripens") 47,12. *cp. next.*

pariṇāma, *m.* (= *sa.*) change, development; digestion; sammā-pariṇāmaṁ (*acc.*) gaccheyya, 78,16 (can be fully digested).

paritassati (& paritasati), *vb.* (*sa.* pari-√tras) to be frightened or alarmed, to tremble; *pr. 3. sg.* na ~ati (sabbasaṁyojanaṁ chetvā) Dh. 397 ("after cutting all fetters he does not tremble"); but we had perhaps better to translate "he does not feel any desire", and take paritassati = *sa.* pari-√tṛsh, to be afflicted by thirst, *metaph.* to feel desire or longing; the explanation Dhpd. (1855) p. 428 : taṇhāya na bhāyati (he does not fear on account of thirst) and on several other passages in the commentaries is probably due to a confusion of those two verbs, of which *pp.* paritasita (*cp.* tasita) frequently occurs; paritassanā, *f.* seems to have both significations : fear & longing; *cp.* Mil. p. 253,26 (goṇo chāto paritasito), *Rhys Davids,* Dial. of the Buddha (1899) p. 53.

paritoseti, *vb.* (*sa.* pari-√tush, *caus.* paritoshayati) to satisfy completely, to appease (*acc.*); *part. med. m.* ~ayamāno (aṅke nisinnaṁ puttaṁ) 38,15 ("cherishing").

paritta¹. *mfn.* (*sa.* paritta) limited, small, little; *n.* ~aṁ (udakaṁ) 4,5; parittaṭṭhakathā, *f.* a concise commentary, *acc.* ~aṁ, 113,24.

*paritta[2], *n.* (*cp. sa.* paritrāṇa, *fr.* pari-√trā) protection, an amulet; °-sutta, *n.* a thread for defence, a charming thread, 111,11 (°-tejena).

paridahati, *vb.* (*sa.* pari-√dhā) to put on (clothes, *acc.*); *fut. 3. sg.* ~dahessati (kāsāvaṁ vatthaṁ) Dh. 9.

parideva, *m.* (= *sa.*) lamentation; *instr. pl.* ~ehi, 70,29; *gen. pl.* ~ānaṁ (soka-°) 90,17; soka-° (*dvandva comp.*) 66,10-17. *cp.* pariddava.

paridevati, *vb.* (*sa.* pari-√div) to lament, cry, groan; *part. m.* ~anto, 30,23; *f.* ~antī, 31,3; *gen. pl.* ~antānaṁ, 47,31; *part. med. m.* ~māno, 30,15; *aor. 3. sg.* paridevi, 24,7. parideva, *m.* & paridevana, *n.* (*q. v.*).

paridevana, *n.* (= *sa.*) lamentation, groaning; °-sadda, *m.* "the sound of groaning", *nom.* ~o, 23,33. *cp.* parideva & *next.*

*pariddava, *m.* (*sa.* *paridrava, √dru; this word is formed after the analogy of upaddava (*q. v.*) and may probably be due to an old confusion with parideva (*v. above*), by which it is generally explained in the commentaries (Tr.); it is only found in *comp.* with soka-°) lamentation; tiṇṇasoka-°, *mfn.* "who has crossed the flood of sorrow"? Dh. 195.

*pariniṭṭhiti, *f.* (*fr.* pari-ni-√sthā, *cp.* niṭṭhita) completion, accomplishment; *acc.* ~iṁ (gatesu, fulfilled) 114,31.

parinibbāti, *vb.*, *v.* parinibbāyati.

parinibbāna, *n.* (*sa.* parinirvāṇa) complete extinction of individuality, so that one shall not be born again; attainment of Nirvāṇa; *abl.* ~ā, 80,19; °-mañcamhi nipanno, 110,19.

parinibbāyati & parinibbāti, (*sa.* parinirvāti, √vā) to be extinguished, to attain Nirvāṇa; *pr. 3. pl.* ~āyanti (Tathāgatā) 76,28; ~anti, Dh. 126; *aor. 3. sg.* ~āyi, 29,18; 80,19 (Bhagavā); *pp. v.* parinibbuta. *cp.* parinibbāna, *n.*

parinibbuta, *mfn.* (*pp. sa.* parinirvṛta, √vṛ, but as to the signification belonging to parinir-√vā, *v.* parinibbāyati, *cp.* nibbuta) completely extinguished or liberated (from the saṁsāra); *m.* ~o, 80,11; *loc.* ~e, 80,19; *pl. m.* ~ā (loke, "even in this world") Dh. 89.

paripakka, *mfn.* (*sa.* paripakva) completely cooked; quite ripe, accomplished; *m.* ~o (vayo) Dh. 260.

paripucchati, *vb.* (*sa.* pari-√prach) to put questions to (*acc.*); *inf.* ~ituṁ, *comp.* °-kāma, *mfn.* who wishes that questions shall be put to himself, *m.* ~o, 84,7; *grd. m.* ~itabbo, ib.

paripuṇṇa, *mfn.* (*sa.* pari-pūrṇa) quite full; accomplished, perfect; *n.* ~aṁ (candamaṇḍalaṁ, "the full moon") 32,30; *sabbākāra-°, *mfn.* altogether perfect, *acc. m.* ~aṁ (purisaṁ) 10,26; *°-gabbhā, *f. adj.* (*v.* gabbha).

paripūrati, *vb.* (*sa.* pari-√pṝ) *intr.* to become full (completely); to become perfect; *pr. 3. sg.* ~ati (paññā) Dh. 38; *pp.* paripuṇṇa (*q. v.*).

paripphoseti, *vb.* (*caus.* pari-√prush) to besprinkle, water (*acc.*); *ger.* ~itvā ([bhūmiṁ] udakena) 84,22.

pariplava, *mfn.* (= *sa.*) swimming round; unsteady; *°-pasāda, *mfn.* "whose peace of mind is troubled", *gen. m.* ~assa, Dh. 38.

pariphandati, *vb.* (*sa.* pari-√spand) to tremble all over; *pr. 3. sg.* ~ati (idaṁ cittaṁ) Dh. 34 (*cp.* phandana).

paribbajati, *vb.* (*sa.* pari-√vraj) to wander about (*esp.* as a religious mendicant, *cp.* paribbāja(ka)); *pr. 3. pl.* ~anti (etam [bandhanaṁ] chetvāna) Dh. 346; *pot. 3. sg.* paribbaje (kāme pahatvāna anāgāro) Dh. 415.

paribbaya, *m.* (*sa.* parivyaya) payment, salary; travelling expenses or travelling cash; *acc.* ~aṁ, 18,23; 48,18.

paribbājaka, *m.* (& paribbāja;

sa. parivrāja(ka)) a religious mendicant, ascetic; *nom.* ~o (Uttiyo) 89,19; *acc.* ~aṁ, 29,22; °-ārāma, *m.* (*v. h.*). — °-vesena, in the character of a p. 110,29.

paribhāvita, *mfn.* (*pp.* paribhāveti; = *sa.*, *caus.* pari-√bhū) prepared, treated; *n.* ~aṁ (cittaṁ, "highly cultivated") 105,2; *acc. f.* ~aṁ (mānusivācaṁ, karuṇāya, "filled with compassion") 22,3.

paribhāsati, *vb.* (*sa.* pari-√bhāsh) to blame, censure, abuse (*acc.*); *pr. 3. sg.* ~ati (bhikkhū) 84,29.

paribhuñjati, *vb.* (*sa.* pari-√bhuj) to eat, enjoy (*acc.*); *pr. 3. sg.* ~ati (dadhiṁ) 35,22; 97,9 ("makes use of it"); *3. pl.* ~anti, 21,6; *inf.* ~ituṁ (kāme) 69,27; *ger.* ~itvā, 36,35; *pp.* paribhutta, *n.* ~aṁ (yassa, "when he has eaten it") 78,16. *cp. next.*

paribhoga, *m.* (= *sa.*) enjoyment, use; *devatā-°, *mfn.* 36,31. (*v. h.*).

parimajjati, *vb.* (*sa.* pari-√mṛj) to cleanse, wipe; to touch, stroke (*acc.*); *pr. 2. sg.* ~asi (bāhiraṁ) 106,11 = Dh. 394; *part. f.* ~anti (piṭṭhiṁ) 46,8.

parimaṇḍala, *mfn.* (= *sa.*) round, circular; *n.* ~aṁ, 36,33, *adv.* ~aṁ, all around, 82,27; *su-parimaṇḍalaṁ, *adv.* completely, 113,7.

parimaddati, *vb.* (*sa.* pari-√mṛd) to rub, stroke (*acc.*); *ger.* ~itvā (hatthena tassa sarīraṁ, "passed his hand over") 24,23.

parimāṇa, *n.* (= *sa.*) circumference, extent; *acc.* ~aṁ (rajja-°) 43,29.

pariyatti, *f.* (*sa.* paryāpti) learning, *esp.* study of the holy texts; the texts themselves handed down through oral tradition (= tipiṭaka); *nom.* ~i, 102,10; °-antaradhāna, *n.* 'the disappearance of learning', name of a chapter of Anāgata-vaṁsa (*q. v.*) 102,2.

pariyanta, *mfn.* (*sa.* paryanta) ended, ceased; far, remote; — *m.* end, circumference, edge, border, outskirt; *acc.* ~aṁ (parisa-°, *v.* parisā) 87,23; *loc.* ~e (udaka-°) 4,2; (sara-°) 5,17; *pl.* hattha-pāda-pariyantā (the hoofs) 5,27.

pariyāti, *vb.* (*sa.* pari-√yā) to go round (*acc.*); *pr. 3. sg.* ~āti (rājanivesanaṁ) 31,3.

pariyādāna, *n.* (*buddh. sa.* paryādāna) consuming, consumption, exhaustion, destruction, end; *abl.* ~ā (tassa, "when that has been consumed") 95,8.

***pariyāpanna**, *mfn.* (*fr.* pari-ā-√pad) included, contained in; patta-pariyāpannaṁ, *n.* "what has been put in the bowl", 83,2.

pariyāya, *m.* & *n.* (*sa.* paryāya) 'going round', encompassing (also a synonym); turn, succession, series, enumeration (also a religious discourse in general, *opp.* nippariyāya, a discourse delivered on some particular occasion); way, manner, order, method, precision; view or point of view; *nom. n.* āditta-pariyāyaṁ ("the sermon of the burning") 71,18; *instr.* ~ena (aññena = aññenākārena, in another way, from a different point of view o: wrongly?) 91,11-32; aneka-pariyāyena, *adv.* in many ways, 69,18.

pariyesati, *vb.* (*sa.* pari-√ish) to seek or search for, inquire, investigate (*acc.*); *part. m.* ~anto (gocaraṁ) 14,29; (phalāphalāni) 35,32; *part. med. m. pl.* ~mānā (mige, in order to find) 6,8; *fut. 1. sg.* ~issāmi, 14,32; (dibbakāme) 45,5; *inf.* ~ituṁ, 43,3; *ger.* ~itvā (core) 30,30.

***pariyogāḷha**, *mfn.* (*pp.* pariyogāhati, to inquire into, penetrate; *sa.* *paryava-√gah, *cp.* ava-gāḍha); °-dhamma, *mfn.* who has penetrated the truth, *m.* ~o, 69,13. *cp. next.*

***pariyogāha**, *m.* (*fr.* pari-ava-√gāh) inquiring into, penetrating; *duppariyogāha, *mfn.* (*q. v.*).

***pariyodapana**, *n.* (*fr. next*) cleansing, purification; sacitta-°, Dh. 183 (*v.* citta[1]).

***pariyodapeti**, *vb.* (*caus.* pari-ava-√dai) to cleanse, purify (*acc.*); *pot. 3. sg.* ~eyya (metrically = paryodapeyya, attānaṁ) Dh. 88.

pariyosāna, *n.* (*sa.* paryavasāna) end, conclusion; *loc.* ~e, 29,17 (sacca-°, *q. v.*); 34,19 (jīvita-°); *e. c. mfn.* = ending with: gala-°, 18,7; maraṇa-°, 86,16; vipatti-°, 47,16 (*v. h.*).

pariḷāha, *m.* (*sa.* paridāha) burning, heat; pain, suffering, sorrow; *nom.* ~o, Dh. 90; sa-pariḷāha, *mfn.* filled with pain, *n.* ~aṁ, 94,2.

parivajjeti (& **parivajjayati**) *vb.* (*sa.* parivarjayati, *caus.* pari-√vṛj) to avoid (*acc.*); *pr. 3. sg.* ~eti (pāpāni) Dh. 269; *imp. 2. sg.* (*med.*) ~ayassu (kulāvakā (*acc. f.* or *n. pl.*?) "dont disturb the birds' nests") 60,16; *pot. 3. sg.* ~aye, Dh. 123.

parivattati, *vb.* (*sa.* pari-√vṛt) to turn, change (*intr.*), to change into (*nom.*); *pot. 3. sg.* ~eyya (khīraṁ, dadhi ~) 99,28; *ger.* ~itvā, 47,12; — *caus. v. next.*

parivatteti, *vb.* (*sa.* parivartayati, *caus.* pari-√vṛt) [1]) to overthrow, turn topsy-turvy; also *intr.* to rush, hurtle (on account of confusion): *part. m. pl.* ~entā, 60,8. — [2]) to repeat, rehearse, recite (*acc.*); *pr. 3. sg.* ~eti (Pātañjalī-mataṁ) 113,7; *pot. 2. sg.* ~eyyāsi (mantaṁ) 52,26; *ger.* ~etvā, 32,10. — [3]) to translate (*acc.*); *imp. 2. sg.* ~ehi (taṁ, Māgadhānaṁ niruttiyā) 113,33; *aor. 3. sg.* ~esi, 114,27.

parivāra, *m.* (= *sa.*) suite, retinue, followers; *e. c. mfn.*, surrounded by; *instr.* ~ena (mahantena) 7,5. 62,8; pañcasata-bhikkhu-°, *mfn.* 87,3; pañcasata-miga-°, *mfn.* 5,29; pañcasugandhika-°, *mfn.* prepared with five kinds of fragrant substances, *n.* ~aṁ (tambūlaṁ) 41,13; sa-parivāra, *mfn.* together with the retinue, *acc. m.* ~aṁ, 110,25.

parivāreti, *vb.* (*sa.* parivārayati, *caus.* pari-√vṛ) to surround, encompass (*acc.*); *without obj.* to stand around; *aor. 3. sg.* ~esi, 36,23; *fut. 3. pl.* ~essanti, 35,15; *ger.* ~etvā (ambarukkhaṁ, "round the Mango tree") 37,19; *pp. m.* parivārito (amacca-°) 112,26. *cp.* parivāra, *m.* & parivuta, *mfn.*

***parivitakketi**, *vb.* (*fr.* pari-vi-√tark) to reflect, ponder; *aor. 3. sg.* ~esi, 53,33.

parivisati, *vb.* (*sa.* pari-√vish, but as to the formation confounded with pari-√viç) to serve, wait on (*acc.*); *imp. 2. sg.* parivisa (maṁ tena, "serve me with it") 78,8; *aor. 3. sg.* parivisi, 78,11; *ger.* ~itvā, 87,17; *part. f.* ~antī (rājānaṁ, suvaṇṇa-kaṭacchuṁ gahetvā) 53,32.

parivuta, *mfn.* (*sa.* parivṛta, *pp.* pari-√vṛ) surrounded by (*instr.* or *e. c.*); *m.* ~o (deva-gaṇena) 60,23; 36,28; 74,17; 7,28 (miga-gaṇa-°); *acc. m.* ~aṁ (amacca-gaṇa-°) 39,28; *f. pl.* ~ā (dāsi-gaṇa-°) 21,1.

***parisaṁvuta**, *mfn.* (*sa.* *parisaṁvṛta) covered, hidden, guarded; restrained, controlled; su-parisaṁvuta, Dh. 234 (*q. v.*).

parisappati, *vb.* (*sa.* pari-√sṛp) to run about; *pr. 3. pl.* ~anti, Dh. 342. The common form of this verb is pari-sakkati, *cp.* osakkati, nissakkana *etc.*

parisā, *f.* (*sa.* parishad) an assembly; multitude, group, crowd; *nom.* ~ā (assa, "his followers") 40,3; *acc.* ~aṁ, 88,25; *instr.* ~āya, 74,17; *gen. dat.* ~āya, 6,32; 86,10 (sampatta-°, the assembly present); *loc.* ~āyaṁ, 87,25; *comp.* catu-°, *f.* (*v. h.*); at the beginning of *comp.* generally shortened to parisa-, 87,23 (°-pariyantaṁ); °-majjhe, 10,21. 42,4. 51,15.

parisuddha, *mfn.* (*sa.* pariçuddha, √çudh) clean, pure; a-parisuddha, *mfn.* 41,1 (*q. v.*).

parissaya, *n.* (& *m.*) (*sa.* pariçraya, *m.* (?) *Weber*, Ind. Str. III, 395; as to the signification nearly agreeing with parissama (*sa.* pariçrama) by which it is sometimes replaced in the manuscripts; *Fausbøll*, Dhpd. (1855) p. 407 & Gloss. Sn., derives it from *sa.* *parismaya, √smi, which can hardly be possible) danger; pain, trouble, annoyance; *n. pl.* ~āni (sabbāni) Dh. 328. [Physically parissaya seems to mean 'the internal heat of the body', as it is sometimes in the comm. explained by kammaja-tejo; perhaps it ought to be derived from pari + √çri = √çrā (or √çram), *cp.* utu-parissaya-vinodana, MN. I p. 10,17.]

pariharati, *vb.* (*sa.* pari-√hṛ) 1) to carry (round), to wear (*acc.*); *pr. 1. sg. med.* ~hare (muñjaṁ, *q. v.*) 103,33; *ger.* ~itvā (kucchiyā Bodhisattaṁ) 62,3. — 2) to protect, take care of, be the leader of; *fut. 1. sg.* ~issāmi (bhikkhu-saṁghaṁ) 74,23; *inf.* ~ituṁ, 74,24; *cp.* parihāra.

parihāna, *n.* (*sa.* parihāṇa) the being deprived of, falling away from; *dat.* ~āya (abhabbo) Dh. 32.

parihāyati, *vb.* (*sa.* pari-hīyate, *pass.* pari-√hā, *cp.* jahāti) to be deprived of; to fall away from (*abl.*), disappear, vanish, decrease, *etc.*; *pr. 3. sg.* ~ati (saddhammā) Dh. 364; *aor. 3. sg.* ~hāyi, 18,29; *fut. 3. sg.* ~issati, 102,10; — *pp.* parihīna, *loc. m.* ~e, 102,10; *n.* ~aṁ n'atthi (*w. abl.* 'has not been neglected') 37,27; a-parihīna, *mfn.* unbroken (*v. h.*).

parihāra, *m.* (= *sa.*) 'carrying round', protection, taking care of, the making much of anything; *abl.* ~ato (porāṇaka-°, as hitherto) 37,27; *gabbha-°, *m.* (*q. v.*) 42,23 (laddha-°).

parihīna, *mfn.* (*pp.* parihāyati, *q. v.*).

***parūpakkama**, *m.* (*fr.* para + upakkama) approaching or attack of others (external enemies); *instr.* ~ena, 76,27 (*cp.* an-upakkamena).

***parūpaghātin**, *mfn.* (*fr.* para + upaghātin) who strikes or injures others; *nom. m.* ~ī, Dh. 184.

pareta, *mfn.* (= *sa. pp.* parā + √i) reached, approached; *e. c.* = followed by, overcome with; *soka-°, *mfn.* overcome with sorrow, *gen. m.* ~assa, 104,17.

parodati, *vb.* (*sa.* pra-√rud) to begin to weep or lament; *aor. 3. sg.* parodi (mahantena saddena) 16,31.

pary-, *v.* pariy-.

palavati (or pilavati, plavati), *vb.* (*sa.* plavati, √plu) to float, swim; *pr. 3. sg.* ~ati (hurāhuraṁ) 107,30 = Dh. 334 (metri causa ~atī); *aor. 1. sg.* a-plaviṁ (phalakena) 20,23.

***palāpeti**, *vb.* (*caus.* palāyati, *q. v.*) to drive away (*acc.*); *imp. 2. sg.* ~ehi (te) 35,12; *2. pl.* ~etha, 52,20; *aor.* ~esi, ib.; *inf.* ~etuṁ, 8,1.

palāyati (& paleti), *vb.* (*sa.* palāyati) to flee or fly away, escape; *pr. 3. sg.* paleti, 106,3 = Dh. 49; *2. sg.* ~āyasi, 54,21; *3. pl.* ~āyanti, 6,31; *1. pl.* ~āyāma (let us escape), 21,30; *aor. 3. sg.* ~āyi, 10,23; *3. pl.* ~āyiṁsu, 30,30; *fut. 3. pl.* ~issanti, 35,14; *1. pl.* ~issāma, 21,32; *inf.* ~ituṁ, 21,27; *ger.* ~itvā, 60,31; — *caus.* *palāpeti (*v. h.*).

palāsa, *m. & n.* (*sa.* palāça) 1) *m.* a leaf; paṇḍu-palāso, Dh. 235 (*q. v.*). — 2) *n.* (*coll.*) leaves, foliage; sākhā-palāsaṁ, 95,22 (*q. v.*); apagata-°, *mfn.* 95,23.

paḷi- or **pali-**, *prp.* = pari- (*q. v.*) *cp. next etc.*

paḷigha, *m.* (*sa.* parigha [& paligha]) a bolt or bar of a door; an obstacle, hindrance; *ukkhitta-°, *mfn.* Dh. 398 (*v. h.*).

palita, *mfn.* (= *sa.*, but often spelled with ph through confusion with phalita, *q. v.*); 1) grey, greyhaired; *n.* ~aṁ (siro) Dh. 260 (ph°); *-kesa, *mfn.* greyhaired, *acc. m.* ~aṁ, 63,9. — 2) *n.* grey hair (*sg.* & *pl.*); *nom. sg.* ~aṁ (ekaṁ) 44,26 (ph°); 46,24 (eka-p°); 46,27 (ekaṁ p°); *pl.* ~āni, 46,23; 44,23 (ph°); — *phalita-pātubhāva, *m.* 44,32 (*v.* pātubhāva).

***palipatha**, *m.* (read: pali-°; *fr.* pra-√lip. *w. suff.* -atha) mud, mire; *acc.* ~aṁ (duggaṁ) Dh. 414 (this miry road, which is difficult to pass?)

cp. Tr. PM. p. 80–81 Notes; JPTS. '84, p. 86. *Childers & Fausbøll* derive it from pari-patha (-pantha), "adversary".

palibuddha, *mfn.* (probably identical with *sa.* pari-ruddha, through dissimilation (?) or from *pra-vi-ruddha by metathesis; in palibodha, *m.* hindrance, we could suppose influence from *sa.* pari-√bādh (Tr. PM. p. 66) or pari-√bandh (*Leumann*); from palibuddha we have verb. denom. palibuddhati, to check, restrain; to urge, dun; to seize upon, usurp) checked, restrained; *m. pl.* ~ā (titthiyā, 'there was put a stop to their mischief') 74,14. (*cp.* also *sa.* pary-ava-rodha.)

palujjati, *vb.* (*pass. sa.* pra-√ruj) to be broken, destroyed; to fall off; *pot. 3. sg.* ~eyya (sākhāpalāsaṁ), 95,32; *3. pl.* ~eyyuṁ (tacapapaṭikā) ib.

paleti, *vb.* = palāyati (*q. v.*).

palepana, *n.* (*sa.* pralepana) the act of smearing; *gāḷha-°, *mfn.* 92,7 (*v. h.*).

palobheti, *vb.* (*sa.* pralobhayati, *caus.* pra-√lubh) to allure, seduce (*acc.*); *ger.* ~etvā (vāṇije) 21,13.

pallaṁka, *m.* (*sa.* paryaṅka & palyaṅka) a couch or sofa; a throne or palanquin; the sitting cross-legged (as in meditation), in the phrase: pallaṁkena (*instr.*) or ~e (*loc.*) nisīdati, 17,35. 65,4. 66,4 (eka-°, *q. v.*); 53,23 (*loc.*); °-majjhe, 39,26 ("on the royal throne"); kañcana-°, 42,9 (*v. h.*); nisinna-pallaṁkato, *abl.* "from the couch on which he was sitting", 65,27 (vuṭṭhāya).

pallala, *n.* (*sa.* palvala) a small pond or lake; *acc.* ~aṁ, Dh. 91; *loc.* ~e, 21,36.

pavaḍḍhati, *vb.* (*sa.* pra-√vṛdh) to grow up, increase; *pr. 3. sg.* ~ati, Dh. 282; *3. pl.* ~anti, 107,32 = Dh. 335.

pavattati, *vb.* (*sa.* pra-√vṛt) [1]) to arise, set out, break forth; *aor. 3. sg.* pavatti (mahānadī) 36,25; (udānaṁ) 65,12. — [2]) to become, appear; to be, exist; *pr. 3. sg.* ~ati (ratho'ti nāmaṁ) 98,24; (Sīhalesu ~ati, "is extant among the S.") 113,31; *fut. 3. sg.* ~issati (manussesu catuppādikā gāthā) 102,22. *caus. v.* pavatteti; *cp. next.*

pavattar, *m.* (rather fr. *sa.* pravaktṛ than fr. pra-vartitṛ, *cp. next*) one who tells or relates, expounder, teacher; *acc.* ~āraṁ (nidhīnaṁ, "who tells of hidden treasures") Dh. 76.

pavatti, *f.* (*sa.* pravṛtti) appearance, what appears or happens, news, tidings, *etc.*; *acc.* ~iṁ (ārocesi) 6,21; tatr'assa ~iṁ na jānāma, "we dont know what happened afterwards", 73,23.

pavatteti, *vb.* (*caus.* pavattati, *sa.* pravartayati) to cause to arise, send forth (*acc.*); *ger.* ~etvā (mahoghaṁ) 35,19.

pavara, *mfn.* (*sa.* pravara) the choicest, best; noble, excellent; *acc. m.* ~aṁ, Dh. 422.

pavassati, *vb.* (*sa.* pra-√vṛsh) to rain, begin to rain; *imp. 2. sg.* pavassa (deva!) 104,22; *aor. 3. sg.* pāvassi (mahāmegho) 105,21.

pavāti (& pavāyati), *vb.* (*sa.* pra-√vā) to blow through, pervade (*acc.*); *pr. 3. sg.* ~āti (sabbā disā) Dh. 54.

pavādin, *m.* (*sa.* pravādin) a disputer, polemic; *acc. pl.* ~ino (āhiṇḍanto) 113,5. *cp.* parappavāda.

pavāḷa (& pavāla), *m. n.* (*sa.* pravāḍa & pravāla) [1]) coral; *comp.* -ppavāḷa-, 27,28; [2]) a sprout, a young leaf or branch; kāḷā-°, 47,20 (*q. v.*).

pavāsa, *m.* (*sa.* pravāsa) absence from home, departure; *abl.* ~ā (āgato) 9,27. *cp.* cira-ppavāsin, *mfn.*

pavijjhati, *vb.* (*sa.* pra-√vyadh) to hurl or cast down (*acc.*); *aor. 3. sg.* pavijjhi (mahantaṁ silaṁ) 75,35.

paviṭṭha, *mfn.* (*pp.* pavisati, *sa.* pra-vishṭa) entered, one who has entered or come into (*acc.* or *abl.*); *m.* ~o (himagabbhaṁ) 16,9; *acc.* ~aṁ (ādittapaṇṇasālaṁ) 44,20; mukhe

~aṁ (ambaphalaṁ) 37,34; (ñāṇa ālassa anto ~) 86,28; *comp.* kucchiṁ paviṭṭha-sadiso, 61,21; gahanaṭṭhāna-paviṭṭha-maggaṁ, "the path by which they had turned into the jungle", 34,11.

pavibhajati, *vb.* (*sa.* pra-vi-√bhaj) to divide, distribute, arrange (*acc.*); *aor. 3. pl.* ~ajjiṁsu (Satthusāsanaṁ) 109,32 (incorrect spelling instead of pavibhajiṁsu); *ger.* ~ajja, 110,1. *cp.* vibhajana.

paviveka, *m.* (*sa.* praviveka) solitude; *°-rasa, *m.* "the sweetness of solitude", Dh. 205 (*acc.* ~aṁ).

pavisati, *vb.* (*sa.* pra-√viç) to enter, go to, come into (*acc.* [or *loc.*]); *pr. 3. pl.* ~anti (nagaraṁ) 90,36; (antojālaṁ) 88,35; *part. m. instr.* ~antena, 83,31; *imp. 2. sg.* pavisa (udakaṁ, dive into) 13,1; (aggiṁ) 51,12; *fut. 1. sg.* ~issāmi (aggiṁ, *i. e.* I will pay with my life for it) 54,4; *aor.* a) (*w. augm.*) *3. sg.* pāvisi, 13,2 (~ī, metri causa), 33,25; b) *3. pl.* pavisiṁsu, 53,4. 60,22; *2. pl.* ~ittha (mā) 27,30; *inf.* ~ituṁ, 13,15; *comp.* ~itu-kāma, *mfn.* 82,24. 83,27 (*m.* ~o, *w. acc.*); *ger.* a) pavissa, Dh. 127; b) ~itvā, 6,7. 14,15. 37,12; *grd.* ~itabbaṁ, *n.* 83,31; *pp.* paviṭṭha (*q. v.*); *caus.* paveseti & pavesāpeti (*q. v.*) *cp. next.*

*pavisana, *n.* (*nom. act. fr.* pavisati, *cp.* pavesana) entering, coming in; °-kāle (*w. acc.* aggiṁ) 51,14; 73,12 (do. nagaraṁ); °-velāyaṁ (tesaṁ, "as they came in") 53,4.

pavuccati, *vb.* (*pass.* pra-√vac) to be called; *pr. 3. sg.* dhammaṭṭho 'ti ~ati, Dh. 257; taṇhā ~ati, 103,26.

pavedeti (~ayati), *vb.* (*caus.* pra-√vid, *sa.* pravedayati) to communicate, relate, teach (*acc.*); *pr. 3. pl.* ~ayanti (*sc.* dhammaṁ) Dh. 151; *pp.* pavedita, taught; *acc. m.* ~aṁ (isi-pp°, maggaṁ) Dh. 281; *loc. m.* ~e (ariya-°, dhamme) Dh. 79.

pavedhati, *vb.* (*fr. sa.* pra-√vyath, but arisen as a new simplex to *caus.* *pra-vyāthayati > pavedheti; *cp.* Tr. PM. 76,25) to tremble, quiver; *part. med. acc. m. f.* ~mānaṁ, 47,22. 63,9.

paveṇi & paveni (or ~ī), *f.* (*sa.* praveṇī) 'a long braid of hair', hence [1]) race, lineage, *esp.* breed of cattle, cattle for breeding; *pl.* ~iyo (godharaṇiyo, *q. v.*) 105,11-14. (Comm. on Sn. v. 26 : vayappattā balivaddehi saddhiṁ methunapatthana-gāvo); [2]) tradition, traditional custom or doctrine (also = the holy scriptures) *cp.* Tr. PM. p. 69,7-44.

*pavellati, *vb.* (*fr.* pra-√vell) to shake or swing to and fro, to sway; *part. med. f.* ~mānā, 47,20.

pavesana, *n.* (*sa.* praveçana) [1]) entering (*cp.* pavisana); [2]) placing or putting on, application; daṇḍe pavesana-vasena (*v.* vasa) "according as you fit it to the handle", 35,5.

*pavesāpeti, *vb.* (*caus. II.* pavisati) to cause one (*acc.*) to enter (*acc.*); *pr. 3. sg.* ~eti (mātugāmaṁ aggiṁ) 51,20.

*pavesetar, *m.* (*nom. agentis fr. next*) one who allows to enter, who gives admittance; *nom.* ~ā (ñātānaṁ) 90,33.

paveseti, *vb.* (*caus.* pavisati; *sa.* praveçayati) to cause or allow to enter (*acc.*) into (*acc.* or *loc.*), to put on, introduce; *pr. 3. pl.* ~enti, 49,1; *fut. 3. sg.* ~essati, 102,27; *ger.* ~etvā (bahumige uyyāne) 6,5; (migagaṇaṁ uyyānaṁ) 6,13; (uggahaṇa-rajjukaṁ gīvāya) 14,32; (nagaraṁ) 73,26; *caus. II.* pavesāpeti (*q. v.*) *cp.* pavesana, *n.*, pavesetar, *m.*

pasaṁsati, *vb.* (*sa.* pra-√çaṁs) to praise (*acc.*); *pr. 3. pl.* ~anti (appamādaṁ) Dh. 30; Dh. 229. 366; na-ppasaṁsanti, Dh. 177; *ger.* ~itvā, 3,28; *pp.* pasaṁsita, *m.* ~o, Dh. 228–30. *cp. next.*

pasaṁsā, *f.* (*sa.* praçaṁsā) praise; nindā-pasaṁsāsu, *loc. pl.* (blame and praise) 106,30 = Dh. 81.

pasanna, *mfn.* (*pp.* pasīdati; *sa.* prasanna) [1]) clear, bright; placid, tranquil; pleased, happy (*w. gen.* or *loc.*); *m.* ~o, (te) 7,13; (tassā) 31,14; (Buddhasāsane) Dh. 368; 114,1; *instr.* ~ena, 8,2; Dh. 2 (manasā). — [2]) who is clear in his persuasion, believing, full of faith or devotion, pious; *m.* ~o, 28,3. 102,32; evaṁ ~o ahaṁ, 79,27; *pl.* ~ā, 76,32 (*opp.* a-ppasanna, *q. v.*); *°-citta, *mfn.* with a pious mind, believing, *acc. m.* ~aṁ, 68,22.

pasavati, *vb.* (*sa.* pra-√sū) to procreate, produce (*acc.*); *pr. 3. sg.* ~ati (veraṁ) Dh. 201; *pp.* pasūta (*q. v.*).

pasahati, *vb.* (*sa.* pra-√sah) to conquer, overcome (*acc.*); *pr. 3. sg.* ~ati (*metri causa* ~atī) Dh. 7 (taṁ); Dh. 8 (na-ppasahati); 104,5 (taṁ senaṁ); *pot. 3. sg. med.* ~etha (na-pp°) Dh. 128.

pasāda, *m.* (*sa.* prasāda) [1]) brightness, purity; [2]) favour, kindness (*opp.* kopa); [3]) conviction, persuasion, faith (*opp.* ñāṇa); *abl.* ~ā, 79,29; *°-mattā, *f.* a minute portion of faith (Gotamassa, "on G.") 94,23; *pariplava-°, *mfn.* Dh. 38 (*v. h.*).

pasādana, *n.* (*sa.* prasādana) [1]) clearing, calming, propitiating; [2]) = *prec.* *yathā-pasādanaṁ, *adv.* according to one's favour, pleasure, or faith, Dh. 249.

pasādhana, *n.* (*sa.* prasādhana) decoration, vesture; ~aṁ (uracchada-°, *q. v.*) 23,32; (yakkharāja-°) 112,32; *instr. pl.* ~ehi, 112,33.

pasādheti, *vb.* (*sa.* pra-√sādh) to adorn, decorate, array (*acc.*); *aor. 3. sg.* ~ayi (bhaccaṁ, pasādhanehi) 112,33; *pp.* pasādhita, *m.* ~o (maṇḍita-°, "dressed and arrayed") 41,10. *cp. prec.*

pasāreti, *vb.* (*sa.* prasārayati, *caus.* pra-√sṛ) to stretch or spread out, to open (*acc.*); *aor. 3. sg.* ~esi (āpaṇaṁ, "opened a shop") 48,31; *ger.* ~etvā (pakkhe) 10,14; (hatthaṁ) 62,18; *pp.* pasārita, outstretched, °-gīvā, *f.* 17,22 (*v. h.*).

pasibbaka, *m.* (*sa.* prasevaka, *cp. Fausbøll*, Dhpd. (1855) p. 268; *fr.* *pra-sīvyaka (?) *Childers*) a bag, sack, purse; *acc.* ~aṁ, 12,31; 13,5 (chinna-°); *loc.* ~e, 12,24; tambūla-°, 57,33 (*q. v.*).

pasīdati, *vb.* (*sa.* pra-√sad) to become clear, tranquil, or pleased (*w. gen.*); *pr. 3. sg.* ~ati (cittaṁ) 103,21; *ger.* ~itvā (tassa) 37,17; *pp.* pasanna (*q. v.*) *cp.* pasāda & pasādana.

pasu, *m.* (*sa.* paçu) cattle; puttapasu-°, Dh. 287 (children and cattle).

pasuta, *mfn.* (*sa.* prasita, *pp.* pra-√sā, si) intent upon, devoted to (*gen.* or *loc.*, or *e. c.*); *m.* ~o (migavadha-°) 5,32; (gocara-°) 13,13; (sadattha-°) Dh. 166; *pl.* ~ā (sa-kicca-°) 86,23; (jhāna-°) Dh. 181.

pasūta, *mfn.* (*pp.* pasavati, *sa.* prasūta, √sū) procreated, brought forth; *n.* ~aṁ (bahuṁ apuññaṁ) 76,3.

passa, *n.* (*sa.* pārçva) side; *instr.* ~ena (nipajjāpetvā, "upon his side") 13,17; *loc.* ~e (piṭṭhi-°, brāhmaṇassa, "behind") 50,18; *loc. pl.* ~esu (ubhosu) 40,5; — *sammaṭṭha-°, *mfn.* 47,19 (*v. h.*).

passati, *vb.* (*sa.* √paç) to see, look at, consider, perceive, notice, find out (*acc.*) *cp.* dissati [2]); *pr. 3. sg.* ~ati (paññāya, understands) 107,11 = Dh. 277; (rājānaṁ, comes to see, visits) 52,24; *2. sg.* ~asi, 10,13. 73,6. 85,16. 111,19; *1. sg.* ~āmi, 31,35. 97,30; 42,17 (~ vo'haṁ attānaṁ, 'an example thereof I am myself'?); *3. pl.* ~anti, 63,10. 110,12 (find); *1. pl.* ~āma, 73,22; *part. m.* [a]) passaṁ (evaṁ, 'considering this') 71,4; a-passaṁ, Dh. 114; [b]) passanto, 14,27. 46,4 (a-°, not seeing); *gen.* [a]) passato, 96,8. Dh. 114; [b]) passantassa (*gen. abs.*) 17,24; *instr.* passatā (intelligent) Dh. 245; *pl.* a-passantā, 30,31; *f.* a-passantī, 68,29; *gen.* ~antiyā, 64,17; — *imp. 2. sg.* passa, 2,1. 5,7 (pass'); 11,17. 19,23. 103,24; *2. pl.* ~atha, 18,6. 51,19. 88,3; — *pot. 3. sg.* [a]) passe, Dh. 76. 170; [b]) passeyya, 16,14 (find); 69,1; 90,34 (look for); — *fut. 1. sg.*

~issāmi, 65,26; — *aor. 3. sg.* passi, 28,8. 36,7. 54,8 (mahājano mā ~); a-passi, 111,17; *3. pl.* ~iṁsu, 27,1; *1. pl.* ~imha, 54,13; — *inf.* passituṁ, 4,13; — *ger.* a-passitvā (not seeing) 13,5; — *pass. v.* dissati [1]); — *caus. v.* dasseti.

passāsa, *m.* (*sa.* praçvāsa) breathing in, inhaling; *nom.* ~o (assāsa-°, *q. v.*) 80,32.

pahaṁsati [1]; *vb.* (*sa.* pra-√ghṛsh) to rub, stroke (*acc.*); *ger.* ~itvā (pharasuṁ hatthena) 35,8. *cp.* parighaṁsati.

[pahaṁsati [2]] *vb.* (*sa.* pra-√hṛsh) to rejoice, be glad; *pp. v.* pahaṭṭha.

pahaṭa, *mfn.* (*pp.* paharati, *q. v.*).

pahaṭṭha, *mfn.* (*sa.* prahṛshṭa, *pp.* pra-√hṛsh) erect (as the hairs of the body *etc.*); delighted, glad, pleased; °-kaṇṇa-vāla, *mfn.* with the tail and ears erect, *m.* ~o, 76,21.

pahata, *mfn.* (*sa.* prahata, √han; sometimes confounded with pahaṭa, *sa.* prahṛta, *v.* paharati) beaten, killed, severely hurt; *m.* ~o, 30,23. *cp. next.*

pahatvāna, *ger. v.* pajahāti (Dh. 243. 415–16 = Sn. 639–40; the Birm. reading is always pahantvāna, *fr.* pra-√han).

paharati, *vb.* (*sa.* pra-√hṛ) to beat, strike, cut; to strike at, hit, attack (*w. acc.*, or rarely *w. loc.* or *gen.*); *pr. 3. sg.* ~ati (kaṇṇaṁ, "reaches his ear") 22,24; *part. m. pl.* ~antā (bhūmiṁ, muggarehi) 6,11; *imp. 2. sg.* ~āhi, 50,17; *pot. 3. sg.* ~eyya (brāhmaṇassa, B. has hareyya) Dh. 389; *aor. 3. sg.* pahari (taṁ mukhe) 12,10; 13,20. 50,19 (sīse kapparena); 89,8; *1. sg.* ~iṁ, 51,8; *3. pl.* ~iṁsu, 52,18; *inf.* ~ituṁ, 7,36; *comp.* ~itukāma, *mfn.* desiring to beat, *m.* ~o, 29,25 ("to butt"); *f.* ~ā, 50,16; *ger.* ~itvā; 13,21. 23,9. 36,3. 41,18. 50,9; — *caus. II.* *pahārāpeti, to let strike; *imp. 2. sg.* ~ehi (etaṁ katipayehi pahārehi) 55,8; *aor. 3. sg.* ~esi (ubhosu passesu) 55,14; *ger.* ~etvā (jāraṁ tava sīse) 51,1; — *pp.* pahaṭa, *m.* ~o, 12,11; *n. pl.* ~āni (loṇajala-°, cakkhūni, "injured") 24,16; *cp.* pahata, pahāra.

pahassatha, pahātave, pahātuṁ, *v.* pajahāti.

pahāna, *n.* (*sa.* prahāṇa) abandoning, giving up; *nom.* ~aṁ (sabbassa dukkhassa) Dh. 331.

pahāya, *ger.*, *v.* pajahāti.

pahāra, *m.* (*sa.* prahāra) [1]) a stroke, blow; *nom.* ~o (thaddho) 50,22; *acc. pl.* ~e, 55,15; *instr. pl.* ~ehi, 55,8; pahāra-sate (*loc.*) 55,12 (a hundred stripes); eka-ppahāren'eva (*instr.*) *v.* eka [3]); daḷha-pahāraṁ (*acc.*) 30,13 = su-ppahāraṁ, ib.; pāṇi-ppahāra-saddena (*instr.*) "at the clapping of the hands", 18,18. — [2]) the mark of a blow, wound; *acc.* ~aṁ, 50,24. 52,33; *acc. pl.* ~e, 6,21.

pahiṇāti (& ~ati) *vb.* (*sa.* pra-√hi) to send, send away (*acc.*); *aor.* [a]) (*augm.*) *3. sg.* pāhesi (paṇṇaṁ) 36,22; (dārakaṁ) 81,12 [hence we have by false analogy a new verb pāheti, *pr. 3. sg.*]; [b]) *3. sg.* pahiṇi, 48,29; 64,6 (sāsanaṁ); *3. pl.* pahiṇiṁsu (paṇṇākāre) 58,22; *pp. v. next.*

pahita, *mfn.* (*pp.* pahiṇāti, *sa.* prahita) sent, directed towards; *acc. m.* ~aṁ (paṇṇākāraṁ) 58,23; — pahitatta, *mfn.* (*sa.* prahitātman, *cp.* attan) whose mind is intent upon, energetic, resolute; *acc. m.* ~aṁ, 103,17; padhāna-°, 103,2 (*v. h.*); *pl. m.* ~ā, 104,9; *acc. pl.* ~e, 108,19 (sāvake).

pahīna, *mfn.* (*pp.* pajahāti; *sa.* prahīna, √hā) thrown off, abandoned, ceased; *n.* ~aṁ (taṁ rūpaṁ Tathāgatassa) 95,10; *puñña-pāpa-°, *mfn.* "who has ceased to think of good and evil", *gen. m.* ~assa, Dh. 39; *sabbagantha-°, *mfn.* Dh. 90 (*v.* gantha); *°-māna, *mfn.* free from pride, *gen. m.* ~assa, Dh. 94.

pahūta, *mfn.* (*sa.* prabhūta, *pp.* pra-√bhū) much, abundant; *n.* ~aṁ (sūkaramaddavaṁ) 78,2; (puññaṁ) 103,9.

pākaṭa (or pākata) *mfn.* (*fr.* pakati, *q. v.*; *sa.* prākṛta, *cp. sa.* prakaṭa) 'natural', vulgar, universal; known, widely known, famous; *m.* ~o (sakalakappaṁ) 16,15; 38,17; *n.* ~aṁ (bhikkhusaṁghe) 29,28; *comp.* °-bībhaccha-sambādha-ṭṭhānā (disclosed) 65,7.

pākāra, *m.* (& *n.*?) (*sa.* prākāra) a wall, rampart; ~aṁ (*n.*? perhaps we have to read: sabbaso vā pana tesaṁ pākāro na hoti, "or else [because] those [towns] have no fortification at all") 91,19; thira-°, & daḷha-° (*v. h.*); — *°-parikkhitta, *mfn.* surrounded by a wall, *n.* ~aṁ (nagaraṁ) 23,26; *°-vivara, *n. acc.* ~aṁ, 90,34 = pākārassa chinnaṭṭhānaṁ, 91,30; *°-sandhi, *f.*, *acc.* ~iṁ, 90,34 = dvinnaṁ iṭṭhakānaṁ apagataṭṭhānaṁ, 91,29.

pācana (rarely pājana) *n.* (*sa.* prājana) a goad; *°-yaṭṭhi, *f.* 71,29 (= patoda-laṭṭhi, 98,6) *v.* yaṭṭhi. *cp.* pāceti.

pācīna, *mfn.* (*sa.* prācīna) eastern; °-loka-dhātu, 32,30 (*v. h.*); *°-sīsaka, *mfn.* with the head turned towards the east, *n.* ~aṁ (dibbasayanaṁ) 61,16.

*pāceti (& pājeti) *vb.* (*sa.* *pra-√aj, *caus.*) to drive (as cattle, *acc.*); *pr. 3. sg.* ~eti (gāvo) Dh. 135. *cp.* pācana.

pāṭali, *f.* (= *sa.*) the trumpet flower tree (Bignonia suaveolens); *Citta-°, *f.* 59,29 (*q. v.*).

pāṭha, *m.* (= *sa.*) reading, lecture; the text of a book, passage, lectio varians; Khuddaka-°, *m. nom. pr.* (*q. v.*).

pāṇa, *m.* (& rarely *n. pl.* (*sa.* prāṇa) breath, life; a living being; *pl.* & *sg. coll.* living beings; *nom.* ~o, 17,29; *acc.* ~aṁ, 60,17 (= jīvitaṁ, 60,14); eka-pāṇaṁ, 27,23; *coll.* 97,10. Dh. 246; *n. pl.* ~āni, Dh. 270; *gen. pl.* ~ānaṁ (sabba-°) ib.; *°-vadhakamma, *n.* destroying life, *acc.* ~aṁ, 60,13. *cp. next etc.*

pāṇaka, *m.* (*sa.* prāṇaka) a little animal, a worm or insect; *pl.* ~ā, 16,5.

*pāṇaghātin, *m*(*fn*). (*cp. sa.* prāṇa-ghātaka) one who kills or murders; *m. nom.* ~ī, 17,29.

pāṇātipāta, *m.* (*sa.* prāṇātipāta) destroying life, taking animal life; *nom.* ~o, 97,15; *acc.* ~aṁ, 15,31. 17,26; *abl.* ~ā, 17,31; 81,33 (veramaṇī). *cp.* pāṇaṁ atimāpeti, Dh. 246.

pāṇi, *m.* (= *sa.*) the hand; *instr.* ~inā, 112,28; Dh. 285; *loc.* ~imhi, 44,26; *comp.* °-ppahāra-saddena, 18,18 (*v. h.*) *cp.* tamba-paṇṇī (*v.* tamba).

pāṇin, *mfn.* (*sa.* prāṇin) living; *subst. m.* a living being; *acc.* ~inaṁ, 17,29; *gen. pl.* ~inaṁ (= pāṇīnaṁ) Dh. 135 (*cp. Kuhn,* Beitr. p. 81).

pāṇupeta, *mfn.* (*sa.* prāṇôpeta) living, "while one's life lasts"; *acc. m.* ~aṁ (maṁ, saraṇaṁ gataṁ) 69,20 (*cp.* upeta).

pāta, *m.* (= *sa.*) falling (down or into); *v.* piṇḍapāta, *m.* 83,12.

*Pātañjalī-mata, *n.* the doctrine of Patañjali (*q. v.*); *acc.* ~aṁ 113,6. (Pātañjalī- must either be *adj.* = *Pātañjaliya or *subst.* = Patañjali; *cp. sa.* Pātañjala, *mfn.* & Pātañjali = Patañjali.)

pātarāsa, *m.* (*sa.* prātar-āça) morning meal, breakfast; *acc.* ~aṁ, 8,20; *°-bhattaṁ, 57,9 (id.); bhutta-°, *mfn.* one who has eaten his breakfast. *m.* ~o, 22,22. *cp.* pāto.

pāti, *f.* (*sa.* pātrī) a cup, bowl; *acc.* ~iṁ, 56,25; tuccha-°, 56,27; puṇṇa-°, 27,18; bhatta-°, 34,13; *loc.* ~iyā, 56,26; *pl.* ~iyo (suvaṇṇa-rajata-°) 61,27; *instr.* ~īhi (id.) ib.

pātimokkha, *n.* (*buddh. sa.* prātimoksha, *m.*, *fr.* prati-√muc, *cp.* SBE. XIII, p. XXVI) the moral law, the title of the oldest collection of moral precepts of the Buddhists; *loc.* ~e (saṁvaro, "living restrained under the law") Dh. 185. 375 (*cp.* SBE. X. p. 51 Note; *Hardy,* Eastern Monachism p. 8; a translation of the Pātimokkha-precepts is given by *Rhys Davids* & *Oldenberg*, SBE. XIII. p. 1–69.)

pātu-, *indecl.* (before vowels: pātur-; *sa.* prādur) forth, in sight (only prefixed to the verbs karoti & bhavati and their derivatives) *v. below.*

pātuṁ, *inf.*, *v.* pivati.

pātu-bhavati, *vb.* (*sa.* prādur-√bhū) to become visible or clear, appear; *pr. 3. pl.* ~anti, 66,20; *aor. 3. sg.* pātur-ahosi, 67,31; *pp.* pātu-bhūta, *n.* ~aṁ, 45,4. *cp. next.*

pātu-bhāva, *m.* (*sa.* prādur-bhāva) becoming visible, manifestation, appearance; *acc.* ~aṁ (phalita-⁰) 44,32.

pāteti, *vb.* (*caus.* patati; *sa.* pātayati) to cause to fall, let fall, drop, loose, throw down (*acc.*); *part. m.* ~ento (daṇḍakaṁ) 13,21; *aor. 3. sg.* ~esi, 29,27. 36,1; *fut. 2. sg.* ~essasi, 4,29; *ger.* ~etvā, 4,23. 12,31. 23,9; *pp.* pātita, *m.* ~o, Dh. 407.

pāto, *adv.* (*sa.* prātar, *cp.* pātarāsa above) in the early morning; ~ va (nikkhamitvā) "quite early in the morning", 14,21; ~ va tāva hotu, "let it be till to-morrow", 15,16.

pātheyya, *n.* (*sa.* pātheya; *cp.* patha) provisions for a journey, viaticum; ~aṁ, Dh. 235.

pāda, *m.* (= *sa.*; *cp.* pada) [1]) the foot or leg (of a person or an animal), the foot (of a mountain, tree *etc.*), basis, foundation (?); *nom.* ~o (pabbata-⁰) 14,9; *instr.* ~ena (gacchantassa) 97,35; *loc.* ~e, 76,1; *pl.* ~ā, 97,36; hattha-⁰, 99,13 (hands and feet) *comp.* 5,27; *acc. pl.* ~e, 49,6. 57,16. 62,28; *instr.* ~ehi, 40,25; pacchima-⁰, 24,26 (hind feet); *loc.* ~esu, 59,8. 75,22 (sirasā nipatitvā) *cp.* pāda-mūle (*loc.*) "at one's feet", 49,5. 36,27; – pādodaka, *n.*, *⁰-kathalika, *n.*, *⁰-paṁsu, *n.* = ⁰-raja, *n.*. ⁰-paricārikā, *f.*, ⁰-pīṭha, *m.*, ⁰-saññata, *mfn.* (*v. h.*). – *thira-pākāra-pāda, *mfn.* whose fortifications have a strong foundation; *n.* ~aṁ, 91,20 (comment on daḷhuddāpaṁ). – [2]) the fourth part of a verse; *abl. pl.* ~ehi, 114,21. *cp.* catuppādika, *mfn.*

pādaka, *mfn.* (= *sa.*) having feet (*e. c.*); *sarabha-⁰, *mfn.* 42,9 (*q. v.*).

pādukā, *f.* (= *sa.*) a shoe, slipper; *acc. pl.* ~āyo (suvaṇṇa-⁰, "gilt slippers") 68,2; *abl. pl.* ~āhi (do.) 68,16.

pāna, *n.* (= *sa.*) drinking, a drink; *instr.* ~ena (*opp.* anna) 20,26; *comp.* ⁰-bhojana, *n.* (drink and food) *loc.* ~e, Dh. 249; dibba-⁰, *n.* 59,25 (*i. e.* the liquor of the Devas); surā-⁰, surā-meraya-⁰ (*q. v.*).

pānaka, *n.* (= *sa.*) a drink, beverage; *sakkharā-pānakādīhi (*instr. pl.*) "sugar-water and the like", 18,27.

pānīya (or pāniya), *n.* (= *sa.*) a drink, *esp.* water, drinking water; *acc.* ~aṁ, 1,13; *instr.* pāniyena, 83,13; *⁰-tittha, *n.* a watering-place, 11,28 (*loc.* ~e); vāsita-⁰, *n.* 41,11 (*q. v.*).

pāpa, *mfn.* (= *sa.*) bad, evil, wicked; *m.* ~o, Dh. 119 (*opp.* bhadra); *n. subst.* evil-doing, sin, crime (often *esp.* of sexual intercourse); *nom.* ~aṁ (mayā kata-⁰) 17,17; *acc.* ~aṁ, Dh. 117 (*opp.* puñña); 48,7 (unchastity); 59,21; 85,26 (mukhasā); 104,34; *gen.* ~assa (phalaṁ) 17,26; Dh. 183 (sabba-⁰); *abl.** ~ā, Dh. 116; *loc.* ~asmiṁ, ib.; *pl.* ~āni, Dh. 119. 265; *gen. pl.* ~ānaṁ, Dh. 265. 333 (pāpān'); – *cp.* nippāpa, *mfn.*, bāhita-⁰, *mfn.* (*v. h.*); puñña-pāpa-pahīna, *mfn.* (*v.* pahīna); ⁰-vagga, *m.* the 9th chapter of Dh. – *compar.* ~iyo (or ~iya) *v. h. cp. next etc.*

pāpaka, *mfn.* (= *sa.*) bad, evil, wicked; *f.* ~ikā (gatī) Dh. 310; *acc.* ~ikaṁ (diṭṭhiṁ) 91,16. Dh. 164; *n.* ~aṁ (diṭṭhigataṁ) 90,24; (kammaṁ) 100,6; *abl. pl.* ~ehi (kammehi) 100,8; *n. subst.* ~aṁ, evil-doing, 59,21.

pāpa-kamma, *n.* (*sa.* pāpa-karman) wickedness, sin, crime; *nom.* ~aṁ, 51,7; *acc.* ~aṁ (vācāya) 85,34; 99,13. (Satthārā kata-⁰) 73,27; *abl.* ~ā, Dh. 127.

pāpa-kammin, *mfn.* (*sa.* pāpakarmin) evil-doing; *m. pl.* ~ino, Dh. 126.

pāpa-kārin, *mfn.* (= *sa.*) = *prec.*; *m.* ~ī, Dh. 15.

pāpimat, *mfn.* (*sa.* pāpman) wicked, sinful; *m. subst.* 'the wicked one', *i. e.* Māra; *nom.* ~mā, 71,27 (Māro); *gen.* ~mato (Mārassa) 71,24; *voc.* ~ma, 71,31.

pāpiya(*s*), *compar. fr.* pāpa (*sa.* pāpīyas) worse; [*m.* ~o; *n.* ~aṁ &] pāyiyo, Dh. 42. 76 (*opp.* seyyo).

pāpuṇāti (& pappoti) *vb.* (*sa.* pra-√āp) to arrive at, attain to, reach, obtain (*acc.* or *gen.* (*dat.*)); *pr. 3. sg.* pappoti (sukhaṁ) Dh. 27; *3. pl.* pāpuṇanti (maraṇaṁ) 6,22; *imp. 3. sg.* ~ṇātu (vāro, mama parisāya (*gen. dat.*) *cp.* 6,32) 6,26; *pot. 3. sg.* ~ṇe, Dh. 138; *aor. 3. sg.* ~ṇi, 6,32 (*w. gen. dat.*); 20,8 (rukkhassa santikaṁ); 42,32; 89,16; *1. sg.* ~ṇiṁ, 17,7; *fut. 3. pl.* ~ṇissanti, 34,19; *2. pl.* ~ṇissatha (vināsaṁ) 32,28; *ger.* patvā, 17,11 (dukkhaṁ); 23,21 (dīpaṁ); 30,4. 38,11. 45,29. 87,23. 110,18; *pp.* patta (*q. v.*) as finite tense: *m.* ~o, 30,23; *n.* ~aṁ, 43,8 (= pāpuṇi); *caus. v. next. cp.* patti, *f.*

pāpeti, *vb.* (*caus.* pāpuṇāti; *sa.* prāpayati) to cause one (*acc.*) to reach or attain (*acc.* or *gen. dat.*); *pr. 3. sg.* ~eti (nāvaṁ vināsaṁ) 27,12; *imp. 2. sg.* ~ehi (vāraṁ aññassa) 7,8; *fut. 1. sg.* ~essāmi (taṁ vināsaṁ) 5,10; *inf.* ~etuṁ (vāraṁ aññesaṁ) 6,35; *ger.* ~etvā (taṁ jīvitakkhayaṁ) 4,22.

pāmado, *aor. 2. sg.* (*v.* pamajjati.)

*pāmokkha, *mfn.* (*fr.* pamukha, *q. v.*) eminent, famous; chief, principal; disā-°, *mfn.* (*v. h.*); brāhmaṇa-pāmokkhe (*acc. pl.* the most eminent among the Br.) 61,24; Mahākassapa-pāmokkhā therā. the Theras whose chief was M., 110,15.

*pāmojja, *n.* (*fr.* pamodati; *cp. sa.* pramoda) joy, delight; *acc.* ~aṁ (pīti-°, "happiness and joy") Dh. 374; °-bahula, *mfn.* full of delight, *m.* ~o, Dh. 376.

pāyāsa, *m. n.* (*sa.* pāyasa) rice boiled in milk, milk-porridge; *gen.* ~assa (vara-°, excellent milk-porridge) 61,26.

pāyāsi, pāyiṁsu, *aor.*, *v.* payāti.

pāyeti, *vb.* (*caus.* pivati; *sa.* pāyayati) to give to drink (*w. double acc.*), to give suck (*acc.*); *pr. 1. sg.* ~emi (naṁ) 58,33; *imp. 2. sg.* ~ehi, ib.; *ger.* ~etvā (asure dibbapānaṁ) 59,25.

pāra, *n.* (= *sa.*) the opposite bank or shore, the other side; the highest end, *metaph.* = Nibbāna; ~aṁ (*prp. w. gen.*) on the other side, beyond; 2,11 (samuddassa); *comp.* °-Gaṅgāya (*loc.*), on the other side of the Ganges, 1,14; nadī-pāre (*loc.*) 56,21; *acc.* ~aṁ (essanti) Dh. 86 (perhaps to be taken as one word: pāram-essanti, "will pass over", SBE. X. p. 25); *abl.* (*adv.*) pārato, *v. below*; pāraṁ a-pāraṁ vā, 'neither the further nor the hither shore', Dh. 385, & pārâpāraṁ, 'both shores', ib. seem to be used *metaph.* in the sense of 'this and the future existence, the whole existence' (?) *cp.* orapāraṁ, *adv.* 108,26 (*v. h.*).

pāra-ga, *mfn.* (= *sa.*) going to the opposite shore, crossing over, who has overcome or mastered, knowing thoroughly, versed in (*gen.* or *loc.*); *m.* ~o (tisu vedesu) 113,8; *pl.* ~ā (jāti-maraṇassa) 105,26. *cp.* pāra-gū.

pāra-gata, *mfn.* (= *sa.*) who has reached the opposite shore (*i. e.* Nibbāna); *m.* ~o, Dh. 414.

*pāra-gavesin, *mfn.*, looking for the other shore; *m. pl.* ~ino, Dh. 355.

pāra-gāmin, *mfn.* (= *sa.*) passing over to the opposite shore; *m. pl.* ~ino, Dh. 85.

pāra-gū, *mfn.* (= pāra-ga, *q. v.*) *nom. sg. m.* ~ū (tiṇṇaṁ vedānaṁ, brāhmaṇo) 16,23; (bhavassa) Dh. 348; (dvayesu dhammesu) Dh. 384.

pārato, *adv.* (*sa.* pāratas; *abl. fr.* pāra, *q. v.*) on or to the further side; 83,21 (*opp.* orato).

*pāramī, *f.* (& pāramitā, *f.*; *buddh. sa.* id.) perfection, accomplishment; virtue (*esp. pl.* ~iyo, the ten virtues : dāna, sīla, nekkhamma, khanti, mettā, paññā, viriya, sacca, adhiṭṭhāna, upekkhā); sacca-°, 108,31; – pāramīgata, *mfn.* having attained to perfection; *m. pl.* ~ā (*w. loc.* saddhamme) 109,21.

*Pāricchattaka, *m.* (*cp. sa.* pārijātaka) *nom. pr.* of a tree in Devaloka, under which Sakka's throne (paṇḍukambalasilāsana) is placed; ~o, 59,28.

pāruta, *mfn.* (*sa.* prāvṛta, *pp.* prā-√vṛ) covered, dressed; put on; *m.* ~o (sīhacammena) 8,28; su-pāruta, *mfn.* duly dressed (*i. e.* according to the rules of the order) *acc. m.* ~aṁ (pabbajitaṁ) 63,30. *cp. next.*

pārupati, *vb.* (*sa.* prā-√vṛ) to cover, dress; put on (*acc.*); *ger.* ~itvā (gadrabhaṁ sīhacammena) 8,18; (saṁghāṭiyo) 82,28; *pp.* pāruta (*q. v.*) *cp.* pārupana, *n.* [Tr. PM. p. 63; *cp.* apāruta & avāpurāpeti.]

pārupana (or pāpuraṇa) *n.* (*sa.* prāvaraṇa) an upper garment; *nom.* ~aṁ, 29,23 (*cp.* nivāsana).

pāla(ka), *m.* (= *sa.*) guard, protector keeper (*e. c.*); *v.* uyyāna-°, khetta-°, & gopāla(ka), *cp.* Dhanapālaka & Saṁghapāla, *m. nom. pr.*

pāli (often written pāḷi) *f.* (= *sa.*) a line, row, series; a holy text, reading or passage of the holy text; *nom.* sāṭṭhakathā pāli (the text together with the commentary) 102,3; *acc.* ~iṁ (viya, "as the text itself") 114,30; ~iṁ (abhidhammassa, "a passage from the A.") 113,15; *pl. abl.* ~īhi (the verses ?) 114,21; pāli-mattaṁ, the text alone without the Comm. 113,26. [Tr. PM. p. 69; *Franke,* Anzeige, BB. XXII. 296.].

pāvaka, *m.* (= *sa.*) fire; *nom.* ~o (bhasmāchanno) 106,23 = Dh. 71; aggī ~o, Dh. 140 ("lightning-fire" ?).

pāvacana, *n.* (*sa.* pravacana) speaking, recitation, discourse, *esp.* the words of Buddha, the holy scriptures (the suttas); *nom.* ~aṁ (atītasatthukaṁ) 79,3; ~aṁ (Gotamassa) 95,25.

Pāvā, *f. nom. pr.* of a city of the Mallas (near Vesāli); *nom.* ~ā, 77,16; *acc.* ~aṁ, 77,21; *loc.* ~āyaṁ. 77,19.

pāvisi, *aor.*, *v.* pavisati.

pāsa, *m.* (*sa.* pāça) [1]) a snare, trap; *acc.* ~aṁ (oḍḍetvā) 11,29; *loc.* ~e, 11,30. – [2]) = pāsaka (*v. next*).

pāsaka, *m.* (*sa.* pāçaka, *cp.* prāsaka) a die; *acc. pl.* ~ake (suvaṇṇa-°, khipati) 48,8; pāse = pāsake, 50,39; °-khipana, *n.* throwing the dice, 48,23.

pāsāṇa, *m.* (*sa.* pāshāṇa) a stone, rock; *nom.* ~o, 3,1; *voc.* ~a, 3,7; *acc.* ~aṁ, 2,33. 104,13; *instr.* ~ena, 3,6; kāḷa-°, a black rock, 24,21; *piṭṭhi-° (*v. h.*); °-tale, 10,7; °-ppamāṇa, *n.* 3,2; °-piṭṭha, *n.* 17,20; *°-sakalikā, *f.* 17,22 (*q. v.*).

pāsāda, *m.* (*sa.* prāsāda) a platform or terrace, the upper story of a house, a lofty building, palace; *nom.* ~o (Vejayanta-°, *q. v.*) 60,34; *acc.* ~aṁ, 63,14; *abl.* ~ā, 67,24; *loc.* ~e, 50,6; *pl.* ~ā, 67,22; *loc. pl.* ~esu, 76,29; °-talato, 65,34 (*v.* tala); upari-°, 64,12 (*v. h.*); *metaph.* paññā-°, Dh. 28 (*v. h.*).

pāsādika, *mfn.* (*sa.* prāsādika; *cp.* pasāda) kind, amiable; graceful, beautiful; *m.* ~o, 24,11.

pāhesi, *aor.*, *v.* pahiṇāti.

pi, *indecl.* (*enclit.* form of api. *q. v.*) [1]) and, also; 2,25 (punadivase pi); 4,26 (tam pi); 5,31 (añño pi); 5,32 (so pi); 6,33 (aham pi); 7,17 (etesam pi); 26,10 (tato pi); 29,32 (pubbe pi) *etc.*; *w. negation* : nâpi, 16,1 (*neque*); 97,15 (nor). – [2]) *emphatically* : very, even, although; 9,1 (ciram pi); 7,13 (manussesu pi); 27,27; 53,16; 68,24 (seyyathā pi nāma);

106,2 (yathāpi); 112,15 (idhāpi, *cp.* idha); — 20,29. 22,18. 24,17. 31,13. 41,33. 57,3 *etc.*; *pleonast. repeated* 114,22 (potthakesu pi tīsu pi); *w. negation*: 4,25 (eka-macchaṁ pi na); 16,10. 17,18. 18,30. 27,23. (*cp.* kiñcâpi). — [3]) Similarly used after word expressing 'quantity' (numerals *etc.*) implying the notion of totality: sabbe pi, 3,24; ubho pi, 5,12; tayo pi, 11,26 (*cp.* te pi tayo, 13,6); dvīhi pi, 12,2; cattāro pi, 14,10; sakalo pi, 16,13 *etc.* — [4]) but (*vero*; after a new subject at the beginning of a sentence): 9,3. 10,28. 13,6. 23,16. 79,24 (but then). — [5]) perhaps, probably, may be (*w. foll. fut.* or *pot.*): 7,16. 35,19; 13,15. 87,15. — [6]) *repeated*: [a]) both - - and; 4,14 (jale pi thale pi); 9,16. 67,8. 76,12; [b]) either - - or: 6,22. 35,5; 17,14 (whether - - or). — [7]) *prp.* (prefix to verbs) *v.* pidahati (pithīyati), pilandhati (~āpeti).

piṁsati, *vb.* (*sa.* √pish, pinashṭi) to crush, pound; to hurt, injure (*acc.*); *part. med. n.* ~ mānaṁ (tassa matthakaṁ) 24,5.

piṭaka, *n.* (= *sa.*) a basket; a collection of sacred books ('a basket of oral tradition', *cp.* Tr. PM. p. 67—68). The Buddhist canonical works are divided in 3 great collections: ti-piṭaka, *n.* (*q. v.*, *cp.* tepiṭaka) *viz.* [a]) Vinaya-piṭaka, 102,16-17; [b]) (Sutta-) or Suttanta-p. 102,13 (which is also named āgama-p. 110,3); [c]) Abhidhamma-p. 102,13 (*cp.* dhamma[3b])). The term piṭaka is also applied to the last book of the Sutta-piṭaka: Cariyā-piṭaka (*q. v.*). — *Piṭaka-ttaya, *n.* = ti-piṭaka, *acc.* ~aṁ, 113,18. 114,11; *loc.* ~e, 114,25.

piṭṭha, *n.* (& piṭṭhi, *f.*, *v. next*) (*sa.* pṛshṭha) the back; the hinder part or upper side of anything, top, surface; pāsāṇa-°, *n.* the top of a rock, *acc.* ~aṁ, 17,20; kavāṭa-°, *n.* 84,12 (*v. h.*; in this *comp.* and in piṭṭha-saṁghāṭa(ka) *n.* 91,21 (*comm.* on toraṇa) piṭṭha seems to have the signification of 'post, door-post'; *cp.* sayana-piṭṭhaṁ, 'bed-side', 41,30); *instr.* & *loc.* (at the end of *comp.*) are often used prepositionally = along, over; beside, on *etc.*; *instr.* ~ena (samudda-° gacchanto, "passing the ocean") 23,21. 60,6; (udaka-°) 28,10; *loc.* piṭṭhe, 5,17 (paṁka-°); 16,18 (taruṇa-dabbatiṇa-°); 20,7. 41,25. 65,4 (sayana-°); 23,11. 59,32 (samudda-°); 45,22 (hatthi-°). *cp.* SBE. XX. 105.

piṭṭhi, *f.* (*sa.* pṛshṭha & pṛshṭhi) = piṭṭha [*cp.* Tr. PM. p. 55; *Franke*, Anzeige, BB. XX. 287]; *nom.* ~i (rucirā) 10,19; *acc.* ~iṁ, 1,17. 46,8; *abl.* ~ito, 2,5. 8,17; *adv.* ~ito ~ito (upajjhāyassa, 'hot-foot upon') 83,28; *loc.* ~iyaṁ, 52,33. 55,12; *°-passe, behind (*w. gen.*) 50,18 (*v.* passa); *~pāsāṇa, *m.* a rock in the surface of the water, or a flat rock, a bare rocky ground; ~o, 2,22; *loc.* ~e, 2,31. 10,29 (*cp.* pāsāṇa-piṭṭha, 17,20).

piṇḍa, *m.* (= *sa.*) a lump of food, alms of food (received by the Buddhist monks in their alms-bowl); *acc.* ~aṁ (raṭṭha-°, "the charity of the land") 107,2 = Dh. 308; *dat.* ~āya (for alms) 76,17. 86,5. — *piṇḍa-cāra, *m.* wandering about for alms, 85,2 (°-atthāya). — piṇḍa-pāta, *m.* the food received in the alms-bowl, 83,12. 97,8; °-paṭikkanta, *m.* one who has returned from seeking alms, 86,5 (~o). *cp. next.*

piṇḍi, *f.* (*sa.* piṇḍī) a ball, lump; a cluster or bunch of fruits; *acc.* ~iṁ (amba-°) 15,2; *comp.* pakka-phala-°, 2,1.

pitar, *m.* (*sa.* pitṛ) father; *nom.* pitā, 87,10. 108,15; (*acc.* ~araṁ, *loc.* ~ari); the weak stem is pitu (or piti), hence *gen.* (*dat.*) *sg.* pitu, 24,13. 56,31. 87,14 & pituno, 69,22 (after the analogy of u-stems); *pl. nom. acc.* ~aro, 22,13 (mātā-°, parents); *gen.* ~unnaṁ (do.) 31,18; *loc.* ~ūsu (do.) 7,24; pitāputte, *acc. pl.* a father and a son, 32,18; pitu-hadayaṁ, a father's heart, 64,17. *cp.* petteyyatā, *f.*

pitta, *n.* (= *sa.*) bile; *nom.* ~aṁ, 82,4 = 97,22; 103,20.

pithīyati, *vb.* (*pass.* pidahati; *sa.* (a)pi-√dhā; the Burmese write pidhīyati, v. Tr. PM. p. 62(17)) to be covered or shut; to shut, close (*intr.*); *pr. 3. sg.* ~ati, Dh. 173; *aor. 3. pl.* ~iṁsu (akkhīni) 3,19.

pidahati, *vb.* (*sa.* (a)pi-√dhā) to cover, conceal; to shut, close (*acc.*); *part. med. f.* ~mānā (tassa akkhīni) 50,14; *inf.* ~ituṁ (mukhaṁ) 13,18; *ger.* pidhāya (dvāraṁ) 6,14; *pass.* pithīyati, *pp.* pihita (*q. v.*).

pipati, *vb.*, *v.* pivati.

pipāsā, *f.* (= *sa.*) thirst; *v.* khuppipāsā.

pipīlikā, *f.* (= *sa.*) an ant; *nom.* ~ā (ekā) 53,19; *pl.* ~ā, 53,30; *gen. pl.* ~ānaṁ, 53,16. *cp.* kipillikā.

piya, *mfn.* (*sa.* priya) beloved, dear; pleasant, agreeable; *n.* ~aṁ, 55,1; *abl.* ~ato, Dh. 212 ("from pleasure"); *n. pl.* ~āni (beloved objects or pleasures) 55,1; piyā = piyāni, 55,2; *instr. abl.* ~ehi, 67,10. 106,25 = Dh. 210; *gen.* ~ān[aṁ] 106,26; — *subst. m.* = friend, *acc.* ~aṁ, Dh. 220; — *comp.* piyāpāya, *m.* (*v.* apāya); piyappiyaṁ, *n.* pleasant and unpleasant, Dh. 211 (*cp.* a-ppiya, *mfn.*); piya-ggāhin, *mfn.* grasping at pleasure, *m.* ~ī, Dh. 209; °-bhaṇḍa, 54,34; °-mātulaka, 5,5; °-saṁvāsa, 11,27 (*v. h.*); Piya-vagga, *m.* the XVIth chapter of Dh. — *compar.* piyatara, *mfn.* 54,33 (*m.* ~o) *cp. next.*

piyāyati, *vb.* (*denom. fr.* piya; *sa.* priyāyate) to be fond of, love, fondle; *part. med. f.* ~mānā, 9,22.

***pilandhati**, *vb.* (*denom. fr.* pilandha = *sa.* pi-naddha, api-√nah) to dress, deck, decorate (*w. double acc.*); to deck oneself with (*acc.*); *ger.* ~itvā (pupphāni) 41,7. — *caus.* *pilandhāpeti; *ger.* ~etvā (maṁ pupphāni) 33,3. *cp.* onaddha, upa-nayhati, san-nayhati. (Tr. PM. p. 55.)

pilavati, *vb.*, *v.* palavati.

***pilotikā**, *f.* (rarely *n.*) cloth, stuff (made of hair, worn by poor people; felt?) *n. pl.* ~āni (jiṇṇakāni) 57,5. If this word is not a loanword [*Trenckner* refers to Syriac *piloto* fr. Greek πιλωτής (?)] then it is probably derived from *sa.* plota = prota, *mn.*

pivati (or pipati) *vb.* (*sa.* √pā, pibati) to drink; *pr. 3. sg.* ~ati (majjaṁ) 97,11; *2. sg.* ~asi (suraṁ) 74,7; *part. nom. m.* [a]) pivaṁ, Dh. 205; [b]) pivanto, 45,28; *pl.* ~antā, 74,4; *imp. 2. sg.* piva, 22,30. 111,20; *2. pl.* ~atha, 21,5; *fut. 2. sg.* ~issasi, 56,22; *1. sg.* ~issāmi. 22,32; *inf.* pātuṁ, 11,30; *ger.* [a]) pītvā, Dh. 205; [b]) pivitvā, 1,12 *etc.*; *pp.* pīta (*q. v.*); *caus.* pāyeti (*q. v.*) *cp.* pāna, pānīya. pītin, pipāsā.

pihaka, *n.* (*sa.* plihan, *m.*) the spleen; *nom.* ~aṁ, 82,3 = 97,21.

pihita, *mfn.* (*pp.* pidahati; *sa.* pihita) covered, shut, closed; *°-dvāra, *mfn.* whose doors are barred, *loc. n.* ~e (bhavane) 41,29.

piheti (or pihayati) *vb.* (*sa.* √spṛh, spṛhayati) to desire (*acc.* or *gen.*); to envy (*gen. pers.*); *pr. 3. sg.* ~eti (pihet'attānuyoginaṁ, *gen. pl.*) Dh. 209; *3. pl.* ~ayanti, Dh. 94; Dh. 181 (according to the metre: pihenti); *part. nom. m.* ~ayaṁ (aññesaṁ) Dh. 365.

pīṭha(ka), *n.* (= *sa.*) a chair, stool; *nom.* ~aṁ. 84,13; *acc.* ~aṁ, 83,18 (heṭṭhā-°, *v. h.*); 83,29 (jantāghara-°, *v. h.*); *loc.* ~ake, 87,17; — pāda-°, *n.* a foot-stool, *nom.* ~aṁ, 83,6.

pīṇita, *mfn.* (*pp.* pīṇeti; *sa. caus.* prīṇayati, √prī) satisfied, pleased, delighted; *f.* ~itā (yakkhī) 111,35. *cp.* piya, pīti.

pīta, *mfn.* (*pp.* pivati; = *sa.*) drunk or having drunk; *gen. m.* ~assa (yāguṁ) "when he has drunk it", 82,20.

pīti, *f.* (*sa.* prīti) pleasure, joy; *acc.* ~iṁ (buddhārammaṇaṁ) 28,6 (*cp.* ārammaṇa); °-pāmojja, *n.* Dh. 374 (*v. h.*); *°-bhakkha, *mfn.* "feeding on happiness", *pl. m.* ~ā (devā yathā) Dh. 200; *°-somanassa-jāta, *mfn.*

64,13 (*v.* jāta); — *dhamma-pīti, *f.* delighting in the dhamma, Dh. 205 (⁰-rasaṁ); *dhamma-pīti, *m(fn)*. id. Dh. 79 (so all Mss; the comm. takes it = dhamma-pītin (*i. e.* pāyako, pivanto), but I dont know whether the word pītin (drinking) is found elsewhere in the Pāli texts).

pītin, *mfn.* (*sa.* pītin, *e. c.*) drinking (*v.* pīti & dhamma-⁰).

pīḷeti, *vb.* (*sa.* √pīḍ, pīḍayati) to press, squeeze, wring; to hurt, annoy, oppress (*acc.*); *ger.* ~etvā (pabbataṁ) 16,16; (coḷakaṁ) 84,21; 45,1 (without *obj.* oppressing); *pp.* pīḷita, vexed, annoyed, *m.* ~o (suṁsumārena) 108,25.

puggala, *m.* (*sa.* pudgala) a person; personality, individuality, the Ego or individual soul; *nom.* ~o, 3,24. 92,6; na h'ettha ~o upalabbhati, 97,2. *cp.* paṭipuggala & *next*.

Puggala-paññatti, *f. nom. pr.* of a canonical Pāli work, the 4th part of the Abhidhamma-piṭaka; 102,12.

pucimanda, *m.* (*sa.* picumanda or ⁰-marda) another name of the Nimb tree (*v.* nimba); *acc. pl.* ~e, 38,1; *⁰-parivāra, *mfn.* surrounded by Nimb trees, *m.* ~o (ambo) 37,33.

pucchati, *vb.* (*sa.* √prach, pṛcchati) to ask, question (*acc. pers. & rei*); *pr. 3. sg.* ~ati, 91,14; *3. pl.* ~anti, 21,9; *2. pl.* ~atha, 88,9; *part. m.* ~anto, 9,25; *pl.* ~antā (Mahāsattaṁ samuddassa nāmaṁ) 25,24; *imp. 2. pl.* ~atha, 79,18; *pot. 3. sg.* ~eyya, 94,32-34; *2. pl.* ~eyyātha (maṁ imaṁ kāraṇaṁ) 17,1; 79,24; *fut. 1. sg.* ~issāmi, 56,7; *aor. 2.–3. sg.* apucchi, 91,10 (Bhagavantaṁ pañhaṁ); 112,8; pucchi, 9,17; *3. pl.* apucchisuṁ, 110,30; pucchiṁsu, 4,8; *ger.* ~itvā, 29,31; 43,26 (vayaṁ); 86,32 (kumārikaṁ pañhe); 109,15; *grd. m.* ~itabbo (upajjhāyo pāniyena, he ought to be offered water to drink) 83,13; *cp.* a-puccha, *mfn.*; — *pp.* a) puṭṭha, *m.* ~o, 25,28 (evaṁ tehi ~); 85,14 (katakammaṁ); 90,26 (pañhaṁ); *f.* ~ā, 73,13; b) pucchito, *m.* 54,27; 91,15; *comp.* mayā pucchita-pañho, 88,11. *cp.* pañha & *next*.

pucchā, *f.* (*sa.* pṛcchā) question; *acc.* ~aṁ, 91,15; *gen. pl.* ~ānaṁ (sabba-⁰) 91,14.

pujja, *mfn.* (*grd.*, *v.* pūjeti).

puñja, *m.* (= *sa.*) a heap, mass, quantity, multitude; *loc.* ~e (paduma-⁰) 16,7; *comp.* ratta-kambala-⁰, 5,27.

puñña, *n.* (*sa.* puṇya) virtue, good work, moral or religious merit (*opp.* pāpa); *nom. acc.* ~aṁ, Dh. 196. 331; 103,9; 107,27 = Dh. 18; 106,6 = Dh. 267; *instr.* ~ena, 103,14; *pl.* ~āni (katvā) 8,13; dānādīni ~, 17,34; 103,7; *gen. pl.* ~ānaṁ (phalaṁ) 58,12; 103,15 (read: puññena?). — *comp.* kata-puñña, *mfn.* one who has done good, virtuous, *m.* ~o, 107,26 = Dh. 18; *acc.* ~aṁ, Dh. 220; — ⁰-pāpa-pahīna, *mfn.* (*v.* pahīna); — *⁰-pekha, *mfn.* (*v. h.*).

puññavat, *mfn.* (*sa.* puṇyavat) full of merit, virtuous, fortunate; *f.* ~vatī, 56,1.

puṭṭha¹, *mfn.* (*pp. v.* pucchati).

puṭṭha², *mfn.* (*sa.* pushṭa. *pp.* √push; *cp.* posāpeti) nourished, fed; *m.* ~o (nivāpa-⁰, *q. v.*) Dh. 325. *cp.* phuṭa & phuṭṭha.

puṇṇa, *mfn.* (*pp.* pūrati, pūreti; *sa.* pūrṇa) full; ⁰-ghaṭa, 62,6 (*q. v.*); ⁰-pāti, 27,18.

Puṇṇa, *m. nom. pr.* of a thera; *nom.* ~o (dhammakathikānaṁ [aggo]) 109,9.

puṇṇa-canda, *m.* (*sa.* pūrṇa-candra) the full moon; *acc.* ~aṁ, 42,3; *⁰-mukha, *mfn.* with a face splendent like the full moon, *m.* ~o (Gotamabuddho) 87,6.

puṇṇamā, *f.* (*sa.* pūrṇimā (pūrṇamā)) the day of full moon; *gen.* ~āya, 61,3; puṇṇamuposathadivasa, 22,19 (*v.* uposatha).

putta, *m.* (*sa.* putra) a son, *pl.* children (also the brood of animals); *acc.* ~aṁ, 7,29; *pl. nom.* ~ā, 105,5; *acc.* ~e, 13,4; *instr.* ~ehi, 105,28; at the end of *comp.* it is often used as designation of family or caste, as metronymic or patronymic, *v.* kammāra-°, kula-°, khara-°, deva-°, rāja-°, ludda-°, seṭṭhi-°, Māluñkyā-°; *cp.* ayya-putta, bhagini-putta; *dvandva*: °-dāra, *m.* (*q. v.*); °-dhītāsu (*loc. pl.*, *v.* dhītar); °-pasu-, Dh. 287; pitā-putte, *acc. pl.* 32,18.

puttaka, *m.* (*sa.* putraka) a little son or child; *nom.* ~o (eka-°, an only son) 23,6; *acc.* ~aṁ, 6,35; *acc. pl.* ~e, 12,35 (young ones).

*puttimat, *mfn.* (probably arisen by confusion between *sa.* putrin & *putra-mat = putravat) having sons; *nom. m.* ~mā, 105,28-31.

puthu, 1) *mfn.* (*sa.* pṛthu) extensive, broad, large; manifold, diverse, common, general; *acc. m. pl.* ~ū (samaṇa-brāhmaṇe) 19,2. – 2) *indecl.* (*adv.*) extensively, far and wide, all round; 104,8 (*cp. sa.* pṛthak & *next.*)

puthujjana, *m.* (*sa.* pṛthag-jana) a vile or ignorant person, a fool; *coll.* common people, the vulgar; *loc.* ~e (andhabhūte) Dh. 59; a-puthujjanasevita, Dh. 272 (*q. v.*); °-kālakiriyā, *f.* 87,29 (*q. v.*) *cp.* pothujjanika.

puna (& punaṁ) *adv.* (before vowels also pun' or punar-, punad-; *sa.* punar) back, again; ~ gantvā, 4,23; ~ ānetvā, 4,17; at the beginning of a sentence: 53,29; 63,19 (pun'ekadivasaṁ); puna pi, again, once more, 3,8. 53,31; punar eva (do.) Dh. 338; puna . . . va, again as before, 38,4; *w. negation*: na punaṁ, not again, no more, Dh. 238. 348; puna-nâsakkhi, 55,17; na . . . vā puna (nor yet) Dh. 271; puna asūrānaṁ an-āgamanatthāya, in order that they might not come back again, 60,26. The enclitic form of this word is pana (*q. v.*) *cp. next etc.*

*puna-divasa, *m.* the next day; *loc.* ~e, 2,25.

punappuna(ṁ), *adv.* (*sa.* punaḥpunar) again and again, repeatedly; 25,18. 73,4; ~aṁ, 52,23. 108,5.

punabbhava, *m.* (*sa.* punarbhava) new birth, transmigration; *nom.* ~o, 108,15. *cp.* pono(b)bhavika.

*puna-vāre, *adv.* (*loc.*, *cp.* vāra) another time, the next time; 18,17.

puppha, *n.* (*sa.* pushpa) a flower; *acc.* ~aṁ, 106,2 = Dh. 49; *pl.* ~āni, 33,3; 37,16 (akāla-°); 41,6 (nānā-°); Dh. 47 (~ān'eva); *instr.* ~ehi, 20,9 (dibba-gandha-°); 34,6 (vana-°); *gen.* ~ānaṁ, 65,29; – *comp.* pupphantarehi, 62,12 (*v.* antara); *°-kaṇṇikasadisa, *mfn.* 7,29 (*v.* kaṇṇikā); *°-gandha. *m.* the scent of flowers, ~o, Dh. 54; *°-rāsi, *m.* a heap of fl., Dh. 53 (*abl.* ~imhā); *°-vagga, *m.* the IVth chapter of Dh.

pupphati, *vb.* (*denom. fr.* puppha; *sa.* pushpyati) to flower, blossom; *pr. 3. sg.* ~ati, 59,31; *pp.* ~ita, *gen. f.* ~āya, 59,29; – *caus.* *pupphāpeti, to cause to flower or blossom; *part. m.* ~ento (akāla-pupphāni) 37,16.

pubba¹, *m.* (*sa.* pūya) pus, purulent matter; *nom.* ~o, 82,4 = 97,32.

pubba², *mfn.* (*sa.* pūrva) first, former; except *loc.* pubbe (*adv. q. v.*) it is only used in *comp.* like °-kamma, *n.* & °-nimitta, *n.* (*q. v.*) and *esp.* at the end of *adj. comp.* whose first part is a past participle, implying the sense of 'before', with a negation: 'not before, never': diṭṭha-pubba, *mfn.* seen before. *m.* ~o (na mayā, I have never seen (before this day)) 7,13; ito me tiṇṇaṁ saṁvaccharānaṁ matthake Satthā ~o, it is three years since I saw the master, 87,8; the same *comp.* is also used in an active sense (*w. obj. acc.*): aññapurisaṁ diṭṭhapubbaṁ itthiṁ, a woman who has seen another man before, 48,13 (but this construction may probably have arisen through a dissolution of a longer *comp.* *añña-purisa-diṭṭha-pubba, *mfn.*); dinnapubba, *mfn.* given before, *v.* a-dinna; *cp.* a-pubba, anu-pubba & *next.*

pubbaṅgama, *mfn.* (*sa.* pūrvaṁgama) preceeding, going before, leading, chief; *v.* mano-°.

pubbaṇha, *m.* (*sa.* pūrvāhṇa) morning, forenoon; *°-samaya, *m.* id.; *acc.* ~aṁ, in the morning, 76,15; rattindivam-pubbaṇhâdisu (*loc.*) 88,22.

pubbāpara, *mfn.* (*sa.* pūrvāpara) being before and after; successive; *n. pl. acc.* ~āni (*scil.* akkharāni, in the right order) Dh. 352; °-vasena, according to the consecutive order, 114,20 (*cp.* vasa).

pubbe, *adv.* (*loc. fr.* pubba, *cp. sa.* pūrvaṁ) before, formerly, in times past; 28,15 (~ pi); 54,13; 69,28; 85,13; 86,7 (~ va). – *°-nivāsa, *m.* (*cp. sa.* pūrva-nivāsa) 'former habitation', *i. e.* former existences, *acc.* ~aṁ, Dh. 423.

pura, *n.* (= *sa.*) a city, town; *nom.* ~aṁ (yakkha-°) 112,12; *acc.* ~aṁ (deva-°) 27,31. *cp.* antopura.

pura(s), *indecl.* (*sa.* puras) at the beginning of *comp.* pura-° or puro-° (*v. below*) = pure (*q. v.*) *cp.* purato, purima.

purakkhata, *mfn.* (*sa.* puraskṛta) 'placed before', followed by, filled with, attacked or injured by (*gen.* or *instr.*); *f.* ~ā (pajā, tasiṇāya) Dh. 342.

purato, *adv.* & *prp.* (*w. gen.*) (*sa.* puratas) before (of place), in front of; forward, further; ~ ṭhapetvā, 35,27; ~ paṭicchādetvā (*opp.* pacchato) 83,32; after *gen.* assa ~, 23,1; tesaṁ ~, 42,3; rathassa ~, 54,9; mātu ~, 62,23; 76,36. 94,29.

puratthā, *adv.* (*sa.* purastāt) before, in front; hence: *puratthima, *mfn.* eastern; *acc. f.* ~aṁ (disaṁ) 95,5 (*opp.* pacchimaṁ).

purāṇa, *mfn.* (= *sa.*) ancient, old; °-gāma, *m.* 35,22 (a ruined village); °-jaṭila, *m.* who has been Jaṭila before, 70,22; °-seṭṭhikula, *n.* 55,31 (*q. v.*); *n. pl.* purāṇāni, events of the past, Dh. 156. *cp.* porāṇaka.

***purima**, *mfn.* (*fr.* pura(*s*), *cp.* pure) former, previous, first; the same as before; *instr. m.* ~ena (kathāsallāpena) 94,22; *gen.* ~assa, 101,22; *loc.* ~e (yāme, the first watch) 99,19; *comp.* °-bhave, in a previous existence, 58,11; °-nayen'eva, *v.* naya; °-sadisa, *mfn.* happening as before (or above), *n.* ~aṁ (sabbaṁ) 31,28.

purisa (rarely pūrisa), *m.* (*sa.* purusha) a man, person; *nom.* ~o, 92,7; Dh. 117 (pūriso); 36,3 (rukkhe nisinna-°); 86,19 (bhīta-°); sap-puriso, Dh. 54 (*cp.* sat & santa[3]); *voc.* ~a, 23,34. 101,6; 76,3 (mogha-°); *acc.* ~aṁ, 10,26; *gen.* ~assa, 9,13; *pl.* ~ā (rāja-°, royal servants) 40,8. 74,7; Dh. 235 (Yama-°, *q. v.*); *acc. pl.* ~e, 74,4; – *comp.* purisādhama, *m. acc. pl.* ~e, low people, Dh. 78 (*cp.* adhama); *purisājañña, *m.* a remarkable man, supernatural person (*i. e.* Buddha) Dh. 193 (*cp.* ājañña); purisuttama, *m. acc. pl.* ~e, the best people, Dh. 78 (*cp.* uttama); purisantara, *m.*, *v.* antara[2]; *°-gabbha, *m.* (*q. v.*); °-vadha, murder, 74,14 (°-daṇḍa, *q. v.*); °-sahassaṁ, *n.* a thousand men, 34,9; – eka-purisikā, *f.* & nip-purisa, *mfn.* (*v. h.*) *cp.* porisa & posa.

pure, *adv.* (*sa.* puras) in front, before, formerly; ~ ca pacchā ca majjhe ca, Dh. 421; munca ~ ("give up what is before") Dh. 348; of time: 37,30. 47,1. 61,8. Dh. 326 (once, formerly); 108,15 (in former births); 85,5 (id. = pubbe atītajātiyaṁ, 85,12). *cp.* pura(*s*) (pura-, puro-) & *next.*

purekkhāra, *m.* (*sa.* puraskāra) 'placing before', intention; giving preference to, preference, precedence; *acc.* ~aṁ (bhikkhusu) Dh. 73. *cp.* purakkhata.

***pure-dvāra**, *n.* the front door of a house (*opp.* pacchima-dvāra); *instr.* ~ena (nikkhamantaṁ, by the front door) 12,10; *loc.* ~e (dārūni nikkhipitvā) 57,13.

purohita, *m.* (= *sa.*) a family priest, a king's domestic chaplain; ~o, 48,9; *instr.* ~ena, 48,5; *gen.* ~assa, 45,21; *°-brāhmaṇa, *m.* id.; *gen.* ~assa, 51,19; *°-ṭṭhāna, *n.* the rank or situation of a p., *loc.* ~e, 45,29 (*cp. Fick*, Soc. Glied. p. 107–117).

pūjana, *n.* & pūjanā, *f.* (*sa.* pūjana, *n.*) worship, homage, adoration; *nom.* ~ā (sā) Dh. 106.

pūjā, *f.* (= *sa.*) worship, honour, care, *etc.*; *acc.* ~aṁ, 37,31; *acc. pl.* ~ā, Dh. 73; – pūjāraha, *mfn.* (*sa.* pūjārha) deserving homage; *acc. pl. m.* ~e, Dh. 195 (*cp.* araha).

pūjeti, *vb.* (*sa.* pūjayati, √pūj) to honour, worship, revere (*acc.*); *part. gen. m.* ~ayato (pūjārahe) Dh. 195; *pot. 3. sg.* ~aye (bhāvitattānaṁ) Dh. 106; *aor. 3. pl.* a-pūjesuṁ (kākaṁ maṁsena) 18,33; *ger.* ~etvā, 34,7; *pp.* pūjita, *m.* ~o, Dh. 303; *grd.* pujja, *mfn.*, *v.* a-pujja. *cp.* pūjana (~ā), pūjā.

pūti, *mfn.* (= *sa.*) stinking, foul, putrid; *f.* stink, stench; *°-sandeha, *m.* a heap of corruption, ~o, 107,8 = Dh. 148.

*pūti-latā, *f.* name of a certain kind of creeper or shrub; *acc.* ~aṁ, 105,19; according to the comment Jāt. I. p. 177,6 & Dbpd. (1855) p. 313,3 [read : taruṇā pi galocilatā pūtilatā] it is another name of the young (or soft) galoci-creeper.

pūraṇa, *mf*(~ī)*n.* (= *sa.*) filling, completing; *v.* Manoratha-pūraṇī.

pūrati, *vb.* (*pass.* √pṝ, pūr, *sa.* pūryate & ~ti) to be filled; *pr. 3. sg.* ~ati, Dh. 121–22; *pp.* puṇṇa & *caus.* pūreti (*q. v.*).

pūrisa, *m.* = purisa (*q. v.*).

pūreti, *vb.* (*caus.* √pṝ, pūr, *sa.* pūrayati) to fill (*acc.*) with (*gen.* or *instr.*); to fulfill, complete (*acc.*); *part. m.* ~ayanto, 105,21; *part. med. m.* ~ayamāno (saggapathaṁ) 34,29; *aor. 3. sg.* ~esi (tuccha-pātiṁ yāguyā) 56,28; devanagaraṁ, devapuraṁ, saggapadaṁ (or saggapathaṁ) pūresi is a frequently occurring expression for 'going to heaven', or 'attaining heavenly bliss' : 17,34. 27,31. 44,15 (34,29); *aor. 3. med.* (= *aor. 3. pass.*) pūrayittha ("was filled with", *instr.*) 28,29; *ger.* ~etvā (pātiyo pāyāsassa) 61,27; (sīlaṁ, "fulfilling the moral law") 16,19; *pp.* pūrita, filled, *n.* ~aṁ (uyyānam) 6,16; *pass.* pūrati (*v. above*).

pūva (rarely pūpa), *m.* (& *n.*) (*sa.* pūpa, *m.*) a cake; *acc.* ~aṁ (a rice-cake) 57,19-21; °-khaṇḍa, *m. n.* 53,18 (*v. h.*).

pe, *indecl.*, a syllable indicating abbreviation = 'and so on' (in the same way); 92,4 (*cp.* 89,25, *etc.*); 92,32-33. 93,1-5 (*cp.* 89,28-30, *etc.*); 93,29-31. 94,4 (do.); 96,19-21 (= 66,13); 100,23-24 (= 100,12); instead of pe we find also frequently pa or la (*q. v.*), and in the Birm. Mss. gha is similarly used (probably arisen through corruption of the letters pe or pa-la). According to the native comm. pe is an abridgment of peyyāla, *m. n.*, which most likely is another form of pariyāya (*q. v.*) *i. e.* 'repetition' [*paliyāya, *payyāla] *cp. Oldenberg*, KZ. 25,324; Tr. PM. p. 66. *Buddh. sa.* peyāla & preyāla, *v. Windisch*, Māra und Buddha, p. 315.

pekkha(ka), *mfn.* (*e. c.* = *sa.* prekshā, *f.* & prekshaka, *mfn.*) seeing, regarding, looking at; *puññapekha, *mfn.* aiming at merit, Dh. 108.

pekkhati, *vb.* (*sa.* pra-√īksh) to look at, regard, wiew (*acc.*); *part. nom. m.* ~aṁ (attham anāgataṁ, foreseeing) 112,4; *part. med. m.* ~māno (ti ~) 47,26. *cp. prec.*

*pekkhuṇa (or pekhuṇa), *n.*, a tail feather (*esp.* that of a peacock); *pl.* ~āni (vyāmamattāni) 10,20; citra-°, *mfn.* 10,10 (*v. h.*). – The etymology of this word is unknown; but it may be akin either to pakkha (*q. v.*), or to piñja, *n.* (*cp. sa.* piccha), by which it is explained in the comm. Jāt. I, 207,27 & VI, 218,29. *Pischel*, Gr. § 89, refers to *sa.* preṅkhaṇa, *Prâkr.* pehuṇa; *cp. Weber*, Ind. Str. III. 396.

pekha, pekhuṇa, *v.* pekkha, pekkhuṇa.

pecca, *adv.* (*orig. ger. fr.* pra-

√i, *sa.* pretya) after death, in the next world; 74,3; 107,26 = Dh. 18 (*opp.* idha). *cp. next.*

peta, *mfn.* (*sa.* preta, *pp.* pra-√i) dead, deceased; *m.* the spirit of a dead person, a ghost, demon; *nom.* ~o, 84,33; *acc.* ~aṁ, 85,3; *sūkara-mukha-⁰, a peta with a pig's mouth, 84,27; *sūkara-peta-vatthu, the story of that peta, 86,10. petī, *f.* (*q. v.*).

Peta-vatthu, *n. nom. pr.* of a canonical Pāli-book (a section of the Khuddaka-Nikāya); specimen thereof (with the comm. of Dhammapāla [Paramattha-dīpanī]) p. 84,25–86,10.

***petī**, *f.*, a female peta (*q. v.*); *pl. acc.* ~iyo, 23,16–23.

***petteyyatā**, *f.* (*fr.* pitar through *petteyya, *mfn.*) the state of a father; Dh. 332. *cp.* matteyyatā, *f.*

pema, *n.* (*sa.* preman, *m. n.*) love, affection; *abl.* ~ato, Dh. 213.

peyyāla, *m. n.*, *v.* pe.

***pesakāra**, *m.* (*fr. sa.* *peçaskāra?) a weaver; ⁰-geha, *n.* 88,5; ⁰-dhītar, *f.* 86,13; ⁰-sālā, *f.* 88,5 (*v. h.*) *cp. Fick,* Soc. Gl. p. 211.

***pesanaka**, *mfn.* (*fr.* pesaṇa, *n.* 'sending', errand, commission; *sa.* preshaṇa) one who sends a message; only in the *comp.* ⁰-corā, *m. pl.* robbers who use to despatch one to fetch the ransom, 32,15, *etc.*

pesala, *mfn.* (*sa.* peçala), beautiful, lovely; skilful, clever; su-pesalo, *m.* (catuppado) 30,8.

pesi, *f.* (*sa.* peçī) a small piece of flesh or meat; the foetus shortly after conception; *gen.* ~iyā, 99,11.

pesikā, *f.* (*sa.* peçikā) a piece, stick (*esp.* of bamboo); *instr.* ~āya (veḷu-⁰) 52,31.

pesuñña, *n.* (*sa.* paiçunya) backbiting, calumny; *⁰-kāraka, *m.* a slanderous person, *gen.* ~assa, 42,7.

peseti, *vb.* (*sa.* preshayati, *caus.* pra-√ish) to send, send forth or away (*acc.*); *pr. 3. sg.* ~eti (paṇṇākāraṁ) 64,27; *3. pl.* ~enti, 32,18; *imp. 2. pl.* ~etha (macchaṁ) 4,14; *part. m.* ~ento, 37,4; *aor. 3. sg.* ~esi, 24,30; *ger.* ~etvā, 65,26. *cp.* pesanaka.

pokkhara, *n.* (*sa.* pushkara, *cp.* paushkara) a lotus-flower, *esp.* the blue lotus; *acc. pl.* ~e (= pokkharāni?) 111,9; ⁰-patta, *n.* a lotus-leaf, *loc.* ~e, Dh. 401.

pokkharaṇī, *f.* (*sa.* pushkariṇī & paushkariṇī) a lotus-tank; *acc.* ~iṁ, 58,28. 111,7; *loc.* ~iyaṁ, 52,28.

***pokkharatā**, *f.* (*fr.* pokkhara) beauty; *instr.* ~āya (vaṇṇa-⁰, beauty of complexion) Dh. 262.

Poṭṭhapāda, *m.* (*cp. sa.* proshṭapāda) *nom. pr.* of a parrot; *nom.* ~o, 9,8.

pota(ka), *m.* & **potikā**, *f.* (= *sa.*) a young animal; assa-pota-⁰, 2,18; assa-potaka-⁰, 5,29; suka-potaka, *m. acc. pl.* ~e, 9,11; supaṇṇa-potakā, *pl.* 60,8; haṁsa-potakassa, *gen. m.* 10,21; ⁰-potikā, *f.* 10,4.

potthaka, *m. n.* (*sa.* pustaka) a book or manuscript; *acc.* ~aṁ, 114,16; *acc. pl.* ~e, 114,8; *loc. pl.* ~esu, 52,11 (porāṇa-⁰); 52,14. 114,22; ⁰-dvayaṁ, 114,18 (two books); ⁰-ttayaṁ, 114,19 (three books).

***pothujjanika**, *mfn.* (*fr.* puthujjana) vulgar; *m.* ~o, 66,26 (*synon.* hīna, gamma).

potheti, *vb.* (*sa.* √puth, *caus.* pothayati) to strike, beat, cudgel (*acc.*); *pot. 3. sg.* ~eyya (maṁ) 87,15; *ger.* ~etvā, 8,29. 39,15. 51,26.

pono[b]bhavika, *mfn.* (*sa.* paunar-bhavika) causing new births; *f.* ~ā (taṇhā) 67,13 (*cp.* punabbhava).

porāṇa, *mfn.* (*sa.* paurāṇa) relating to the past, ancient; *n.* (*subst.*) ~aṁ, "an old saying", Dh. 227 (*opp.* ajjatana); ⁰-potthakesu, *loc. pl.* in the old manuscripts, 52,11. *cp.* purāṇa & *next.*

porāṇaka, *mfn.* (*sa.* paurāṇika) ancient, former, old; what has been hitherto, usual; *comp.* ⁰-uyyānapāla, *m.* 37,17; ⁰-parihāra, *m.* 37,27.

porisa, *m.* (*fr.* purisa; *sa.* paurusha) a man; *nom.* ~o (uttama-⁰, *q. v.*) Dh. 97. *cp. next.*

*pôsa, *m.* (= purisa, porisa; arisen by contraction, perhaps influenced by the verb poseti, *v. next*) a man; *nom.* ~o, Dh. 228; purisa (metrically = posa) *voc.* Dh. 248; *gen.* ~assa, Dh. 104.

*posāpeti, *vb.* (*caus. II.* poseti, to feed, nourish; *sa.* poshayati, √push) to rear, bring up (*acc.*); *ger.* ~etvā (kumārikaṁ) 48,20. *cp.* puṭṭha, *mfn.*

plavati, *vb.*, *v.* palavati (pilavati).

Ph.

phandana, *mfn.* (*sa.* spandana) moving (suddenly), quivering, trembling; *n.* ~aṁ (cittaṁ) Dh. 33 (*synon.* capala). *cp.* pari-phandati.

pharati, *vb.* (*sa.* √sphar (sphur)) to spread, extend (*trans. & intr.*); to pervade, suffuse, fill up (*acc.*); *aor. 3. sg.* phari (hatthiṁ mettena cittena) 76,34; *ger.* ~itvā (rasaharaṇiyo) 57,23; *pp.* phuṭa & phuṭṭha (*q. v.*).

pharasu, *m.* (*sa.* paraçu) an axe; *nom.* ~u, 35,5; *acc.* ~uṁ, 35,7; — *dim.* *pharasuka, *m.* 35,5 (vāsi-⁰, *q. v.*).

pharusa, *mfn.* (*sa.* parusha) harsh, cruel; *acc. f.* ~aṁ (vedanaṁ) Dh. 138; *n.* ~aṁ, Dh. 133 (of speech); *instr. m. pl.* ~ehi (yakkhehi) 41,34.

phala, *n.* (= *sa.*) fruit; *metaph.* consequence, result (good or bad), retribution, reward, advantage; [1]) *pl.* ~āni, 2,23; 1,13 (kasaṭa-⁰); *gen. pl.* ~ānaṁ (madhura-⁰) 1,15; pakka-phala-⁰, ripe fruits, 2,1; ⁰-rukkha, *m.* a fruit tree, *instr. pl.* ~ehi, 2,20; *cp.* phalāphala below; — [2]) *nom. acc.* ~aṁ, 17,26 (pāpassa); 29,10 (sīlassa); 58,13 (puññānaṁ); 42,14 (kataviriyassa, samijjhati); 42,18 (viriya-⁰); *⁰-paṭisedhana, *n.* (*q. v.*); sakadāgāmi-⁰, 29,17 & sotāpatti-⁰, 87,1 (*v. h.*); magga-phala-nibbānāni, *n. pl.* (*dvandva comp.*) *v.* nibbāna; — at the end of *adj. comp.* phala is often spelled with 'pph', *v.* kaṭuka-pphala, madhura-⁰, maha-⁰, *cp.* a-phala & sa-phala, *mfn.*

phalaka, *n.* (= *sa.*) a board, plank; *nom.* ~aṁ (apassena-⁰, *q. v.*) 84,16; *instr.* ~ena, 20,23; *loc.* ~e, 20,1; 48,8 (*rajata-⁰, a silver table for dicing).

phalati, *vb.* [1]) (*sa.* √phal) to burst open, split asunder; *aor. 3. pl.* ~iṁsu (devadundubhiyo) 80,30; *pp.* phalita (*q. v.*); *caus.* phāleti (*q. v.*). — [2]) (sometimes written phallati; *sa.* phalati, ~te, *denom. fr.* phala) to bear fruit, ripen; *pr. 3. sg.* phallati (dummedho, phalāni kaṭṭhakassêva) Dh. 164.

*phalāphala, *n.* (*sg. & pl.*) various kinds of fruits (*cp.* phala); ~aṁ, 1,15; 2,7 (tava ~ taṁ eva hotu, 'only keep all those fruits to yourself'); *instr.* ~ena, 18,15. *cp.* maggāmagga [Tr. PM. p. 74].

phaḷika, *m.* (*sa.* sphaṭika) crystal; *⁰-vimāna, *n.* a crystal palace; 23,15.

phalita, *mfn.* [1]) (*pp.* phalati; = *sa.*) burst, split; bearing fruit; *instr. n.* ~ena (hadayena) 59,10. — [2]) grey; *n.* grey hair (through confusion with palita (*q. v.*), because the grey hairs split and fall off).

phallati, *vb.*, *v.* phalati.

phassa, *m.* (*sa.* sparça) touch, contact; *nom.* ~o, 66,8 (saḷāyatana-paccayā); ⁰-nirodha, *m.* 66,14 (*v. h.*); ⁰-paccayā, 66,8 (*v.* paccaya). *cp.* phusati.

phāṇita, *n.* (= *sa.*) the juice of the sugar cane, molasses, sugar; *⁰-bindu, *n.* a drop of molasses, 53,18; *⁰-sakaṭa, *n.* a cart-load of m., 53,20; *dvandva-comp.* madhu-phāṇitehi (*instr. pl.*) 53,17; madhu-phāṇita-pūve (*acc. pl.*) 53,21.

*phāli-, only in *comp.* phāli-phulla, *mfn.*, which seems to be either an intensive formation of *vb.* phalati, or a *dvandva-comp.* phālin (= *sa.* phalin, bearing fruit) + phulla (= *sa.* flowery); at any rate, preceeded by words like sabba or eka as it is always found, it means 'flowery all over', or 'with fruits and flowers all over'; sabbaṁ eka-phāliphullaṁ [*scil.* Lumbini-vanaṁ] ahosi ɔ: it was in full blow, 62,11.

phāleti, *vb.* (*caus.* phalati; *sa.* phālayati) to split, break (*trans. w. acc.*); *part. m.* ~ento (hadayaṁ) 27,5; *ger.* ~etvā (pasibbakaṁ) 12,31.

***phāsu**, *n.* [& *adj.*?] (either from *prāsu, *i. e.* pra + asu, or from *ved. sa.* prāçu, quick) health, healthiness; ease, comfort; Vin. I, 92,24. Jāt. II, 394,18. *cp. next.*

***phāsuka**, *mfn.* (*fr. last*) agreeable. comfortable, pleasant; °-ṭṭhāne (*loc.*) on a pleasant spot, 35,26; a-phāsuka, *mfn.* (*v. h.*). The etymology of phāsu & phāsuka has often been discussed; *Childers* derives it from *sa.* spārha (√spṛh), but see the objections of *Weber*, Ind. Str. III, 396, and *Sénart*, Journ. As. 1876, II, 485 (referring to *Buddh. sa.* sparça); *Trenckner*, PM. p. 81,20, takes it = *ved. sa.* prāçu; *Jacobi* refers to *Prâkr.* phāsuya, *sa.* prāsuka (from pra + asu) ZDMG. 34, p. 311; *Pischel*, Gr. § 208, to √spṛç, *sparçuka.

phāsukā, *f.* (*sa.* parçukā, pārçukā & pārçvaka, *m.*) a rib; *pl.* ~ā, Dh. 154 (*metaph.* said of the rafters of a house).

phuṭa, *mfn.* (*pp.* pharati, *cp. sa.* sphuṭa; it is often written puṭṭha & phuṭṭha, *q. v. cp.* MN. I, 276, Note) thrilled, pervaded, filled with (*instr.*); *m.* ~o (manasā, thoughtful? = pūrito, Comm.) Dh. 218.

phuṭṭha, *mfn.* [1]) = phuṭa (*v. above*); *m.* ~o (mettena cittena) 76,35. – [2]) = phusita (*pp.* √spṛç, sprshṭa) touched; *m. pl.* ~ā (sukhena) Dh. 83; tamba-bhūmi-rajo-°, 112,29 (*v.* corrections). *cp.* phusati, phoṭṭhabba.

phulla, *mfn.* (= *sa.*) blown (as a flower); *v.* phāli-° *above*, *cp.* phalati.

phusati, *vb.* (*sa.* √spṛç) to touch; to reach, attain (*acc.*); *pr. 1. sg.* ~āmi (nekkhamma-sukhaṁ) Dh. 272; *3. pl.* ~anti (nibbānaṁ) Dh. 23; *pot. 3. pl.* ~eyyu, Dh. 133; *pp. v. next*; *grd. v.* phoṭṭhabba; *cp.* phassa & phuṭṭha.

phusita, *mfn.* (= phuṭṭha, *pp.* phusati, *q.v.*) touched, reached, attained; *m.* ~o (mayā, maggo) 108,14.

pheggu, *f.* (? = *sa.* phalgu; *cp. sa.* velli = valli, Tr.) brittle or weak wood, fibrous wood, bast (?); *nom.* ~u, 95,22; apagata-phegguka, *mfn.* "free from the unsound wood", *m.* ~o, 95,24.

pheṇa, *m.* (*sa.* phena & pheṇa) foam, scum; pheṇūpama, *mfn.* (*sa.* phenopama) resembling scum; *acc. m.* ~aṁ (kāyaṁ) Dh. 46.

phoṭṭhabba, *m.* (& *n.*) (*orig. grd. fr.* phusati, *q. v.*; *sa.* sprashṭavya, *n.*) touch, contact; *pl.* the objects of contact; *nom. pl.* ~ā, 70,32; *loc.* ~esu, 71,10. *cp.* phassa.

B.

baka, *m.* (= *sa.*) a heron, crane; *nom.* ~o, 4,1 *etc.* – °-jātaka, *n.* 3,28.

bajjhati, *vb.* (*pass.* bandhati; *sa.* badhyate) to be bound or tied, to be ensnared or caught; *ger.* ~itvā (pāse) 11,30.

baddha, *mfn.* (*pp.* bandhati; = *sa.*) bound. tied; ensnared, caught; *m.* ~o (bandhanāgāre) 46,20; Dh. 324; *f.* ~ā, 104,30; *°-rāva. *m.* the cry of one who has been caught, *acc.* ~aṁ (ravi) 11,30; *āḷhā-°, *mfn.* 111,10 (*q. v.*); *bhaṇḍika-°, *mfn.* 34,12 (*q. v.*).

bandha, *m.* (= *sa.*) binding, bond; emprisonment; vadha-°, Dh. 399 (*v. h.*); hatthi-bandha, *v.* bhaṇḍa.

bandhati, *vb.* (*sa.* √bandh) to bind, tie; catch, ensnare; to bind round, put on (*acc.*), bandage (*acc. & instr.*); *imp. 3. pl.* ~antu (paṇṇasaññaṁ)

8,8; *aor.* *3. sg.* bandhi (mukhaṁ) 50,14; *3. pl.* ~iṁsu (veraṁ, aññamaññaṁ, "nursed enmity") 11,20; *ger.* ~itvā (dvāraṁ) 6,5; (te devasaṁkhalikāya) 21,14; (rājānaṁ gāḷhabandhanaṁ) 39,31; (mukhaṁ sāṭakena) 50,12; (kāyabandhanaṁ) 82,28; *caus. II.* bandhāpeti, *pass.* bajjhati, *pp.* baddha (*q. v.*) *cp.* bandha, bandhana, *etc.*

bandhana, *n.* (= *sa.*) binding, bond, fetter; *nom.* ~aṁ, 64,7; 23,32 (pañcaṅgika-⁰, *q. v.*); *abl.* ~ā, 33,2; Dh. 276 (Māra-⁰); *pl.* ~āni, 105,19; kāya-⁰, *n.* (*q. v.*); *gāḷha-⁰, *mfn.* (*q. v.*); *paṇṇa-bandhana-sañña, *n.* (*v.* paṇṇa); bandhanāgāra, *n.* a prison; *abl.* ~ato, 32,1; *loc.* ~e, 46,20.

bandhava, *m.* (*sa.* bāndhava) a kinsman, relative; *pl.* ~ā, Dh. 288.

*bandhāpeti, *vb.* (*caus. II.* bandhati) to cause to bind or bandage (*acc.*); *ger.* ~āpetvā (mukhaṁ) 50,15.

bandhu, *m.* (= *sa.*) a kinsman, relative; a friend; *voc.* ~u, 103,13 (pamatta-⁰, *q. v.*); *instr.* ~unā, Dh. p. 94, v. 3 (ādicca-⁰, *q. v.*).

babbaja, *m.*, *v.* pabbaja.

bala, *n.* (= *sa.*) power, strength, force; military force, army; *nom.* ~aṁ, Dh. 109; 13,35 (yaṁ ~aṁ ahuvamhase, "according to what power we had"); *acc.* ~aṁ, 10,18; 60,20 (reinforcement); *instr.* ~ena (mahantena) 36,28; *e. c. mfn. v.* khanti-⁰, nāga-⁰, *cp.* a-bala, dub-bala, *etc.* – *balappatta, *mfn.* mighty (*i. e.* by wisdom), *m.* ~o (Tathāgato) 80,25; – balānīka, *mfn.* 'who has strength for his army', strongminded; *acc. m.* ~aṁ, Dh. 399. *cp. next etc.*

*bala-vāhana, *n.* military force, army; *acc.* ~aṁ, 39,8; *instr.* ~ena, 38,24.

balava (& balava*t*), *mfn.* (*sa.* balavat) powerful, strong; ~aṁ (mayā katapāpaṁ) 17,17.

bali*n*, *mfn.* (= *sa.*) powerful, strong; *m.* ~ī, Dh. 280.

balivadda, *m.* (*sa.* balivarda) a bull, ox; *nom.* ~o, Dh. 152; *acc. pl.* ~e, 71,31; *instr. pl.* ~ehi, 71,32.

balya, *n.* (*sa.* bālya) foolishness, stupidity; *nom. acc.* ~aṁ, 54,21. Dh. 63. *cp.* bāla.

bahala, *mfn.* (= *sa.*) thick (of consistence), dense, compact, firm, deep (as water) *etc.*; ati-bahala, *mfn.* (*q. v.*).

bahi, *adv.* (*sa.* bahis) out, outside; ~ nikkhante, 50,6; 52,2 (apart from that place, *viz.* khāditaṭṭhānaṁ; but here bahi is perhaps an error for bahu. *cp.* bahu-tiṇassa, 51,33); *comp.* bahinagare (*loc.*) outside the city, 39,20. 43,9. 73,34 (*opp.* antonagare); *bahivalañjanaka, *m. pl.* out-door people, *acc.* ~e, 43,8 (*v.* valañja). *cp.* bāhira & *next.*

bahiddhā, *adv.* (*sa.* bahirdhā) outside (*abl.*), from outside; *⁰-samuṭṭhāna, *mfn.* 'originating from outside', resulting in outward behaviour (*i. e.* in good manners); *n.* ~aṁ (ottappaṁ) 10,16 (*opp.* ajjhatta-⁰).

bahu, *mfn.* (= *sa.*) much (many), great, frequent, abundant; *n.* ~u & ~uṁ, Dh. 258 (bahu bhāsati); ~uṁ (dhanaṁ) 23,6; (apuññaṁ) 76,3; (nāvaṭṭhaṁ) 111,32; taṁ ~ yaṁ hi jīvasi, it is a wonder that you are still alive, 13,29; *instr. m.* ~unā, Dh. 166; *n. pl.* ~ūni, 49,16; *m. pl.* ~ū (macchā) 3,33; ~avo, Dh. 307; *instr. pl.* ~ūhi, 91,22; *gen. pl.* ~unnaṁ, 23,27; ~ūnaṁ, 108,21; *comp.* bahumige, 6,5; ⁰-bhattaṁ, 57,11, *etc.* (*v. below*); *cp.* bahuka, bahula, bāhu-⁰, bhiyyo (*compar.*), bhiyyoso, yebhuyyena.

*bahu-abhiññāta, *mfn.* highly esteemed; *m. pl.* ~ā (sāvakā) 109,19.

bahuka, *mfn.* (= *sa.*) much, many; *acc. m.* ~aṁ (janaṁ) 108,12.

bahu-jana, *m.* (= *sa.*; sometimes written bahujjana, metri causa or after the analogy of puthujjana; *Fausbøll*, Das. Jāt. p. 28) many people; *nom.* ~o, 88,32; Dh. 320 (-jj-).

*bahu-jāgara, *mfn.*, very watchful, awake; *m.* ~o (*opp.* sutta) Dh. 29. *cp.* jāgarati.

bahujjana, *v.* bahu-jana.

bahu-tiṇa, *n.* (*sa.* bahu-tṛṇa) abundant grass, beautiful pasture; *gen.* ~assa, 51,33 (= manāpassa tiṇassa 52,3).

*bahu-dvāra, *mfn.*, having many doors or gates; *loc. n.* ~asmiṁ (nagare) 91,22.

*bahu-buddhi, *mfn.*, wily, cunning, crafty; *f. gen. pl.* ~īnaṁ (thīnaṁ) 51,30.

*bahu-bhāṇin, *mfn.*, who speaks much; *acc. m.* ~inaṁ, Dh. 227.

*bahu-bhāva, *m.*, quantity, abundance; *acc.* ~aṁ, 49,19.

bahula, *mfn.* (= *sa.*) much, large, abundant; *e. c.* abounding in; pāmojja-°, *mfn.* full of delight, *m.* ~o, Dh. 376. *cp.* sambahula.

*bahu-saṁkappa, *mfn.*, having many purposes, full of schemes; *acc.* ~aṁ (kāyaṁ) Dh. 147.

bahussuta, *mfn.* (*sa.* bahu-çruta) very learned; *m.* ~o (Ānando) 109,18; *acc.* ~aṁ, Dh. 208; *gen. pl. m.* ~ānaṁ, 109,7. *cp.* bāhusacca.

*bahūpakāra, *mfn.*, very useful (*v.* upakāra); *m.* ~o (amhākaṁ, sakuṇo) 18,12.

bādhita, *mfn.* (= *sa.*; *pp.* bādhati, √bādh, to press, pain, vex) pained, oppressed; *m.* ~o (saso, "a snared hare") Dh. 342. *cp.* bībhaccha.

Bārāṇasī (& ~i), *f.* (*sa.* Vārāṇasī) *nom. pr.* of the city Benares; *abl.* ~iyā (avidūre) 36,20; *loc.* ~iyaṁ, 1,2; °-rājā (~i) the king of B., 5,32, *etc.*; °-rajja, *n.* (~i) the kingdom of B., 38,23; °-rajja-sāmika, *m.* king of B., 43,22.

bāla, *mfn.* (= *sa.*) ignorant, foolish; *m.* ~o, 2,7. 54,16; *voc.* ~a, 44,30; *acc.* ~aṁ (yathā) 75,23; 106,22 = Dh. 71; *pl.* ~ā, 54,12; *gen. pl.* ~ānaṁ, 107,10 = Dh. 60; *comp.* °-suṁsumāra (*voc.*) 2,5; °-rājā, 54,6; °-mahājano (many unconverted) 74,14; *andha-°, *mfn.* (*v. h.*); *°-saṅgatacārin, *mfn.* "walking in the company of fools", *m.* ~ī, Dh. 207; °-vagga, *m.* the fifth chapter of Dhpd. – *compar.* bālatara, *mfn.* 54,22 (*m.* ~o) *cp. next* & balya, *n.*

bālatā, *f.* (= *sa.*) stupidity, foolishness; *instr.* ~āya (attano, on account of their foolishness) 5,9.

*bālisika (& bāḷisika), *m.* (*fr.* balisa or baḷisa, *m.* a fish-hook; *sa.* baḍiça & vaḍiça) a fisherman, angler; *nom.* ~o, 14,22.

*Bāveru, *f.* (?) *nom. pr.* of a city (perhaps = Babylon, *cp. Minayeff,* Bull. de l'Acad. de St. Pétersbourg, T. 17, p. 70 (Mél. As. VI 591): *Morris,* JPTS '91–93. p. 25; *Franke,* ZDMG. 47. Bd. p. 606); *acc.* ~uṁ, 18,34; °-jātaka, *n.* 18,1; °-raṭṭha, *n.* the kingdom of B. 18,4-5.

bāhā, *f.* (= bāhu, *sa.* bāhu, *m.*) the arm; *pl. acc.* ~ā, 30,19; *instr.* ~āhi, 20,6; *pacchā-bāhaṁ, *adv.* (*v. h.*) *cp. Franke,* Pāli u. Sanskr. p. 102.

bāhita, *mfn.* (*pp.* bāheti, *q. v.*) removed; *°-pāpa, *mfn.* 'who has got rid of evil', *m.* ~o ti brāhmaṇo (intended to be the etymology of the word brāhmaṇa. *cp. Franke,* Pāli u. Sanskr. p. 117) Dh. 388.

bāhira, *mfn.* (*fr.* bahi; *sa.* bāhya. *cp.* bāhīka) being outside (one's self, one's body, house, or family); being outside the Buddhistic order, non-Buddhistic; *n.* ~aṁ, the exterior (*opp.* abbhantaraṁ) 106,11 = Dh. 394; *m.* ~o (samaṇo n'atthi, "there is no Samaṇa beyond the order" [just as there is no path through the air]) Dh. 254–55 (*var.* bāhire, *loc. adv.*) *cp.* bāhiya (~ika), Jāt. I 421,23 & III 432,23, which probably is a *nom. pr.* (*cp. Müller,* Pāli Gr. p. 31.)

bāhu, *m.* & *f.* (also bāhā, *f.* (*q. v.*); *sa.* bāhu. *m.*) the arm; *v.* Sīhabāhu, *nom. pr.*

*bāhusacca, *n.* (*fr.* bahussuta, *sa.* bahu-çruta, rather than fr. *bahusati (*sa.* *bahu-smṛti) which is not found in Pāli) much learning, erudition; *instr.* ~ena, Dh. 271 (*cp.* Dhpd. (1855) p. 381; Tr. PM. p. 75, corrections).

bāheti, *vb.* (*sa.* barhayati. *caus.* √bṛh (Tr.), if not *denom. fr.* bahi (*Weber*, ZDMG. 14,82) *cp.* also √bādh & √vāh) to tear out, eradicate, remove (*acc.*); *ger.* ~etvā (puññañ ca pāpañ ca) 106,6 = Dh. 267; *pp.* bāhita (*q. v.*).

bindu, *m.* & *n.* (= *sa.*) a drop; *nom.* ~u (uda-°) 108,2 = Dh. 336; ~uṁ (madhu-°, phāṇita-°, *q. v.*) 53,18; uda-bindu-nipātena, Dh. 121.

bimba, *m. n.* (= *sa.*) an image (as a picture or statue); *acc.* ~aṁ (said of the human body) Dh. 147.

biḷāra, *m.* (*sa.* biḍāla) a cat; *°-nissakkana-matta, *mfn.* just large enough that a cat can sneak out through it, *n.* ~aṁ (pākāra-vivaraṁ) 90,35.

bībhaccha, *mfn.* (*sa.* bībhatsa) loathsome, disgusting; °-sambādhaṭṭhāna, *n.* 65,7 (*q. v.*).

bīraṇa, *n.* (*sa.* vīraṇa) name of a fragrant grass (Andropogon Muricatum); ~aṁ, 107,33 = Dh. 335 (its root is called usīra, 108,4).

bujjhati, *vb.* (*sa.* √budh) to know, perceive, understand (*acc.*), to be conscious of; *pr. 3. sg.* ~ati (*w. part.* pāpāni kammāni karaṁ, "when he commits evil deeds") Dh. 136; (do. rahokammaṁ āvikubbaṁ, "when he openly does what ought to be secret") 54,17; (antarāyaṁ) Dh. 286; *pp.* buddha, *mfn.* intelligent, wise, enlightened (*esp. subst. m. & nom. pr.*, *v. next*); *acc.* ~aṁ, Dh. 398. *cp.* buddhi, bodhi, *etc.*

Buddha, *m.* (= *sa*; *pp.* bujjhati, *q. v.*) a Buddha, *i. e.* a person who has attained to infinite knowledge, and who is liberated from all existence, so that he shall not be born again; *nom. pr.* 'the Buddha' (*i. e.* Gotama, *q. v.*) mostly mentioned by epithets like Bhagavat, Satthar, Sugata (*q. v.*) *cp.* Tathāgata & Sammāsambuddha; ~o (viya) 113,21; yadi ~o tiṭṭheyya ("if the B. were alive") 98,33; ~o bhagavā, 66,2; ~o dhammarājā pabhaṁkaro, 19,1; ~o bhavissati loke vivattacchaddo, 61,33; ~o tapati tejasā, 107,25 = Dh. 387; mahā-Gotama-°, 87,8; *acc.* ~aṁ (anantagocaraṁ) Dh. 179; *gen.* ~assa (viya) 113,20; *loc.* ~e (in the formula B., dhamma, saṁgha, *cp.* 107,17) 79,17; *pl. instr.* ~ehi, 102,34; *gen.* ~ānaṁ, 68,22. 74,15. 86,24. 108,20 (metri causa: Buddhāna). *comp. v. next etc.*

*Buddha-gata, *mfn.*, directed to Buddha; *f.* ~ā (sati) Dh. 296.

*Buddha-ghosa, *m. nom. pr.* of a Buddhist teacher, author of several commentaries on canonical books (living about 420 A. D.); *nom.* ~o (ti naṁ viyākaruṁ, Buddhassa viya gambhīraghosattā) 113,21.

*Buddha-desita, *mfn.*, taught by the Buddha; *acc. m.* ~aṁ (dhammañ ca vinayañ ca) 109,25.

*Buddhantara, *n.*, a period between two Buddhas; *acc.* ~aṁ (ekaṁ) 84,30. (*cp.* antara.)

Buddha-manta, *m.* (*sa.* °-mantra) a sacred text of the Buddha; ~o, 113,16.

*Buddha-līḷhā, *f.*, the grace or charm of a Buddha; *instr.* ~āya (dhammaṁ desetvā) 7,27. 47,17.

*Buddha-vagga, *m.*, the title of chapter XIV. of Dhpd.

Buddha-vacana, *n.* (= *sa.*) the word of the Buddha, the holy texts; *acc.* ~aṁ (karotha) 108,6; *loc.* ~e (tepiṭake) 102,2.

*Buddha-vīra, *m.*, 'the enlightened hero' (Buddha); *voc.* ~a, 108,11.

*Buddha-seṭṭha, *m.*, 'the best of Buddhas' (Buddha); *gen.* ~assa, 109,23.

*Buddhārammaṇa, *mfn.*, *v.* ārammaṇa.

buddhi, *f.* (= *sa.*) intelligence, insight; *v.* dubbuddhi & babubuddhi, *mfn. cp. next.*

buddhimat, *mfn.* (= *sa.*) endowed with insight, wise; *m.* ~mā, 113,24; *pl.* ~manto, 76,32.

***Buddhuppāda**, *m.*, the appearance or birth of a Buddha, the period after the appearance of a Buddha; *gen.* ~assa abhāvā, because the Buddha had not appeared, 63,31; *loc.* ~e (imasmiṁ) in the present Buddha-period, 84,31.

bubbula, *m.* & *n.* (*sa.* budbuda) a bubble; *dimin.* bubbulaka, *m.* & *n.*, id., *acc.* ~aṁ, Dh. 170; (*cp. Morris,* JPTS. '84,89).

bojjhaṅga, *m.* (*sa.* bodhy-aṅga, *n.*) one of the seven faculties necessary for attaining perfect knowledge (or Buddhahood), *viz.* sati, dhamma-vicaya, viriya, pīti, passaddhi, samādhi, upekhā; *pl.* ~ā (satta) 82,12; *acc. pl.* ~e, 91,8. *cp.* sambodhi-aṅga.

bodhi, *m.* & *f.* (= *sa.*) [1]) *f.* perfect knowledge (possessed by a Buddha), Buddhahood; *v.* bojjhaṅga, *cp.* sambodhi; [2]) *m.* the sacred tree under which Buddhahood is achieved, a Bo-tree; °-rukkha-mūle, *loc.* at the foot of the Bo-tree, 66,3; *cp.* Mahābodhi & *next.*

***Bodhimaṇḍa**, *m.* or *n.* (?) the terrace of the great Bo-tree in Magadha; °-samīpambhi (*loc.*) near B., 113,2.

Bodhisatta, *m.* (*sa.* Bodhisattva) one who is destined to become a Buddha, the Buddha in any of his anterior births; ~o, 1,3; *acc.* ~aṁ, 2,27; *gen.* ~assa, 1,6; *abl.* ~ato, 8,10.

***bondi**, *f.* (& *m.*) (probably akin to *sa.* budhna) the body; *nom.* ~i (mahatī) 2,12 (= sarīra, 2,7). *cp. Prákr.* boṁdi, buṁdi; *Kuhn,* Beitr. p. 41; *Morris,* JPTS. '89,207.

bya- *etc.*, *v.* vya-.

brahma-cariya, *n.* (*sa.* brahmacarya) a holy or religious life, holiness, purity, chastity (sometimes = the Buddhism or the Buddhist religious system and practice); *nom.* ~aṁ (vusitaṁ) 71,15; *acc.* ~aṁ (cara, "lead a holy life") 70,16. 92,3; *°-vāsa, *m.* the living a religious life; *nom.* ~o, 92,27; *gen.* ~assa (kālo) 46,35. — *°ādi-brahmacariyika, *mfn.* (*v.* ādi [1])) *cp. next etc.*

brahmacariyavat, *mfn.* (*sa.* brahmacaryavat) who leads a holy life, practising chastity; *nom. m.* ~vā, 106,6 = Dh. 267.

brahmacārin, *m.* (= *sa.*) one who leads a religious life, who practises chastity, a priest; *nom.* ~ī, 30,19. Dh. 142; sa-brahmacārī (*m. pl.*) 96,30 ("fellow-priests").

brahmaññatā, *f.* (*sa.* brahmaṇyatā) [1]) friendliness towards Brahmans; [2]) the state of a Brahman; *nom.* ~tā, Dh. 332.

brahma-daṇḍa, *m.* (= *sa.*) name of a certain kind of punishment imposed by the order on a Bhikkhu; *nom.* ~o, 79,13-14 ("the Bhikkhus should neither speak to him, nor exhort him, nor admonish him", 79,15) *cp.* Vin. II p. 290; *Kern,* Manual of Indian Buddhism, p. 87.

Brahma-datta, *m.* (= *sa.*) *nom. pr.* of several mythic kings in Benares; *loc.* ~e, 1,2. 2,17, *etc.*; °-kumāro, 42,34; °-mahārājā, 43,22.

Brahman, *m.* (= *sa.*) the god Brahma; *nom.* ~ā, 110,11; ~ Sahampati, 80,21; *instr.* ~unā, Dh. 105; Mahā-°, *id.* (*v. h.*) *cp.* sa-brahmaka, *mfn.* & *next.*

Brahma-loka, *m.* (= *sa.*) the world or heaven of Brahma; *loc.* ~e, 45,16; *°-ûpaga, *mfn.* going to B.; *m.* ~o, 45,18 (*cp.* upaga); *°-parāyana, *mfn.* destined for B.; *m.* ~o, 47,33.

brahma-vihāra, *m.* (= *sa.*) one of the four perfect states of mind (*viz.* mettā, karuṇā, muditā, upekhā); *acc. pl.* ~e (bhāvetvā) 45,15-18.

brāhmaṇa, *m.* (= *sa.*) a man belonging to the priestly caste, a Brāhman; *nom.* ~o, 9,9. 92,10; 106,8 = Dh. 393 *etc.* (in a moral sense); *acc.*

~aṁ, 30,9; *gen.* ~assa, 9,9. 66,20; *voc.* ~ā (metri causa), 30,12; *pl.* ~ā, 61,30; *gen.* ~ānaṁ, 61,26; purohita-°, 51,19 (*q. v.*); *°-pāmokkha, *mfn.* (*q. v.*); *°-māṇava, *m.* a young Br., *nom.* ~o, 113,2; *°-vesena (*instr.*) in the disguise of a Br., 15,10; *°-vagga, *m.* title of Dhpd. ch. XXVI; – *dvandva comp.* samaṇa-°, 19,2; amacca-°-gahapatike, 42,3; °-gahapatikesu, 7,25 (*cp.* gahapati); sa-ssamaṇa-brāhmaṇa, *mfn.* (*q. v.*).

brāhmaṇī, *f.* (= *sa.*) a Brāhman's wife, 9,10; *acc.* ~iṁ. 9,14.

brūti, *vb.* (*sa.* brūte & bravīti, √brū) to say, reply; to speak to (*acc.*); to tell (*acc.* & *gen.*); to call (*w. double acc.*); *pr. 1. sg.* brūmi (tan te, = kathemi) 85,25-28; 106,13 (taṁ brāhmaṇaṁ) = Dh. 395; 106,34; *aor. 3. sg.* a) a-bravi (Māraṁ) 103,12; b) a-bruvi, 110,31; 111,9.

brūheti, *vb.* (*sa.* bṛṁhayati, *caus.* √bṛṁh) to increase, further, promote, cherish, practise (*acc.*); *imp. 2. sg.* ~aya (santimaggaṁ) Dh. 285.

Bh.

bhakkha, 1) *mfn.* (*e. c.*; *sa.* bhaksha) eating or drinking; *lohita-°, *mfn.* blood-drinking; *gen.* ~assa. 13,28; *pīti-°, *mfn.* (*q. v.*). – 2) *m.* (*sa.* bhaksha, *m.* or bhakshya, *grd.*) food; ~o si mama ("thou art my prey") 111,10.

bhakkheti, *vb.* (*sa.* bhakshayati, √bhaksh) to eat, devour; *inf.* ~etuṁ, 111,11; *pp.* ~ita, *m. gen. pl.* ~ānaṁ (vāṇijānaṁ) 111,32; bhakkha. *mfn.* (*v. above*).

bhagavat, *mfn.* (= *sa.*) illustrious, venerable, holy; *esp. m.* used as a term of veneration by Buddhists when speaking of Buddha, "the Blessed one"; *nom.* Buddho bhagavā or only Bhagavā, 66,2-3-5. 104,23. 108,17; *acc.* ~vantaṁ, 68,17. 104,11; *instr.* ~vatā, 69,18; *gen. abl.* ~vato, 76,1; 68,11; *loc.* ~vati, 74,32; 92,2 ("under the Blessed one").

bhaginī, *f.* (= *sa.*) a sister; also used as a term of address to any woman (or said of a woman of the order); *voc.* ~i, 73,5; *instr.* ~iyā (kaniṭṭha-°) 56,36; *°-~i-putta, *m.* a nephew; *v.* ati-bhagini-putta. *cp.* bhāgineyya.

bhagga, *mfn.* (*pp.* bhañjati; *sa.* bhagna) broken; *n.* ~aṁ, 30,17. 53,30; *f. pl.* ~ā, Dh. 154.

bhaṅga, *m.* (= *sa.*) breaking, breach; bending, fold; *nom.* ~o, 83,11; *acc.* ~aṁ (sarīra-°) 47,16.

bhacca, *m.* (*sa.* bhṛtya, *grd.* √bhṛ) a servant, attendant; *acc.* ~aṁ (taṁ taṁ) 112,23; *pl.* ~ā, 111,18; *acc. pl.* ~e, 111,19; *instr. pl.* ~ehi, 111,20.

bhajati, *vb.* (*sa.* √bhaj) to partake of, recur to, keep company with, frequent, follow, practise (*acc.*); *pr. 3. sg.* ~ati (padesaṁ) Dh. 303; *part. med. gen. m. sg.* ~mānassa, Dh. 76; *imp. 2. sg. med.* ~assu (mitte) Dh. 375; *pot. 3. sg.* bhaje, Dh. 76. 78; *3. sg. med.* ~etha, Dh. 78. 208; *caus.* bhājeti (*q. v.*).

bhañjati, *vb.* (*sa.* √bhañj) to break, bend; to defeat (*acc.*); *pr. 1. sg.* ~āmi (senaṁ) 104,6; *part. m. pl.* ~antā (aṭṭhīni) 8,29; *aor. 3. sg.* (mā) bhañji (vo) 108,5; *pp.* bhagga (*q. v.*) *cp.* bhaṅga, *m.*

bhaññati, *vb.* (*pass.* bhaṇati. *q. v.*).

bhaṇati, *vb.* (*sa.* √bhaṇ) to speak, say; to recite, propound (*acc.*); *pr. 3. sg.* ~ati (musā) 97,11; *1. sg.* ~āmi (do.) 98,21; *1. sg. med.* bhaṇe (*v. next*); *part. m.* ~aṁ, 103,11 (imā gāthā); Dh. 264 (alikaṁ); *part. med. m.* ~ māno, 83,4; *gen.* ~ mānassa, 83,3; *imp. 2. sg.* bhaṇa, 11,13; *pot. 3. sg.* bhaṇe (saccaṁ) Dh. 224; *1. sg.* bhaṇeyy'āhaṁ, 11,11; *aor. 1. sg.* abhāṇiṁ (an old augmented formation) 47,8; *pass.* bhaññati, *loc. n. part.* bhaññamāne (veyyākaraṇasmiṁ) 71,17;

pp. n. bhaṇitaṁ (alikaṁ tassa, *scil.* mayā) 108,30. *cp.* bhāṇaka, bhāṇin.

bhaṇe, *indecl.* (*orig. pr. 1. sg. med. fr.* bhaṇati) *lit.* 'I say', look here! my friends! a term of address used by a superior to inferiors (the latter answer with 'bhante', *q. v.*); mayaṁ kho ~, 76,10; tena hi ~, 76,12.

bhaṇḍa, [1]) *n.* (*sa.* bhāṇḍa) *sg.* & *pl.* goods, wares, things; utensils, implements, instruments, ornaments, *etc.*; *nom.* ~aṁ, 30,17; *acc.* ~aṁ (appaggha-°, "wares of a little value") 26,2; (piya-°, "anything that is dear") 54,34; *pl.* ~āni (turiya-°, "musical instruments") 65,5. — [2]) *m.* (*c. c.* = bandha) a keeper, groom (*cp. sa.* bhaṇḍa); *hatthi-°, *m.* an elephant-keeper (= *hatthi-bandha, *cp. sa.* açva-bandha) *pl.* ~ā, 76,15; *acc. pl.* ~e, 76,10. *cp.* SBE. XVII, 141, Note [2].

bhaṇḍaka, *n.* (*sa.* bhāṇḍaka) = bhaṇḍa, *n.*; *assa-°, 65,17 (horse-trappings).

bhaṇḍikā, *f.* (*sa.* bhāṇḍikā) a bundle, a small packet; *acc.* ~aṁ, 8,17. 33,7; sahassa-°, a purse of 1000 pieces, 23,1 (*cp.* sahassa-ṭhavika, 102,24); — *bhaṇḍika-baddha, *mfn.* packed, bundled up; *gen.* ~assa (dhanassa) 34,12.

bhata, *mfn.* (*sa.* bhṛta, *pp.* bharati) 'born', brought up, reared, supported; *f.* ~ā (bhariyā) 51,4; *atta-vetana-°, *v.* attan.

bhataka, *m.* (*sa.* bhṛtaka) a servant; *nom.* ~o, 105,8.

bhati, *f.* (*sa.* bhṛti) wages, hire, support; service for wages; *instr.* ~iyā, 105,9.

bhatta, *n.* (*sa.* bhakta) a meal, ration; food, *esp.* boiled rice; *nom. acc.* ~aṁ, 78,3; 21,5. 33,25. 53,30. 70,10. 76,11; bahu-°, 57,11; *pacchā-°, 86,5; *pātarāsa-°, 57,9; *mataka-°, 16,23 (*v. h.*); *ratti-°, 15,19; *loc.* ~e, 57,27; ~asmiṁ, Dh. 185; *pl.* ~āni, 111,33; — *comp.* *bhatta-kāraka, *m.* (*sa.* bhatta-kāra) a cook; *nom.* ~o, 6,20; — bhatta-kicca, *n.* preparations for a meal; °-âvasāne, *loc.* (*v.* avasāna) after the meal, 86,15; — *bhatta-pāti, *f.* a rice-bowl, *acc.* ~iṁ, 34,13; — *bhatta-sakaṭa, *n.* a cart-load of rice, 53,30.

bhadanta, *m.* (= *sa.*) a venerable person, a term esp. used in addressing (or mentioning) a Buddhist priest, often equal to *pron. 2. pers.* (but with the verb in *3. sg.*); kathaṁ ~o ñāyati, "how is your reverence named", 96,29. [bhadanta (also often written bhaddanta) seems to be a later formation from the *voc.* bhadante, which has probably arisen from the phrase bhaddaṁ (or bhadraṁ) te (*q. v.*) and has been contracted into bhante (*v. below*); *cp. Windisch* Māra und Buddha, p. 68; Tr. PM. p. 69–70; *Weber*, Bhag. II, 155 & I, 418; *Sénart*, Kacc. p. 115 (II, 4,35); *Pischel*, Gr. § 366[b].]

bhadda (& **bhadra**), *mfn.* (*sa.* bhadra) happy, good, pleasant, beautiful; *m.* ~ro (a good man, *opp.* pāpo), Dh. 120; *acc.* ~raṁ (assaṁ) Dh. 380; *f.* ~ā (mātā) 20,25; *voc. f.* ~e (my dear!) 1,8; *n.* ~raṁ, happiness, Dh. 119; *pl.* ~rāni (good things) Dh. 120; *n.* ~aṁ is often used with *gen. pron. 2. pers.* parenthetically in a sentence, meaning 'if you please', 'let it be said with all deference', 'sit venia verbo' and the like: na me ruccati bhaddaṁ vo, 11,16; taṁ vo vadāmi bhaddaṁ vo, 108,3 (*cp. sa.* bhadraṁ te (vaḥ) & bhadanta *above*).

bhaddaka, *mfn.* (*sa.* bhadraka) = bhadda: *m.* su-bhaddako (catuppado), very pleasant or lovely, 30,8.

bhanta, *mfn.* (*pp.* bhamati; *sa.* bhrānta) wandering, moving, or rolling about (unsteadily); *acc. m.* ~aṁ (rathaṁ) 106,33 = Dh. 222.

***bhante**, *indecl.* (*fr.* bhadanta, *q. v.*) a term of address to superiors or venerable persons: reverend sir, your reverence! [1]) = *voc.* 28,12 (to

Buddha); 35,8 (tāpasa); evaṁ ~, 76,14 (Devadatta); 79,10 (an elder bhikkhu ought to be addressed by bhante or āyasmā); 85,29 (Nārada); kinnāmo si ~, 96,29; – 2) = *nom.* ~ Bhagavā, 69,4 (with *3. sg.* of the verb). [bhante has generally been considered as a Magadhism, from *sa.* bhavant- (*Weber, Trenckner & Franke,* KZ. XIV, p. 419), from which also bhadanta (*v. above*) possibly might have arisen through insertion of an inorganic 'd'; but I think it will be impossible to arrive at a true historical view of the various terms of address, bhagavā, bhavaṁ (bhonto, *etc.*), bhadanto (~te), bhante, bhaṇe, which seem to be connected with one another phraseologically as well as etymologically.]

bhabba, *mfn.* (*grd.* bhavati; *sa.* bhavya) future, what probably will be or ought to be, suitable, proper; *w. inf.* being able to; *m.* ~o (kāme paribhuñjituṁ) 70,1; a-bhabba, *mfn.* (*q. v.*).

bhamati, *vb.* (*sa.* √bhram) to wander about, to move to and fro (on account of perplexity); *caus.* bhameti, to swing, agitate, perplex; *imp. 2. sg. med.* bhamassu, Dh. 371, seems to be used as *imp. 3. sg.*, but perhaps we have here an old error; the Mss. Khar. reads mā te kāmaguṇā bhamemsu cittaṁ, which seems to prove that we ought to read kāmaguṇā bhamiṁsu (*aor. 3. pl.*) or bhamesuṁ (*aor. 3. pl. caus.*).

bhamara, *m.* (*sa.* bhramara) a bee; ~o, 106,3 = Dh. 49; °-gaṇā, swarms of bees, 62,13 (pañcavaṇṇa-°).

bhaya, 1) *n.* (= *sa.*) fear, danger; *nom.* ~aṁ, 53,10. 110,32. Dh. 283; *instr.* bhayena, from fear, 13,15. 43,7, often at the end of *comp.*: geha-patana-°, 19,16; niraya-°, 17,30; maraṇa-°, 6,21; rukkha-nibbattana-°, 37,5 (*q. v.*) *cp.* a-kuto-bhaya, a-bhaya, mahā-bhaya, *mfn.*; – *°-janana, *mfn.* (*q. v.*); – bhayaṭṭha, *mfn.* (*sa.* bhaya-stha) terrified, *f.* ~ā, 111,26; – *°-tajjita, *mfn.* (*q. v.*); – °-dassin & *°-dassivas, *mfn.* seeing danger, fearing; *nom. m.* ~vā, Dh. 31; *pl.* ~ino, Dh. 317; – *°-bhīta, *mfn.* & *°-saṅkita, *mfn.* frightened, alarmed (*v. h.*) – 2) *mfn.* dangerous; *acc. m.* ~aṁ (maggaṁ) Dh. 123.

bharati, *vb.* (*sa.* √bhṛ) to bear, support, hire; *cp. next etc.*, bhāra, bhacca, bhata(ka), bhati.

bharita, *mfn.* (= *sa.*) filled with (*e. c.*); vippaviddha-nānākuṇapa-°, *mfn.* 65,10 (*v. h.*).

bhariyā, *f.* (*sa.* bhāryā) a wife; *nom.* ~yā, 1,5. 51,4; *acc.* ~yaṁ, 101,18; *gen.* (*dat. loc.*) ~yāya, 1,22; 54,29 (metri causa contracted to bhariyā); 58,2 (dovārika-°).

Bharukaccha, *n.* (*sa. id.* & Bhṛgukaccha) *nom. pr.* of a seaport-town in Western India (Baroach, Βαρυγαζα); *nom.* ~aṁ (nāma paṭṭanagāmo) 24,9; *°-paṭṭanaṁ, 25,12; *°-payāta, *mfn.* 20,22 (*v.* payāti); *°-vāṇija, *m.* 19,24 (*q. v.*).

*Bharu-raṭṭha, *n. nom. pr.* of a country; *loc.* ~e, 24,9. – *Bharu-rājan, *m.* the king of that country; *nom.* ~ rājā nāma, 24,9.

bhava, *m.* (= *sa.*) 1) coming into existence, birth; existence, any mode of existence, being, life; *nom.* ~o (upādāna-paccayā) 66,9; °-paccayā (jāti) 66,10; *gen.* ~assa (pāragū) Dh. 348; *loc.* ~e (purima-°, in a former life) 58,11; *pl.* tayo bhavā, "the three modes of existence", *viz.* sensual, corporeal, formless existence, or existence in the three worlds kāma-, rūpa-, arūpa-loka, 65,11 (*cp.* kāma. bhava, vibhava 67,14); – *°-taṇhā, *f.* thirst for existence, 67,14; *°-nirodha, *m.* cessation of ex., 66,18; *°-sallāni, *n. pl.* "the thorns of life", Dh. 351; kāmā-°, taṇhā-°, nandī-° (*v. h.*) – 2) increase, welfare, prosperity (*opp.* vibhava, *q. v.*); *dat.* ~āya, Dh. 282. – *cp.* bhāva, punabbhava, *etc.*

bhavaṁ, *pron.* (*orig. part.* bhavat

fr. next; *sa.* bhavān, *m.* & bhavatī, *f.*) thou, you (used as a respectful term of address, often comb. with the name of the person addressed, but mostly with the *3. pers.* of the verb); *nom.* ~aṁ (Gotamo) 90,19. 93,27; (*acc.* bhavantaṁ); *instr.* bhotā (Gotamena) 90,15; *gen.* bhoto (Gotamassa) 94,6; (*loc.* bhavati); *pl. nom. voc. acc.* bhonto (or bhavanto, *nom.*, bhavante, *acc.*) : suṇantu me ~o, 97,3; (*instr. pl.* bhavantehi; *gen. pl.* bhavantānaṁ, or bhavataṁ). As *voc. sg.* & *pl.* we have a contracted form bho (*q. v. separately below*).

bhavati, *vb.* (*sa.* √bhū; very often contracted to hoti, *q. v.*) to be, exist, stay, become, arise, come into, *etc.* (also used as auxiliary verb); *pr. 3. sg.* ~ati, Dh. 375; *3. pl.* ~anti (jāti-paccayā) 66,11; 111,4; *pr. 1. pl. med.* bhavāmase, 105,26; *part. v.* bhavaṁ *above*; *imp. 2. sg.* bhava (*cp.* hohi) Dh. 236; *2. pl.* bhavātha (*var.* ~atha) Dh. 143; *pot. 3. sg.* bhaveyya, 1,25; *1. sg.* ~eyyaṁ, 56,5; *2. sg.* ~eyyāsi, 86,3; *aor.* ahu, ahosi, *etc.*, *v.* hoti; *fut. 3. sg.* bhavissati (*cp.* hessati) = will be, 'must be', or 'is probably', 'is certainly' : 32,26. 87,3. 99,7, etc.; 12,27. 34,3 (vassāpitaṁ ~); 40,22 (gahito ~); 56,30 (laddhaṁ ~ maññe); also in questions and answers : kiṁ- ~ (supinaṁ) 61,29; kin nu kho ~ (kumārikā) "how may she be"? 86,29; evaṁ ~, 56,15; *fut. 2. sg.* ~issasi, 46,14. 56,12; *1. sg.* ~issāmi, 23,29; *3. pl.* ~issanti, 6,28. 21,11-27. 33,27 (imaṁ dhanaṁ dve koṭṭhāsā ~, *pl.* instead of *sg.*); *1. pl.* ~issāma, 21,12; – *cond. 3. sg.* a-bhavissa, 42,11. 92,28; bhavissa, 29,8; – *inf.* bhavituṁ, 24,24. 56,4; – *ger. v.* hutvā (under hoti); – *grd.* bhavitabba, *mfn.* (*cp.* hotabba & bhabba) *n.* ~aṁ (used like *fut.* in *pass.* construction) 24,2 (iminâpi āgatena ~ = ayam pi āgato bhavissati); 34,4-10. 47,13. 48,26. 91,23, *etc.*; *acc. n.* ~am ev'etaṁ kathesi, "you tell of what must be", 47,11 (*cp.* kālikaṁ, 47,10); – *pp.* bhūta (*q. v.*); – *caus.* bhāveti (*q. v.*) *cp.* bhava. bhāva, *m.*, bhavana, *n.*

bhavana, *n.* (= *sa.*) house (palace), home, abode (world); *acc.* ~aṁ (attano) 19,18; *loc.* ~e, 41,29; asura-°, tāvatiṁsa-°, nāga-°, Sakka-°, supaṇṇa-° (*v. h.*).

bhasta, *m.* (*sa.* basta) a he-goat; *acc.* ~aṁ, 54,16 (*cp.* Jāt. VI, 12,2; Abhidh. has vasso).

bhasma, *n.* (*sa.* bhasman) ashes; *°-âchanna, *mfn.* 106,22 (*v.* āchanna).

bhassati, *vb.* (*sa.* √bhraṁç) to fall down, drop; to swoop down, go on shore; to take a road, lounge about; *aor. 3. sg.* bhassi (adho Gaṅgaṁ) 14,24; (tassa matthakaṁ) 24,5; *aor. 3. sg. med.* a-bhassatha (vīṇā kacchā) 104,17 (*cp. Kuhn*, Beitr. p. 110).

bhāga, *m.* (= *sa.*) 1) a part, fraction (often *comp. v.* numbers, *v.* catu-bhāga, ti-bhāga & sahassa-°); – 2) a portion, share, lot; task, business, wages, salary; (*v.* ācariya-°); – 3) place, region, side, quarter (*v.* upari-°, kaṇṇa-°, bhūmi-°, *cp.* sabbato-bhāgena, *instr. adv.*); – 4) time, division of time (*v.* ratti-°, *cp.* aparabhāge, *loc. adv.*) *cp.* bhaga, *etc.*, sobhagga.

*bhāgavat, *mfn.* (*fr. prec.*) partaking of, having a share in (*gen.*); *nom. m.* ~vā (sāmaññassa) Dh. 19. 20.

bhāgineyya, *m.* (*sa.* bhāgineya) a sister's son, nephew; °-haṁsapotakassa (*gen.*) a young haṁsa, a nephew of his, 10,21. *cp.* bhaginī.

bhājana, *n.* (= *sa.*) a vessel, an earthen jug; *acc.* ~aṁ, 82,19.

bhājeti, *vb.* (*caus.* bhajati; *sa.* bhājayati) to divide, distribute (*acc.*); *inf.* ~etuṁ (matamanussaṁ) 40,32; *ger.* ~etvā, 27,29. *cp.* bhāga, bhājana.

bhāṇaka, *m.* (= *sa.*; *fr.* bhaṇati) a reciter, repeater, declarer; *Dīgha-°, *m.* (*q. v.*).

bhāṇavāra, *n.* (& *m.*) a section

of the holy texts, which are divided into such sections for purpose of recitation; paṭhamaka-°aṁ, the first section of Dhpd. containing ch. I–XIV; Dh. 196.

*bhāṇin, *mfn.* (*fr.* bhaṇati) saying, speaking; *v.* bahu-°, mañju-°, manta-°, mita-°, *mfn.*

bhātar, *m.* (*sa.* bhrātṛ) a brother; *nom.* ~tā, 108,15; 9,7 (kaniṭṭha-°); *acc.* ~taraṁ, 31,30; *instr.* ~tarā, 31,31; *nom. pl.* ~taro, 31,13. 34,32.

bhātika, *m.* (*sa.* bhrātṛka) a brother; *acc.* ~aṁ (jeṭṭhaka-°) 32,21; *gen.* ~assa (jeṭṭha-°) 35,20.

bhāyati, *vb.* (*sa.* √bhī, bibheti & bhayate) to fear, be afraid of (*gen.*); *pr. 3. pl.* ~anti (maccuno) Dh. 129; *aor. 2. sg.* (mā) bhāyi, 1,10. 4,30. 75,20; *2. pl.* (mā) bhāyittha, 32,24. 76,26; *pp.* bhīta (*q. v.*); *ger.* bhāyitvā (kassa) 98,13. *cp.* bhaya, bhiṁsanaka, bhīru, bherava.

bhāra, *m.* (= *sa.*) burden, load; trouble, labour; task, charge; *nom.* ~o (mayhaṁ ~, or mayhaṁ esa ~, "let it be my charge, leave that to me") 42,6. 49,30; imassa sukha-dukkhaṁ tava ~o, "look after him in better and worse", 28,20; khāri-°, *m.* & panna-°, *mfn.* (*v. h.*).

bhāraka, *m.* (?) (= *sa.*) burden, load; only in the *comp.* *gadrabha-°, *m.* (?) [1]) an ass-driver; [2]) goods carried by an ass, *instr.* ~ena vohāraṁ karonto, 8,16.

bhāva, *m.* (= *sa.*) [1]) being, becoming, appearance, state, condition, nature; *nom.* ~o (thīnaṁ) 51,31. — [2]) do., at the end of *comp.* (*subst. m.*): [a]) *w. adj.*: tittaka-°, duggata-°, dubbaca-°, nihata-māna-°, paṇḍita-°, bahu-°, sapariggaha-apariggaha-°, samāna-vaya-°, sassāmika-°, sithila-°, suddha-° (*q. v.*); — [b]) *w. adv.*: tathā-° (*q. v.*); — [c]) *w. subst.* (*cp.* dhamma): atta-°, mitta-°, sotthi-°, & likewise with the verb atthi, *3. sg.*: atthi-° (*q. v.*) — khuracakka-° (= "that it was") 24,6; yakkhini-°, 21,26 (do.) *cp.* hāva-bhāva (*q. v.*) 21,13; — [d]) *w. pp.* or *grd.* (which in English is expressed by a full sentence: "that it was . . .", or "that it ought to be"): āgata-°, gata-°, gahita-°, bhinna-°, mārita-°, vañcita-°, hattha-gata-°; chaḍḍetabba-° (*q. v.*); — [e]) *similarly w. nom. actionis*: avattharaṇa-°, āgamana-°, an-āgamana-°, gamana-°, nikkhamana-°, maraṇa-° (*q. v.*) *cp.* tuṇhī-bhāva & pātu-bhāva, *m.*; a-bhāva, *m.* & an-abhāva-kata, *mfn.*

bhāvanā, *f.* (= *sa.*) [1]) producing, acquiring, mastering, developing (one's own mental faculties), meditation; *acc.* ~aṁ (anuyuñjati, "applies himself to meditation") 97,9; *loc.* ~āya (attanā bhāvita-°) 29,2; (rato mano) Dh. 301; — [2]) veneration, respect, praise, reputation; *acc.* ~aṁ (asataṁ, metri causa bhāvan') Dh. 73.

bhāvita, *mfn.* (*pp. fr. next*; = *sa.*) produced, developed, cultivated, practised; *f.* ~ā (maraṇa-sati) 86,20; °-bhāvanāya (pattiṁ, "the powers I have developed") 29,2; — bhāvitatta(*n*), *mfn.* (*sa.* bhāvitātman) one who has trained himself (by meditation); *acc.* ~ānaṁ, Dh. 106. *cp.* a-bhāvita, su-bhāvita, *mfn.*

bhāveti (& bhāvayati), *vb.* (*caus.* bhavati; *sa.* bhāvayati) to produce, develop, cultivate, apply oneself to (*acc.*); *pr. 3. sg.* ~eti (metri causa bhāvayati) Dh. 350 (asubhaṁ); *imp. 2. pl.* (or *pot. 3. sg. med.*) ~etha (mettaṁ) 40,8; (maraṇa-satiṁ) 86,17; *pot. 3. sg. med.* ~etha (paṇḍito) Dh. 87; *aor. 3. sg.* ~esi, 86,25; *inf.* ~etuṁ, ib.; *ger.* ~etvā (brahma-vihāre) 45,15; (bojjhaṅge) 91,8; *pp.* bhāvita, *v. above*; bhāvanā, *f.* (*q. v.*).

bhāsati, *vb.* (*sa.* √bhāsh) to speak, talk; to say, pronounce, recite (*acc.*); *pr. 3. sg.* ~ati, 22,3; Dh. 1–2 (metrically = ~atī; Dh. 258; *2. sg.* ~asi (alikaṁ) 97,31; *part. m.* ~māno, 103,4; Dh. 19; *imp. 2. sg. med.* bhāsassu, 98,20; *pot. 3. sg.* bhāse (gāthā sataṁ) Dh. 102; *fut. 1. sg.* ~issāmi (gāthaṁ) 87,1; *aor. 3. sg.* abhāsi, 13,30. 80,22; *3. sg. med.* abhāsatha, 105,22; *pp.* bhāsita (*q. v.*) *cp. next.*

bhāsā, *f.* (*sa.* bhāshā) language (*esp.* vernacular), dialect; *loc.* ~āya (Sīhala-°, in the Sinhalese language) 113,31; mūla-bhāsāya (*abl.* or *instr.*?) 114,28 (*v.* mūla); sabba-bhāsa, *mfn.* (*v. h.*).

bhāsita, *mfn.* (*pp.* bhāsati) said, spoken; *n.* ~aṁ, 98,28; *gen.* ~assa (atthaṁ) 90,30. *n. subst.* ~aṁ, speech, word, Dh. 363; 93,18; *cp.* dubbhāsita, subhāsita, *mfn.*

*bhiṁsanaka, *mfn.* (*fr. sa.* bhīshaṇa & bhīshma) terrible; *m.* ~o, 27,6 (saddo); 80,20 (bhūmicālo); *n.* (*subst.*?) ~aṁ, 81,3.

bhikkhati, *vb.* (*sa.* √bhiksh, bhikshate) to beg, ask for, *esp.* to beg alms (from, *acc.*); *pr. 3. sg. med.* ~ate (pare, "others") 106,4 = Dh. 266. *cp. next etc.*

bhikkhā, *f.* (*sa.* bhikshā) the act of begging alms; *dat.* ~āya (caranto) 29,24.

bhikkhu, *m.* (*sa.* bhikshu) a mendicant, a Buddhist monk or priest; *nom.* ~u, 79,8. 106,4 = Dh. 266; Dh. 75 (Buddhassa sāvako); *acc.* ~uṁ, Dh. 362; *instr.* ~unā, 79,8; *gen.* ~uno, 79,12; eka-bhikkhussa, 79,17; *pl. nom.* ~ū, 29,28; ~avo, 109,16; *voc.* ~ave, 29,30. 70,25; ~avo, Dh. 243; *acc.* ~ū, 66,24; *instr.* ~ūhi, 79,15; — *°-vagga, *m.* title of Dhpd. ch. XXV; — °-sata, *n.* 79,33; °-sahassa, *n.* 70,22 (*q. v.*); °-saṁgha, *m.* the congregation of Buddhist monks, the Buddhist brotherhood; *gen.* ~assa, 72,27; *instr.* ~ena, 70,21; *loc.* ~e, 29,27; *pl.* ~ā, 109,2.

bhikkhunī, *f.* (*sa.* bhikshuṇī) a Buddhist nun; *instr.* ~iyā, 98,28.

bhiṁkāra, *m.* (*sa.* bhṛṅgāra) a pitcher, bowl or vase (golden); *instr.* ~ena (suvaṇṇa-°) 41,11.

bhijjati, *vb.* (*pass.* bhindati) to be broken or wrecked; to be scattered or dispersed; *pr. 3. sg.* ~ati, 107,8 = Dh. 148; *fut. 3. sg.* ~issati (nāvā) 19,30; *1. pl.* ~issāma (tattha tatth'eva) 11,8.

bhitti, *f.* (= *sa.*) a wall; *nom.* ~i (kaṇṇakitā) 84,20.

*bhindāpeti, *vb.* (*caus. II.* bhindati) to cause to be broken (*acc.*); *fut. 1. sg.* ~essāmi (sīlaṁ assā) 48,26.

bhindati, *vb.* (*sa.* √bhid) to break, cut asunder, destroy, disturb, violate (*acc.*); *part. m.* ~anto (ghaṭaṁ) 16,29; (sotāni) 27,5; *pot. 3. sg.* ~eyya (mettiṁ) 53,9; *aor. 3. sg.* bhindi (nāvaṁ) 20,1; ~ituṁ (rañño vacanaṁ, to disobey) 40,8; (itthiyā sīlaṁ, to seduce) 48,28; ~itvā, 10,14 (hirottappaṁ); 50,5. 58,28 (dvidhā); *pp.* bhinna; *grd.* bhejja; *caus. II.* bhindāpeti (*q. v.*) *cp.* bheda.

bhinna, *mfn.* (*pp.* bhindati; = *sa.*) [1]) broken, destroyed, violated; wrecked; *n.* ~aṁ (bhaṇḍaṁ) 30,17; *f.* ~ā (nāvā) 20,23. 28,22; *loc.* ~āya (nāvāya) 28,16; bhinna-nāva, *mfn.* (*cp. sa.* bhinnanau) shipwrecked; *m. pl.* ~ā, 21,9; *gen.* ~ānaṁ, 20,33. — [2]) separate, different, deviating; *-rūpa, *mfn. id.*; *m. pl.* ~ā (ācariya-vādā, "the schismatic doctrines of old teachers"?) 113,27.

bhiyyo, *adv.* (*sa.* bhūyas; *compar. fr.* bahu) [1]) more, still more; ~ cittaṁ pasīdati, 103,21; ~ nandati, 107,27 = Dh. 18; — [2]) once more, again; ~ opammaṁ karohi ("give another illustration") 99,27. *cp. next* & yebhuyyena.

bhiyyoso, *adv.* (*sa.* bhūyaças) still more; only in the *comp.* *bhiyyosomattāya (*v.* mattā, *f.*, *cp. buddh. sa.* bhūyasyā mātrayā) in still higher degree, 65,8.

bhisakka, *m.* (*sa.* bhishaj) a physician; *acc.* ~aṁ, 92,8. (As to the form *cp. sa.* a-tvak-ka) *cp.* bhesajja.

bhisi, *f.* (*sa.* bṛsī) a cushion, roll, pad; *nom.* ~ī, 104,30 (baddhā hi ~ susaṁkhatā; in this sentence bhisi seems to be somewhat ambiguous; could it also mean a sort of cushion, made of twisted grass. used instead of a swimming-girdle? *Fausbøll*, SBE. X, (2) p. 4, translates it by 'raft'; *cp.* SBE. XX, p. 163. Note 3); *instr.* ~iyā, 104,31.

bhīta, *mfn.* (*pp.* bhāyati; = *sa.*) frightened, terrified (*w. gen.* or *e. c.*); *m.* ~o (tāsaṁ) 21,33; (maraṇa-bhaya-°) 8,26; 75,17; *m. pl.* ~ā, 40,10; 17,31 (niraya-bhaya-°); bhīta-tasitā, *m. pl.* *dvandva comp.* 27,5; °-puriso, 86,19 (āsīvisaṁ disvā ~).

bhīru, *mfn.* (= *sa.*) timid, cowardly; *subst. f.* bhīrū, cowardice, 103,27 (chaṭṭhā [senā Mārassa]). *cp.* bherava.

bhuñjati, *vb.* (*sa.* √bhuj) to enjoy, eat (*acc.*, rarely *instr.*), to take a meal; to swallow, devour (*acc.*); *pr. 3. sg.* ~ati (vinā maṁsena na ~) 6,1; Dh. 324; *3. pl.* ~anti, 57,10; *part. gen. m.* ~antassa (sāyamāsaṁ) 53,29; *imp. 2. pl.* ~atha (bhattaṁ) 21,5; *pot. 3. sg.* ~eyya, 101,3. 107,2 = Dh. 308; *3. sg. med.* ~etha, Dh. 70; *aor. 3. sg.* bhuñji, 41,10. 57,15; *1. sg.* bhuñjiṁ, 101,8; *3. pl.* a-bhuñjisuṁ, 111,34; *ger.* [a]) bhutvā, 15,15; [b]) bhuñjitvā, 21,7 (khāditvā ~); 57,15; 61,7 (bhojanaṁ); 78,29 (bhattaṁ); [c]) bhuñjiya, 111,35; *pp.* bhutta (*q. v.*); *grd. v.* bhojanīya; *caus.* bhojeti (*q. v.*) *cp.* bhoga[2], bhojana.

bhutta, *mfn.* (*pp.* bhuñjati; *sa.* bhukta) [1]) enjoyed, eaten; *m. pl.* ~ā (me kāmā) 45,5; *m.* ~o (ayoguḷo, "swallowed") 107,1 = Dh. 308; *°-pātarāsa, *mfn.* (*v. h.*); — [2]) one who has eaten; *gen. sg.* ~assa (*w. instr.* sūkaramaddavena) 78,31.

***bhuttāvi(n)**, *mfn.* (*fr. last*) one who has enjoyed or eaten (*acc.*), who has finished the meal; *gen. m.* ~vissa (bhattaṁ) 78,24; 83,14.

bhutvā, *ger. v.* bhuñjati.

bhumma, [1]) *mfn.* (*sa.* bhūmya, *cp.* bhauma) belonging to the earth. — [2]) *comp.* = bhūmi, *f.* (arisen through bhummi? or from the old *loc.* bhumyā, Jāt. I, 507,12. V, 84,12, *etc.*); *bhumma-ṭṭha, *mfn.* standing on the ground; *acc. m. pl.* ~e, Dh. 28; — *bhumma-ttharaṇa. *n.*. 'floor covering', a carpet; ~aṁ, 84,17. *cp.* bhūma.

bhusa[1], *mfn.* (*sa.* bhṛça) strong, vehement, excessive; *m. pl.* ~ā (sotā) Dh. 339.

bhusa[2], *n.* (*sa.* busa) chaff; ~aṁ (viya) 53,2; yathā ~aṁ, 106,17 = Dh. 252.

bhūta, *mfn.* (*pp.* bhavati; = *sa.*) [1]) being, existing, real, true; become, happened; *n.* ~aṁ, 9,29 (*opp.* a-bhūtaṁ, *q. v.*); 101,30. — [2]) *subst. m. n.* any living being; *pl. m.* ~ā (sabbe) 80,23; *n.* ~āni, Dh. 131; *loc.* ~esu. Dh. 405. — [3]) *e. c.* being, being like (sometimes almost pleonast.): [a]) *agārika-°, *aṇḍa-°, *andha-°, *tanu-°, *saṁkāra-°, *mfn.* (*v. h.*); [b]) -ī-bhūta: *v.* tuṇhī-°, *samaṅgi-°, sammukhī-°, sīti-°; *cp.* yathā-bhūta (°-bhucca) & pahūta.

°**bhūma** & °**bhūmaka**, *mfn.* (only *e. c.* = bhūmi, *cp. sa.* bhūmikā & bhumma *above*): satta-bhūmaka, *mfn.* (*sa.* sapta-bhūma. & °-bhūmika) having 7 stories; *n.* ~aṁ (gehaṁ) 48,31.

bhūmi, *f.* (= *sa.*) [1]) the earth, soil, ground; *nom.* ~i (acalā) 110,7; *acc.* ~iṁ, 6,11; (otiṇṇā, gone on shore) 112,27; *loc.* ~iyā (on the ground) 61,25. 83,19. 97,34; ~iyaṁ, 5,12. 53,19. 56,27 (katvā); tamba-°, 112,29 (*q. v.*); *°-cāla, *m.* (*cp. sa.* bhūmi-cala) an earthquake; *nom.* ~o (mahā-°) 80,19. — [2]) the floor of a house; 84,21; story (of a house) *v.* bhūma. — [3]) a territory, country; *v.* *ariya-°, *uyyāna-°, paccanta-°, Suvaṇṇa-°. — [4]) place; *°-rāmaṇeyyaka, *n.* a delightful place, Dh. 98 (*q. v.*); ukkāra-°, 18,31 (*q. v.*); °-bhāga, *m.* place, quarter, stall (of a horse); *loc.* ~e, 65,19. — [5]) step, stage; *acc.* ~iṁ (yathāviditaṁ, "stage of knowledge") 69,23. [Burm. writing bhummi; *cp.* bhumma & bhūma *above*.]

bhūri, [1]) *mfn.* (= *sa.*) much, great (only at the beginning of *comp.*). — [2]) *f.* knowledge, intelligence; *nom.* ~ī, Dh. 282 (yogā jāyati); *°-saṁkhaya, *m.* loss of knowledge, *nom.* ~o, Dh. 282.

*bhūsita, *mfn.* (*pp.* °bhūseti, √bhūsh) adorned, decorated; *f.* ~ā (sabbābharaṇa-°) 112,1.

bhejja, *mfn.* (*grd.* bhindati; *sa.* bhedya) to be broken or destroyed; a-bhejja, *mfn.* 39,12 (*q. v.*).

bheda, *m.* (= *sa.*) breaking, destroying, dissolving; *abl.* ~ā (kāyassa), "when this body is dissolved", 7,26. Dh. 140.

bhedana, *n.* (= *sa.*) = *prec.*; *acc.* ~aṁ (sarīrassa) "injury of the body", Dh. 138.

bherava, *mfn.* (*fr.* bhīru; *sa.* bhairava) terrible; *n. subst.* horror, terror; *~rava, *m.* a cry of horror; *acc.* ~aṁ (ravantā) 86,19.

bheri, *f.* (= *sa.*) a drum, kettle-drum; *acc.* ~iṁ, 35,13; (carāpetvā) 42,2. 102,26 (used generally by proclamations); *gen.* ~iyā, 36,15; °-tale, 35,21.

bhesajja, *n.* (*sa.* bhaishajya) medicament, medicine; *comp.* gilāna-paccaya-°, 97,8. *cp.* bhisakka.

bho, *indecl.* (*sa.* bhos) a vocative particle, orig. *voc.* of bhavaṁ (*q. v.*), used in addressing one or more persons: O! Hallo! I say, look here! [1]) *with a foll. voc.* bho pāsāṇa, 3,7; kiṁ bho pāsāṇa (vānarinda) 3,9-11; bho purisa, 23,34. 101,6; bho corā, 32,34; bho yakkhā, 40,36; [2]) *without voc.* ehi bho, 24,3; aho vata bho, 42,17; dhi-r-atthu vata bho, 63,13; upaddutaṁ vata bho, 65,12; nâhaṁ bho gāmaṁ jhāpemi, 101,7; ayaṁ bho ko nu dīpo, 110,31; – bhovādin, *v. below. cp.* ambho & hambho.

bhoga[1], *m.* (= *sa.*) a curve, fold; *acc.* ~aṁ (orato katvā) 83,21. *cp.* obhoga & bhogga.

bhoga[2], *m.* (= *sa.*) enjoyment, use, advantage; wealth, riches, treasures; *pl.* ~ā, Dh. 355; *gen.* ~ānaṁ, Dh. 139; °-taṇhā, *f.* "thirst for riches", Dh. 355 (*instr.* ~āya); yaso-bhoga-samappita, *mfn.* (*q. v.*).

*Bhoga-nagara, *n. nom. pr.* of a town (from bhoga[1], in the sense of 'serpent'); *loc.* ~e, 77,15.

bhogga, *mfn.* (*sa.* bhugna) bent, crooked; gopānasī-bhogga-sama, *mfn.* 47,22 (*q. v.*).

bhojana, *n.* (= *sa.*) [1]) enjoying, eating; *vikāla-°, eating at forbidden times; *abl.* ~ā. 81,24 (*cp.* vikāla). – [2]) a meal, food (*esp.* boiled rice); *acc.* ~aṁ, Dh. 70; 20,7 (dibba-°); 41,9 (nānaggarasa-°); 61,7 (vara-°); pāna-bhojanaṁ, food and drink. Dh. 249; – *pariññāta-°, *mfn.* (*q. v.*).

bhojaniya, *n.* (*sa.* bhojanīya; *grd.* bhuñjati) soft food (as boiled rice, gruel, soft cake, meat *etc.*, *opp.* khādaniya, *q. v.*); *acc.* ~aṁ, 78,2; khādaniya-°, 18,30.

bhovādin, *mfn.* (= *sa.*) one who addresses another person by 'bho' (as non-Buddhists used to address Buddha; hence sometimes = a Brahman); *m.* ~ī (bhovādi nāma) Dh. 396. *cp.* Tr. PM. p. 70; differently *Weber*, Ind. Str. I, 181.

M.

m, [1]) by sandhi instead of ṁ: vuddhim anvāya, 2,18; āgacchantam eva, 2,31, *etc.* – [2]) an old m (ṁ) is sometimes preserved by sandhi, *e. g.* tuṇhīm āsīnaṁ, Dh. 227. – [3]) inserted in *comp.*: nāga-m-āsado, 77,3; okam-okato. Dh. 34; do. metri causa: bhūmiṁ-rāmaṇeyyakaṁ, Dh. 98; *cp.* aññam-aññaṁ. – [4]) inserted between two words (not *comp.*): jeyya-m-attānaṁ, 107,4 = Dh. 103; apassi-m-uttiṇṇapadaṁ, 111,17; idh'eva-m-eso, Dh. 247; sammati-m-eva, Dh. 390; *cp.* saṅgaṁ, Dh. 412 (Tr. PM. 82). – [5]) m', abbreviation of me = mama, 112,20. [*Windisch*, Ber. d. sächs. Ges. 1893, p. 228.]

maṁsa, *n.* (*sa.* māṁsa) flesh, meat; *nom.* ~aṁ, 82,2 = 97,20; *acc.*

~aṁ, 1,7 (hadaya-⁰); 15,7 (sarīra-⁰); *instr.* ~ena. 6,1; 18,14 (maccha-⁰); *loc.* ~e. (hadaya-⁰) 1,6; — *maṁsa-sūla, *n. & m.* a spit with roasted meat, or 'a bit of roasted meat' (*cp. sa.* çūlya-māṁsa, *n.*; *Morris*, JPTS. '84,91); *n. pl.* ~āni, 14,29; *m. pl.* ~ā, 15,20; *acc. m. pl.* ~e, 14,32; — maṁsa-lohita-, flesh and blood. Dh. 150 (*v.* lepana).

makara, *m.* (= *sa.*) a certain sea monster or fabulous fish (delphin, sword-fish; corresponding to the capricorn of the zodiac); *nom.* ~o, 20,1; *instr. pl.* ~ehi (bhinnā nāvā) 20,23.

makasa, *m.* (*sa.* maçaka) a mosquito, gnat, fly; *andhaka-⁰, *m.* (*q. v.*).

makkaṭa, *m.* (*sa.* markaṭa) a monkey; *nom.* ~o, 14,10.

makkaṭaka, *m.* (*sa.* markaṭaka) a spider; *nom.* ~o. Dh. 347.

makkha, *m.* (*sa.* mraksha & maksha) hypocrisy, dissimulation; *nom.* ~o, 103,28. Dh. 150. 407.

makkhikā, *f.* (*sa.* makshikā) a fly; *acc.* ~aṁ, 53,23; nimmakkhika, *mfn.* (*q. v.*).

makkhita, *mfn.* (*pp. fr. next*; *sa.* mrakshita) smeared (with *instr.* or *e. c.*); *n.* ~aṁ (lohita-⁰, mukhaṁ) 12,21; *m. pl.* ~ā (asucinā) 62,26, *opp.* a-makkhito, 62,29; *instr.* ~ehi (kaddama-⁰, "mud-stained") 71,29.

makkheti, *vb.* (*caus.* √mraksh) to besmear (*acc.*) with (*instr.*); *ger.* ~etvā (mukhaṁ mattikāya) 83,32; *pp.* makkhita, *v. above*; *cp.* makkha.

*Makhādeva, *m. nom. pr.* of a king; ~o (rājā Mithilāyaṁ) 44,19; *voc.* ~a, 44,31; ⁰-amba-vana (& -vanuyyāna), 45,7-14 (*q. v.*).

magga, *m.* (rarely *n.*) (*sa.* mārga) [1]) track, road, way; *nom.* ~o (gamana-⁰, way to go or escape) 3,14; *acc.* ~aṁ (āgacchanto, "on the way") 28,12; 62,6; (ācikkhitvā) 56,34; (tiṁsa-yojana-⁰ āgato) 87,19; (Jetavana-⁰) 73,15; *instr.* ~ena (aññena, "by another way") 12,30; *abl.* ~ā (uyyāhi, "make way") 44,3; *loc.* ~e, 33,18; (sakaṭa-⁰, "carriage-road") 43,18; (gamana-⁰) 60,7; *gen. pl.* ~ānaṁ (metri causa maggān') Dh. 273; — mahā-⁰, *m.* a highroad; *instr.* ~ena, 34,4. 43,14: *loc.* ~e, 34,5; — hatthi-⁰, *m.* an elephant track. 35,11. — [2]) *in the dogmatics*: the path or way (leading to emancipation from the misery of existence; *nom.* ~o (ariyo aṭṭhaṅgiko, "the holy eightfold path") 67,3, etc.; ~o visuddhiyā. "the way that leads to purity", 107,12 = Dh. 277 (*cp.* Visuddhi-magga); *acc.* ~aṁ (nibbānagamanaṁ) Dh. 289; *loc.* ~e (the fourth link of the series: Buddha. dhamma, saṁgha, *etc.*, *cp.* paṭipadā) 79,18; *dvandva comp.* ⁰-phala-nibbānāni, 97,10; ⁰-vagga, *m.* title of Dhpd. ch. XX; santi-maggaṁ (*acc.*) "the path of peace", Dh. 285. *cp. next.*

*maggāmagga, *m.* (*sg.* or *comp.*) 'various paths', the various parts of 'the path' (or the best of paths?); *gen.* ~assa (kovidaṁ) Dh. 403. [*cp.* phalāphala; I think that *Trenckner*, PM. p. 74, is right in tracing this sort of *dvandva comp.* "to a drawing together of phrases like gamā gamaṁ, dumā dumaṁ"; by the commentaries it is generally explained by magga + a-magga, "the right way and the wrong", SBE. X p. 93.]

Maghavat (or -van?) *m.* (= *sa.*) the chief of the gods, Sakka or Indra; *nom.* ~vā (devānaṁ) Dh. 30.

maṁku, *mfn.* (= *sa.*) dejected, despondent, dispirited; *m.* yo ~u bhavati (*w. loc.*) Dh. 249. (*cp. sa.* manyu, *m.*; Dhpd. (1855) p. 375.)

maṅgala, *n.* (= *sa.*) a festival or solemn ceremony (*comp.* = anything auspicious or solemn); *acc.* ~aṁ (kāresi) 58,30: āvāha-⁰, *n.* (*q. v.*); *kata-maṅgala-sakkāra, *mfn.* (*q. v.*); *maṅgalassa, *m.* a state horse, 24,29; *⁰-sindhava, *m. id.* 63,5 (*q. v.*); *⁰-ratha. *m.*, a state chariot, 25,1; *⁰-sāla-vana, *n.*, a pleasure-grove of Sal-trees, 62,10; *⁰-hatthin, *m.*, a state elephant; 24,20. *cp.* a-maṅgala. *mfn.*

mañgura, *m.* (*sa.* madgura & mañgura) a kind of fish; *°-cchavi, *mfn.* having the colour of that fish (yellow?), 92,13.

macca, *m.* (*sa.* martya) mortal, a man, person; *acc.* ~aṁ, Dh. 141; *instr.* ~ena, Dh. 53; *gen. pl.* ~ānaṁ (metri causa ~āna) Dh. 182.

maccu, *m.* (*sa.* mṛtyu) ¹) death; *gen.* ~uno, Dh. 21. — ²) Death personified, the king of death (= Māra, *q. v.*); *nom.* ~u, Dh. 47 = 287; °-rāja(*n*), *m.* (*sa.* mṛtyu-rāj) id.: *acc.* ~rājānaṁ, 44,29; *gen.* ~rājassa, Dh. 46; — *°-dheyya, *n.* the dominion of death, the world of death (*i. e.* saṁsāra) Dh. 86 (~aṁ suduttaraṁ). (*cp.* *Windisch*, Māra, p. 186.)

maccha, *m.* (*sa.* matsya) a fish; *acc.* ~aṁ (kāṇa-mahā-°) 4,15; (eka-°) 4,25; *gen.* ~assa, 51,31; *pl.* ~ā, 4,1; *acc.* ~e, 4,1; 14,23 (rohita-°); *gen.* ~ānaṁ, 4,10; *khīna-°, *mfn.* (*q. v.*); *°-gahaṇa, *n.* catching fish, ~niyāmena, 25,35 (*v.* niyāma); °-gandha & °-maṁsa, *m.* (*q. v.*).

macchaka, *m.* (*sa.* matsyaka) a little fish; *acc. pl.* ~e (sabba-°, all the poor fishes?) 4,24.

maccharin, *mfn.* (*sa.* matsarin) stingy, niggardly; *m.* ~ī, Dh. 262.

macchera, *n.* (*sa.* mātsarya) stinginess, niggardliness; ~aṁ, Dh. 242.

majja, *n.* (*sa.* madya) spirituous liquor, any intoxicating drink (*cp.* surā, meraya); *acc.* ~aṁ, 97,11; surā-meraya-°, 81,23.

majjati, *vb.* (*sa.* √mad) to be drunk or mad; *aor. 2. sg.* mado (mā) 77,5; *pp.* matta (*q. v.*) *cp.* pamajjati.

majjha, *n.* (*sa.* madhya, *mfn.*) ¹) the middle, centre, the interior of anything; *acc.* ~aṁ (janapada-°) 39,18; *instr. adv.* ~ena, midway, 96,17 (ubho ante anupagamma); *loc. adv.* majjhe, in the middle (of, *gen.* or *e. c.*) : ~ ṭhite mige, 6,8; ~ katvā, 6,10; ~ janapadaṁ hanāpesi, 39,4; pure ca pacchā ca ~ ca. Dh. 421; mā ~ bhañgo ahosi, 83,11; sakuṇānaṁ ~, 10,12; sayanassa ~, 47,35; *comp.* agāra-°, 46,18; nadī-°, 2,32; nagara-°, 60,23; parisa-°, 10,21 (*etc.* *v.* parisā); mahājana-°, 51,16; lekhā-°, 59,7; sakuṇa-saṁgha-°, 10,18; samudda-°, 28,16. Dh. 127; — ²) the middle of the body, waist; *v.* su-majjha, *mfn.* — *cp.* vemajjha, *next etc.*

***majjhantika**, *m.* (*sa.* *madhyantika; probably transformation of *sa.* madhyaṁdina or madhyāhna) midday, noon; *°-samayaṁ, *acc.* "in the middle of the day", 97,34; °-suriyo viya, "like the sun at midday", 26,4 (*cp.* Tr. PM. 75,16.)

majjhima, *mfn.* (*sa.* madhyama) being in the middle, middlemost, intermediate, central; *m.* ~o (puriso, "of the middle height") 92,13; *f.* ~ā (paṭipadā, *q. v.* *cp.* *Windisch*, Māra, p. 303) 66,28; *loc. m.* ~e (yāme, "in the middle watch") 99,20; *comp.* °-taṇḍula, *m.* (*v. h.*); °-tāpasa, *m.* the second brother, 36,14; *°-desa, *m.* (*sa.* madhyadeça) the midland; also *nom. pr.* of the midland country between Himalaya & Vindhya; *loc.* ~e, 91,18.

Majjhima-nikāya, *m. nom. pr.* of a Pāli work, the second of the five Nikāyas (*q. v.*); *nom.* ~o, 102,15; specimens thereof : 92,1—95,33; commentary : Papañca-sūdanī (*q. v.*).

mañca, *m.* (= *sa.*) a bed, bedstead; *nom.* ~o, 84,11; *acc.* ~aṁ (heṭṭhā-°, under the bed) 83,18; *loc.* ~amhi (parinibbāna-°) 110,19; — *°-paṭipādaka, *m.* (*v. h.*).

mañcaka, *m.* (= *sa.*) a bed or couch; a bier, litter; *acc.* ~aṁ, 73,26; *loc.* ~e (khuddaka-°) 42,1.

mañju, *mfn.* (= *sa.*) beautiful, lovely; *°-bhāṇin, *mfn.* lovely-voiced; *gen. m.* ~ino (sikhino) 18,32.

maññati, *vb.* (*sa.* √man) to think, reflect; to suppose, imagine; to believe, consider; to know, understand (*acc.*); *pr. 3. sg.* ~atī (bālyaṁ. "knows his foolishness") Dh. 63; *2. sg.* ~asi,

69,34. 94,29 (taṁ kiṁ ~); *pr. 1. sg. med.* maññe (*v. below*); *part. m. med.* maññamāno, 44,30; *imp. 3. pl.* ~antu, Dh. 74; *pp.* mata (*q. v.*) *cp.* maññita, maññeti; munāti; mati, manas, *etc.*

*maññita, *n* (?) (*fr.* maññati) imagining; *gen. pl.* ~ānaṁ (sabba-°) 94,11.

maññe, *indecl.* (*orig. pr. 1. sg. med.* maññati; *sa.* manye) certainly, to be sure; as it were; I think, suppose, or dare say (sometimes ironically): 3,25. 5,7. 38,28. 56,14-30. 67,31.

*maññeti, *vb.* (rarely instead of maññati, perhaps arisen through influence by maññe, *v. above*) to think, imagine, *etc.*; *aor. 2. sg.* ~esi, 50,33.

maṇi, *m.* (= *sa.*) a precious stone, gem, jewel; *acc.* ~iṁ, Dh. 161; nīla-° & indanīla-°, *m.* sapphire, 26,23. 28,29; — °-kuṇḍala, *n. pl.* (*dvandva*) *q. v.*; — °-kkhandha, *m.* a large gem, *acc.* ~aṁ. 35,23; *gen.* ~assa, 35,34; *°-guḷa, *m.* jewel, pearl, 5,26. 18,7; — *°-tālavanta, *n.* (*v.* tāla); — °-ratana, *n.* a most excellent jewel, 62,30 (*cp.* ratana); — *°-vaṇṇa-gīva, *mfn. v.* gīva; — *°-vimāna, *n.* (*q. v.*); — °-sāra, *m.* = maṇi-ratana, 24,20 (°-ādīni).

maṇḍa, *m. n.* (= *sa.*) scum, cream, essence (*e. c.* implying 'choiceness'); *Bodhi-°, the terrace of the Bo-tree, 113,2 (contracted of mandira?).

maṇḍana, *n.* (= *sa.*) ornament, decoration; °-vibhūsana-, 81,25.

maṇḍala, *n.* (= *sa.*) a circle, disk (*esp.* the orb of the sun or the moon); *nom.* ~aṁ, 32,31 (canda-°); *loc.* ~e, (do.) 16,16; āpāna-°, jūta-° (*q. v.*) *cp.* ti-maṇḍala, pari-maṇḍala.

*maṇḍu, *m.* (?) name of a certain plant (perhaps shortened from maṇḍuka = *sa.* maṇḍūka); °-kaṇṭakena, with a maṇḍu thorn, 37,5.

maṇḍita, *mfn.* (*pp.* maṇḍeti) adorned, dressed; °-pasādhita, *mfn.* 41,10 (*q. v.*).

maṇḍeti, *vb.* (*sa.* √maṇḍ, *caus.* maṇḍayati) to adorn, decorate (*acc.*); *ger.* ~etvā, 16,26; *pp.* maṇḍita (*q. v.*) *cp.* maṇḍana.

mata¹, *mfn.* (*pp.* maññati, = *sa.*) thought, imagined; known, understood; honoured, esteemed; *subst. n.* opinion, view, doctrine, belief; *acc.* ~aṁ (sakaṁ, otāresi) 113,12; Pātañjali-° (*q. v.*); Sambuddha-mata-kovida, *mfn.* 114,13 (*v.* kovida).

mata², *mfn.* (*pp.* marati; *sa.* mṛta) dead; *m.* ~o, 34,5. 36,4; *pl.* ~ā (bhavissanti) 21,11; *acc. f.* ~aṁ, 89,9; *comp.* °-manussaṁ. 40,31; *n. subst.* ~aṁ, death, 7,34. 103,34 (*opp.* jīvitaṁ); *cp.* a-mata, an-amatagga & *next.*

mataka, *mfn.* (*sa.* mṛtaka) dead; *m.* a dead man; *°-bhatta, *n.* a feast for the dead; *acc.* ~aṁ (dassāmi) 16,23.

*matatta, *n.* (*sa.* *mṛtatva) the being dead; *abl.* ~ā (mātāpitunnaṁ) "as my parents are dead", 31,18.

mati, *f.* (= *sa.*) understanding, knowledge, intellect; mahā-°, *mfn.* eminently wise, *m.* ~i, 114,2; dummati, *m*(*fn*). (*q. v*); *vajja-mati, *mfn.* (*q. v.*).

matimat, *mfn.* (= *sa.*) wise, intelligent; *instr. m.* ~matā (metri causa: matī-°) 113,28.

matta¹, *mfn.* (*pp.* majjati; = *sa.*) overjoyed, drunken, mad, furious; *m.* ~o (vedanā-°) 24,7; *acc. m. pl.* ~e (asure). 59,25; *gen. f. pl.* ~ānaṁ (uttama-yobbana-vilāsa-°) 47,15; °-vāraṇa, *m.* a rut elephant, *acc. pl.* ~e, 39,9; °-vara-vāraṇa, *m.* "a royal elephant in his pride", 45,31.

matta², *n.* (*sa.* mātra; only *e. c.* = mattā. *q. v.*) measure, quantity (*e. c.* the exact measure, a small quantity, as much as, only, mere, *etc.*): ¹) *subst. n.* ammaṇa-mattena, *instr.* in a measure of an ammaṇa (*q. v.*) 65,29; — nāma-mattaṁ, a mere name, 97,3; — pāli-mattaṁ, the text only, 113,26; — mānusa-matte, *loc. abs.*, a mere mortal, 19,30; — lomakūpa-mattam pi . . . na, not even a pore of the skin, 16,10; — vidatthi-mattaṁ, as much as one vidatthi (*q. v.*); 87,11; – (na) sīlabbata-mattena, *instr.* ("not) only by discipline and vows", Dh. 271; – [2]) *mfn.* of that measure or number, as large as, just large enough : [a]) aṭṭhūsabha-matta (*v.* aṭṭha[1]); aḍḍhanāḷika-matta (*v.* aḍḍha); aṇu-matta (*q. v.*); catusaṭṭhi-matta (*q. v.*); biḷāranisakkana-matta (*v.* biḷāra); yojana-matta (*q. v.*); sahassa-matta (*q. v.*); – [b]) *comp. w. a past part.*, in English often translated by a subordinate (temporal) clause : an-okkanta-matta, (*v.* okkamati); āgata-matta, at one's arrival, 33,28; (mukhe) ṭhapita-matta (*v.* ṭhapita); ṭhita-mattam eva (*acc.*, *w. prec. ger.* bhattaṁ otāretvā, instantly after he had put it on the ground, *cp.* ṭhita & ṭhapita) 33,33; visaṭṭha-matta (*q. v.*); vutta-matta, when thus addressed, in conformity to the command : *m.* ~o (Sakkena) 110,28; *f.* ~ā, 111,30. – *cp.* *appa-mattaka (*mfn.*) *next etc.*

*mattaññu, *mfn.* (*sa.* *mātrajña) moderate; *acc. m.* ~uṁ (bhojanamhi, moderate in his food) Dh. 8. *a-mattaññu, *mfn.* (*q. v.*).

*mattaññutā, *f.* (*fr. last*), moderation; *nom.* ~ā (bhattasmiṁ) Dh. 185.

mattā, *f.* (*sa.* mātrā) = matta[2]; *°-sukha, *n.* a small pleasure, *acc.* ~aṁ, Dh. 290; °-sukha-pariccāgā, by leaving a small pleasure; ib.; – *pasāda-°, *f.* (*q. v.*); – *bhiyyoso-mattāya (*instr. adv.*) 65,8 (*v.* bhiyyoso).

mattikā, *f.* (*sa.* mṛttikā) earth, clay; ~ā (temetabbā; "the face was besmeared with moistened clay in order to protect it from the heat", SBE. XIII, 157) 83,28; *instr.* ~āya, 83,31.

*matti-sambhava, *mfn.* of (good) maternal extraction; *acc.* ~aṁ, Dh. 396. ('matti' may either be another form of mātu- (*v.* mātar) or contracted of mattika, *mfn.* (*sa.* mātṛka) maternal.)

*matteyyatā, *f.* (*fr.* mātar through *matteyya, *mfn.* who loves his mother) the state of a mother, motherhood; ~ā (sukhā) Dh. 332. (*cp.* petteyyatā).

matthaka, *m.* (*sa.* mastaka) [1]) the head, skull; *acc.* ~aṁ, 3,21. 24,4; *loc.* ~e, 65,30 *etc.*; °-majjhe, 41,17. – [2]) the upper part of anything, surface, top, end (mostly *e. c.*); *instr.* matthaka-matthakena (samuddassa, along the crests of the ocean) 60,5; Himavanta-°, over the H., 36,5; *loc.* ~e (ito tiṇṇaṁ saṁvaccharānaṁ, after 3 years) 87,8; ito saṁvacchara-°, 33,14.

matthaluṅga, *n.* (*sa.* mastu-° & mastaka-luṅga) the brain; matthake ~aṁ, 82,6 = 97,23.

mathita, *mfn.* (= *sa. pp.* √math) churned; shaken, agitated; *n. subst.* agitation; *gen. pl.* ~ānaṁ (sabba-°) 94,11.

mado, *aor. 2. sg.*, *v.* majjati.

maddati, *vb.* (*sa.* √mṛd) to tread upon, crush, trample (*acc.*); *part. m.* ~anto (paṭhaviṁ) 28,14; *ger.* ~itvā (tiṇi pi ekato) 57,28; (vālikā) 97,35.

maddava, *mfn.* (?) (*sa.* mārdava, *n.*) soft, putrid, withered; *n. pl.* ~āni (pupphāni) Dh. 377; – *subst. n.* 'softness, mildness'; *comp.* *sūkara-maddava, *n.* a kind of meat, generally transl. by "hog's flesh (lard or bacon)", "a dried boar's flesh" (*Rhys Davids*), but *Neumann* (in his German translation of MN. p. XX–XXI) is perhaps right in translating it by "Eberlust, eine essbare Pilzart" (*cp. Fr. Zimmermann,* Buddhistischer Katechismus, p. 26 ff.; "in this case probably connected with √mṛd"?) *nom.* ~aṁ, 78,11-14; *instr.* ~ena (vyādhi ppabāḷhā udapādi Satthuno) 78,31.

madhu, *n.* (= *sa.*) honey; *comp.* *°-cāṭi, *f.* & °-paṭala, *n.* (*q. v.*); *°-bindu, *n.* a drop of honey, 53,18; *dvandva-comp.* °-phāṇita-°, 53,17-20; °-lāja-°, 18,27; sappi-°, 61,26. *cp.* madhuvā.

madhura, *mfn.* (= *sa.*) sweet;

pleasant, charming; *acc. m. n.* ~aṁ (paṁsuṁ) 38,3; (bhāsitaṁ) Dh. 363; (varadhammaṁ) 87,9; *f. pl.* ~ā, 52,7; *n. pl.* ~āni (phalāni) 37,3; *comp.* °-gīta-sadda, *m.* sound of sweet song, 23,33; °-phalānaṁ, *gen. pl.* sweet fruit, 1,15; °-phala, *mfn.* bearing sweet fruit, *m.* ~o (ambo) 37,32; °-rasa, *m.* sweetness, 38,4; °-ssara. *m.* sweet voice, *instr.* ~ena. 5,20 (*cp.* sara). a-madhura, *mfn.* (*q. v.*).

madhuvā, *adv.* (*sa.* madhu-vat) like honey; Dh. 69.

mana(s). *n.* (*sa.* manas) 1) the mind, the internal organ or mental powers in general (often *esp.* from a moral point of view); 2) *in the psychology*: the faculty of thought or organ of thought, considered as the sixth organ of sense (*cp.* āyatana), whose objects are dhammā (*v.* dhamma 4); *nom.* a) mano (sometimes *masc. generis* and considered as a-stem) 70,32 (āditto); Dh. 116; Dh. 300–01 (rato); b) manaṁ (santaṁ, declined like a-stems) Dh. 96; *instr.* manasā, Dh. 1–2. 233. 281; manasâkāsi, *v. next*; *gen.* manaso, Dh. 390; *loc.* a) manasi, *v. next*; b) manasmiṁ, 71,11; – *comp.* mano-°, *v. below*, *cp.* manāpa, manuñña; *e. c.* °-mana & °-manas, *v.* atta-°, dummana (domanassa), sumana (somanassa); paṭibaddha-°, vyāsatta-°, saṁsanna-saṁkappa-°, *mfn.*; hiṁsa-°, *n.* (*q. v.*) *cp.* °-mānasa, *mfn.*

manasi-karoti, *vb.* (*sa.* manasi-kṛ) to bear in the mind, think over, meditate upon, remember (*acc.*); *aor. 3. sg.* manasâkāsi (contraction of manasi akāsi) 66,6 (paṭiccasamuppādaṁ); *ger.* manasikatvā (*sc.* dhammaṁ) 71,23.

***manāpa**, *mfn.* (*sa.* *mana-āpa) 'gaining the mind', pleasant, charming; *f.* ~ā (gopī) 104,33; *gen. n.* ~assa (tiṇassa) 52,3; °-ssavana, *mfn.* flowing with pleasure (*cp.* savana); *m. pl.* ~ā (sotā) Dh. 339.

manuja, *m.* (= *sa.*) a man; *gen.* ~assa, 107,29; *pl.* ~ā, 74,2. 110,32. *cp.* manussa.

manuñña, *mfn.* (*sa.* manojña) 'agreeable to the mind', pleasing, lovely, beautiful; *n.* (*adv.*) ~aṁ (rudaṁ) 10,19.

manussa, *m.* (*sa.* manushya) a man, human being; *pl.* men, beings; *pl. nom.* ~ā, 6,3. 25,26; *acc.* ~e, 21,3; *gen.* ~ānaṁ, 6,1; *loc.* ~esu, 7,13. 102,29; – *comp.* °-satāni (satta) 27,13; sassa-kārake-°, ārakkha-°, (*q. v.*): *manussâvāsa, *m.* (*v.* āvāsa); *°-ghātaka, *m(fn).* a manslayer; *nom.* ~o (hatthī) 76,9; *°-paṭilābha, *m.* obtaining birth as a human being, Dh. 182; *°-bhūta, *mfn.* being a man (ɔ: enjoying the benefit of having been born among men) *m.* ~o, 41,33; *°-vāsa, *m.* abode of men, *acc.* ~aṁ. 21,2; *°-saṇṭhāna, *mfn.* of human form or figure, 85,21; *°-samāna-sarīra, *mfn.* with body like men, 25,33; *cp.* a-manussa, mānusa & *next*.

manussatta, *n.* (*sa.* manushyatva) manhood, the state or condition of man; *nom.* ~aṁ (dullabha-°, *q. v.*) 22,15.

***mano-duccarita**, *n.* the sins of the mind, Dh. 233.

***mano-pakopa**, *m.* anger of the mind, Dh. 233.

***mano-pubbaṅgama**, *mfn.* 'having the mind (or thought) going before', resulting from mind; *m. pl.* ~ā (dhammā), Dh. 1.

***mano-maya**, *mfn.* consisting of mind (or thought), spiritual; *m. pl.* ~ā (dhammā) Dh. 1.

***Manoratha-pūraṇī**, *f.* 'fulfilling desires', *nom. pr.* of a Pāli book. being the Comm. on Aṅguttara Nikāya; specimen thereof: 91,13-33.

manorama, *mfn.* (= *sa.*) pleasant, beautiful; *n.* ~aṁ (padumaṁ) Dh. 58; *subst. n.* a comfortable abode, 15,25; *cp.* ati-manorama.

***mano-viññāṇa**, *n.* 'consciousness of mind', the thinking faculty. 70,33.

***mano-samphassa**, *m.* 'contact of mind', perception through the sense of thought, 70,33; °-viññāṇâyatana, the sense of thought, 72,5 (*cp.* āyatana).

Manosilā, *f.* (*sa.* manah-çilā, 'red arsenic') *nom. pr.* of a place in Himavanta near the Anotatta lake; °-tale (*loc.*) "on the M. table-land", 61,11.

***mano-susaṁvuta**, *mfn.* "well restrained in mind"; *m.* ~o, Dh. 281 (*cp.* manasā saṁvuto. Dh. 233).

***mano-seṭṭha**, *mfn.* having mind for the best or essential part; *m. pl.* ~ā (dhammā) Dh. 1.

mano-hara, *mfn.* (= *sa.*) 'seizing the mind', ravishing, fascinating, charming; *n.* ~aṁ (rūpaṁ) 111,36.

manta, *m.* (*sa.* mantra) [1]) deliberation, counsel; [2]) a sacred text, a mystical verse, charm, spell; *nom.* ~o, 32,2; 53,14 (anaggha-°); *acc.* ~aṁ, ib.; *instr.* ~ena, 55,15; *pl.* ~ā, Dh. 241; jānana-°. a spell of knowledge, 53,36; 53,14 (sabba-ruta-°); °-lobhena, through greed for the charm, 55,13; jāti-mantūpapanna, *mfn. v.* upapanna; [3]) knowledge, doctrine, wisdom (also *f.* mantā) : *nom.* ~o, 113,16 (Buddha-°); *cp. next etc.*

***mantajjhāyaka**, *m(fn).* versed in mystic knowledge (the Vedas); *comp.* °-brāhmaṇo, 17,5 (probably *fr.* manta + jhāyaka, *v.* jhāyati [2]).

***mantatthin**, *mfn.* desirous of knowledge; *m.* ~ī, 113,18.

***mantabhāṇin**, *mfn.* speaking wisely; *m.* ~ī, Dh. 363 (mantā vuccati paññā, Comm., *cp.* manta [3]).

manteti, *vb.* (*sa.* √mantr) to consult, deliberate, discuss (*acc.*); *part. m. pl.* ~entā; *aor. 3. pl.* ~ayiṁsu, 11,32. 72,30.

manda, *mfn.* (= *sa.*) [1]) slow; scarce, small (of quantity); *m.* ~o (gocara) 4,5; *n.* ~aṁ (udakaṁ) 3,32; *n. pl.* ~āni (sitthāni) 56,28; [2]) weak, tender; *f.* ~ā, 28,8; *m.* ~o, 99,4; [3]) fool, stupid; *m.* ~o, Dh. 325. *cp. next.*

mandakkhī, *adj. f.* (*sa.* mandāksha, *mfn.*) looking with softness, tenderness, or bashfulness, languishing or bashful (?), 20,27. *cp.* akkhi.

mama, *gen. pron. 1. pers.*, *v.* ahaṁ; *cp. next etc.*

mamāyati, *vb.* (*denom. fr. prec.*; *sa.* mamāyate) to treat anything as if it were one's own property, to love, fondle, to be attached or devoted to; *pp.* *mamāyita, being one's own, beloved, dear; *n. sg.* & *pl.* one's own property, beloved or desired objects; yassa n'atthi ~itaṁ (*w. loc.* nāmarūpasmiṁ, "who has no desire at all for name and form", free from selfishness) Dh. 367; *cp.* Sn. v. 119.

***mamiṁkāra**, *m.* (*fr.* *mamīkāra; *cp.* niraṁkaroti = nirākaroti, *sa.* mama-kāra) the false view that anything belongs to one's self; sabba-ahiṁkāra-°, 94,11 (comm. = taṇhā). *cp.* ahiṁkāra.

°maya, *mfn.* (= *sa.*) only *e. c.* = made of, consisting of; *v.* amha-°, indanīlamaṇi-°, kaṭṭha-°, muñja-°, rajata-°, vaddha-°, suvaṇṇa-° & sovaṇṇa-°.

mayūra, *m.* (= *sa.*) a peacock; °-rājan, *m.* an excellent or magnificent peacock, *acc.* ~ānaṁ. 18,17. *cp.* mora.

maraṇa, *n.* (= *sa.*) the act of dying, death; *nom. acc.* ~aṁ, 67,9. 103,5; 6,22. 7,10. *instr.* ~ena, 70,29; *gen.* ~assa, 103,6; *abl.* ~ā, 17,15: ~ato, 87,32; *comp.* *°-kāle, 89,13; *°-dukkha, *n.* 7,9; maraṇanta, *mfn.* (= *sa.*) ending in death, 107,8; *°-pariyosāna, *mfn.* id. 86,16; °-bhaya, *n.* the fear of death, °-tajjita. *mfn.* 5,14; °-bhīta. *mfn.* 27,13; °-bhāva, *m.* (*q. v.*); *°-sati. *f.* thinking of death, calling to one's mind that death is inevitable, 86,17-18; *dvandva comp.* jarā-°, 66,10; jāti-°, 105,26; vyādhi-°, 108,22; *cp.* param-maraṇā, *adv.* (*q. v.*).

marati (& **mīyati** (**miyyati**) *q. v.*), *vb.* (*sa.* √mṛ) to die; *part. m. instr.* marantena, 49,27; *m. pl.* ~antā 5,11; *pot. 2. sg.* ~eyyāsi. 53,15; *aor.*

3. sg. mari, 9,3. 24,33; *3. pl.* ~iṁsu, 16,5; *fut. 1. sg.* marissāmi, 88,23; *1. pl.* ~issāma, 5,12; *pp.* mata, *mfn.* (*q. v.*); *grd.* maritabba, *n.* ~aṁ (mayā) 86,16; *loc.* ~e (sati) 6,24; *cp.* macca, maccu, maraṇa; *caus.* māreti (*cp.* Māra, māraṇa) & mārāpeti, *q. v.*

marīci & marīcikā, *f.* (= *sa.*) a mirage, vapour like a surface of water, often appearing in deserts; *acc.* ~ikaṁ, Dh. 170; *⁰-dhamma, *mfn.* like a mirage; *acc. m.* ~aṁ, Dh. 46.

maruvā, *f.* (Birm. reading: muruvā, *sa.* mūrvā) a sort of hemp, from which bowstrings are made; *gen.* ~āya, 92,17.

marū, *m. pl.* (*sa.* marutas) gods, deities (= devatā), 114,18.

mala, *n.* (= *sa.*) dirt, impurity; spot, taint; fault, sin; *nom. acc.* ~aṁ, 106,19 = Dh. 240; Dh. 239. 241. 242 (mal'itthiyā); 243; *abl.* ~ā (malataraṁ) Dh. 243; *comp.* mānusa-⁰, 61,13; *niddhanta-⁰, *mfn.* (*q. v.*); *vanta-⁰, *mfn.* free from impurity, Dh. 261; vīta-⁰, *mfn.* id. 68,26; *asajjhāya-⁰, *mfn.* whose fault is non-repetition, *m. pl.* ~ā (mantā) Dh. 241; *an-uṭṭhāna-⁰, *mfn.* (*v. h.*) *cp.* nim-mala, *mfn.*; Mala-vagga, *m.* the title of Dh. XVIII.

*malatara, *mfn.* (*compar.* of mala) more impure; *n.* ~aṁ, a greater or worse taint, Dh. 243.

mallaka, *m.* (= *sa.*) an earthen vessel or bowl; *nom.* ~o (khela-⁰, *q. v.*) 84,15.

*Mallika, *m. nom. pr.* of a king; *nom.* ~o (Kosalarājā) 43,15; ⁰-rañño, *gen.* 43,20; ⁰-mahārājā, 43,23.

mallikā, *f.* (= *sa.*) Jasminum Zambac; *comp.* sumana-mallikādīnaṁ pupphānaṁ, 65,29; tagara-⁰, Dh. 54 (*q. v.*).

mahaggha, *mfn.* (*sa.* mahārgha) of great price; *n.* ~aṁ, 25,5 (*cp.* aggha).

mahagghasa, *m.* (*sa.* mahāghasa) a great eater, Dh. 325.

mahaddhana, *mfn.* (*sa.* mahādhana) having much money, carrying much wealth; *m.* ~o (vāṇijo) Dh. 123.

mahat, *mfn.* (= *sa.*) great, large, high, numerous, important, eminent, *etc.*; *m.* mahā, 3,4. 37,1. 55,19. 95,21. 112,15, *etc.*; (*acc.* mahantaṁ); *n. nom. acc.* mahantaṁ, 2,8. 5,29. 17,17. 71,28; *f. nom.* mahatī, 2,12. 101,20; *instr. m.* mahatā, 70,21; *f.* mahatiyā, 74,17; *gen. m. n.* mahato, 10,14; the strong stem mahanta is also used in *nom. m.* and sometimes in the weak cases: *nom. m.* mahanto, 4,6. 99,5; *instr.* mahantena, 7,5; *loc.* mahante, 10,7; mahantamhi, 110,20; at 75,35 mahantaṁ seems to be *acc. f.* (silaṁ); *cp.* ati-mahanta, kīva-mahanta & *compar.* mahantatara, *m.* ~o, 74,15. – At the beginning of *comp.* we generally find mahā (*v. below*), whose ā in most cases is contracted with a foll. vowel (or elided, *v.* mahānubhāva, mahāraha, mahiddhika, mahesi, mahogha, *etc.*, *cp.* mahaggha), but sometimes the ā is shortened before a doubled consonant (*v.* mahagghasa, mahaddhana, mahapphala); *cp.* mahallaka, *mfn.*

mahanta & mahantatara, *mfn.*, *v.* mahat.

mahapphala, *mfn.* (*sa.* mahāphala) bearing much fruit, bringing great reward; *n.* ~aṁ, 14,18. Dh. 312. 356.

mahallaka, *mfn.* (= *sa.*) old; grown, adult; elder (of two); *m.* ~o, 45,4. 74,21; 55,21; *gen.* ~assa, 43,27; *f.* ~ikā, an old woman, 46,23. 57,9.

mahā-⁰, *mfn.* = mahat, at the beginning of *comp.*: ⁰-uposatha-divasa, *m.* 22,20 (*q. v.*); ⁰-gaṇin, *m.* 109,17 (*q. v.*); ⁰-jana, *m.* (*q. v.*); ⁰-tala, *n.* a royal hall, *acc.* ~aṁ, 39,29. 65,10; *loc.* ~e, 39,26. 53,17; ⁰-thera, *m.* 109,11. 113,8 (*q. v.*); ⁰-dāna, *n.* 61,6 (*q. v.*); ⁰-nadī, *f.* 35,18, *etc.* (*q. v.*); ⁰-nāda, *m.* 6,13 (*q. v.*); ⁰-nāvā, *f.* 28,27 (*q. v.*); ⁰-nāsa, *m.* 34,18 (*q. v.*); ⁰-pañña, *mfn.* very wise, of profound knowledge, *m.* ~o, 113,9 (*cp.* paññā);

°-patha, *m.* Dh. 58 (*q. v.*); °-bhaya, *mfn.* awful, *m.* ~o (saddo) 27,6; °-bhūmicāla, *m.* 80,19 (*v.* bhūmi); °-magga, *m.* 34,4 (*q. v.*); °-maccha, *m.* 4,15 (kāṇa-°, *q. v.*); °-mati, *mfn.* very clever, eminently wise, 114,9; °-muni, *m.* the great sage, *i. e.* Buddha, 105,24. 110,20; °-megha, *m.* 105,21 (*q. v.*); °-yogga, *n.* 58,19 (*q. v.*); °-yodha, *m.* 39,12 (*q. v.*); – °-rava, *m.* 60,8 (*q. v.*); °-varāha, *m.* Dh. 325 (*q. v.*); °-virava, *m.* 40,21 (*q. v.*); °-sadda, *m.* 16,33 (*q. v.*); °-samudda, *m.* 10,27. 95,13 (*q. v.*); °-sampatti, *f.* 58,8 (*q. v.*); °-sayana, *n.* 41,36 (*q. v.*); °-sara, *m. n.* 4,9 (*q. v.*); °-sāla-rukkha, *m.* 61,11 (*q. v.*); °-soka, *m.* 89,10 (*q. v.*); °-sobbha, *m.* 27,3 (*q. v.*); °-hasita, *n.* 16,29 (*q. v.*); *cp.* also *next etc.*

Mahā-kassapa, *m.* (*sa.* °-kāçyapa) *nom. pr.* of a thera (president of the first Buddhist council); °-thero, 109,17 = Kassapo, 109,6; °-pāmokkhā therā, 110,15 (*v.* pāmokkha).

mahā-nāga, *m(fn).* (= *sa.*) most eminent, heroic (? *cp.* nāga[2]); *m. pl.* ~ā (kuñjarā) Dh. 322.

mahânubhāva, *mfn.* (= *sa.*) of great might, powerful; *m.* ~o (Bhagavā), 75,30; *gen.* ~assa (rañño) 62,14 (*cp.* anubhāva).

*Mahā-pakaraṇa, *n.* (*sa.* *°-prakaraṇa) 'the great work', *i. e.* Paṭṭhāna (*q. v.*); *nom.* ~aṁ, 102,11.

Mahā-pajāpatī Gotamī, *f.* (*sa.* °-prajāpatī Gautamī) *nom. pr.* of Buddha's aunt and foster-mother; gāthās of hers: 108,11–22.

*Mahā-padāna, *n.* (*sa.* *°-pradāna) name of a chapter (sutta) in Dīgha-Nikāya (DN. XIV); *loc.* ~e, 63,12.

*Mahā-padhāna-ghara, *n.* *nom. pr.* the Mahāpadhāna Hall (in Mahāvihāra, *q. v.*); *acc.* ~aṁ, 114,4.

Mahā-bodhi, *m.* (= *sa.*) *nom. pr.* [1]) the Bo-tree at Buddha Gaya; *acc.* ~iṁ (vandituṁ Jambudīpam upāgami) 114,32; [2]) the Bo-tree at Anurādhapura (Ceylon); °-samīpamhi, 114,14. (*cp.* bodhi[2]).

Mahā-brahman, *m.* (= *sa.*) *nom. pr.* the god Brahma, ruler in the Brahmaloka; *pl.* °-brahmāno (cattāro) 62,22 (*i. e.* four Mahābrahmas of different cakkavālas, *q. v.*).

mahâbhinikkhamana, *n.* (*sa.* °-abhinishkramaṇa) 'the great retirement', 65,13 (*v.* abhinikkhamana).

Mahā-māyā, *f.* (= *sa.*) *nom. pr.* of Buddha's mother; (devī) 61,3.

mahâraha, *mfn.* (*sa.* mahârha) precious, splendid; *v.* araha.

mahā-rājan, *m.* (= *sa.*) [1]) a great king or supreme sovereign (*opp.* uparājan); *nom.* °-rājā, 43,23 (Mallika-°); *voc.* °-rāja, 7,16. 96,30. 97,19 (~ā'ti); – [2]) *pl.* °-rājāno (cattāro) 61,9, the four lokapālas or guardians of the world, *viz.* Dhataraṭṭha (in the North), Virūḷha (South), Virūpakkha (West), Vessavaṇa (East).

mahā-rajja, *n.* (*sa.* °-rājya) the title or position of a supreme sovereign; *acc.* ~aṁ (katvā) 44,21.

Mahā-vaṁsa, *m.* (= *sa.*) name of a Pāli work, being a chronicle of Ceylon, written in the 5th century by Mahānāma; specimens thereof: 110,17–114,33.

Mahā-vihāra, *m.* (= *sa.*) *nom. pr.* of a Buddhist monastery (vihāra) at Anurādhapura, Ceylon; *acc.* ~aṁ, 114,3.

Mahā-satta, *m.* (*sa.* °-sattva) 'the great creature', *synon.* Bodhisatta (*q. v.*); *nom.* ~o. 7,33; *acc.* ~aṁ, 25,24.

*Mahā-sīlava, *m.* *nom. pr.* of a king; °-rājā, 38,11; °-jātaka, *n.* 38,7. *cp.* Sīlava.

*mahiddhika, *mfn.* of great power, mighty; 75,30. 109,20 (*cp.* iddhi & iddhika).

Mahinda, *m.* (*sa.* Mahendra) *nom. pr.* of a prince, son of king Asoka (he transplanted Buddhism into Ceylon, in the last half of the 3rd century BC.); *instr.* ~ena (matīmatā) 113,28.

mahisa, *m.* (*sa.* mahisha) a buffalo; *gen.* ~assa, 92,21; vana-mahisaṁ (*acc.*) a wild buffalo, 13,22.

mahī, *f.* (= *sa.*) 1) the earth; °-tale, "throughout the world", 113,21; 2) *nom. pr.* of a river; *gen.* Mahiyā, 104,21; Mahiy', 104,24.

mahesakkha, *mfn.* (*sa.* maheçākhya, *i. e.* mahā-īça-ākhya; differently Tr. Mil. p. 422 (65,14)) eminent, mighty; *m.* ~o (putto) 62,24.

mahesi, *m.* (*fr.* mahā + isi, *sa.* maharshi) the great sage (*i.e.* Buddha); *acc.* ~iṁ, Dh. 422; *instr.* ~inā, 77,13.

mahesī, *f.* (*sa.* mahishī, a buffalo-cow) a queen; agga-°, *q. v.*

mahogha, *m.* (*sa.* mahaugha) a mighty flood, *v.* ogha.

*mahodaka, *mf*(~ikā)*n.* abounding with water, *v.* udaka.

*Mahosadha, *m.* (*fr. sa.* mahā + aushadha) *nom. pr.* of a prince (Bodhisatta); *nom.* ~o, 55,24.

mā, *indecl.* (= *sa.*) a negative particle, generally used in prohibitive (or consecutive) sentences: 'not, that not, lest', and joined with *aor.* of the verb (augmentless or augmented), but also frequently with *imper.* or *pot.*, and even with *indic.* of *pr.* & *fut.*; mā 'ti paṭisedhe nipāto, 85,33. — 1) *w. aor.* ~ bhāyi, 1,10. 4,30; ~ āsaṁkittha, 7,11; ~ karittha, 39,2; ~ mariṁsu, 16,5, *etc.*; augmented: ~ akāsi (= mā karohi) 86,1; ~ ahosi (*3. sg.*) 83,11; ~ ahesuṁ (mā-y-ime, *i. e.* mā ime, to be scanned: *may-me) 60,17; ~ acāvayi (*3. sg.*) 104,4. — 2) *w. imper.* ~ gaccha, 7,31; ~ detha, 52,20; ~ karontu, 8,7; ~ kilamantu, 60,12; *imper.* & *aor.* alternatively, *v.* Dh. 371. — 3) *w. pot.* ~ anuyuñjetha, Dh. 27; ~ vadetha, 55,26. — 4) *w. pr. 3. sg.* ~ h'evaṁ kho . . . paṭilabhati, 90,24. — 5) *without verb*: vanaṁ chindatha, mā rukkhaṁ. Dh. 283.

Māgadha, *mfn.* (= *sa.*) relating to the Magadha country; *m. pl.* the inhabitants of that country, *gen.* ~ānaṁ, 113,32; *instr. f.* ~āya (niruttiyā) the M. dialect, *i. e.* Pāli, 114,28.

māṇava, *m.* (= *sa.*) a youth, *esp.* a young Brāhman; *nom.* ~o, 19,11; °-vesena, in the disguise of a young Br., 19,10; brāhmaṇa-°, 113,2. — *dimin.* 1) māṇavaka, *m.* id.; *pl.* ~ā, 16,31; *acc. pl.* ~e (nāga-°, "Nāga youths") 53,1; — 2) māṇavikā, *f.* a young girl, *acc.* ~aṁ, 48,24; nāga-°, a Nāga girl, 52,28; *acc.* ~aṁ, 52,25; *instr.* ~āya, 52,27; *loc. pl.* ~āsu, 52,24.

mātaṅga, *m.* (= *sa.*) an elephant: *nom.* ~o (mātaṅg'araññe va nāgo) Dh. 329.

mātar, *f.* (*sa.* mātṛ) a mother; *nom.* mātā, 20,25; 59,23 (dāraka-°); 64,5 (Rāhula-°, *q. v.*); *acc.* ~araṁ, 23,9; *instr.* ~arā, 23,8; *gen.* mātu, 9,12, or mātuyā (Bodhisatta-°) 62,31, [after the analogy of u-stems, also used for other oblique cases] or mātāya (Rāhula-°) 65,27 [after the analogy of ā-stems]; *loc.* ~ari, Dh. 284; — *dvandva comp.* mātā-pitaro, *m. pl.* parents, 22,13 (*v.* pitar); mātā-puttā, *m. pl.* mother and son, 49,8; mātu-dhītaro, *f. pl.* a mother and her daughter, 32,20 (instead of mātā-° ?); — at the begin. of other *comp.* we find the weak stem mātu- [or māti-]: °-hadaya, *n.* a mother's heart, *nom.* ~aṁ, 59,12; a-mātuhadayaṁ. ib.; *cp.* matti-sambhava, matteyyatā & mātugāma *below*.

Mātali, *m.* (= *sa.*) *nom. pr.* of the charioteer of Sakka (Indra); ~i, 60,18 (*nom.*); 60,12 (*voc.*); *acc.* ~iṁ, 60,9.

mātu, *etc.*, *v.* mātar.

mātu-gāma, *m.* (*sa.* mātṛ-grāma) womankind, the female sex, any being of the female sex, woman; *nom.* ~o, 50,34; *acc.* ~aṁ, 48,12. 50,32; *°-vasika, "being in the power of womankind", *m.* ~o (rājā) 54,3.

mātula(ka), *m.* (= *sa.*) a maternal uncle (also used as a term of familiar address); *voc.* ~a, 5,4; piya-mātulaka, *mfn.* who loves his uncle, *m.* ~o (atibhaginiputto, *q. v.*) 5,5.

m ā n a, *m.* (= *sa.*) pride, arrogance; *nom.* ~o, Dh. 74. 407; *acc.* ~aṁ, Dh. 221; °-diṭṭhi-ādi, 64,21; *°-ânusaya, *m.* 94,11 (*v. h.*); *nihata-°, *pahīna-°, *mfn.* (*q. v.*).

m ā n a s a, *n.* (= *sa.*) the mind; *e. c. mfn.*, *v.* tuṭṭha-°, vimutta-°, viratta-°, saṁvigga-°.

m ā n i n, *mfn.* (= *sa.*) thinking, imagining; paṇḍita-°, *mfn.* (*q. v.*).

m ā n u s a, *mfn.* (= *sa.*) human; °-mala-, 61,13 (human stain); a-mānusa, *mfn.* (*q. v.*); — *m.* a man, human being; *pl.* ~ā (gandhabba-°) Dh. 420; *acc.* ~e, 107,3 = Dh. 103; °-matta, *n.* (*v.* matta²); *f.* mānusī, a woman, *pl.* ~iyo, 21,29; *comp. w. subst. f.* mānusi-vācā, human speech, *acc.* ~aṁ, 22,3.

m ā n u s a k a, *mfn.* (= *sa.*) human; *acc. m.* ~aṁ (yogaṁ) Dh. 417; *pl. m.* ~ā (kāmā) 45,5.

m ā p e t i (or māpayati), *vb.* (*sa.* māpayati, *caus.* √mā) to make, prepare, create (by supernatural power, *w. acc.*); *aor. 3. sg.* ~esi (sarīraṁ mahānāvaṁ katvā, changed his own body into a large ship) 28,28; (sayanaṁ) 112,1; *ger.* ~etvā (aṅgārarāsiṁ. attano ānubhāvena) 16,3; ~ayitvā (rūpaṁ, nagaraṁ) 111,36. 112,25. *cp.* mita, *mfn.* & atimāpeti.

M ā y ā, *f.* (= *sa.*) *nom. pr.* of the mother of Gotama Buddha; ~ā (janayi Gotamaṁ) 108,21; Mahā-°, 61,3.

M ā r a, *m. nom. pr.* (= *sa.*) Death, the Tempter, the Evil One; *nom.* ~o, 103,11. 108,5; 71,27 (pāpimā); *acc.* ~aṁ, 103,12; *gen.* ~assa, 71,24; °-jāla, *n.* & °-bandhana, *n.* (*v. h.*) *cp.* samāra-ka, *mfn.* & Namuci, *m.* — *Māradheyya, *n.* the realm of M., the world of death, ~aṁ, Dh. 34 (*cp.* *maccudheyya).

m ā r a ṇ a, *n.* (= *sa.*) killing, death; *māraṇantika, *mfn.* ¹) 'bordering on death', being on the point of killing, almost mortally; *acc. m.* ~aṁ (ābādhaṁ) 78,30; *pl. f.* ~ā (vedanā), 78,25; ²) which is to end at death; *n.* ~aṁ (nāmarūpaṁ) 101,12 (*cp.* maraṇanta).

*m ā r ā p e t i, *vb.* (*caus. II.* marati, *cp. next*) to cause to be killed or murdered; *pp.* ~ita, *f.* ~ā, 74,9 (kehi ~, "who bade you to kill her"); 74,12.

m ā r e t i, *vb.* (*caus.* marati, *sa.* mārayati, √mṛ) to kill, murder (*acc.*); *pr. 1. sg.* ~emi (taṁ) 111,26; *3. sg.* ~eti, 97,15; *part. loc. m.* ~ente (& a-mārente) 17,14; *fut. 1. sg.* ~essāmi, 2,8. 12,28; *inf.* ~etuṁ, *comp.* ~etu-kāma, *mfn.* (*v.* kāma²); *ger.* ~etvā, 9,23; *pp.* mārita, *f.* ~ā, 74,8; °-bhāva, *m.* the having been killed, *acc.* ~aṁ (aññehi) 74,3.

*m ā ḷ a ¹, *m.* a pavilion, a thatched hut; *acc.* ~aṁ, 101,8.

°m ā l a ² & °m ā l i (*n*) = mālā (*e. c.*).

m ā l ā, *f.* (= *sa.*) a wreath, garland; *acc.* ~aṁ, 16,25; °-dāma, *n.* id.; *pl.* ~āni, 37,2; °-guṇa, *m.* a garland of flowers (by the lover cast over his bride), *acc. pl.* ~e, Dh. 53; *°-kacavara, *m.* (*q. v.*); *dvandva comp.* °-gandha-, 61,4. 73,11. 81,26; gandha-°, 49,14 (perfumes and flowers); *e. c.* māla or māli(*n*), *v.* Aggi-°, Kusa-°, Khura-°, Dadhi-°, Nala-°.

*M ā l u ṅ k y ā p u t t a, *m. nom. pr.* of a thera; *nom.* ~o, 93,18; *voc.* ~a, 92,2; his gāthās from Theragāthā: 107,29–108,9.

*m ā l u v ā, *f.* name of a certain creeper, 107,29 = Dh. 334 (*cp. sa.* mālu).

m ā s a, *m.* (= *sa.*) a month; *loc.* ~e (māse māse, month after month) Dh. 70. 106; *acc. pl.* ~e (cattāro) 25,21; (dasa-°) 62,2; °-addha-māsa-, a month and a half, 20,11 (*v. h.*).

m i g a, *m.* (& *f.* ~ī) (*sa.* mṛga) a deer, antelope; *acc. pl.* ~e (bahu-°) 6,5; 6,18 (suvaṇṇa-°); *instr. pl.* ~ehi, 8,12; *gen. pl.* ~ānaṁ, 6,4; *f. gen.*

~iyā (gabbhinī-°) 6,31; *comp.* kuruṅga-°, *m.* (*q. v.*); Nigrodha-° & Sākha-°, *m. nom. pr.* (*q. v.*); °-gaṇa. *m.* 6,10; *°-dhenu, *f.* 7,29; °-yoni, *f.* 5,25 (*v. h.*); °-rājan, *m.* 7,3; *°-luddaka, *m.* 11,27 (a hunter); °-vadha, *m.* hunting, 5,32 (°-pasuta, *mfn. q. v.*) *cp. next etc.*

migadāya, *m.* (*sa.* mṛgadāva) a deer-park; *nom.* ~o, 68,7; *loc.* ~e (Isipatane) 66,24.

migava, *m.* (?) (*sa.* mṛgayā, *f.* & mṛgavya, *n.*) hunting; *acc.* ~aṁ (gacchati) 6,2.

micchā, *adv.* (*sa.* mithyā) wrongly, falsely; ~ carati (kāmesu) commits immorality, 97,11; *comp.* °-diṭṭhi, *f.* false doctrine, Dh. 167; 316 (°-samādāna, *mfn. q. v.*); *°-paṇihita, *mfn.* (*q. v.*); *°-laddha, *mfn.* falsely obtained, *m.* ~o (yaso) 103,29; *°-saṁkappa, *m.* wrong thought or study (*opp.* sammā-°) Dh. 11 (°-gocara, *mfn. q. v.*).

miñjā, *f.* (*sa.* majjā, *cp.* majjan, ~as, & Prākr. mijjā) marrow; *aṭṭhi-°, *f.* the marrow of bones, 82,3. 97,31.

mita, *mfn.* (= *sa.*, *pp.* mināti, √mā) measured, moderate, little; *°-bhāṇin, *mfn.* speaking little, *acc. m.* ~inaṁ, Dh. 227.

mitta, *m.* (*sa.* mitra) a friend, companion; *acc. pl.* ~e, Dh. 78. 375; *comp.* ñāti-mittā, *pl.* kinsmen and friends, Dh. 219; mittâmaccā, *pl.* (*v.* amacca); °-bhāva, *m.* friendship, ~o, 52,16 (nāgarājena saddhiṁ); *°-dhamma, *m. id.* ~o, 14,3; a-mitta, *m.* (*v. h.*) *cp.* metta, metti & paccāmitta.

*Mittavindaka, *m. nom. pr.* of a merchant's son; 22,13, *etc.*

Mithilā, *f.* (= *sa.*) *nom. pr.* of a city, the capital of the Videha country; *loc.* ~āyaṁ, 44,19.

mithuna, *n.* (= *sa.*) a pair, couple (male and female); copulation; *v.* methuna.

middha, *n.* (= *sa.*) the state between sleeping and waking, drowsiness, indolence; *dvandva comp.* thīna-°, 103,27 (*q. v.*) *cp. next.*

*middhin, *mfn.* (*fr. prec.*) drowsy, indolent; *m.* ~ī, Dh. 325.

mināti, *vb.* (*sa.* √mā. mi, *cp.* √mī) to measure; *pp.* mita (*q. v.*); *caus.* māpeti (*q. v.*).

Milinda, *m.* (= *sa.*) *nom. pr.* of the Greek king Menander; 96,24, *etc.* – °-pañha, *m.* title of a Pāli book, containing a conversation between king M. and the Buddhist sage Nāgasena; specimens thereof: 96,23–101,33.

mīyati (& miyyati) = marati (*q. v.*; *sa.* √mṛ) to die; *pr. 3. pl.* ~anti, Dh. 21.

mukha, *n.* (= *sa.*) [1]) mouth (of men or animals); *nom. acc.* ~aṁ, 3,16. 5,27. 41,12; *instr.* ~ena, 5,14. 35,24; *mukhasā = mukhena, 85,26-34; *abl.* ~ato, 13,21; *loc.* ~e, 37,24; *comp.* mukhodaka. *n.* (*v.* udaka); °-tuṇḍaka, *n.* (?) a beak, *acc.* ~aṁ, 18,7; *instr.* ~ena, 4,8; °-vivaṭe, *loc. abs.* = mukhe vivaṭe, 3,17; *°-saññata, *mfn.* who controls his mouth, *m.* ~o, Dh. 363; vivaṭa-°, *mfn.* with the mouth open, *f. pl.* ~ā, 65,7; sūkara-°, *mfn.* (*v. h.*). – [2]) face, head, front; ~aṁ, 11,6. 83,32. 85,5; *abl.* ~ato, 50,23; *loc.* ~e, 12,10; *comp.* *°-dhovana, *n.* (*v. h.*); assu-°, *mfn.* (*q. v.*); ohitāmukha, *mfn.* (*v.* ohita); *puṇṇacanda-°, *mfn.* (*q. v.*); sa-mukha-veṭhita, *mfn.* (*v. h.*) *cp.* abhimukha, pamukha, & sammukha. – [3]) entrance, opening; edge, brim; aṭavi-°, 30,30 (*q. v.*); āvāṭa-°, 40,28 (°-vaṭṭi, *q. v.*); uyyoga-°, Dh. 235 (*q. v.*). – [4]) way, method; cause, means; *instr.* ~ena, *adv.* (*e. c.*) by means of: īsā-°, 60,16 (*q. v.*); phala-paṭisedhana-°, 86,4 (*v.* paṭisedhana); *loc.* ~e, *adv.* (*e. c.*) by way of, like, as: dāna-mukhe, 16,6 ("as a free gift"). *cp. next.*

mukhara, *mfn.* (= *sa.*) garrulous, loquacious; *m.* ~o, 86,2.

mugga, *m.* (*sa.* mudga) a sort of bean (Phaseolus Mungo); *pl.* ~ā, 16,1.

muggara, *m.* (*sa.* mudgara) a mallet, mace, club, stick; *instr. pl.* ~ehi, 6,11; muggarâdi-⁰, 6,7.

muccati[1], *vb.* (*pass.* muñcati, *sa.* mucyate) to be loosed, released, liberated; to escape (from, *abl.*); *pr. 3. sg.* ~ati (jālato) 88,34; *aor. 3. pl.* ~iṁsu (sedā sarīrā, "rolled down") 45,1; [a]) *fut. 2. sg.* mokkhasi (me) 72,1 ("escape from me"); *3. pl.* ~anti, Dh. 37; [b]) *1. sg.* muccissāmi, 16,28; *inf.* muccituṁ (maraṇā) 17,15; *pp.* mutta (*q. v.*).

muccati[2], *vb.* (*sa.* √mūrch; probably instead of mucchati through confusion with muccati[1]) to congeal, coagulate, turn sour (as milk); *pr. 3. sg.* ~ati (khīraṁ va, pāpaṁ kammaṁ, with both significations : to loosen & to turn sour) 106,21 = Dh. 71. *cp. next.*

muccheti, *vb.* (*caus.* √mūrch) to strain, strengthen; to tune (a stringed instrument, *acc.*); *ger.* ~etvā (vīṇaṁ) 19,32. (*Morris*, JPTS. '84,92.)

muñcati, *vb.* (*sa.* √muc) to loose, release, set at liberty; to leave, give up; to send forth, utter (*w. acc.*); *intr. med.* & *act. w. abl.* or *gen.* (*dat.*) to free one's self from, to make resistance against (Dh. 389?); *pr. 3. sg.* ~ati (assa) Dh. 389; *part. m.* ~anto (obhāsaṁ) 26,4; *imp. 2. sg.* muñca (pure, *q. v.*) Dh. 348; *pot. 3. sg.* ~eyya (pāpakammā) Dh. 127 (*w. intrans.* sense; B. has the *pass.* mucceyya); *pot. 3. sg. med.* ~etha (assa) Dh. 389; *aor. 3. pl.* ~iṁsu (atikaruṇa-saraṁ, uttered) 27,15; *ger.* ~itvā, 17,18. 76,13; *pass. v.* muccati[1]; *pp.* mutta (*q. v.*); *caus.* moceti (*q. v.*) *cp.* mutti.

muñja, *m.* (= *sa.*) name of a sort of grass or rush; *acc.* ~aṁ (paribare, "I wear m.-grass", a token of sacrificing one's self in battle : saṁgāmâvacarā anivattino purisā attano anivattanakabhāvaṁ ñāpanatthaṁ sīse vā dhaje vā āvudhe vā muñja-tiṇaṁ bandhanti, Comm.) 103,33; ⁰-kesa, *mfn.* with hair like m., 21,35; ⁰-maya, *mfn.* made of m., *m. pl.* ~ā (dāmā) 105,17.

muṭṭhi, *f.* (*sa.* mushṭi) the clenched fist; a handful, a small bundle; *acc.* ~iṁ (akāsi, closed his hand) 56,8.

muṇḍa(ka), *mfn.* (= *sa.*) shaved; *subst. n.* muṇḍaka, tonsure, *instr.* ~ena, Dh. 264.

mutiṅga, *m.* (*sa.* mṛdaṅga) a small drum, tabour; *acc.* ~aṁ, 67,29 (*cp.* Tr. PM. p. 62, 64; 78–79).

mutta[1], *mfn.* (*sa.* mukta; *pp.* muñcati) loosed, released, freed (from, *abl.*); *m.* ~o, 54,21. Dh. 172 (abbhā); 100,8 (pāpakehi kammehi); *comp.* jāla-⁰, 88,30; vana-⁰, Dh. 344; *m. pl.* ~ā (dukkhato) 31,30.

mutta[2], *n.* (*sa.* mūtra) urine; *nom.* ~aṁ, 82,5. 97,23.

muttā, *f.* (*sa.* muktā) a pearl; at the beginning of *comp.* we find sometimes mutta-⁰ : *⁰-sāra, *m.* 24,20; muttā-hāra, *m.* a necklace of pearls, *acc.* ~aṁ, 64,26.

mutti, *f.* (*sa.* mukti) liberation, deliverance (from, *abl.*); 67,16 (taṇhāya); 87,32 (maraṇato).

mudu, *mfn.* (*sa.* mṛdu) soft, mild, gentle; *instr. m.* ~unā (aṁkena) 20,24; *n.* 44,1 (~unā muduṁ, *sc.* jeti); ~uṁ, "something soft", 104,14; *⁰-citta, *mfn.* 'soft-minded', impressible; *acc. m.* ~aṁ, 68,23.

muduka, *mfn.* (*sa.* mṛduka) soft, mild, tender; *m.* ~o (hattho) 50,22; *n.* ~aṁ (mātuhadayaṁ, *w. loc.* dārake) 59,12.

muddā, *f.* (*sa.* mudrā) [1]) a seal, seal-ring; [2]) reckoning or speaking by means of the fingers, signal made by the hand, at 56,7 called *hatthamuddā, *instr.* ~āya (pucchissāmi).

muddhan, *m.* (*sa.* mūrdhan) the head; [*nom.* ~ā]; *acc.* ~aṁ, Dh. 72; *loc.* ~ani, 77,8.

munāti, *vb.* (= maññati, √man (*Kuhn*, Beitr. p. 99) or rather *fr.* √mi (*Trenckner*, *cp. Pischel*, Gr. § 489)) to understand, to know (*acc.*);

pr. 3. sg. ~āti (ubho loke; etymology of muni, *q. v.*) Dh. 269. (*cp.* Dh. (1855) p. 380.)

muni, *m.* (= *sa.*) a sage; *nom.* ~i (mahā-⁰, Buddha) 110,20; *voc.* 105,24 (do.); ~ī (metri causa) 80,33 (Buddha); 106,3 = Dh. 49; Dh. 268–69; *pl.* munayo, Dh. 225. *cp.* mona, *n.*

mummura, *m.* (?) (*sa.* murmura) embers, ashes; *loc.* ~e (upakūḷito) 9,32.

muyhati, *vb.* (*sa.* √muh) to be confused or bewildered; *pp. v.* mūḷha; *cp.* mogha, moha.

muḷāli, *m.* [& muḷāla, *m. n.*] (*sa.* mṛṇāla, *n.*) a lotus-fibre or -root (edible); *acc. pl.* ~ayo, 111,8.

musā, [1]) *adv.* (*sa.* mṛshā) falsely; ~abhāṇiṁ, 47,8 (I told a lie); ~ bhaṇati, 97,11; *comp.* ⁰-vāda, *m.* lying, lie; *acc.* ~aṁ (katvā) 46,24; (bhāsati) Dh. 246; 97,32; *abl.* ~ā, 81,23; ⁰-vādi(*n*), *mfn.* who speaks falsely; *gen. m.* ~issa, 106,14 = Dh. 176. – [2]) *musā, *subst. f.* falsehood, lie, 51,32 = musāvādo, 52,1.

muhutta, *m.* (*sa.* muhūrta) a moment, instant; *acc.* (*adv.*) ~aṁ, for a moment, awhile, 64,32 (niddaṁ okkami); 50,15 (naccitvā); 83,8; ~aṁ api, but for a moment, Dh. 65. 106.

mūla, *n.* (= *sa.*) [1]) the root (of plants); foot, bottom, base; *metaph.* cause, origin; *nom.* ~aṁ (mūlena. *instr.* "root with root") 37,34; *pl.* ~āni (mūlehi, do.) 37,20; sāla-⁰, 62,16; *metaph.* Dh. 247; taṇhāya ~aṁ, 108,4 = Dh. 337; vināsa-⁰, 33,26; *abl.* ~ato paṭṭhāya, "from the ground", 62,10; *loc.* ~e (rukkha-⁰) 4,23; (pāda-⁰, at one's feet) 36,27. 49,5; ~amhi (rukkha-⁰) 111,6; ~asmiṁ (do.) 112,2; *comp.* *⁰-taṇḍula, *m.* (*v. h.*); *⁰-bhāsā, *f.* the original language (or the chief of all languages?), *instr.* ~āya (sabbesaṁ, *i. e.* Māgadhā nirutti, *q. v.*) 114,28; *ucchinna-⁰, *mfn.* (*v. h.*). – [2]) price, payment, money; *nom.* ~aṁ, 57,4; 49,19 (bahuṁ); 49,15 (agahetvā, "gratis"); 49,2 (gandha-puppha-⁰, "money to buy flowers and perfumes"); *instr.* ~ena (gaṇhatha, "take it at a price") 18,10; (kammaṁ n'atthi, *v.* kamma [2]) 57,4; *comp.* sahassa-mūla, *mfn.* (*q. v.*) *cp. next.*

*mūla-ghaccaṁ, *adv.* radically (extirpated); ~ samūhataṁ, "taken out with the very root", Dh. 250 (*cp.* ghacca).

mūḷha, *mfn.* (*pp.* muyhati; *sa.* mūḍha) confused, bewildered, stupid: *acc. m.* ~aṁ, 75,24; *gen.* ~assa, 69,16; *comp.* *⁰-rūpa, *mfn.* foolish; *m.* ~o, Dh. 268. *cp.* mogha, moha.

mūsika, *m.* (*sa.* mūshika) a mouse, rat; *⁰-cchinna, *mfn.* cut by mice, *n.* ~aṁ (ṭhānaṁ) 25,7.

me = mama, *gen. pron. 1. pers.*, *v.* ahaṁ; – 'me = ime, *pl. pron. demonstr.*, *v.* ayaṁ.

megha, *m.* (= *sa.*) a cloud; *nom.* ~o (mahā-⁰, "a shower") 105,21.

*meṇḍa(ka), *m.* (*cp. sa.* meṇḍa, meṇḍha, meṇḍhra, meṭha, meṇṭha) a ram; *instr.* ~ena, 30,22; *comp.* ⁰-vara, *m.* 30,9 (*q. v.*); meṇḍako. 30,14 (*cp.* eḷaka).

metta, [1]) *n.* & mettā, *f.* (*sa.* maitra, *n.*) friendship, kindness; *acc.* ~aṁ, 40,7; *comp.* khanti-mettânuddaya-⁰, 7,12. 38,15 (*v. h.*); *mettā-vihāri*n*, *mfn.* "who behaves with kindness", *m.* ~ī, Dh. 368. – [2]) *mfn.* friendly, kind, benevolent; *instr. n.* ~ena (cittena) 76,34; ⁰-citta, *mfn.* friendly, benevolent, *m. pl.* ~ā, 35,14.

mettī, *f.* (*sa.* maitrī) = *prec.*; *nom.* ~ī, 18,12; *acc.* ~iṁ, 53,9.

Metteyya, *m.* (*sa.* Maitreya) *nom. pr.* of the future Buddha; *nom.* ~o, 114,24.

methuna, *n.* (*sa.* maithuna) copulation, love, marriage; *⁰-dhamma, *m.* id., *acc.* ~aṁ, 54,11.

meda, *m.* (*sa.* meda, *m.* & medas. *n.*) fat; ~o, 82,5. 97,23; – ⁰-vaṇṇa, *mfn.* "looking like (a lump of) fat", *acc. m.* ~aṁ (pāsāṇaṁ) 104,13.

*medhaga (or medhaka) *m. n.* (*cp. ved. sa.* mṛdh & medhayu) quarrel, strife; *pl.* ~ā, Dh. 6 (= kalaha, Comm.) *cp.* Sn. v. 893–94; Vin. II, 88.

medhā, *f.* [& medhas, *n.*] (= *sa.*) intelligence, prudence; *instr.* ~āya, 91,27. *cp.* dummedha, sumedha, sumedhasa, *mfn.* & *next.*

medhāvin, *mfn.* (= *sa.*) intelligent, wise; *nom. m.* ~ī (dovāriko) 90,33. 91,27; *acc.* ~iṁ, Dh. 76.

°medhin, *mfn.* (*e. c.* = *sa.*) id.; *v.* dummedhin.

meraya, (*n.*) (*sa.* maireya) a kind of strong drink; *dvandva comp.* surā-°, 81,23. Dh. 247 (°-pānaṁ).

mokkhati, *fut.*, *v.* muccati.

Moggallāna, *m.* (*sa.* Maudgalyāyana) *nom. pr.* of one of Buddha's most famous pupils; Sāriputta-Moggallānā, *pl.* S. & M. 74,30 (~êva); *gen. pl.* ~ānaṁ, 74,27.

mogha, *mfn.* (= *sa.*) vain, useless; foolish; *n.* ~aṁ (aññaṁ) 89,23; °-purisa, *voc.* O foolish one! 76,8; *°-jiṇṇa, *mfn.* grown old in vain, *m.* ~o, Dh. 260.

moceti, *vb.* (*caus.* muñcati; *sa.* mocayati) to cause to be loose, let go (*acc.*); to liberate, save (*acc.* & *abl.*); *aor. 3. sg.* ~esi (jane dukkhā) 31,25; *inf.* ~etuṁ, 40,20; *ger.* ~etvā (maṁ bandhanā) 33,2; (asse) 44,12; (sāṭakaṁ) 50,24; (puttaṁ) 59,11.

modati, *vb.* (*sa.* √mud) to be glad or happy, to delight; *pr. 3. sg.* ~ati (*opp.* socati) Dh. 16.

mona, *n.* (*sa.* mauna) silence; *instr.* ~ena, Dh. 268.

mora, *m.* (= mayūra, *q. v.*) a peacock; *nom.* ~o, 10,13; *voc.* ~a, 10,11; *gen.* ~assa, 92,30; °-yoni, *f.* 18,3 (*v. h.*); *dvandva comp.* haṁsamorâdayo, 10,6.

moha, *m.* (= *sa.*) bewilderment, infatuation, delusion, folly; *acc.* ~aṁ (in the series: rāga, dosa, moha) Dh. 20. *comp.* mohaggi, *m.* the fire of delusion, 64,20; *°-dosa, *mfn.* damaged by delusion, *f.* ~ā (pajā) Dh. 358; *vīta-°, *mfn.* free from delusion, *loc. pl.* ~esu, Dh. 358.

Y.

y, 1) on account of sandhi inserted in mā-y-ime, 60,17; mama-y-idaṁ, 72,20. 2) instead of i or e, *v.* ty' (= ti, te) *cp.* tv'.

ya-, base of the *pron. relat.* (= *sa.*); *nom. acc. n.* yaṁ (*sa.* yad): 56,11. 72,20. 78,8 *etc.*; 78,7 (yan); the old form yad is sometimes preserved by sandhi: Dh. 345; yad-idaṁ, 97,3; yad-eva, 91,9; *m.* yo, 30,9 *etc.*; with elision of the vowel: y'assa, Dh. 389; y'āyaṁ (*i. e.* yo ayaṁ) Dh. 56; *f.* yā, 47,27, *etc.*; 67,12 (yâyaṁ); yā ce = yañ ce, Dh. 104 (*v.* yañce); as for the rest the declension is like that of *pron. demonstr.* taṁ: *acc. f.* yaṁ, 67,10. 87,18; *gen. m.* (*n.*) yassa, 3,26 (yass'ete); *gen. f.* yassā, 64,15 (yassâyaṁ); *instr. m. n.* yena, 1,9. 103,13 (yen'atthena, *v.* attha 1); yen'eva (*n.*) 96,27; *f.* yāya, 92,16 (yāy'); Dh. 408; *abl. m.* (*n.*) a) yamhā, Dh. 392; b) yasmā (*v. separately*); *loc. m.* (*n.*) a) yamhi, 106,9 = Dh. 393; 108,26 (yamh'okāse); b) yasmiṁ, 84,7; *pl. n.* yāni, 2,11; *m.* ye, 75,3; *gen.* yesaṁ, 86,20; 86,18 (yesañ hi); 92,31 (yes'-āhaṁ, *i. e.* yesaṁ ahaṁ); *loc. f.* yāsu, 51,30. — 1) who, which, what (often *corresp. with foll. demonstr.*, *cp.* taṁ): 68,22. 78,7-8 *etc.*; yaṁ yeva ... taṁ yeva (the same .. as) 99,30; yasmiṁ vihāre ... sace so vihāro, 84,7; yo yaso ... esā te senā, 103,29-31; yo ... taṇhāya ... nirodho (*after prec.* idaṁ) 67,15; yâyaṁ taṇhā, 67,12 (do.); esā yā (gehe vasato, *part. gen.*) rati, 47,27; *w. pot. of the verb.*: yo evaṁ vadeyya, 99,30; anavakāso yo (do.) 76,26 (*v.* an-avakāsa); yaṁ balaṁ (*q. v.*) 13,25. — 2) *repeated*: whatever, whichever; yaṁ yaṁ, 50,3; yā yā, 50,3. — 3) *combined with other pron.* a) *w. pron. demonstr.* = whatever, whichsoever: yan taṁ, Dh. 42; yad-idaṁ, 70,26; yena tena, 1,9; ye te, 76,30. b) *in the same sense w. pron. indef.*: yo koci, 110,8; yaṁ kiñci, 68,27; yo añño, 34,24; *likewise followed by* pi: yam pi ... tam pi, 67,10; c) *w. pron. 1. pers.* (*foll. by 1. pers. of the verb.*): yo'haṁ, 75,24; ye mayaṁ (we who, since we) 105,23; yesan no (*gen. pl.*) n'atthi kiñcanaṁ, though we have nothing at all, Dh. 200. — 4) *pleonastic* or *omitted*: yad-idaṁ 'Nāgaseno' ti, this word N., 97,2; yaṁ bhiṁsanakaṁ (*v. h.*) 81,3; [yo] jaññā, Dh. 352; [yo] udīraye, Dh. 408. — 5) *several cases are used as indecl.* (*conj.*): *n. acc.* yaṁ, *instr.* yena, *abl.* yasmā, *v. separately. cp.* yato, yattaka, yattha, yathā, yadā, yadi, yāva *etc.* & yebhuyyena.

yaṁ, *indecl.* (*conj.*) (*acc. n. fr.* ya-; *sa.* yad) 1) that (*quod*); taṁ bahuṁ yaṁ hi jīvasi, 13,29 (*v.* bahu); 2) when, if (*quum* in its different meanings): 80,33 (yaṁ kālam akarī munī); 97,18 (yaṁ vadesi); 90,19 (yaṁ pan'); 54,26 (yan nu, even if); 3) as, since, because: 76,3. 95,7 (yaṁ hi); 51,8 (anacoluthic = as (for instance?)); 4) *comb. w.* nūna (in optative sense like Germ. *dass. w. pron. 1. pers. and pot. of the verb*): yan nūnâhaṁ, what if I? = let me! 33,27. 46,33. 68,35. 71,26 *etc.*; yan nūna mayaṁ, 6,3; 5) *comb. w.* ce, *v.* yañce.

yakana, *n.* (*sa.* yakṛt, yakan) the liver; *nom.* ~aṁ, 82,3. 97,21.

yakkha, *m.* (*sa.* yaksha) name of certain superhuman beings (as goblins or ogres), who are the enemies of men; *nom.* ~o (*i. e.* Māra) 104,18; *gen.* ~assa. 112,13; *pl.* ~ā (inhabitants of Laṅkā) 112,10; *acc. pl.* ~e, 112,9 (to be corr. into yakkhā); 112,21 (sabba-0); *gen. pl.* ~ānaṁ (they eat dead corpses) 40,31; 0-nagara, *n.* 20,32 = 0-pura, *n.* 112,12 (Sirīsavatthu); 0-rāja-0, 112,22.

yakkhinī (or yakkhī), *f.* (*sa.* yakshiṇī & yakshī) a female yakkha; *nom.* ~inī, 58,30; 21,22 (jeṭṭha-0); 59,19 (~ini-mhi = ~inī amhi); ~ī, 111,35. 112,11; *acc.* ~iṁ, 111,23; *instr.* ~iniyā, 59,7; *gen.* ~iniyā, 21,25; *pl.* ~iniyo, 20,33; 0~ini-bhāva, *m.* (*q. v.*); paricārika-0, *f.* (*v.* paricārikā).

yajati, *vb.* (*sa.* √yaj) to sacrifice; *pot. 3. sg. med.* ~etha (sahassena, "with a thousand") Dh. 106. *cp.* yiṭṭha.

*yañce (or yañ ce), *indecl.* (*i. e.* yaṁ + ce, *q. v.*) than, than if; mataṁ seyyo ~ jīvitaṁ, 7,34; 103,34. Dh. 106–07; by attraction to a *subst. f.* we have yā ce = yañce, Dh. 104 (seyyo yā c'āyaṁ itarā pajā) *cp.* yañ ce, Dh. 229 (*v.* ce).

yaṭṭhi, *f.* (*sa.* yashṭi) 1) a stick, staff; *acc.* ~iṁ (pācana-0, a goad) 71,29; 2) name of a certain measure of length = 7 hatthas or ratanas (about $3^1/_2$ metres) *v.* yojana. *cp.* laṭṭhi.

yato, 1) *indecl.* (*adv. & conj.*; *abl. of pron. rel.* ya-, *correl. of* tato; *sa.* yatas) a) whence, wherefrom, where, 31,35 (~ sodariyam ānaye); b) since when, 27,22 (~ sarāmi attānaṁ); c) since, because, 66,21. 112,29; d) *repeated*: yato yato, as soon as, according to, *w. foll.* tato tato: the more — the more, Dh. 374. 390. — 2) *gen. part.*, *v.* yāti.

*yattaka, *mfn.* (*correl. of* ettaka, kittaka, *q. v.*) however much, as much as (*quantus*); *pl. m.* ~ā, as many as, 57,10 (*fr. sa.* yāvat, *v.* Tr. PM. p. 30).

yattha (& yatra), *adv.* (*sa.* yatra) in or to what place, where, whither; 56,17 (gatā); 63,13 (yatra, *sc.* jātiyā, jātassa); 104,10 (~ gantvā); *comp.*, *v. next etc.*

yattha-kāmaṁ, *adv.* (*sa.* yatra-kāmam) whereever one plases, according to one's wish; Dh. 326; *comp.* yatthakāma-nipātin, *mfn.* (*v.* nipātin).

*yatthaṭṭhita, *mfn.* (*cp. sa.*

yatra-stha) where staying; *m.* ~o, Dh. 127; *acc.* ~aṁ, Dh. 128.

yatra, *adv.* (= *sa.*) *v.* yattha.

yathā, *indecl.* (*conj.*; = *sa.*; *correl.* of tathā) [1]) as, like (with full sentence, *corr. w. demonstr.* tathā, evaṁ, *etc.* or before nouns; at the beginning of *comp. v. below*): [a]) *w. full sentence* (*pres.*): 5,8 (tathā); 34,22 (evam eva); ~ (kho) pana ... na evaṁ, 62,25. 79,6; tādiso vaṇṇo yathā passasi, 85,16; sometimes at the beginning of a sentence (*w. pot.*) by giving an illustration: "it is as if", 100,11 *etc.*; [b]) *before nouns*: 3,26 (~ tava); 26,5. 51,32. 63,11 (na ~ aññesaṁ); 75,23 (~ bālaṁ, *acc.* like a fool). — [2]) so that, in order that (*ut*; yathā na, *ut non, ne*); that (*quod*); 12,6 (*w. fut.*); 12,2 (*w. pres. ind.*); 13,18. 22,23. 39,33 (do.); 68,36 (*w. pot.*); 70,8 (*quod*). — [3]) as soon as, 18,17 (*w. pres. ind.*). — *comp.*: *yath'icchitaṁ, *adv.* (or *adj. n.*) according to one's desire, 111,28; — yathā-kammaṁ, *adv.* according to one's deeds, 8,13. 13,7. 22,18; — °-diṭṭha, *mfn.* as seen, *acc. f.* ~aṁ (bhūmiṁ) 69,23; — *°-paññatta, *mfn.* 84,17 (*v. h.*); — °-padese, *loc.* (*sa.* yathā-pradeçaṁ) 47,1 (*v.* padesa); — *°-pasādanaṁ, *adv.* Dh. 249 (*v. h.*); — *°-'bhirantaṁ. *adv.* 70,20. 77,15 (*v.* abhiramati); — *°-bhucca, *mfn.* (*fr.* yathā-bhūtaṁ) according to the fact, real; *n.* ~aṁ (ajānantī. "the truth") 108,16; — °-bhūtaṁ, *adv.* according to the fact, rightly, truly, 91,8. 96,8. Dh. 203; — *°-vācaṁ, *adv.* (*cp. sa.* °-vacanaṁ) according to one's words, 108,30; *°-vātaṁ. *adv.* by the wind, 20,2 (gacchanto); — °-vidita, *mfn.* (*sa.* °-vitta) as found or understood; *acc. f.* ~aṁ (bhūmiṁ) 69,23; — °-saddhaṁ, *adv.* according to faith, Dh. 249; — °-sukhaṁ, *adv.* according to one's pleasure, 2,13. Dh. 326. *cp.* seyyathā.

yad-, by sandhi = yaṁ (*v.* ya-).

yadā, *indecl.* (*conj.* = *sa.*; *correl. of* tadā) when, whenever; from what time, as soon as; *w. aor.* 18,34 (āgamā, *w. foll.* atha); 68,21 (do.); 99,4. 108,24; *w. pot.* 35,7. 44,22 (*w. foll.* atha); *w. pr. indic.* 66,20 (atha); 76,12 (tadā); 107,11 (atha).

yadi, *indecl.* (*conj.* = *sa.*) if; *w. pot.* 98,33. 100,8; *w. pres. ind.* 100,7; yadi evaṁ (without verb, "if so") 5,15; yadi vā or yadivā (after *prec.* vā, = "or") Dh. 98; yadiva (shortened of yadi vā) Dh. 195 ("or"); yadi vā (repeated, without verb, = whether — or) 92,15 *etc.*

yanta, *n.* (*sa.* yantra) a vice, press, machine; *loc.* ~e (pakkhipitvā viya) 40,18.

yanti, *pr. 3. pl.*, *v.* yāti.

yan nūna, *v.* yaṁ.

Yama, *m. nom. pr.* (= *sa.*); the king of hell or god of death; *gen.* ~assa (santike, "near to the death") Dh. 237; — °-purisa, *m.* a servant of Y., messenger of death, *pl.* ~ā, Dh. 235; — °-loka, *m.* the world of Y., *acc.* ~aṁ, Dh. 44–45.

Yamaka, *n. nom. pr.* (lit. "the twofold") of a Pāli work, the sixth book of Abhidhamma-Piṭaka; ~aṁ, 102,11. — °-vagga, *m.* name of the first chapter of Dh. (lit. "double-verses").

[**yamati**], *vb.* (*sa.* √yam) [to hold, support; hold back, restrain; *intr.* to leave off, to cease (*i. e.* "to decease"?)]; *imper.* (*injunctive*) *1. pl. med.* yamāmase, Dh. 6 (the meaning is uncertain; perhaps "to subdue one's self" or "to be subdued" as by Yama?). (*cp. Franke*, WZKM. 1901; Dhpd. (1855) p. 110.)

yava, *m.* (= *sa.*) barley; *acc.* ~aṁ, 9,1; °-khetta, *n.* a field of barley, 8,18 (sāli-°); — °-majjhaka, *mfn.* having barley(-fields) in the middle, or being situated amidst the barley-field? *comp.* *Uttara-yavamajjhaka, *m. nom. pr.* of a village, 55,30.

yasa (& yasas, *comp.* yaso-) *m.* (*sa.* yaças) [1]) honour, glory, reputation, celebrity; *nom.* ~o (mahā) 55,19;

103,29; Dh. 24; *acc.* ~aṁ, 42,12. 45,29. 54,34; *instr.* ~ena. 64,10; *comp.* yaso-bhoga-samappita, *mfn.* endowed with glory and fortune, *m.* ~o, Dh. 303. — [2]) Yasa, *nom. pr.* of a man; *nom.* ~o (kulaputto) 67,21 *etc. cp. next.*

yasassin, *mfn.* (*sa.* yaçasvin) glorious, famous, celebrated; *nom. m.* ~ī, 30,9.

yasmā, *indecl.* (*abl. fr.* ya-) since, because (*corr. w.* tasmā) 85,29. 91,18 (*cp.* yato).

yāgu, *f.* (*sa.* yavāgu) rice-gruel; *nom.* ~u, 56,29. 82,19-20; *acc.* ~uṁ, 21,5; *instr.* ~uyā, 56,28; °-ghaṭa, *m.* (*q. v.*) 56,24.

yācaka, *m.* (= *sa.*) a beggar; *acc. pl.* ~e, 14,19; *gen. pl.* ~ānaṁ, 15,5.

yācati, *vb.* (*sa.* √yāc) to ask or beg (for, *acc.*); *pr. 1. sg.* ~āmi, 31,5; *2. pl.* ~atha (etaṁ) 18,28; *aor. 3. sg.* yāci (jīvitaṁ) 111,26; *ger.* ~itvā (*w. doubl. acc.*) 7,23. 89,16; — *pass.* yāciyati; *part. pass. m.* [a]) yāciyamāno, 25,18. 46,15; [b]) *yāciyanto, 111,12; — *pp.* yācita, *m.* ~o (tena) 28,17; Dh. 224 (*w. loc.* appasmi); yācaka, *m. v. above.*

yāti, *vb.* (*sa.* √yā) to go, walk; *pr. 3. sg.* yāti, Dh. 29. 179. 294; *2. sg.* yāsi, 49,14; *3. pl.* yanti, Dh. 126 (saggaṁ); *part. gen. m.* yato (ito paraṁ, "when he is passing from hence") 77,4; *imp. 2. sg.* yāhi, 13,1. 32,19. 38,21.

yāna, *n.* (= *sa.*) a carriage, any vehicle or draught-animal; *instr. pl.* ~ehi, Dh. 323.

yāma, *m.* (= *sa.*) a night-watch (three hours); *acc.* ~aṁ (tiṇṇam aññataraṁ) Dh. 157; (paṭhamaṁ, during the first watch) 66,5; *loc.* yāme (paṭhama-°) 11,30; (purime, id.) 99,19; (majjhime, in the middle w.) 99,20; (pacchime, in the last w.) 99,23.

yāva (or yāvaṁ, by sandhi yāvad-) *indecl.* (*sa.* yāvat) [1]) *conj.* as long as, until (*corr. w.* tāva); *w. pres. ind.*: 23,19. 48,21. 102,3. 110,4. Dh. 72 (yāvad-eva). Dh. 119; *w. aor.* 33,21. 77,8; yāva na, while not, before, *w. pres. ind.* 19,1. 92,9. Dh. 284 (yāvaṁ); *w. fut.* 92,3. — [2]) *prp. w. abl.* 12,17 (aruṇuggamanā); 62,6; *w. acc.* 43,13 (paccantabhūmiṁ); 62,10 (aggasākhā); ~ tatiyaṁ (up to the third time) 3,7. 102,26; ~ dutiyaṁ, 102,26. *cp.* °-jarā, °-jīvaṁ.

*yāva-jarā, *adv.* (*fr.* yāva + jarā, the last being either *contr.* of jarāya (?) *abl.* of jarā. *f.* (?) or *abl.* of the base jara, *q. v.*) until old age, Dh. 333.

yāva-jīvaṁ, *adv.* (*sa.* yāvajjīvaṁ) during all the life, Dh. 64.

yāvat, *mfn.* (= *sa.*) as great, as much; *pl.* as many; *m. pl.* yāvanto, 108,3 = Dh. 337 (yāvant' ettha samāgatā). *cp. next etc.*

*yāvataka, *mfn.* (*correl.* of tāvataka) = *prec.*; *acc. pl.* ~e, 81,17.

yāvatā, *indecl.* (*instr. fr.* yāvat, = *sa.*) as far as, inasmuch as, because; 106,4 = Dh. 266 (*corr. w.* tena & tāvatā); *cp. next.*

*yāvatāyukaṁ, *adv.* (*cp. sa.* yāvadāyushaṁ) all one's life long; ~ ṭhatvā, after having lived out one's term of life, 8,11, 34,28. 38,5.

yiṭṭha, *mfn.* (*pp.* yajati; *sa.* ishṭa) sacrificed; *n. subst.* ~aṁ (yajetha) Dh. 108 (offering, sacrifice).

yuga, *n.* (= *sa.*) a yoke; ~aṁ, 98,5.

yujjhati, *vb.* (*sa.* √yudh) to fight (against, *acc.*; with, *instr.* or *prp.*); *part. m. med.* ~māno, 60,3; *ger.* ~itvā (corehi saddhiṁ) 33,19; (aññamaññaṁ) 33,20. *cp. next* & yuddha, yodha.

*yujjhana, *n.* (*fr. prec.*) fighting; °-ṭṭhāna, *n.* fighting ground, 29,24.

*yuñjati, *vb.* (*sa.* √yuj) [1]) to yoke, harness, join; to prepare, arrange; [2]) *med.* & *act. w.* attānaṁ, to apply or give one's self to (*loc.*); *pr. 3. sg. med.* ~ate (Buddhasāsane) Dh. 382; *part. m.* yuñjaṁ (attānaṁ, ayoge) Dh. 209; *pp.* yutta (*q. v.*); *caus.* yojeti & *yojāpeti (*q. v.*) *cp.* yuga, yoga, yogga, yojana, *etc.*, yotta.

yutta (& *yuttaka), *mfn.* (*pp.* yuñjati; *sa.* yukta) [1]) joined, yoked; 54,9 (rathe °-sindhavā); [2]) prepared, arranged; *acc. f.* ~aṁ (dhajiniṁ) 104,8; [3]) proper, fit (*w. inf.*); right; *m.* ~o (maṅgalasso bhavituṁ) 24,31; *comp. w. grd.* *kattabba-°, *mfn.* right to do, *n.* ~aṁ, 54,32; kātabba-yuttakaṁ karissanti, 39,34 (*v.* karoti, *grd.*); *ṭhapetabba-yuttaka, *mfn.* fit to be set in a place (*loc.*); *acc. m.* ~aṁ (rājaṭṭhāne) 11,1.

yuddha, *m. n.* (= *sa.*; *pp. fr.* yujjhati) battle, war; *acc.* ~aṁ (detu, let him fight) 36,21. 39,30; *dat.* ~āya (paccuggacchāmi), 104,4.

yuvan, *mfn.* (= *sa.*) young, *nom. m.* ~vā, Dh. 280 (a youth). *cp.* yobbana.

yūsa, *m. n.* (*sa.* yūsha) juice, gravy; ~aṁ (amba-°, *q. v.*) 37,24.

ye, *pl. m. pron. rel.*, *v.* ya-.

yena, *indecl.* (*conj.*; *instr. fr. pron. rel.* ya-, *corr. w. demonstr.* tena) [1]) in what direction, where; 68,5 *etc.* (*cp.* yena, *sc.* maggena, 104,2). — [2]) (so) that (*ut*); 77,6 (tathā karissasi ~ gamissasi). — [3]) because; Dh. 256 (*w. pot.*); 260. 270 (*w. pres.*).

***yenicchakaṁ**, *adv.* (*fr.* yena + icchā) where one likes; Dh. 326.

***yebhuyyena**, *adv.* (*instr. of* yebhuyya, *mfn.* numerous, much; *fr.* ye = yaṁ (Magadhism) & bhiyyo (Tr. PM. p. 75); *cp. sa.* yad-bhūyas) generally, entirely, always, upon the whole, in all; 73,33. 96,7-11. (*cp. Franke*, KZ. n. F. XIV, 420.)

yeva, *indecl.*, *v.* eva.

yesaṁ, **yehi**, **yo**, *v.* ya-.

yoga, *m.* (= *sa.*) [1]) junction, union, combination; *acc.* ~aṁ (mānusakaṁ, "bondage") Dh. 417; *comp.* sabba-°-visaṁyutta, *mfn.* (*v. h.*); nakkhatta-°, *m.* conjunction of stars, constellation (*v. h.*). — [2]) application of the mind, exertion, devotion, meditation *etc.*; *abl.* ~ā, Dh. 282; *loc.* ~asmiṁ, Dh. 209; *comp.* *aññatra-°, *mfn.* (*q. v.*); yoga-kkhema, *m.* 'tranquillity of devotion', complete happiness (= Nibbāna); *acc.* ~aṁ (anuttaraṁ, nibbānaṁ) Dh. 23; *gen.* ~assa (pattiyā) 103,3; a-yoga, *m.* (*q. v.*).

yogga, *n.* (*sa.* yogya) a carriage, vehicle; *loc.* ~e (mahā-°, a chariot of state) 58,19.

yojana, *n.* (= *sa.*) 'yoking, harnessing', a measure of distance (the length of an Indian yojana is variously indicated, varying between 4—18 miles; according to some = 21,400 Metres (about 12 miles) = 4 gāvutas, one gāvuta being 80 usabhas à 20 yaṭṭhis à 7 ratanas (or hatthas, $^1/_2$ Metre) à 2 vidatthis à 12 aṅgulas (inches)); *nom.* ~aṁ, 107,9 = Dh. 60; *loc.* ~e (addha-°, *q. v.*) 63,19; *comp.* *°-ppamāṇa, & *°-matta, *mfn.* having an extent of a yojana, 63,28; 6,8; *°-sahass'-ubbedha, *mfn.* (*v.* ubbedha); ti-yojana-satika, *mfn.* (*q. v.*); tiṁsa-°, & diyaḍḍha-° (*v. h.*).

yojanā, *f.* (= *sa.*) 'union, conjunction', grammatical construction; in the comment style: what is to be supplied or understood; 'mukhena sūkara-sadiso āsin' ti yojanā, 'I was like a pig by my mouth', so is to be understood, 85,22.

yojanika, *mfn.* (*e. c.* = *sa.*) so many yojanas long; saṭṭhi-°, 61,10; satta-°, 61,11.

yojāpeti, *vb.* (*caus. II.* yuñjati) 'to cause to be joined or fixed', to apply, employ, prepare (*acc.*); *ger.* ~etvā (dvāraṁ) 6,7.

yojeti, *vb.* (*caus.* yuñjati; *sa.* yojayati) [1]) to harness; to make ready (*acc.*); *ger.* ~etvā (sindhave), 63,5; *imp. 2. sg.* ~ehi (rathaṁ) 63,3; [2]) to fasten, hold fast, grapple, attack (*acc.*); *pot. 3. sg. med.* ~etha (Māraṁ) Dh. 40; *w.* attānaṁ: to apply or give one's self to (*loc.*), *part. m.* a-yojayaṁ (attānaṁ yogasmiṁ, who does not give one's self to meditation) Dh. 209.

yotta, *n.* (*sa.* yoktra) a rope, cord; *acc.* ~aṁ, 25,35; *pl.* ~āni, 28,30.

yodha, *m.* (= *sa.*) a warrier, soldier; *pl.* °-mahā-yodhā, 39,12.

Yona(ka), *mfn.* (*sa.* Yavana) Ionian, Greek; *pl.* the Greeks (in Bactria), ~kā, 97,4. (*cp. Weber,* Ind. Str. II, 321.)

yoni, *f.* (= *sa.*) the womb, uterus; source, origin; *e. c.* a class or kind of living beings; *loc.* yoniyaṁ (kapi-° nibbattitvā, having been born as an ape) 1,3; (miga-°) 5,25. *cp. next etc.*

yonija, *mfn.* (= *sa.*) born from the womb, born in a certain class of beings; *acc. m.* ~aṁ (na brāhmaṇaṁ brūmi, "on account of his birth") Dh. 396.

yoniso, *adv.* (*sa.* yoniçaṣ) 'by the source', radically, thoroughly, deeply (wisely); Dh. 326 (*cp.* SBE. X. 79).

yobbana, *n.* (*fr.* yuvan; *sa.* yauvana) youth; *loc.* ~e, Dh. 155; uttama-yobbana-vilāsa-matta, *mfn.* 47,14 (*v.* vilāsa, *cp.* matta[1]).

R.

r, sandhi-consonant, inserted between vowels (like *sa.* siddhi-r astu, 114,33) : dhi-r-atthu, 63,13. 103,33; usabho-r-iva, 105,19; āragge-r-iva, Dh. 401; sāsapo-r-iva, Dh. 407 (*cp.* Tr. PM. p. 82; *Windisch,* Ber. d. sächs. Ges. 1893).

raṁsi, *f.* (*sa.* raçmi, *m.*) [1]) a string, line, rein, bridle (*v.* rasmi *below*). — [2]) a ray of light, splendour; *gen. pl.* ~īnaṁ (chabbaṇṇānaṁ, *q. v.*) 87,33.

rakkhaka, *mfn.* (*sa.* rakshaka) guarding, watching; *m.* a watchman; khetta-°, *m.* a field-watcher, *pl.* ~ā, 8,18.

rakkhati, *vb.* (*sa.* √raksh) to guard, watch, protect; to keep, observe; to beware of (*acc.*); *pr. 3. sg.* ~ati (sīlaṁ) 38,14. 97,9; (dhanaṁ) Dh. 26; *part. m.* ~anto, 33,24; *gen.* ~ato, Dh. 241; *imp. 2. sg.* rakkha, 22,16. 110,25; *pot. 3. sg.* rakkhe, Dh. 40; rakkheyya (kāya-ppakopaṁ) Dh. 231; Dh. 157 (metri causa : ~eyyā); *3. sg. med.* ~etha, Dh. 36; *inf.* ~ituṁ, 20,29; *grd.* rakkhitabba (to be observed) 14,12; a-rakkhiya, *mfn.* difficult to watch, *m.* ~o (mātugāmo) 52,8; *pp.* rakkhita, & *caus.* *rakkhāpeti (*v. below*) *cp.* rakkhaka, rakkhana, rakkhā, dūrakkha.

rakkhana, *n.* (*sa.* rakshaṇa) guarding, protecting; °-atthāya, 52,25 (*v.* attha[1]); sassa-rakkhan'atthaṁ, 8,7.

rakkhā, *f.* (*sa.* rakshā) protection; *acc.* ~aṁ (Laṅkā-°) 110,27.

***rakkhāpeti**, *vb.* (*caus. II.* rakkhati) to watch; *aor. 3. sg.* ~esi, 73,32.

rakkhita, *mfn.* (*pp.* rakkhati; *sa.* rakshita) guarded, protected; *comp.* °-gopita-vatthumhi (*loc., v.* vatthu) 58,13; a-rakkhita, su-rakkhita, *mfn.* (*q. v.*).

racchā, *f.* (*sa.* rathyā) a carriage-road, street; *acc.* ~aṁ, 76,18. (*cp.* ratha).

raja(s), *m.* (*sa.* rajas, *n.*) vapour, dust; dirt, impurity (*metaph.* of passions); *nom.* ~o, 108,8 (pamādânupatito, "defilement"); (sukhumo) Dh. 125; *acc.* ~aṁ, Dh. 313; 58,5 (pāda-°, "the dust at his feet", *cp.* pāda-paṁsūni, 77,7); *instr.* ~ena, 84,23; *comp.* rajo-° (originally *n.*) 112,29 (tambabhūmi-°); *cp.* rajovajalla *below.*

rajata, *n.* (= *sa.*) silver; *nom.* ~aṁ, 26,16; *gen.* ~assa, Dh. 239; *comp.* *°-dāma-vaṇṇa, *mfn.* like a silver chain, 61,19; *°-phalaka, *n.* 48,8 (*v. h.*); °-maya, *mfn.* made of silver, 28,30; *°-vaṇṇa, *mfn.* silver-coloured, 5,27; *°-vimāna, *n.* 23,22 (*v. h.*); *dvandva comp.* suvaṇṇa-°, 61,27; jātarūpa-°, 81,26. — **Rajatapabbata**, *m. nom. pr.* of a mountain (in Himavanta), 'Silver-Hill'; *nom.* ~o, 61,15.

rajana, *n.* (= *sa.*) colouring, dye; *acc.* ~aṁ, 68,25. *cp.* ratta[1].

***rajovajalla** (or rajojalla), *n.* (*fr.* raja(*s*) & *jalla, avajalla = smut, soot (?) *cp. sa.* jhallikā & *Childers s. v.*) "dust and dirt", or "rubbing with dust". Dh. 141 (SBE. X, 38; Dhpd. (1855) p. 306; *Trenckner* refers to jāleti, *denom. fr.* jāla, to cover, which is found in Pāli, *cp.* Dhātup. XXXII,10; the Birm. reading is rajojallaṁ, which is always found elsewhere: Jāt. V, 421,29; Mil. p. 133 *etc.*; rajovajall(aṁ) might be due to tmesis = rajo va [= vā] jallaṁ; *cp.* rajojallika, *mfn.* covered with dust, Jāt. I, 390,18, & Sn. v. 198. 249).

rajja, *n.* (*sa.* rājya) sovereignty, government; kingdom; *nom.* ~aṁ, 112,9; *acc.* ~aṁ, 1,2. 8,3 *etc.* (~ karoti, to be king); *instr.* ~ena, 59,25; *loc.* ~e, 42,26; *comp.* *rajjatthika, *mfn.* (*v.* atthika); °-parimāṇa, *n.* 43,29 (*q. v.*); *°-sāmika, *m.* king, 43,32 (Bārāṇasi-°); °-sīmā, *f.* 39,15 (*q. v.*) *cp.* eka-°, opa-°, mahā-°, & raṭṭha.

rajju, *f.* (rarely *m.* = *sa.*) a rope; *nom.* ~u (ālambanī, *q. v.*) 47,27; *acc.* uṁ (cīvara-°, *q. v.*) 83,21; *instr.* ~uyā, 54,20. *cp. next.*

rajjuka, *m.* (*dimin. fr. last*; = *sa.*) a rope, string; *acc.* ~aṁ (uggahaṇa-°, *q. v.*) 14,32.

raññā, raññe, rañño, *v.* rāja(*n*).

raṭṭha, *n.* (*sa.* rāshṭra) kingdom, realm, country; *abl.* ~ā, 38,21; ~ā ~aṁ (*acc.* from kingdom to kingdom) 104,8; *loc.* ~e, 18,24; *comp.* °-janapada-vāsino, 102,5 (*v. h.*); °-piṇḍa, *m.* 107,2 (*v. h.*); Kāsi-°, Kosala-°, Bāveru-°, Videha-° (*q. v.*) *cp.* rajja.

rata, *mfn.* (*pp.* ramati; = *sa.*) delighting in (*loc.* or *e. c.*); *m.* ~o, Dh. 181. 300; ajjhatta-°, Dh. 362; taṇhakkhaya-°, Dh. 187; dhamma-°, Dh. 364 (*q. v.*); *pl.* ~ā (gocare) Dh. 22.

ratana[1], *n.* (*sa.* ratna) a jewel, *e. c.* a valuable or precious thing; *pl.* ~āni, 33,6; *instr. pl.* ~ehi, 27,29; 28,28 (sattahi, the 7 precious things, *i. e.* gold, silver, *etc.*) *cp.* satta-ratana-vicitta, *mfn.* ornamented with the 7 jewels, 18,26, & satta-ratana-vassa, *n.* 32,11 (*v.* vassa); *gen. pl.* ~ānaṁ (tiṇṇaṁ, the 3 jewels, *metaph.* of Buddha, Dhamma, Saṁgha) 28,26; *e. c.* assa-°, 24,19; kambala-°, 25,5; nīlamaṇi-°, 26,23; maṇi-°, 62,30; hatthi-°, 24,19 (*q. v.*) (*cp.* JRAS. XII (1880) p. 178).

ratana[2], *n.* (or ratani, *f.*; *sa.* ratni, aratni) a certain measure of length = 2 vidatthi (*q. v.*) *cp.* yojana.

rati, *f.* (= *sa.*) pleasure, delight (often *esp.* of love); *nom.* ~i, 47,27. Dh. 149; ~ī, Dh. 310; *acc.* ~iṁ, Dh. 187; *abl.* ~iyā, Dh. 214; *comp.* kāma-°, kilesa-°, dhamma-° (*v. h.*) *cp.* a-rati.

ratta[1], *mfn.* (*pp.* √rañj, rajjati, rañjati, rajati; *sa.* rakta) coloured, dyed (*esp.* with red colour); *metaph.* affected with (*e. c.*); *comp.* °-kambala, 5,27 (*v. h.*); rāga-°, *mfn.* subject to passion, *pl.* ~ā, Dh. 347; sāratta-°, *mfn.* Dh. 345 (*v. h.*) *cp.* rajana, rattatā.

ratta[2], *m. n.* (*e. c.* = ratti; *sa.* rātra) night; aḍḍha-°, 40,8 (*q. v.*); aho-°, Dh. 226 (*q. v.*); *cp.* dīgharattaṁ, *adv.*

rattatā, *f.* (*sa.* raktatā) redness; *instr.* ~āya (akkhīnaṁ) 59,5.

ratti, *f.* (*sa.* rātri) night; *nom.* ~ī (dīghā) 107,9 = Dh. 60; *acc.* ~iṁ, 58,17; 22,21 (sabba-°); *adv.* by night 9,16 (*opp.* divā); 112,7 (*cp.* rattindiva); *gen. loc.* ~iyā. 66,5. 78,1; 41,28. 42,1; an old *loc.* is ratto (*sa.* rātrau) Dh. 296; *pl. acc.* ~iyo (sabba-°) 67,27; *comp.* °-khitta, *mfn.* (*q. v.*); *°-bhatta, *n.* evening meal, 15,19; *°-bhāga, *m.* the night time, 21,23; eka-ratti-°, 104,24 (*v.* eka[2]); *aho-°, *f.* day & night (*v. h.*); at the end of *comp.* we find sometimes the a-stem ratta[2] (*q. v.*) *cp. next.*

rattindiva, *m.* & *n.* (*sa.* rātriṁdiva) night and day; *acc. adv.* ~aṁ 88,22 (*comp.* ~am-).

ratto, *adv.*, *loc.* ratti (*q. v.*).

ratha, *m.* (= *sa.*) a chariot; *nom.* ~o, 60,5; 25,1 (maṅgala-°, *q. v.*); *acc.* ~aṁ, 7,5; 63,4 (uttama-°); *instr.* ~ena (pāyāsi) 54,4; 98,2; 60,4 (Vejayanta-°, *q. v.*); *pl.* ~ā (rāja-°) Dh. 151; *comp.* *°-daṇḍaka, *m.* the banner-staff of a chariot, 98,5; *°-pañjara, *n.* 98,5 (*v. h.*); °-vara, *m.* an excellent ch., 64,10 (*acc.* ~aṁ); °-vega-, 60,10 (*q. v.*) *cp.* racchā.

randheti (or randhayati) *vb.* (*caus.* √randh) to make subject to, bring to (*acc.* & *dat.*); *aor. 3. pl.* ~ayuṁ (mā taṁ dukkhāya) Dh. 248.

°**rama**, *mfn.* (*e. c.* = *sa.*) pleasing, delighting; *v.* dū-rama, mano-rama.

ramaṇīya, *mfn.* (*grd. fr. next*; = *sa.*) pleasant, delightful, beautiful; *n.* ~aṁ (uyyānaṁ) 37,16; *loc. m.* ~e, 65,19; *n. pl.* ~ān[i] (araññāni) Dh. 99. *cp.* rāmaṇeyyaka.

ramati, *vb.* (*sa.* √ram) to be glad, to delight in (*loc.*); *pr. 3. sg.* ~ati, Dh. 79; 99 (metri causa ~atī); *1. sg. med.* rame (gahe) 47,26; *3. pl.* ~anti, Dh. 91; *1. pl.* ~āma (kilesaratiyā) 53,24; *fut. 1. pl.* ~issāma ("we will enjoy ourselves") 53,27; *fut. caus.* (= *simplex*) *3. pl.* ~essanti, Dh. 99; *pp.* rata (*q. v.*, *cp.* ramita); *grd.* ramaṇīya & ramma (*q. v.*); — *caus. II.* ramāpeti, to gladden, delight; *ger.* ~etvā (taṁ kilesaratiyā) 73,18.

ramita, *mfn.* (*pp. caus.* √ram; = *sa.*) delighted, happy; *m.* ~o, Dh. 305.

ramma, *mfn.* (*grd.* √ram; *sa.* ramya) delightful, beautiful; *loc.* ~e, 109,31.

rava, *m.* (= *sa.*) a roar, cry; song, sound; *nom.* ~o, 60,10; *acc.* ~aṁ, 53,31; 8,25 (gadrabha-°); 60,8 (mahā-°); *loc.* ~e (gadrabhānaṁ) 113,11; *gīta-°, *m.* 112,7 (*q. v.*); *bherava-°, *m.* 86,19 (*q. v.*).

ravati, *vb.* (*sa.* √ru, rauti, ravīti) to roar, cry, to set up a cry (*acc.*); *part. m. pl.* ~antā (bherava-ravaṁ) 86,19; *part. med. m.* ~māno, 9,2; *aor. 3. sg.* ravi, 8,25. 11,30; *3. pl.* ~iṁsu, 60,8; *cp.* rava, rāva, ruta.

rasa, *m.* (= *sa.*) juice, essence; taste, flavour (*esp.* agreeable), sweetness; *acc.* ~aṁ, 37,9. 106,8 = Dh. 49; Dh. 354; 16,16 (pabbata-°); *pl.* ~ā, 70,32; *loc. pl.* ~esu, 71,9; °-haraṇī, *f.* (*v. h.*); dhamma-°, & dhammapīti-° (*q. v.*); nānagga-° (*v.* nānā); paviveka-° (*q. v.*); madhura-° (*q. v.*); sadisa-°, *mfn.* of the same taste, 37,32 (nimba-paṇṇa-°); sūpa-° (*q. v.*); *dvandva comp.* vaṇṇa-gandha-°, 37,30 (°-rasūpeta, *mfn.*).

rasmi, *f.* (& *m.*) = raṁsi (*sa.* raçmi); *pl.* ~iyo, 98,6 (the reins); °-ggāha, *m.* holder of the reins (*opp.* sārathi) 106,34 = Dh. 222.

rassa, *mfn.* (*sa.* hrasva) short; *m.* ~o (puriso; *opp.* dīgho) 92,12; *n.* ~aṁ, Dh. 409.

rahada, *m.* (*sa.* hrada) a lake, pool; *nom.* ~o, Dh. 82 (metrically: rhado); Dh. 95.

rahassa, *n.* (*sa.* rahasya) a secret; *acc.* ~aṁ, 46,9. *cp. next.*

raho. *adv.* (*sa.* rahas) in secret, privately; 54,13; *°-kamma, *n.* what is to be done in secret, *acc.* ~aṁ, 54,17.

rāga, *m.* (= *sa.*) [1]) colour, dyestuff (*cp.* rajana, ratta[1], & vaṁsarāga); [2]) *metaph.* passion, lust; *nom.* ~o, 106,32 = Dh. 14; *comp.* °-aggi, *m.* the fire of lust, *loc.* ~imhi. 64,20 (in the series: rāga, dosa, moha); *°-dosa, *mfn.* damaged by passion, *f.* ~ā, Dh. 356 (*cp.* dosa[1]); *°-nissita, *mfn.* devoted to passions, Dh. 339 (*v. h.*); *°-sama, *mfn.* like passion, Dh. 202; *tibba-°, & *vīta-°, *mfn.* (*v. h.*); *dvandva comp.* nandi-rāga-°, 67,13.

rāja(n), *m.* (*sa.* rājan) a king, prince, chief; *nom.* ~ā, 6,3; *voc.* ~a (mahā-°) 7,16; *acc.* ~ānaṁ, 6,14; *instr.* raññā, 48,21; *gen.* (*dat.*) rañño,

6,5; *abl.* ~ato, Db. 139; *loc.* raññe, 52,14; *pl. nom. acc.* ~āno, 102,4. Dh. 294; *gen.* ~ūnaṁ, 37,4; – in *comp.* we have the base rāja-°, °-rāja (*e. c.* also frequently rāja*n*): agga-°, *m.* (*nom.* ~ rājā, 98,13); aja-°, *m.* (*voc.* ~ rāja, 54,26); assa-°, *m.* (*acc.* ~ānaṁ, 65,19); kapi-°, *m.* (*gen.* ~assa, 1,7); kumbhīla-°, *m.* (*voc.* ~ rāja, 1,16); Kosala-°, *m.* (*gen.* ~rañño, 31,2); cora-°, *m.* (*gen.* ~rañño, 39,35); Tamba-°, *m.* (*nom.* ~ rājā, 19,6; *instr.* ~ rājena, 19,10); deva-°, *m.* (*nom.* ~ rājā, 45,30); dhamma-°, *m.* (*nom.* ~ rājā, 19,1); nāga-°, *m.* (*nom.* ~ rājā, 28,27; *instr.* ~ rājena, 52,15); maccu-°, *m.* (*acc.* ~ānaṁ, 44,29); mahā-°, *m.* (*q. v.*); yakkha-°, *m.* (~rāja-°, 112,22); sasa-°, *m.* (*acc.* ~ rājaṁ, 15,9); Sīlavamahā-°, *m.* (*gen.* ~ rājassa, 39,11); supaṇṇa-°, *m.* (*nom.* ~ rājā, 19,15; *gen.* ~rañño, 20,10; ~ rājassa, 20,3); haṁsa-°, *m.* (*nom.* ~ rājā, 10,5; *cp.* rāja-haṁsa, 10,3); – rāj'-aṅgaṇa, *n.* (*q. v.*); °-âbhisekha, *m.* (*v.* abhisekha); °-ûpaṭṭhāna, *n.* (*v.* upaṭṭhāna); °-ovāda-jātaka, *n.* (*v.* ovāda); °-kula, *n.* (*q. v.*); *°-ñātaka, *m.* (*q. v.*); °-tanaya, *m.* (*q. v.*); °-nandana, *m.* (*v.* nandanā); °-nivesana, *n.* (*q. v.*); °-putta, *m.* a prince, a person of the royal family; *gen.* ~assa, 45,23; *instr.* ~ena, 111,8; °-purisa, *m.* a royal servant, *pl.* ~ā, 40,3. 74,7; °-ratha, *m.* a royal chariot, *pl.* ~ā, Dh. 151; *°-rathūpama, *mfn.* like a royal chariot, Dh. 171; °-seṭṭha, *m.* the best among kings, *voc.* ~a, 47,8; °-haṁsa, *m.* a kind of swan, 10,3 (suvaṇṇa-°, 'golden king-swan').

Rājagaha, *n.* (*sa.* Rājagṛha) 'the king's house', *nom. pr.* of a city, the capital of the Magadha country; *acc.* ~aṁ, 76,9; *loc.* ~e, 76,8; °-samīpe, near to R., 84,31.

Rādha, *m.* (= *sa.*) *nom. pr.* of a parrot (Bodhisatta); *nom.* ~o, 9,7; °-jātaka, *n.* 9,5.

rāmaṇeyyaka, *n.* (*fr.* ramaṇīya; *sa.* rāmaṇīyaka) loveliness, beauty; *comp.* *bhūmiṁ-°, *n.* (with ṁ inserted) a delightful place, Dh. 98 (*cp.* Tr. PM. p. 55–56).

rāva, *m.* (= *sa.*) a cry, roar; *acc.* ~aṁ (baddha-°, *q. v.*) 11,30; *instr.* ~ena (gadrabha-°, *q. v.*) 113,10. *cp.* rava.

rāsi, *m.* (*sa.* rāçi) a heap, quantity, multitude; *acc.* ~iṁ (dhanassa) 34,12; 16,3 (aṅgāra-°); 5,8 (kaṇṭaka-°); 51,11 (dāru-°); *abl.* ~imhā (puppha-°) Dh. 53; *loc.* ~imhi (aṅgāra-°) 16,7.

Rāhula, *m.* (= *sa.*) *nom. pr.* [1]) of Gotama Buddha's son [Lāghula in the Açoka Inscr. (Bhabra text)]; *nom.* ~o, 64,7 (explained by bandhanaṁ, 'a bond, fetter, impediment', *cp. Weber,* Ind. Stud. III, 130 & 149) = *°-kumāro, 64,9; *°-mātar, *f.* the mother of R., whose name according to later Buddhist tradition was Yasodharā; *nom.* ~ā, 64,5; *gen.* ~āya, 65,27; – [2]) of a sāmaṇera (*q. v.*) of Sāriputta; *nom.* ~o, 81,14.

rukkha, *m.* (*sa.* ruksha & vṛksha; *cp. Pischel,* Gr. § 320; *Wackernagel,* Gr. I, § 184, b.) a tree; *nom.* ~o, 36,36; *abl.* ~ā, 12,32; ~ato, 11,31; *loc.* ~e, 2,3; *comp.* rukkhagge, *loc.* at the top of a tree, 11,35 (*v.* agga); *°-koṭṭhaka, *m.* a woodpecker (*q. v.*); °-devatā, *f.* a dryad, 3,31; °-mūla, *n.* the foot of a tree (*q. v.*); *dvandva comp.* °-gumbâdayo, 6,11; *cp.* ārāma-°, udumbara-°, kappaṭṭhiya-°, nigrodha-°, phala-°, bodhi-°, mahā-sāla-°, varaṇa-°, susira-°.

ruci, *f.* (= *sa.*) liking, pleasure; wish, desire; *acc.* ~iṁ (uppādeti, *w. loc.* to take pleasure in, take a fancy to) 10,12. 64,2; *loc.* ~iyā (assa sati, "at his command") 39,11. *cp.* *aññarucika, *mfn.*

rucita, *mfn.* (*pp.* ruccati; = *sa.*) being at one's pleasure, agreeable; *citta-°, *mfn.* (*q. v.*).

rucira, *mfn.* (= *sa.*) beautiful, lovely; *f.* ~ā (piṭṭhi) 10,19; *n.* ~aṁ (pupphaṁ) Dh. 51.

ruccati (& °-rocati), *vb.* (*sa.* √ruc)

to please, to be agreeable to (*gen.*); *pr. 3. sg.* ~ati (no, mayhaṁ) 11,3-18; *pot. 3. sg.* ~eyya (mama) 55,25; *aor. 3. sg.* rucci (mā te ~) 74,24; *pp.* rucita (*q. v.*); *caus.* roceti (*q. v.*) *cp.* ruci, rucira.

rujati, *vb.* (*sa.* √ruj) to cause pain, ache; *pr. 3. pl.* ~anti (pādā, gacchantassa (te)) 97,36. *cp.* palujjati & roga, *m.*

ruta, *n.* (= *sa.*) cry, voice (of animals); sabba-°-jānana-manta, *m.* a spell giving knowledge of all sounds, 53,13.

***ruda**, *n.* (*cp. sa.* rud, *f.* & *prec.*) cry, voice (of animals); *nom.* ~aṁ (manuññaṁ) 10,19.

rudati (& rodati, *q. v.*), *vb.* (*sa.* √rud) to cry, weep; *part. acc. m.* ~antaṁ, 111,13.

rudda, *mfn.* (*sa.* rudra) furious, cruel, formidable; °-dassana, *mfn.* of dreadful appearance, *m.* ~o (kumbhīlo) 108,27; *cp.* ludda.

ruha, *mfn.* (*e. c.* = *sa.*) growing; *uttamaṅga-°, *v.* aṅga. *cp.* rūhati.

ruhira, *n.* (*sa.* rudhira) blood; *nom. acc.* ~aṁ, 76,7. 76,4. *cp.* rohita, lohita.

rūpa, *n.* (& *m.*) (= *sa.*) [1]) form, appearance, *esp.* handsome form, grace, beauty; *acc.* ~aṁ (manoharaṁ) 111,36; *instr.* ~ena (soṇi-°, *q. v.*) 111,2; *gen.* ~assa (ādīnavaṁ) 47,23; *comp.* *rūpagga-ppatta, *mfn. v.* agga[1], *cp.* patta[3]; *°-ppatta, *mfn.* beautiful, *f. pl.* ~ā, 64,30; °-sampatti, *f.* beauty, *acc.* ~iṁ, 19,11; °-siri, *f.* (*dvandva*) "beauty and majesty", *acc.* ~iṁ. 64,13; *uttama-rūpa-dhara, *mfn.* endowed with the highest beauty, *f.* ~ā, 19,7; *e. c.*, *v.* anurūpa, *mfn.*, abhirūpa, *mfn.*, evarūpa, *mfn.*, *kalyāna-°, *mfn.*, jāta-°, *n.*, tathā-°, *mfn.*, *bhinna-°, *mfn.*, *mūḷha-°, *mfn.*, *sādhu-°, *mfn.* — [2]) *in the dogmatics*: material form, body; idaṁ ~aṁ, 107,7 = Dh. 148 (*synon.* ayaṁ kāyo, 107,5); *esp.* as one of the five constituent elements of an individual (*v.* khandha): 94,8, *etc.*; *pl.* visible things, objects to cakkhu: ~āni, 69,17; *m. pl.* ~ā, 70,25. 71,32; *loc.* ~esu, 71,5; *°-saṁkhā-vimutta, *mfn.* "released from what is styled form", *m.* ~o (Tathāgato) 95,12; *dvandva comp.* nāma-rupa, *n.* (*v. h.*) *cp.* nāmañ ca rūpañ ca, 82,9.

rūpaka, *n.* (= *sa.*) an image, *esp.* a statue; *kañcana-°-paṭibhāga, *mfn.* 47,14 (*v.* paṭibhāga).

rūḷha, *mfn.* (*pp.* rūhati; *sa.* rūḍha) sprung up, grown; °-tiṇa, *mfn.* abounding with grass, *loc.* ~e (kacche) 104,27.

rūhati, *vb.* (*sa.* rohati, ruhati, √ruh) to grow; *pr. 3. sg.* ~ati (rukkho) Dh. 338; *pp.* rūḷha (*q. v.*); *caus.* ropeti, ropāpeti (*q. v.*) *cp.* ruha.

Revata, *m. nom. pr.* of a thera; *nom.* ~o (mahāthero) 113,8.

roga, *m.* (= *sa.*) disease; *abl.* ~ā (jigacchā paramā ~, hunger is worse than disease) Dh. 203; paṇḍu-°, *m.* (*q. v.*); *°-niḍḍa, *n.* (*v. h.*) *cp.* aroga & niroga, *mfn.*

roceti, *vb.* (*caus.* ruccati; *sa.* rocayati) to find pleasure in, to choose (*acc.*); *part. f.* ~entī (sāmikaṁ) 10,12; *aor. 3. sg.* ~esi (moraṁ) 10,10; *ger.* ~etvā (ulūkaṁ) 11,3.

rodati, *vb.* (sometimes also rudati (*q. v.*); *sa.* √rud) to cry, weep; *part. m.* [a]) ~anto, 17,9. 89,11; [b]) rodaṁ. Dh. 67; *part. med. f.* ~mānā, 58,13. 59,11; *aor. 2. sg.* rodi, 16,32; *1. sg.* rodiṁ, 17,13. 58,14 (rodin ti); *inf.* ~ituṁ, *ger.* ~itvā, 49,10.

***ropāpeti**, *vb.* (*caus. II.* rūhati) to cause to be planted (*acc.*); *ger.* ~etvā, 36,35.

ropita, *mfn.* (*fr. caus.* ropeti; = *sa.*) planted; *n.* ~aṁ, 37,6; *m. pl.* ~ā, 100,14.

***ropima**, *mfn.* planted, raised, cultivated (*opp.* kaccha, sayaṁjāta); *acc.* ~aṁ (kaṇḍaṁ) 92,19.

ropeti, *vb.* (*caus.* rūhati; *sa.* ropayati) to plant, sow (*acc.*); *aor. 3. sg.* ~esi, 37,10; *ger.* ~etvā (nivāpatiṇaṁ) 6,6; *pp.* ropita (*q. v.*) *cp.* ropima.

roruva, *m.* (*sa.* raurava, *cp.* ruru) a kind of savage animal, the Ruru-deer; *gen.* ~assa, 92,22.

rohita, *mfn.* (= *sa.*) red; °-macche, 14,23. (*cp.* lohita).

L (-ḷ-).

ḷ, Sandhi-Consonant (*sa.* -ḍ-), preserved in cha-ḷ-abhiñña, sa-ḷ-āyatana (*q. v.*).

la, *indecl.*, a syllable indicating abbreviation, = *etc.* 70,31 (*cp.* pa, pe).

***lakana(ka)**, *n.* & **lakāra**, *m.*, *v.* laṅkara.

lakkhaṇa, *n.* (*sa.* lakshaṇa) a mark, sign, attribute; a lucky mark, mark of beauty; *acc.* ~aṁ (sasa-°, the sign of a hare) 16,16; sabba-° -sampanna, *mfn.* endowed with all marks of beauty, *f.* ~ā, 55,32.

laggati, *vb.* (*sa.* √lag) to adhere, stick in (*loc.*); *aor. 3. sg.* laggi (gale) 13,11; (jāle) 36,32; *caus. v. next.*

***laggāpeti**, *vb.* (*caus. II.* laggati) to tie (*acc.*), to lay to, bring to (as a ship); *ger.* ~etvā (nāvaṁ) 25,35.

laggeti, *vb.* (*caus.* laggati; *sa.* lāgayati) to tie (*acc.*, to : *loc.*); *aor. 3. sg.* ~esi, 12,25; *ger.* ~etvā (suttaṁ hatthesu) 111,1.

Laṅkā, *f.* (= *sa.*) *nom. pr.* of the capital of Ceylon; *acc.* ~aṁ, 110,33; *loc.* ~āyaṁ, 110,34; *°-dīpa, *m.* Ceylon, 110,31; °-nagara, *n.* 112,13 (°-vāsinī, *f.*, *v.* vāsin); °-rakkhā, *f.* (*q. v.*).

***laṅkāra**, *m.* (Birm. reading of lakāra; lakana(ka) *n.* is also found) *prob.* an anchor (= *arab. pers. mahratt.* lankar, langar); *nom.* ~o, 28,30. (*cp.* Jāt. Transl. II, 78; Tr. PM. 62,16).

laṁghati, *vb.* (*sa.* √laṅgh) to leap over, spring up, ascend; *ger.* ~itvā, 16,6.

lajjati, *vb.* (*sa.* √lajj) to be ashamed (*w. gen .pers.* & *instr.* or *loc. rei*); *pr. 2. sg.* ~asi, 50,13; *1. sg.* ~āmi (*w. duo loc.*) 50,12; *3. pl.* ~anti (lajjitāye) Dh. 316. *3. pl. med.* ~are, ib.; *ger.* ~itvā, 10,22; *pp. m.* ~ito (filled with shame) 10,16; *grd.* lajjitabba (what one ought to be ashamed of) of which an elder form is found Dh. 316 : lajjitāye, *loc. n.* & a-lajjitāye (*cp.* Tr. PM. p. 66,43).

lajjā, *f.* (= *sa.*) shame; *instr.* ~āya (from shame) 46,6.

lajjita, & ~**āya**, *v.* lajjati.

***lajjin**, *mfn.* (*fr.* lajjā) endowed with the sense of shame, modest, well-conducted; *m. pl.* ~ino, 102,17.

laṭṭhi, *f.* (= yaṭṭhi (*q. v.*); *sa.* yashṭi) a stick, goad; patoda-°, *f.* (*v. h.*).

latā, *f.* (= *sa.*) a creeping plant, creeper; *nom.* ~ā, Dh. 340; *comp.* *pūti-°, & vijjullatā (*q. v.*).

laddha, *mfn.* (*pp.* labhati; *sa.* labdha) taken, obtained; arrived; *n.* ~aṁ (dukkhaṁ) 16,30; *acc. m.* ~aṁ (yasaṁ) 54,34; it is often used as finite tense : *n.* ~aṁ, 22,16. 52,23. 56,30; *f.* ~ā, 58,11; *w. auxiliary verb* : 56,30. 58,12 (~ bhavissati); in *duo loc.* 7,14 (abhaye ~e); 87,20 (okāse); sometimes it is even used in active sense: 'has got, obtained' : na kho tvaṁ ... patiṭṭhaṁ laddho, 28,15; – *comp.* *°-âbhaya, *mfn.* (*v.* a-bhaya); *°-ovāda, *m.* (admonition obtained from, *abl.*) 8,11; *°-kahāpaṇa, *m.* (money received or gained, *i. e.* blood money) 74,6; *°-gabbha-parihāra, *mfn.* (*v. h.*); *°-pabbajjūpasampada, *mfn.* (*v.* upasampadā); °-vijayo, 112,22 (*v.* Corrections); *cp.* *micchā-°, & su-laddha, *mfn.*

°**laddhaka**, *mfn.* (*sa.* labdhaka) = *prec.* (only *e. c.*); *abhaya-°, *mfn.* (*v.* a-bhaya).

laddhā, *ger.* & **laddhuṁ**, *inf.*, *v.* labhati.

***lapa**, *mfn.* (*fr. next*) talking, speaking (*esp.* falsely), hypocritical; *°-sakkhara, *mfn.* speaking sweetly, wheedling, *f. pl.* ~ā, 51,34.

lapati, *vb.* (*sa.* √lap) to talk, prate; *caus.* lapayati (lapeti) id.; *pr. 3. pl.* ~ayanti, Dh. 83; *cp.* lapa, lapana.

lapana, *n.* (= *sa.*) talking, speaking; niratthaka-°, *n.* nonsense; *instr.* ~ena, 52,6.

labuja, *m.* (*sa.* lakuca & likuca, *cp.* libujā) the bread-fruit tree (Artocarpus Lacucha); amba-labujâdīnaṁ (*gen. pl.*, *v.* ādi) 1,14 (*cp.* panasa).

labbha, *mfn.* (*grd.* labhati; *sa.* labhya) obtainable, attainable, possible; *n. pl.* ~ā (piyā) 55,2; hence *labbhā, *indecl.* (probably originally *subst. f.*) frequently used in passive constructions like sakkā (*q. v.*).

labbhati, *pass.*, *v.* labhati.

°labha, *mfn.* (*e. c.* = *sa.*), *v.* dullabha.

labhati, *vb.* (*sa.* √labh) to take, catch, find; to get, obtain, receive (*acc.*); to be allowed, or have opportunity of (doing anything, *w. foll. inf.*); *pr. 3. sg.* ~ati (paharituṁ) 8,4; (icchaṁ) 67,10; (okāsaṁ) 87,19; metri causa ~atī, Dh. 374; *1. sg.* ~āmi (*hist. pr.*) 108,25; *2. pl.* ~atha (khāadituṁ) 8,6; *3. sg. med.* ~ate, Dh. 131. 103,32 (sukhaṁ); *part. m.* ~anto, 48,34; a-labhanto, 3,7; *f.* ~antī (a-°) 46,3; *f. pl.* ~antiyo, 21,16; *part. med. m.* ~māno, 37,31; *f.* ~mānā (a-°) 6,36; *imp. 3. pl.* ~antu (tāva, be it then that they obtain) 7,18; *1. pl. med.* (injunctive) labhāmase, 13,26; *pot. 1. sg.* ~eyyaṁ, 15,11. 70,15; ~eyyâhaṁ, 70,14; *3. sg. med.* ~etha, Dh. 328; *aor. 1. sg.* labhiṁ (jīvitaṁ, saved my life) 12,33; *3. pl.* ~iṁsu, 28,16; *fut. 3. sg.* [a]) labhissati (jīvitaṁ) 12,3; *1. sg.* ~issāmi, 1,10. 4,36, *etc.*; *3. pl.* ~issanti (abhayaṁ) 7,16; *2. pl.* ~issatha, 18,10; [b]) *2. sg.* lacchasi, 2,30; *inf.* laddhuṁ, 11,1; *ger.* [a]) ~itvā, 6,21, 28,13 (patiṭṭhaṁ); 60,21 (balaṁ); a-labhitvā, 10,22. 73,4. 102,27; [b]) ~itvāna, 54,29; — *pass.* (to be found, obtained, acquired) *pr. 3. sg.* labbhati (yassa mittadhammo ~, whose friendship is acquired) 14,3; *part.* labbhamāne (*loc. m.*) 48,7; *pp.* laddha (*q. v.*); *grd.* labbha (*q. v.*) *cp.* °labha, lābha.

lasikā, *f.* (*sa.* lasīkā) the lubricous fluid of the joints, synovial fluid; 82,5 = 97,23.

lahu, *mfn.* (*sa.* laghu) light, quick; inconstant, flighty; *gen. n.* ~uno (cittassa) Dh. 35; *n.* (*adv.*) lahuṁ, quickly, Dh. 369.

lākhā, *f.* (*sa.* lākshā) lac; *°-parikamma-kata, *mfn.* lacquered, 5,28.

lāja, *m.* (= *sa.*) [1]) fried or parched grain; *dvandva comp.* madhulāja-°, 18,27. — [2]) a kind of flowers (of Dalbergia arborea, *Childers*); lājâdībi, 61,24 (*v.* ādi).

lābha, *m.* (= *sa.*) obtaining, acquisition, gain, profit; *nom.* ~o, 18,35; *dat.* ~ā (shortened of lābhāya, *cp. Kuhn,* Beitr. p. 71; *Weber,* Ind. Str. III, 371) 70,7. 105,25, if not we have here *pl.* = *sg.*, *cp.* Dh. 204 : ārogyaparamā (*q. v.*) lābhā, which must be *nom. pl.*; but ārogya-paramā might perhaps be an old error for ārogyaṁ paramā (or paramaṁ); if ~aṁ lābhā is the true reading, we have to translate : health is better than gain, and lābhā would be *abl.* (*cp.* rogā, Dh. 203), parama being used in the sense of a *comparative*; — *comp. v.* *a-puñña-°, *m.*; *appa-°, *mfn.*; salābha, *m.* (*v.* sa-[4]); lābhagga, *n.* the highest gain (*v.* agga[3]); *dvandva* : °-sakkāra, *m.* gain and honour, *nom.* ~o, 18,29; *loc.* ~e, 72,28; *hata-°-sakkāra, *mfn.* who has lost his gain and honour, *m. pl.* ~ā, 72,28; *cp.* *lābhūpanisa, *mfn.* (? *v.* upanisā).

Lāḷa, *m.* (*sa.* lāṭa) *nom. pr.* of a country in India (*cp. Westergaard,* Buddha's Dødsaar, Overs. Vid. Selsk. Forh. Copenh. 1860, p. 162); °-visaya, *m.* 'who has L. for his dominion', i. e. king of the Lāḷa Country, 110,22 (Vijayo).

lālā, *f.* (= *sa.*) saliva, spittle;

°-kilinna-gatta, *mfn.* whose body is wet with spittle, *f. pl.* ~ā, 65,5.

lippati, *vb.* (*pass.* limpati, to besmear, taint, defile; *sa.* √lip) to adhere, cling to (*loc.*); *pr. 3. sg.* ~ati (kāmesu) Dh. 401. *cp.* lepana.

līna, *mfn.* (= *sa.*; *pp.* √lī) 'adhering'; dissolved, melted; slothful; modest, humble, dispirited (often *opp.* uddhata); *a-līna, *mfn.* free from attachment, or: undaunted, confident, cheerful; Dh. 245 (*cp. J. J. Meyer*, Daçakumāracarita, p. 8–9, note).

***līḷhā**, *f.* (*prob. fr.* √lih: 'delicate taste, delicacy') grace, charm, graceful power (*cp. sa.* līlā); *instr.* ~āya (Buddha-° dhammaṁ desetvā) 7,27. 47,17; (kinnara-°, *q. v.*) 49,12.

luñcati, *vb.* (*sa.* √luñc) to pluck, pull out (*acc.*); *ger.* ~itvā (palitaṁ, kesaṁ) 46,28–29.

ludda[1], *mfn.* (*sa.* rudra) furious, cruel; *cp.* rudda; *n. pl. acc.* ~āni, cruelties, 13,28 (*cp. next*).

ludda[2], *m.* (*sa.* lubdha, confounded with rudra = ludda[1]) a hunter; ~o, 12,8; *gen.* ~assa, 12,7; *°-putta, *m.* a person who is by caste a hunter, *acc.* ~aṁ, 12,22. (*cp.* Tr. PM. p. 59,19. 63,31; *Fausbøll*, 5 Jāt. p. 38.)

luddaka, *m.* (*sa.* lubdhaka) a hunter; *nom.* ~o, 9,8; 11,27 (miga-°).

Lumbini-vana, *n. nom. pr.* of a grove between Kapilavatthu and Devadaha (the birthplace of Gotama-Buddha); ~aṁ, 62,9–13.

lekhā, *f.* (= *sa.*) a line, stroke; *acc.* ~aṁ (kaḍḍhitvā) 59,6; °-majjhe, 59,7.

leḍḍu (or leṇḍu, Birm. also leṭṭu) *m.* (& *n.*) (*sa.* leshṭu, *cp.* leṇḍa) a clod or lump of earth; °-ādīhi, 52,17 (*cp.* ādi).

lepana, *n.* (= *sa.*) smearing, plastering; maṁsa-lohita-°, *mfn.* plastered with flesh and blood, *n.* ~aṁ (aṭṭhīnaṁ nagaraṁ) Dh. 150.

loka, *m.* (= *sa.*) 1) the universe, a region or sphere of the universe; the world, the earth; *acc.* ~aṁ, 86,28; (saggaṁ, heaven) 7,26; *loc.* ~e, 3,23. 61,33. 69,21; ~asmiṁ, Dh. 247; metri causa ~asmi, Dh. 143; °-dhātu, *f.* (*v. h.*); °-nāyaka, *m.* (*v. h.*); *°-sannivāsa, *m.* (*q. v.*); *cp.* deva-°, para-°, Brahma-°, Yama-°; 2) the life in this world, this existence (= bhava, saṁsāra); ayaṁ ~o, 96,7; *abl.* ~amhā, 91,5. Dh. 175; *loc.* ~e, 96,8–10; *°-nirodha, *m.* & *°-samudaya, *m.* (*q. v.*); °-vagga, *m.* name of ch. XIII of Dh.; *°-vaddhana, *mfn.* supporting or cherishing this existence, *m.* ~o, Dh. 167; *cp.* vanta-lokāmisa, *mfn.* & sabba-lokābhibhū (*v.* abhibhū); — 3) mankind, people, men; ayaṁ ~o, 88,29 = ayaṁ lokamahājano, 88,31; sabbo ~o, 90,22; jīva-°, *m.* living beings, 47,17.

loṇa, *n.* (*sa.* lavaṇa) salt; °-jala, *n.* salt water, 24,16 (°-pahaṭa, *mfn.*).

lobha, *m.* (= *sa.*) cupidity, covetousness, greediness; *nom.* ~o (ca nām' esa vināsamūlaṁ, now, 'covetousness is the root of ruin' [proverbially], lit. 'this very covetousness') 33,25; Dh. 248; *acc.* ~aṁ (imassa karissāmi, excite his senses) 47,4; *instr.* ~ena, 25,33; (dhana-°) 22,22; *dvandva comp.* icchā-lobha-°, Dh. 264.

lobhayati, *vb.* (= *sa.*, *caus.* √lubh) to cause to desire, to excite lust; *part. f.* ~ ayantī (va naresu gacchati, she walks among men as it were in order to excite their senses) 47,20.

loma, *m.* (& *n.*) (*sa.* loman) the hair of the body; *pl.* ~ā, 82,2 = 97,19; lomantaresu, 16,5 (*v.* antara); °-kūpa, *m.* (*q. v.*). *cp.* anuloma, paṭiloma, viloma & *next*.

loma-haṁsa & **-haṁsana**, *mfn.* 'causing erection of the hairs of the body', *i. e.* terrible (*subst. n.* terror); *m.* ~ haṁso (bhūmicālo) 80,20; *n.* ~ haṁsanaṁ, 81,3.

lola, *mfn.* (= *sa.*) wanton, lustful; itthi-°, *mfn.* (*v.* itthī); a-lola, *mfn.* (*q. v.*).

loha, *n.* (= *sa.*) iron, any metal;

*°-guḷa, *m.* an iron-ball, Dh. 371; *°-nigaḷa-sadisa, *mfn.* like an iron chain, 11,28.

lohita, [1]) *mfn.* (= *sa.*) red; °-candana-vilepana, *n.* 23,33 (*v. h.*); *cp.* rohita. — [2]) *n.* blood; *nom.* ~aṁ, 23,32. 103,19. 82,5 = 97,22; *loc.* ~e, 103,20; *°-pakkhandikā, *f.* dysentery, 78,24; *°-bhakkha, *mfn.* (*q. v.*); *°-makkhita, *mfn.* (*q. v.*); *dvandva comp.* °-maṁsa-. 41,33 (°-khādaka, *mfn. q. v.*); maṁsa-°, Dh. 150 (°-lepana, *n. q. v.*). *cp.* sālohita.

V.

va, *indecl.* [1]) enclitic particle, shortened of iva (*q. v.*), only after words ending with a long vowel : like, as if; 9,32. 20,16. 47,20. 88,30-33 (vā'ti); 104, 6-13 (°~aṁ va); 108,5 (do.); 111,10. Dh. 28; as conjunction with full sentence : Dh. 240 (*corr. w. foll.* evaṁ). — [2]) do. = eva (*q. v.*), after long vowels : just, even, only, *etc.* : 5,32, 22,1. 55,2. 69,21; 2,32. 6,20-29. 10,22. 17,20; 22,25. 86,7; — 30,25. 32,5. 33,31. 37,31; 44,31. 57,25, etc. etc. — [3]) do. rarely = vā, 'or' : 26,5 (aggīva suriyo va); 26,13-20-27; Dh. 195 (yadiva = yadi vā).

vaṁsa, *m.* (*sa.* vaṁça) [1]) bamboo; *cīvara-°, *q. v.*; *°-rāga-, the colour of bamboo, 26,31 (°-veḷuriyaṁ, *q. v.*). — [2]) race, lineage, family; *acc.* ~aṁ, 45,17. — [3]) tradition, list of teachers; genealogy, history, chronicle; *v.* Anāgata-vaṁsa, Dīpavaṁsa, Mahāvaṁsa.

vakka, *n.* (*sa.* vṛkka) kidney; *nom.* ~aṁ, 82,3 = 97,21.

vagga, *m.* (*sa.* varga) [1]) a division, class, group, multitude; [2]) a chapter or section of a book; *°-paññāsaka, *mfn.* (*v. h.*); *esp.* of the sections of Dīgha-Nikāya; the chapters of Dhpd. are likewise named vagga. *cp.* pañcavaggiya, *mfn.*

vaṁka, *mfn.* (*sa.* vakra, *cp.* vaṅkya) crooked, curved, wry; *acc. m.* ~aṁ, 63,9; °-gati, *mfn.* having a winding course, *f.* ~ī (nadī) 48,6; *vaṁkoṭṭha, *mfn.* 54,20 (*v.* oṭṭha).

Vaṅgīsa, *m.* (*cp. sa.* vāg-īça) *nom. pr.* of a thera, 109,8 (~o paṭibhānavā).

vaca(*s*), *m.* & *n.* (*sa.* vacas, *n.*) speech; *acc. n.* ~o, 110,26; dubbaca, *mfn.* (*q. v.*) *cp.* vacī, vācā, vācasika, & *next.*

vacana, *n.* (= *sa.*) speaking. speech, word; advice, instruction; *acc.* ~aṁ (sutvā) 6,17; ~aṁ karoti, to follow one's advice, 4,8. 32,25; ~aṁ bhindati, to disobey, 40,2; ~aṁ agaṇhantiṁ, disobeying, 52,32; eka-vacanena, *instr.* 57,31 (*v.* eka[3]); — °-kara. *mfn.* obedient, *acc. m. pl.* ~e, 21,33; Buddha-°, *n.* (*q. v.*); *cp.* paṭi-vacana.

*vacī, *f.* (mostly at the beginning of *comp.*) speech, word; °-duccarita, *n.* misbehaviour in speech, 86,8 (°-sannissita, *mfn. q. v.*); °-pakopa, *m.* anger of speech, *acc.* ~aṁ, Dh. 232; °-sucarita, *n.* good conduct in speech, 86,8 (°-paṭisaṁyutta, *q. v.*).

vaccha, *m.* (*sa.* vatsa) [1]) a calf; *nom.* ~o, Dh. 284; °-danta, *m.* a kind of arrow, *acc.* ~aṁ, 92,24 (a calf-tooth arrow). — [2]) *nom. pr.*, *v. next.*

*Vacchagotta, *m. nom. pr.* of an ascetic (paribbājaka); *nom.* ~o, 93,22; *voc.* Vaccha, 94,7.

vajati, *vb.* (*sa.* √vraj) to go, walk, wander; to go away; to enter into, attain (*acc.*); *pr. 3. pl.* ~anti, 47,28 = Dh. 347; Dh. 83; (sugatiṁ) 77,5; (devalokaṁ) Dh. 177.

vajira, *n.* (rarely *m.*; *sa.* vajra) [1]) a diamond; *nom.* ~aṁ, 25,32. Dh. 161; *pl.* ~āni, 27,29; *°-samudda, *m.* a diamond sea, 25,33; °-sāra, *m.* a good deal of d., *acc.* ~aṁ, 26,1. — [[2]) a thunderbolt.]

Vajirā, *f. nom. pr.* of a bhikkhunī, contemporary of Buddha; *instr.* ~āya, 98,28.

vajja[1], *n.* (*sa.* vadya & vādya) speech, speaking; *v.* sacca-°.

vajja[2], *n.* (*sa.* varjya) 'to be shunned', *i. e.* fault, sin; *nom.* ~aṁ, 106,16 = Dh. 252; *acc. abl.* ~aṁ ~ato ñatvā, considering sin what is sin, Dh. 319; *pl.* ~āni, 106,17; *⁰-dassin, *mfn.* seeing fault, pointing out what is sin, *acc. m.* ~inaṁ, Dh. 76; *⁰-mati, *mfn.* seeing sin, *m. pl.* ~ino, Dh. 318 (avajje); para-⁰, the faults of others, Dh. 253 (⁰-anupassin, *q. v.*); *cp.* a-vajja.

vajjha, *mfn.* (*sa.* vadhya, *grd.* vadhati) to be killed; *subst. n.* (or ~ā, *f.*) killing, execution; *⁰-ppatta, *mfn.* sentenced to death, *m. pl.* ~ā, 40,14.

vañcana, *n.* [or ~ā, *f.*] (= *sa.*) deception, fraud; *nom.* ~aṁ, 51,35.

vañceti, *vb.* (*caus.* √vañc, *sa.* vañcayati) 'to cause to go astray', i. e. to deceive, trick (*acc.*); *aor. 1. sg.* ~esiṁ (taṁ) 2,7; *inf.* ~etuṁ (attano sāmikaṁ, seems to be a gloss inserted into the text) 51,27; *comp.* vañcetu-kāma, *mfn.* (*v.* kāma[2]); *ger.* ~etvā (macche) 4,2; (padaṁ, picked up his heels) 12,30; *grd.* ~etabba, *mfn.* to be tricked, *m.* ~o, 3,15; *pp.* vañcita, *mfn.* tricked, *m.* ~o, 51,25. 2,13; ⁰-bhāva, *m.* the being tricked, *acc.* ~aṁ (mayā) 5,11. *cp.* vañcana.

vaṭṭa, *n.*, *v.* vatta.

vaṭṭaka, *m.* (*sa.* vartaka) a certain kind of bird, a quail; *loc. pl.* ~esu, 88,34.

vaṭṭati, *vb.* (*sa.* √vṛt) [1]) to turn, roll; to take place, be found; to live; in this sense it is nearly always written vattati (*q. v.*); [2]) *pr. 3. sg.* [a]) *impersonally*: must, ought; may, is permitted, advisable, sufficient, *etc.* (*w. inf.*, the subject of which, if added, is put into *instr.* or *gen.*); kin te . . . khādituṁ ~ (had you not better to eat) 1,16; amhākaṁ . . . laddhuṁ ~, 11,1; amhehi palāyituṁ ~, 21,27; mayā ~. 35,26-36. 36,8. 43,3. 64,24. 65,14 ("it behoves me"); mayā ettha kiṁ kātuṁ ~ ("what can I do about that?") 73,7; tava gantuṁ ~, 50,8; imāya me paricārikāya bhavituṁ ~, 56,4; *without subject* (& *object*): idaṁ kātuṁ ~, 44,13; laddhaṁ yasaṁ pahātuṁ na ~, 54,35; dametuṁ ~ ("it will be worthy [of me] to convert [him]") 113,9. — [b]) *personally*: ought to take place, is good, is sufficient; appatissavāso na ~, 10,31; eko va [dovāriko] ~, 91,23. — *caus.* vaṭṭeti, to cause to turn, to upset; *pp.* vaṭṭita (*v. below*).

vaṭṭi, *f.* (*sa.* varti) [1]) a roll, tuft (*esp.* the wick of a lamp), a lump, mass; [2]) rounding, edge, rim, brim, *esp. comp. w.* mukha-⁰; *āvāṭa-mukhavaṭṭiyaṁ, *loc.* "at the brink of the pit", 40,28.

vaḍḍhati, *vb.* (sometimes spelt vaddhati; *sa.* √vṛdh) to grow, increase; *pr. 3. sg.* ~ati (udakaṁ, *opp.* hāyati) 3,4; 48,21 (grows up); 107,29 (taṇhā); *3. pl.* ~anti, Dh. 109; *part. m.* ~anto, 24,12; *aor. 3. pl.* ~iṁsu, 37,20; *pp.* [a]) vaddha & vuḍḍha (*q. v.*); [b]) vaḍḍhita, *m.* ~o (sammā, grown properly) 24,33; *caus. v. next etc. cp.* vaddhana. vaḍḍhi & vuddhi.

vaḍḍhāpeti, *vb.* (*caus. II.* vaḍḍhati; *sa.* vardhāpayati) to cause to increase, raise (*acc.*); *inf.* ~etuṁ (vetanaṁ) 76,12.

vaḍḍhi, *f.* (*cp.* vuddhi; *sa.* vṛddhi) growth, increase; prosperity, success; gain, profit; *acc.* ~iṁ. 34,18.

vaḍḍheti, *vb.* (*caus.* vaḍḍhati; *sa.* vardhayati) to cause to grow, increase; to foster, bring up; to prepare, make ready, bring, deliver (a discourse *etc.*) (*w. acc.*); *pr. 1. sg.* ~emi (yāguṁ) 56,36; *aor. 3. sg.* ~esi (Bodhisattaṁ) 45,25; (tasaraṁ), 87,17; *ger.* ~etvā. 18,11-26. 63,18. 87,12.

vaṇa, *m.* (& *n.*) (*sa.* vraṇa) a wound; ~o, Dh. 124; *cp.* a-bbaṇa, *mfn.* & vaṇita.

vaṇijjā, *f.* (*sa.* vaṇijyā) trade; *acc.* ~aṁ (karoti) 30,2; *cp.* vāṇija.

vaṇita, *mfn.* (*sa.* vraṇita) wounded; *m. pl.* ~ā, 6,28.

vaṇṭa, *n.* (*sa.* vṛnta) the footstalk of a leaf (or flower); tāla-⁰, *n.* (*q. v.*).

vaṇṇa, *m.* (*sa.* varṇa) [1]) form, shape, appearance; *instr.* ~ena (nāvāya, "in ship-shape") 29,11; kassaka-°, the appearance of a ploughman, *acc.* ~aṁ. 71,28; — [2]) complexion, colour (also: tribe, caste); *nom.* ~o, 85,16; °-gandha, *m.* (*dvandva*) colour and scent, 37,30; 106,2; °-pokkharatā, *f.* (*q. v.*); °-sadda, *m.* the word vaṇṇa, 85,22; very frequently at the end of *comp. mfn.* = having the colour of . . ., coloured, *v.* añjana-°, kāḷa-° (°-kata, 84,21), kāḷa-pāsāṇa-kūṭa-°, 24,21; kumuda-patta-°, nīla-°, meda-°, rajata-°, rajata-dāma-°, 61,19; rattakambala-puñja-°, 5,27; suvaṇṇa-°; *chabbaṇṇa, *mfn.* of six colours (*q. v.*); pañca-°, *mfn.* of five colours, 4,9 (°-paduma-); 62,12 (°-bhamara-gaṇā); — [3]) beauty; ~o, Dh. 109; *gen.* ~assa, Dh. 241; chavi-°, 18,7; sarīra-°, 47,5; — [4]) praise, glory; *v.* a-vaṇṇa. — *cp.* Uppala-vaṇṇa, dubbaṇṇa, vevaṇṇiya, suvaṇṇa (sovaṇṇa), *next etc.*

vaṇṇanā, *f.* (*sa.* varṇanā) explanation, commentary; 86,10 (Sūkarapeta-vatthu-°).

vaṇṇavat, *mfn.* (*sa.* varṇavat) of beautiful colour; *n.* ~vantaṁ (puppham) Dh. 51.

vaṇṇita, *mfn.* (*sa.* varṇita) praised; *loc. m.* ~e (guṇe) 47,3; Satthu-°, *mfn.* praised by the Master, *m. pl.* ~ā, 109,19.

°vaṇṇin, *mfn.* (*sa.* varṇin; only *e. c.*) having the colour of °, like, resembling; *m. pl.* ~ino (devakumāra-°) 45,26.

vaṇṇeti, *vb.* (*fr.* vaṇṇa; *sa.* varṇayati) to colour, depict, describe; to praise (*acc.*); *aor. 3. sg.* ~esi, 4,18. 37,13. 64,1; *fut. 1. sg.* ~essāmi, 47,5.

vata[1], *adv.* (= *sa.*) a particle inserted after the first word of a sentence, often followed by bho (*q. v.*): [1]) expressing asseveration or admission: certainly, indeed, truly; 2,12. 30,8 (vat'ayaṁ); 34,17. 42,13. 90,25. 105,23; — [2]) expressive of [a]) astonishment: aho vata bho, 42,17; [b]) of satisfaction or hopefulness: ~bho, 76,31–33; [c]) of delight: sobhati vatâyaṁ dārako, what a pretty little child! 58,31; [d]) of regret or hopelessness: dhi-r-atthu ~bho, 63,18; upaddutaṁ ~bho, 65,12; aciraṁ vat'ayaṁ, 107,5 = Dh. 41.

vata[2], *n.* (*sa.* vrata) observance, religious duty, a religious vow; ~aṁ, Dh. 312; *cp.* a-bbata, su-bbata, sīla-bbata & *next.*

vatavat, *mfn.* (*sa.* vratavat) dutiful, performing the religious duties; *acc. m.* ~vantaṁ, Dh. 208. 400.

vati, *f.* (*sa.* vṛti) a hedge, fence; *acc.* ~iṁ, 8,7.

vatta (& vaṭṭa), *n.* (*sa.* vṛtta) a circle; practice, custom; good conduct, politeness; business, duty, service; *comp.* vatta-paṭivattaṁ, every single duty, 36,7 (tāpasassa akāsi, he rendered him every service). *cp.* paṭi & *next.*

***vatta-kata** (or °-gata), *mfn.* round, circular; wide-open; *instr.* ~ena (mukhena) 5,13.

vattati, *vb.* (= vaṭṭati, *q. v.*) to take place, set in; to be found; to live; *pr. 3. sg.* ~ati (ravo, is heard) 60,10; *3. pl.* ~anti (kharā vedanā, set in) 13,13; 78,25 (*w. gen.* came upon him); *fut. 1. sg.* ~issāmi (guṇesu, live a good life) 43,4; — *mcd. pr. 3. sg.* vattate (ussavo mahā) 112,16. *cp.* vatta (vaṭṭa) *n.*

vattabba, **vattuṁ**, *v.* (vadati &) vuccati.

vattha, *n.* (*sa.* vastra) cloth, garment, dress; *nom.* ~aṁ (suddhaṁ) 68,34; *acc.* ~aṁ (dibba-°) 61,13; *instr.* ~ena, 20,26; *loc.* ~e (Kāsika-°, *q. v.*) 62,29; *pl.* ~āni (ahata-°, *q. v.*) 27,18. 33,3; *instr. pl.* ~ehi (dibba-°) 20,8; *comp.* ahata-vattha-°, 61,28; apagata-°, *mfn.* with the dress fallen apart, *f. pl.* ~ā, 65,7.

vatthu, *n.* (*sa.* vastu [& vāstu]) [1]) site, place, ground (of a building *etc.*) *v.* Kapila-°, Sirīsa-°, & a-vatthu-kata, *mfn.* — [2]) thing, object, matter (of a story *etc.*); property;

nom. ~uṁ (a tale, story) 89,17; *loc.* ~umhi (parassa rakkhita-gopita-°, "in protecting and guarding the property of others") 58,13; sūkara-peta-°, 86,10 (*q. v.*) *cp.* Kathā-vatthu.

vatvā, *ger.*, *v.* (*next* &) vuccati.

vadati & ***vadeti**, *vb.* (*sa.* √vad; suppletive of vuccati, *q. v.*) to say, speak (*acc.*), answer; to speak to (*acc.*), to tell (*acc. gen.*), to declare; — A) vadati, *3. sg.* 73,18. 85,29; *2. sg.* ~asi, 24,1. 88,7; *1. sg.* ~āmi, 70,30. 94,13; (saccaṁ) 38,28; (taṁ) 108,3; (naṁ, speak to her) 9,18; *3. pl.* ~anti, 21,6. 72,30; *part. acc. m.* ~antaṁ, 22,18, *loc.* ~ante. 9,3, *pl.* ~antā, 74,11; *part. med. m.* ~ amāno, 99,31; *pot. 3. sg.* ~eyya, 79,15. 92,2; *2. sg.* ~eyyāsi, 35,8. 99,14; *3. pl.* ~eyyuṁ (guṇaṁ, praise) 43,8; *aor.* [a]) *2. sg.* vādi (mā) 9,19; [b]) *3. sg.* vadi (taṁ) 108,28; *3. pl.* ~iṁsu, 24,27. 73,31. — B) vadeti. *pr. 2. sg.* ~esi, 17,14; *1. sg.* ~emi, 88,19; *imp. 2. sg.* ~ehi, 51,15; *2. pl.* ~etha (mā kiñci rañño ~) 55,26; *aor. 2. sg.* ~esi, 88,13. 93,31; *1. sg.* ~esiṁ, 88,24. — *caus.* vādeti (*q. v.*). As to the wanting forms of this verb (*act.* & *pass.*) *v.* vuccati (√vac); *cp.* vajja, vadana, vāda, vādin.

vadana, *n.* (= *sa.*) 'speaking, mouth'; speech, communication, injunction; *acc.* ~aṁ (avoca) 110,31.

***vadeti**, *vb.* = vadati (*q. v.*).

vaddha[1], *m.* [or *n.*?] (*sa.* vardhra) leather, a leathern strap or thong; *acc.* ~aṁ, 12,30; — *°-maya. *mfn.* leathern, *acc. m.* ~aṁ (pāsaṁ) 11,29. *cp.* varattā.

vaddha[2], *mfn.* (also spelt vuḍḍha [or vuddha], *pp.* vaḍḍhati; *sa.* vṛddha) grown; old; *comp.* *vaddhāpacāyin. *mfn.* (*v.* apacāyin).

vaddhati, *vb.*, *v.* vaḍḍhati.

°vaddhana, *mfn.* (*e. c.*, *sa.* vardhana) causing to increase; *loka-°, *mfn.* (*q. v.*).

vadha, *m.* (= *sa.*) killing, destroying; murder; execution or corporal punishment; *comp.* miga-°, 5,32; pāṇa-°, 60,13 (*q. v.*); purisa-°, 74,14 (*q. v.*); *dvandva*: vadha-bandha, *m. acc.* ~aṁ, Dh. 399 ("stripes and bonds").

vadhaka, *mfn.* (= *sa.*) killing or intending to kill; *°-citta, *mfn.* with murderous intent, 75,24; *satthu-°, *mfn.* 108,27 (*v.* satthar).

vadhati, *vb.* (*sa.* √vadh) to kill, murder (*acc.*); *aor. 3. sg.* a-vadhi, Dh. 3; *ger.* ~itvā, 13,23. 22,11. *cp.* vajjha, vadha, vadhaka.

vana, *n.* (rarely *m.*; = *sa.*) [1]) a forest, grove; *acc.* ~aṁ, 5,20; *loc.* ~e, 15,15; ~asmiṁ, 106,13 = Dh. 395; ~asmi, 107,30 = Dh. 334; *pl.* vanā (sabbe) 48,6; ~āni, Dh. 188; *comp.* °-gumba, *m.* (*q. v.*); *°-cāraka. *m.* a forester, *acc. pl.* ~e, 36,34; °-puppha, *n.* a wild flower, *instr. pl.* ~ehi, 34,6; *°-mahisa, *m.* (*q. v.*); °-saṇḍa, *m.* (*q. v.*); *cp.* amba-°, Cittalatā-°, tāla-°, naḷa-°, nāga-°, maṅgala-sāla-°, Lumbini-°, veḷu-°, Simbali-°. — [2]) lust, desire (*cp. ved. sa.* vanas); *acc.* ~aṁ, *abl.* ~ato, Dh. 283; vanante, *loc.* "at the end of desires", Dh. 305 (*cp.* anta); *°-ādhimutta, *°-mutta, *mfn.* (*v. h.*) Dh. 344. *cp. next* & nibbana.

***vanatha**, *m.* (*cp.* vana[2] & *sa.* √van) lust, desire; *nom.* ~o, Dh. 284; *acc.* ~aṁ, Dh. 283 (vanaṁ ~añ ca, "the forest of desires and its undergrowth").

vanta, *mfn.* (*sa.* vānta; *pp.* vamati) vomited; ejected, put away; *°-kasāva, *mfn.* (*q. v.*); *°-dosa, *mfn.* (*v.* dosa[2]); *°-mala, *mfn.* (*q. v.*); *°-lokāmisa, *mfn.* "who has rejected the baits of the world", Dh. 378 (*cp.* āmisa); *°-āsa, *mfn.* (*v.* āsā).

vandati, *vb.* (*sa.* √vand) to praise, worship; to salute, greet (*acc.*); *ger.* ~itvā. 28,10. 32,23 (ācariyaṁ); *inf.* ~ituṁ (Mahābodhiṁ) 114,32. *cp. next.*

vandanā, *f.* (= *sa.*) praise, worship; *nom.* ~ā (Buddhāna[ṁ]) 108,20.

vapati, *vb.* (*sa.* √vap) to sow,

strew, throw (*acc.*); *ger.* ~itvā (nivāpaṁ) 6,4.

vapayāti. *vb.* (*sa.* vi-apa-√yā) to go away, pass away, vanish; *pr. 3. pl.* ~ayanti (kaṅkhā) 66,21 (*cp. Kuhn,* Beitr. p. 96–97).

vamati, *vb.* (*sa.* √vam) to vomit; *pp.* vanta (*q. v.*).

vaya[1], *m.* (& vaya(*s*), *n.*; *sa.* vayas) age, vigorous age, youth, ripe age, old age; *nom.* ~o (paripakko) Dh. 260; *acc.* ~aṁ, 43,26; *acc. n.* vayo (anuppatto) 74,21; *loc.* ~e (pariṇamante) 47,12; *comp.* vaya- & vayo-: *~a-ppatta, *mfn.* grown up, marriageable; *m.* ~o, 8,15; *f.* ~ā, 101,16; *samāna-vaya-bhava, *m.* the being of equal age, *acc.* ~aṁ, 43,29; *~o-hara, *mfn.* indicating or disclosing old age, *m. pl.* ~ā, (uttamaṅgaruhā) 45,11; upanīta-vaya, *mfn.* (*q. v.*).

vaya[2] (or vyaya), *m.* (*sa.* vyaya) perishing, decay, destruction; *⁰-dhamma, *mfn.* perishable, transitory; *pl. m.* ~ā (saṁkhārā) 80,8 (*cp.* dhamma[4]); *uppāda-vaya-dhammin, *mfn.* (*q. v.*); *dvandva comp.* udaya-vyaya, *m.* origin and destruction, *acc.* ~aṁ, Dh. 113. 374 (*v. l.* udayabbayaṁ).

vara, [1]) *mfn.* (= *sa.*) best, choicest, excellent; *acc. n.* ~aṁ (vadanaṁ) 110,21; Dh. 268 (ādāya); repeated: ~aṁ ~aṁ (*w. gen.*) 51,33. 52,3; *acc. m.* ~aṁ ~aṁ (præstantissimum quemque) 109,4; most frequently *comp. w. subst.* (before or after): [a]) ⁰-sūra, 39,12; ⁰-vāraṇa, 45,31. 61,17; ⁰-bhojana, 61,7; ⁰-dhamma, 87,9; *etc.* — [b]) meṇḍa-⁰, 30,9; ratha-⁰, 64,10; pāsāda-⁰, 64,12; *etc.*; sabb'-ākāra-var'-ūpeta, 81,4 (*v.* ākāra). — [2]) *m.* choice, wish, boon, gift; *nom.* ~o (mayā dinno) 8,2; *acc.* ~aṁ (tassā adāsi) 10,4; *comp.* *gāma-vara, *m.* the grant of a village (perhaps a landed property of a certain measure, if not simply 'an excellent village'?) *acc.* ~aṁ (datvā) 45,3. — [3]) *n.* varaṁ, *indecl.* rather, better (than: *abl.* or *instr.*); ~ mayhaṁ udumbaro (is better to me) 2,11; ~ assatarā dantā, Dh. 322; *w. abl.* tato ~, ib.; *w. instr.* Dh. 178.

varaṇa, *m.* (= *sa.*) name of a certain tree (Cratæva Roxburgh.); ⁰-rukkhe, *loc.* 4,21.

varattā. *f.* (*sa.* varatrā) a strap. thong (of leather); *acc.* ~aṁ, Dh. 398 (*metaph.* of attachment); 12,7 (camma-⁰); *pl.* ~ā (sesa-⁰) 12,20. *cp.* vaddha[1].

varāha. *m.* (= *sa.*) a hog; *nom.* ~o (mahā-⁰) Dh. 325.

*valañja, *m.* (& *n.*) [1]) use, daily expenditure (also of excrements); [2]) a mark (from scratching or scraping); pada-⁰, footprint, *acc.* ~aṁ, 11,28. Hence valañjaka, *mfn. c. c., v.* anto-⁰, bahi-⁰ (*cp. Fausbøll,* JRAS. 1870, p. 13, & Ten Jāt. p. 90 [√lañj & lāñch]).

Vaḷabhāmukha, *m.* (?) (*sa.* Vaḍabāmukha) the entrance to the infernal regions at the South pole; *⁰-samudda, *m.* the Southern sea. *acc.* ~aṁ, 27,1-11; *⁰-mukhi(*n*), *m.* id. 27,9.

valaya, *n.* (& *m.*) (= *sa.*) a bracelet, ring; *nārāca-⁰, 111,23 (*q. v.*).

valāha(ka), *m.* (*sa.* balāhaka) a cloud; *nom.* ~ako (vāta-cchinna-⁰) 40,28; *valāhassa, *m.* a flying horse (*cp.* assa[1]) 21,34 (⁰-yoni).

vallī, *f.* (= *sa.*) a creeper; *loc.* ~iyā (a stalk of a creeper, a withe) 14,23; ~iyaṁ, 14,27; *pl.* ~iyo (paggava-⁰, *q. v.*) 37,19.

vavatthāpeti, *vb.* (*sa.* vyavasthāpayati, *caus.* vi-ava-√sthā) to settle, determine, distinguish, understand; *pp.* ~ita, 3,2 (tassa su-vavatthāpitaṁ, very well known to him).

vasa, [1]) *m.* (*sa.* vaça) wish, will, power; *loc.* ~e (ṭhapeti, to bring into one's power) 48,14; *instr.* vasena is used as *prp. w. gen.* or more frequently at the end of *comp.* with the meanings: by, by way of, on account of, according to, with regard to; hatthīnaṁ ~, 35,12; ovāda-⁰, 14,13; kilesa-⁰, 20,11; daṇḍe pavesana-⁰, 35,5; udāna-⁰, 42,14; chandâdi-⁰, 42,27; kammassa vipāka-⁰, 84,32; aniccâdi-⁰,

88,32 (*v.* a-nicca); pubbāpara-°, 114,20; – attha-vasa, *m.* the power of the matter, *acc.* ~aṁ (etaṁ, the meaning of this) Dh. 289. – 2) *mfn.* subdued, subject to; ~aṁ (kurute) Dh. 48, which may also be *subst.* ('into his power'). *cp.* ativasa, vasiṁ & vasika.

vasati, *vb.* (*sa.* √vas) to stay, dwell, live; *pr. 3. sg.* ~ati, 2,27 (*w. loc.* nadiyā); 35,35 (idha); *1. sg.* ~āmi. 49,13. 73,14; *3. pl.* ~anti, 14,15; *part. m.* ~anto, 20,29; 58,25 (*w. acc.* samaggavāsaṁ); 114,26; *loc.* ~ante, 25,12; *gen.* ~ato, 47,27; *pl.* ~antā, 7,21; *part. med.* ~māna, *f. gen.* ~āya (kinnaraḷīḷhāya, endowed with grace) 49,12; – *imp. 2. sg.* vasa, 15,15. 23,20 (vasā ti); – *aor. 3. sg.* vasi, 1,5; *3. pl.* ~iṁsu (piyasaṁvāsaṁ, *acc.* lived together in amity) 11,27; 20,33; – *fut. 1. sg.* ~issāmi (vassaṁ, during the rainy season) Dh. 286; – *inf.* ~ituṁ, 9,34; – *ger.* ~itvā, 2,25 etc.; 112,24 (vasitv'ettha). – (*pass.* vussati); *pp.* vussita (vuttha, vasita) *q. v.*; – *caus. II.* *vasāpeti (*q. v.*) *cp.* vāsa, vāsika, vāsin & *next.*

vasana, *n.* (= *sa.*) dwelling, residence; *comp.* *°-gāma, 12,7; *°-gumba, 14,27; *°-ṭṭhāna, 2,24. 65,27 (*q. v.*).

vasā[1], *f.* (*sa.* vaçā) a cow; *pl.* ~ā, 105,11.

vasā[2], *f.* (= *sa.*) serum, lymph; *nom.* ~ā, 82,5 = 97,23.

***vasāpeti**, *vb.* (*caus. II.* vasati) to cause to dwell, lodge; *ger.* ~etvā (taṁ ghare, received her into his house) 48,18.

vasiṁ, *indecl.* (*sa.* vaçī-) only combined with karoti, to subdue (*acc.*); ~ karitvā (saṁkappaṁ) 104,7; [also *comp.* vasī-karoti, *etc.*]

°**vasika**, *mfn.* (*sa.* vaçika) being in one's power: taṇhā-°, 23,20; mātugāma-°, 54,3 (*v. h.*).

vassa, *n.* (*sa.* varsha) 1) rain, a shower (*cp.* vuṭṭhi); *kahāpaṇa-°, Dh. 186 (*q. v.*); *dhana-°, 33,15; satta-ratana-°, 32,11. *nom.* – 2) the rainy season; *acc.* ~aṁ, Dh. 286. – 3) a year; *pl. acc.* ~āni, 86,37. 104,11; °-sataṁ, *n.* a century, Dh. 106. 110; soḷasa-vassa-kāle, in his 16th year, 24,13; soḷasa-vassa-padesika, °-uddesika (*v. h.*); caturāsīti-°sahassāni, 44,20 (*q. v.*). *cp.* vassika.

vassati[1], *vb.* (*sa.* √vāç) to cry, screech (as birds); *pr. 3. sg.* ~ati, 18,18; *part. m.* ~anto, 18,31; *ger.* ~itvā, 12,9.

vassati[2], *vb.* (*sa.* √vṛsh) to rain; *pr. 3. sg.* ~ati (vassaṁ) 32,11; (devo, the god, *i. e.* the sky rains) 102,6; *part. m. gen.* vassato (devassa) 105,22; *caus. II.* *vassāpeti, *v. below*; *cp.* vassa, vuṭṭhi, & *next.*

***vassāpanaka**, *mfn.* (*fr. nom. act. of next*) bringing about rain; dhana-°-nakkhattayoga, *m.* a conjunction of stars bringing about a shower of money, 32,25.

***vassāpeti**, *vb.* (*caus. II.* vassati[2]) to cause to rain or pour down, call down a shower; *aor. 3. sg.* ~esi, 33,11 (dhanaṁ); *2. pl.* mā ~ayittha, 32,27; *fut. 1. sg.* ~essāmi, 33,13 (dhanavassaṁ); *2. pl.* ~essatha, 32,27; *ger.* ~etvā, 32,33; *pp.* ~ita (ācariyena dhanaṁ ~itaṁ, *n.*) 34,3.

vassika, *mfn.* (*sa.* vārshika) 1) belonging to the rainy season; *m.* ~o (*scil.* pāsādo) 67,23; – 2) *e. c.* being so many years old; soḷasa-°, *n.* ~aṁ (rūpaṁ) 111,36.

vassikā & ~**kī**, *f.* (*sa.* vārshikī. *cp.* varshika, *n.* & vṛshaka, *n.*) a sort of jasmine; Dh. 55. 377.

vaha, *m.* (= *sa.*) a river, stream, wave; *pl.* ~ā, Dh. 339 (in stead of vāhā, *cp.* SBE. X. p. 82).

vahati, *vb.* (*sa.* √vah) to draw, convey, carry away (*acc.*); *pr. 3. sg.* ~ati, 29,11; *2. sg.* ~asi, 54,22; *3. pl.* ~anti, Dh. 339; *part. m. gen.* ~ato (of the draught animal) Dh. 1. *cp.* vaha, vāha, vāhana.

vā, *indecl.* (= *sa.*) a disjunctive particle (sometimes *comb. w.* other particles): 1) 'or', used (*enclitically*) in combinations of two sentences or links of a sentence: asassato loko ti vā, 92,30; yāvatake vā pana (or else) 81,17; *after prec. negation*: na . . . vā puna (nor yet) Dh. 271. — [2]) *repeated* = 'either — or' (after two or more links): 9,14. 9,29. 31,31. 92,10. etc.; *w. negation* = 'neither — nor': 7,36. 8,1 (*v.* corrections); 56,11; vā . . . yadivā [before the last link] Dh. 98; vâpi . . . vā, 114,20 (*w. foll.* n'eva); athavā [before the first link] . . . vā, Dh. 271. — [3]) *corresp. w. foll.* ca (in the same sense): Māro vā Brahmā ca . . . na passanti, 110,11. — [4]) sometimes shortened to va (*q. v.*).

*vākkaraṇa, *n.* (*sa. vāk + karaṇa) vociferation; na°-mattena, "not by means of much talking only", Dh. 262 (*cp.* matta[2]).

vākya, *n.* (= *sa.*) speech, sentence; *v.* *ati-vākya.

*vācasika, *mfn.* (*fr.* vaca[s]) concerning the speech; *instr. m.* ~ena (saṁvarena) 85,19.

vācā, *f.* (*sa.* vāc & vācā) speech, words; *nom.* ~ā (pacchimā, Tathāgatassa) 80,3; Dh. 51—52; 67,4 (sammā-°, *q. v.*); *acc.* ~aṁ (karuṇaṁ) 103,4; 22,3 (mānusi-°, *v.* mānusa. *mfn.*); *instr.* ~āya, 84,29. Dh. 232. — *vācânurakkhin, *mfn.* watching one's speech, *m.* ~ī. Dh. 281; *yathāvācaṁ, *adv.* (*v.* yathā); *santa-vāca, *mfn.* (*q. v.*), *cp.* vākkaraṇa, vaca(*s*) & *next.*

°vācika & °vāciya, *mfn.* (*sa.* vācika), verbal; only *e. c.*, *v.* eka-vāciya, te-vācika.

vāceti, *vb.* (*caus.* √vac, *v.* vuccati; *sa.* vācayati) to read out, recite (*acc.*); *aor. 3. pl.* ~ayiṁsu, 114,19; *inf.* ~etuṁ, 114,14.

vājita, *mfn.* (= *sa.*; √vaj, Dhātup. 32,74) having feathers, feathered; *acc.* ~aṁ (pattehi, kaṇḍaṁ) 92,19.

vāṇija, *m.* (= *sa.*) a merchant; ~o, 8,16; *pl.* ~ā. 18,4; °-kula, *n.* (*q. v.*) 30,2. *cp.* vaṇijjā. — vāṇijaka, *m.* (= *sa.*) id.; *acc. pl.* ~e, 18,8.

vāta, *m.* (= *sa.*) [1]) the wind; *acc.* ~aṁ, 19,15; *instr.* ~ena, 106,29; *nom.* ~o, 103,18 (here we have a pun: the wind as drying up humours & the asceticism destructive of lust); *comp.* *°-cchinna, *mfn.* (*v.* chinna); *°-vega, *m.* (*q. v.*); *akāla-°, *n.* "unseasonable wind", ~aṁ, 25,21; *nāsā-°, *m.* (*q. v.*); *cp.* paṭivātaṁ, yathāvātaṁ. — [2]) rheumatism (cause of disease or pain) *v.* kammaja-vātā, *pl.* 62,19. — *cp.* nivātaka.

vāti, *vb.* (*sa.* √vā) to blow; to smell; *pr. 3. sg.* ~ti (gandho timīrānaṁ) 20,16; Dh. 56.

vāda, *m.* (= *sa.*) [1]) speech; *v.* musā-°; [2]) addressing; *v.* āvuso; [3]) doctrine, system; *acc.* ~aṁ, 113,14; agga-°, 109,30 (*q. v.*) = thera-° (*q. v.*); ācariya-° (*q. v.*); dhuta-°, *m.* (*q. v.*); [4]) discussion, controversy; sabba-vāda-°, 113,4 (°-visārada, *q. v.*). *cp. next.*

*vādatthin, *mfn.* (*cp.* atthin) desirous of dispute; *m.* a disputant; ~ī, 113,5.

vādi, *aor.*, *v.* vadati.

vādita, *n.* (= *sa.*) music; *pl.* ~āni (nacca-gīta-°) 64,31; *cp.* 81,21.

vādin, *mfn.* (= *sa.*) speaking (mostly *e. c.*); *acc. m.* ~inaṁ (tathā, or *comp.* tathā-°, *q. v.*) 103,12; *cp.* a-bhūta-°, alika-°, niggayha-°, bho-°, musā-° (*gen.* °-vādissa, 106,14), sacca-°, Dh. 217.

vādeti, *vb.* (*caus.* vadati; *sa.* vādayati) to cause to speak or sound, to play musical instruments (*acc.*); *part. m. pl.* ~entā (bheriyo, "beating drums") 8,24; *loc. pl.* ~entesu (viṇaṁ) 50,10; *aor. 3. sg.* ~esi, 50,11, = a-vādesi, 51,3. *cp.* vādita, *n.*

vānara, *m.* (= *sa.*) a monkey, ape; ~o, 3,9. 107,30; vānarinda, *m.* (*v.* inda).

vāma, *mfn.* (= *sa.*) left, sinister; °-hatthena, "with his left hand", 111,24 (*opp.* dakkhiṇa).

vāmanaka, *mfn.* (= *sa.*; *fr.* vāmana, a dwarf) dwarfish, deformed (lame or halting?); (pacchā-)vāmanaka-dhātuka, *mfn.* (*q. v.*) 24,24-26.

vāyamati, *vb.* (*sa.* vi + ā-√yam) to struggle, strive, endeavour; *imp. 2. sg.* vāyama, Dh. 236 (khippaṁ). *cp.* vāyāma.

vāyasa, *m.* (= *sa.*) a crow; ~o, 104,13; *gen.* ~assa, 18,35 (*synon.* kāka).

vāyāma, *n.* (*sa.* vyāyāma) endeavour, effort; ~o (sammā-⁰, *q. v.*) 67,5; *acc.* ~aṁ (karissati) 34,35.

vāra, *m.* (= *sa.*) time, turn, lot; ~o, 6,25-26; *acc.* ~aṁ (gacchati, to take one's turn) 6,33; *loc.* ~e (catutthe, tatiye, for the 4th, 3rd time) 58,7. 114,17; *comp.* eka-vāraṁ, *adv.* once, 50,16; puna-vāre, *adv.* the next time, 18,17; *⁰-ppatta, *mfn.* whose turn it is, on whom the lot falls; *m.* ~o, 6,27. *cp.* bhāṇavāra.

vāraka, *m.* (= *sa.*) a pot, vessel; dadhi-⁰, *m.* 14,30 (*q. v.*).

vāraṇa, *m.* (= *sa.*) an elephant; ~o (seta-vara-⁰) 61,17; *acc.* ~aṁ, 24,31; *gen.* ~assa (matta-⁰) 45,31; *loc.* ~e (do.) 39,9.

vāri, *n.* (= *sa.*) water; *nom.* ~i, Dh. 401; *acc.* ~iṁ, 13,3. 111,9. — ⁰-ja, *m.* 'born in water', *i. e.* a fish (or a lotus); *nom.* ~jo, Dh. 34.

vāreti, *vb.* (*caus.* √vṛ; *sa.* vārayati) ¹) to keep back, prevent, prohibit (*acc.*); *aor. 3. sg.* ~esi, 23,7; *fut. 1. sg.* ~essāmi, 23,8; *inf.* ~etuṁ, ib.; *ger.* ~etvā (mige) 8,6; *pass.* vāriyati, *part. m.* ~anto, 111,3. — ²) to choose, ask for (*acc.*); *aor. 3. sg.* ~esi (sāmikaṁ) 10,5; *ger.* ~etvā, 101,15; *pp.* vāritā, *f.* 101,20 (dārikā). — ³) to cast lots (*acc.*, salākaṁ); *part. pass.* vāriyamānā, *f.* (salākā) 23,12. *cp.* vāra.

vāḷa, *mfn.* (*sa.* vyāḍa & vyāla) fierce, cruel; *subst. m.* a beast of prey, a snake; *pl.* ~ā, 51,34 (*cp.* 52,6).

vāla, *m.* (= *sa.*) the hair (*esp.* of a horse's tail); the tail (of a horse or other animals); *pahaṭṭha-kaṇṇa-⁰, *mfn.* 76,21 (*q. v.*) *cp. next etc.*

vāladhi, *m.* (= *sa.*) a tail (*esp.* of a horse, a deer, or an ox); *nom.* ~i, 5,28; *acc.* ~iṁ, 22,6.

*vāla-vedhin, *m(fn).* (*sa.* *vālavyādhin) hair-splitting; *m.* ~ī, "skilled in hair-splitting" (sophist) 110,9.

vālikā (or vālukā), *f.* (*sa.* vālukā) sand, gravel; *instr. loc.* ~āya, 14,24; 97,35; *pl. acc.* ~ā (in *dvandva comp.*) ib.

vāsa, *m.* (= *sa.*) ¹) dwelling, abode; *nom.* ~o, Dh. 237; *acc.* ~aṁ (manussa-⁰) 21,2; ~aṁ kappeti, to live, 1,4. 2,25; *comp.* *a-ppatissa-vāsa, *m.* (*v.* patissava); *eka-rati-⁰, *mfn.* (*v.* eka²); *brahmacariya-⁰, *m.* (*q. v.*); *samagga-⁰, *m.* (*q. v.*); *samāna-⁰, *mfn.* (*q. v.*) *cp.* saṁvāsa, vāsika, vāsin. — ²) perfume; *v.* vāsita.

vāsi, *f.* (*sa.* vāçī) a small axe, knife, razor; *⁰-pharasuka, *m.* a "razor-axe" (daṇḍe pavesanavasena vāsi pi hoti pharasu pi) 35,4-5.

vāsika, *mfn.* (*sa.* vāsaka; *fr.* vāsa¹) dwelling, living (*e. c.*); katthavāsikā, *m. pl.* 21,8 (*v.* kattha).

vāsita, *mfn.* (= *sa.*; *pp.* vāseti, √vās, *cp.* vāsa²) perfumed, scented; ⁰-udakaṁ, 41,2; ⁰-pānīyaṁ, 41,11 (ṭhapita-⁰, *q. v.*).

vāsin, *mfn.* (= *sa*; *fr.* vāsa¹) dwelling, living (in: *loc.*, but mostly *e. c.*); *f.* ⁰-vāsinī (Laṅkānagara-⁰) 112,13; *m. pl.* ~ino (gāma-⁰, the villagers) 8,23-29; (Bārāṇasi-⁰, the inhabitants of B.) 20,12; (nagara-⁰) 58,21; *gen. pl.* ~īnaṁ (do.) 58,24. 62,9; *comp.* Kāsiraṭṭha-vāsi-manusso. 35,28.

vāha, *m.* (= *sa.*) lit. 'drawing, flowing', *i. e.* ¹) a draught-animal, a horse; ²) a cart-load, a certain measure; ³) a current (of water), stream; *pl.* ~ā, Dh. 339 ("waves").

vāhana, *n.* (= *sa.*) any animal for riding (a horse, an elephant); any vehicle or chariot; army or military force (*cp. sa.* vāhanā, *f.*); *instr.* ~ena, 98,2 (riding? *cp.* rathena, ib.); *bala-⁰, *n.* (*v. h.*); sa-vāhana. *mfn.* together with one's army, *acc. m.* ~aṁ (Māraṁ) 104,3. Dh. 175.

vi-, *indecl.* (= *sa.*) prefix to verbs and nouns, implying 'asunder, out, away, about'; 'in various directions' (or 'contrarily', often *metaph. cp.* vivadati, vicinteti); with nouns it often denotes 'negation' or 'separation' (*opp.* sa-, *cp.* a-[4]), *v.* vikāla, vimala, virāga, visoka, *etc.*; with verbs (and their derivatives) it is sometimes used to denote 'intensity' (*cp.* vinassati, vipassati) or 'opposition' (*cp.* vivarati, vijjhāpeti). — Before vowels we have vy- (viy-) : vyaya (& vaya), viyūhati, or more frequently v- (by elision & contraction), *esp.* before other verbal prefixes beginning with a vowel : vi + ati (*v.* vītināmeti, vītisāreti); vi + apa (*v.* vapayati, *cp.* vyapānudi); vi + ava (*v.* vavatthāpita, voropeti, *etc.*); vi + ā (*v.* vāyamati, *cp.* vyākaroti (viyākāsi), vyāpajjati); vi + ud (*v.* vuṭṭhāti, *etc.*); vi + upa (*v.* vūpasama); *cp.* vippa-, vippaṭi- (*sa.* vi + pra, vi + prati).

vikāla, *m.* (= *sa.*) afternoon, evening; wrong time; *loc.* ~e (kāle ~, "in season and out of season") 9,12; *°-bhojana, *n.* 81,24 (*v. h.*).

vikāseti, *vb.* (*caus.* vi + √kas, *sa.* vikāsayati) to cause to be opened (*acc.*); *aor. 3. sg.* ~esi (hatthaṁ, she opened her hand, in order to make him know that she was unmarried, *cp. Meyer,* Daçakum. p. 98) 56,9.

*vikulāva, *mfn.*, deprived of one's nest, homeless; *pl.* ~ā (dijā) 60,17 (*v.* kulāvaka).

vikūjati, *vb.* (*sa.* vi-√kūj) to chirp, sing, warble (as birds); *part. m. pl.* ~antā (sakuṇasaṁghā) 62,13.

vikesika, *mfn.* (*sa.* vikeça) having dishevelled hair; *acc. f.* ~aṁ, 67,30.

*vikkhāleti, *vb.* (*fr.* vi-√kshal) to wash off, rinse (*acc.*); *ger.* ~etvā (mukhaṁ) 41,12. 56,33.

vikkhīṇa, *mfn.* (*sa.* vikshīṇa, *pp.* vi-√kshi) destroyed; *m.* ~o (jātisaṁsāro) 108,18.

*vikkheḷika, *mfn.*, having saliva flowing from the mouth; *acc. f.* ~aṁ, 67,30 (*cp.* kheḷa).

vigata, *mfn.* (= *sa.*) gone away; *vigaticcha, *mfn.* (*v.* icchā); *°-kathaṁkatha, *mfn.*, *°-khila, *mfn.*, & *°-surā-pāna, *mfn.* (*v. h.*); *cp.* vīta, Dh. 356.

vighāta, *m.* (= *sa.*) destruction, ruin, pain; sa-vighāta, *mfn.* "coupled with ruin" (*synon.* sa-dukkha) 94,2.

*vicakkhu-kamma, *n.*, 'making blind', the making one's sight wrong, perplexing, bewildering; *dat.* ~āya, ("in order to perplex him") 71,27. (*cp. sa.* vi-cakshus).

vicarati, *vb.* (*sa.* vi-√car) to wander about, go away; *pr. 3. sg.* ~ati. 8,16; *3. pl.* ~anti (fly about) 62,13; 73,35; *part. m.* ~anto, 5,6; *acc.* ~antaṁ, 73,6; *f.* ~antī, 20,4; *aor. 3. sg.* vicari, 17,19; *fut. 1. sg.* ~issāmi, 17,16; *cond. 1. sg.* vicarissaṁ (unaugmented = *fut.*) 104,8; *ger.* ~itvā, 25,32; *caus. v. next.*

vicāreti, *vb.* (*caus.* vicarati; *sa.* vicārayati) 'to cause to go about', *i. e.* to arrange, manage, administer, control (*acc.*); *pr. 3. sg.* ~eti (*v. l.* ~esi, *aor.*) 55,20; *part. f.* ~entī (kuṭumbaṁ, "managing the property") 22,15.

vicikicchati, *vb.* (*sa.* vicikitsati, *desid.* vi-√cit) to be uncertain, to doubt; *pr. 3. sg.* ~ati, 96,14. *cp. next.*

vicikicchā, *f.* (*sa.* vicikitsā) doubt; *nom.* ~ā (sattamī senā Mārassa) 103,28; *tiṇṇa-vicikiccha, *mfn.* 69,13 (*v. h.*).

vicitta & vicitra, *mfn.* (*sa.* vicitra) variegated, ornamented, beautiful; satta-ratana-vicitta, *mfn.*, *loc.* ~e, 18,26; *vicitra-kathin, *mfn.* eloquent, *m.* ~ī, 109,9 (Kumārakassapo, *cp.* Mil. p. 196,7).

vicināti (or vicinati), *vb.* (*sa.* vi-√ci) [1]) to search for, investigate, inquire (*acc.*): *imp. 2. pl.* ~atha(naṁ)

73,24; *part. m.* ~anto. 19,23. 34,14; *pl.* ~antā, 73,25; *ger.* vicinitvāna, 109,4. — [2]) to gather, collect, pick up, heap up (*acc.*); *part. f.* ~antī (ūkā, *q. v.*) 46,26; *ger.* ~itvā (saṁkāraṁ, to heap up) 84,23.

vicinteti, *vb.* (*sa.* vicintayati) to think, reflect; *pr. 3. sg.* ~eti, Dh. 286.

*vicuṇṇa, *mfn.*, pushed or hurt on all sides, only *comp. w.* cuṇṇa, 1,25 (*q. v.*).

vicuṇṇita, *mfn.* (*sa.* vicūrṇita) crushed all over; ratha-vega-⁰ (by the course of the chariot) 60,10.

vijaya, *m.* (= *sa.*) [1]) victory; ⁰-ante, *loc.* 60,25 (*v.* anta[1], *cp.* Vejayanta, *nom. pr.*); laddha-⁰, *mfn.* victorious, 112,22 (but see corrections). — [2]) Vijaya, *m. nom. pr.* of a prince, conqueror of Ceylon, ~o (Lāḷavisayo, *q. v.*) 110,22, *etc.*; ⁰-ppamukhā, *pl. m.* (*v.* pamukha).

vijahāti (or ~ati), *vb.* (*sa.* vi-√hā) to leave, quit, abandon (*acc.*); *inf.* ~ituṁ (etā) 21,31; *ger.* ~itvā, 52,29.

vijāta, *mfn.* (*pp.* vijāyati, *q. v.*).

vijānāti, *vb.* (*sa.* vi-√jñā) to know, understand, comprehend, perceive (thoroughly) (*acc.*); *pr. 3. pl.* ~anti, Dh. 6; *imp. 2. sg.* ~ahi, 20,27. 54,19. 54,26; *part. gen. pl.* vijānataṁ, Dh. 171 ("the wise"); Dh. 374 (amataṁ, "who know Nibbāna"); a-vijānataṁ (saddhammaṁ) 107,10 = Dh. 60; *pot. 3. sg.* ~eyya, Dh. 392; *ger.* [a]) viññāya, Dh. 186; [b]) vijāniya, 113,8; *pp.* viññāta (*q. v.*) *cp.* viññāṇa, *etc.*

vijayati, *v.* vijeti.

vijāyati, *vb.* (*sa.* vi-√jan) to bear, generate, produce (*acc.*, rarely in *pass.* sense: to be born); *fut. 3. sg.* ~issati (dhītaraṁ) 48,17; *aor. 3. sg.* vijāyi (puttaṁ) 7,29; *part. med. f.* ~ mānā (etaṁ) 24,25; *ger.* ~itvā, 6,33; *pp.* vijāta, *f.* ~ā (puttaṁ, has born a son) 64,5; vijāta-kāle, after her delivery, 48,18.

vijita, [1]) *mfn.* (= *sa.*: *pp.* vijeti) conquered; *n.* ~aṁ (raṭṭhaṁ) Dh. 329. — [2]) *subst. n.* a conquered country, realm, kingdom; *loc.* ~e, 8,4. *cp. next.*

*vijitāvin, *m(fn).*, victorious; conqueror; *acc. m.* ~inaṁ, Dh. 422.

vijeti (or vijayati), *vb.* (*sa.* vi-√ji) to conquer, defeat, subdue (*acc.*); *fut. 3. sg.* ~essati (paṭhaviṁ) Dh. 44; *pp.* vijita (*q. v.*) *cp.* vijaya.

vijjati, *vb.* (*pass.* vindati; *sa.* vidyate) to be found; to be, exist; *pr. 3. sg.* ~ati (attho na ~, "is of no use". *w. instr.*) 103,14. 104,31; *3. pl.* (*med.*) vijjare, 104,27. 113,27; *part.* (*med.*) vijjamāna, 18,15 (sakuṇānaṁ a-⁰-ṭṭhāne, on a place where there were no birds); *loc. m.* ~amhi (gāmamhi, "where there is a village") 111,4.

vijjā, *f.* (*sa.* vidyā) knowledge, science; *instr.* ~āya, 108,9; aṅga-vijjā, *f.* 'knowledge of limbs' *i. e.* chiromantia, prognostication, *loc.* ~āya, 48,16; *dvandva comp.* *⁰-sippa-kalā-vedin, *mfn.* accomplished in science and arts, *m.* ~ī, 113,3; ⁰-caraṇa, knowledge & behaviour, theory & practice, Dh. 144 (sampanna-⁰, *q. v.*) *cp.* a-vijjā.

vijjullatā, *f.* (*sa.* vidyul-latā; *cp.* latā) a flash of lightning; 3,21.

vijjotati, *vb.* (*sa.* vi-√dyut) to flash forth, lighten; *part. med. m.* ~ māno (springing forth [like lightning]) 3,21; *caus.* vijjoteti, to illuminate, enlighten (*acc.*) 85,8 (sabbā disā; *synon.* pabhāseti (*q. v.*); the reading of B. pabhāsati vijjotati seems to be preferable, on account of the foll. explanation of obhāsate as having a causative meaning).

vijjhati, *vb.* (*sa.* √vyadh) to pierce, wound or kill (as by arrows or lances, *etc.*) (*w. acc.*); *part. m.* ~anto (taṁ tuṇḍena) 4,22; *imp. 3. pl.* ~antu, 6,25; *ger.* ~itvā, 6,19. 37,6; *pp.* viddha (*q. v.*) *cp.* vedhin.

*vijjhāpeti, *vb.* (*caus.* *vijjhāyati, to burn out, go out, become extinct; √kshai, *v.* jhāyati [1]) to put out, extinguish (*acc.*); *ger.* a-vijjhāpetvā (aggiṁ, without putting it out) 100,25; *pp.* ~ita, *m.* a-vijjhāpito (aggi) 100,28.

viññāṇa, *n.* (*sa.* vijñāna) consciousness; *nom.* ~aṁ. 94,10 (one of the 5 khandhas (*q. v.*)); 66,7 (originating from saṁkhārā); *instr.* ~ena, 95,19; *comp.* °-paccayā (*q. v.*) 66,7; °-nirodha. *m.* (*q. v.*) 66,12; viññāṇañcāyatana, *n.*, *v.* ānañca & āyatana; *°-saṁgaha, *m.* aggregation of consciousness, *acc.* ~aṁ (pacchima-°) 99,26; — *apeta-°, *mfn.* (*v. h.*); *kāya-°, *cakkhu-°, *mano-°, the consciousness of body, eye, mind, *i. e.* mental impressions through those organs, or: the sense of touch, the faculty of sight, thought, 70,26-33. 98,1 (dukkha-sahagataṁ kāya-viññāṇaṁ uppajjati, a feeling of pain arises).

viññāta, *mfn.* (*pp.* vijānāti; *sa.* vijñāta) known, understood; *sammāviññāta-samaya, *mfn.* perfectly knowing the religious precepts, *m.* ~o. 113,4.

viññāpana, *mf*[ī]*n.* (*sa.* vijñāpana) instructive; *acc. f.* ~aniṁ (giraṁ) Dh. 408.

viññāya, *ger.*, *v.* vijānāti.

viññutā (& viññūtā) *f.* (*sa.* vijñatā) intelligence; *acc.* ~aṁ. 27,22.

viññū, *m*(*fn*). (*sa.* vijña) intelligent, clever; *m.* ~ū, Dh. 65; *m. pl.* ~ū (purisā) 90,29; Dh. 229.

viṭapa, *m.* (= *sa.*) a forked branch; °-antare (*q. v.*) 4,21 (in a fork of the tree).

vitakka, *m.* (*sa.* vitarka) [1]) deliberation, consideration; [2]) doubt, uncertainty; *°-ûpasama, *m.* Dh. 350 (*v.* upasama); *°-pamathita, *mfn.* Dh. 349 ("tossed about by doubts").

vitāna, *m. n.* (= *sa.*) a canopy, baldachin; *gen.* ~assa (sumana-paṭṭa-°, *q. v.*) 65,18; *°-samalaṁkata. *mfn.* 112,3 (*v. h.*).

vitiṇṇa, *mfn.* (*pp.* vitarati, to cross, pass over; *sa.* vitīrṇa) who has crossed or passed over, also *metaph.* (only *comp.*) who scouts, or does not believe in . . .; *°-paraloka, *mfn.* who does not believe in another world, *gen.* ~assa, 106,15 = Dh. 176; a-vitiṇṇakaṁkha, *mfn.* Dh. 141 (*v. h.*).

vittiṇṇa, *mfn.* (once instead of vitthiṇṇa = vitthaṭa (& ~ta), *pp.* vittharati, to spread out, extend, vi-√stṛ; *sa.* vistīrṇa) broad, large; *f.* ~ā (Gaṅgā) 1,16. *cp. next.*

vitthāra, *m.* (*sa.* vistāra) extension, diffuseness; *abl.* ~to (*adv.*) fully, in detail, 41,31 (kathesi).

vidatthi, *f.* (*sa.* vitasti) a certain measure of length, equal to 12 angulas (inches, *q. v.*), a span; °-mattaṁ, 87,11 (*v.* matta [2]) *cp.* yojana.

[vidati], *vb.* (*sa.* √vid) to know, understand (*acc.*); this present-formation is only ficticious or made for etymological purpose; forms generally met with are: *aor. 3. sg.* vedi (avedi), Dh. 419. 423; *3. pl.* (vidu); *fut. 1. sg.* (vedissāmi); *ger.* viditvā (etaṁ atthaṁ) 66,19; 70,12; *grd.* (veditabba &) vedaniya (*q. v.*); *pp.* vidita, known, understood; *comp.* *°-dhamma. *mfn.* "having penetrated the truth", *m.* ~o, 69,12; yathā-°, *mfn.* (*v. h.*). — (*caus.* vedeti, vedayati, [a]) to know, understand; [b]) to feel, experience, suffer (*acc.*); the *caus. pass.* vediyati [to be known, to be felt] is also generally used in the same active sense). *cp.* veda, vedanā, vedayita, vedin, & vindati.

vidu (& vidū), *mfn.* (*sa.* vidvas & vidus) knowing, wise; *m.* sabbavidū ('ham asmi) Dh. 353. *cp.* viddasu.

vidūra, *mfn.* (= *sa.*) very distant, far; only used with the prefixes a-° & su-° (*synon.* dūra): a-vidūre, *loc. adv.* not far away, near to (*w. gen.* or *abl.*), 48,31 (gharato); 95,31 (gāmassa). *cp.* atidūra.

videsa, *m.* (*sa.* videça) a foreign country, far distant region; *acc.* ~aṁ, 27,25.

Videha, *m.* (*pl.*) (= *sa.*) *nom. pr.* of a country and its inhabitants, in the eastern North-India; °-raṭṭha, *n.* the V. kingdom, *loc.* ~e, 44,19 (its capital was Mithilā).

viddasu, *mfn.* (*sa.* vidvas, *cp.* vidu *above*) wise, intelligent; a-viddasu, *mfn.* Dh. 268 (*v. h.*); viddasu is a curious formation, that looks as if it had been formed with the suffix -vas repeated (Tr.), *cp. Kuhn*, Beitr. p. 69 & avidvā (*gen.* aviddasuno) MN. I, p. 311,7-23.

viddha, *mfn.* [1]) (= *sa.*; *pp.* vijjhati) pierced, wounded; *m.* ~o (sallena) 92,7-10. — [2]) (*sa.* vīdhra. *cp.* vyabhra) clear, pure; *v. Morris*, JPTS. '85, p. 52.

viddhaṁseti, *vb.* (*sa.* vidhvaṁsayati, *caus.* vi-√dhvaṁs) to crush, destroy, disperse, split (*acc.*); *imp. 2. pl.* ~etha (taṁ bhusaṁ viya) 53,2.

vidhavā, *f.* (= *sa.*) a widow; *nom.* ~ā (itthī) 31,13.

vidhāvati, *vb.* (*sa.* vi-√dhāv) to run; *pr. 3. sg.* ~ati (ito c'ito ca) 36,2.

vidhunāti, *vb.* (*sa.* vi-√dhū, dhunoti) to shake (*acc.*); *ger.* vidhūnitvā (or vidhunitvā) 16,6 (sarīraṁ); 18,20 (pakkhe, flapping the wings).

vinuddha, *mfn.* (= *sa.*; *pp.* vi-√nah) covered all over; *pl. m.* ~ā, 37,21.

vinaya, *m.* (= *sa.*) discipline, *esp.* the rules of the Buddhist order; *nom.* ~o, 79,5; *acc.* ~aṁ, 109,15-25; *loc.* ~e, 109,7. — Vinaya, *m.* & Vinaya-piṭaka, *n.*, the first section of the Buddhist holy scriptures; dhamma-vinaya-saṁgaha, *m.* the collection of Dhamma & Vinaya, 109,13; *vinaya-dhara, *mfn.* knowing the V., *pl.* ~ā, 109,26; °-piṭakaṁ, *acc.* 102,17; °-piṭakena, *instr.* 102,16. Specimens p. 66–71,18; 74,16–77,13; 81,6-28; 82,15 –84,24.

vinayaṁ, *part.*, *v.* vineti.

vinassati, *vb.* (*sa.* vi-√naç) to perish; to be lost or forgotten; *pr. 3. sg.* ~ati, 110,4; *imp. 3. pl.* ~antu, 23,13; *fut. 3. sg.* ~issati, 34,25; *caus.* vināseti (*q. v.*), *cp.* vināsa, vināsana.

vinā, *adv.* & *prp.* (= *sa.*) without, except; usually combined with *acc.* or *instr.* (before or after), rarely with *abl.*; ~ maṁsena na bhuñjati (he took no meal in which meat was wanting) 6,1.

vināsa, *m.* (*sa.* vināça) destruction, ruin; annihilation, death; *acc.* ~aṁ (pāpeti, lit. to cause to go to destruction) 5,10. 27,13. 29,32; *instr.* ~ena, 55,7; *°-ppaccaya, *m.* cause of destruction, 34,24; *°-mūla, *n.* id. 33,26. *cp. next.*

vināsana, *n.* (*sa.* vināçana) = *prec.*; *instr.* ~ena (dhanassa), 52,5; a-vināsana, *mfn.* (*q. v.*).

vināseti, *vb.* (*caus.* vinassati; *sa.* vināçayati) to cause to be destroyed or lost; to forget (*acc.*); *pp.* vināsita, destroyed, *n.* ~aṁ, 34,17.

vinicchaya, *m.* (*sa.* viniçcaya) decision, judgement; justice, procedure, court of justice; *acc.* ~aṁ (anusāsati, *q. v.*) 42,27; *loc.* ~e, 59,6; *instr.* ~ena (dhamma-°, "discernment of the law") Dh. 144; °-atthāya, for the sake of litigation, 42,31 (*cp.* attha [1]); *°-ṭṭhāna, *n.* the place where court is held, ib.

vinicchinati, *vb.* (*sa.* vi-niç-√ci) to settle, decide (*acc.*); *aor. 3. pl.* ~iniṁsu (vohāraṁ) 42,28; — *pass.* vinicchiyati; *part. loc. pl.* ~mānesu (vohāresu) 42,29.

viniddisati, *vb.* (*sa.* vi-nir-√diç) to point out, assign, distribute (*acc.*); *aor. 3. sg.* viniddisi (taṇḍulādi) 111,31.

vinipāta, *m.* (= *sa.*) lit. 'falling down', state of suffering (*esp.* in a lower existence); *a-vinipāta-dhamma, *mfn.* (*v. h.*) *cp.* dhamma [4].

*vinīvaraṇa-citta, *mfn.*, whose mind is free from obstacles; *acc. m.* ~aṁ, 68,23. (*cp.* nīvaraṇa).

vineti, *vb.* (*sa.* vi-√nī) [1]) to lead away, remove, dispel (*acc.*); *ger.* vineyya (oghaṁ, *q. v.*) 104,30; — [2]) to train, educate (*acc.*); *part. m.* vinayaṁ (sāvake) 104,8.

vinodeti, *vb.* (*caus.* vi-√nud, *sa.* vinodayati) to drive away or out, to send away, dismiss (*acc.*); *pot. 3. sg.* ~aye (tasinaṁ) Dh. 343.

vindati, *vb.* (= *sa.*; √vid, *cp.* vidati) to find (*acc.*); *pr. 3. sg.* ~ati (maggaṁ) Dh. 57; *pot. 1. pl.* ~ema (muduṁ) 104,14; *pass.* vijjati (*v. h.*).

vipatti, *f.* (= *sa.*) misfortune, calamity; *°-pariyosāna, *mfn.* having a dreary end, *m.* ~o (jīvaloko) 47,16.

*[viparakkamati], *vb.* (*sa.* vi-parā-√kram) to strive, make efforts, exert oneself; only *ger.* viparakkamma (jhāyantaṁ) 103,8.

vipassati, *vb.* (*sa.* vi-√paç) to see (clearly), to understand, to be intelligent; *pr. 3. sg.* ~ati (tanuk'ettha) 88,32-33; *part. gen. m.* vipassato (dhammaṁ) Dh. 373.

vipāka, *m.* (= *sa.*) ripening, maturing (*esp.* of actions, *i. e.* result, reward or punishment); tass'eva kammassa vipāka-vasena, because that action had just been ripe (for punishment) 84,32; *nom.* ~o (kammānaṁ) 97,14; *acc.* ~aṁ, Dh. 67.

vipāteti, *vb.* (*caus.* vi-√pat, *sa.* vipātayati) to break, split (*acc.*); *part. m.* vipātayaṁ (muddhaṁ) Dh. 72.

vipula, *mfn.* (= *sa.*) large, great; *n.* ~aṁ (sukhaṁ) Dh. 27. 290.

vippakāra, *m.* (= *sa.*) 'bad manner', improper proceeding; shame, disgrace; outrage; *acc.* ~aṁ, 65,8.

vippakiṇṇa, *mfn.* (*sa.* vi-prakīrṇa) strown all round about; *acc. n.* ~aṁ, 34,2.

vippajahāti, *vb.* (*sa.* vi-pra-√hā) to give up, abandon (*acc.*); *pot. 3. sg.* ~jaheyya (mānaṁ) Dh. 221; *ger.* vippahāya, Dh. 87.

vippaṭisārin, *mfn.* (*sa.* vipratisārin) filled with regret, repentant; *m.* ~ī, 20,28; *pl.* ~ino (pacchā-°. *q. v.*) 79,18.

vippanaṭṭha, *mfn.* (*sa.* vipranashṭa, √naç) perished, disappeared; *instr.* (or *loc.*) *f.* ~āya (nāvāya) 25,31.

vippamuñcati, *vb.* (*sa.* vi-pra-√muc) to liberate, send away, shake off, to liberate oneself from (*acc.*); *pot. 2. pl.* ~etha (rāgaṁ) Dh. 377; *pp.* vippamutta, liberated, free from (*abl.*); *gen. m.* ~assa, Dh. 90. 212 (piyato).

vippayoga, *m.* (*sa.* viprayoga) separation (from: *instr.*); *nom.* ~o (piyehi) 67,10.

vippalapati, *vb.* (*sa.* vi-pra-√lap) to mutter, talk (wildly, in one's sleep); *part. f. pl.* ~antiyo, 65,6. 67,30.

vippaviddha, *mfn.* (*sa.* vipraviddha, √vyadh) thrown away, scattered about; °-nānā-kuṇapa-bharita, *mfn.* filled with various dead bodies scattered about, *n.* ~aṁ (āmakasusānaṁ) 65,10.

*vippasanna, *mfn.* (*pp. fr. next*) clear, serene, placid; *m.* ~o (yathāpi rahado) Dh. 82; *acc.* ~aṁ (candaṁ va) Dh. 413; *instr. n.* ~ena (cetasā) Dh. 79.

*vippasīdati, *vb.* (*sa.* *vi-pra-√sad) to be thoroughly clear or tranquil; *pr. 3. pl.* ~anti (paṇḍitā) Dh. 82.

vippahāya, *ger.*, *v.* vippajahāti.

vipphandita, *mfn.* (*pp.* vi-√spand) trembling, moving unsteadily; *n. subst.* ~aṁ, agitation, distortion, perversion (?); *diṭṭhi-°, *n.* uncertainty in views, or confusion on account of false views, 94,1.

Vibhaṅga, *m.* (= *sa.*) lit. 'division', or 'explanation', *nom. pr.* 1) of a Pāli work, the 2. part of the Abhidhamma-piṭaka; *nom.* ~o, 102,12; — 2) of the 2. section of Vinaya-piṭaka.

vibhajati, *vb.* (*sa.* vi-√bhaj) 1) to divide, distribute (*acc.* & *gen.*); *ger.* ~itvā, 41,19; *pp.* vibhatta (*q. v.*); — 2) to explain (*cp. next*).

vibhajjana, *n.* (wrong spelling of vibhajana, = *sa.*) 'separation', distinction, explanation; *loc.* ~amhi, 109,10. (*cp.* pavibhajati).

vibhatta, *mfn.* (*pp.* vibhajati; *sa.* vibhakta) divided, distributed; sama-vibhattaṁ, *n.* an equal part, 41,18; su-°, well arranged, 110,14.

vibhava, *m.* (= *sa.*) 1) 'development', prosperity, power, wealth; *loc.* ~e, 48,10; *comp.* *°-taṇhā, *f.* thirst for prosperity, 67,14; *dvandva comp.* siri-⁰, majesty and power, 47,32 (*acc.* ~aṁ); *asītikoṭi-⁰, *mfn.* (*v. h.*). — [2]) (as *opp.* to bhava) loss, destruction; *dat.* ~āya, Dh. 282.

vibhūti, *f.* (= *sa.*) abundance, splendour; *⁰-sampanna, *mfn.* brilliant, 61,4 (mālā-gandha-⁰, with garlands and perfumes).

vibhūsana, *n.* (*sa.* vibhūshaṇa) ornament, decoration; ⁰-ṭṭhāna, *n.* 81,25 (*v.* ṭhāna [7]).

vibhūsita, *mfn.* (*sa.* vibhūshita) adorned, decorated; *f.* ~ā (sabbālaṁkāra-⁰) 61,7.

vimati, *f.* (= *sa.*) doubt, uncertainty; *nom.* ~i, 79,17.

vimala, *mfn.* (= *sa.*) spotless, clean, bright; *acc. m.* ~aṁ, Dh. 413.

vimāna, *n.* (= *sa.*) seat, throne; place, abode; house, mansion, palace; *acc.* ~aṁ, 29,15; *abl.* ~ā, 20,4; *loc.* ~e (phalika-⁰, crystal-palace) 23,15; 23,22-23 (rajata-⁰, maṇi-⁰, kanaka-⁰, *q. v.*); deva-⁰, the palace of the gods, or a divine chariot (or throne), 63,6 (⁰-sadisaṁ rathaṁ); Tusita-⁰, *n.* 87,31 (*v. h.*, *cp.* corrections).

vimuccati, *vb.* (*pass.* vi-√muc) to become free, to be delivered (*esp.* from the bonds of existence, *abl.*); *pr. 3. sg.* ~ati (virāgā) 71,14; *aor. 3. sg.* vimucci (āsavehi) 69,24; *3. pl.* ~iṁsu, 71,18; — *pp.* vimutta, *mfn.* released, delivered; *m.* ~o (anupādā, *v.* upādiyati) 94,12; 71,15 (vimutt'-amhi); Dh. 353 (*w. loc.* taṇhakkhaye, "free through the destruction of thirst"); *loc.* ~asmiṁ (ñāṇaṁ hoti, when delivered, he comprehends that he has become free) 71,14; *n.* ~aṁ (cittaṁ) 69,36. 105,3; *comp.* *⁰-citta, *mfn.* one whose mind has been delivered. 94,13; *su-vimutta-citta, *mfn.* id. Dh. 20; *⁰-mānasa, *mfn.* id. Dh. 348. *cp. next etc.*

vimutti, *f.* (*sa.* vimukti) liberation, emancipation (Nibbāna); ⁰-sukha, *n.* the bliss of emancipation, 66,4.

vimokha, *m.* (*sa.* vimoksha) = *prec.*; *nom.* ~o (cetaso), 80,35. Dh. 92.

viy-⁰, *cp.* vy-⁰.

viya, *indecl.* = iva (*q. v.*): 2,14. 3,7. 5,28. 111,6, *etc.*; sometimes limiting the predicate of a clause: ahaṁ viya sūkaramukho ahosi, 86,1; *do. w. negation*: kappanā viya na hoti (scarcely any) 65,22; *cp.* kassakā viya hotha, 31,1.

viyākāsi, *aor.*, *v.* vyākaroti.

viyūhati, *vb.* (*sa.* vi-√ūh) to remove (*acc.*); *ger.* ~itvā (vālikaṁ) 14,25; (paṁsuṁ) 40,29 (*cp.* apabbūhati).

viraja, *mfn.* (= *sa.*) free from dust or impurity, pure, blameless; *acc. m.* ~aṁ, 68,26. Dh. 386. 412.

virajjati, *vb.* (*sa.* vi-√rañj) to change disposition or affection, to become free from passion (or from pleasure); *pr. 3. sg.* ~ati, 71,14; — *pp.* viratta, *mfn.* having aversion to (*loc.*); *m.* ~o (kāmesu) 65,9; *⁰-mānasa, *mfn.* id. 64,19 (*gen.* ~assa (kilesesu)); *⁰-cittatā, *f.* aversion to (*loc.*), *instr.* ~āya (kilesesu) 64,32. *cp.* virāga.

viramati, *vb.* (*sa.* vi-√ram) to give up, abstain from, leave off (*abl.*); *aor. 3. pl.* ~iṁsu (pāṇātipātā) 17,31. *cp.* veramaṇī.

virava, *m.* (= *sa.*) roaring, crying; a roar; *acc.* ~aṁ (mahā-⁰) 40,21; (eka-⁰) 60,11 (viravanti).

viravati, *vb.* (*sa.* vi-√ru) to roar, cry; *pr. 3. pl.* ~anti (*w. acc.* ekaviravaṁ) 60,11; *part. m.* ~anto (gadrabharāvena, "braying like an ass") 113,10; 11,18; *f.* ~antī, 53,21; *aor. 3. sg.* viravi, 40,21. 55,15; *3. pl.* ~iṁsu, 53,31; *ger.* ~itvā (ti ādīni) 73,30.

virāga, *m.* (= *sa.*) lit. 'the being decoloured', change of colour, play of colours (or simply: colour); most frequently *metaph.* of aversion, indifference (to pleasures), absence of passion; *nom.* ~o (seṭṭho dhammānaṁ) Dh. 273; *dat.* ~āya (saṁvattati), 93,8; *abl.* ~ā (by absence of passion) 71,14. 94,12; — in the *comp.* asesavirāga-nirodha, _m._ complete and trackless destruction, 66,12 (avijjāya) virāga seems to be _adj._ 'without colour' (_i. e._ leaving no track, _cp._ rāga); differently _Rhys Davids_: "the destruction of ignorance, which consists in the complete absence of lust".

viriccati, _vb._ (_sa._ vi-√ric, _pass._ viricyate; it seems to be _pass._ of the _caus._ vireceti, _sa._ virecayati, to purge) to be purged; _part. m._ ~māno, 78,32.

viriya, _n._ (_sa._ vīrya) strength, power, energy; _nom._ ~aṁ, 103,16; Dh. 112 (vīryaṁ); _acc._ ~aṁ (karoti, to persevere) 42,11-18; kata-°, _mfn._ persevering, energetic, _gen._ ~assa, 42,18; *āraddha-°, _mfn._ id. 108,19. Dh. 8 (°-vīriyaṁ), _opp._ hīna-vīriya, _mfn._ weak, Dh. 7. 112; °-phala, _n._ result of energy, 42,18; *°-bala, _n._ perseverance, _instr._ ~ena, 42,11. _cp._ vīra, vīrya.

virujjhati, _vb._ (_pass._ vi-√rudh) to be opposed, to be at variance with, contend against (_instr._); _pr. 3. sg._ no ~ati (is patient) Dh. 95; _pp._, _v. next etc._

viruddha, _mfn._ (_pp. fr. last_; = _sa._) opposite, hostile, intolerant; _loc. pl._ ~esu, Dh. 406; a-viruddha, _mfn._ (_v. h._).

virodha, _m._ (= _sa._) opposition, contradiction; _acc._ ~aṁ (dassayi, "pointed out in what respect they were fallacious") 113,18.

vilāsa, _m._ (= _sa._) sport, play, routine; coquetry, dalliance; grace, charm, beauty; _instr. pl._ ~ehi (at the end of a _dvandva-comp._) 21,13; uttama-yobbana-vilāsa-matta, _mfn._, _gen. f. pl._ ~ānaṁ, 47,14 ("drunken with the pride of their glorious youth").

vilimpati, _vb._ (_sa._ vi-√lip) to smear, anoint (_acc._), anoint oneself, perfume oneself (sometimes with _acc._ of the name of the perfume); _ger._ ~itvā (sakalasarīraṁ) 57,29; (gandhe, _acc. pl._) 41,5; _part. gen._ ~antassa (_without obj._) 53,26; – _caus. II._ *vilimpāpeti, to cause to be anointed or perfumed; _ger._ ~etvā (maṁ gandhehi) 33,8. _cp._ vilepana.

vilumpati, _vb._ (_sa._ vi-√lup) to rob, plunder (_acc._); _ger._ ~itvā (manusse), 30,30; – _caus. II._ *vilumpāpeti, to let plunder; _aor. 3. sg._ ~esi (_without obj._) 39,6.

vilepana, _n._ (= _sa._) anointing; ointment, perfume; _nom._ ~aṁ (lohita-candana-°, _q. v._) 23,33; _dvandva-comp._ mālā-gandha-°, 73,11. 81,25.

viloma, _mfn._ (= _sa._) lit. 'against the hair', contrary, wrong; _n. pl._ ~āni (_subst._) faults, perversities, Dh. 50.

vivaṭa, _mfn._ (_pp._ vivarati; _sa._ vivṛta, √vṛ) uncovered, open; _f._ ~ā (_opp._ channa) 104,35; *°-mukha, _mfn._ with open mouth; _f. pl._ ~ā, 65,7, mukhavivaṭe, _loc. abs._ 3,17. _cp. next._

vivatta, _mfn._ (_sa._ vivṛtta) turned round or away, opened, developed; *vivatta-cchadda, _m._ 'dispeller of delusion', an epithet of a Buddha, 61,34; this word seems to be _sa._ *vivṛtta-chadman, one who has rolled away the cloud or veil (_i. e._ the delusion of this world?), but we find it spelt in different ways: vivaṭa- (vivaṭṭa-, vivatta-) cchadda (-cchada, -cchadana, -ccheda), so that it very well might represent _sa._ *vivarta-chada, or °-cheda, _cp.. sa._ vivarta & _Childers s. v._

vivadati, _vb._ (_sa._ vi-√vad) to contradict, contest; dispute, quarrel; _part. med. pl._ ~ mānā, 101,8.

vivara, _m. n._ (= _sa._) aperture, breach, fissure, hole, cleft; fault; _acc._ ~aṁ (pabbatānaṁ) Dh. 127; pākāra-° (of a wall) 90,34; _cp._ 91,30.

vivarati, _vb._ (_sa._ vi-√vṛ) to open, reveal (_acc._); _pot. 3. sg._ ~eyya (paṭicchannaṁ) 69,16; _aor. 3. sg._ vivari (mukhaṁ) 3,18; (dvāraṁ) 65,28; _3. pl._ ~iṁsu, 68,3; _ger._ ~itvā, 3,16; _pp._ vivaṭa, _q. v._ _cp._ vivara.

vivāha, _m._ (= _sa._) marriage; _acc._ ~aṁ (karoti, to marry a wife) 101,17 (_cp._ āvāha).

vivicca, _ger._ & _grd._ (_fr._ vi-√vic,

to separate) in the *comp.* *viviccasayana, *n.* sleeping alone, Dh. 271 (*instr.* ~ena). *cp.* viveka.

vividha, *mfn.* (= *sa.*) manifold, various; *n.* ~aṁ, 111,32.

viveka, *m.* (= *sa.*) separation, seclusion, solitude; *acc.* ~aṁ. Dh. 75; *loc.* ~e, Dh. 87.

visa. *m. n.* (*sa.* visha) poison, venom; *acc.* ~aṁ (bhatte pakkhipitvā) 33,30; Dh. 123; sa-visa, *mfn.* poisoned, poisonous; *instr.* ~ena (sallena) 92,7. *cp.* visattikā.

visaṁyutta (**visaññutta**), *mfn.* (*sa.* visaṁyukta) detached, delivered (from: *instr.* or *e. c.*); *acc. m.* ~aṁ, Dh. 385. 397. 402. 410; 417 (sabbayoga-⁰). *cp.* saṁyoga.

***visaṁkhāra-gata**, *mfn.*, who is free from predispositions (saṁkhāra, *q. v.*), approaching Nibbāna; *n.* ~aṁ (cittaṁ) Dh. 154.

***visaṁkhita**, *mfn.* (*pp.* visaṁkharoti, to take to pieces; *sa.* *visaṁ-√kṛ) taken asunder; *n.* ~aṁ (gahakūṭaṁ) Dh. 154.

visaññutta, *v.* visaṁyutta.

visaṭṭha, *mfn.* (*sa.* visṛshṭa) set free, released; *⁰-matta, *mfn.* (*v.* matta[2-2b]), *m.* ~o (at the moment he was set free) 17,20.

***visattikā**, *f.* (*prob. fr.* visatta, *sa.* vi-shakta, √sañj, adhering to, extended over, *w. loc.*), desire, lust, longing for (often *w. loc.* loke and coordinate with taṇhā (*q. v.*), to which it sometimes has been taken as *adj.* in the sense of "poisonous" on account of its resemblance to visa); *nom.* ~ā (jālinī ~ taṇhā) Dh. 180; (jammī taṇhā loke ~) 107,31 = Dh. 335.

visada, *mfn.* (*sa.* viçada) clear, pure, spotless; even, smooth; *m.* ~o, 62,29.

visaya, *m.* (*sa.* vishaya) sphere, dominion, country; Lāḷa-⁰, *m.* 110,22 (*v. h.*).

visahati, *vb.* (*sa.* vi-√sah) to be able or capable to; to dare, venture (*w. inf.*); *pr. 3. sg.* ~ati [*scil.* paṭivacanaṁ dātuṁ] 90,26; *1. sg.* ~āmi, 13,15; *3. pl.* ~anti, 8,1; *part. m.* a-visahanto (gantuṁ, not venturing to go, *i. e.* to enter on that expedition) 39,4.

visārada, *mfn.* (*sa.* viçārada) wise, skilled or versed in; bold, confident; *m.* ~o (devindo) 110,26; (sabba-vāda-⁰) 113,4. *cp.* vesārajja.

visīdati, *vb.* (*sa.* vi-√sad) to sink down, be immersed in; to despond, despair; *pr. 3. pl.* ~anti, Dh. 171.

***visīveti**, *vb.* (*caus. fr. sa.* *vi + √çyai) to remove cold, thaw up, warm oneself; *ger.* ~etvā, 100,25. *cp.* *Morris*, JPTS. '84. p. 72.

visujjhati. *vb.* (*sa.* vi-√çudh) to become pure; *pr. 3. sg.* ~ati, Dh. 165; *caus.* visodheti (*q. v.*) *cp. next.*

visuddhi, *f.* (= *sa.*) purification, purity, holiness; *dat. gen.* ~iyā (sattānaṁ) 90,17; (maggo) 107,12. Dh. 274—77; *kamma-⁰, *f.* (*q. v.*). — *Visuddhi-magga, *m. nom. pr.* of a work of Buddhaghosa (lit. 'way of purity'); *acc.* ~aṁ, 114,12.

***visūka**, *n.* (*fr. sa.* *vi-√sūc, or = viçoka, *cp. Kuhn*, Beitr. p. 29, Tr. PM, 78,33) show, spectacle, play; only in the foll. two *comp.*; *diṭṭhi-visūka, *n.* a puppet-show of heresy, 94,1; *visūka-dassana, *n.* seeing spectacles, *abl.* ~ā, 81,24. *cp.* visoka, *mfn.*

visesa, *m.* (*sa.* viçesha) difference, species; distinction, excellence; *abl.* (*adv.*) visesato, especially, distinctively, emphatically; 114,23. Dh. 22.

visoka, *mfn.* (*sa.* viçoka) free from sorrow; *gen. m.* ~assa, Dh. 90. *cp.* visūka, *n.*

visodheti. *vb.* (*caus.* visujjhati; *sa.* viçodhayati) to purify, keep clear (*acc.*); *pot. 3. sg.* ~aye, Dh. 165. 281. 289.

visoseti, *vb.* (*caus.* vi-√çush, viçoshayati) to make dry, dry up (*acc.*); *pot. 3. sg.* ~aye (nadīnaṁ sotāni) 103,18; *pp.* visosita, dried up. *f.* ~ā (taṇhā) 108,13. *cp.* sussati.

vissa, *mfn.* (*sa.* viçva?) whole,

entire; *acc. m.* ~aṁ (dhammaṁ) 106,5 = Dh. 266; (vissa in the sense of *sa.* viçva seems not to occur elsewhere in Pāli; the Comm. Dhpd. 1855. p. 379 takes it apparently = *sa.* visra, *mfn.* (smelling like raw meat), and explains it by visama, vissa-gandha, which occurs sometimes in the commentaries. *e. g.* Vin. III, 288,2).

vissajjana, *n.* (*sa.* visarjana) sending forth, abandoning, giving up; *nom. acc.* ~aṁ, 4,31; 47,4 (imassa ~aṁ kariṁ, "I have caused him to leave me").

***vissajjāpeti**, *vb.* (*caus. II.* vissajjati) to send, throw, thrust away (*acc.*); *aor. 3. sg.* ~esi, 55,17; *ger.* ~etvā, 23,9. 51,21 (hatthaṁ).

vissajjeti, *vb.* (*caus.* vissajjati, *sa.* visarjayati, vi-√sṛj) [1]) to emit, send (forth, away); to let go, set at liberty (*acc.*); *pr. 3. pl.* ~enti (mātaraṁ) 32,20; *imp. 2. sg.* ~ehi (maṁ sarasmiṁ, put into) 5,16; *pot. 1. sg.* ~eyyaṁ, 4,9; *aor. 3. sg.* ~esi, 4,17. 31,19; 36,24 (dadhighaṭaṁ, overturned); *3. pl.* ~esuṁ, 32,23; *fut. 3. sg.* ~essati. 4,32; *ger.* ~etvā, 4,16. 59,14; 61,6 (satasahassāni, dispensing); *pp.* vissajjita, *m. pl.* ~ā (macchā) 4,27. — [2]) to explain, answer (a question, *acc.*); *pr. 3. sg.* ~eti (pañhaṁ puṭṭho) 90,26; *part. m.* ~ento, 85,14; *gen. f.* ~entiyā, 86,32; *ger.* ~etvā (tam atthaṁ) 85,24; *pp.* vissajjita, *m.* ~o (pañho) 88,12; *n. pl.* ~āni, 98,33.

vissaṭṭha, *mfn.* (*pp.* vissajjati = vissajjeti; *sa.* visṛshṭa) sent away, loosed, released; *m.* ~o. 4,23 (put down).

vissamati, *vb.* (*sa.* vi-√çram) to rest, repose; *ger.* ~itvā, 9,24; *pp.* vissamita, *comp.* tesaṁ °-kāle, 21,7 ("taking their rest").

vissasati, *vb.* (*sa.* vi-√çvas) to trust or confide in (*loc.* (or *gen.*, *acc.*)); *pot. 3. sg.* vissase (tāsu) 51,4. *cp. next.*

vissāsa, *m.* (*sa.* viçvāsa) trust, confidence; *acc.* ~aṁ (achinditvā, "in unbroken amity") 13,7; ~aṁ āpajjati (*v. h.*) 30,12; Dh. 272 (metri causa vissāsa-māpādi); *comp.* *°-paramā ñāti, Dh. 204 ("trust is the best of relationships", *cp.* parama & lābha *above*).

vissāsika, *mfn.* (*sa.* viçvāsika) [1]) confident, trustful; [2]) intimate, familiar, confidant; *m.* ~o ("confidential adviser") 38,22.

vihaññati, *vb.* (*pass.* vi-√han) to be anxious or frightened, to be afflicted or grieved, mourn; *pr. 3. sg.* ~ati, 34,20. Dh. 15. 62; *part. m.* avihaññamāno ("without complaint") 78,26.

viharati, *vb.* (*sa.* vi-√hṛ) to dwell, stay, live; *pr. 3. sg.* ~ati, 2,19. 66,2. 75,6. 84,8 (vihāre); *1. pl.* ~āma, Dh. 197; *part. m.* ~anto, 28,2; *gen.* ~ato, 103,23; *imp. 3. sg.* ~atu, 74,22; *ger.* ~itvā, 70,20; *fut. 2. sg.* vihāhisi (sukhaṁ) Dh. 379 (if not better from vijahāti (*sa.* vi-√hā), *cp. Kuhn*, Beitr. p. 116). *cp. next* & saddhi-vihārika.

vihāra, *m.* (= *sa.*) [1]) passing the time agreeably, pleasure; sukhavihāra, happiness, 74,22 (diṭṭha-dhamma-°, *q. v.*); brahma-°, *v. h.* — [2]) pleasure-ground, place of recreation, home, *esp.* a Buddhist monastery or cloister; *nom.* ~o, 84,8; ~aṁ, 22,20. 114,3; *loc.* ~e, 84,7; Aggāḷava-°. Mahā-°. *nom. pr.* (*q. v.*).

vihārin, *mfn.* (= *sa.*) dwelling, living, delighting in; mostly *e. c.*, *v.* *a-ppamāda-°, *mettā-°, *sādhu-°, *mfn.* Dh. 57. 329. 368.

vihāhiti, *fut.*, *v.* viharati (& vijahāti).

vihiṁsati, *vb.* (*sa.* vi-√hiṁs) to injure, hurt (*acc.*); *pr. 3. sg.* ~ati (bhūtāni daṇḍena) Dh. 131. *cp. next.*

viheṭheti, *vb.* (*sa.* vi-√heṭh) to annoy, injure, insult (*acc.*); *part. m.* ~ayanto. Dh. 184 (paraṁ); *ger.* ~etvā, 73,6; *pass. fut. 3. sg.* viheṭhiyissati (nāgena) 76,31; *pp.* ~ita, *pl.* ~ā, 73,5 (viheṭhit' attha). [This verb is confounded with the *synon.* verb viheseti, which seems to be identical with *sa.* vibhīshayati or vihiṁsayati. Tr.] *cp. F. W. Thomas,* JRAS. '04. p. 749.

vīci, *f.* (= *sa.*) a wave; *acc. pl.* ~ī, 28,7.

vīṇā, *f.* (= *sa.*) a certain stringed instrument, a lute; *nom.* ~ā, 104,17; *acc.* ~aṁ, 19,31. 50,10. 67,29.

vīta, *mfn.* (*pp.* vi-√i; = *sa.*) gone away; very frequently at the beginning of *comp.* = free from, without; °-taṇha, *mfn.* Dh. 351 (*v.* taṇhā); *°-dosa, *mfn.* Dh. 357 (*v.* dosa[2]); *vīta-ddara, *mfn.* fearless, Dh. 385 (*fr.* dara, *q. v.*, *cp.* nid-dara); °-mala, *mfn.* 68,26 (*v. h.*); *°-moha, *mfn.* Dh. 358 (*v. h.*).

*vītināmeti, *vb.* (*sa.* *vi-ati-√nam) to spend time, pass away time (*acc.*); *ger.* ~etvā (divasaṁ) 22,23.

vītisāreti, *vb.* (*caus.* vi-ati-√sṛ; *Buddh. sa.* vyatisārayati) to finish (Comm. = pariyosāpeti); only in the usual phrase: sammodanīyaṁ kathaṁ sārāṇīyaṁ ~, to exchange the usual ceremonious greetings, 89,31 (*ger.* ~etvā); the same phrase is put into metre Sn. v. 419 (*cp.* Jāt. IV, 98,18).

vīthi, *f.* (= *sa.*) a row; a street, road, passage; *loc.* ~iyaṁ (antara-°, *q. v.*) 39,6; *loc. pl.* ~īsu (nagara-°) 73,29; *°-sabhāga, *m.* a neighbour (living in the same street), *gen. pl.* ~ānaṁ, 57,7.

vīmaṁsati, *vb.* (sometimes spelt vi-°; *sa.* vi-√mṛç, but perhaps confounded with mīmāṁsate) to investigate, examine, *esp.* to put to the test (*acc.*); *pr. 1. sg.* ~āmi (naṁ) 3,6; *part. m.* ~anto, 57,17; *imp. 2. pl.* ~atha, 58,4; *pot. 3. sg.* ~eyya (maṁ dānena) 16,13; *fut. 1. sg.* ~issāmi, 13,23. 15,9; *inf.* ~ituṁ, 114,8; *ger.* ~itvā, 58,15. *cp. next.* [The grammarians derive this verb from *desider.* √man, *cp. Childers & Sénart,* Kacc. p. 232 (434), *Pischel,* Gramm. § 251; on account of its signification (it has usually a personal object) I think it is preferable, as do *Trenckner & Fausbøll* (5 Jāt. p. 37), to derive it from vi-mṛç°, although √mṛç with other *prp.* becomes masati.]

vīmaṁsana, *n.* (*sa.* vimarçana, but *v. above*) trying, testing; *comp.* °-atthāya, 16,12; °-atthaṁ, 57,23 (*cp.* attha[1]).

vīra, *m.* (= *sa.*) a brave or eminent man, hero; *acc.* ~aṁ, Dh. 418; °Buddha-°, *m.* (*q. v.*); °-sena, *m. nom. pr.*, name of a man, 97,1. *cp. next,* vera & verin.

vīriya, *n.*, *v.* viriya.

vīsaṁ, *indecl.* (& vīsati or °-tiṁ, *nom. acc. pl.*; *sa.* viṁçati (viṁçat)) *num.* '20'; ~ satasahassaṁ, 20,00,000, 23,3.

vīsatima, *mfn.* (*sa.* viṁçatama) twentieth; *m.* ~o (vaggo) Dh. ch. XX; ekūna-°, *q. v.*

vuccati, *vb.* (*pass.* √vac, *sa.* ucyate) to be said, told, spoken (of or to); to be requested; to be called or named; *pr. 3. sg.* ~ati (is called): 25,31. 82,14. 106,7. 109,14; (is spoken of) 96,5; *3. pl.* ~anti (are called) 32,17; *pp.* vutta (*v. below*). From this a number of active forms have been preserved, but the active present tense is taken from the suppletive verb vadati (*vadeti) *q. v.*; *aor.* [a]) avaca, *3. sg.* 51,15. 64,8; *2. sg.* 22,18 (mā maṁ kiñci ~); avacaṁ, *1. sg.* 55,6; — [b]) avoca, *3. sg.* 2,9 (imā gāthā); 68,13 (etad); 76,2 (Devadattaṁ); 110,21; *2. sg.* voca (unaugmented after mā) Dh. 133; *3. pl.* avocuṁ, 76,23; [*aor.* [c-d]) avacāsi, avocāsi are also found; *fut.* vakkhāmi]; *inf.* vattuṁ, 87,21. 103,15; *ger.* vatvā, 2,8. 3,7 *etc.*; a-vatvā; 44,5 (alternating with vutte, *abs. loc.*); *grd.* vattabba, *m.* ~o (bhikkhūhi, to be spoken to) 79,15; *n.* ~aṁ, 88,5; 88,6 (~siyā); *caus.* vāceti (*q. v.*) *cp.* vacana, vācā, *etc.*

vuṭṭhahati & vuṭṭhāti, *vb.* (*sa.* vi-ud-√sthā) to rise, arise, get up (from, *abl.*); *aor. 3. sg.* vuṭṭhāsi, 111,9; *ger.* [a]) vuṭṭhāya (sayanā) 41,27. 65,14; [b]) vuṭṭhahitvā, 80,4; *pp.* vuṭṭhita, *loc. m.* ~e, 82,22. *cp. next.*

vuṭṭhāna, *n.* (*sa.* vyutthāna) rising up; *gabbha-⁰, *n.* 62,21 (*v. h.*).

vuṭṭhi, *f.* (*sa.* vṛshṭi) rain; *nom.* ~i, 106,31 = Dh. 14; *acc.* ~iṁ, 104,28.

vuḍḍha, *mfn.* (*pp.* vaḍḍhati, *cp.* vaddha[2]; *sa.* vṛddha) grown, old; *m.* ~o, 74,21.

vutta, *mfn.* (*pp.* vuccati; *sa.* ukta) said, told, spoken; addressed, answered, requested, proposed; *m.* ~o, 113,12; (samāno, being requested) 98,16; *f.* ~ā, 31,32. 111,31; *n.* ~aṁ (tena ~, on that account it is said) 51,29; (idaṁ) 84,28; ~aṁ ~aṁ ("each of his propositions") 113,13; *loc. abs.* ~e (ti ~, evaṁ ~) 1,19. 79,20, *etc.*; alternating with vatvā (*ger.*) 44,5; *m. pl.* ~ā, 33,9. 73,23; *comp.* *vutta-matta, *mfn.* (*v.* matta[2,2b]); *heṭṭhā-vutta-⁰ (*q. v.*) 63,22 (⁰-nayen'eva, *v.* naya).

***vuttari-bhāveti**, *v.* uttari-⁰.

vutti, *f.* (*sa.* vṛtti) mode of life, conduct, behaviour; *a-cchidda-⁰, *mfn.* Dh. 229; *paṭisanthāra-⁰, *mfn.* Dh. 376 (*v. h.*).

vuddha, *mfn.* (*pp.* vaḍḍhati) = vuḍḍha & vaddha (*q. v.*).

vuddhi, *f.* (*sa.* vṛddhi) growth, increase; *acc.* ~iṁ, 2,18. 18,3. (*cp.* vaḍḍhi).

vusita, *mfn.* (*pp.* vasati; *sa.* ushita) lived, past, completed; *n.* ~aṁ (brahmacariyaṁ) 71,15.

vūpasama, *m.* (*sa.* vyupaçama) cessation, pacification; ~o, 80,29.

ve, *indecl.* (*sa.* vai) a particle of affirmation: 'indeed', 'certainly'; 106,7 = Dh. 267; Dh. 234; 108,6 (ve mā); na ve, 55,1; inserted in the relative sentence: yo ve, 106,33 = Dh. 222. *cp.* have.

***vekaṇḍa**, *m.* (?), a kind of arrow; *acc.* ~aṁ, 92,23 (not found elsewhere).

vega, *m.* (= *sa.*) haste, speed, quickness, rapidity; *instr.* (*adv.*) ~ena (gantvā) 7,4; 60,6; *comp.* asani-⁰, 12,22; vāta-⁰, 12,30; ratha-vega-⁰, 60,10.

Vejayanta, *m.* (*sa.* Vaijayanta) *nom. pr.* of the palace of Sakka (Indra); *nom.* ~o, 60,25 (vijayante uṭṭhitattā); ⁰-pāsādo, 60,24; *⁰-ratha, *m.* Sakka's chariot (chariot of victory) 60,4 (*instr.* ~ena).

veṭhita, *mfn.* (*pp.* veṭheti, √veshṭ; *sa.* veshṭita) enveloped, covered; *m.* ~o (samukha-⁰, *q. v.*) 51,8.

vetana, *n.* (= *sa.*) hire, wages; salary, payment; subsistence, livelihood, earning; *acc.* ~aṁ, 76,12; (~ khaṇḍetvā, *q. v.*) 19,25; *atta-vetana-bhata, *mfn.* 105,5 (*v.* attan).

vetta, *m. n.* (*sa.* vetra) a reed, stick, staff; ⁰-agga, *n.* the point of a reed, 62,17 (susedita-⁰, *q. v.*).

veda, *m.* (= *sa.*) knowledge, perception, emotion, pleasure; *pl.* the (three) Vedas (*viz.* Irubbeda, Yajubbeda, Sāmaveda); *gen. pl.* ~ānaṁ (tiṇṇaṁ) 16,22; *loc. pl.* ~esu (tīsu) 113,3.

vedanā, *f.* (= *sa.*) [1]) feeling, sensation (*in the dogmatics*: the second of the five khandhā, *q. v.*); *nom.* ~a, 66,8 (phassa-paccayā); 94,9. 95,16; *instr.* ~āya, 95,15; *gen.* ~āya, 94,9; ⁰-nirodha, *m.* 66,15 (*q. v.*); *⁰-saṁkhāvimutta, *mfn.* "released from what is styled sensation", 95,17; *pl.* tisso vedanā, the three perceptions (*viz.* dukkhā, sukhā, adukkha-m-asukhā) 82,9; uttama-vedanaṁ (*acc. sg.*) 103,23, seems to be the last of those three. — [2]) pain, suffering; *acc.* ~aṁ, 80,34; *pl.* ~ā (kharā) 13,12; (pabāḷhā) 78,24; *comp.* *vedanaṭṭa, *mfn.* 50,20 (*v.* aṭṭa[1]); *⁰-matta, *mfn.* "maddened with the pain", *m.* ~o, 24,7; *acc.* ~aṁ, 30,15.

vedaniya, *mfn.* (*grd.* √vid; *sa.* vedanīya) to be known, intelligible; *paṇḍita-⁰, *mfn.* 94,26 (*v. h.*).

Vedabbha, *m(fn).* (*sa.* Vaidarbha) relating to the country Vidarbha; *acc. m.* ~aṁ (mantaṁ, name of a certain spell) 32,9; ⁰-brāhmaṇa, *m.* a Brahman knowing that spell, 32,16, *etc.*; 34,21 (Vedabbhaṁ); — ⁰-jātaka, *n.* 32,7.

***vedayita**, *n.* (*fr.* vedeti, *v.* [vidati]) sensation, perception of the senses, impression on the senses; ~aṁ,

70,27; saññā-vedayita-nirodha, *m.* 80,10 (*q. v.*).

*vedalla, *n.* (*sa.* *vaidalya; the native grammarians derive it from veda with the suffix -lla) one of the nine divisions of Buddha's doctrine (navaṅgaṁ Satthu-sāsanaṁ); ∼aṁ, 109,34 (jātak'-abbhuta-°).

vedi, *aor.*, *v.* [vidati].

vedin, *mfn.* (= *sa.*) knowing, feeling (*e. c.*); *m.* ∼ī (vijjā-sippakalā-°) 113,3.

vediyati, vedeti, *v.* [vidati].

vedhin, *mfn.* (*sa.* vedhin & vyādhin) piercing, perforating; *vāla-°, *mfn.* (*q. v.*).

vema, *m.* (= *sa.*) a loom; *acc.* ∼aṁ, 89,7; *°-koṭi, *f. ib.* (*v. h.*).

*vemajjha, *n.* (*cp. sa.* vimadhya) the middle, or more correctly: the interior of anything between its centre and its outskirt (or not far away from its limits); *acc.* ∼aṁ (gata-kāle, *i. e.* before he had got as far as mid-river) 28,7; *loc.* ∼e (nadiyā, not far from the bank in the river) 2,19.

veyyaggha, *mfn.* (*sa.* vaiyāghra? *cp.* vyaggha below) belonging to a tiger, tiger-like, *i. e.* eminent (?); °-pañcamaṁ, 'an eminent man besides' (*lit.* as the fifth) Dh. 295. SBE. X. p. 71–72. *cp.* JRAS. V. 229. (*Fausbøll*, Dhpd. 1855. p. 391, takes it from *sa.* vaiyagra (vy-agra).)

*veyyattiya, *n.* (*fr.* vyatta) intelligence, cleverness; *instr.* ∼ena, 91,26.

veyyākaraṇa, *n.* (*sa.* vaiyākaraṇa, *mfn.*) exposition, explanation; *nom.* ∼aṁ, 109,33 (one of the nine divisions of Buddha's doctrine); *loc.* ∼asmiṁ, 71,17. (*cp.* vyākaroti).

vera, *n.* (*sa.* vaira) enmity, anger, hatred; *acc.* ∼aṁ, Dh. 201; 11,20 (∼ bandhati, *q. v.*); *instr.* ∼ena, 106,23 = Dh. 5; *abl.* ∼ā, Dh. 291; *pl.* ∼āni, 106,23; *comp.* *°-saṁsaggasaṁsaṭṭha, *mfn.* Dh. 291 (*v. h.*); *cp.* a-vera, vīra, verin.

*veramaṇī, *f.* (*fr.* viramaṇa, vi-√ram) abstinence (from, *abl.*); *nom.* ∼ī (pāṇātipātā) 81,22, *etc.*

verin, *mfn.* (*sa.* vairin) hostile, hating; sinful; *nom. m.* ∼ī, Dh. 42 (var. lect.; *cp. next*); *acc.* ∼inaṁ, ib.; *loc. pl.* ∼inesu, Dh. 197. *cp.* a-verin.

verivat (= veravat), *mfn.* (*sa.* vaira-vat) = *prec.*; *nom. m.* ∼vā, Dh. 42 (but the reading: verī vā seems to be preferable). *cp.* puttimat.

velā, *f.* (= *sa.*) [1]) limit, boundary, coast, shore; *°-anta, *m.* (*q. v.*), *loc.* ∼e, 20,4 ("on the edge of the shore"); — [2]) time; *loc.* velāya(ṁ), at that time, on that occasion (mostly *e. c.*): aruṇa-°, 12,18; āgata-°, 20,10; jūta-kīḷana-°, 20,14; pavisana-°, 53,4; tāyaṁ ∼, 66,19; velāyam eva, *adv.* = to morrow (soon) 14,27–15,3. — Uru-°, *nom. pr.* (*q. v.*) = *sa.* °-vilvā.

veḷu, *m.* (once *n.*) (*sa.* veṇu) bamboo; *nom. n.* ∼uṁ, 26,27; °-vana, *n.* a bamboo-grove, 26,25 (*cp. below*); *°-pesikā, *f.* 52,31 (*q. v.*).

veḷuriya, *n.* (*sa.* vaiḍūrya) the cat's-eye-gem, lapis lazuli, βερυλλος; *°-vaṇṇūpanibha, *mfn.* 10,19 (*v.* upanibha); *vaṁsa-rāga-°, "coral of the colour of bamboo" (Jāt. Transl. vol. IV. p. 89) 26,31. *cp.* JRAS. XII (1880) p. 178.

Veḷuvana, *n.* (*sa.* veṇu-vana; *cp.* veḷu *above*) *nom. pr.* of a bamboo-grove and a monastery near Rājagaha, presented to Buddha by King Bimbisāra; *loc.* ∼e, 84,27.

vevaṇṇiya, *n.* (*sa.* vaivarṇya) change of colour, loss of beauty; *acc.* ∼aṁ, 47,16.

vesa, *m.* (*sa.* veça, vesha) dress, ornament, appearance, disguise; mostly *e. c.*: *acc.* ∼aṁ (itthi-°) 58,31; (tunnavāya-°) 58,16; *instr.* ∼ena (aññātaka-°, in disguise) 43,12; (aññatara-°) 55,29; (brāhmaṇa-°, disguised as a Br.) 15,10; (māṇava-°) 19,10; (paribbājaka-°) 110,29.

vesārajja, *n.* (*fr.* visārada; *sa.* vaiçāradya) clearness of intellect, expertness; *°-ppatta, *mfn.* who has gained full knowledge or confidence; *m.* ~o, 69,13.

vessa, *m.* (*sa.* vaiçya) a man of the third caste; *nom.* ~o, 92,10.

*Vessantara, *m.* (*cp. Buddh. sa.* Viçvantara; Jāt. VI. p. 485,18) *nom. pr.* of a king (= Buddha in his last existence but one); °-jātaka, *n.* the last tale in the Jātaka-book, 102,19.

vehāsa (& vehāsaya), *m.* or *n.*(?) (*sa.* vaihāyasa) sky, atmosphere; *comp.* *vehāsaṁ-gama, *mfn.* able to fly through the air, 21,35 (*cp. sa.* vihaṁgama).

vo, *pron. 2. pers., gen. dat. pl., v.* tvaṁ.

*vokāra, *m.* (= okāra, *q. v.*) vileness, worthlessness; anekākāra-°, *mfn.* 86,8 (*v.* an-eka).

voca, *aor., v.* vuccati.

vodaka, *mfn.* (*sa.* vy-udaka) waterless, dry; *acc. m. n.* ~aṁ, 83,15. 84,2. (*cp.* sa-udaka).

voropeti, *vb.* (*sa.* vy-ava-ropayati, *caus.* √ruh) to deprive of (*abl.* & *acc. pers.*); *pot. 3. sg.* ~eyya (Tathāgataṁ jīvitā) 76,27; *aor. 2. sg.* ~esi, 75,31; *fut. 1. sg.* ~essāmi, 75,32; *3. pl.* ~essanti, 75,3; *inf.* ~etuṁ, 75,30; *ger.* ~etvā, 75,8.

*vosāna, *n.* (*fr.* vy-ava-√so) conviction, determination; consummation, perfection; sabba-vosita-°, *mfn.* altogether perfect, *acc. m.* ~aṁ, Dh. 423. *cp. next.*

vosita, *mfn.* (*sa.* vyavasita, *pp.* vy-ava-√so) perfect, determined; *abhiññā-°, *mfn.* Dh. 423 (*v. h.*) *cp.* vosāna.

vohāra, *m.* (*sa.* vyavahāra) [1]) practice, affair, business, trade; *acc.* ~aṁ (karoti) 8,16. 23,2-4; *°-karaṇatthāya, "for business", 9,11; — [2]) lawsuit, litigation; *acc.* ~aṁ, 42,28; *loc. pl.* ~esu, ib.; — [3]) mode of expression, appellation, name; *nom.* ~o, 97,2.

vyaggha, *m.* (*sa.* vyāghra) a tiger; *gen.* ~assa, 8,27. *cp.* veyyaggha.

vyañjana, *n.* (= *sa.*) [1]) ornament, sign, mark, *etc.*; — [2]) a letter, syllable, *esp.* consonant; *instr. abl. pl.* ~ehi, 114,21; — [3]) condiment, sauce; *acc.* ~aṁ, 57,21; *aneka-sūpa-°, *mfn.* 57,11 (*v.* an-eka); *cp.* sa-vyañjana, *mfn.*

vyatta, *mfn.* (*sa.* vyakta) [1]) evident, clear; [2]) learned, clever, intelligent; *m.* ~o (dovāriko) 90,32. 91,26; *instr.* ~ena (bhikkhunā) 81,16. *cp.* veyyattiya.

vyanti-karoti, *vb.* (*sa.* vyantī-√kṛ) to put an and to, remove (*acc.*); *fut. 3. sg.* ~kāhiti (Mārabandhanaṁ) Dh. 350 (metrically = viyanti-kāhiti).

vyapanudati, *vb.* (*sa.* vy-apa-√nud) to drive away, remove (*acc.*); *aor. 3. sg.* (augmented) vyapānudi (dukkhakkhandhaṁ) 108,22.

vyaya, *m.* = vaya [2] (*q. v.*).

vyasana, *n.* (= *sa.*) destruction, ruin; misfortune, calamity; *acc.* ~aṁ (ajjhagu) 34,21; °-ppatta, *mfn.* "come to grief", *acc. m.* ~aṁ, 8,30.

vyākaroti, *vb.* (*sa.* vy-ā-√kṛ) to declare, explain, elucidate, reveal (*acc.*); to give an explanation or answer; to call, name (*acc.*); *pot. 2. sg.* ~eyyāsi (kiṁ) 94,28. 95,6; *1. sg.* ~eyyaṁ (evaṁ), 94,35; *aor. 3. sg.* vyākāsi, 91,12; viyākāsi, 113,13; *3. pl.* viyākaruṁ (naṁ Buddhaghoso'ti) 113,20; *fut. 3. sg.* ~issati, 92,3; *pp.* vyākata, explained, elucidated, revealed, *n.* ~aṁ, 90,16. 93,3; *abl.* ~ato, ib. (*v.* dhāreti) *cp.* a-vyākata, *mfn.* & veyyākaraṇa, *n.*

vyādhi, *f.* (= *sa.*) disease, sickness; *nom.* ~i (dukkhā) 67,9; (pabāḷhā) 78,31; *dvandva comp.* °-maraṇa-°, 108,22.

vyādhita, *mfn.* (= *sa.*) diseased; *acc. m.* ~aṁ (purisaṁ) 63,21.

vyāpajjati, *vb.* (*sa.* vy-ā-√pad) to fall into misfortune, come to a harm; *pr. 3. sg.* ~ati, 25,14. *cp. next.*

vyāpatti, *f.* (= *sa.*) misfortune, ruin; *nom.* ~i (nāvāya) 24,16.

vyāma, *m.* (= *sa.*) a fathom; °-matta, *mfn.* of a fathom's length, *n. pl.* ~āni (pekkhuṇāni) 10,20.

vyāsatta, *mfn.* (*sa.* vyāsakta) attached or devoted to, occupied with; *comp.* *°-manas (or °-manasa? *cp.* °mānasa) *mfn.* whose mind is distracted, *acc. m.* °-manasaṁ, Dh. 47. 48. 287.

S.

sa-[1], *indecl.* (= *sa.*) prefix to nouns, mostly implying 'conjunction' or 'possession' (*cp.* saha-, saṁ-) and *opp.* to a-[4] and other negative prefixes (*cp.* sa-kubbato, Dh. 52 (var. lect.) *opp.* a-kubbato, Dh. 51; sa-ce, *indecl.*, *opp.* no-ce (*q. v.*)); it is often contracted with a foll. vowel (*v.* sāṭṭhakatha, *etc.*, sodariya), but also uncontracted: **sa-udaka**, *mfn.* (*sa.* sodaka) containing water, *m.* ~o (patto) 82,26. – ***sa-upāyāsa**, *mfn.* (*v.* upāyāsa). – **sa-kala**, *mfn.* & **sakad-°**, **sakiṁ**, *v. below.* – ***sa-kiñcana**, *mfn.* wealthy, *m.* ~o, Dh. 396 (*opp.* a-kiñcana). – **sa-gandhaka**, *mfn.* (*sa.* sa-gandha) fragrant, full of scent, *n.* ~aṁ (pupphaṁ) Dh. 52. – ***sa-guṇaṁ**, *adv.* (?), only in the phrase ~ katvā, duly arranged (duly folded or laid together?) 82,25 (= ekato katvā, Comm.). – **sajju**, **sattha**, **sadisa**, *v. below.* – **sa-dukkha**, *mfn.* (*sa.* sa-duḥkha) accompanied with misery, *n.* ~aṁ, 94,2. – **sa-devaka**, *mfn.* (= *sa.*) together with the gods (*comb. w.* loka) 78,15. 87,21. 104,5. Dh. 44. – **sa-dhana**, *mfn.* (= *sa.*) wealthy, 52,4. – **santara**, **santika**, *v. below.* – **sa-pajāpatika**, *m(fn).* (*sa.* °-prajāpatika) together with one's wife, *m.* ~o, 2,26. – ***sa-pariggaha**, *mfn.* married, 56,6 (*comp.* °-a-pariggaha-bhāva, *m.*). – ***sa-pariḷāha**, *mfn.* accompanied with pain, *n.* ~aṁ, 94,2. – **sa-parivāra**, *mfn.* (= *sa.*) *v.* parivāra. – **sa-phala**, *mfn.* (= *sa.*) fruitful, *f.* ~ā (vācā) Dh. 52. – **sa-brahmaka**, *mfn.* (= *sa.*) together with Brahman, *loc.* ~e (loke) 78,15. – **sa-brahmacārin**, *m.* (= *sa.*) fellow-student or -priest, *pl.* ~ī, 96,30. – **sa-bhāga**, *mfn.* (= *sa.*) having a share, *v.* vīthi-°, 57,7. – **sa-māraka**, *mfn.* (= *sa.*) including Māra, *loc.* ~e (loke) 78,15. – **sa-rājaka**, *mfn.* (= *sa.*) including the king, *loc. f.* ~ikāya (parisāya) 74,18 (*i. e.* king Bimbisāra and his retinue). – ***sa-vighāta**, *mfn.*, *v.* vighāta. – **sa-visa**, *mfn.* (*sa.* sa-visha) poisoned, *instr.* ~ena (sallena), 92,7. – **sa-vyañjana**, *mfn.* (= *sa.*) together with condiments, *acc.* ~aṁ (yāguṁ) 57,22. – **savhaya**, *v. below.* – ***sa-ssamaṇa-brāhmaṇa**, *mfn.* including Samaṇas and Brahmans, *loc. f.* ~iyā (pajāya) 78,15. – ***sa-ssāmika-bhāva**, *m.* the being married (to a husband), 56,8. (*cp.* sāmin & sāmika). – ***sa-hetu-dhamma**, *m.*, *v.* dhamma[4]. – ***sāṭṭhakathā**, *adj. f.* together with the commentary, 102,2 (pāli). – **sātthika**, *v. below.* – ***sādāna**, *mfn.* filled with affection or desire, greedy, *loc. pl.* ~esu, Dh. 406 (*opp.* an-ādāna, *cp.* ādāna). – **sādhāraṇa**, *v. below.* – **sānucara**, *mfn.* (= *sa.*) having followers, *n.* ~aṁ (raṭṭhaṁ, "with all its subjects") Dh. 294. – **sāmacca**, *mfn.* (*sa.* sāmātya) together with ministers, *acc.* ~aṁ (rājānaṁ) 40,4. – **sālohita**, **sodariya**, *v. below.*

sa-[2], *num.* (= cha, *q. v.*) in the *comp.* saḷāyatana, soḷasa, *etc.* (*cp.* saṭṭhi).

sa[3], *mf.* (= *sa.*) base of *pron. demonstr. nom. sg.*, *v.* taṁ[1].

sa[4], *mfn.* (*sa.* sva) one's own (also referring to *1.* & *2. pers.*); *instr. pl.* sehi (kammehi) Dh. 136; very commonly the first part of *comp.*: sa-kicca, °-citta, °-nāma (*v. h.*); sa-mukha, 51,3 (°-veṭhito, who has let his own face be enveloped); °-lābha, Dh. 365–66 (*v. h.*); sajjhāya, sadattha-, & sabhāva, *v. below.* *cp.* saka, *mfn.*

saṁ-°, *indecl.* (*sa.* saṁ) prefix to verbal roots, implying 'conjunction', 'completeness', *etc.* (*opp.* vi-⁰), before vowels sam-⁰, and by assimilation also sañ-⁰, sañ-⁰, saṇ-⁰, sal-⁰, before r sometimes sā-⁰ (*cp.* sāratta, sārambha).

saṁyata, *mfn.*, *v.* saññata.

saṁyutta (or saññutta), *mfn.* (*sa.* saṁyukta, √yuj) united, combined, collected; – Saṁyutta-nikāya, *m.* (*cp. buddh. sa.* saṁyuktāgama) name of a canonical Pāli work, the third of the five nikāyas (*q. v.*), consisting of 55 Saṁyuttas or collections of short Suttas, *nom.* ~o, 102,15; *acc. m.* saṁyuttaṁ (*adj.*) 110,2 (saddhammaṁ, *i. e.* "according to Saṁyuttas"). Specimens thereof : 66,22–67,19; 71,19–72,25; 96,1–22.

saṁyoga, *m.* (= *sa.*) union, conjunction; bond, attachment; *pl.* ~ā, Dh. 384. *cp. next.*

saṁyojana & saññojana, *n.* (*sa.* saṁyojana) = *prec.*; *acc.* ~aṁ, Dh. 31; 397 (sabba-⁰); *dvandva comp.* ⁰-saṅga, Dh. 342 (⁰-sattaka, *mfn. q. v.*); – diṭṭhi-⁰, *n.* a clog of theory, 94,2.

saṁvacchara, *m.* & *n.* (*sa.* saṁvatsara) a year; *acc.* ~aṁ ("for a whole year") Dh. 108; *loc.* ~e (tatiye) 36,36; *n. pl.* ~āni, 21,11; *gen. pl.* ~ānaṁ, 87,8; *comp.* ⁰-matthake, 33,14 (*v. h.*).

saṁvattati, *vb.* (*sa.* saṁ-√vṛt) 'to roll together', come to an end, be finished or destroyed; *w. dat.* : to conduce, tend to; *pr. 3. sg.* ~ati (nibbānāya) 66,30. 93,9.

saṁvara, *m.* (= *sa.*) self-control, restraint; *nom.* ~o (pātimokkhe) Dh. 185. 375; (cakkhunā, *etc.*) Db. 360–61; *instr.* ~ena (kāyikena) 85,18; 85,19 (a-saṁvarena); *dat.* ~āya, 75,26. *cp.* saṁvuta.

saṁvasati, *vb.* (*sa.* saṁ-√vas) to dwell, live (with, *instr.*); *pot. 3. sg.* saṁvase (pamādena) Dh. 167. *cp. next.*

saṁvāsa, *m.* (= *sa.*) dwelling together, living with (also of sexual intercourse); *nom.* ~o (bālehi, company with fools) Dh. 207; ([a]samāna-⁰, *q. v.*) Dh. 302; (dhīra-⁰, instead of sukha-⁰) Dh. 207 (*cp.* note ib.); *acc.* ~aṁ (katvāna tāya) 112,5.

*saṁvāsiya, *mfn.* (= ~ika) living together with; *f.* ~iyā (gopī) 104,33.

saṁvigga, *mfn.* (*sa.* saṁvigna) agitated, terrified; ⁰-mānasa, *mfn.* agitated in mind, *m.* ~o, 41,32; *⁰-hadaya, *mfn.* agitated in heart, *m.* ~o, 63,14. *cp.* saṁvega.

saṁvidahati, *vb.* (*sa.* saṁ-vi-√dhā) to place, put; dispose, arrange, prescribe (*acc.*); *ger.* ~itvā, 48,15 (ārakkhaṁ); 63,23.

saṁvuta, *mfn.* (*sa.* saṁvṛta) self-controlled, restrained; *m.* ~o (saṁvarena) 85,18; Dh. 231 (kāyena); *m. pl.* ~ā, Dh. 225. 234. a-saṁvuta, Dh. 7; su-saṁvuta (*q. v.*); sīla-⁰, *mfn.* (*v. h.*) *cp.* saṁvara & saññata.

saṁvega, *m.* (= *sa.*) emotion, agitation; terror; *acc.* ~aṁ, 44,30; *⁰-ppatta, *mfn.* moved, agitated, *m.* ~o, 53,11. *cp.* saṁvigga & *next.*

*saṁvegin, *mfn.* filled with emotion, ardent, eager; *m. pl.* ~ino, Dh. 143.

saṁsagga, *m.* (*sa.* saṁsarga) conjunction, contact, intercourse, company with; *nom.* ~o, 29,6; *instr.* ~ena (amadhura-⁰) 37,21; (madhura-rasa-⁰) 38,4; *vera-⁰-saṁsaṭṭha, *mfn.* Dh. 291 (*v. next*).

saṁsaṭṭha, *mfn.* (*sa.* saṁsṛshṭa) connected, mixed with, entangled; *m.* ~o (*vera-saṁsagga-⁰, "entangled in the bonds of hatred") Dh. 291; *m. pl.* ~ā, 37,20; *cp.* a-saṁsaṭṭha.

saṁsati, *vb.* (*sa.* √çaṁs) to say, tell, speak to, call upon (*acc.*); *aor. 3. sg.* asaṁsi (maṁ) 108,28.

saṁsandeti, *vb.* (*caus.* ⁰-sandati, *sa.* saṁ-√syand) 'to let run together', *i. e.* to sum up, to compare (*acc.*, with: *instr.*); *ger.* ~etvā (niyyāmakasuttena, gāthaṁ āha) 25,28 (*i. e.* comformably to his mariner's lore).

saṁsanna, *mfn.* (*pp.* saṁsīdati,

to sink, go down; *sa.* saṁ-√sad) depressed, without energy; *°-saṁkappamana(*s*), *mfn.* Dh. 280 ("whose will and thought are weak"). *cp.* saṁsādeti.

saṁsaya, *m.* (*sa.* saṁçaya) doubt; *v.* nis-saṁsayaṁ, *adv.*

saṁsarati, *vb.* (*sa.* saṁ-√sṛ) to go about (unvoluntarily), toss the body about, *esp.* to pass from existence to existence; *part. loc. m.* ~ante (aparāparaṁ) 40,24; *aor. 1. sg.* ~sari, 108,16 (saṁsari'haṁ). *cp.* saṁ-carati & saṁsāra.

saṁsādeti, *vb.* (*caus.* saṁsīdati; *sa.* saṁsādayati) 1) 'to cause to sit down or sink', to embarrass, perplex; 2) *intr.* to be embarrassed or perplexed; *pr. 3. sg.* ~eti, 90,26. *cp.* saṁsanna.

saṁsāra, *m.* (= *sa.*) the revolution of being, transmigration or passing through a succession of existences, the life in this world; *nom.* ~o (dīgho bālānaṁ) 107,10 = Dh. 60; *acc.* ~aṁ, Dh. 414; *loc.* ~e (anamataggasmiṁ, *q. v.*) 89,13; *pl.* ~ā, Dh. 95; *jāti-°, *m.* id. 108,18.

saṁharati, *vb.* (*sa.* saṁ-√hṛ) to draw together, collect, fold up (as clothes, *acc.*); *part. m. instr.* ~antena (cīvaraṁ) 83,10; *ger.* ~itvā, 41,4; *grd. n.* ~itabbaṁ, 83,9. *cp.* saṁhīra.

saṁhita, *mfn.* (= *sa.*) put together, joined, accompanied by (*e. c.*); attha-°, *mfn.*, *v.* attha 3, an-attha-°, *mfn.* (*q. v.*) *cp.* upasaṁhita & sahita.

saṁhīra, *mfn.* (contracted of saṁhāriya (*saṁhera), *grd.* saṁharati, *sa.* saṁhārya) to be removed, shaken or corrupted; *a-saṁhīra, *mfn.* (*v. h.*) *cp.* Tr. PM. 78,28. *Pischel*, Gramm. § 537.

saka, *mfn.* (*fr.* sa 4; *sa.* svaka) one's own (referring also to *1.* & *2. pers.*); *acc. m. n.* ~aṁ (parijanaṁ) 67,28; (mataṁ) 113,13; (vādaṁ, referring to *2. pers.*) 113,14; *loc.* ~e (ṭhāne) 77,9; very often at the beg. of *comp.* °-sarīra, 16,6; °-raṭṭha, 42,7 (*cp. Fleet*, JRAS. '04, 708); °-nagara, 44,16; °-ṭṭhāna, 55,9; °-kammāni, *n. pl.* 106,20; repeated (with distributive meaning): saka-saka-ṭṭhānesu (each on his own place) 22,9.

sakaṭa, *m. n.* 1) (*sa.* çakaṭa) a carriage; a cart-load; *n.* ~aṁ (phāṇita-°, pūva-°, bhatta-°, *q. v.*) 53,20-30; *°-magga, *m.* a highroad, *loc.* ~e, 43,18. — 2) wrong reading instead of kasaṭa (*q. v.*).

sakad-āgāmin, *mf*(*n*). (*buddh. sa.* sakṛd-āgāmin) *lit.* 'returning only once more', *i. e.* a person who is to be re-born only once in the world of men, who has reached the second stage of sanctification (*cp. Childers s. v.* & magga); °-phale patiṭṭhahi, "he entered on the fruit of the second path", 29,17. *cp.* sakiṁ, *adv.*

sakala, *mfn.* (= *sa.*) whole, all; *m.* ~o, 16,13; *n.* ~aṁ, 62,13; *comp.* °-gāma-vāsino, all the villagers, 8,23; °-kappa, 16,15; °-Jambudīpa, 39,11; °-sarīra, 57,29; °-nagara, 65,24. *cp. next.*

***sakalikā**, *f.* (prob. *fr.* sakala, but other spellings: sakkalikā, sakkhalikā seem to show confusion with sakkarā or sakkharā, *q. v.*) a piece, mass, splinter; pāsāṇa-°, a splinter of rock, 17,22.

sakiṁ, *adv.* (*sa.* sakṛt) once (*lat.* semel); 56,17-18; on account of old sandhi we have sakid-, or sakad-, *cp.* sakad-āgāmin, *mfn.*

sakuṇa, *m.* (*sa.* çakuna) a bird; *nom.* ~o, 12,9; *pl.* ~ā, 10,3; *gen. pl.* ~ānaṁ, 10,12; *comp.* *°-gaṇa, *°-saṁgha, *m.* (*q. v.*); *java-°, *rukkhakoṭṭha-° (*q. v.*) *cp.* sākuṇika & *next.*

sakunta, *m.* (*sa.* çakunta) = *prec.*; *nom.* ~o, 88,30; *gen. pl.* ~ānaṁ, Dh. 92.

Sakka, *m.* (*sa.* Çakra) *nom. pr.* of Indra; *nom.* ~o, 16,3. 45,30 (devarājā); 59,31 (jara-°, old Sakka); 80,26 (devānaṁ indo); *acc.* ~aṁ, 110,21; *instr.* ~ena, 110,28; *gen.* ~assa, 15,7; *pl.* ~ā (aññehi cakkavāḷehi, from other worlds) 60,20; °-bhavana, *n.* the heaven or palace of S., 65,9 (°-sadisa). *cp.* sakkatta, *n.*

sakka, *mfn.* (*sa.* çakya) possible, *v.* sakkā, *indecl.*

sakkaccaṁ, *indecl.* (orig. *ger. fr.* sakkaroti, to honour, revere; *sa.* sat-kṛtya) devotedly, zealously, eagerly, assiduously; Dh. 392. (*cp.* sakkāra.)

Sakkatta, *n.* (*sa.* Çakratva) Sakkaship; *acc.* ~aṁ (pāpuṇi, was born as S.) 35,1; (kāresi) 52,15.

sakkarā, *f.*, *v.* sakkharā.

*sakkā, *indecl.* (perhaps orig. *f. sg. fr.* sakka, (*grd.* sakkoti) *cp. sa.* çakyam) mostly used in impersonal sentences, followed by *inf.* (often with *pass.* or *intr.* meaning, but sometimes with *obj.* added in *acc.*), the agens, if expressed, being put generally into *instr.* (but sometimes also *nom.*), to be translated by 'it is possible', *generally w. negation*: 'it is not possible', 'cannot', or 'it is of no use'; [a]) *without subj.*: na ~ tava vāraṁ (*acc.*) aññesaṁ pāpetuṁ, it is not possible to transfer your turn to others, 6,34; yācakānaṁ tiṇāni dātuṁ na ~, 15,5; tumhākaṁ raṭṭhe āgantuṁ na ~, 18,24; na ~ maṁ vāretuṁ, 23,8; appen'eva balavāhanena ~ B.rajjaṁ gaṇhituṁ, 38,24; na ~ dātuṁ, 53,36; nanu na ~ vissajjetuṁ, surely he cannot answer, 91,16; na ~ itoparaṁ. 112,17; *w. auxiliary verb*: sakkā siyā, 56,5; — [b]) *with subj. instr.*: na ~ mayā . . . pakkhipituṁ (I cannot) 7,8; mayā imasmiṁ ṭhāne vasituṁ na ~, 9,34; na ~ mayā maraṇā muccituṁ (I cannot be delivered from death) 17,14; marantenâpi [*sc.* mayā] tuyhaṁ kathetuṁ na ~, 49,27; — [c]) *with subj. nom.* (& *instr. as subj. of the inf.*): mātugāmo kucchiyaṁ pakkhipitvā carentenâpi rakkhituṁ na ~ (a woman you cannot be certain of, even if you walk about having her inside you) 50,31 (here we could also have *acc.* mātugāmaṁ); the *subj.* being expressed by a *relat.* clause: yo koci samaṇo . . . samāgato na ~ paṭivattetuṁ, 110,10. Besides this *indecl.* sakkā we find in some few instances *grd.* sakka, *mfn.* construed with *subj. nom.* (as in *sa.*, *cp. Speyer,* Ved. u. Sa. Synt. § 220 & *Childers s. v.*). Quite parallel to *sakkā is *labbhā (*q. v.*); both forms have been variously explained; on account of the predominant construction with *instr.* it seems evident that the instinct of speech has connected these forms with the *pass. grd.* of sakkoti (√çak); therefore it is difficult to judge, whether *Pischel,* Gr. § 465, is right in taking them as old optatives (*aor.*); *cp. Franke,* Pāli u. Sanskr. p. 103.

sakkāra, *m.* (*sa.* sat-kāra) honour, reverence, worship; reputation; *nom.* ~o, 18,35. 19,4. 37,1. 74,15; *acc.* ~aṁ, Dh. 75; °-atthaṁ, 62,31 (*v.* attha [1]); *kata-maṅgala-°, *mfn.* (*q. v.*); *dvandva comp.* lābha-° (*v. h.*).

sakkoti (later form: sak(k)uṇoti or sak(k)uṇāti) *vb.* (*sa.* √çak) to be able to (*inf.*); to dare, venture, persuade oneself to (*inf.*); *pr. 3. sg.* ~oti (gocaraṁ gaṇhituṁ na ~) 13,12; *2. sg.* ~osi, 46,34; *1. sg.* ~omi, 31,30. 48,28; *3. pl.* ~onti, 8,19; *2. pl.* ~otha, 31,30; *1. pl.* ~oma, 40,33; *part. m.* ~onto, 98,20; *f. gen. sg.* ~ontiyā, 59,9; a-sakkonto, 37,25; *pl.* ~ā, 8,23. 40,23. 102,18; *aor. 3. sg.* a-sakkhi, 16,8. 55,18; *2. sg.* id. 44,31; *1. sg.* a-sakkhiṁ, 20,29; *1. pl.* sakkhimhā, 79,20; a later form is sakuṇi, *3. sg.* 111,11; *fut.* [a]) sakkhati, *2. sg.* ~asi, 48,27; [b]) sakkhiti, *3. pl.* ~inti, 105,18; [c]) sakkhissati, 89,10; *2. sg.* ~asi, 4,34; *1. sg.* ~āmi, 48,13; *3. pl.* ~anti, 34,10; *1. pl.* ~āma, 1,9. 21,31; [d]) sakkuṇissāma, *1. pl.* 73,2; *grd.* sakka, *mfn.* (*q. v.*) *cp.* sakkā.

sakkharā, *f.* (sometimes spelt sakkarā, in the beg. of *comp.* also ~a; *sa.* çarkarā) [1]) gravel, pebble, small stone; °-a-kaṭhala-vālikā (*pl. dvandva comp.*) 97,35. — [2]) sugar; *nom.* ~ā, 52,7; *dvandva comp.* sappi-madhu-sakkarā-°,

61,26; °-ôdaka, *n.* sugar-water, 38,3; *°-pānaka, *n.* id. 18,27; *lapa-°, *mfn.* (*v. h.*).

sakkhiti, sakkhissati, *fut., v.* sakkoti.

Sakya, *m.* (*pl.*) (*sa.* Çākya) *nom. pr.* of a tribe in Kapilavatthu (from which Gotama Buddha was descended); °-putta, *m.* a man of that tribe (*esp.* of Gotama); °-puttiya, *m.* (*sa.* °-putrīya) a follower of Gotama. *gen. pl.* ~ānam (samaṇānaṁ, the Buddhist monks) 73,30.

sagga, *m.* (*sa.* svarga) [1]) heaven; *acc.* ~aṁ (yanti) Dh. 126; *dat.* ~āya (gacchati) 88,30. 89,1; *gen.* ~assa (gamana) Dh. 178; saggaṁ (*adj.*) lokaṁ (*acc.*) id. 7,26; *comp.* *°-kathā, *f.*, a discourse about heaven, 68,30 (~aṁ pakāsesi); °-patha, °-pada, *m.* the way to heaven, 34,29. 44,15 (*cp.* pūreti); saggâpāya, *m.* (*dvandva comp.*) Dh. 423 (*v.* apāya). — [2]) *Sagga, *m. nom. pr.* of a Gandharva, 19,20. 20,4-20.

saṁkaḍḍhati, *vb.* (*sa.* saṁ-√kṛsh) to draw together, gather, collect, pick up (*acc.*); *ger.* ~itvā (dārūni) 15,32: 33,6; 49,35 (kacavaraṁ, to sweep together).

saṁkappa, *m.* (*sa.* saṁkalpa) will, thought, intention, desire; *nom.* ~o (sammā-°, right aspiration) 67,4; Dh. 74; *acc.* ~aṁ, 104,7; *pl.* ~ā, Dh. 339; *saṁsanna-saṁkappa-mano, Dh. 280 (*v. h.*); micchā-°, Dh. 11 (*v. h.*); *bahu-°, *mfn.* Dh. 147 (*q. v.*).

saṁkamati, *vb.* (*sa.* saṁ-√kram) to go away, enter, go to; *fut. 1. pl.* ~issāma, 77,17.

saṁkampati, *vb.* (*sa.* saṁ-√kamp) to shake, quake, tremble; *aor. 3. sg.* ~pi, 110,7.

saṁkara, *m.* (= *sa.*) confusion, turmoil; *dūra-°, *mfn.* secluded, solitary, tranquil; *loc.* ~e (vihāre) 114,26.

***saṁkassara,** *mfn.* (prob. *fr. sa.* *saṁ-kasvara, *cp.* saṁkasuka) bad, impure; unsteady, of doubtful character; *n.* ~aṁ (brahmacariyaṁ) Dh. 312. (*cp. Weber,* Ind. Str. I, 167; *Kern,* Bijdr. (Amsterdam 1886) p. 57; *Morris,* Introd. to AN. I p. IX (1883); SBE. XX, 300.) *cp.* a-saṁkusaka, Jāt. VI. 297,33.

saṁkāra, *m. n.* (= *sa.*) sweepings; *nom. n.* ~aṁ, 84,23; *°-dhāna, *n.* a dunghill, *loc.* ~asmiṁ, Dh. 58; *°-bhūta, *mfn.* being like sweepings, *loc. pl.* ~esu, Dh. 59.

saṁkita, *mfn.* (*sa.* çaṁkita) anxious, alarmed; *bhaya-°, *mfn.* 111,15 (*v. h.*).

saṁkiliṭṭha, *mfn.* (*pp. fr. next; sa.* saṁklishṭa) impure, sinful, depraved, corrupt; *n.* ~aṁ (vataṁ) Dh. 312; *instr. m.* ~ena, Dh. 244.

saṁkilissati, *vb.* (*sa.* saṁ-√kliç, *pass.* °-kliçyate) to be impure, become defiled (by carnal lust); *pr. 3. sg.* ~ati (attanā) Dh. 165; *pp.* saṁkiliṭṭha (*q. v.*) *cp. next.*

saṁkilesa, *m.* (*sa.* saṁkleça) contamination, impurity, sinfulness; *acc.* ~aṁ, 68,30.

***saṁkuppa,** *mfn.* (*grd.* saṁkuppati; *sa.* saṁ-√kup) to be shaken or moved; *a-saṁkuppa, *mfn.* (*v. h.*).

saṁkha, *m.* (*sa.* çaṁkha) a conch-shell, trumpet; *acc. pl.* ~e (dhamentā) 8,23.

saṁkhata, *mfn.* (*sa.* saṁskṛta) put together, constructed, prepared; *f.* ~ā (su-°) 104,30. *cp.* saṁkhāta *below.*

saṁkhaya, *m.* (*sa.* saṁkshaya) destruction; *nom.* ~o (bhūri-°) Dh. 282; *loc.* ~amhi (jīvita-°) Dh. 331.

***saṁkhalikā,** *f.* (*fr. sa.* çṛṅkhala, or ~ā) a chain, fetter; *instr.* ~āya (deva-°) 21,14.

saṁkhā, *f.* (*sa.* saṁkhyā) reckoning; consideration, deliberation; name, appellation; *nom.* ~ā, 97,1; *acc.* ~aṁ (gacchati, to be called) 95,9; *instr.* ~āya. (*v.* saṁkhāti *below*); *comp.* *rūpa-saṁkhā-vimutta, *mfn.* "released from what is styled name", or: 'up to the very name' *i. e.* 'totally released from' (Tr.), 95,12 ff.

saṁkhāta, *mfn.* (*sa.* saṁkhyāta.

pp. saṁ-√khyā) reckoned, considered, weighed; called, named; known, visible; *°-dhamma, *mfn.* "who has well weighed the law", *gen. pl.* ~ānaṁ, Dh. 70 (wrong spelling: saṁkhata-°); *paññā-°, 91,37 (*v. h.*).

[**saṁkhāti**], *vb.* (*sa.* saṁ-√khyā) to reckon; to consider, weigh; to call, name; *inf.* ~ātuṁ (to measure) Dh. 196; *ger.* ~āya ("with care") 106,7 = Dh. 267; *pp.* ~āta, *v. above.*

saṁkhāra, *m.* (*sa.* saṁskāra) 'putting together', composition, aggregation; mostly in *pl.* ~ā: [1]) all existing things or substances, created things or creatures; [2]) (*in the dogmatics:*) the fourth of the five khandhā (constituents of the human being, 94,8-10), *viz.* states of mind, predispositions, conformations (originating from avijjā, and causing viññāṇa, 66,6-7) left from actions in former existences, and therefore denoting any action, speech, or thought, the vital functions *etc.*, *practically* = moral constitution (Karma, *v.* kamma[3]); *nom. pl.* ~ā, 94,10; 80,2 (vayadhammā); 80,28. 107,11 = Dh. 277 (aniccā); 107,13 (dukkhā); Dh. 255 (sassatā n'atthi); *instr.* ~ehi, 95,19; *comp.* °-nirodha, *m.* (*q. v.*) 66,12; *°-ûpasama, *m.* Dh. 368 (*q. v.*) *cp.* vi-saṁkhāra-gata, *mfn.* For signification *cp.* dhamma[4].

saṁkhitta, *mfn.* (*pp. fr. next*; *sa.* saṁkshipta) contracted, abbreviated; *instr. n.* (*adv.*) ~ena, briefly, concisely, 67,11.

saṁkhipati, *vb.* (*sa.* saṁ-√kship) to throw or draw together (*acc.*), to contract, shorten; *part. med. m. pl.* ~mānā (mige) 6,9; *pp.* ~khitta (*v. above*).

saṅga, *m.* (= *sa.*) clinging to, attachment; hindrance, bond, fetter; *nom.* ~o, Dh. 171; *acc.* ~aṁ (ubho, *q. v.*) Dh. 412; *comp.* saṅgâtiga, *mfn.* Dh. 397 (*v.* atiga); pañca-saṅga-°, Dh. 370 (the 5 fetters, *i. e.* the senses, pañcindriyāni, Comm.); saññojana-°, *q. v.*, *cp.* sajjati.

saṁgaṇhāti (or ~ati), *vb.* (*sa.* saṁ-√grah) to gather, collect, to take hold of, take care of, help; to win (one's favour) (*w. acc.*); *aor. 3. sg.* ~gaṇhi (nagaraṁ) 58,24; *ger.* ~gahetvā (Piṭakattayaṁ), 114,12; *pp.* ~gahīta, *m. pl.* eka-saṁgahītā (sabbe, unified) 99,16; *cp.* saṁgaha, saṁgāhaka.

saṅgata, *n.* (= *sa.*) association, intercourse; *bāla-°-cārin, *mfn.* Dh. 207 (*v. h.*).

saṁgaha, *m.* (once *n.*; *sa.* saṁgraha) collection, aggregation; redaction, text; *nom.* ~o (dhamma-vinaya-°) 109,13; (therehi kata-°) 109,14; *nom. n.* ~aṁ, 110,4; *acc.* ~aṁ, 110,6; (dhamma-°) 109,16. 110,16; (viññāṇa-°, *q. v.*) 99,26; antevāsikānaṁ ~aṁ (collecting, *i. e.* teaching of pupils) 102,9.

saṁgahīta, *pp.* & °-gahetvā, *ger.*, *v.* saṁgaṇhāti.

saṁgāma, *m.* (*sa.* saṁgrāma) battle; *loc.* ~e, 103,34. 107,3 = Dh. 103; — °-ji, *mfn.* (*sa.* °-jit) victorious, in the *comp.* saṅgāmajuttama, *m.* "the greatest of conquerors", 107,4 = Dh. 103 (*cp. sa. superl.* saṁgrāmajittama). *cp. next.*

saṁgāmeti, *vb.* (*denom. fr.* saṁgāma; *sa.* saṁgrāmayate) to battle or fight with (*instr.*); *fut. 3. sg.* ~essati (nāgena) 76,33.

saṁgāhaka, *m.* (*sa.* saṁgrāhaka) [1]) a collector, compiler; [2]) a charioteer; *nom.* ~o (Mātali) 60,18.

saṅgīti, *f.* (= *sa.*) [1]) singing together, music; [2]) collection or recension of the holy texts, or a Buddhist council held for that purpose; *°-ttaya, *n.* the three councils (or recensions), 113,29.

saṁgha, *m.* (= *sa.*) [1]) a collection, assemblage, multitude, crowd; *acc.* ~aṁ (sakuṇa-°) 10,9; *pl.* ~ā (do.) 62,12; — [2]) the congregation or order of the Buddhist monks (also a chapter or a certain number of monks, elected and assembled for any religious purpose); *nom.* ~o. 79,11; *acc.* ~aṁ (in the formula Buddha, Dhamma, & Saṁgha, *cp.* ratana[1]) 107,17 = Dh. 190; 114,7; *instr.* ~ena (bhikkhu-⁰) 70,21; *gen.* ~assa (do.) 102,8; *loc.* ~e (do.), 29,28; *pl.* ~ā (bhikkhu-⁰) 109,2 (combined with the *prec. n. pl.* satta satasahassāni); — *⁰-gata, *mfn.* directed to the S., Dh. 298 (*f.* ~ā, sati); *⁰-sammata, *n.* (*v. h.*).

saṁghaṭṭati, *vb.* (*sa.* saṁ-√ghaṭṭ) to strike or knock against, to rub, *etc.*; *part. m. instr.* ~antena (a-⁰) 84,12.

*Saṁghapāla, *m. nom. pr.* of a thera in Mahāvihāra (Ceylon); *gen.* ~assa, 114,4.

saṁghāṭa, *m.* (= *sa.*) the timber or frame work of a house; *piṭṭhasaṁghāṭaka, *n.* (*adj.* in the *comp.* thira-⁰, comm. on toraṇa) 'with strongly constructed doorpost and lintel', 91,21. (*cp.* SBE. XX. p. 105).

saṁghāṭi, *f.* (= *sa.*) an upper garment, one of the three robes of a Buddhist monk; *nom.* ~i. 84,3; *pl.* ~iyo, the two uppers garments, 82,25.

*sace, *indecl.* (*fr.* ce with the *indecl. pref.* sa-, *q.v.*) if; even if, though; this particle is always used at the beginning of a conditional period, the verb of both sentences being put usually either in *fut.* (sometimes *pres.*) or *pot.*, nearly in conformity to the use of the *indic.* & *conjunctive* modes in Latin in such sentences; the second sentence is often beginning with a *pron. demonstr.*, but a particle corresponding with sace is not required; [a]) *w. fut.* (in both sentences): 1,9. 2,2. 35,18. 56,7; sac'āhaṁ: 25,32. 54,1. 65,31; [b]) *w. pres.* & *fut.* (or *grd.*) : 1,17. 82,19-23; [c]) *w. pot.* (in both sentences): 1,24. 4,7. 53,11. 56,5. 86,9; [d]) like yadi evaṁ & noce (*q. v.*) without full sentence: 'if so', 'in that case'. 97,14-15 (sace bhante Nāgasena yo tumhe māreti n'atthi tassâpi pāṇātipāto).

sacca, [1]) *mfn.* (*sa.* satya) true; *n.* ~aṁ (giraṁ) Dh. 408; idaṁ eva ~, 89,24 (*opp.* mogha). — [2]) *n.* (*subst.*) [a]) truth; *nom.* ~aṁ, 51,33 (*opp.* musā); *acc.* ~aṁ (katheti, vadati) 24,27. 32,1; *⁰-sadisa, *mfn.* having the appearance of truth. 52,1; *sacc-ûpasaṁhita, *mfn.* true, 9,31 (*cp.* upasaṁhita); — [b]) speaking the truth, truthfulness, veracity; *nom.* ~aṁ, 3,27; Dh. 261; 106,9 = Dh. 393; *instr.* ~ena, 44,9. 108,31; *dvandva comp.* dama-⁰, Dh. 9 (*q. v.*); — [c]) a solemn asseveration, oath (*cp.* sacca-kiriyā, & ⁰-vajja *below*); *instr.* iminā ~ena ("so truly") 51,18; — [d]) *in the dogmatics* (mostly *pl.*) : the four cardinal truths of Buddhism (*cp.* ariyasacca); ~āni, 29,16; sacca-parivosāne, "at the conclusion of the Truths", 29,17; — [e]) *n.* (*adv.*) truly, indeed, verily; justly, by rights; 54,16 (~ evam āhaṁsu paṇḍitā). [*cp.* bāhusacca, *fr.* bahussuta].

sacca-kiriyā, *f.* (*sa.* satya-kriyā) a solemn asseveration, oath; *nom.* ~ā (bhinnā, is rendered of no effect) 51,22; *acc.* ~aṁ (karoti) 27,20. 51,10; *instr.* ~āya, 27,16.

*sacca-pāramī, *f.* (*Buddh. sa.* satya-pāramitā) truthfulness (one of the ten virtues, *v.* pāramī) 108,31.

*sacca-vajja, *n.* (*fr. sa.* satyavāda) [1]) truthfulness; [2]) solemn asseveration (*cp.* sacca-kiriyā); *instr.* ~ena (etena) 27,24.

sacca-vādin, *mfn.* (*sa.* satyavādin) speaking the truth; *acc. m.* ~inaṁ, Dh. 217.

sacchi-karoti, *vb.* (*fr. sa.* sākshāt-√kṛ, by analogy of other *comp.* of karoti *w. indecl.* ending in 'i') to make visibly present before the eyes, to realize, attain (*acc.*); *pr. 3. sg.* ~oti (magga-phala-nibbānāni) 97,10. *cp. next.*

sacchi-kiriyā, *f.* (*sa.* sākshātkriyā) realization; *dat.* ~aya (nibbānassa) 90,19.

sajjati, *vb.* (*sa.* √sañj; *pass.* sajjate) to cling, adhere; to be attached to (*loc.*); *part. med. acc. m.* a-sajjamānaṁ (nāmarūpasmiṁ) Dh. 221;

pp. satta (*q. v.*); *cp.* saṅga. (The secondary verbal-forms sajjeti & sajjāpeti seem to be *denom. fr.* sajja, sajya. *v. below*).

*sajjāpeti, *vb.* (*caus. II.* sajjeti) to make ready, prepare festively, adorn (*acc.*); *ger.* ~etvā (nagaraṁ) 45,30; (jūtamaṇḍalaṁ) 50,28.

sajju, *adv.* (*sa.* sa-dyas) instantly, immediately; 106,21 = Dh. 71. — *sajjukaṁ, *adv.* id. 110,28.

sajjeti, *vb.* (*denom. fr. sa.* sajja, sajya; *cp. Weber,* Ind. Str. I. p. 243) to make ready, prepare (*acc.*); *imp. 2. pl.* ~etha (nāṭakāni) 63,17; *ger.* ~etvā, 25,13 (nāvaṁ); *caus. II.* sajjāpeti (*v. above*); *pp.* sajjita, *v.* susajjita. (*Fausbøll,* Ten Jāt. p. 99 traces this verb back to √sṛj; but the signification of that root in Pāli is always 'to throw away, leave off' and *caus.* is never used, except vissajjeti, Tr.).

sajjhāya, *m.* (*sa.* svādhyāya) repetition (of sacred texts); *v.* a-sajjhāya.

saṁcarati, *vb.* (*sa.* saṁ-√car) to walk about, pass, move, rock (to and fro, said of voluntary movements, *cp.* saṁsarati); *part. m.* ~anto (aparāparaṁ) 40,27.

saṁcicca, *indecl.* (*ger. fr.* saṁ-√ci(t); *sa.* saṁ-citya, & °-cintya) intentionally; 27,23.

sañchanna, *mfn.* (= *sa.*; *pp.* saṁ-√chad) covered all over; paduma-°, 4,9-27.

*sañjānana, *n.* (*nom. act. fr. next*) understanding, considering, thinking; tesaṁ . . . sañjānan'-atthaṁ, "in order that they might think", 21,8.

sañjānāti, *vb.* (*sa.* saṁ-√jñā) to understand, perceive, recognize (*acc.*); to conceive, imagine; *aor. 3. sg.* ~jāni (Mahāsattaṁ) 58,9; *ger.* [a]) saññāya (sīho ti) 8,19; 30,4; [b]) sañjānitvā, 20,5. 41,27. *cp.* *sañjānana, saññā, saññin.

saññata (or saṁyata), *mfn.* (*pp.* saṁ-√yam, saṁyata) restraining oneself, self-controlled; *m.* ~o, 84,29. Dh. 362 (*w. instr.* kāyena, vācāya); *gen.* ~assa, Dh. 24; a-saññata, *mfn.* (*q.v.*); pāda-°, *mfn.* controlling one's feet, Dh. 362; mukha-°, *mfn.* Dh. 363; hattha-°, *mfn.* Dh. 362; *°-cārin, *mfn.* living under restraint, *gen. m.* ~ino, Dh. 104; *saññatuttama, *mfn.* very well restrained, *m.* ~o, Dh. 362.

saññama, *m.* (*sa.* saṁyama) restraint, self-control; *nom.* ~o, Dh. 261; *instr.* ~ena (saññato) 85,17; Dh. 25.

(saññamati) *vb.* (*sa.* saṁ-√yam) to control, restrain; *pp.* saññata (*q. v.*); *caus.* [a]) saññameti, id. (*acc.*); *fut. 3. pl.* ~essanti (cittaṁ) Dh. 37; [b]) saññāmeti, id. (*acc.*); *imp. 2. sg.* saññāmay[a] (attānaṁ) Dh. 380. *cp.* saññama, *m.*

saññā, *f.* (*sa.* saṁjñā) [1]) understanding, conception; perception (*in the dogmatics*: the third of the five khandhā, *q. v.*); in this last sense: 94,10; 95,18 (*instr.* ~āya); 80,8-10, *etc.* (*comp.* neva-saññā-nâsaññā, *q. v.*, *cp.* a-saññā); *acc.* ~aṁ (karoti, to think, imagine) 5,7; tumhehi ārocitasaññāya (*instr.*) 25,18 (*v.* āroceti). — [2]) sign, mark, name; *acc.* ~aṁ (adāsi, "made a sign to", *gen.*) 50,18; (adatvā, "telling nothing about it") 55,29; *comp.* paṇṇa-bandhana-° (*n.?*) 8,9 (*v.* paṇṇa).

saññāṇa, *n.* (*sa.* sañjnāna) = saññā [2]; *instr.* ~ena, 87,32 (olokita-°, = olokitākārena, 87,25; *v.* ākāra).

saññāmeti, *vb. caus.*, *v.* saññamati.

saññāya, *ger.*, *v.* sañjānāti.

saññin, *mfn.* (*sa.* saṁjñin) conscious, perceiving; thinking, imagining; *m.* ~ī (ahosi, "you believed, imagined") 2,6; *ujjhāna-°, *mfn.* (*v. h.*).

saññojana, *n.*, *v.* saṁyojana.

saṭṭhi, *f. num.* (*sa.* shashṭi) sixty; *°-yojanika, *mfn.* sixty yojanas long, *loc. n.* ~e (Manosilā-tale) 61,10; *cp.* catu-saṭṭhi.

saṭha, *mfn.* (*sa.* çaṭha) dishonest, deceitful, fraudulent; *m.* ~o (naro) Dh. 262; kitavāsaṭho, Dh. 252 (*v.* kitava).

saṭhila, *mfn.* (an older form of sithila, *sa.* çithila; the orig. base was *çṛthila or *çṛthira. *cp. sa.* çratha, çlatha, & *ved. sa.* çrathayati) loose, relaxed; *metaph.* careless, or carelessly performed; *m.* ~o (paribbājo) Dh. 313; *n.* ~aṁ (kammaṁ) Dh. 312 (var. lect. in both places : sithila); *cp. Kern,* Verkl. p. 58.

***saṇikaṁ** (or sanikaṁ), *adv.* (*fr. sa.* çanais through saṇiṁ) slowly, gradually; softly, gently; cautiously, accurately; 14,4. 35,32. 50,18. 54,23. (In spite of Abh. v. 1153 & *Childers* this word has never the signification 'quickly', *v.* Nord. Tidsskr. f. Filol. 3. R. V, p. 51—52; *cp. Pischel,* Gr. § 84.)

***saṇṭha**, *m.* or *n.*? (*cp. sa.* çrantha) bark-strips or fibres of bamboo(?) from which bowstrings were made (= veṇuvilīva, Comm.); *gen.* ~assa, 92,17. (*cp. D'Alwis,* Introd. p. 103.)

saṇṭhapeti, *vb.* (*caus. fr. next*; *sa.* saṁ-sthāpayati) to cause to stand firm, restore, establish (*acc.*); *aor. 3. pl.* ~esuṁ. 114,18; *inf.* ~etuṁ (kuṭumbaṁ) 56,6.

saṇṭhāti (saṇṭhahati, or santiṭṭhati), *vb.* (*sa.* saṁ-√sthā) to remain, stand firm or still; *aor. 3. sg.* ~āsi (nibbidāya, *dat.* (?), *v.* nibbida) 67,33; *caus.* saṇṭhapeti (*q. v.*) *cp. next.*

saṇṭhāna, *n.* (*sa.* saṁsthāna) shape, form, appearance; state, condition; *loc.* ~e (chavi-⁰, complexion) 85,23; *instr. pl.* ~ehi (hattha-pāda-mukha-⁰) 49,8; *manussa-⁰, *mfn.* of human form, 85,21; *sūkara-⁰, *mfn.* 85,31 (*q. v.*) *cp.* su-saṇṭhāna, *mfn.*

saṇḍa, *m*(*n*). (*sa.* shaṇḍa, *cp.* sāndra; *Weber,* Ind. Str. I. 237) a group of trees or plants, a wood, thicket; vana-⁰, id., *acc.* ~aṁ, 15,1.

saṇḍāsa, *m.* (*sa.* saṁdaṁça) a pair of tongs or nippers; a vice; *instr.* ~ena, 5,13; 5,2 (kammāra-⁰); 44,27 (suvaṇṇa-⁰). *cp.* ḍasati.

saṇha, *mfn.* (*sa.* çlakshṇa) smooth, gentle, mild; small, fine; *instr. m.* ~ena (aṁkena) 20,21.

saṇhaka, *n.* (*sa.* çlakshṇaka) betel-nut (?); ⁰-sadisa, *mfn.* like betel, *instr. pl.* ~ehi (kesehi, = paṇḍara, white?) 47,12 (the Birman reading sāṇavāka-sadisehi (like hempen cloth, *sa.* *sāṇavalka) seems to be an improvement of the text).

sat, *mfn.* (= *sa.*; *part. fr.* atthi. *q. v.*) [1]) being; *v.* atthi; [2]) good, right, righteous; *acc. m.* santaṁ (padaṁ, *i. e.* Nibbāna) Dh. 368; *nom. pl.* santo, Dh. 83. 151. 304; *instr. pl.* sabbhi, Dh. 151. 29,12 (sabbhi-r-eva); *gen. pl.* sataṁ, Dh. 54. 77. 151. *cp.* santa[3] (santaka), samāna, a-sat, a-santa; sak-kaccaṁ, sak-kāra, sad-dhamma, sap-purisa, & satta[2].

sata[1], *n.* (*sa.* çata) a hundred; [a]) *appositive to a subst.* : gāthā ~. 100 verses, Dh. 102; [b]) *w. subst. gen.*, or at the end of *subst. comp.* : *acc.* ~aṁ (kahāpaṇa-⁰) 18,13; (vassa-⁰, for 100 years) Dh. 106. 110; *instr.* ~ena (for a hundred *scil.* pieces of money, kahāpaṇa-⁰ being understood) 18,11; *loc.* ~e (pahāra-⁰) 55,12; [c]) *comp. w. other numerals,* usually *mfn. pl.* (but also *sg.*, *cp.* aṭṭha-sataṁ bhattaṁ, Mil. 88,4) : satta-satāni, *n. pl.* 111,14 (without *subst.*); aḍḍhateyya-⁰, "250", *nom. m. pl.* ~satā, 21,31; *acc. m. pl.* ~sate, 21,33; pañca-⁰, "500" (*v. h.*); in this sort of *comp.* sata is often separated from the first number and put at the end of a *subst. comp.* : satta manussa-satāni, "700 men", 27,13 (for more exx. see pañcasata); *cp.* sattāmacca-satānuga (*v.* anuga) 110,23; [d]) *at the beg. of comp.* : sata-sahassa, *n.* "100,000", 23,3; *pl.* ~āni, 109,2; *comp.* *⁰-agghanaka, *mfn.* & *⁰-uṭṭhāna, *mfn.* (*q. v.*); — *sataṁsamaṁ, ("for a hundred years") Dh. 106, may be *adv.* with ṁ inserted (Fsb.), if not an old error for sataṁ samā (?), *v.* samā. — *cp.* satika, satima.

sata[2], *mfn.* (*sa.* smṛta) recollecting, conscious, thoughtful, attentive; *m.* ~o, 78,35 (*synon.* sampajāna); *gen. pl.* ~ānaṁ, Dh. 293; *sadāsata, *mfn.*

"always reflecting", Dh. 350. *cp.* sati[2], sarati.

satataṁ, *adv.* (= *sa.*) continually, constantly; *v.* sātacca & sātatika.

satapatta, *m.* (*sa.* çatapattra) a woodpecker; *nom.* ~o, 11,25.

sati[1], *part. loc.*, *v.* sat (atthi).

sati[2], *f.* (*sa.* smṛti) recollection, thoughtfulness, attention, thinking of; *nom.* ~i, 103,22. Dh. 293; *acc.* ~iṁ, 104,7; ~iṁ karoti, to think of (*gen.*) 63,18; maraṇa-°, *f.* 86,20 (*q. v.*); sammā-°, *f.* right recollection. 67,5; *sati-paṭṭhāna, *n.* (*cp. Buddh. sa.* smṛtyupasthāna & upaṭṭhāna *above*) fixing the attention, earnest meditation (being fourfold, *viz.* meditation on the evils of body, sensation, mind, and existence, *Childers*); *loc. pl.* ~esu (catūsu) 91,7. *cp.* satima*t* & sarati.

°**satika**, *mfn.* (*sa.* çatika) containing or concerning a hundred (only *e. c.*); ti-yojana-°, & diyaḍḍha-yojana-°, *mfn.* (*v. h.*).

***satima**, *mfn.* (*cp. sa.* çatatama) the 100th; pañca-°, *v.* pañca-sata.

satima*t*, *mfn.* (*sa.* smṛtimat) full of attention, whose thoughts are well collected; *nom. m.* ~mā, 109,18. Dh. 379; *gen.* ~mato, 104,12. Dh. 24 (metri causa : satī-°); *pl.* ~manto, Dh. 91 (do.); *gen. pl.* ~mataṁ, Dh. 181 (do.).

satta[1], *mfn.* (*pp.* sajjati; *sa.* sakta) adhering or attached to; hence °-sattaka, *mfn.* (*e. c.*) id.; *m. pl.* ~ā (saññojana-saṅga-°, "held in fetters and bonds") Dh. 342; *cp.* a-satta.

satta[2], *m.* (& *n.*) (*sa.* sattva) a living being, creature, mortal, person; *nom.* ~o, 86,7. 89,1. 113,9; *gen.* ~assa. 103,24; *pl.* ~ā, 17,25. 27,14. 62,25. Dh. 316; *acc.* ~e (sabba-°) 38,16; *gen.* ~ānaṁ, 2,6. 54,33 (imesaṁ); nerayika-°, Bodhi-°, Mahā-° (*v. h.*); — *sattāvāsā, *m. pl.* (*v.* āvāsa); *sattūpaladdhi, *f.* human knowledge, imperfect understanding, or: false opinion concerning the real existence of 'satta' (?) [*cp.* Mil. 268. SBE. XXXVI. 103]; *loc.* ~iyaṁ (ṭhatvā) 91,12-32.

satta[3], *num.* (*sa.* sapta) seven; *nom.* & *acc.* satta, 14,23. 25,20. 82,11. 91,8; 109,2 (satt'); *instr.* ~ahi, 28,28; *loc.* ~asu, 50,33; *comp.* °-aṭṭha (*v. h.*), seven or eight, 35,1; sattāhaṁ, seven days (*v.* aha), 23,16; °-dvāra-koṭṭhaka, *mfn.* (*q. v.*); °-bhūmaka, *mfn.* (*q. v.*); °-yojanika, *mfn.* (*q. v.*); °-ratana (*q. v.*); °-sata, *n.* '700' (*v. h.*). *cp.* sattama, *etc.*

Sattapaṇṇa-guha, *nom. pr.* of a cave near Rājagaha, *prob.* incorrect spelling instead of sattapaṇṇi-guhā. *f.* (*sa.* *saptaparṇī-°, *cp.* Vin. III, p. 287,17); *loc.* ~e, 109,31.

sattama, *mfn.* (*sa.* saptama) the seventh; *loc. m.* ~e (divase) 23,10-18; *f.* ~ī, 103,28; *comp.* °-divasato, 61,3.

sattarasa, *num.* (*sa.* saptadaça) '17'; sattarasama. *mfn.* (*sa.* saptadaçama) the 17th; Dh. XVII. *cp.* dasa.

sattāvāsā, *v.* satta[2].

sattāhaṁ, *v.* satta[3].

satti, *f.* (*sa.* çakti; *cp.* çastrī) [1]) power, energy; [2]) a spear; 6,12 (asi-°); [3]) a hunting knife; *acc.* ~iṁ, 12,8.

***sattūpaladdhi**, *f.*, *v.* satta[2].

sattha[1], *n.* (*sa.* çastra) a weapon; a-sattha, *mfn.* (*q. v.*).

sattha[2], *m.* (*sa.* sārtha) a caravan, troop, company; *v.* *appa-sattha.

satthar, *m.* (*sa.* çāstṛ) a teacher. *esp. nom. pr.* of Buddha ("the master"); *nom.* ~ā (teacher) 79,4; 28,2 (Buddha); *acc.* ~āraṁ, 28,10; *instr.* ~ārā, 73,27; *gen.* [a]) ~u (sāsane) 69,14; [b]) ~uno, 78,31. 86,6. 110,5; *loc.* ~ari, 84,26; — *comp.* Satthu-°, *v.* °-kappa, *mfn.*; °-gārava, *m. n.*; °-vaṇṇita, *mfn.*; — *°-vadhaka, *mfn.* having murderous intent against the Master, *m.* ~o, 108,27; *°-sāsana, *n.* the doctrine of the Master, 109,32 (navaṅga, *q. v.*). *cp.* satthuka.

satthi, *n.* (*sa.* sakthi) the thigh or thigh-bone; *nom.* ~i (bhaggaṁ) 30,17.

°satthuka, *mfn. e. c.* (*sa.* çāstṛka), *v.* atīta-°.

*sadattha-pasuta, *mfn.* (*fr.* sa[4] + attha[1] with 'd' inserted) intent upon one's own aim or sake; *m.* ~o, Dh. 166. *cp.* atta-d-attha.

sadā, *adv.* (= *sa.*) always, ever; 109,27. Dh. 30. 79. 206. 226. 296; *comp.* *sadāsata, *mfn.*, *v.* sata[2].

sadisa, *mfn.* (*sa.* sadṛça) like, similar (*w. gen.*, or *instr.*, or both); Tathāgatassa paññāya añño sadiso n'atthi, 91,24; *acc. m.* ~aṁ (attano) Dh. 61; most frequently *e. c. mfn.*, *e. g.* puppha-kaṇṇika-°, 7,29; loha-nigaḷa-°, 11,29; maṇi-guḷa-°, 18,7; *etc. etc.*; eka-sadisa, *mfn.* identical, *pl.* ~ā, 49,8; purima-°, *mfn.* "as above", *n.* ~aṁ, 31,28; *comp. w. a past part.*: paviṭṭha-sadiso ahosi, "seemed to enter", 61,21 (*cp.* pubba); *°-rasa, *mfn.* (*q. v.*).

sadda, *m.* (*sa.* çabda) a sound, tone, noise; voice, cry; a word; *nom.* ~o, 97,30. 112,16; 98,30 (~ ratho iti, the word ratha); 23,33 (paridevana-°, madhuragīta-°); kiṁ-saddo, 60,9. 112,8 (*v.* kiṁ[1]); *acc.* ~aṁ, 31,4. 53,16; 40,10 (akaṁsu); 89,6 (do.); 59,4 (kalaha-°); 112,7 (turiya-°); *instr.* ~ena, 11,31. 16,31; 18,17-18 (accharā-°, pāṇippahāra-°); *pl.* ~ā, 70,31; *loc. pl.* ~esu, 71,8. – *cp.* nissadda, *mfn.*

saddahati (& ~āti), *vb.* (*sa.* çrad-√dhā) to believe (*w. gen. pers.* & *acc. rei*); *pr. 2. pl.* ~atha (sarassa atthibhāvaṁ mayhaṁ) 4,13; *part. acc. m. pl.* ~ante (mayhaṁ) 4,12; *aor. 3. sg.* saddahi, 74,14; *ger.* ~itvā, 1,18 (taṁ); 4,14 (tassa); a-saddahitvā (attano) 49,9; – *caus.* saddahāpeti (*sa.* çraddhāpayati) to make one believe (*acc.*); *fut. 1. sg.* ~essāmi (tumhe) 51,10. *cp.* saddhā (& saddha).

saddha, *mfn.* (*sa.* çrāddha) faithful, believing; *m.* ~o, Dh. 303; *acc.* ~aṁ, 28,3. Dh. 8; *m. pl.* ~ā, 76,32; a-ssaddha, *v.* saddhā.

sad-dhamma, *m.* (*sa.* sad-dharma) the sacred doctrine, the true law or faith; *acc.* ~aṁ, 107,10 = Dh. 60. 38; 110,1; *abl.* ~ā, Dh. 364; *loc.* ~e, 109,31; *pl.* ~ā, 110,4; a-saddhamma, *m.*, *v.* a-sat; °-desanā, *f.* Dh. 194; °-savana, *n.* Dh. 182.

saddhā, *f.* (*sa.* çraddhā) faith, religious belief; *nom.* ~ā, 103,16. Dh. 333; *instr.* ~āya, Dh. 144; *gen.* ~āya. 29,10; yathā-saddhaṁ, *adv.* (*v.* yathā); a-ssaddha, *mfn. v. h.*

saddhiṁ, *adv.* & *prp.* (*sa.* sadhri, *cp.* sadhryac, Tr.) along, together; with, together with, accompanied by (*w. instr.* before or after, sometimes *w. gen.* or other cases); pāsāṇena ~ kathento, 3,6; mayā ~, 4,13; 15,13. 61,10. 70,21. 72,32; ~migehi. 8,12; ~ bhikkhu-saṁghena, 78,4. *cp. next.* [*Childers* takes it = *sa.* sārdhaṁ, but see *Pischel*, Gr. § 103.]

*saddhiṁ-cara, *mfn.* walking together with; *acc. m.* ~aṁ (sahāyaṁ), Dh. 328.

*saddhi-vihārika, *m.* (*cp. Buddh. sa.* sārdhaṁ-vihārin) *lit.* 'living in the same vihāra', *i. e.* the famulus of a thera, a pupil, disciple; *instr.* ~ena, 82,16. *cp.* saddhiṁ *above.*

sanantana, *mfn.* (*sa.* sanātana), eternal, permanent; *m.* ~o (dhammo) 106,24 = Dh. 5.

sanikaṁ, *v.* saṇikaṁ.

santa[1], *mfn.* (*sa.* çānta, *pp.* √çam, *cp.* sammati) appeased, pacified, tranquil; *n.* ~aṁ, *f.* ~ā, Dh. 96; *comp.* *°-kāya, *°-vāca, *mfn.* Dh. 378 (*v.* kāya & vācā); *°-citta, *mfn.* tranquil-minded, Dh. 373. *cp.* santavat, *mfn.*

santa[2], *mfn.* (*sa.* çrānta, *pp.* √çram) tired, fatigued; *gen. m.* ~assa, 107,9 = Dh. 60.

santa[3], *mfn.* (*part.*, *sa.* sat) being, existing, true, good; *v.* sat & atthi.

*santaka, *mfn.* (*fr.* santa[3]) belonging to, dependent, due to (*gen.* or *e. c.*); *n.* ~aṁ (tassā) 7,10; mama ~ (my property) 57,27; kula-°, *mfn.* (*q. v.*); para-°, *mfn.* (*v. corrections*); *cp.* a-santa.

santati, *f.* (= *sa.*) continuity, succession, series; *v.* dhamma-°.

santappeti, *vb.* (*caus.* saṁ-√tṛp, *sa.* santarpayati) to satisfy, gladden (*acc.* & *instr.*); *aor. 3. sg.* ~esi, 61,28; *pp.* santappita, *gen. pl.* ~ānaṁ (sabbakāmehi) 61,29.

santara, *mfn.* (*sa.* sāntara, *fr.* sa[1] + antara) having interval or anything within; *°-bāhiraṁ, *adv.* within and without, Dh. 315 (guttaṁ ~).

***santavat**, *mfn.* (*fr.* santa[1], √çam) tranquil; *m.* ~vā, Dh. 378.

santasati, *vb.* (*sa.* saṁ-√tras) to tremble (with fear); *pr. 3. pl.* ~anti, 86,22. *cp. next* & santāsa.

***santasana**, *n.* (*nom. act. fr. last*) trembling; *v.* a-santasana.

santānaka, *n.* (= *sa.*) anything spreading, *e. g.* membrane, film, cream, tissue of roots, *etc.*; a cobweb (*cp. sa.* santānikā, *f.*); *nom.* ~aṁ, 84,18.

santāsa, *m.* (*sa.* santrāsa) trembling, fear; *°-ppatta, *mfn.* frightened, *m. pl.* ~ā, 86,19; *cp.* a-santāsin.

santi[1], *f.* (*sa.* çānti) tranquillity, peace; enternal rest, Nibbāna; *acc.* ~iṁ, 80,33. 110,18; *°-magga, *m.* the road of peace, Dh. 285; *°-para, *mfn.* (*v.* para[2]).

santi[2], *pr. 3. pl.*, *v.* atthi.

(***santika**, *mfn.*, near, proximate; *prob. fr.* sa[1] + antika): several cases from this stem are used as *adv.*, or *prp. w. gen.* or *e. c.* (*cp. sa.* antikam, *etc.*): [1]) santikaṁ, near; to the presence of, to; 1,12 (gantvā): *w. gen.* 3,16. 7,30. 15,16. 24,30. 38,30. 73,14. 87,25; [2]) santikā, from; 6,36. 48,29. 114,4 (*w. gen.*); [3]) santike, near; in the presence or vicinity of, by, with, before, among; 4,17. 17,1. 32,12. 37,14. 103,5 (*w. gen.*); *comp.* dhana-santike, 33,26; susāna-°, 56,19, nibbāna°-, Dh. 372; santike may also be used in the sense of santikā: 70,15. 109,23; 109,28 (agga-santike), or of santikaṁ: 81,11. Dh. 237.

santiṭṭhati, *v.* saṇṭhāti.

santuṭṭhi, *f.* (*sa.* saṁ-tushṭi) satisfaction, contentment; *nom.* ~ī, Dh. 204. 375.

santusita, *mfn.* (= santuṭṭha, *pp.* saṁ-√tush) contented, pleased; *m.* ~o, Dh. 362.

santo, *pl. m.*, *v.* sat.

santhata, *mfn.* (*pp.* santharati, saṁ-√stṛ; *sa.* saṁstṛta) strewn, covered; *subst.* (*n.*) a cover, couch; *comp.* dhamani-°, *mfn.* (*q. v.*).

santhana, *n.* (*sa.* çranthana, √çrath) the being loosened or removed; salla-°, Dh. 275 (*v. h.*).

santhambhati, *vb.* (*sa.* saṁ-√stambh) to stand firm, take courage, restrain oneself; *inf.* ~ituṁ, 34,10.

santhava, *m.* (*sa.* saṁstava) acquaintance, familiarity, intimacy; *acc.* ~aṁ (sabbhi kubbetha) 29,12; Dh. 27 (kāma-rati-°, *q. v.*).

sandasseti, *vb.* (*caus.* saṁ-√dṛç, *sa.* sandarçayaṭi) to enlighten, instruct (*acc.*); *pr. 3. sg.* ~eti, 71,22; *aor. 3. sg.* ~esi, 77,25; *ger.* ~etvā, 78,23; *pp. m.* ~ito, 77,27.

sandahati, *vb.* (*sa.* saṁ-√dhā) [1]) *trans.* to put together, unite, reconcile; to direct, level, aim; to think on, comprehend, understand; [2]) *intr.* (*cp.* paṭi-sandahati): to stand, be the case ('sich verhalten'), or: to take place, arise (?), or: to be comprehended (in a certain way?); *pr. 3. sg.* ~ati (dhamma-santati, *q. v.*) 99,25; (apubbam acarimaṁ viya) 99,26 (*v.* a-pubba); — *ger.* sandhāya (*q. v.*); *pp.* saṁhita (*q. v.*); *cp.* sandhi.

sandāna, *n.* (= *sa.*) a rope, bond, fetter; *acc.* ~aṁ, Dh. 398.

sandeha, *m.* (= *sa.*) [1]) conglomeration (of material elements); *nom.* ~o (pūti-°, *q. v.*) 107,8 = Dh. 148; — [2]) doubt, uncertainty; *acc.* ~aṁ (janassa) 110,16.

sandhāya, *indecl.* (*ger.* sandahati, *q. v.*) [1]) *ger.* directing; dhanuṁ ~, 111,22 ("bending or seizing his bow"); [2]) *prp. w. acc.* towards, in that direction or meaning, with reference to, concerning; sarīraṁ ~, 85,29.

sandhāvati, *vb.* (*sa.* saṁ-√dhāv) to run through (*acc.*); *cond. 1. sg.* ~issaṁ (anekajāti-saṁsāraṁ) Dh.

153 (in the sense of a *futurum in præterito*: "I should run through", like adhigacchissaṁ, 104,12 (*q. v.*), *cp.* SBE. X. p. 43; Tr. PM. 56; *Childers*, JRAS. V. (1871) p. 222).

sandhi, *m.* (= *sa.*) 1) junction, union; agreement; joint; 2) interval, crevice, hole; *acc.* ~iṁ (pākāra-°, *q. v.*) 90,34. 91,28–29; *āloka-°, *m.* (*v. h.*). — sandhi-ccheda, *mfn.* cutting over the ties, or making hole; *m.* a hole or breach in a wall; Dh. 97. ~o (naro).

sanna, *mfn.* (*pp.* sīdati; = *sa.*; *cp.* nisinna) set down, sunk down (into, *loc.*); *m.* ~o (paṁke) Dh. 327.

sannaddha, *mfn.* (*pp. fr. next*; = *sa.*) armed, mailed; *m.* ~o (khattiyo) 107,24 = Dh. 387.

sannayhati, *vb.* (*sa.* saṁ-√nah) to bind, put on, gird on (weapons, *acc.*); *ger.* ~itvā (khaggaṁ) 33,29. 41,19; (dhanukalāpaṁ) 75,16; *pp.* sannaddha (*q. v.*).

sannicaya, *m.* (= *sa.*) gathering, heaping together, accumulation (of provisions); *nom.* ~o, Dh. 92.

***sanniṭṭhāna**, *n.* (*sa.* *saṁnishṭhāna) resolution, determination, conviction; *acc.* ~aṁ (katvā) 43,27.

sannipatati, *vb.* (*sa.* saṁ-ni-√pat) to come together, assemble; *aor. 3. sg.* sannipati, 17,23; *3. pl.* ~iṁsu, 10,7; *ger.* ~itvā, 10,25. 72,29; *pp.* sannipatita, *loc. m.* ~e, 18,19; *m. pl.* ~ā, 31,22; *caus.*, *v. below*; *cp. next*.

sannipāta, *m.* (= *sa.*) union, collection, assembly; *acc.* ~aṁ (akkharānaṁ) Dh. 352; *loc.* ~amhi (devatā-°) 110,30.

sannipāteti, *vb.* (*caus.* sannipatati) to collect, call together, assemble (*acc.*); *ger.* ~etvā, 6,3; *caus. II.* *sannipātāpeti, id.; *aor. 3. sg.* ~esi, 10,6; *ger.* ~etvā, 8,5. 42,3.

°**sannibha**, *mfn.* (*e. c.* = *sa.*) like, similar; *m.* ~o (uttatta-kanaka-°) 85,7.

sannivāsa, *m.* (= *sa.*) living together, company with (*gen.*); *nom.* ~o, Dh. 206; *instr.* ~ena (sataṁ) 29,13; 37,35. — *loka-°, *m.* the society of men, all the world, *nom.* ~o (sakalo) 16,13.

sannisinna, *mfn.* (*sa.* saṁ-nishanna, √sad) sitting together; *m. pl.* ~ā, 29,31.

sannissita, *mfn.* (*Buddh. sa.* saṁ-ni-çrita) connected with; *acc. m.* ~aṁ (vacīduccarita-°) 86,8.

sanneti, *vb.* (*sa.* saṁ-√nī) to mix, knead (*acc.*); *grd.* ~etabba, *n.* ~aṁ (cuṇṇaṁ) 83,27.

sapatha, *m.* (*sa.* çapatha) an oath; *acc.* ~aṁ (katvā) 41,36; (yakkhiṁ akārayi, "made her take an oath") 111,29.

sappa, *m.* (*sa.* sarpa) a snake, serpent; *nom.* ~o, 52,17; *acc.* ~aṁ (udaka-°) 52,28.

sappi, *n.* (& *m.*?) (*sa.* sarpis) clarified butter, ghee; *dvandva comp.* °-madhu-°, 61,26.

sappurisa, *m.* (*sa.* satpurusha; *cp.* sat) a good man; *nom.* ~o, Dh. 54; *acc.* ~aṁ, Dh. 208.

sabba, *mfn.* (*sa.* sarva) whole, entire, all, every; *m.* ~o, 85,6; 90,22 (loko, 'all men'); *acc.* ~aṁ, 4,16; *f.* ~ā (nadī) 48,6; *n.* ~aṁ, everything, 55,19; 70,24 (ādittaṁ); 96,15 (~atthi); 20,5. 31,28 ('the whole story'); *pl. m.* ~e, 3,24; *f.* ~ā, 66,21 (*nom.*); 85,4 (*acc.*); *instr.* ~ehi, 11,10; 70,22; *gen.* ~esaṁ, 11,3. 114,26; most frequently at the beg. of *subst. comp.*: 4,24. 7,33. 10,6, *etc. etc.*; sabbaṅga-°, *v.* aṅga; °-gandhāpana, *v.* āpaṇa; °-loka, *v.* abhibhū, ādhipacca, hita; sabbālaṁkāra-°, *v.* alaṁkāra; sabbākāra-°, *v.* ākāra; sabbābharaṇa-°, *v.* ābharaṇa; sabbitthiyo, *v.* itthī; *cp. next etc. etc.*

***sabba-cetaso**, *adv.*, *v.* cetas.

***sabbañjaha**, *mfn.* (*sa.* *sarvaṁjaha; *cp.* jahāti) 'having left all', *m.* ~o, Dh. 353.

sabbaññū, *m.* (*sa.* sarva-jña) omniscient (said of a Buddha); hence *sabbaññutā, *f.*, omniscience; *instr.* ~āya (Satthu) 110,14.

sabbato, *adv.* (*sa.* sarvatas) from all sides, entirely; *°-bhāgena, *adv.* on every side, 27,2–3 (*cp.* bhāga).

sabbattha, *adv.* (*sa.* sarvatra) everywhere; Dh. 83. 193. 348. 361.

sabbadā, *adv.* (*sa.* sarvadā) always; at any rate; 108,8; Dh. 207; 340 (*v. l.* sabbadhi, 'everywhere', 'in every direction').

***sabbadhi**, *adv.* (*fr. sa.* *sarvadha (= viçvadha), *Weber*, Ind. Str. III, 392; *cp.* sarvadry-añc) on all sides, in every respect; Dh. 90; 340 (*v. l.*).

***sabba-bhāsa**, *mfn.* (*cp.* bhāsā, *f.*) speaking all languages; *gen. pl.* ~ānaṁ (sattānaṁ, "all people of different tongues") 114,29.

***sabbavidu**, *mfn.* (*cp.* vidu, vidū; *sa.* sarva-vid) all knowing; *m.* ~ū ('ham asmi) Dh. 353.

***sabba-sāmukkaṁsika**, *mfn.*, *v.* sāmukkaṁsika.

sabba-seta, *mfn.* (*sa.* sarva-çveta) white all over; *m.* ~o, 21,34.

sabbaso, *adv.* (*sa.* sarvaças) wholly, entirely; at all, at any rate, always (*w. negation*: not at all, never); 34,25. 91,19. 93,33. 114,5; Dh. 265. 367. 419.

sabba-sovaṇṇa, *mfn.* (*sa.* sarva-sauvarṇa) entirely of gold, golden all over; *m.* ~o (kāyo) 84,26. 85,4–6.

sabbābhibhū, *m(fn).* (*sa.* sarvābhibhū) who has conquered all; Dh. 353.

sabbha, *mfn.* (*sa.* sabhya) polite, honorable; *v.* a-sabbha.

sabbhi, *v.* sat.

sabhā, *f.* (= *sa.*) an assembly or meeting; a large room or hall; dhamma-°, *f.* (*q. v.*).

sabhāga, *mfn.*, *v.* sa[1].

sabhāva, *m.* (*sa.* sva-bhāva) natural state or disposition, nature; *comp.* *asantasana-°. *mfn.* (*v.* a-santasana).

sama[1], *m.* (*sa.* çama) tranquillity, equanimity, absence of passion; *acc.* ~aṁ carati, to lead a life of tranquillity. 7,26. Dh. 142 (in this construction difficult to be distinguished from sama[2], *m.*); *sama-cariyā, *f.* the living in tranquillity; ~ā, *instr.* (shortened of ~āya) Dh. 388. *cp.* samatha, sammati, *etc.*

sama[2], *mfn.* (= *sa.*) [a]) like, equal to (*gen.* or *e. c.*); *m.* ~o (me saccena) 108,31; *pl.* ~ā (bhavanti) 74,2; °-vibhatta, *n.* (*q. v.*); gopānasī-bhogga-°, 47,22 (*q. v.*); dosa-°, rāga-°, *mfn.* Dh. 202; paṭhavī-°, Dh. 95; — [b]) even; *acc. m.* ~aṁ (maggaṁ kāretvā) 62,6; — [c]) just, impartial; *m. subst.* impartiallity, justice (*synon.* dhamma); *instr.* ~ena (nayati pare) Dh. 257; dhammena ~ena, 42,26 (*cp.* sama[1]). *cp.* samā, *f.* & samāna, *mfn.*

samagga, *mfn.* (*sa.* samagra) [1]) all, entire; [2]) agreeing, harmonious; *acc. m. pl.* ~e (sāvake) 108,20; *gen. pl.* ~ānaṁ, Dh. 194; *-vāsa, *m.* living together in unity & harmony, *acc.* ~aṁ (vasanto, tāya saddhiṁ) 58,35; *loc.* ~e, 46,17. *cp.* sāmaggi.

samaṅgin, *mfn.* (= *sa.*) & *samaṅgi-bhūta, *mfn.* endowed with, possessed of (*instr.*); *gen. m.* ~bhūtassa (kāmaguṇehi) 67,25.

samaññā, *f.* (*sa.* samājñā) name, appellation, term; *nom.* ~ā, 97,1.

samaṇa, *m.* (*sa.* çramaṇa) an ascetic, mendicant monk. *esp.* (by non-Buddhists) said of the Buddhist mendicants & even of Buddha himself, but also of the monks of other sects; *nom.* ~o (Gotamo) 71,25. 110,8; Dh. 265. 388 (false etymology: samitattā, samacariyā, *v. h.*); Dh. 254—55 (n'atthi bāhiro. *v. h.*); *gen. pl.* ~ānaṁ (Sakyaputtiyānaṁ) 73,30; — *comp.* *°-dhamma, *m.* the ascetic duties, *acc.* ~aṁ, 15,12. 45,7; pacchā-°, *m.* (*q. v.*); mahā-°, *m.* the great S. (*i. e.* Gotama Buddha) 76,31; *dvandva comp.* °-brāhmaṇā, *m. pl.* 104,1; *acc.* ~e, 19,2. *cp.* sāmañña, sāmaṇera.

samatikkanta, *mfn.* (*pp.* samati-kkamati; *sa.* √kram, samatikrānta) transgressed, surpassed, overcome;

e. c. free from : *papañca-⁰, Dh. 195 (*q. v.*) *cp. next.*

samatikkama, *m.* (*sa.* samatikrama) transgressing, surpassing, overcoming; *dat.* ~āya (soka-paridevānaṁ) 90,17.

*samativijjhati, *vb.* (*sa.* *sam-ati-√vyadh) to pierce or break through, penetrate (*acc.*); *pr. 3. sg.* ~ati (agāraṁ vuṭṭhi) 106,31 = Dh. 14.

samattha, *mfn.* (*sa.* samartha) able to, capable of (*inf.*); venturing (do.); knowing to behave, or capable of finding a way; *m.* ~o (jale pi thale pi) 4,14; 27,16. 35,19. (*w. inf.*); ~o n'āhosi (do. 'did not venture') 40,2; *f.* ~ā, 27,11; *pl.* ~ā, 39,12. *cp.* sāmatthiya.

samatha, *m.* (*sa.* çamatha) = sama [1]; *acc.* ~aṁ (gatāni, "subdued") Dh. 94.

samanantara, *mfn.* (= *sa.*) immediately following; ~ā, *adv.* (*cp. sa.* samanantaraṁ) immediately after, 80,18.

samanta, *mfn.* (= *sa.*) being on every side, whole, entire; *abl. adv.* [a]) ~ā, on all sides, around, completely; 38,2; 90,33 (*w. gen.*, nagarassa); 104,3; [b]) ~ato, id.; 63,23. 85,8. *cp.* sāmantā.

samannāgata, *mfn.* (*sa.* samanvāgata) attended by, endowed with, possessed of (*instr.* or *c. c.*); *m.* ~o (dhammehi) 3,24; (dasahi aṅgehi) 82,14; 85,19. 91,26-27; *f. pl.* ~ā (asaddhamma-⁰) 51,26.

*samannāharati, *vb.* (*sa.* *sam-anu-ā-√bhṛ) to direct one's whole attention to (*acc.*); *ger.* ~itvā (sabbacetaso, "seizing upon it with their whole minds") 71,24.

samappita, *mfn.* (*pp. fr. next*; *sa.* samarpita) delivered over to (*loc.*); endowed with (*instr.* or *c. c.*); *m. pl.* ~ā (nirayamhi) 108,7 = Dh. 315; *gen. m.* ~assa (kāmaguṇehi) 67,25; *comp.* yaso-bhoga-⁰, *mfn.* Dh. 303.

samappeti, *vb.* (*sa.* samarpayati, *caus.* sam-√ṛ) to deliver over, consign (*acc.* & *gen.*); *aor. 3. sg.* ~appayi, 110,27.

samaya, *m.* (= *sa.*) [1]) time, occasion, season; *nom.* ~o (pabbajjā-⁰) 45,12; *acc.* ~aṁ (ekaṁ, "once") 66,23. 71,20; paccūsa-⁰ ("at dawn") 68,9; pubbaṇha-⁰, 76,15; majjhantika-⁰, 97,34; *instr.* ~ena (tena) 5,32. 71,21. 74,17; aparena ~, "afterwards", 95,23. 101,16; *loc.* ~e (ekasmiṁ, once upon a time) 30,28; tasmiṁ ~, 40,30. 62,10; aḍḍharatta-⁰, "at midnight", 40,8; nidāgha-⁰, 3,32; sāyaṇha-⁰, 2,32; 14,11. — [2]) view, doctrine, system, religious persuasion; *sammā-viññāta-⁰, *mfn.* 113,4 (*v.* viññāta).

samalaṁkata, *mfn.* (*sa.* samalaṁkṛta) well adorned, decorated; *n.* ~aṁ (vitāna-⁰, *q. v.*) 112,2.

samassattha, *mfn.* (*sa.* samāçvasta, *pp.* sam-ā-√çvas) revived, recovered; ⁰-kāle, when he was recovered, 20,7. *cp. next.*

samassāseti, *vb.* (*caus.* sam-ā-√çvas) to reanimate, comfort (*acc.*); *imp. 2. sg.* ~ehi (naṁ) 46,11; *aor. 3. sg.* ~esi, 46,12; *ger.* ~etvā, 1,11. 57,36. 89,12.

samā, *f.* (= *sa.*) a year (= vassa); sataṁ-samaṁ, Dh. 106 (*v.* sata [1]).

samāgacchati, *vb.* (*sa.* sam-ā-√gam) to come together, assemble, arrive; *w. instr.* to meet with, to be united with, cling to; *aor. 2. sg.* ~gañchi (piyehi) 106,25 = Dh. 210; *ger.* ~gantvā, 10,7. 75,38; *pp.* ~gata, *m.* ~o, 110,9; *pl.* ~ā, 108,3. 109,2. *cp. next.*

samāgama, *m.* (= *sa.*) coming together, meeting with; assembly; *nom.* ~o, 20,20. 112,16. Dh. 207.

samādapeti, *vb.* (*caus.* samādiyati; *sa.* samādāpayati) to incite, arouse (*acc.*); *pr. 3. sg.* ~eti, 71,22; *aor. 3. sg.* ~esi, 77,25; *ger.* ~etvā, 78,22; *pp. m.* ~ito, 77,27.

samādāna, *n.* (= *sa.*) taking upon oneself, undertaking; a vow;

micchā-diṭṭhi-⁰, *mfn.* "embracing false doctrines", *pl.* ~ā, Dh. 316.

samādiyati, *vb.* (*sa.* sam-ā-√dā, *cp.* ādiyati) to take upon oneself, adopt (*acc.*); *ger.* a) ~ādāya (vissaṁ dhammaṁ) 106,5 = Dh. 266; b) ~ādiyitvā (sīlaṁ) 14,18; *caus.* samādapeti (*q. v.*); samādāna, *n.*, *v. above.*

samādhi, *m.* (= *sa.*) tranquillity of mind, meditation, self-concentration, the highest stage of jhāna (*q. v.*); *nom.* ~i, 103,22; sammā-⁰, 67,5 (right meditation); *acc.* ~iṁ (adhigacchati) Dh. 249. 365; *instr.* ~inā, Dh. 144; *comp.* *⁰-jhāna, *n.* 109,21.

samāna[1], *mfn.* (= *sa.*) like, equal; same, alike; *comp.* *samāna-balâdi-padesa, *mfn.*, 43,31 (*v.* padesa); *⁰-vaya-bhāva, *mfn.* 43,29 (*v.* vaya[1]); *⁰-vāsa, *mfn.* dwelling with equals, *m.* ~o, 104,21; *⁰-saṁvāsa, *m.* the dwelling together with equals (family-life), *nom.* ~o, Dh. 302 (2. ed. [a]-samāna-vāso ?); *manussa-samāna-sarīra, *mfn.* with body like men, *m. pl.* ~ā (macchā) 25,23. *cp.* sama, samāniya.

*samāna[2], *mfn.* (*part. med. fr.* atthi) being (*pleonast.* added mostly to *past part.*. or sometimes to *adj.*); *m.* ~o (puṭṭho) 90,4; (vutto) 98,16; (andho) 25,15; *acc. pl. m.* ~e (matte) 59,26. *cp. Pischel,* Gr. § 561.

*samāniya, *mfn.* (*fr.* samāna[1], *cp. sa.* samānyā, *adv.*) joined, assembled; *m. pl.* ~ā (puttā me, "my children are all about me") 105,5.

samāneti, *vb.* (*sa.* sam-ā-√nī) to collect, assemble (*acc.*); *ger.* ~etvā (saṅghaṁ) 114,7.

samāpajjati, *vb.* (*sa.* sam-ā-√pad) to attain, arrive to, enter into (*acc.*); *aor. 3. sg.* ~pajji (catuttha-jjhānaṁ) 80,5. *cp. next etc.*

samāpatti, *f.* (= *sa.*) 'attainment', one of the eight successive states of the ecstatic meditation; *abl.* ~iyā (ākāsānañcāyatana-⁰, *q. v.*) 80,6, *etc.*

samāpanna, *mfn.* (*pp.* samāpajjati; = *sa.*) arrived to, entered into (*acc.* or *e. c.*); *m.* ~o, 80,18; icchā-lobha-⁰, Dh. 264.

samāraddha, *mfn.* (*sa.* samārabdha) undertaken, begun; su-⁰, *mfn.* Dh. 293 (*q. v.*).

[samāsati], *vb.* (*sa.* sam-√ās) to sit together, associate with (*instr.*); *pot. 3. sg. med.* samāsetha (sabbhir eva) 29,12.

samāsato, *adv.* (*abl.* samāsa, *m.* abridgement; *sa.* samāsatas) concisely, briefly, in an abridged form, 114,12.

samāhita, *mfn.* (= *sa.*) put together, collected, composed, *e. c.* furnished with; *m.* ~o, Dh. 362 (collected in mind); *paññā-sīla-⁰, *mfn.* Dh. 229 (*q. v.*); a-samāhita, su-samāhita, *mfn.*, *v.* a-⁰, su-⁰.

samijjhati, *vb.* (*sa.* sam-√ṛdh) to prosper, succeed, flourish, ripen; *pr. 3. sg.* ~ati (viriya-phalaṁ) 42,14-19. *cp.* samiddhi.

*samiñjati, *vb.* (a secondary formation of sam-√iṅg) to tremble, falter; *pr. 3. pl.* ~anti, 106,29 = Dh. 81. (*cp. Weber,* Ind. Str. III, 397; *Oldenberg,* KZ. XXV (1881) 324.)

*samitatta, *n.* (*fr.* samita, *pp.* sameti; *sa.* *çamita-tva) the being appeased or quieted; *abl.* ~ā (pāpānaṁ) Dh. 265.

samiti, *f.* (= *sa.*) coming together, meeting; battle, war; *acc.* ~iṁ, Dh. 321.

samiddhi, *f.* (*sa.* samṛddhi) success, increase, perfection, welfare; *acc.* ~iṁ (attano) Dh. 84.

samīpa, *n.* (= *sa.*) nearness, proximity; only used adverbially in oblique cases: 'near', 'in the vicinity', 'towards' (often *e. c.*); *acc.* ~aṁ, 56,10; 8,24 (khetta-⁰); 65,14 (dvāra-⁰); *instr.* ~ena, 49,3 (āpaṇa-⁰); *loc.* ~e, 44,29; 21,18 (nagara-⁰); 73,20 (gandhakuṭi-⁰); 84,31 (Rājagaha-⁰); ekasmiṁ gāma-samīpe, in the vicinity of a certain village, 33,23; ~amhi (Bodhimaṇḍa-⁰) 113,2; – samīpa-ṭṭha, *mfn.*, standing near; *acc. m.* ~aṁ, 110,21.

samīrati, *vb.* (*pass.* sam-√īr,

prob. contraction of *samiriyati) to be moved or shaken; *pr. 3. sg.* ~ati (vātena) 106,29 = Dh. 81.

samukkaṁsati, *vb.* (*sa.* sam-ut-√kṛsh) to elevate, praise, extol (*acc.*); *pot. 3. sg.* ~kaṁse (attānaṁ) 103,30. *cp.* sāmukkaṁsika.

samugga, *m.* (*sa.* samudga) a box, casket; *acc.* ~aṁ (catujāti-gandha-°) 41,5; *loc.* ~e (suvaṇṇa-°) 41,6.

samucchinna, *mfn.* (= *sa.*; *pp.* samucchindati) uprooted, destroyed; *n.* ~aṁ, Dh. 250 = 263.

samuṭṭhāna, *n.* (*sa.* samutthāna) rise, origin; *°ajjhatta-°, & *°bahiddhā-°, *mfn.* (*v. h.*).

***samuṭṭhāpana**, *n.* (*nom. act. fr. next*) the causing to rise or start; kathā-°, 54,10 (°-atthaṁ, "for sake of starting talk").

samuṭṭhāpeti, *vb.* (*caus.* samuṭṭhāti, √sthā; *sa.* samutthāpayati) to cause to rise (*acc.*); *aor. 3. sg.* ~esi (vātaṁ) 19,15; *3. pl.* ~esuṁ (kathaṁ, "they discussed the matter") 29,28.

samuṭṭhita, *mfn.* (*pp.* samuṭṭhāti, √sthā; *sa.* samutthita) risen, sprung from; *n.* ~aṁ (ayasā, *v.* ayas) 106,19 = Dh. 240.

samuttejeti, *vb.* (*caus.* *sam-ut-√tij; *Buddh. sa.* samuttijayati) to incite, inflame (*acc.*); *pr. 3. sg.* ~eti, 71,22; *aor. 3. sg.* ~esi, 77,25; *ger.* ~etvā, 78,22; *pp. m.* ~ito, 77,27.

samudaya, *m.* (= *sa.*) rise, origin, cause; *nom.* ~o (rūpassa) 94,8; (dukkha-kkhandassa) 66,12; *°-dhamma, *mfn.*, subject to birth, *n.* ~aṁ, 68,27 (*opp.* nirodha-dhamma); dukkha-°, *m.* the cause of suffering; ~aṁ ariya-saccaṁ, 67,12, *cp.* dukkha-nirodha.

samudācarati, *vb.* (*sa.* sam-ud-ā-√car) to appear, behave; to follow, attack, treat, overcome; to speak to, address (*acc.*); *pr. 3. pl.* ~anti (aññamaññaṁ āvuso-vādena) 79,7; 96,30; *grd.* ~itabba, 79,7-10.

samudāhaṭa, *mfn.* (*sa.* samudāhṛta, √hṛ) mentioned, named; *acc. m. pl.* ~e (potthake) 114,17.

samudda, *m.* (*sa.* samudra) the sea, ocean; *nom.* ~o (mahā-°) 95,13; *acc.* ~aṁ, 20,19; *gen.* ~assa, 2,11; *loc.* ~e (mahā-°), 10,28; *gen. pl.* ~ānaṁ (catunnaṁ) 89,14; ku-samudda, *m.*, *v.* ku-; °-tira, *n.*; °-devatā, *f.*, °-piṭṭhe & °-majjhe, *loc.* (*q. v.*); dakkhiṇa-°, *m.* & *pakati-°, *m.* (*v. h.*).

samuppāda, *m.* (*sa.* samutpāda) rise, origin; *dukkha-°, *m.* the origin of pain; *acc.* ~aṁ, 107,19 = Dh. 191 (*synon.* dukkha-samudaya, 67,12); paṭicca-°, *m.* 66,5 (*v. h.*).

samussaya, *m.* (*sa.* samucchraya) collection, accumulation, *esp.* the aggregation of the elements (mental and material) of a human being; existence, birth, body; *nom.* ~o (antimo, the last existence) 108,17; *acc.* ~aṁ, 80,23. *cp. next.*

samussita, *mfn.* (*pp.* sam-ud-√çri; *sa.* samucchrita) collected, joined together; or, elevated, arrogant (?) Dh. 147.

samūhata, *mfn.* (*pp. fr. next*; *sa.* samuddhata) done away, pulled out, extirpated; *n.* ~aṁ (mūlaghaccaṁ) Dh. 250.

***samūhanti**, *vb.* (*sa.* *sam-ud-√han) to lift up, throw away, abolish (*acc.*); *imp. 3. sg.* ~antu (sikkhāpadāni, saṁgho) 79,12. *pp.*, *v. above.*

samūheti, *vb.* (*caus.* sam-√ūh; *sa.* samūhayati) to collect, assemble (*acc.*); *ger.* ~etvā (saṁghaṁ) 114,13.

samekkhati, *vb.* (*sa.* sam-√īksh) to investigate, examine, consider, ponder (*acc.*); *ger.* samekkhiya (kathā-maggaṁ) 113,30.

sameti[1], *vb.* (*sa.* sam-√i) 'to come together', agree with (*instr.*); *pr. 3. sg.* ~eti (sutaṁ diṭṭhena) 54,15.

sameti[2], *vb.* (*caus.* sammati; *sa.* çamayati) to appease, quiet (*acc.*); *pr. 3. sg.* ~eti (pāpāni) Dh. 265; *pp.* samita, *v.* samitatta, *n.*

***samodhāneti**, *vb.* (*denom. fr.* samodhāna, *sa.* samavadhāna) to put together, connect, compare; to enumerate, calculate, sum up (*acc.*); *aor. 3. sg.* ~esi (jātakaṁ, *q. v.*) 29,17.

*****sampajāna**, *mfn.* (*nomen agentis fr.* sam-pra-√jñā) conscious, selfpossessed; *m.* ~o, 78,25; *gen. pl.* ~ānaṁ, Dh. 293 (*synon.* sata[2]).

sampajjati, *vb.* (*sa.* sam-√pad) 1) to prosper, succeed; *pr. 3. sg.* ~ati (takes root) 37,7; *part.* ~anta, flourishing, 102,7 (a-sampajjantesu, *loc. pl.*); *fut. 3. pl.* ~issanti (sassāni) ib.; 2) to become, turn into (*nom.*); *pot. 3. sg.* ~eyya (dadhi) 101,27; — *pp.* sampanna (*q. v.*), *caus.* sampādeti (*q. v.*), *cp.* sampatti.

*****sampaṭicchati**, *vb.* (*sa.* sam-prati-√ish) to receive, accept; consent, agree to (*acc.*); *aor. 3. sg.* ~icchi (sādhū'ti) 5,1. 6,29. 53,16; 46,15; *3. pl.* ~icchiṁsu (taṁ silaṁ) 75,36; *ger.* ~icchitvā, 1,18. 14,14-20. 62,23; *pp.* ~icchita, 55,23 (*loc. abs.* tena ~e, when he had consented).

sampatta, *mfn.* (*sa.* sam-prāpta) reached, attained; who has reached, arrived, come to; *m.* ~o (*w. acc.* Mahāvihāraṁ) 114,3; *m. pl.* ~ā (used as *tempus finitum* 'came') 20,13. 62,22; *acc. pl. m.* ~e (yācake) 14,19; *comp.* °-nāvā (a ship arrived there), 27,13 (*acc.* ~aṁ); °-parisā (the assembly present there) 86,10 (*dat.* ~āya).

sampatti, *f.* (= *sa.*) success, prosperity; excellence, perfection; pleasure, bliss; magnificence, glory; *nom.* ~i, 58,11; 42,10; *acc.* ~iṁ, 4,18. 63,17; rūpa-°, beauty, 19,11; dibba-°, divine bliss, 23,17.

sampanna, *mfn.* (= *sa.*; *pp.* sampajjati) 1) complete, perfect, excellent; °-sassa, *n.* excellent crops, 26,18; *°-vijjā-caraṇa, *mfn.* perfect in knowledge and behaviour, *m. pl.* ~ā, Dh. 144; *°-sīla, *mfn.* perfect in virtues, *gen. pl.* ~ānaṁ, Dh. 57; sabbaṅga-°, *mfn.* (*v.* aṅga); — 2) endowed with, possessed of, full of (*w. instr.* or more frequently *c. c.*); *m.* ~o (phalarukkhehi) 2,20; *comp.* *thāma-°, 1,3; pakka-phala-piṇḍi-°, 2,1; khanti-mettânuddaya-°, 7,12; āṇā-°, 10,26; sara-°, 18,34; ñāṇa-°, 24,14; ānubhāva-°, 35,23; sīla-°, 41,35; sabba-lakkhaṇa-°, 55,32; mālā-gandha-vibhūti-°, 61,4; parideva-soka-°, 69,32; sīla-dassana-°, Dh. 217 (*v. h.*).

sampayāta, *mfn.* (*sa.* samprayāta) come together, having advanced towards; *m.* ~o (Yamassa santike) Dh. 237.

sampayoga, *m.* (*sa.* samprayoga) joining, conjunction, connection (with, *instr.*); *nom.* ~o (appiyehi) 67,9.

[**samparivatta**, *m.*] (*sa.* samparivarta) turning or rolling round; only in *comp.* *°-sāyin, *mfn.* "rolling oneself about". *nom. m.* ~ī, Dh. 325.

samparivāreti, *vb.* (*caus.* sampari-√vṛ) to surround (*acc.*); *ger.* ~ayitvā (naṁ) 64,30.

*****sampavedhin**, *mfn.* (*fr.* sampavedhati. to tremble, shake, swing to and fro; *sa.* sam-pra-√vyath) shaking, trembling; only in *comp.* a-sampavedhin, *mfn.* (*v. h.*).

sampassati, *vb.* (*sa.* sam-√paç) to look upon, regard, consider (*acc.*); *part. m.* ~passaṁ (vipulaṁ sukhaṁ) Dh. 290; *part. med. m.* ~passamāno (ādīnavaṁ) 93,32 (considering it dangerous).

sampahaṁseti, *vb.* (*sa.* sampraharshayati, *caus.* sam-pra-√hṛsh) to make glad (*acc.*); *pr. 3. sg.* ~eti (bhikkhū) 71,23; *aor. 3. sg.* ~esi, 77,25; *ger.* ~etvā, 78,22; *pp.* ~ito, *m.* 77,27.

sampādeti, *vb.* (*caus.* sampajjati; *sa.* sampādayati) to bring about, produce, supply, prepare (*acc.*); *intr.* to go to work, endeavour, strive; *pr. 3. sg.* ~eti (rathaṁ) 98,17; *imp. 2. pl.* ~etha (appamādena) 80,2; *ger.* ~etvā, 6,4. 57,21; *pp.* sampādita, prepared, 41,9.

sampāpuṇāti, *vb.* (*sa.* sam-pra-√āp) to reach, come to, arrive at (*acc.*); *aor. 3. sg.* sampāpuṇi, 29,25; *3. pl.* ~iṁsu, 59,27.

sampuṇṇa, *mfn.* (*sa.* sampūrṇa).

complete, accomplished; *°-pada, *mfn.* complete up to the single words; *n.* (*adv.*) ~aṁ (correctly, perfectly) 113,7.

samphassa, *m.* (*sa.* saṁsparça) touch, contact; *nom.* ~o (*cakkhu-°) 70,26; (*mano-°, *q. v.*) 70,33; *acc.* ~aṁ (hattha-°) 51,9. *cp.* vedayita, viññāṇa.

samphusati, *vb.* (*sa.* saṁ-√spṛç) to come in contact with, touch; suffer, endure (*acc.*); *aor. 3. sg.* ~usī (metri causa) 78,30 (ābādhaṁ).

sambandha, *m.* (= *sa.*) connexion, conjunction; relationship (with, *instr.*); *abl.* ~ā (tena, on account of the relationship with him) 112,32.

sambahula, *mfn.* (= *sa.*) numerous; *instr. pl.* ~ehi (bhikkhūhi) 76,16.

sambādha, *m.* (= *sa.*) a narrow place; press, crowd; *°-ṭṭhāna, *n.* the interstice between the legs, in the *comp.* pākaṭa-bībhaccha-°, *mfn.* having the loathsome parts of the body disclosed, *f. pl.* ~ā, 65,8.

***sambāhati** (& *sambāheti), *vb.* (*sa.* sam + √vāh (bāh)) to rub (*acc.*); *aor. 3. sg.* ~bāhi (pahāraṁ) 50,24.

sambuddha, 1) *mfn.* (= *sa.*) awakened, clear in insight; *nom. m.* ~o, 80,25; *gen. pl.* ~ānaṁ, Dh. 181; 2) *m.* a Buddha; *gen.* ~assa, 104,12; *loc.* ~e, 81,4; *°-mata, *n.* the doctrine of the Buddha, 114,13 (°-kovida); sammā-°, *m.* the enlightened one, the supreme Buddha, *instr.* ~ena, 88,3; *gen.* ~assa, 81,5; Kassapa-°, 28,18 (*q. v.*).

sambodhi, *f.* (= *sa.*) perfect knowledge, supreme wisdom (of a Buddha); *dat.* ~āya, 66,30. 93,8; *°-parāyana, *mfn.* destined to obtain supreme wisdom, *m.* ~o, 79,34; *°-aṅga, (*m.*) i. e. sambojjhaṅga = bojjhaṅga (*q. v.*); Dh. 89 (*loc. pl.* ~esu).

sambhata, *mfn.* (*sa.* sam-bhṛta) collected, produced, earned; *gen. n.* ~assa (dhanassa) 52,5.

sambhava, *m.* (= *sa.*) birth, origin; being, existence; *nom.* ~o (*jāti-°, existence) 17,28; *instr.* ~ena (mātu-kucchi-°, on account of the sojourn in the mother's womb) 62,28; atta-°. & *matti-°, *mfn.* (*q. v.*).

sambhāra, *m.* (= *sa.*) bringing together; *abl.* ~ā (aṅga-°, *q. v.*) 98,30.

sambhūta, *mfn.* (= *sa.*) produced, arisen, come into being; *n.* ~aṁ, 99,33.

samma-, shortened of sammā (*q. v.*).

***samma**, *indecl.*, a term of familiar address to inferiors or equals (not to women), sometimes also with plural ending (sammā): friend! my dear! [possibly some derivate from √çam, or çam, *indecl.* (*ved. sa.*), *cp.* çamya, çāmya, *etc.*, if not, after all, akin to sammā (*v. below*); it is by some considered as related to *sa.* saumya; *Fausbøll*, Five Jāt. p. 37, hesitatingly, refers to *sa.* çarman; *Pischel*, KZ (BB.) I. p. 176, to *sa.* *çamba]; 1,20. 6,23; *w. foll. voc.*: ~ kumbhīla, 3,16; ~ mora, 10,11; ~ kappaka, 44,23.

sammajjati, *vb.* (*sa.* sam-√mṛj) to sweep, cleanse, scrub (*acc.*); *grd. m.* ~itabbo (deso) 82,23; *f.* ~ā, 84,32; *pp. v. next.*

sammaṭṭha, *mfn.* (*pp.* sammajjati; *sa.* sam-mṛshṭa) cleansed, smooth; *°-passa, *mfn.* well-formed, beautiful, *acc. f.* ~aṁ (kumāriṁ) 47,19.

sammata, *mfn.* (= *sa.*) 1) considered as, so called; sutta-°, 110,3; 2) elected, authorized; *m.* (& *n.*?) a deputy; a select committee; *saṁgha-°, 109,5.

sammati, *vb.* (*sa.* √çam) to become quiet, appeased; to cease; to rest, dwell; *pr. 3. sg.* ~ati, Dh. 3; 390 (sammati-m-eva); *3. pl.* ~anti (verāni) 106,23-24 = Dh. 5; *caus.* sameti, *pp.* santa (*q. v.*) *cp.* sama, samatha.

sammatta, *mfn.* (= *sa.*) inebriated, maddened, mad with joy, love &; *m. pl.* ~ā (macchā) 19,33; *putta-pasu-°, *mfn.* one who is fully engaged in taking care of his children and cattle, Dh. 287.

sammad-, sandhi-form of sammā (*q. v.*) *cp. next etc.*

***samma-d-akkhāta**, *mfn.* (*fr.* sammā + akkhāta; *sa.* *samyag-ākhyāta) well preached; *loc.* ~e (dhamme) Dh. 86.

samma-d-aññā, *f.* (*sa.* samyag-ājñā) perfect knowledge; *°-vimutta, *mfn.* (*v.* aññā) Dh. 57. 96.

***samma-ppajāna**, *mfn.* (*fr.* sammā + pajāna, *q. v.*) possessed of complete knowledge, *m.* ~o, Dh. 20.

***samma-ppaññā**, *f.* (*fr.* sammā + paññā, *q. v.*) complete knowledge, clear understanding; *instr.* ~āya, 107,18 = Dh. 190.

sammasati, *vb.* (*sa.* sam-√mṛç) to take hold of, grasp; to consider, meditate, perceive fully (*acc.*); *pr. 3. sg.* ~ati (khandhānaṁ udayavyayaṁ) Dh. 374.

sammā, *indecl.* (*sa.* samyak) completely, wholly, truly, properly, duly, correctly, clearly; at the beg. of *comp.* it is shortened to samma-° before double cons. (*v.* samma-ppajāna, *etc.*), and before vowels an euphonical -d- generally is inserted (*v.* samma-d-akkhāta, *etc.*); likewise before a foll. eva: samma-d-eva, 68,25; a) *beyond comp.*: 24,32 (vaḍḍhito); 82,16 (? sammā-vattitabbaṁ, *v.* sammā-vattati *below*); 99,31 (vadeyya); 102,6-7 (vassati, sampajjissanti); Dh. 89 (subhāvitaṁ); Dh. 373 (vipassato); b) *at the beg. of comp., v. separately.*

sammā-ājīva, *m.* (*sa.* samyag-ājīva) right living, 67,4.

sammā-kammanta, *m.* (*sa.* samyak-karmānta) right conduct, 67,4.

sammā-diṭṭhi, *f.* (*sa.* samyag-dṛshṭi) right belief, 67,3. 96,5.

***sammā-paṇihita**, *mfn., v.* paṇihita.

***sammā-pariṇāma**, *m., v.* pariṇāma.

sammā-vattati, *vb.* (probably to be read in two words) to observe a right conduct (towards, *loc.*); *grd. n.* ~itabbaṁ, 82,16. *cp. next.*

***sammā-vattanā**, *f.* right conduct or behaviour; 82,17.

sammā-vācā, *f.* (*sa.* samyag-vāc) right speech, 67,4.

sammā-vāyāma, *m.* (*sa.* samyag-vyāyāma) right endeavour, 67,5.

***sammā-viññāta**, *mfn.* perfectly known or understood; °-samaya, *mfn.* having a perfect knowledge in religious doctrines, 113,4.

sammā-saṁkappa, *m.* (*sa.* samyak-saṁkalpa) right aspiration or resolve, 67,4; *°-gocara, *mfn.* "following true desires" (*opp.* micchā-°) Dh. 12.

sammā-sati, *f.* (*sa.* samyak-smṛti) right recollection, 67,5.

sammā-samādhi, *m.* (*sa.* samyak-°) right meditation, 67,5.

sammā-sambuddha, *m.* (*sa.* samyak-°) *v.* sambuddha.

sammukha, *mfn.* (= *sa.*) being face to face with (*gen.*); present; suitable; *m. pl.* ~ā, 79,20; *abl.* (*adv.*) ~ā (Bhagavato, in the presence of) 98,29; 109,34 (sutvā, "having heard it from B. himself"); *comp.* *°-ciṇṇa, *n.* a manifest suitable deed; *instr.* ~ena, 14,3. *cp. next* & samukha-veṭhita, 51,8 (*v.* sa-4).

sammuti, *f.* (*sa.* sammati) custom, general or current opinion (or expression), name, appellation, phrase; hoti satto'ti sammuti, 98,31 ("we use the phrase a living being").

sammodati, *vb.* (*sa.* sam-√mud) to exchange friendly greetings; *aor. 3. sg.* sammodi (Bhagavatā saddhiṁ) 89,20; *part. med.* ~ modamāna, dwelling friendly and harmonious together, 16,19; *grd.* sammodanīya, in the phrase: sammodanīyaṁ kathaṁ *etc.* 89,20. 93,24. 96,26 (*v.* vītisāreti). *cp.* paṭi-sammodati.

sammoha, *m.* (= *sa.*) confusion; *acc.* ~aṁ (āpādiṁ, *v.* āpajjati) 94,22; *dat.* ~āya (alaṁ, *q. v.*) 94,24.

saya, *mfn.* (*sa.* çaya) lying, sleeping; *v.* guhā-°, darī-°.

. **sayaṁ**, *indecl.* (*sa.* svayaṁ) self, by one's self, spontaneously; 7,2. 33,32. 46,16; sayam eva, 55,25. 85,28; sayam pi, 112,32; *comp.* °-kata, *mfn.* Dh. 347 (*v. h.*); °-jāta, *mfn.* 'self-born', growing wild, 22,1 (°-sāli). *cp.* sāmaṁ.

sayati, *vb.*, *v.* seti.

sayana, *n.* (*sa.* çayana) lying, sleeping; bed, couch; *acc.* ~aṁ, 112,2; *instr.* ~ena, 20,26. 61,10; Dh. 271 (vivicca-°, *q. v.*); *abl.* ~ā, 41,27; (uccā-°-mahā-°) 81,26; ~ato, 16,4 (dabbatiṇa-°); *gen.* ~assa, 47,25; *loc.* ~e (pupphānaṁ ammaṇamattena abhippakiṇṇa-°) 65,30; 41,36 (mahā-°) *cp.* siri-sayana; *°-gabbba, *m.* bed-chamber, 46,3; *°-gumba, *m.* 14,33 (*v. h.*); °-piṭṭha (*q. v.*) *cp. next.*

sayanāsana, *n.*, *v.* senāsana.

sayani-ghara, *n.* (*sa.* çayanagṛha, *cp.* çayanīya-gṛha) a bed-chamber; *acc.* ~aṁ, 52,22.

sara[1], *m.* (*sa.* çara) an arrow; *acc.* ~aṁ, Dh. 320; *pl.* ~ā, Dh. 304.

sara[2], *m. n.* (*sa.* sara & saras) a lake, pond; *acc.* ~aṁ, 4,13; 3,30 (paduma-°); *gen.* ~assa, 4,12; *loc.* ~e, 3,33. 21,36 (Tambapaṇṇi-°); ~asmiṁ, 5,16 [*loc.* also sarasi from saras]; °-tīra, °-pariyanta (*v. h.*).

sara[3], *m.* (*sa.* svara) sound, voice, cry; *acc.* ~aṁ (atikaruṇa-°) 27,14; (aṭṭa-ssaraṁ, *v.* aṭṭa[1]) 40,21; (gīta-°) 19,32; *instr.* ~ena (madhurena) 17,27; (madhura-ssarena) 5,20. 62,13; °-sampanna, *mfn.* having a melodious voice, *m.* ~o (moro) 18,34.

saraka, *m. n.* (= *sa.*) a drinking vessel or cup; *instr.* ~ena (suvaṇṇa-°) 41,11.

saraṇa, *n.* (*sa.* çaraṇa) refuge; *acc.* ~aṁ, Dh. 188; 192 = 107,21; ~aṁ gacchati (upeti), to take refuge in (*acc.*): 69,19. 105,24. 107,17 = Dh. 190; *pl.* ~āni (tīṇi = ratanāni, *v.* ratana) 28,25.

sarati, *vb.* (*sa.* √smṛ) to remember (*acc.* or *gen.*), to think of (with sorrow or regret); *pr. 1. sg.* ~āmi (attānaṁ) 27,22; an earlier form of *pr. 3. sg.* sumarati is found Dh. 324 (*w. gen.* nāgavanassa); *pp. v.* sata[2]; *cp.* sati[2] & sārāṇiya.

sarabha, *m.* (*sa.* çarabha) a kind of deer; *°-pādaka, *mfn.* with legs of that deer, *loc.* ~e (kañcana-pallaṁke) 42,9.

sarita, *mfn.* (= *sa.*; *pp.* √sṛ) moving, going, running; *n. pl.* ~āni (somanassāni) Dh. 341 ("extravagant"). *cp.* sārin.

sarīra, *n.* (*sa.* çarīra) the body; *nom.* ~aṁ, 2,7; *acc.* ~aṁ, 1,6; 16,6 (saka-°); 57,29 (sakala-°); *instr.* ~ena, 89,9 (do.); *abl.* ~ā, 45,1; ~ato, 23,32; *loc.* ~e, 15,33; *°-paṭijaggana, *n.*, *°-bhaṅga, *m.*, *°-maṁsa, *n.* (*v. h.*); *antima-°, *mfn.* (*q. v.*); *obhagga-°, *mfn.* one whose body is bent or crooked, 63,9; *manussa-samāna-°, *mfn.* (*q. v.*); mahā-°, *mfn.* having a great body, 1,3; *cp.* a-sarīra, *mfn.*

salākā, *f.* (*sa.* çalākā) a small stick or twig, a piece or splint of bamboo and the like, used as ticket or ballot (by casting of lots); *v.* kālakaṇṇi-°, 23,12.

saḷāyatana, *n.* (*sa.* shaḍ-āyatana) the six organs of sense; *nom.* ~aṁ, 66,8; °-nirodha, *m.* 66,14 (*q. v.*) *cp.* āyatana.

salla, *n.* (*sa.* çalya) a stake or thorn, an arrow; a wound; *nom.* ~aṁ, 92,9; *acc.* ~aṁ (attano, *metaph.* of passions) 108,9; *instr.* ~ena, 92,7; *pl.* ~āni (*bhava-°, *q. v.*) Dh. 351; *°-santhana, *n.*, "the removal of the thorns" (*metaph.*) Dh. 275. *cp. next.*

salla-katta, *m.* (*sa.* çalya-karttṛ) a surgeon; *acc.* ~aṁ, 92,8.

sallakkheti, *vb.* (*sa.* saṁ-√laksh) to notice, observe. think of, consider (*acc.*); *ger.* ~etvā, 84,17; a-sallakkhetvā (taṁ kāraṇaṁ) 3,18; (*w. gen.* tassā) 89,5.

sallapati, *vb.* (*sa.* saṁ-√lap) to talk together, converse, speak to, address; *part. m.* ~anto (tena saddhiṁ) 13,34; *f.* ~antī, 73,4. *cp. next.*

sallāpa, *m.* (*sa.* saṁlāpa) conversation; allāpa-⁰, *m.* id., *acc.* ~aṁ, 56,22; *kathā-⁰, *m.* id., *instr.* ~ena, 94,22.

sallīna, *mfn.* (*sa.* saṁ-līna, *pp.* saṁ-√lī) bent down, depressed; *a-sallīna, *mfn.* (*v. h.*).

savati, *vb.* (*sa.* √sru) to flow, stream; *pr. 3. pl.* ~anti (sotā) Dh. 340; *cp.* savana², sota².

savana[1], *n.* (*sa.* çravaṇa) hearing, learning; dhamma-⁰, sad-dhamma-⁰ (*q. v.*); su-ssavana, *n.* (*v.* su-⁰).

savana[2], *n.* (*sa.* sravaṇa) flowing, streaming; *manāpa-⁰, *mfn.* (*v. h.*).

savhaya, *mfn.* (*e. c.*) (*fr.* sa¹ + avhaya; *sa.* sāhvaya) named, called; Ānanda-⁰, *m. acc.* ~aṁ, 109,15.

sasa, *m.* (*sa.* çaça) a hare; *nom.* ~o, Dh. 342; *⁰-paṇḍita, *m.* the wise hare, 14,12; *⁰-yoni, *f.* (*q. v.*); *loc.* ~iyaṁ (nibbattitvā, having been born as a hare) 14,8; *⁰-rāja, *m.* (*v.* rājan); ⁰-lakkhaṇa, *n.* the sign of a hare, *acc.* ~aṁ, 16,16.

sassa, *n.* (rarely *m.*) (*sa.* sasya or çasya) corn, crop; *nom.* ~o, 26,20; *acc.* ~aṁ, 8,5; 26,18 (sampanna-⁰, *q. v.*); *pl.* ~āni, 7,35. 102,7; *⁰-kāraka-manussa, *m.* a husbandman, *pl.* ~ā, 8,7; *⁰-rakkhana, *n.* protection of fields, 8,7 (⁰-atthaṁ).

sassata, *mfn.* (*sa.* çāçvata) eternal; *m.* ~o (loko) 89,24; a-sassato, 89,26 (*q. v.*); *m. pl.* ~ā (saṁkhārā, n'atthi) Dh. 255.

saha, *prp.* (= *sa.*) with, together with, simultaneously with (*instr.* or *abl.*); ~ kheḷena, 57,24; ~ Brahmunā, Dh. 105; ~ parinibbānā (*abl.*) 80,19; *cp. next etc.*

saha-gata, *mfn.* (*e. c.*; = *sa.*) accompanied by; dukkha-⁰, *mfn.* 97,36; nandi-rāga-⁰, *mfn.* 67,13.

***sahanukkama**, *mfn.* (saha + anukkama) together with all pertaining; *n.* ~aṁ (sandānaṁ) Dh. 398.

***saha-semāna**, *mfn.* (*v.* seti [sayati]) lying or reposing with; *acc. f.* ~aṁ (yakkhiniṁ) 112,8.

sahati, *vb.* (*sa.* √sah) to overcome, conquer; to bear, endure (*acc.*); *pr. 3. sg.* ~atī (metri causa) 107,31 = Dh. 335; *part. m.* a-sahanto (dukkhaṁ) 32,26; *pot. 3. pl.* ~eyyuṁ (vuṭṭhiṁ) 104,28; *cp.* sahasā, sāhasa.

Sahampati, *m.* (*Buddh. sa.* Sahāpati) an epithet of Brahman (*cp.* SBE. XIII, p. 86); *nom.* Brahmā ~, 80,21.

sahasā, *indecl.* (= *sa.*) by violence; unexpectedly, inconsiderately; Dh. 256 (atthaṁ naye); *cp.* a-sāhasena.

sahassa, *n.* (*sa.* sahasra) a thousand (*w. nom.* [or *gen.*] *pl.* of the things numbered, or *e. c.*); *nom. acc. sg.* ~aṁ (datvā, 1000 pieces of money) 37,10; (vācā, gāthā) Dh. 100. 101; purisa-⁰, 33,22. 34,9; *instr.* ~ena (at the rate of) 18,28; Dh. 106; amacca-⁰ (saddhiṁ) 39,26; kahāpaṇa-⁰ (do.) 57,32; bhikkhu-⁰ (do.) 70,22; sahassaṁ sahassena mānuse (*acc. pl.*) 1000 times 1000 men, 107,3 = Dh. 103; — *comp. w. other numerals*: sata-sahassaṁ, *n.* 23,3 (vīsaṁ); *pl.* ~āni (cattāri) 61,6; (satt'eva) 109,2; *⁰-agghanaka, *mfn.* (*v. h.*); caturāsīti-vassa-sahassāni, 44,20; asīti-⁰, *mfn.* eighty thousands, *m. pl.* ~ā (bhikkhū) 97,4; — *at the beg. of comp.*: *⁰-kahāpaṇa, *m.* (*sg.*) 1000 pieces of money, *acc.* ~aṁ (imaṁ) 102,25; *⁰-thavikā, *f.* (*q. v.*); *⁰-bhaṇḍikā, *f.* (*q. v.*); ⁰-bhāga, *m.* the thousandth part, or (perhaps better): with 1000 parts; *nom.* ~o (maraṇassa, "is the property of death"; perhaps we ought to correct: sahassabhāge maraṇaṁ, *cp. Windisch*, Māra, p. 4) 103,6; *⁰-matta, *mfn.* being a number of 1000, *m. pl.* ~ā, 39,12; ⁰-mūla, *mfn.* worth a thousand pieces, *acc. m.* ~aṁ (sāṭakaṁ) 31,10; (paṇṇākāraṁ) 58,21; ⁰-vagga, *m.* the eighth chapter of Dh.; *yojana-sahass'-ubbedha, *mfn.* (*v.* ubbedha).

sahāya, *m.* (= *sa.*) a companion, friend; *nom.* ~o, 12,8; *acc.* ~aṁ,

47,30. Dh. 328; *gen.* ~assa, 12,34; *pl.* ~ā, 11,27. *cp. next etc.*

sahāyaka, *m.* (= *sa.*) = *prec.*; *nom.* ~o, 79,24; *gen.* ~assa, ib.; *gen. pl.* ~ānaṁ, 55,29.

sahāyatā, *f.* (= *sa.*) companionship; *nom.* ~ā (n'atthi bāle) Dh. 61. 330.

*sahāyikā, *f.* (*fr.* sahāyaka) a female companion or friend; *voc.* ~e, 58,31; *instr. pl.* ~āhi, 57,34.

sahita, *mfn.* (= *sa.*) [1]) joined, connected, sensible (?); *n.* ~aṁ (bahuṁ, bhāsamāno, speaking many sensible words?) Dh. 19 (*cp. Childers* sub voce, SBE. X. p. 8); [2]) *e. c.* accompanied by, endowed with (*cp.* saṁhita).

sā, *f. pron. demonstr.*, *v.* taṁ [1].

sākuṇika, *m.* (*sa.* sākunika) a fowler, bird-catcher; *instr.* ~ena, 88,33 (chekena).

Sākha, *m.* (*sa.* çākha-[0]), *nom. pr.* of a deer ("Branch-deer", *cp. next*); *acc.* ~aṁ, 7,33; *loc.* ~asmiṁ, 7,34; [0]-miga, *m.* id. (*sa.* [0]-mṛga). *nom.* ~o, 5,31; *dvandva comp.* Nigrodhamiga-[0], 6,9 (*gen. pl.*).

sākhā, *f.* (*sa.* çākhā) a branch; *nom.* ~ā (sāla-[0]) 62,17; *acc.* ~aṁ, 62,19; *loc.* ~āya, 13,13; ~āyaṁ (sāla-[0]) 62,17; *pl.* ~ā (sākhāhi, *instr.*, branch with branch) 37,20; 62,11 (agga-[0], *q. v.*); sākhagge, sākhaggesu, on the top of the branch(es), 13,22; 1,25 (*cp.* agga [4]); sākhantarehi, 62,11 (*v.* antara); [0]-palāsa, *n. dvandva comp.* branches and leaves, 95,22; apagata-[0], *mfn.* 95,25 (*v.* apagacchati).

sāṭaka, *m.* (*sa.* çāṭaka) cloth; dress, clothes; robe, skirt, gown; *nom.* ~o, 87,11 (*v. corrections*); *acc.* ~aṁ, 31,4-10. 50,23. 57,32; 50,13 (ghana-[0], *q. v.*); *instr.* ~ena, 50,19; *loc.* ~e, 58,29; *pl.* ~ā, 45,1; *acc. pl.* ~e, 41,4; *camma-[0], *m.* (*q. v.*).

sāṭī (or sāṭikā), *f.* (*sa.* çāṭī; *cp. prec.*) a robe, skirt, gown; *ajina-[0], *f.* (*q. v.*); *sāṇa-[0], *f.* (*q. v.*).

sāṭṭhakathā, *v.* sa [1].

sāṇa, *mfn.* (*sa.* çāṇa) made of hemp; *[0]-sāṭī-nivattha, *mfn.* wearing a skirt or tunic of hempen cloth, *m.* ~o, 71,29.

sāṇi, *f.* (*sa.* çāṇī) cloth of hemp (used for tents or curtains); *acc.* ~iṁ (curtain) 62,20; *instr.* ~iyā, 112,8; *paṭa-[0], *f.* 37,3 (*q. v.*).

sāta, *n.* (*sa.* çāta) joy, pleasure; *a-sāta, *mfn.* (*q. v.*); *[0]-sita, *mfn.* bound to pleasure, given up to pleasure, *pl.* ~ā, Dh. 341.

*sātacca-kārin, *mfn.* (*sa.* *sātatya-[0]; *cp.* satataṁ *above*) persevering; *m. pl.* ~ino (*w. loc.* kicce) Dh. 293.

*sātatika, *mfn.* (*fr. sa.* satata) = *prec.*; *m. pl.* ~ā, Dh. 23.

sātthaka, *mfn.* (*sa.* sārthaka) useful, successful, beneficial; *f.* ~ikā (desanā) 86,10. 87,2. 89,3.

sāda, *m.* (*sa.* svāda) taste; *appassāda, *mfn.* Dh. 186 (*v. h.*).

*sādāna, *mfn.* (*sa.* sa + ādāna) *v.* sa-[1].

sādhana, *n.* (= *sa.*) accomplishment, establishment, demonstration; [0]-atthaṁ, 31,11 ("in order to enforce this truth").

sādhayati, or sādheti, *vb.* (*sa.* √sādh, *caus.* sādhayati) to direct, set right, accomplish, prepare (*acc.*); *ger.* ~ayitvāna (bhattāni) 111,33.

sādhāraṇa, *mfn.* (= *sa.*) common, belonging to all; *instr. n.* ~ena (rajjena) 59,25.

sādhu, [1]) *mfn.* (= *sa.*) good, excellent, right, honorable; *n.* ~u (hoti) 2,30; *acc.* ~uṁ (sādhunā [*instr.*] jeti, "pays good with goodness") 44,2 (*cp.* a-sādhu); *m.* ~u (damatho) Dh. 35; *instr. pl.* ~uhi (therehi) 109,13; *gen. pl.* ~ūnaṁ (sabba-[0], all good men) 114,3. – [2]) *indecl.* [a]) *adv.* well, rightly; ~ jānāsi, 98,24; [b]) *interj.* very well! well done! ~ū'ti (sampaṭicchitvā) 1,18; 5,1. 53,16; (paṭisuṇitvā) 16,26; *w. foll. voc.* sādhu deva! 65,17; *repeated*: sādhu sādhu Nāgasena! 98,34. *cp. next etc.*

*sādhukaṁ, *adv.* (*fr.* sādhu [2])

well, rightly, properly, thoroughly; 82,21. 110,25.

sādhu-kāra, *m.* (= *sa.*) approval; ~aṁ dadāti, to consent, applaud, 5,19. 34,27. 87,1. 98,18.

*__sādhu-rūpa__, *mfn.* respectable, comely, sympathetic; *m.* ~o (naro) Dh. 262.

*__sādhu-vihārin__; *mfn.* living righteously; *m. acc.* ⁰-vihāri (formally in one word with the foll. dhīraṁ) instead of ⁰-vihāriṁ (or ⁰-vihārinaṁ) Dh. 328–29.

sāma, *mfn.* (*sa.* çyāma) dark-coloured; *m.* ~o (puriso) 92,13.

*__sāmaṁ__, *indecl.* (*pron.*), self, one's self (said of all persons) (= sayaṁ, to which it seems to be related in some way; possibly from *sayamaṁ, 'ipsissimum', Tr. ?); 6,19 (~ gantvā āneti); 68,31 (sāmaṁ yeva); 85,28 (sāman 'ti sayam eva).

sāmaggi, *f.* (*fr.* samagga; *sa.* sāmagrī) [1]) totality, complete collection, completeness; [2]) concord, harmony; *nom.* ~ī (saṁghassa) Dh. 194.

sāmañña, [1]) *n.* (*fr.* samaṇa, *q. v.*; *sa.* çrāmaṇya) the state of a samaṇa, asceticism; *nom.* ~aṁ (dupparāmaṭṭhaṁ) Dh. 311; *gen.* ~assa, Dh. 19; *cp. next.* – [2]) *mfn.* (*sa.* sāmānya) common; *n.* community.

*__sāmaññatā__, *f.* = sāmañña [1]; Dh. 332.

sāmaṇera, *m.* (*sa.* çrāmaṇera) a Buddhist monk in his noviciate, pupil, novice; *nom.* ~o, 81,15; *pl.* ~ā, 81,14; *acc.* ~e, 81,17; *instr.* ~ehi, 81,21; *gen.* ~ānaṁ, 81,18.

sāmatthiya, *n.* (*fr.* samattha; *sa.* sāmarthya) ability, competence, qualification; *acc.* ~aṁ (tava dassehi) 114,9.

sāmanta, *mfn.* (*fr.* samanta; = *sa.*) being on all sides, near; *n.* neighbourhood; *abl.* (*adv.* & *prp.*) ~ā, near, round (*w. gen.* (*acc.*) or *e. c.*): āpatti-⁰, 83,4 (*v. h.*).

sāmika, *m.* (*fr. next*; *sa.* ⁰svāmika) an owner, lord, husband; *nom.* ~o, 14,26. 100,18 (amba-⁰). 100,26 (khetta-⁰); 10,10; *acc.* ~aṁ, 10,5; *gen.* ~assa, 58,5; *loc.* ~amhi, 31,9; *pl. acc.* ~e, 21,22; *gen.* ~ānaṁ, 21,10; *comp.* *⁰-acchādana, *n.* (*v. h.*); *rajja-⁰, *m.* king, 43,22-23 (Bārāṇasi-⁰, Kosala-⁰); *sa-ssāmika, *mfn.*, *v.* sa-[1].

sāmin, *m.* (*sa.* svāmin) an owner, master, lord, husband; *nom.* ~ī, 87,6; *voc.* sāmi, 1,7. 5,14. 7,15, *etc.* (at the beginning, after the opening word, or at the end of the sentence); *gen.* [a]) sāmino, 112,9; [b]) sāmissa (Dhamma-⁰, *q. v.*) 114,6; *pl.* ~ino, 43,31. *cp. next* & *prec.*

sāminī, *f.* (*sa.* svāminī) mistress, lady; *nom.* ~ī. 111,5.

*__sāmukkaṁsika__, *mfn.* (*Buddh. sa.* sāmutkarshika; *cp.* samukkaṁsati, *vb.*) most excellent, most essential (or principal); *f.* ~ā (dhammadesanā buddhānaṁ) 68,28; *acc. m.* ~aṁ (sabba-⁰, pañhaṁ) 90,25. [*cp.* SBE. XIII, p. XXVI.]

sāyaṁ, *adv.* (= *sa.*) in the evening, at evening time; 2,24. 57,9. 73,11; ajja .. ~ .. eva, even this very evening, 2,30. *cp. next etc.*

sāyaṇha, *m.* (*sa.* sāyāhna) evening: ⁰-samaye (*loc.*) 2,32. 14,11.

sāyataraṁ, *adv.* (*compar.*; *sa.* sāyatare) late or later in the evening, 57,14.

sāyam-āsa, *m.* (*sa.* sāyam-āça) evening meal, supper; *acc.* ~aṁ (bhuñjantassa) 53,29.

sāyikā, *f.* (*sa.* çāyikā) lying, sleeping; *v.* thaṇḍila-⁰, Dh. 141.

sāyin, *mfn.* (*sa.* çāyin) lying; *v.* samparivatta-⁰, Dh. 325.

sāra, *m.* (= *sa.*) strength; the essential part of anything, a precious thing, reality, quintessence; *loc.* ~e (patiṭṭhito) 95,24; *acc.* & *abl.* sāraṁ sārato ñatvā, knowing what is essential in its essence, Dh. 12; – *sāra-mati(*n*), *mfn.* imagining to find the essence; *pl.* ~ino (asāre) Dh. 11; *cp.* a-sāra; – *e. c.* maṇi-⁰, mutta-⁰, choice gems, pearls, 24,20; vajira-°, 26,1. (*cp.* ratana).

*sāratta-ratta, *mfn.* (*sa.* *saṁrakta-rakta) passionately enamoured or devoted to; *f.* ~ā (apekhā, "passionately strong") Dh. 345.

sārathi, *m.* (= *sa.*) a charioteer; *nom. voc.* ~i, 43,20-21; *acc.* ~iṁ, 63,2. 106,24 = Dh. 222; *instr.* ~inā, Dh. 94.

sārada, *mfn.* (*sa.* çārada) autumnal, mature, new, fresh (not too old; *cp.* Mil. transl. II. p. 79, note 2, where it is taken = sāra-da, which can hardly be possible); – *m. subst.* (= sarada) autumn; *loc.* ~e, Dh. 149.

sāradika, *mfn.* (*sa.* çāradika) autumnal; *acc.* ~aṁ (kumudaṁ) Dh. 285.

sārambha, *m.* (*sa.* saṁrambha) quarrel, brawling; abuse, brutality; anger, fury; *nom.* ~o, Dh. 134; *°-kathā, *f.* abusive or angry speech, Dh. 133.

*sārāṇiya, *mfn.* (either from √sṛ, *caus.* kathaṁ sāreti, *cp.* vītisāreti & Tr. PM. 75,22, or from √smṛ, *Childers*) usual, customary, traditional (or introductory ?); *acc. f.* ~aṁ (sammodanīyaṁ kathaṁ, the usual (introductory) compliments) 89,20-21.

sārin, *mfn.* (= *sa.*) flowing, running, wandering about; *in the comp.* anoka-°, *mfn.*, *v.* an-oka.

Sāriputta, *m.* (*Buddh. sa.* Çāriputra) *nom. pr.* of one of Buddha's most famous pupils; *nom.* ~o, 29,18; *gen.* ~assa (āyasmato) 81,11; °-Moggallānā, *m. pl.* (*dvandva*) 74,26-30.

sāla, *m.* (*sa.* çāla) the Sāl tree (shorea robusta); *acc.* ~aṁ, Dh. 162; °-rukkha, *m.* id. 61,11 (mahā-); 95,21; °-vana, *n.*, a grove of sāl trees, 62,10 (maṅgala-°), 62,15 (°-kiḷaṁ), 62,16; °-sākhā, *f.* 62,17 (*q. v.*) *cp. next.*

sālā, *f.* (*comp.* also sāla-°; *sa.* çālā) a house, mansion, workshop; *acc.* ~aṁ, 87,10; 88,5 (pesakāra-°, *q. v.*); sāla-dvārena (gacchanti, pass by the house-door) 59,3; *cp.* assa-°, dāna-°, paṇṇa-°, hatthi-°.

sāli, *m.* (*sa.* çāli) rice, paddy, grains of rice; *acc.* ~iṁ, 100,23; 22,1 (sayaṁ-jāta-°, *q. v.*); *°-yava-khetta, *n.* 8,18 (*q. v.*).

sālohita, *m.* (*Buddh. sa.* id.; *fr. sa.* sa-lohita) a kinsman; *pl.* ~ā (ñāti-°, *dvandva*, "relatives and kinsmen") 92,8.

sāvaka, *m.* (*sa.* çrāvaka) "a hearer", a disciple, pupil, *esp.* a believing Buddhist; *nom.* ~o (sammāsambuddha-°) Dh. 59; *pl.* ~ā (Gotamassa) 73,26. Dh. 296 ff.; *acc. pl.* ~e, 104,8. 108,20; *gen. pl.* ~ānaṁ, 90,16; 74,18 (Gotama-°); *ariya-°, *m.* (*v. h.*).

Sāvatthi, *f.* (*sa.* Çrāvastī) *nom. pr.* of a city, the capital of North-Kosala (the exact position of which seems to be rather doubtful; according to Dhpd. (1855) p. 232 seven yojanas north of Sāketa (Oudh ?)); *nom.* ~i, 81,8; *loc.* ~iyaṁ, 29,24; °-vāsino, *m. pl.* the inhabitants of S., 73,32.

*sāvanā, *f.* (*sa.* çrāvaṇa, *n.*) announcement, proclamation; *acc. pl.* ~ā, 11,4; tatiya-sāvanāya (*instr.*) 11,5; *cp.* savana.

sāveti, *vb.* (*caus.* suṇāti; *sa.* çrāvayati) to cause to be heard, teach; to announce, proclaim (*acc.*); *part. m. gen.* ~entassa, 11,4; *aor. 3. sg.* ~esi ("made a proclamation") 11,4; 64,22 (su-ssavanaṁ); *ger.* ~etvā (sa-nāmaṁ) 111,22; *cp.* sāvanā, *f.*

sāsana, *n.* (*sa.* çāsana) 1) order, instruction, message; *nom. acc.* ~aṁ, 36,22. 64,6; 2) teaching, doctrine, religion; *nom.* 110,5-24. Dh. 183. 185 (Buddhāna ~); 109,32 (Satthu-°); *loc.* ~e (Satthu) 69,14; 109,6 (Jina-°, *q. v.*); Kassapassa Bhagavato sāsane, at the time when K. B. preached his doctrine, 84,28; *sāsana-kāraka, *m.* one who acts according to the order or doctrine, *pl.* ~ā (mama) 104,9; *sāsanâraha, *mfn.* worthy of the sacred doctrine, 110,8 (*cp.* araha).

sāsapa, *m.* (*sa.* sarshapa) a mustard-seed; *nom.* ~o, Dh. 401.

sāhasa, *n.* (= *sa.*) violence, cruelty; *v.* a-sāhasa.

si = asi, *v.* atthi.

sikkhati, *vb.* (*sa.* √çiksh) to learn, study (*acc.*); to practise or exercise oneself (in : *loc.*); *pr. 3. sg.* ~ati (sippaṁ) 99,12; *grd. n.* ~itabbaṁ (kattha amhehi ~, in what have we to exercise ourselves?) 81,20; *inf.* ~ituṁ (tesu, used in a passive sense *w. instr.* sāmaṇerehi) 81,21; *pp.* sikkhita, learned, studied; trained, educated; *m.* ~o, 99,12; su-sikkhita, *mfn.* (*v.* su-⁰); *caus. v.* *sikkhāpeti, *cp.* sekha & *next.*

sikkhāpada, *n.* (*sa.* çikshā-pada) a moral precept; *nom.* ~aṁ, 81,15; *pl.* ~āni, 79,19. 81,19; (dasa) 81,21.

***sikkhāpana**, *n.* (*nom. actionis fr. next*) the giving instruction; ⁰-atthāya. "in order to give (her) a lesson", 53,8.

***sikkhāpeti**, *vb.* (*caus.* sikkhati) to cause to learn, train, instruct (*acc.*); *aor. 3. sg.* ~esi (paricārikaṁ) 51,13; *ger.* ~etvā, 18,18; *cp.* *sikkhāpana.

sikkhita, *mfn.*, *v.* sikkhati.

sikhā, *f.* (*sa.* çikhā) a lock of hair, crest; a flame; aggi-⁰, *f.* 107,1 (*q. v.*), *cp. next.*

sikhin, *mfn.* (*sa.* çikhin) having locks, crests or flames; *m.* ¹) fire; ²) a peacock; *gen.* ~ino, 18,33 (= morassa).

sigāla, *m.* (*sa.* sṛgāla) a jackal; *nom.* ~o, 14,10.

siṅga, *n.* (*sa.* çṛṅga) the horn of an animal; *instr.* ~ena, 12,31; *pl.* ~āni, 5,26.

siṅghāṇikā, *f.* (*sa.* çṛṅkhāṇikā, siṅghāṇikā) the mucus of the nose, 82,5. 97,23.

siñcati, *vb.* (*sa.* √sic) to besprinkle, water; to pour out, empty, bale out (a ship, *acc.*); *pr. 3. pl.* ~anti, 37,1; *imper. 2. sg.* ~a (nāvaṁ) Dh. 369; *pp.* sitta (*v. below*); *caus.* *siñcāpeti, to water; *aor. 3. sg.* ~esi (aṭṭhiṁ khīrodakena) 36,36.

sita, *mfn.* (= *sa.*) bound; *v.* sāta-⁰.

sitta, *mfn.* (*pp.* siñcati; *sa.* sikta) poured out, emptied; *f.* ~ā (nāvā) Dh. 369.

sittha, *n.* (*sa.* siktha) a grain or lump of boiled rice; *nom.* ~aṁ (ekaṁ) 53,29; *pl.* ~āni, 56,28.

sithila, *mfn.* (*sa.* çithila; *cp.* saṭhila *above*) loose, relaxed; *m.* ~o (paṁsu) 40,34; *n.* ~aṁ (bandhanaṁ, yielding, elastic?) Dh. 346; ⁰-bhāva, *m.* the being loosened, *acc.* ~aṁ, 40,26. *cp. next.*

***sithila-hanu**, (*m.*) lit. 'loose-jaw', name of a certain bird; *gen.* ~uno, 92,20.

Siddhattha, *m.* (*sa.* Siddhārtha) *nom. pr.* of Gotama Buddha before his pabbajjā; ⁰-kumāro, 64,26; ⁰-kumārassa, 63,7.

siddhi, *f.* (= *sa.*) accomplishment, success, prosperity, result; siddhi-r-astu, 114,25.

***Sineru**, *m. nom. pr.* of a mythical mountain (*sa.* Meru, or Sumeru, of which sineru is possibly only a variation; the short forms Neru and Meru are also found in Pāli); *nom.* ~u, 110,10; *acc.* ~uṁ, 60,3; *gen.* ~ussa, 59,27; ⁰-papāta, *m.* (*q. v.*).

sineha, *m.* (*sa.* sneha) affection, love, attachment; *acc.* ~aṁ, Dh. 285.

sinehita, *mfn.* (*sa.* snehita) connected with love or lust; *n. pl.* ~āni (somanassāni) Dh. 341.

sindhava, *m.* (*sa.* saindhava) 'coming from Indus or Sindh', a horse; *nom.* ~o, 54,24; *pl.* ~ā (rathe yutta-⁰) 54,9. Dh. 322; *acc. pl.* ~e (maṅgala-⁰, *q. v.*) 63,5.

sinna, *mfn.* (*sa.* svinna, *pp.* √svid) wet, sweating, wet with perspiration; *n.* ~aṁ (cīvaraṁ) 83,8; *cp.* sedita.

sippa, *n.* (*sa.* çilpa) art, discipline, learning; *acc.* ~aṁ (uggaṇhāti) 32,13; (sikkhati) 99,12; *gen.* ~assa (upacāro, *q. v.*) 55,7; *loc. pl.* ~esu (sabba-⁰, all branches of learning) 38,10;

niyyāmaka-⁰, *n.* 24,13 (*q. v.*); *dvandva comp.* vijjā-⁰ (*v. h.*) *cp. next.*

sippavat, *mfn.* (*sa.* çilpa-vat) skilled in art (or science), well-educated; *nom. m.* ~vā, 99,8.

sibbati, *vb.* (*sa.* √siv) to sew (*acc.*); *fut. 1. sg.* ~issāmi, 57,5; *grd. n.* ~itabbaṁ (kiñci) 57,3.

simbali, *m.* or *f.* (*sa.* çālmali, *cp.* simbala) the silk-cotton tree; *loc.* ~ismiṁ, 60,16 (= Simbali-vane); *Simbali-vana, *n.* name of a forest in heaven, 60,6-11.

siyā, *pot.*, *v.* atthi.

siras, *n.* (*sa.* çiras) the head; *nom.* siro (phalitaṁ) Dh. 260; *instr.* sirasā (nipatitvā) 75,22; *loc.* sirasmiṁ, 44,22; *cp.* sīsa.

sirī (*comp.* siri-⁰), *f.* (*sa.* çrī) beauty, welfare, success, glory, dignity, majesty, *etc.*; *acc.* ~iṁ (rūpa-⁰, "beauty and majesty") 64,18; generally at the beg. of *subst. comp.*: *siri-gabbha, *m.* a royal bed-chamber, 41,22. 61,8; *⁰-vibhava, *m.* majestic power, 47,22; *⁰-sayana, *n.* a royal bed, *loc.* ~e, 53,3. 64,28; ⁰-piṭṭhe, 41,25; *⁰-sobhagga, *n.* majestic glory, *instr.* ~ena, 64,10.

***Sirisavatthu**, *n.* (*sa.* *çirīsha-vastu) *nom. pr.* of a fabulous town; *nom.* ~u (yakkha-puraṁ) 112,12; ~uṁ (yakkha-nagaraṁ, Tambapaṇṇidīpe) 20,32.

silā, *f.* (*sa.* çilā) a stone, rock; *acc.* ~aṁ, 75,35; paṇḍu-kambala-⁰, *f.* a sort of stone, of which Sakka's throne (paṇḍu-kambala-silâsana, *n.* 15,8) is said to be made (*cp.* āsana). *cp.* sela, *m.*

siloka, *m.* (*sa.* çloka) fame, reputation, praise; a verse; *nom.* ~o, 103,29.

sivikā, *f.* (*sa.* çibikā, çivikā) a palanquin, litter; *loc.* ~āya (sovaṇṇa-⁰) 62,7.

sīgha, *mfn.* (*sa.* çīghra) quick, rapid; *n.* (*adv.*) ~aṁ, quickly, 63,17. 111,32; 87,12 (sīgham eva); — *comp.* sīgh'-assa, *m.* a race-horse, Dh. 29.

sīta, *mfn.* (*sa.* çīta) cold, cool; *n.* ~aṁ (odakaṁ) 15,26; *⁰-cchāya, *mfn.* yielding cool shadow, *n.* ~aṁ (manoramaṁ) 15,25; — *subst. n.* ~aṁ, coolness; cold water, 83,35 (*opp.* uṇhaṁ); *instr.* ~ena, ib.; *cp. next.*

sītala, *mfn.* (*sa.* çītala) cold, cool; *n.* ~aṁ (sarīraṁ), 21,26; *ati-sītala, *mfn.* (*q. v.*).

sītibhūta, *mfn.* (*sa.* çītī-bhūta) become cold, *metaph.* tranquillized; *acc. m.* ~aṁ, Dh. 418.

sīmā, *f.* (*sa.* sīmā, *f.* & sīman, *m.*) boundary, border, limit; *acc.* ~aṁ, 39,17; *abl.* ~ato (paccanta⁰-, *q. v.*) 43,14; *sīmantarikā, *f.* 40,32 (*v.* antarikā).

sīla, *n.* (*sa.* çīla) ¹) morality, virtue; *acc.* ~aṁ, 15,1. 48,26; *loc.* ~e, 17,32; 29,2 (attanā rakkhita-⁰); *comp.* *sīlācāra, *sīlaguṇācāra, *m.* (*v.* ācāra); *sīlānisaṁsa, *m.* (*v.* ānisaṁsa); *⁰-kathā, *f.* the duties of morality, *acc.* ~aṁ (pakāsesi) 68,19; *⁰-gandha, *m.* "the perfume of virtue", Dh. 55; *⁰-teja, *m.* "splendid display of virtue", *instr.* ~ena, 15,7; sīlabbata, *v. below*; *⁰-saṁvuta, *mfn.* well behaved, Dh. 289; *⁰-sampanna, *mfn.* virtuous, 41,35. 42,18 = *sampanna-sīla, *mfn.* Dh. 57; *dvandva comp.* ⁰-dassana, Dh. 217 (⁰-sampanna, *mfn.* possessing virtue and intelligence); paññā-⁰, Dh. 229 (⁰-samāhita, *mfn.*). — ²) moral precept, *esp. pl.* pañca sīlāni (= the first five of the dasa sikkhāpadāni, 81,21); *loc. pl.* pañcasu ~esu, 7,24. — ³) nature, quality (good or bad), mostly *e. c.*; *v.* *kujjhana-⁰, *dus-⁰, *dhorayha-⁰, *mfn.* (*cp. next etc.*).

***sīlabbata**, *n.* (*sa.* *çīla-vrata) mere ceremonial practices or rites (probably ironically said of brahmanical rites); ⁰-mattena, Dh. 271 ("not only by discipline and vows", *cp.* matta ²). (*cp. Childers s. v.* & Dhamma-saṅgaṇi, transl. by *C. Rhys Davids*, p. 260–61).

sīlavat, *mfn.* (*sa.* çīlavat) moral, virtuous; *nom. m.* ~vā, 15,31. 99,9;

acc. m. ∼vantaṁ, Dh. 400; *gen. pl.* ∼vataṁ, Dh. 56; at the beg. of *comp.* sīlava-⁰ : *Sīlava-kumāra, *m. nom. pr.* of a prince, 38,9; *Sīlava-[mahā-]rājan, *m.* = Mahāsīlava (*q. v.*) 40,4-5.

sīlavanta, *mfn.* = *prec.*; *gen. m.* ∼assa, Dh. 110; *compar.* sīlavantatara, *gen. m.* ∼assa, 43,32.

sīlin, *mfn.* (*sa.* çīlin) virtuous (only *e. c.*); *v.* abhivādana-⁰.

sīsa, *n.* (*sa.* çīrshan) the head; *acc.* ∼aṁ, 5,12. 65,15; *instr.* ∼ena, 36,3. 57,12. *abl.* ∼ato, 46,28; *loc.* ∼e, 46,28; ∼amhi, 47,1; ⁰-ccheda, *m.* cutting off the head, *acc.* ∼aṁ, 17,7; *kāka-⁰, *mfn.* & Gayā-⁰, *n.* (*v. h.*); *cp.* ussīsaka, *n.* & *pācīna-sīsaka, *mfn.*

sīha, *m.* (*sa.* siṁha) a lion; *nom.* ∼o, 8,22. 13,22; *acc.* ∼aṁ, 10,2. 112,31; *gen.* ∼assa, 8,27. 13,10; ⁰-camma, *n.* (*q. v.*) *cp. next etc.*

*sīha-pañjara, *n.* (*cp.* pañjara) a window; *loc.* ∼e, 46,1.

Sīhabāhu, *m.* (*sa.* Siṁha-bāhu) *nom. pr.* of a king, father of Vijaya (*q. v.*); 112,31; ⁰-narinda-ja, *m.* son of king S. (Vijaya), 110,22.

Sīhala, *m.* (*sa.* Siṁhala) Ceylon; *pl.* ∼ā, the people of Ceylon, 112,32; ∼o (*m. sg.*) = Sīhabāhu (sīham ādinnavā iti, *i. e.* so called on account of his having split a lion) 112,31-32; — *⁰-aṭṭhakathā, *f.* & *⁰-bhāsā, *f.* (*v. h.*).

Sīhasena, *m.* (*sa.* Siṁhasena) *nom. pr.* of a man; *nom.* ∼o, 97,1.

su-, *indecl.* (= *sa.*) prefix to *subst.*, implying the sense of 'good, right, excellent', or to *adj.* & *adv.*, 'well, rightly, very, greatly, beautifully, easily', *etc.* (*opp.* du- (dur-)); before vowels sv- (or suv-) *cp.* svākkhāta *below*, or contracted, *cp.* sotthi.

su-kaṭa (or su-kata), *mfn.* well done (*opp.* dukkaṭa, *q. v.*) 97,14; *n.* a good deed, Dh. 314. — ⁰-kara, *mfn.* easy to do, Dh. 163. — ⁰-kumāra, *mfn.* very tender or delicate, *f. pl. gen.* ∼ānaṁ, 47,14 (= sukhumāla, *q. v. separately*). — sukha, *v. sep.* — ⁰-gata, *mfn.* wellfaring, Dh. 419; Sugata, *m. nom. pr.* = Buddha, 72,24; *instr.* ∼ena, Dh. 285; *loc.* ∼e, 105,25. — ⁰-gati, *f.* (sometimes spelt suggati after the analogy of duggati) happiness, bliss, 77,4; *acc.* ∼iṁ, 7,26. 77,5. 89,1; 107,27 = Dh. 18 (-gg-). — *⁰-gatin, *mfn.* righteous, *pl.* ∼ino, Dh. 126. — ⁰-gandha, *mfn.* fragrant, *f.* ∼ā, 53,27; ⁰-gandhaka, *mfn.* id.; *f.* ∼ikā, fragrant substance (?) 41,13 (pañca-sugandhika-parivāra, *mfn.*). — ⁰-gahaṇa, *n.* 4,35 (*q. v.*). — ⁰-gahita, *mfn.* firmly seized or held, *acc.* ∼aṁ, 4,30 *etc.* — ⁰-carita, *mfn.* good, right; *acc. m.* ∼aṁ (dhammaṁ, righteousness, virtue) Dh. 168; *n.* good conduct, 86,8 (vacī-⁰, *q. v.*); Dh. 231. — ⁰-citta, *mfn.* (*v.* citta [2]). — *⁰-cchanna, *mfn.* well thatched, *acc.* ∼am (agāraṁ) Dh. 14 = 106,31. — ⁰-jīva, *mfn.* easy to live, *n.* ∼aṁ (jīvitaṁ) Dh. 244 (*w. instr.*). — ⁰-tanu, *mfn.* having a very slender or beautiful body, *acc. f.* ∼uṁ (kumāriṁ) 47,19. — ⁰-danta, *mfn.* well tamed, restrained; *m.* ∼o, Dh. 159; *n.* ∼aṁ (cittaṁ) 105,2; *instr.* ∼ena, Dh. 323; *m. pl.* ∼ā (assā) Dh. 94. — ⁰-dassa, *mfn.* easily perceived, *n.* ∼aṁ, 106,16 = Dh. 252. — ⁰-duttara, *mfn.* very difficult to be passed, *n.* ∼aṁ (Maccudheyyaṁ) Dh. 86. — ⁰-duddasa, *mfn.* very difficult to be observed, *n.* ∼aṁ (cittaṁ) Dh. 36. — ⁰-dullabha, *mfn.* very difficult to be found, 51,30. — *⁰-desita, *mfn.* well shown, well taught, *n.* ∼aṁ (dhammapadaṁ) Dh. 44. — *⁰-dhammatā, *f.* honesty (or generosity ?) *loc.* ∼āya, 1,22. — *⁰-nipuṇa, *mfn.* very skilful, very subtile, *n.* ∼aṁ (cittaṁ) Dh. 36. — *⁰-nivattha, *mfn.* carefully dressed, 63,30. — ⁰-paṭicchanna, *mfn.* well protected, 110,14. — ⁰-paṇṇa, *v. below sep.* — ⁰-patiṭṭhita, *mfn.* standing firm; *m.* ∼o, 110,10; *f.* ∼ā, Dh. 333; *acc.* ∼aṁ (satiṁ) 104,7; *comp.* *⁰-citta, *mfn.* firm-minded, *pl.* ~ā, 91,7. — *°-parikkhitta, *mfn.* well covered or overspread. *n.* ~aṁ (sayanaṁ) 112,3. — *°-parimaṇḍalaṁ, *adv.* completely, 113,7. — *°-parisaṁvuta, *mfn.* well controlled, *pl.* ~ā, Dh. 234. — *°-pāruta, *mfn.* 63,30 (*v. h.*). — °-pesala, *mfn.* very handsome or skilful, *m.* ~o, 30,8. — °-ppabuddhaṁ, *adv.* ~ pabujjhanti, "are well awake", Dh. 296. — °-ppahāra, *m.* a well dealt blow, *acc.* ~aṁ, 30,18. — *°-bbata, *mfn.* pious, virtuous, dutiful, *m.* ~o, Dh. 95; *pl.* ~ā, 104,2. (*cp.* vata[2]). — subha, *v. below sep.* — *°-bhaṇa, *mfn.* well spoken, salutary (*synon.* niyyānika), *n.* ~aṁ (giraṁ) 9,31. (*cp.* bhaṇati). — °-bhaddaka, *mfn.* 30,8 (*v. h.*). — °-bhāvita, *mfn.* well developed or cultivated, *n.* ~aṁ (cittaṁ) 106,32 = Dh. 14. — °-bhāsita, *mfn.* well spoken, *f.* ~ā (vācā) Dh. 51. — °-majjha, *mfn.* having a slender waist, *acc. f.* ~aṁ (kumāriṁ) 47,19. — °-mana, *mfn.* well pleased, cheerful, *m.* ~o, Dh. 68 (*cp.* somanassa & mana(*s*)). — °-manā, *f.*, *v. below sep.* — °-medha, *mfn.* wise, *acc. m.* ~aṁ, Dh. 208 (*cp.* medhā). — °-medhasa, *mfn.* wise, *m.* ~o, Dh. 29. — °-rakkhita, *mfn.* well protected, Dh. 157. — *°-laddha, *mfn.* well obtained, *n.* ~aṁ, "a high bliss", 70,8. — °-vaṇṇa, *v. below sep.* — *°-vavatthāpita, *mfn.* (*v.* vavatthāpeti). — °-vinīta, *mfn.* well disciplined, *f.* ~ā (parisā) 40,3. — °-vibhatta, *mfn.* well arranged, 110,14. — *°-vimuttacitta, *mfn.* (*v. h.*). — °-saṁvuta, *mfn.* well controlled, Dh. 8. 281. — °-saṁkhata, *mfn.* well constructed, 104,30. — *°-sajjita, *mfn.* well prepared or decorated, 62,14. — °-saṇṭhāna, *mfn.* well formed or made, 105,17. — °-samāraddha, *mfn.* (*q. v.*) well undertaken, well composed, Dh. 293. — °-samāhita, *mfn.* well collected, very intent upon (*loc.*), Dh. 10. 378. — *°-sikkhita, *mfn.* well trained, very skilled or perfect (in: *loc.*) 18,21. 64,29. — °-sukhaṁ, *adv.* very pleasantly, comfortably, happily, Dh. 197. — *°-sedita, *mfn.* well soaked (or heated?) 62,17. — *°-ssavana, *n.* a good lesson, 64,32 (*v.* savana[1]). — °-hajja, *v. sep. below.* — °-hita, *mfn.* very pleased, 41,30.

sumsumāra, *m.* (*sa.* çiçumāra) a crocodile; *nom.* ~o, 1,5; *voc.* ~a (bāla-°) 2,5; *instr.* ~ena, 108,25. (*cp.* kumbhīla). — *f.* sumsumārī, *acc.* ~iṁ, 1,11.

suka, *m.* (*sa.* çuka) a parrot; °-potaka, *m.* a young parrot, *acc. pl.* ~e, 9,11; °-yoni, *f.* 9,7 (*q. v.*).

sukka, *mfn.* (*sa.* çukla) white, bright, pure (good); *acc. m.* ~aṁ (dhammaṁ, "the bright state of life") Dh. 87 (*opp.* kaṇha); *cp. next.*

*sukkaṁsa, *m.* (*fr. sa.* çukla + aṁça, *v.* aṁsa[2]) the good side or point of a person, *acc.* ~aṁ, Dh. 72.

sukha, [1]) *mfn.* (= *sa.*) pleasant, agreeable, happy; *m.* ~o, 80,29. Dh. 118; *f.* ~ā, Dh. 331—32; *n.* ~aṁ, 70,27; °-vihāra, *m.* 74,28 (*v. h.*); *comp.* sukha-saṁvāsa, *m.* Dh. 207 (wrong reading instead of dhīra-saṁvāsa, *v.* saṁvāsa); a-sukha, unpleasant, 70,28 (a-dukkham-°); — [2]) sukhaṁ, *adv.* pleasantly, happily; 5,21 (~am edhati, *q. v.*); Dh. 79 (~seti); 112,5 (nipajji sayane); *comp.* sukha-payāta, *mfn.* 19,27 (*v.* payāti); yathā-sukhaṁ, *adv.* (*v.* yathā); su-sukhaṁ, Dh. 197; — [3]) *n. subst.* ~aṁ (*opp.* dukkhaṁ) happiness, joy, pleasure, 23,17. 103,32; *kāma-°, *n.* (*q. v.*); *mattā-°, *n.* (*q. v.*); *dvandva comp.* sukha-dukkhaṁ (imassa, tava bhāro) 28,30 (*v.* bhāra); vimutti-°, *n.* (*q. v.*); *-kāma, *mfn.* (*v. h.*); °-vagga, *m.* title of Dhpd. ch. XV; °-āvaha, *mfn.* (*v. h.*), *cp. next* & sukhesin.

sukhin, *mfn.* (= *sa.*) possessing happiness, blessed; *m.* ~ī, Dh. 177. 206. 393.

sukhuma, *mfn.* (*sa.* sūkshma) small, fine, light; *m.* ~o (rajo) Dh. 125.

sukhumāla, *mfn.* (= su-kumāra, *q. v.*, through confusion with sukhuma); *m.* a delicately nurtured youth; *nom.* ~o, 67,22; accanta-°, 97,34 (*q. v.*); *khattiya-°, 97,33 (*q. v.*).

sukhesin, *mfn.* (*sa.* sukhaishin) seeking pleasure; *m. pl.* ~ino, Dh. 341.

suñka, *n.* (or *m.*) (*sa.* çulka) price, toll, customs, nuptial gift (for purchase of a bride); *acc.* ~aṁ (datvā) 101,15; *dinna-suñkā, *adj. f.* (a maid) for whom the purchase-money has been paid, 101,20 (mayā).

suci[n], *mfn.* (*sa.* çuci & çucin) clear, bright, pure; *m.* ~ī, 106,9 (= Dh. 393 : sukhī); *°-kamma, *mfn.* whose deeds are pure, *gen. m.* ~assa, Dh. 24; *°-gandha, *mfn.* having a pure scent, *n.* ~aṁ (padumaṁ) Dh. 58; *°-gavesin, *mfn.* looking for what is pure, *instr. m.* ~inā, Dh. 245.

*Sujā, *f. nom. pr.* of Sakka's wife; *acc.* ~aṁ (asura-kaññaṁ) 54,7.

suñña, *mfn.* (*sa.* çūnya) empty, void; °-āgāra, *n.* an empty house, *acc.* ~aṁ, Dh. 373 (*cp.* agāra).

*suññata, *mfn.* (*fr. prec. w. pleonastic ending?*) empty, i. e. indiscriminate or destitute of all characteristics, said of Nibbāna; *m.* ~o (animitto ca vimokho) Dh. 92.

suṭṭhu, *adv.* (*sa.* sushṭu) duly, well; ~ te kataṁ, 15,29; ~ ñatvā, 49,4; ~ paṇḍita-°, 91,24.

suṇāti, *vb.* (*sa.* √çru) to hear, listen to (*acc.*), to hear or learn from (*w. gen.* of the person speaking); *pr. 1. sg.* suṇāmi (dhammaṁ) 87,14; (tassā pāpaṁ) 104,34; *3. pl.* suṇanti (dhammaṁ) 71,21; *part. m.* suṇanto (taṁ, *n.*) 54,23; *imper. 2. sg.* suṇāhi, 22,17; 44,7; *3. pl.* suṇantu (me) 97,3; *aor. 1. pl.* assumha, 54,13; *fut. 1. sg.* sossāmi, 87,16; *inf.* sotuṁ, 65,35. 87,9; *comp.* sotu-kāma, *mfn.* wishing to hear (*acc.*), *f.* ~ā, 87,13; *ger.* sutvā (tassa kathaṁ) 4,18; 49,29; (devassa vassato) 105,22; (tassā) 112,21; sutvāna, Dh. 82. 259; *pass. 3. sg.* suyyati, 27,6 (suyyat'); *pp.* suta (*v. below*); *caus.* sāveti (*q. v.*) *cp.* savana, sāvanā, sāvaka, sota[1].

suta, *mfn.* (*pp.* suṇāti; *sa.* çruta) heard, learnt; *n.* ~aṁ (taṁ no ~, we have heard it) 54,15; (evaṁ me ~, thus I have heard) 66,33. 93,21 (*v. corrections*); ('ti me ~) 78,29; °-divasato, 86,30 (*v.* divasa); *cp.* *appassuta, bahu-ssuta, *mfn.* & *next.*

sutavat, *mfn.* (*sa.* çrutavat) learned, wise; *nom. m.* ~vā, 71,5.

sutta[1], *mfn.* (*pp.* supati; *sa.* supta) sleeping; *acc. m.* ~aṁ (gāmaṁ) Dh. 287; *loc. pl.* ~esu, Dh. 29.

sutta[2], *n.* (*sa.* sūtra) [1]) a string, thread; *acc.* ~aṁ (tesaṁ hatthesu laggetvā) 111,1 (i. e. a charmed thread); *paritta-°, 111,11 (*v.* paritta[2]). — [2]) the thread of tradition, doctrine, scientific system, a single rule, passage, or chapter in the Buddhist holy scriptures (containing a discourse of Buddha himself); *nom.* ~aṁ, 31,14 (of a single gāthā); 109,33 (a part of navañga-Satthusāsana); *°-sammata, *mfn.* known by the name of Sutta, 110,3; *niyyāmaka-°, *n.* "the mariner's lore", 25,28. *cp. next etc.* [Tr. PM. p. 69; *Neumann*, Die Reden des Gotama Buddha, I. p. 505—6.]

*Sutta-nipāta, *m.* name of a collection of old Buddhist Suttas, mostly in verse, forming a section of the Khuddaka-nikāya (*q. v.*); specimens thereof p. 103—5.

suttanta, *n.* (& *m.*) (*Buddh. sa.* sūtrānta, *m.*) [1]) = sutta; Aggi-Vacchagotta-°, *n.* 95,33; [2]) = Sutta-piṭaka, or Suttanta-piṭaka, *n.* (*v.* piṭaka); *loc.* ~e, 102,11; °-piṭakaṁ, 102,13 (the 2. division of the holy scriptures, comprising the five nikāyas).

*sudaṁ, *indecl.*, an enclitic particle used in narrative sentences, mostly after *demonstr.* (or *relat.*) *pron.* or *adv.*, the verb generally following in *pres.*; tatra ~, 70,22. 77,19. 81,9; tā ~, 78,25 (*w. foll. aor.*). [The last part of this word seems to be identical with the last element of idaṁ, the first part with another frequently occurring particle su ('ssu, assu, or sa, 'ssa), probably = *sa.* sma; *cp. sa.* svid, *indecl.*]

sudda, *m.* (*sa.* çūdra) a man of the fourth caste; *nom.* ~o, 92,11.

suddha, *mfn.* (*sa.* çuddha; *pp.* sujjhati, √çudh, *cp.* sodheti) cleansed, pure; faultless, genuine, *etc.*; *m.* ~o, 62,29; (rukkho) 95,24; *gen.* ~assa (posassa) Dh. 125; *f.* ~ā (aṭṭhakathā) 113,28; *n.* ~aṁ (vatthaṁ) 68,24; (pāvacanaṁ) 95,25; *m. pl.* ~ā, 109,3; *°-citta, *mfn.* pure-minded, *pl.* ~ā. 62,22; °-bhāva, *m.* purity, chastity, *acc.* ~aṁ, 58,15; *cp. next etc.*

suddhatā, *f.* (*sa.* çuddhatā) purity; *acc.* ~aṁ, 103,24.

***suddhājīva**, *mfn.* living a pure life (*cp.* ājīva, *m.*); *instr.* ~ena, Dh. 245 (*cp. Kern,* Verkl. p. 59); *acc. pl. m.* ~e, Dh. 375. — *suddhājīvi(*n*), *mfn.* id.; *acc.* ~iṁ, Dh. 366.

***suddhin**, *mfn.* (?) possessed of purity, pure; *nom. m.* ~ī (paccattaṁ, *q. v.*) Dh. 165 (*cp.* a-suddhin).

Suddhodana, *m.* (*sa.* çuddhodana) *nom. pr.* of the father of Gotama Buddha; 62,4. 64,6 (°-mahārāja(*n*)).

sunakha, *m.* (rarely sunaka [perhaps on account of false etymology: su-nakha]; *sa.* çunaka) a dog; *pl.* ~ā, 111,4; *acc.* ~e, 21,4; *cp.* soṇa. [*Pischel,* Gr. § 206; *Trenckner,* PM. p. 59,12.]

sundara, *mfn.* (= *sa.*) good, excellent, beautiful, handsome; *f.* ~ā (yāgu) 57,26; *n. adv.* ~aṁ, well, rightly, 1,24 (~ te kataṁ).

Sundarī, *f.* (= *sa.*) *nom. pr.* of a woman; *nom.* ~ī, 74,11; *voc.* ~i, 73,16; *acc.* ~iṁ, 73,3; *instr.* ~iyā, 73,2; *gen.* ~iyā, 73,31.

supaṇṇa, *m.* (*sa.* suparṇa) a kind of bird (of mythical or fanciful description); *nom.* ~o, 20,18; °-potaka, *m.* 60,8 (*q. v.*); *°-bhavana, *n.* the abode or world of the Supaṇṇas, 19,9; °-yoni, *f.* 19,8 (*q. v.*); °-rājan, *m.* the S.-king, 19,15.

supati, *vb.* (*sa.* √svap) to sleep; *part. acc. m.* ~antaṁ, 67,28; *pp. v.* sutta[1]; *cp. next.*

supina, *m.* (& *n.*) (*sa.* svapna) sleep, sleeping; a dream, vision; *acc.* ~aṁ (addasa) 61,9.

Suppāraka, *m.* (*sa.* çūrpāraka) *nom. pr.* [a]) of a seaport-town (paṭṭana), probably in the western India, [b]) of a man (niyyāmaka): °-kumāro, 24,11; °-paṇḍita, *m.* id. 25,14; °-jātaka. *n.* 24,8.

subha, *mfn.* (*sa.* çubha) splendid, beautiful, handsome; good, agreeable, delightful; happy, auspicious; *acc. f.* ~aṁ (pokkharaṇiṁ) 111,16; *n.* ~aṁ (astu) 114,33; *dvandva comp.* subhāsubhaṁ, Dh. 409 (*cp.* a-subha); — *subhânupassin, *mfn.* looking only for what is delightful, *acc. m.* ~iṁ, Dh. 7; Dh. 8 (a-°); *gen. m.* ~ino, Dh. 349. *cp.* sobhati.

sumanā, *f.* (at the beg. of *comp.* sumana-°; = *sa.*) name of a sort of great flowering jasmine; °-mallikâdīnaṁ, *gen. pl.* (*cp.* mallikā) 65,29; *°-paṭṭa-vitāna, *m. n.* a canopy of cloth with pattern of that flower, *gen.* ~assa, 65,18.

sumarati, *vb.* (*sa.* √smṛ; *v.* sarati) Dh. 324.

suyyati, *vb.* (*pass.* suṇāti, *q. v.*) 27,6.

surā, *f.* (= *sa.*) a kind of spirituous liquor; *acc.* ~aṁ, 74,4; °-pāna, *n.* drinking sp. l., 61,4 (vigata-°, *mfn.*); °-meraya-pāna, *n.* id. Dh. 247; °-meraya-majja-°, 81,23. (*q. v.*).

suriya, *m.* (*sa.* sūrya) the sun; *nom.* ~o, 26,5; (majjhantika-°) 26,4; *loc.* ~e, 32,29. 42,1; *suriyuggamana, *n.* sunrise, 72,29 (°-kāle).

suruṅgā, *f.* (= *sa.*) a subterraneous abode; *loc.* ~āyaṁ, 111,13. (*cp. Weber,* Ind. Str. II, 395. III, 392).

suvaṇṇa, *n.* (*sa.* suvarṇa) gold; *nom.* ~aṁ, 26,9; at the beg. of *subst.*

comp. 'golden' or 'golden coloured', *v.* ⁰-kaṭacchu, ⁰-caṁgoṭaka, ⁰-jāla, ⁰-pañjara, ⁰-pādukā, ⁰-pāsaka, ⁰-bhiṁkāra, ⁰-miga, ⁰-rajata-pātiyo, *f. pl.* (dishes of gold and silver, *cp.* pāti) 61,27, ⁰-rājahaṁsa, ⁰-sandāsa. ⁰-samugga, ⁰-saraka, ⁰-haṁsa; — ⁰-maya, *mfn.* made of gold, *n. pl.* ~āni, 28,30; ⁰-vaṇṇa, *mfn.* golden coloured, of beautiful complexion, *m.* ~o, 5,26. 24,11. 87,8; *cp.* sovaṇṇa & *next.*

*Suvaṇṇa-pabbata, *m.* "Gold-Hill", *nom. pr.* of a (mythical) mountain (in Himavanta); *nom.* ~o, 61,17.

Suvaṇṇa-bhūmi, *f.* (*sa.* Suvarṇa-bhūmi) *nom. pr.* of a country ("the golden land"), probably on the coast of Burma or of the Malay Peninsula; *acc.* ~iṁ, 19,24.

suve, *adv.*, *v.* sve.

susāna, *n.* (*sa.* çmaçāna) a cemetery; *nom.* ~aṁ, 56,18. 67,31; ⁰-santike (*q. v.*) 56,19; *āmaka-⁰, *n.* (*v. h.*).

susira, *mfn.* (*sa.* sushira) perforated, full of holes, hollow; ⁰-rukkha, *m.* a hollow tree, *instr.* ~ena, 25,3.

Susīma, *m.* (= *sa.*) *nom. pr.* of a king; *voc.* ~a, 46,32; ⁰-kumāra, *m.* 45,28; ⁰-jātaka, *n.* 45,19.

sussati, *vb.* (*sa.* √çush) to become dry, dry up; *pr. 3. sg.* ~ati, 103,30; *part. med. loc.* sussamānamhi (lohite) ib.; *cp.* upa-sussati, vi-soseti.

*Sussondī, *f. nom. pr.* of a queen, 19,7. 20,17; *gen.* ~iyā, 19,18; ~i-jātaka, *n.* 19,5. (Among the different *varr. lect.* of this name Sussoṇī (*sa.* su-çroṇī) seems to be worthy of notice.)

suhajja [& suhada], *m.* (*sa.* suhṛdaya [su-hṛd]) a friend; *pl.* ~ā, Dh. 219; *gen. pl.* ~ānaṁ, 47,31 (ñāti-mitta-⁰).

sūkara, *m.* (= *sa.*) a boar, hog, pig; *nom.* ~o, 35,22. 46,33 (-gāma-⁰, *q. v.*); *acc.* ~aṁ, 35,32; *gen.* ~ass[a], 85,5; *⁰-maddava, *n.* (*q. v.*); ⁰-mukha, *n.* a pig's mouth, 84,34 (⁰-sadisa, *mfn.*); *mfn.* having a pig's mouth, 85,26; 84,27 (⁰-peta, *q. v.*); ⁰-sadisa, *mfn.* ressembling a pig, 85,22.

sūpa, *m.* (= *sa.*) sauce, soup; ⁰-rasa, *m.* the taste of soup, *acc.* ~aṁ, Dh. 64; aneka-sūpa-vyañjana, *mfn.* 57,11 (*v.* an-eka).

sūra, *mfn.* (*sa.* çūra) strong, brave, valiant; *m.* ~o (ativiya ~ hutvā, "showing a very bold front") 38,31; *m. pl.* ~ā, 40,14; — *subst. m.* a hero, warrior; abhejja-vara-sūra-mahāyodhā, *pl.* unconquerable excellent heros and great warriors, 39,12; a-sūra, *m.* 103,32 (*q. v.*); *kāka-⁰, *m.* (*q. v.*).

Sūrasena, *m.* (*sa.* Çūrasena) *nom. pr.* of a man (fictitious); *nom.* ~o, 96,31.

sūla, *m. n.* (*sa.* çūla) a pointed stake, spike, pike; a spit (for roasting meat); *maṁsa-⁰, *m. n.* 14,29 (*q. v.*).

sekha, *m.* (*sa.* çaiksha; *cp.* sikkhati) a beginner, pupil, one who has entered the path (*v.* magga [2]), but has not yet become an arahat (*q. v.*); *nom.* ~o, Dh. 45; — *mfn.* (*cp. sa.* çaikshya) belonging to the stage of a pupil, elementary; *instr. n.* ~ena (ñāṇena, dassanena, "an imperfect degree of knowledge, or insight") 69,34-35.

seṭṭha, *mfn.* (*sa.* çreshṭha) most excellent, best (*w. loc.* or *e. c.* best of or among); *m.* ~o (manussesu) Dh. 321; *n.* ~aṁ (dhanaṁ) Dh. 26; *comp.* rāja-⁰, *m.* 47,8 (*voc.* ~a); Buddha-⁰, *m.* 109,23 (*gen.* ~assa). *cp.* seyya & *next.*

seṭṭhatā, *f.* (*sa.* çreshṭhatā) the first rank, superiority; *acc.* ~aṁ (devānaṁ) Dh. 30.

seṭṭhi, *m.* (*sa.* çreshṭhin) the chief of an association (of merchants *etc.*), president of a guild (in later times appointed by the king to this office (which was sometimes heritable)); *nom.* ~i (gahapati) 68,29; *gen.* ~ino, 22,13; ~issa, 69,9; *loc.* ~imhi, 70,13; *⁰-kula, *n.* (purāṇa-⁰, an ancient S. family) 55,31; *⁰-putta, *m.* 67,22 (*q. v.*).

[SBE. XIII, p. 102; *Fick,* Soc. Glied. p. 166.]

seṇi, *f.* (*sa.* çreṇi) a guild or association of traders; *acc. pl.* ~iyo (sabba-°, *opp.* amacca-brāhmaṇa-gahapatike) 42,2.

seta, *mfn.* (*sa.* çveta) white; *m.* ~o (sabba-°, white all over) 21,34; *n. pl.* ~āni, 47,3; *comp.* °-cchatta, *n.* 42,8; °-paduma, *n.* 61,19; °-vara-vāraṇa, *m.* 61,17 (*q. v.*).

seti (& sayati), *vb.* (*sa.* √çī) to lie, lie down, sleep, repose; *pr. 3. sg.* seti, 30,21. Dh. 79. 168. 169 (sukhaṁ, "lives happily"); Dh. 201 (dukkhaṁ); sayati (ekako) 46,19; *1. sg.* sayāmi, 47,26; *3. pl.* senti, Dh. 156; *part. med.* *semāna [*sayamāna, sayāna] *v.* saha-semāna; *pot. 3. sg.* sayetha, 9,33; *ger.* sayitvā, 12,11. 58,17 (tāya saddhiṁ). *cp.* sayana, *etc.*, seyyaka, seyyā.

seda, *m.* (*sa.* sveda) sweat, perspiration; *nom.* ~o, 82,5. 97,22; *pl.* ~ā, drops of perspiration, 45,1. *cp. next.*

sedita, *mfn.* (*pp.* sedeti, to soften, cook, steam; *sa.* svedita) softened; *su-sedita, *mfn.* well-steamed (bent, or crooked) 62,17 (°-vettagga, *q. v.*).

Senaka, *m.* (*sa.* senaka?) *nom. pr.* of a king; *loc.* ~e (Bārāṇasiyaṁ) 52,14; *gen.* ~assa, 52,15.

senā, *f.* (= *sa.*) an army, battle-array; *nom.* ~ā, 103,25; *acc.* ~aṁ, 104,5; *instr.* ~āya (caturaṅginiyā) 35,15; at the end of *comp.* (*nom. pr. m.*) °-sena, *v.* Nāga-°, Vīra-°, Sīha-°, Sūra-°.

senāsana (& sayanāsana), *n.* (*sa.* çayanāsana) *lit.* 'sleeping and sitting', bedding, dwelling, habitation (sometimes = vihāra); 97,8; Dh. 185 (sayanāsanaṁ, pantaṁ, *q. v.*).

***semāna**, *part.*, *v.* seti.

semha, *n.* (*sa.* çleshman, *m.*) phlegm; *nom.* ~aṁ, 82,4. 97,22. 103,20.

***semhāra**, [*m.*] name of a certain animal, according to the comm. a monkey (makkaṭa); *gen.* ~assa, 92,32.

seyya (or seyyas), *mfn.* (*sa.* çreyas) better, preferable; *m.* ~o (attā) 55,2; 107,1 = Dh. 308; *acc.* ~aṁ, Dh. 61; the orig. s-stem is preserved in *n.* seyyo, 7,34. 103,7-34; Dh. 76. 100. 106 (sā pūjanā); 314; further in *seyyaso, *indecl.* = still better, Dh. 43. (*cp.* seṭṭha).

***seyyaka**, *mfn.* (*fr.* seyyā) lying, sleeping (only *e. c.*), *v.* uttāna-°.

***seyyathā**, *indecl.* (Magadhism instead of taṁ-yathā, *Buddh. sa.* tad-yathā, *cp. sa.* sa yathā) just as, as if; *w. foll. nom.* 69,27 (~ pi pubbe agārikabhūto); 95,18 (~ pi mahāsamuddo); at the beg. of full sentence (*w. pot.*): ~ pi puriso sallena viddho assa ("it is as if . . .") 92,6; ~ pi rañño paccantimaṁ nagaraṁ [*scil.* assa, *pot.*] 90,30 (only fancy, for instance, that a certain king has a frontier fortress); ~ pi nāma (*w. foll. pot.* & *corresp.* evam eva) 68,24; — seyyath'idaṁ, that is to say, namely, 67,3. 68,19. [*cp. Trenckner,* PM. p. 75; *Franke,* KZ. (N. F.) XIV. p. 419; differently *Pischel,* Gr. § 423.]

***seyyaso**, *indecl.*, *v.* seyya(*s*).

seyyā, *f.* (*sa.* çayyā) lying, sleeping; a bed, couch; *acc.* ~aṁ (kappeti, *q. v.*) 46,22; *eka-°, *f.* (*q. v.*); gabbha-°, *f.* (*q. v.*); *nanikāma-°, *f.* (*q. v.*) *cp.* uttāna-seyyaka, *mfn.*

***Seruma**, [*m.*] *nom. pr.* of an island; *acc.* ~aṁ, 20,19; °-dīpa, *m.* (= Nāgadīpa, Ceylon?) 19,8.

sela, [1]) *m.* (*sa.* çaila; *cp.* silā) a stone, rock; *nom.* ~o, 106,29 = Dh. 81; *acc.* ~aṁ, 104,16. — [2]) *mfn.* stony, rocky; *acc. m.* ~aṁ (pabbataṁ) Dh. 8.

sevati, *vb.* (*sa.* √sev) to frequent, serve, follow, practise, devote oneself to (*acc.*); *pr. 3. sg.* ~ati (piyāni) 55,1; *3. pl.* ~anti, Dh. 293; *pot. 3. sg.* [a]) seve (paradāraṁ) Dh. 310; [b]) seveyya, 7,33; Dh. 167 (dhammaṁ); *grd.* sevitabba, 66,25 (na ~ā. to be avoided); *pp.* sevita, enjoyed, Dh. 272 (a-puthujjana-°, *q. v.*) *cp. next.*

sevanā, *f.* (= *sa.*) waiting upon, service, honouring; 14,2.

sesa, [1]) *mfn.* (*sa.* çesha) remaining, left, mostly *pl.* = the others, the rest, or at the beg. of *comp.*; *pl. nom. m.* ~ā, 7,16. 40,16; 49,7 (sesâpi); 73,32 (*pleonast.* added after ṭhapetvā ariyasāvake); *acc. pl.* ~e. 21,21; *instr. pl.* ~ehi, 112,23; *gen. pl.* ~ānaṁ, 40,16; *comp.* °-varattā, 12,20; °-vāṇijānaṁ, 21,28; °-âmacce, 40,5. — [2]) *subst. n.* sesa(ka), the rest; *loc.* ~ke, 33,32; *cp.* a-sesa, *mfn.*

so, *pron. demonstr. m.* (= sa[3]), *v.* taṁ.

soka, *m.* (*sa.* çoka) sorrow; *nom.* ~o (mahā-°) 89,10; *acc.* ~aṁ, ib.; *pl.* ~ā, 107,32 = Dh. 335; *instr. pl.* ~ehi, 70,29; *comp.* (*dvandva*): °-parideva-, 66,10. 90,17. 92,31; parideva-soka-sampanna, *mfn.* full of lamentation and sorrow, 69,32; *tiṇṇa-soka-pariddava, *mfn.* (*v.* pariddava); *tanu-bhūta-°, *mfn.* (*q. v.*); *°-pareta, *mfn.* (*q. v.*) *cp.* a-soka, vi-soka (visūka) & *next.*

***sokin**, *mfn.* (*fr.* soka) sorrowing; *acc. f.* ~iniṁ (pajaṁ) Dh. 28.

socati, *vb.* (*sa.* √çuc) to grieve, mourn, suffer pain; *pr. 3. sg.* ~ati, 17,29; 105,31 (puttehi); Dh. 15 (*opp.* nandati, modati); *3. pl.* ~anti, 108,7; *3. pl. med.* socare, 104,10. Dh. 225; *aor. 2. sg.* (mā) soci, 89,12; *cp.* soka, *etc.*, socanā.

socanā, *f.* (= *sa.*) sorrow, suffering; 105,32.

soṇa, *m.* (*f.* ~i, also spelt sona, ~i; *sa.* çvāna, ~ī) a dog; soṇirupena, in the appearance of a bitch, 111,2; *cp.* sunakha.

soṇḍā, *f.* (& soṇḍa, *m.*; *sa.* çauṇḍa, *fr.* çuṇḍā) an elephant's trunk; *acc.* ~aṁ. 76,21; *instr.* ~āya, 61,19.

sota[1], *n.* (*sa.* çrotra) the ear (as organ of hearing, *cp.* kaṇṇa); *nom.* ~aṁ. 70,30; *instr.* ~ena, Dh. 360; *loc.* ~asmiṁ, 71,8; *pl.* ~āni, 27,4; °-samphassa-, 72,9 (*v. h.*); *ohita-°, *mfn.* (*q. v.*).

sota[2], *m.* & *n.* (*sa.* srotas, *n.*) a stream, flood, current; *nom.* ~o, 108,5; *acc.* ~aṁ, Dh. 347 (*metaph.* of the flood of passions); *pl.* ~ā, Dh. 339 (do.); *n. pl.* ~āni (nadīnaṁ) 103,18; *cp.* uddhaṁ-sota, *mfn.* & *next.*

sotāpatti, *f.* (*Buddh. sa.* srotāpatti) the state of a sotāpanna, the first step in sanctification; °-phala, *n.* the advantage of Sotāpannaship, Dh. 178; *loc.* ~e, 87,1; (= „die Hörerschaft", nicht von √sru, sondern von √çru, *Neumann*, Reden des Gotama Buddha, I. p. 505).

sotāpanna, *mfn.* (*Buddh. sa.* srotāpanna) 'who has entered the stream' (*i. e.* of sanctification), a converted who has reached the first stage of sanctification (the three last stages of which are: sakad-āgāmin, an-āgāmin, arahat); *m.* ~o, 28,18. 29,18 (*v. corrections*); 79,33; *pl.* ~ā, 22,13.

sotuṁ, *inf.*, *v.* suṇāti.

sotthi, *f.* & *n.* (*sa.* svasti) welfare, success, prosperity; *acc.* ~iṁ (tesaṁ karissāmi, I will save them) 27,16; amhākaṁ ~iṁ karonto pi tvaṁ ñeva karissasi (you do so, I think, in order to save me) 54,31; ~iṁ gacchati (was saved) 29,13; sotthiṁ, *acc.* (*adv.*) safely, happily. Dh. 219 (~āgataṁ); sotthinā, *instr.* (*adv.*) id. 42,23; sotthi-bhāva, *m.* safety, *acc.* ~aṁ (kātuṁ) 27,15.

sotthiya, *m(fn).* (*sa.* çrotriya) conversant with the sacred doctrine, a brahman (or bhikkhu); *acc. m. pl.* ~e (rājāno, "holy kings") Dh. 295.

sodariya, *m.* (*fr.* sa + udariya; *sa.* sodarya) a uterine brother; *acc.* ~aṁ, 31,35.

sodhana, *n.* (*sa.* çodhana) cleansing, investigation, examination; °-kāle ("when the search was made") 49,36.

sodheti, *vb.* (*sa.* çodhayati, √çudh) to cleanse, purify; to clear up, examine, investigate (*acc.*); *pr. 3. pl.* ~enti (maccaṁ) Dh. 141; *part. instr. m.* ~entena (vihāraṁ) 84,9; *pl.* ~entā, 25,7 (examining);

inf. ~etuṁ, 50,3 (id.); *ger.* ~etvā, 48,34 (id.); *grd. m.* ~etabbo, 84,8; *cp.* suddha & sodhana.

sona, *v.* soṇa.

sobbha, *m.* (*sa.* çvabhra) a hole, pit, abyss; *nom.* ~o, 27,7 (a whirlpool); 27,8 (chinna-taṭa-mahā-⁰); *loc.* ~e, 78,14.

sobhagga, *n.* (*sa.* saubhāgya) welfare, prosperity, auspiciousness; beauty, grace, loveliness; *instr.* ~ena (siri-⁰, *q. v.*) 64,10; *⁰-ppatta, *mfn.* happy, well-to-do, auspicious, lovely; *m.* ~o, 1,4; *acc.* ~aṁ, 10,26; *f.* ~ā, 73,8; (perhaps confounded with sobhā, *f.* (*sa.* çobhā), beauty, *v. next etc.*).

sobhati, *vb.* (*sa.* √çubh) to be bright or splendid, to shine, look beautiful; *aor. 3. sg.* sobhi (Buddho viya) 113,21.

sobhana, *mfn.* (*sa.* çobhana) splendid, beautiful; excellent, good; *n.* ~aṁ (kammaṁ) 100,6.

somanassa, *n.* (*fr.* su-mana(*s*); *sa.* saumanasya) gladness, satisfaction; *pl.* ~āni (pleasures) Dh. 341; *⁰-jāta, *mfn.* glad, delighted, 16,28. 64,13; *⁰-ppatta, *mfn.* id. 15,29.

soḷasa, ¹) *num.* (*mfn. pl.*) (*sa.* shoḍaça) 16; ~ petiyo, 23,23; ⁰-vassa-, 42,25, *etc.* (*v. h.*); *⁰-vassika, *mfn.* being 16 years old, 111,36 (*n.* ~aṁ, rūpaṁ). — ²) *mfn.* the 16th; *acc. f.* ~iṁ (kalaṁ) Dh. 70; — soḷasama, *mfn.* (*sa.* shoḍaçama) id.; ~o (vaggo) Dh. XVI.

sovaṇṇa, ¹) *mfn.* (*fr.* suvaṇṇa; *sa.* sauvarṇa) golden; *m.* ~o (sabba-⁰) 84,26; ⁰-sivikā, *f.* 62,7 (*q. v.*); — ²) *n.* gold; *⁰-maya, *mfn.* made of gold, *m.* ~o, 28,29.

sossati, *fut.*, *v.* suṇāti.

svākkhāta, *mfn.*, *v.* akkhāti.

*svātanāya, *adv.* (an old *dat.* [*scil.* divasāya?] *cp.* ajjatana & *sa.* çvastana, *mfn.*) for the next day, or to-morrow; 77,28. *cp. next.*

sve (& suve), *adv.* (*sa.* çvas) tomorrow; 14,16. 101,26; suve suve, daily, day after day, Dh. 229. *cp. prec.*

H.

h', apparently sandhi-consonant in some few instances (if not shortened of ha, or hi, *q. v.*): no h'etaṁ, (certainly) not so! 70,2; mā h'evaṁ kho, 90,24.

ha, *indecl.* (= *sa.*) an emphatic particle ("indeed", "verily"), mostly used after ti, or na; tasmā ti ha, 93,2 (*q. v.*); *comp.* have (*v. h.*).

haṁsa¹, *m.* (= *sa.*) a goose (or swan); *pl.* ~ā, Dh. 91; ⁰-potikā, *f.* 10,4 (*q. v.*); ⁰-rājan, *m.* 10,5; rāja-⁰, *m.* a special kind of swan, *nom.* ~o, 16,7; *gen.* ~assa, 10,4 (suvaṇṇa-⁰); suvaṇṇa-⁰, *m.* id. 10,3-15.

⁰haṁsa², & ⁰haṁsana, *mfn.* (only *e. c.*; *sa.* harsha, harshaṇa) causing erection (of the hairs), *v.* loma-⁰.

haññati (or ~te), *vb.* (*pass.* hanti; *sa.* hanyate) to be slain or killed; *pr. 3. sg.* ~ate, 30,19.

haññe, *pot.*, *v.* hanti.

*haṭa-haṭa-kesa, *mfn.* (of uncertain derivation; *cp. sa.* haṭha & *mahratt.* haṭahaṭa) having dishevelled hair; *m.* ~o, 71,29.

haṭṭha, *mfn.* (*sa.* hṛshṭa) glad; *m.* ~o, 68,16; *tuṭṭha-⁰, *mfn.* (*q. v.*).

hata, *mfn.* (*pp.* hanti; = *sa.*) beaten, slain, destroyed; *m.* ~o, 30,22; *⁰-lābha-sakkāra, *mfn.* (*v.* lābha); *hatāvakāsa, *mfn.* (*cp.* okāsa, *m.*) who has cut off every occasion (for good and evil), *m.* ~o, Dh. 97 (confounded with haṭa (*pp.* harati) *cp.* pahata); a-hata, *mfn.* (*v. h.*).

hattha, *m.* (*sa.* hasta) the hand (or arm), fore leg (or paw); *nom.* ~o, 50,22; *acc.* ~aṁ, 23,9; *instr.* ~ena, 24,23. 83,17-20; 111,24 (vāma-⁰); *abl.* ~to ("from") 101,25-29; *loc.* ~e; 23,9. 36,21. 58,7. 101,26 (tassa. 'with him'); *acc. pl.* ~e (dve) 62,28; *instr. pl.* ~ehi (ubhohi) 27,20; *loc. pl.* ~esu, 59,8. 111,1; *comp.* ⁰-gata, *mfn.* come to hand, obtained, 37,18 (⁰-bhāva, *m.*, *q. v.*); ⁰-gahaṇa, *n.* seizing one's hand, 51,14; *°-dhovana, *n.* 56,25 (*v. h.*); °-ppatta, *mfn.* (*cp.* patta³) = °-gata; *°-patha, *m.* the reach of one's hand, *acc.* ~aṁ, 62,18; °-pādā, *m. pl.* hands and feet, 99,15; 5,27 (*comp.* hatthapāda-°); *°-muddā, *f.* 56,7 (*v. h.*); *°-saññata, *mfn.* who controls his hands, *m.* ~o, Dh. 362; — daṇḍa-°, *mfn.* (*q. v.*); *nānāvudha-°, *mfn.* armed with weapons of all kind, 6,7 (*cp.* āvudha). *cp. next.*

hatthin, *m.* (*sa.* hastin) an elephant; *nom.* ~ī, 76,8; 24,21 (maṅgala-°, *q. v.*); ~iṁ, 24,26; *gen.* ~issa, 77,1; *pl.* ~ī, 35,21; *instr. pl.* ~īhi, 35,11; *gen. pl.* ~īnaṁ, ib.; *comp.* hatthi-°, *v.* *°-kkhandha, *m.*; °-nāga, *m.* an excellent elephant, *instr.* ~ena, 102,25; *°-pabhinna, *m.* (*q. v.*); °-piṭṭhe (*v.* piṭṭha); *°-bhaṇḍa, *m.* (*q. v.*); *°-magga, *m.* (*q. v.*); *°-ratana, *n.* (*q. v.*); °-sālā, *f.* (*q. v.*).

hadaya, *n.* (*sa.* hṛdaya) the heart; the mind or soul; *nom.* ~aṁ, 1,24. 82,3. 97,21; 59,12 (mātu-°, amātu-°); 64,17 (pitu-°); 64,18 (pajāpati-°); *acc.* ~aṁ, 2,2. 27,5; *instr.* ~ena, 59,10; *pl.* ~āni, 2,1; *comp.* °-maṁsa, *n.*; *thaddha-°, *mfn.*; *saṁvigga-°, *mfn.* (*q. v.*).

hanati, *vb.*, *v.* hanti.

***hanāpeti**, *vb.* (*caus. II.* hanti, √han; *cp.* ghāteti) to cause to be killed, massacred, or devastated (*acc.*); *imper. 2. pl.* ~etha (paccantagāmaṁ) 38,29; *aor. 3. sg.* ~esi (do.) 38,32.

hanu & hanukā, *f.* (= *sa.*; but also hanu, & ~ka, *m. n.*) a jaw; *sithilahanu, *m.* (*q. v.*); *hanukaṭṭhika, *n.* 40,18 (*v.* aṭṭhika).

hantar, *m.* (*sa.* hantṛ) a striker, one who kills; *acc.* ~āraṁ (brāhmaṇassa) Dh. 389.

hanti, *vb.* (& hanati; *sa.* √han) to strike, kill, destroy, devastate (*acc.*); *pr. 3. sg.* ᵃ) hanti, Dh. 72. 355. 405; ᵇ) hanati (pāṇaṁ) 97,10; *3. pl.* hananti, Dh. 355; *2. pl.* hanatha (gāmaṁ) 38,33; *pot. 3. sg.* ᵃ) haññe (pāṇinaṁ) 17,29; ᵇ) haneyya, Dh. 129; *aor. 3. pl.* haniṁsu, 34,21; *ger.* hantvā, Dh. 294; *caus. v.* *hanāpeti & ghāteti; *pass.* haññati, *pp.* hata (*q. v.*) *cp.* ghacca, ghañña, hantar.

handa, *indecl.* (*sa.* hanta) a particle implying resolution or exhortation, followed by *pr. 1. sg.*, *fut. 1. sg.*, or *imper.*, mostly at the beginning of a sentence and often followed by dāni (*v.* idāni) = well then! come! look! 80,1 (~ dāni, *w. pr. 1. sg.*).

hambho, *indecl.* (*cp.* ambho; *sa.* haṁho) a particle implying indignation, anger, *etc.*; or exclamation of surprise; ~ passatha, 88,3. (*cp. Pischel*, Gr. § 267.)

hammiya, *n.* (*sa.* harmya) a large house with more stories, or the topmost story of such a house; *loc. pl.* ~esu, 76,29 ("the balconies", SBE. XX, 248).

°hara, *mfn.* (*e. c.* = *sa.*) bringing, taking, seizing, ravishing; mano-hara, *mfn.* (*q. v.*); *vayo-hara, *mfn.* (*v.* vaya).

°haraṇa, *n.* & *mfn.* (*e. c.* = *sa.*) bringing, taking, removing; mānusamala-°-atthaṁ, "in order to remove every human stain", 61,13.

haraṇi, *f.* (= *sa.*) a passage by which water, *etc.*, passes, a channel, conductor, nerve; *rasa-haraṇi, *f.* a nerve of taste, *acc. pl.* ~iyo, 57,23.

harati, *vb.* (*sa.* √hṛ) to carry, bring, fetch, take (away), remove, destroy (*acc.*); to rob, plunder, attack (*gen.*); *pr. 3. sg.* ~ati, 50,3 (*opp.* āharati); *2. sg.* ~asi, 56,13 (kassa yāguṁ); *1. sg.* ~āmi (pitu tasaraṁ) 87,14; *imper. 2. sg.* hara (mama santikā) 49,15; *pot. 3. sg.* ~eyya (visaṁ pāṇinā) Dh. 124; (brāhmaṇassa ~) Dh. 389 (*var. lect.* pahareyya); *aor. 3. sg.* ahāsi (me) Dh. 3; *fut. 2. sg.* ~issasi, 56,14; *1. sg.* ~issāmi (jīvitaṁ) 4,33; *caus. II.* harāpeti (*q. v.*); (*pp.* haṭa, *cp.* hata); *cp.* hara, haraṇa (~ṇi).

harāpeti, *vb.* (*caus. II.* harati) to cause to be brought or removed, to take away (*acc.*); *ger.* ~etvā (paṁsuṁ) 38,2.

harita, *mfn.* (= *sa.*) green; *acc. m.* ~aṁ (yavaṁ) 9,1; *haritupatta, *mfn.* (*prob. fr.* harita + upatta, *q. v.*) strown or prepared with green leaves, *loc. f.* ~āya (bhūmiyā) 61,24 [different from harita-patta, *mfn.* (*v.* patta[1]) having green leaves, Jāt. III, 495,7, *etc.*].

have, *indecl.* (*sa.* ha vai) particle of asseveration (sometimes used after *relatives*): truly, certainly; yadā ~, 66,20; yo ~, Dh. 382.

hasati, *vb.* (*sa.* √has) to laugh; *part. acc. f.* ~antiṁ (tāpasiṁ) 111,17; *part. f. med.* hasamānā, 58,10; *aor. 3. sg.* hasi, 36,3. 53,22. 65,24 (mahāhasitaṁ, said of a horse: neighed); *2. sg.* hasi, 16,32; *1. sg.* hasiṁ, 17,9. 58,13; *ger.* ~itvā (mahā-hasitaṁ) 16,29; *pp.* hasita (*v. next*); *cp.* hāsa.

hasita, *n.* (= *sa.*) laughing, laughter; *acc.* ~aṁ (mahā-⁰, hasati, to laugh aloud) 16,29. 65,24; ⁰-kāraṇa, *n.* 53,24 (*v. h.*).

hāpeti, *vb.* (*caus.* jahāti; *sa.* hāpayati, √hā) to abandon, neglect, forfeit (*acc.*); *pot. 3. sg.* hāpaye (attadatthaṁ) Dh. 166.

hāyati, *vb.* (*pass.* jahāti; *sa.* hīyate, √hā) to be left or abandoned; to be lost, decrease; to be inferior, be outrun; *pr. 3. sg.* ~ati (udakaṁ) 3,4 (*opp.* vaḍḍhati); *aor. 3. sg. med.* ahāyatha (lābho ca sakkāro) 18,35. 19,4 (*cp. Kuhn,* Beitr. p. 110).

hāra, *m.* (= *sa.*) a garland, necklace; muttā-⁰, *m.* a pearl-necklace, 64,26.

hāva, *m.* (= *sa.*) 'calling', dalliance, blandishment; ⁰-bhāva, *m.* (*dvandva*) coquettish gestures, 21,13.

hāsa, *m.* (= *sa.*) laughter; joy, pleasure; *nom.* ~o, Dh. 146.

hi, *indecl.* (= *sa.*) an enclitic particle, generally joined to the first word of a sentence, with a causal or affirmative meaning, but sometimes denoting only transition, continuation, or emphasis: for, since, indeed (*nam, enim*; *igitur*); sace ~, 1,24; tvaṁ ~, 5,11; 13,1; santi ~, 11,14; yaṁ ~, 13,29 (*q. v.*); yatra ~, 63,13; ahaṁ ~, 73,14; ayaṁ h' ettha attho, 85,29; na ~, 97,19 ("nay verily"); tena hi, "well then", 1,10-19; 90,28 (tena h'); 113,14; at the end of a sentence: 112,10.

hiṁsati, *vb.* (*sa.* √hiṁs) to injure, harm, kill, destroy (*acc.*); *pr. 3. sg.* ~ati (bhūtāni daṇḍena) Dh. 131–32; (pāṇāni) Dh. 270; *pp.* hiṁsita, injured, killed; *n.* ~aṁ (na . . . ekapāṇaṁ pi) 27,23. *cp. next.*

hiṁsā, *f.* (= *sa.*) injury, harm; *comp.* *hiṁsa-mana(*s*), *n.* (?) inclination to injure, *nom.* ~o, Dh. 390. *cp.* a-hiṁsā, *f.*

hita, *mfn.* (*pp.* dahati, √dhā; = *sa.*) [1]) put, set, placed; *v.* ohita, purohita, sahita (saṁhita), su-hita; [2]) good, advantageous, salutary; *n.* ~aṁ, benefit, welfare; sabbaloka-hitaṁ katvā, "having conferred blessings on the whole world", 110,18; *hitāvaha, *mfn.* (*cp.* āvaha) conductive to welfare or blessing, *f.* ~ā, 114,29; 113,33 (sabbaloka-⁰); *cp.* a-hita, *mfn.*

hitvā, *ger.*, *v.* jahāti.

hima, *n.* (= *sa.*) cold, frost; ice, snow; ⁰-gabbha, *m.* an icy or snowy place, *acc.* ~aṁ, 16,9. *cp. next* & hemanta.

Himavanta (or Himavat), *m.* (*sa.* Himavat) 'the snowy mountain', Himālaya; *nom.* ~o, Dh. 304; *acc.* ~aṁ, 46,34; *loc.* ~e, 10,6; *abl.* ~to, 21,35; *comp.* ⁰-padese, 13,9; ⁰-matthakena, 36,5 (*v. h.*).

hiri (or hirī), *f.* (*sa.* hrī) shame, modesty; *nom.* ~i, 10,16 (ajjhattasamuṭṭhānā, *q. v.*); *dvandva comp.* *hirottappa, *n.* (*cp.* ottappa) sense of shame and tact in behaviour, *acc.* ~aṁ (bhinditvā) 10,13; *bhinna-hirottappa, *mfn.* without shame and decency, 10,17; – *hirī-nisedha, *mfn.* Dh. 143 (*v.* nisedha); *cp.* a-hirika (a-hirīka) & *next.*

hirīmat, *mfn.* (*sa.* hrīmat) modest, bashful; *instr. m.* ~matā (dujjīvaṁ) Dh. 245.

hīna, *mfn.* (*pp.* jahāti, *cp.* hāyati, √hā; = *sa.*) [1]) abandoned, left, lost; °-vīriya, *mfn.* weak, feeble, Dh. 7. 112 (*v.* viriya); [2]) inferior, low, vile, bad, mean, base, secular; *m.* ~o, 66,26; *dat. n.* ~āya (āvattitvā, the secular life, the world) 69,27.

huta, *n.* (= *sa.*) an oblation, sacrifice; *nom.* ~aṁ, Dh. 106. 108. (*cp.* juhati).

hutta, *n.* (*sa.* hotra) = *prec.*; only in the *comp.* aggi-° (*q. v.*).

huraṁ, *adv.* (*ved. sa.* huras) only used in old texts, and always *opp.* to idha: 'yonder', *i. e.* in another world, in another existence, Dh. 20 (idha vā ~ vā). Hence *hurāhuraṁ, *adv.* (= huraṁ huraṁ ?) from life to life, hither and thither, 107,30 = Dh. 334. (*cp. Morris*, JPTS. '84, p. 103–05.)

heṭṭhā, *prp. & adv.* (*sa.* adhastāt) [1]) under, beneath, from under (*w. gen.* or *abl.*; or *acc.* in *comp.*); rukkhassa ~, 35,26; setacchattassa ~, 42,9; vitānassa ~, 65,18; ~ pāsādā (*abl.*) 67,24; °-pīṭhaṁ, *adv.* (under the chair) 83,18; °-mañcaṁ, *adv.* (under the bed) 83,18; — [2]) below (*adv.*); 85,30 (*opp.* upari); 'heṭṭhā' in a book is = 'above', the reading (or writing) being considered as a moving upwards, so that a preceding passage consequently is 'below'; °-vutta-nayen'eva, 63,22 ('just in the same manner as mentioned before', *cp.* naya).

***heṭṭhima**, *mfn.* (*superl.* of heṭṭhā; *sa.* *adhastima, *cp. Pischel*, Gr. § 107) lowest; °-tale, 59,27 (*v.* tala).

***heṭheti**, *vb.* (*sa.* √heṭh) to worry, injure (*acc.*); *part. nom. m.* a-heṭhayaṁ (vaṇṇagandhaṁ. "without injuring") 106,2 = Dh. 49. *cp.* viheṭheti.

hetu, *m.* (= *sa.*) cause, reason; *e. c.* (*adv.*) = for one's sake (*sa.* hetoh), *v.* atta-°, parassa-° (para-°); *°-attha, *m.* causative meaning, 85,9 (antogadha-°, *mfn. q. v.*); *°-taṇhā, *f.* 'thirst' as cause [*scil.* sabba-dukkhassa] 108,13; sa-hetu-dhamma, *m.*, *v.* sa-[1], & dhamma[4]. 66,21.

hemanta, *m.* (= *sa.*) winter; °-gimhisu (*loc. pl.*) in winter and summer, Dh. 286 (*v.* gimha); *cp. next.*

hemantika, *mfn.* (*sa.* haimantika) relating to winter; *m.* ~o (pāsādo) 67,22; *loc.* ~e (kāle) 100,24.

hessati, *fut.*, *v.* hoti.

hoti, *vb.* (a contracted form of bhavati, *q. v.*; *sa.* √bhū) to be, exist, become, arise, turn into, *etc.*; *pr. 3. sg.* hoti, 2,6-30. 35,11. 66,12-18. 89,29. 98,30-31. 106,5 = Dh. 266; *3. pl.* honti, 4,1. 6,22. 12,21. 31,15; *2. pl.* hotha, 31,1; *part.*, *v.* bhavaṁ; *imper. 2. sg.* hohi, 25,16. 37,14. 62,24. 105,24; *3. sg.* hotu, 2,7. 6,25. 7,1. 10,10. 64,9. 74,7 (hotu hotu); *2. pl.* hotha. 14,18. Dh. 243; *3. pl.* hontu, 44,6; *pot.*, *v.* bhaveyya; *aor. 3. sg.* [a]) ahu & ahū, 80,32 (nâhu); 94,23. 112,30; Dh. 228 (câhu); 20,20 (ahū); 42,16. 80,35 (ahū'ti); [b]) ahuvā, 37,30; [c]) ahosi, 3,32; 3,3 (assa etad ~, he thought by himself); 23,3. 64,19 (do.); 67,31 (pātur-°, *q. v.*); *2. sg.* [a]) ahū. 85,26. 86,1 (mā . . . ahū'ti); [b]) ahosi, 2,6. 86,2 (mā ~, comm. on mā . . . ahū); *1. sg.* [a]) ahuṁ, 108,15; [b]) ahosiṁ, 52,10; *3. pl.* [a]) ahū (or ahu) 112,29; [b]) ahesuṁ, 5,26; 60,17 (mā ~); 79,21 (tuṇhī ~); *2. pl.* ahuvattha (mā ~) 79,19; *1. pl.* (*med.*) ahuvamhase ("we had", in the sense of abhisambhavati) 13,25 (*cp.* bala); *fut. 3. sg.* (hohiti &) hessati, 54,30. 110,32. Dh. 228 (according to the metre, mss. bhavissati); *inf.*, *v.* bhavituṁ; *ger.* hutvā, 1,4. 2,19, 3,4. 4,18. 12,27. 23,31. 35,18. 38,21, *etc.*; *grd.* hotabba, *n.* ~aṁ. 83,2 (*w. instr.*); *pp. v.* bhūta, *cp.* pa-hūta.

CORRECTIONS AND ADDITIONS.

P. 1 after **a-bhāsi** insert: **a-bhuñjisuṁ**, *v.* bhuñjati.
— 2 read: **a-kataññū**
— — **a-kiñcana** .. *cp.* ākiñcañña.
— — after **a-gata** insert: **a-gati**, *f.*, *v.* gati.
— 3 after **a-disvā** insert: **a-dukkha**. *mfn.* 70,27, *v.* dukkha.
— — ***a-dūbha** .. read: (*cp.* dubbhati).
— 4 ***a-ppatikāraka** ... read: (*v.* patikāra).
— 5 after **a-bhejja** insert: **a-makkhita**, *mfn.* 62,39, *v.* makkhita.
— 6 ***a-vajja** .. read: not to be avoided, *n.* no sin (or fault).
— — after ***a-saṁkuppa** insert: **a-saṁghaṭṭanta**, *v.* saṁghaṭṭati.
— 7 ***a-santasana** ... read: °-sabhāva.
— — after **a-sāhasa** insert: **a-sukha**, *mfn.* 70,27, *v.* sukha.
— 10 ***an-eja** ... (*cp. Leumann, Album-Kern, p.* 393)
— — **akkosati** ... *aor. 3. sg.* akkocchi, Dh. 3.
— 13 after **accaya** insert: **accāsanna**, *mfn.*, *v.* āsanna.
— — **acchati** ... *cp.* āsīna.
— — after **acchādeti** add: (*cp.* āchanna).
acchindati, *vb.*, *v.* chindati.
— 15 **aññā** ... (*cp.* āṇā, *f.*)
— — ***aṭṭiyati** ... (*cp. Kern,* Verkl. p. 68.)

P. 16 ***aṇḍa-bhūta**, *mfn.*... (differently *E. Hardy*, Litt. Centralbl. 1904, p. 507).
— 17 ***ati-dhona-cārin** ... (*cp.* dhona, dhuta).
— 19 after ***attha-pada** insert: **attharaṇa**, *v.* tharaṇa.
— 19—20 **atthi** ... *pr. 2. pl.* 'ttha, 29,30. 31,23; — *pot. 3. sg.* assa, Dh. 376; — *aor.* (*impf.*) *3. sg.* āsi, 81,3 (tadâsi).
— 20 read: **addhagū**.
— 21 **adhipa**, read: **adhipati**
— 26 **andhaka** ... read: *andhaka-makasā
— 27 **aparādha** ought to be put after ***aparabhāge**.
— 29 **abhiññā** ... jhānâbhiññā, read: jhānâbhiññā
— — **abhinikkhamana**, *n.* (*sa.* abhinishkramaṇa)
— 30 ***abhippahāraṇī**, read: °-hāriṇī
— — **abhirūhati** ... (*cp.* Tr. PM. p. 78).
— 31 **abhisaṁkhāra**, *m.*
— — after **amacca** insert: **Amarādevī**, *f. nom. pr.* of a woman, 55,32. 58,32; = Amarā, 56,12.
— — **amba** ... ambapakká. *n. nom.* ~aṁ, 15,25 (ambapakk').
— 33 **ariya** ... (*cp.* kadariya, *mfn.*)
— 34 **avajīyati** ... (*cp.* ojita).
— — **avaharati** ... *caus. v.* ohāreti (*cp.* *ohārin)
— 36 **ākāra** ... (*cp.* paṇṇākāra, *m.*).

P. 37 āgacchati ... *aor. 3. sg.* āgañchi, 20,30.

— — ācikkhati, *vb.* (*sa.* ā-√caksh, or possibly *fr.* ā-√khyā, *redupl.* *ā-cikhyati; *Pischel*, Gr. § 492, *cp. T. Michelson*, Idg. F. XIX, p. 210.)

— 41 ārāma ... (*cp.* dhammārāma, *mfn.*)

— 43 āvuṇāti (or āvunāti, *cp.* Tr. PM. p. 63,45.)

— — *āvuso ... read: *āvuso-vāda, *m.*

— — āsana ... (*cp.* dhammāsana.)

— 44 after āsāḷhi insert: āsi, āsiṁ, *v.* atthi.

— 51 upaga ... (*cp.* Brahmalok'ūpaga, *mfn.*)

— — upaṭṭhāna ... (*cp.* paṭṭhāna & sati-paṭṭhāna.)

— 56 Uruvelā, *f.* (*sa.* Uruvilvā)

— 60 ereti ... or = *sa.* erayati (ā + √ir).

— 63 obhāsati ... (*cp.* vijjotati.)

— 65 kaccha¹ ... read: kakshya (instead of *kākshya).

— — kañña, read: kaññā.

— 69 karaṇa¹ ... (*cp.* *dubbalīkaraṇa. *mfn.*)

— 73 [kāma] ... naccitu-kāma, *mfn.* 50,35.

— — kāma-kāma ... or, perhaps better, *abl. sg.* ("out of desire for sensual gratification", *Morris*, IPTS. 1891–93, p. 39–41)

— 78 kuñjara ... *nom.* ~o, Db. 324.

— 80 kūla ... (*cp.* paṭi-kkūla, *mfn.*)

— 82 khamāpeti ... to ask one's (*acc.*) pardon.

— — khaya, *m.* (instead of *n.*)

— 89 gāma ... *⁰-vara, *m.* (*cp.* vara, *m.*) ... paṭṭana-⁰, *m.* (*q. v.*)

— 96 cāra(ka) ... (*cp.* *piṇḍacāra. *m.*)

— — citta¹ ... (*cp.* sa-⁴, instead of sa-³.)

— 98 cha ... (*cp.* saḷāyatana.)

P. 98 jhāyati¹ ... (*cp.* *vijjhāpeti.)

— — jhāyati² ... (*cp.* ajjhāya & mantajjhāyaka.)

— 107 ⁰-ṭṭha ... (*cp.* bhummaṭṭha, *mfn.*)

— — taṁ ... *loc. f.* tassā, 2,26.

— 108 taṇhā ... add ⁰-nirodha, *m.* 66,15 (*q. v.*)

— 109 after tathā-rūpa insert: tathā-vādi*n*, *mfn.*, *v.* vādi*n*

— 115 terasa ... (*cp. Franke*, Pāli und Sanskrit, p. 104 (so).)

— 116 thera-vāda ... *abl. pl.* 114,21 (instead of *instr. pl.*)

— 122 dugga ... *acc.* ~aṁ (palipathaṁ, instead of saṁsāraṁ.)

— 123 dubbuddhi*n*, read: dubbuddhi.

— 124 dūra ... read: (*cp.* vidūra) instead of (*opp.* vidūra.) — add: *⁰-saṁkūra, *mfn.* (*q. v.*)

— 127 dhana ... read: *⁰-vassāpanaka.

— 129 dhamma-pīti*n* ... (*cp.* pīti.)

— 140 [nibbāna] ... (*cp. F. Otto Schrader*, On the problem of Nirvāṇa, IPTS. 1904–5, p. 157.)

— 146 *pa¹ ... read: (*cp.* la, instead of ḷa.)

— — pakati ... (*cp.* pākaṭa [pākata].)

— 149 pajāpati ... Pajāpatī (= *sa.* prajāvatī, *Oldenberg*, Buddha, p. 112.)

— 151 paṭikkūla ... *instr.* ~ena (if not, as suggested by *E. Olesen*, *adv.* = *sa.* pratikūlaṁ, in inverted order, i. e. with the head turned downwards, head foremost?)

— 154 *paṭisanthāra ... read: (*sa.* *⁰-vṛtti).

— 158 padeti ... to be inserted below after paduma.

— 161 pabhāseti ... (*cp.* vijjotati).

P. 170 read: paveni & paveṇi.
— 187 bāhira ... (*cp.* santara-bāhiraṁ, *adv.*)
— 193 bhāga ... (*cp.* sabhāga, *mfn.*)
— — *bhāṇavāra (instead of bhāṇavāra).
— 200 mati... (*cp.**sāra-mati(*n*))
— 202 madhuvā, *adv.* (or rather *adj. n.* instead of madhuvaṁ (an old error?) *cp.* bhadraṁ, Dh. 119.)
— — manuñña ... read: *n.* (*adj.*) ~aṁ.

P. 203 manta ... *nom.* ~o, 32,9.
— 205 Mahāpajāpatī Gotamī (*fr. sa.* °-prajāvatī, *Oldenberg*, Buddha p. 112, *cp.* Sp. *Hardy*, Manual of Buddhism p. 306.)
— 215 yojana ... (= about $7^1/_2$ miles, IRAS. 1902. p. 284 Note.)
— 245 sa-[1] ... read: sātthaka (instead of sātthika.)
— 246 saṁvāsa ... *acc.* ~aṁ (piya-°, vasiṁsu) 11,27.

SUPPLEMENTARY LIST OF ABBREVIATIONS.

Childers = Dictionary of the Pāli Language; ***Fausbøll***, Bem. = Nogle Bemærkninger om enkelte vanskelige Pāli-Ord i Jātaka-Bogen (Oversigt over det Kgl. Danske Vidensk. Selsk. Forhandl. 1888 p. 7–58); ***Fausbøll***, Das. Jāt. = Dasaratha Jātaka (Copenhagen 1871); Five Jāt. = Five Jātakas (Copenhagen 1861); Ten Jāt. = Ten Jātakas (Copenhagen 1872); ***Fick***, Soc. Gl. = Die sociale Gliederung im nordöstlichen Indien zu Buddha's Zeit (Kiel 1897); ***Jacobi***, Erzähl. = Ausgewählte Erzählungen in Māhārāshtrī (Leipzig 1886); ***Kern***, Bijdr. (or Verkl.) = Bijdrage tot de Verklaring van eenige woorden in Pāli-geschriften voorkomende (Verhandelingen d. Kon. Akad. van Wetenschappen. Afd. Letterkunde XVII. Amsterdam 1888); ***Kuhn***, Beitr. = Beiträge zur Pāli-Grammatik (Berlin 1875); ***Lassen***, IA. = Indische Alterthumskunde; ***Müller***, PGr. = A simplified grammar of the Pāli language (London 1884); ***Pischel***, Gr. = Grammatik der Prākrit-Sprachen (Strassburg 1900); ***Sénart***, Kacc. = Kaccayana et la Littérature grammaticale du Pāli (Paris 1871); ***Wackernagel***, Gr. = Altindische Grammatik (Göttingen 1896 ff.); ***Weber***, Ind. Str. = Indische Streifen; Ind. Stud. = Indische Studien; ***Windisch***, Māra = Māra und Buddha (Leipzig 1895; Abhandl. d. Kön. sächs. Ges. d. Wiss. phil.–hist. Cl. XV.)

BB. = (Bezzenberger's) Beiträge zur Kunde der indogermanischen Sprachen; GGA. = Göttingische gelehrte Anzeigen; Gött. Nachr. = Nachrichten von der Kön. Ges. d. Wiss. zu Göttingen; Idg. F. = Indogermanische Forschungen; Ind. Ant. = The Indian Antiquary; KZ. = (Kuhn's) Zeitschrift für vergleichende Sprachforschung; KZ (BB) = dieselbe vereinigt mit Bezzenberger's Beiträge (Bd. I = Bd. XLI.); Pāṇ. = Pāṇini's Grammatik, herausgeg. von O. Böhtlingk (Leipzig 1887); Tr. PM. = *Trenckner*, Pāli Miscellany, Part 1 (Copenhagen 1879); WZ. or WZKM. = Wiener Zeitschrift für die Kunde des Morgenlandes.

CORRECTIONS TO PART I.

1,14 . . . ciṇṇaṭṭhāne
2,29-30 . . . dohaḷo uppanno
— 33 . . . sāyaṇhasamaye
7,32 . . . ovadantī
8,1 . . . °petuṁ vā na visahanti
9,6 . . . su-
— 9 . . . puttaṭ-
— 14 . . . paṭicchā-
— 15 . . . cari,
15,19 . . . dussaṁ
— 33 . . . dārūni
17,16 . . . appa-
— 18 . . . eḷakaṁ
23,4 . . . uṭṭhāpetvā (*bis* instead of upaṭṭhapetvā)
27,6 . . . saddo (instead of samuddo)
29,18 . . . sotāpanno upāsako
36,28 . . . (in some copies:) nâsakkhi (instead of nâaskkhi)
41,5 . . . catujāti-°
44,1 . . . Malliko,
47,4 . . . 'imassa lobhaṁ
48,7 . . . labbhamāne nimantake
— 32 . . . sattadvāra-°
53,21 . . . tassā ravaṁ
59,7 . . . nipajjāpetvā
60,23 . . . devalokesu
62,32-33 . . . gāhāpesuṁ
66,15-16 . . . (insert after taṇhānirodhā:) upādānanirodho, upādānanirodhā
73,11 . . . mālāgandha-°
75,26 . . . āyatiṁ
76,1 . . . papaṭikā
— 10 . . . etad avoca
83,30 . . . ekena hatthena
85,8 . . . samantato pabhāsati vijjotati
— 32 . . . kiṁ idan ti ce ti āha (corrected by *E. Hardy*).
87,11 . . . parasantako me sāṭako āropito, tassa vidatthimattaṁ aniṭṭhitaṁ (the Cinghalese Edition, Colombo 1898.)
— 11-12 . . . niṭṭhāpessāmi
— 31 . . . Tusitavimāne
89,8 . . . papatā
— 26 . . . aññan" ti
91,19 . . . pākāro na hoti
— 31 . . . pañhaṁ puna pi pucchi
93,21 . . . evam me sutaṁ
96,14 . . . ñāṇam
103,2 . . . Tam [maṁ]
— 6 . . . Sahassabhāge maraṇaṁ, ekaṁse
— 13 . . . sen'atthena
— 14 . . . Aṇumatto pi puññena
— 15 . . . yesañ ca attho puññena
— 31 . . . °-âbhippahāriṇī
104,1 . . . Pagāḷhā ettha [na] dissanti
106,16 . . . pana duddasaṁ
— 18 . . . kitavā saṭho
111,27 . . . Jīvitaṁ dehi
112,9 . . . yakkhā ca ghātiyā
— 22 . . . sayam pi Vijayo laddhā
— 29 . . . Tambabhūmirajophuṭṭhā tambapaṇṇī yato ahū
113,9 . . . satto, dametuṁ

ADDITIONS TO THE NOTES.

Baka-Jātaka . . . translated by *R. Pischel*, Ausland, 1876, p. 757.

Nacca-Jātaka . . . translated by *R. Pischel*, Ausland, 1876, p. 758; translated by *Warren*, Hermes, XXIX, p. 476.

Ucchaṅga-Jātaka . . . translated by *R. Pischel*, Hermes, XXVIII, p. 465 (*cp. Nöldeke*, ib. XXIX, p. 155, & *Zachariae*, Wien. Zeitschr. f. d. Kunde d. Morgenl. XV, p. 72).

Vedabbha-Jātaka . . translated by *J. J. Meyer*, Daṇḍin's Daça-kumāra-caritam. Leipzig 1902, p. 15–19.

Susīma-Jātaka . . . 47,28 = Dh. 347,3-4 (*cp.* 346).

Aṇḍabhūta-Jātaka ... translated with Notes by *R. Pischel*, Philol. Abhandlungen M. Hertz zum 70. Geburtstage von Schülern dargebracht. Berlin 1888, p. 74.

Mahosadha's Marriage .. translated by *J. J. Meyer*, Daṇḍin's Daçakumāra-caritam, p. 96–103.

Mahosadha's Judgement ... *cp. H. Oldenberg*, Die Literatur des alten Indien. Stuttgart 1903, p. 114 (& Note p. 291).

The Great Retirement .. 64,14-15 = As. p. 34,5 (*cp.* Mahāvastu II, 157).

Dhammacakka-pavattana-Sutta ... translated SBE. XI, p. 146 & XIII, p. 94.

Yasapabbajjā .. *cp.* Lalita Vistara ed. by *Rājendralāla Mitra*. Calcutta 1877, p. 251; *Sp. Hardy*, Manual of Buddhism, p. 156 (159); *P. Bigandet*, The Life or Legend of Gaudama. Rangoon, 1866, p. 55; *H. Alabaster*, The Wheel of the Law. London 1871, p. 125.

The Fire-Sermon ... translated by *Oldenberg*, Buddha p. 209.

Māra as Plowman .. translated by *E. Windisch*, Māra und Buddha. Leipzig 1895, p. 104.

Buddha's Death ... = DN. II, p. 154. – 80,28-29 = Jāt. I, p. 392.

The Ten Precepts .. 81,22 (*cp.* Dh. v. 246–47).

The Legend of the Weaver's Daughter, 86,12–89,17 .. Edited: Dhammapadaṭṭhakathā ... by *W. Dhammānanda Thera* & *M. Ñāṇissara Thera*. Colombo 1898, p. 428-31.

The Questions of Uttiya .. *cp.* Mil. ed. by *V. Trenckner*. Copenhagen 1880, Note p. 424. – 89,20-21 *cp.* Sn. v. 419.

Rebirth is not Transmigration .. translated (the beginning only) by *R. Garbe*, Beiträge zur indischen Kulturgeschichte. Berlin 1903, p. 129–30.

Padhāna-Sutta ... translated by *E. Windisch*, Māra und Buddha, p. 3 (= Lalita Vistara, ch. XVIII; Mahāvastu II, 237) *cp.* ib. p. 322. – v. 19 bhañjāmi (Ed. gacchāmi) *cp. R. Pischel*, Indische Miscellen (KZ. (BB) I, p. 182).

Dhaniya-Sutta ... translated by *Pavolini*, Buddismo. Milano 1898, p. 125.

Buddhaghosa .. translated SBE. X. Introduction, p. XXIX–XXXI.

Obs! Several of the Texts above have been printed in: *J. Takakusu*, A Pāli Chrestomathy, with notes and glossary giving Sanskrit and Chinese equivalents. Tokyo 1900.

MISPRINTS

to be corrected in the Pāli Text of Dhammapada, 2. ed. by *V. Fausbøll*. London 1900.

V. 18,4 .. suggatiṁ
— 37,2 .. Mārabandhanā
— 40,2 .. ṭhapetvā
— 41,3 .. apetaviññāṇo
— 69,1 .. Madhuvā
— 86,2 .. suduttaraṁ
— 148,1 .. idaṁ
— 166,2 .. attadattham
— 227,2 .. tuṇhīm
— 251,2 .. nadī
— 253,1 .. paravajjānupassissa
V. 312,2 .. saṁkiliṭṭhañ ca
— 316,3 .. micchādiṭṭhi-°
— 329,1 .. labhetha
— 330,2 .. sahāyatā
— 343,4 .. ākaṁkha
— 369,1 .. bhikkhu
— 370,2 .. pañcasaṅgātigo
— 390,1 .. akiñci
— 391,2 .. brāhmaṇaṁ
— 404,2 .. appicchaṁ
— 414,1 .. palipathaṁ